A Brief Introduction to Law in Canada

SECOND EDITION

John Fairlie

emond ▪ Toronto, Canada ▪ 2021

Emond Montgomery Publications Limited
1 Eglinton Ave E, Suite 600
Toronto ON M4P 3A1
http://www.emond.ca/highered

Printed in Canada.
Reprinted January 2021

We acknowledge the financial support of the Government of Canada and the assistance of the Government of Ontario. Canadä Ontario

Emond Montgomery Publications has no responsibility for the persistence or accuracy of URLs for external or third-party Internet websites referred to in this publication, and does not guarantee that any content on such websites is, or will remain, accurate or appropriate.

Vice president, publishing: Anthony Rezek
Publisher: Mike Thompson
Director, development and production: Kelly Dickson
Developmental editor: Sandy Matos
Production manager: Anna Killen
Production editor: Kimberley Griffiths
Copy editor: Holly Dickinson
Typesetter: SPi Global
Permissions editor: Nadine Bachan
Proofreader: Leanne Rancourt
Indexer: Andrew Little
Cover designer: Jordan Bloom
Cover image: Statue of *Veritas*, Supreme Court of Canada, Ottawa. WorldStock/Shutterstock
Printer: Marquis

Library and Archives Canada Cataloguing in Publication

Title: A brief introduction to law in Canada / John Fairlie.
Names: Fairlie, John, author.
Description: Second edition. | Includes index.
Identifiers: Canadiana 20200353985 | ISBN 9781772557664 (softcover)
Subjects: LCSH: Law—Canada—Textbooks. | LCGFT: Textbooks.
Classification: LCC KE444 .F33 2021 | LCC KF385.ZA2 F33 2021 kfmod | DDC 349.71—dc23

ISBN 978-1-77255-766-4

For my wife, Christine

—JF

Brief Contents

Contents vii

Table of Cases xiii

Preface xvii

About the Author xix

PART I   THEORY AND CONTEXT

1   What Is Law? 3

2   Common Law, Civil Law, and Indigenous Legal Systems 27

3   From the Reception of English and French Law into Canada to the Charter 59

PART II   LAW AND THE CANADIAN CONSTITUTION

4   The Legislature and the Executive: The First and Second Branches
    of Government 89

5   The Judiciary: The Third Branch of Government 127

6   Civil Liberties 159

PART III   KEY SUBJECT AREAS IN LAW

7   Private Law Survey: Tort, Contract, Property, and Family Law 183

8   Business and Consumer Law 229

9   Administrative Law 249

10   Criminal Law 269

PART IV   WORKING WITH THE LAW

11   The Practice of Law: Careers, Education, and Ethics 303

12   Access to Justice and Law Reform 331

APPENDIXES

A   Constitution Act, 1867 351

B   Constitution Act, 1982 363

Glossary 375

Index 383

Credits 397

Contents

Brief Contents v

Table of Cases xiii

Preface xvii

   In Memoriam—A Special Dedication xviii

About the Author xix

PART I
Theory and Context

1 What Is Law? 3

Learning Outcomes 4

Introduction 4

How Law Is Commonly Defined 5

   Types of Rules 5

   Structure of Rules 6

How Law Relates to Other Rules 6

   Law, Morality, and Ethics 6

   Law and Justice 8

   Law and Religion 11

Theories of Law: "Ought" and "Is" 12

   Natural Law Theory 13

   Legal Positivism 14

   Legal Realism 15

   Other Legal Theories 16

Rule of Law 17

   Origins 17

   Basic Principles 18

   Rule of Law in the International Context 20

Divisions of Law 20

Legal Terminology 23

Chapter Summary 24

Key Terms 24

Further Reading 24

Review Questions 25

Exercises 25

2 Common Law, Civil Law, and Indigenous Legal Systems 27

Learning Outcomes 28

Introduction 28

Common Law 30

   Law in Pre-Norman England: Romans and Anglo-Saxons 30

   Origins of Common Law 30

   Chief Features of Common Law 33

   Common Law: A Summary 37

Civil Law 37

   Origins of Civil Law 38

   Civil Law: A Summary 41

Comparison of the Common Law and Civil Law Systems 41

Harmonizing Common Law and Civil Law in Canada 43

Indigenous Law 44

   The Colonial Context 44

   Nature of Indigenous Law 48

   Canadian Law and Indigenous Peoples: A Timeline ... 51

   New Directions for Indigenous Law in Canada 54

Chapter Summary 56

Key Terms 56

Further Reading 57

Review Questions 57

Exercises 58

**3 From the Reception of English
and French Law into Canada
to the Charter** 59

Learning Outcomes 60

Introduction 60

Common Law Rules of Reception of
English Law 60
  Settlement 62
  Conquest or Cession 62
  Adoption 62

Reception of English and French Law
into Canada's Provinces and Territories 63
  Newfoundland and Labrador 63
  Nova Scotia 64
  Prince Edward Island 64
  New Brunswick 65
  Quebec 65
  Ontario 67
  Manitoba 67
  Saskatchewan 68
  Alberta 69
  British Columbia 69
  Yukon 70
  Northwest Territories 70
  Nunavut 70

Prelude to Confederation in 1867 70

Canada Is Born 72
  John A Macdonald and the New
    Federal Government 72

Post-Confederation Problems 73
  Omissions in the BNA Act 73
  Interpreting the Constitution:
    The Role of the Privy Council 75

The Movement to Patriate the Constitution
and Adopt a Charter of Rights 77
  Pierre Trudeau and the Quest for a
    Domestic Amending Formula and
    Charter of Rights 77
  Indigenous Peoples and the Patriation Process 78
  Women and the Patriation Process 81

Patriation and a Revived Constitution 82

Chapter Summary 84

Key Terms 84

Further Reading 84

Review Questions 85

Exercises 85

PART II

Law and the Canadian Constitution

**4 The Legislature and the Executive:
The First and Second Branches
of Government** 89

Learning Outcomes 90

Introduction 90

Legislative Power 90
  Statutes 91
  Subordinate Legislation 106
  Parliamentary Sovereignty 108

Executive Power 109
  Responsible Government 110
  Sources of Executive Power 112
  Limits of Executive Influence 116

Chapter Summary 118

Key Terms 119

Further Reading 119

Review Questions 120

Exercises 120

Appendix 4.1: Reading and Understanding Legislation ... 122

**5 The Judiciary: The Third Branch
of Government** 127

Learning Outcomes 128

Introduction 128

Role of the Judiciary 129

Canadian Courts: Constitutional Basis 129
  Inferior Courts 130
  Superior Courts 131
  The Supreme Court of Canada 132

Canadian Courts: Organization and Function 132
  The Supreme Court of Canada 134
  Provincial Court Systems 138
  Territorial Court Systems 141
  Federal Court System 142
  Military Court System 144

Precedent and Stare Decisis in the Canadian
Court System 144

Judicial Appointments 145
  Superior Court Judges 146
  Inferior Court Judges 149

Public Proceedings 149

Judicial Independence 150

Chapter Summary 153

Key Terms 153

Further Reading 153

Review Questions 154

Exercises 155

Appendix 5.1: Reading and Understanding Case Law. . . 156

6 Civil Liberties 159

Learning Outcomes 160

Introduction 160

The Evolution of Civil Liberties in Canada 161

Protection of Civil Liberties in the Private Sector 163
Provincial and Territorial Legislation 163
Federal Legislation: The Canadian
Human Rights Act 164
Exceptions 166

Protection of Civil Liberties When Governments
Are Involved: The Charter 167
An Overview of the Charter 167

The Future of Civil Liberties in Canada 176

Chapter Summary 178

Key Terms 178

Further Reading 178

Review Questions 179

Exercises 180

PART III
Key Subject Areas in Law

7 Private Law Survey: Tort, Contract, Property, and Family Law 183

Learning Outcomes 184

Introduction 184

Constitutional Basis of Private Law 185

Burden of Proof and Standard of Proof in
Private Law Claims 185

Tort Law 186
Intentional Torts 186
Negligence 189

Strict Liability Torts 193
Miscellaneous Torts 194
Tort Remedies 196

Contract Law 197
Pervasiveness of Contracts 197
Elements of a Valid Contract 197
Duties of Good Faith and Honesty 199
Individually Negotiated Contracts and
Standard Form Contracts 200
Contract Terms and Terminology 201
Excuses for Non-Performance of Contracts 203
Contract Remedies 205

Property Law 207
Real Property 207
Personal Property 213
Intellectual Property 214

Family Law 216
Marriage 216
Marriage Breakdown and Divorce 220
Common Law Marriages and Marriage-Like
Relationships 222

Chapter Summary 224

Key Terms 225

Further Reading 225

Review Questions 225

Exercises 226

8 Business and Consumer Law 229

Learning Outcomes 230

Introduction 230

Business Structures 231
Sole Proprietorships 231
Partnerships 232
Corporations 234

Business Transactions 237

Builders and Repairers: Security for
Services Performed 238

Product Sales and Consumer Protection Legislation . . . 238
Sale of Goods Acts 239
Federal Consumer Protection Legislation 240
Provincial and Territorial Areas of
Consumer Protection 243

Advertising Standards 244

Chapter Summary 246

Key Terms 246

Further Reading 247

Review Questions 247

Exercises 247

9 Administrative Law 249

Learning Outcomes 250

Introduction 250

The Role of Administrative Agencies in Society 251

The Constitutional Basis of
Administrative Agencies 252

   Constitutional Limitations on
     Administrative Tribunals 252

Delegated Power and Functions of
Administrative Agencies 253

   Legislative Functions 254

   Administrative Functions 254

   Quasi-Judicial Functions 256

The Public's Interaction with Administrative Bodies ... 258

   Substantive Rules 258

   Procedural Rules 258

Challenging Administrative Decisions 259

   Internal Means of Challenge 259

   Challenging in the Courts 259

   Jurisdiction of Superior Courts to Review 260

   Privative Clauses 261

   Grounds for Review 261

Chapter Summary 267

Key Terms 267

Further Reading 268

Review Questions 268

Exercises 268

10 Criminal Law 269

Learning Outcomes 270

Introduction 270

Sources of Canadian Criminal Law 271

True Crimes Versus Quasi-Criminal Offences 273

Basic Principles of Criminal Law 275

   The Elements of a Criminal Offence 275

   Burden of Proof and Standard of Proof 275

Organization and Classification
of Criminal Code Offences 276

   Organization of Criminal Code Offences 276

   Summary Conviction Offences 277

   Indictable Offences 279

   Hybrid Offences 279

Police Investigation of Crime 279

   Detention and Arrest 280

   Search and Seizure 280

   Other Aspects of Police Investigation 282

Prosecution of Crime and the Duty to Disclose 283

The Criminal Trial Process 285

   Criminal Courts 285

   Pretrial Procedures 287

   The Trial 289

   Defences 290

   Sentencing 291

Youth Criminal Justice Act 294

Indigenous Peoples and the Criminal
Justice System 295

Chapter Summary 299

Key Terms 299

Further Reading 299

Review Questions 300

Exercises 300

PART IV
Working with the Law

11 The Practice of Law: Careers,
Education, and Ethics 303

Learning Outcomes 304

Introduction 304

Origins and Development of the Legal Profession 305

Legal Practitioners in Canada Today 305

   Judges and Other Adjudicators 306

   Lawyers 306

   Paralegals 308

   Law Clerks 310

   Legal Administrative Assistants and
     Legal Assistants 310

   Notaries 311

   Other Law-Related Positions 312

Ethics and the Practice of Law 313

   Judges 314

   Lawyers 315

   Paralegals, Law Clerks (Ontario), and
     Legal Assistants 324

Notaries 324
Other Legal Professionals 324

Chapter Summary 326

Key Terms 327

Further Reading 327

Review Questions 328

Exercises 328

12 Access to Justice and Law Reform 331

Learning Outcomes 332

Introduction 332

Access to Legal Services 333
Legal Aid Plans 333
Pro Bono Legal Services 334
Increased Use of Paralegals 335
Prepaid Legal Services Plans 335
Legal Scholarship 336

Courts and Alternative Dispute
Resolution Mechanisms 336
Negotiation 336
Mediation 336
Arbitration 337

Public Access to Legal Information 338

Government Measures to Enhance Access to Justice   339
Improving Court Processes 339

Increasing Access to Government Information 340
Creating Public Advocacy Offices 340
Improving Access to Justice for Indigenous Peoples   341

Law Reform 343
Law Reform Commissions 343
Public Inquiries 344
Political Demonstrations 345
National Organizations and Lobbying 345
Public Interest Groups as Interveners 346

Chapter Summary 347

Key Terms 347

Further Reading 347

Review Questions 348

Exercises 348

APPENDIXES

A Constitution Act, 1867 351

B Constitution Act, 1982 363

Glossary 375

Index 383

Credits 397

Table of Cases

Andrews v Law Society of British Columbia, [1989] 1 SCR 143, 1989 CanLII 2 173
Anns v Merton London Borough Council (1977), [1978] AC 728, [1977] 2 All ER 492 (HL) 190
Attorney General of Nova Scotia v Attorney General of Canada,
   [1951] SCR 31, [1950] SCJ No 32 (QL) 253
Baker v Canada (Minister of Citizenship and Immigration), [1999] 2 SCR 817, 1999 CanLII 699 265
Bardal v Globe & Mail Ltd, 1960 CanLII 294, 24 DLR (2d) 140 at 145 (Ont H Ct J) 207
Bebawi, R c, 2020 QCCS 22 235
Bell Canada v Canada (Attorney General), 2019 SCC 66 261
Beckman v Little Salmon/Carmacks First Nation, 2010 SCC 53 53
Bhasin v Hrynew, 2014 SCC 71 200
Big M Drug Mart Ltd, R v, [1985] 1 SCR 295, 1985 CanLII 69 168
Bliss v Attorney General of Canada, [1979] 1 SCR 183, 1978 CanLII 25 82
C (MH), R v, (1988), 46 CCC (3d) 142, 1988 CanLII 3283 (BCCA) 284
Calder v Attorney-General of British Columbia, [1973] SCR 313, 1973 CanLII 4 . . . . 51, 52, 53, 80, 208
Canada (Attorney General) v Bedford, 2013 SCC 72 . . . . 278, 300
Canada (AG) v Lavell, [1974] SCR 1349, 1973 CanLII 175 82
Canada (Director of Investigation and Research) v Southam Inc,
   1991 CanLII 1702 (Comp Trib) 241
Canada (Judicial Council) v Girouard, 2019 FCA 148 314
Canada (Minister of Citizenship and Immigration) v Vavilov, 2019 SCC 65 . . . . 261, 263-64, 268
Canadian National Railway Co v McKercher LLP, 2013 SCC 39 321
Carter v Canada (Attorney General), 2015 SCC 5 172
Casimel v Insurance Corp of British Columbia
   (1993), 106 DLR (4th) 720, 1993 CanLII 1258 (BCCA) 50, 55
Celgene Corp v Canada (Attorney General), 2011 SCC 1, [2011] 1 SCR 3 124
Century 21 Canada Limited Partnership v Rogers Communications Inc, 2011 BCSC 1196 201
Childs v Desormeaux, 2006 SCC 18 226
Citizens' Insurance Co of Canada v Parsons (1881), 7 App Cas 96 (PC) 98
Coldwater First Nation v Canada (Attorney General), 2020 FCA 34 . . . . 100, 209
Collins, R v, [1987] 1 SCR 265, 1987 CanLII 84 281
Cooper v Hobart, 2001 SCC 79 190
Coughlin v The Ontario Highway Transport Board, [1968] SCR 569, 1968 CanLII 2 253
Crookes v Newton, 2011 SCC 47 196
Dagg v Canada (Minister of Finance), [1997] 2 SCR 403, 1997 CanLII 358 340
Daley, R v, 2007 SCC 53 291
Daniels v Canada (Indian Affairs and Northern Development), 2016 SCC 12 53
Daviault, R v, [1994] 3 SCR 63, 1994 CanLII 61 291
Delgamuukw v British Columbia, [1997] 3 SCR 1010, 1997 CanLII 302 . . . . 52, 53, 208-9
Dobson (Litigation Guardian of) v Dobson, [1999] 2 SCR 753, 1999 CanLII 698 191
Doe 464533 v ND, 2016 ONSC 541 188
Donoghue v Stevenson, [1932] AC 562, [1932] All ER 1 (HL) 12, 35, 190
Dunsmuir v New Brunswick, 2008 SCC 9 261
Edwards v Canada (AG), [1930] AC 124, 1929 CanLII 438 (PC) 81

Egan v Canada, [1995] 2 SCR 513, 1995 CanLII 98. 174
Fearon, R v, 2014 SCC 77. 175
First Nations Child and Family Caring Society of Canada v Attorney General of Canada
    (for the Minister of Indian and Northern Affairs Canada), 2016 CHRT 2. 166
Ford v Quebec (Attorney General), [1988] 2 SCR 712, 1988 CanLII 19. 176
Frank v Canada (Attorney General), 2019 SCC 1. 170
Girouard v Canada (Attorney General), 2019 FC 1282 314
Gladue, R v, [1999] 1 SCR 688, 1999 CanLII 679. . . . . 287, 292-93, 296
Grant, R v, 2009 SCC 32, [2009] 2 SCR 353 175
Guerin v The Queen, [1984] 2 SCR 335, 1984 CanLII 25 (SCC) 52, 208
Haida Nation v British Columbia (Minister of Forests), 2004 SCC 73 . . . . 53, 263-64
Honda Canada Inc v Keays, 2008 SCC 39 207
Hong Kong Fir Shipping Co Ltd v Kawasaki Kisen Katsha Ltd,
    [1962] 1 All ER 474, [1962] 2 QB 26 (CA) 34, 35
Ipeelee, R v, 2012 SCC 13. 293
Irwin Toy Ltd v Quebec (Attorney General), [1989] 1 SCR 927, 1989 CanLII 87 . . . . 168, 236
Jarvis v Swan Tours, [1973] 1 QB 233 (Eng CA). 227
Jones v Tsige, 2012 ONCA 32 188
Just v British Columbia, [1989] 2 SCR 1228, 1989 CanLII 16 266
Kazenelson, R v, 2018 ONCA 77. 235
Keegstra, R v, [1990] 3 SCR 697, 1990 CanLII 24. 168
Knight v Indian Head School Division No 19, [1990] 1 SCR 653, 1990 CanLII 138. 265
Krieger v Law Society of Alberta, 2002 SCC 65 284
Ktunaxa Nation v British Columbia (Forests, Lands and Natural Resources Operations),
    2017 SCC 54 171
Law Society of New Brunswick v Ryan, 2003 SCC 20. . . . . 317, 323
London Street Tramways Co v London City Council, [1898] AC 375 (HL) 33
Love v Acuity Investment Management Inc, 2011 ONCA 130. 207
M'Alister (or Donoghue) v Stevenson, [1932] AC 562, [1932] All ER 1 (HL) 12
Marshall, R v; Bernard, R v, 2005 SCC 43 . . . . 53, 58, 208
Metron Construction Corporation, R v, 2013 ONCA 541 235
Miazga v Kvello Estate, 2009 SCC 51 284
Morgentaler, R v, [1988] 1 SCR 30, 1988 CanLII 90. 172
Mustapha v Culligan of Canada Ltd, 2008 SCC 27. 192
Newfoundland Telephone Co v Newfoundland (Board of Commissioners of Public Utilities),
    [1992] 1 SCR 623, 89 DLR (4th) 28 250
Norberg v Wynrib, [1992] 2 SCR 226 226
Oakes, R v, [1986] 1 SCR 103, 1986 CanLII 46. . . . . 168, 169-70
Oickle, R v, 2000 SCC 38 281
Oler, R v, 2019 BCSC 784. 217
Powley, R v, 2003 SCC 43 . . . . 45, 50, 53, 55
Practice Statement, [1966] 3 All ER 77 (HL). 33
Prebushewski v Dodge City Auto (1984) Ltd, 2005 SCC 28 243
Rankin (Rankin's Garage & Sales) v JJ, 2018 SCC 19 190
Reference re Environmental Management Act, 2019 BCCA 181. 100
Reference re Environmental Management Act, 2020 SCC 1. 100
Reference re Remuneration of Judges of the Provincial Court (PEI),
    [1997] 3 SCR 3, 1997 CanLII 317. 151
Reference re a Resolution to amend the Constitution, [1981] 1 SCR 753, 1981 CanLII 25. 112
Reference re Same-Sex Marriage, 2004 SCC 79. . . . . 100, 109
Reference re Section 293 of the Criminal Code of Canada, 2011 BCSC 1588. 217
Richard v Time Inc, 2012 SCC 8 245
Roncarelli v Duplessis, [1959] SCR 121, 1959 CanLII 50. 19

Rylands v Fletcher (1868), LR 3 HL 330. 193-94

Salomon v Salomon & Co Ltd, [1896] UKHL 1, [1897] AC 22. 235

Sauvé v Canada (Chief Electoral Officer), 2002 SCC 68. 170

Scott v Scott, [1913] AC 417 150

Shoppers Drug Mart Inc v 6470360 Canada Inc
 (Energyshop Consulting Inc/Powerhouse Energy Management Inc), 2014 ONCA 85. 235

Sparrow, R v, [1990] 1 SCR 1075, 19960 CanLII 1704. . . . . 52, 55

St Catharines Milling and Lumber Co v R, (1887), 13 SCR 577, 1887 CanLII 3 (SCC) 51, 52

Stinchcombe, R v, [1991] 3 SCR 326, 1991 CanLII 45 . . . . 284, 288

Strother v 3464920 Canada Inc, 2007 SCC 24. 321

Sullivan, R v, 2020 ONCA 333 291

Taku River Tlingit First Nation v British Columbia (Project Assessment Director), 2004 SCC 74. 264

Tatton, R v, 2015 SCC 33. 291

The Queen v Chandler (1869), 12 NBR 556 (SC) 76

Toronto (City) v York (Township), 1938 CanLII 252, [1938] AC 415 (UKJCPC) 132

Truchon v Attorney General of Canada, 2019 QCCS 3792 (CanLII) 172

Tsilhqot'in Nation v British Columbia, 2014 SCC 44 . . . . 53, 208-9

Van der Peet, R v, [1996] 2 SCR 507, 1996 CanLII 216 . . . . 52, 79

Vriend v Alberta, [1998] 1 SCR 493, 1998 CanLII 816 174

Wallace v Canadian Pacific Railway, 2011 SKCA 108 321

Watt v Hertfordshire County Council, [1954] 2 All ER 368, [1954] 1 WLR 835 (CA). 191

Whiten v Pilot Insurance Co, 2002 SCC 18 . . . . 9, 10, 36

Preface

Our objective in writing the second edition of *A Brief Introduction to Law in Canada* is, like that of the first edition, to provide a theoretical basis for understanding the law and its development in the Canadian context and to examine the key features of our legal system. It is based on our more expansive *Introduction to Law in Canada*, also in its second edition (2019).

We have tried to be inclusive, imagining how readers from, or interested in, all parts of Canada would interpret the book's relevance. When citing statutory or case law, for example, we have represented as many regions as possible. And in our discussion of the division of powers under the Constitution, the territories are included alongside the provinces in our explanations of the relevant principles.

We also wanted to reflect Canada's social and cultural diversity. For example, we describe how we are a bijural nation primarily influenced by the common law and civil law traditions; we look at how Indigenous peoples have contributed, and continue to contribute, to our legal heritage; and we examine how the *Canadian Charter of Rights and Freedoms* has shaped equality and other rights.

At the same time, we have been mindful that law is a tool for the regulation of individuals and societies and has a very practical side. As well as introducing the law in a way that is accessible, we have attempted to describe it in sufficient detail to be useful. Part I covers theory and context. Part II examines the Canadian Constitution, including how legislative power is divided between our federal, provincial, and territorial governments; how executive power is used to administer the law; how judicial power is distributed through our system of courts; and, finally, how civil liberties and the guarantee of rights and freedoms under the Charter influence our laws. In Part III, we consider an array of subject areas—including tort law, contract law, property law, family law, administrative law, and criminal law—allowing readers to take the next steps in their studies and providing them with a firm legal grounding wherever their future career paths may take them. Part IV concludes the book by looking at legal professionals and their ethical obligations to the public and others and by examining access to justice and law reform.

In this abridged introduction, however, we have reduced our coverage of some areas. For example, we have limited our discussion of legal systems in other countries; included fewer historical references; shortened our expositions on reading and understanding legislation and case law; and omitted some topics altogether, such as public international law. On the other hand, we have covered new developments in the law, including in the areas of constitutional law and civil liberties, administrative law, criminal law, and access to justice. We have also included a new section in Chapter 2 on Indigenous law.

It is our hope that this text will serve as a useful guide for all students studying the law—including those in legal programs (law, paralegal, notary, law clerk, legal assistant, and related areas), justice studies, criminology, security and policing, border services, social work, history, business, and political science—and for anyone else who is interested in learning how the law operates in Canada.

Our thanks go out to the following reviewers for providing their helpful feedback and suggestions during the development of this edition: Gargi Mukherji, Sheridan College; Katherine Willis, St Lawrence College; Chris Nowlin, Langara College; Sabrina Ngo, University of the Fraser Valley; Ashlyn O'Mara, Seneca College; Aaron Felt, Memorial University; and John Borrows, University of Victoria. We would also like to thank the team at Emond Publishing for helping us put this book together, in particular: Sandy Matos, developmental editor; Holly Dickinson, copy editor; and Leanne Rancourt, proofreader, for their thoughts and contributions during the galley stages; and Kelly Dickson, Kimberley Griffiths, and Mike Thompson for their support and encouragement.

As a final note, although Philip Sworden's name no longer appears on the book cover, I have continued to use the pronouns "our" and "we" throughout most of this edition to reflect the fact that the book started as a joint project with Philip. In this small way, I hope to acknowledge his contributions to the text and our shared vision for an introduction to law and to honour his memory.

John Fairlie
Vancouver, British Columbia

In Memoriam—A Special Dedication

In 2016, Philip Sworden retired from teaching and moved to Australia with his wife to spend more time with his son and grandchildren. Sadly, he passed away unexpectedly in 2018. Philip had a passion for teaching law, Canadian history, and celebrating the diversity of his students and Canada's peoples. His passions are reflected in this book. Philip was also an accomplished painter, inspired by Tom Thomson and the Group of Seven. He will be greatly missed, and this edition is dedicated to his memory.

John and the Emond team

Serene Algonquin by Philip Sworden, 2011.

About the Author

John Fairlie, BMus, LLB, LLM, is a faculty member in the School of Legal Studies at Capilano University in North Vancouver. He was the lead developer of Capilano's Bachelor of Legal Studies (Paralegal) degree, which launched in 2010. He has taught a range of law courses—including introduction to law, jurisprudence, torts, contracts, property, family, company, business, criminal, evidence, and legal research—and was chair of the School of Legal Studies from 2007 to 2019.

He has also lectured at Simon Fraser University in the School of Criminology and at the British Columbia Institute of Technology in the School of Business. His other pursuits have included working as a legal writer and co-running a small importing business.

In addition to this book, John is a co-author of *Introduction to Law in Canada*, also published by Emond (2nd edition, 2019), and the author of *How to Find Canadian Law*, a guide to legal research (1999).

PART I
Theory and Context

CHAPTER 1 What Is Law?

CHAPTER 2 Common Law, Civil Law, and Indigenous Legal Systems

CHAPTER 3 From the Reception of English and French Law into Canada to the Charter

1 What Is Law?

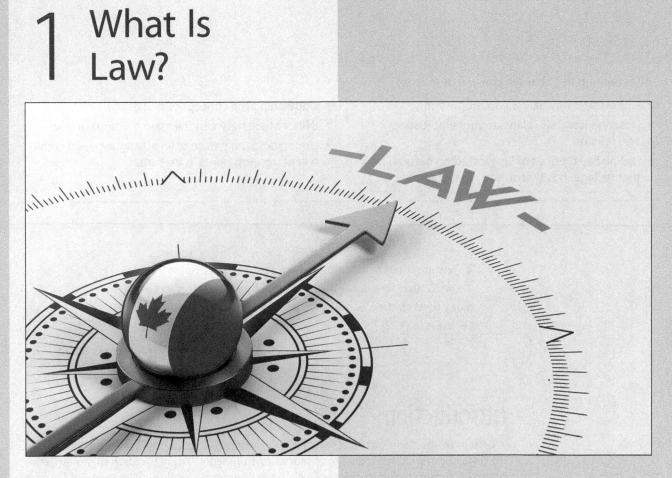

Introduction 4

How Law Is Commonly Defined 5

How Law Relates to Other Rules 6

Theories of Law: "Ought" and "Is" 12

Rule of Law 17

Divisions of Law 20

Legal Terminology 23

Chapter Summary 24

Key Terms 24

Further Reading 24

Review Questions 25

Exercises 25

After reading this chapter, you will be able to:

- Understand how law is commonly defined.
- Describe how law relates to morality, justice, and religion.
- Define key theories of law, including natural law theory, legal positivism, and legal realism.

- Understand the concept of rule of law.
- Differentiate between the main divisions of law.
- Understand the nature of legal language and some recent developments in that area.

> Few questions concerning human society have been asked with such persistence and answered by serious thinkers in so many diverse, strange, and even paradoxical ways as the question "What is law?"
>
> HLA Hart, *The Concept of Law*, 2nd ed
> (Oxford: Oxford University Press, 1994) at 1

Introduction

A defining characteristic of most societies is the existence of an imposed order on what would otherwise be unpredictable and unsafe social environments. One of the instruments societies use to create and maintain order is law.[1] In this chapter, we explore the concept of law at a basic level to set the stage for a more detailed examination of Canadian law in later chapters.

We begin with some definitions of law and then examine the law's relationship to morality and ethics, justice, and religion. Next, we consider some prominent theories of law—including natural law theory, legal positivism, and legal realism—and the rule-of-law doctrine. In the final sections, we look at the divisions of law and at some of the challenges and developments associated with legal terminology.

Exploring these ideas will raise questions that cannot always be answered. Absolutes and certainties are sometimes unavailable, and accepting the limitations of the law can be challenging. However, despite its imperfections, the law is an endlessly rich and fascinating field with the potential to engage you for a lifetime.

---

1 One historian's view is that law, religion, and other social constructs, such as human rights, are "fictions" or "myths" that are not rooted in instinct or objective reality outside of people's imaginations. They are tools used to allow large communities of relative strangers to cooperate and work together toward common goals. These "imagined" orders can be relatively stable if there are enough believers. Changing an imagined order involves the simultaneous substitution of a new order in the consciousness of these believers. This requires a complex catalyst, such as a political, an ideological, or a religious movement. See Yuval N Harari, *Sapiens: A Brief History of Humankind* (Toronto: Penguin Random House Canada, 2016). There are contrary views. For example, in the area of equality rights, there is some evidence that the desire for equal treatment and opportunity is in our biology (a part of our social DNA), so equality is more than a fiction or myth that can be changed with a new system of beliefs. Selfishness and greed, assuming that these traits are also instinctual, must then compete against fairness at a biological and not just an intellectual level.

Definitions of Law

The more laws and restrictions there are, the poorer people become. … The more rules and regulations, the more thieves and robbers.

Laozi (ca. 6th century BCE),
Tao Te Ching

[L]aws were invented for the safety of citizens, the preservation of States, and the tranquility and happiness of human life.

Marcus Tullius Cicero (106–43 BCE),
De Legibus, or *On the Laws*

Law … is nothing else than an ordinance of reason for the common good, made by him who has care of the community, and promulgated.

Thomas Aquinas (1225–1274),
Summa Theologica

Law … is the perfection of reason.

Edward Coke (1552–1634),
Institutes of the Laws of England

No enactment of man can be considered law unless it conforms to the law of God.

William Blackstone (1723–1780),
Commentaries on the Laws of England

[L]aw [may be thought of] as a set of rules which are generally obeyed and enforced within a politically organized society.

Peter Shears & Graham Stephenson,
James' Introduction to English Law, 13th ed
(London, UK: Butterworths, 1996) at 6

How Law Is Commonly Defined

Is the law simply what we say it is, or is there more to it than that? Is it subject to higher standards? Do our legal rules have to meet these standards in order to qualify as law? For example, if our Parliament passed a law providing that all green-eyed babies must be given up for medical stem cell research, would that law be valid? Why or why not?

We will return to these questions later in the chapter, in connection with various conceptions of justice and theories of law. For now, though, we need a basic definition of law to help us get our bearings. There are many definitions available (see Box 1.1). For our purposes, the law can be defined as a system of enforceable rules that governs the relationship between the individual members of a society and between those members and the society itself. The law allows us to live in communities safely and to balance the needs of the individual with the needs of the community.

Types of Rules

The rules that make up the law can be divided into many categories. A good place to start is to say that there are three types of rules:

1. *General norms or standards of behaviour.* These rules usually prohibit certain activities, such as murder or careless driving.
2. *Condition rules.* These rules establish conditions or requirements that must be met before certain activities can be carried out. Licensing requirements for conducting a business, getting married, or driving a car are examples of these rules.

3. *Power-conferring rules.* These rules allow you to define your own legal relationship within certain contexts. The main examples of power-conferring rules are those relating to the law of contract; they allow you to set the terms and conditions that govern your relationship with another person, such as when purchasing or selling property and in business transactions generally. Other examples of power-conferring rules include those relating to wills, which allow you to control how your property is distributed after you die.

Structure of Rules

Whatever the type of rule involved, the form of the rules is relatively standard:

If A, B, and/or C, then X.

A, B, and C are elements (or conditions) that must be present for X (the legal result) to occur. Many legal rules involve three elements (A, B, and C), but some rules may have more elements and some fewer. More complex rules may involve sub-elements.

If the elements are joined by "and" (A, B, *and* C), the list is called "conjunctive." This means that all elements must be satisfied or proved in order for the legal result to occur. If the elements are joined by "or" (A, B, *or* C), the list is called "disjunctive." In this case, only one of the elements must be satisfied or proved in order for the legal result to occur. (Sometimes the elements may be part of a hybrid list, part conjunctive and part disjunctive.)

The crime of murder, simply defined, is structured in the conjunctive form. If an accused engages in behaviour (element A: the *actus reus* element) that causes the death of the victim (element B: the causation element), and if the accused means to cause the death (element C: the intention or *mens rea* element), then the accused is guilty of murder and subject to punishment (X: the legal result).

Now let's look at a motor vehicle accident liability case. Such a case, again, simply defined, is also based on a conjunctive list of elements. If a defendant's driving falls below the standard of a "reasonable motorist" (element A: the standard-of-care element), and this causes a loss to the plaintiff (element B: the causation element), and the loss is a compensable form of injury (element C: the damages element), then the defendant is liable in negligence and obliged to pay damages to the plaintiff (X: the legal result).

Legal claims are based on these underlying rules, regardless of their type or precise form. To succeed with a claim—that is, to obtain a legal result—you must establish all the required elements and sub-elements of the case. This is true whether you are a prosecutor in a criminal case or a plaintiff in a civil case.

How Law Relates to Other Rules

One thing that distinguishes the law from other kinds of rules is its enforceability. This enforcement occurs by way of state-sanctioned mechanisms or institutions such as police forces, regulatory agencies (such as those that license certain activities), and court systems. The state does not enforce other kinds of rules—moral and ethical codes, abstract principles of justice, and religious tenets—until they have been incorporated into or recognized as law.

Law, Morality, and Ethics

Most of us have a sense of right and wrong, and many of us are in general agreement about what is moral or immoral, ethical or unethical. Despite this common ground, ethical and moral disagreements frequently arise. What seems immoral to one person may be acceptable to another. For example, when is it acceptable to lie? Never? Sometimes, depending on the circumstances? Always?

We can define **morality** as a system of values or principles concerning what is right or wrong with respect to human behaviour. Morality can be viewed from two perspectives:

1. descriptive or
2. normative.

morality
standards of right and wrong, often associated with personal character

When we consider morality from a *descriptive* perspective, we are simply observing what a particular community believes to be right or wrong. We are offering no judgments or endorsements of these beliefs. We are describing things as they are.

When we approach a moral system from a *normative* perspective, we believe it to have an objective truth, or to set an ideal standard. We accept it and are invested in it. A moral code viewed in this light tells us how we should behave. Conduct that offends the code is considered immoral.

However, regardless of the perspective, when morality's relationship to law is examined, we are confronted with difficult questions. When is a matter a purely moral issue and therefore outside of the law's reach? When does immoral conduct also become illegal? Whose moral code is the standard?

These questions have been debated for decades. In Britain in the 1960s, Lord Devlin (1905–1992) and HLA Hart (1907–1992) argued opposing views. Devlin's conservative position was that a shared morality is the foundation of society and should be broadly enforced by the law. Hart's more liberal position was that there are many personal moralities that the law should only minimally enforce (when necessary for safe and peaceful cooperation in society).[2] In Canada, Pierre Elliott Trudeau (1919–2000) championed a similar view to Hart's when he stated that "there's no place for the state in the bedrooms of the nation."[3]

More recently, changes to Canada's *Criminal Code*[4] relating to prostitution, the recreational and therapeutic use of cannabis, and assisted dying have sparked similar debates. In general terms, it is fair to say that accepted morality is reflected in the law in some respects and that changing moral views can be a stimulus for legal change.

Ethics also deals with standards of human behaviour—with what is right or wrong, good or bad. Ethics, like morality, can be approached from either a descriptive or a normative point of view. There are many branches and sub-branches of ethics; one of these is meta-ethics. This area deals with basic questions, such as how we determine what is good or bad and the nature of behavioural standards.

ethics
standards of right and wrong, often applied to specific groups—for example, professions

There is no generally accepted distinction between morality and ethics. One view is that morality focuses on personal character and behaviour, whereas ethics focuses on standards of behaviour in defined social settings. The word "ethics" is frequently used in professional contexts to describe standards of conduct. Most professions, including the legal profession, have codes of ethics. Members who offend these codes may be disciplined

---

2   The Hart–Devlin debate took place in the context of calls for the liberalization of laws in the areas of "private" morality, dealing with such things as abortion, prostitution, and homosexuality. Hart's view won the day, and the law was liberalized in these areas. Capital punishment was also abolished.

3   Trudeau made the statement in 1967 as justice minister when questioned about a bill he had introduced in the House of Commons that decriminalized homosexual acts. The bill, which also covered other matters, including the easing of abortion rules, was passed into law (see also Box 1.4).

4   RSC 1985, c C-46.

by their governing bodies. We will examine codes of ethics in the legal profession in more detail in Chapter 11.

Concerning the relationship between law and ethics, Earl Warren (1891–1974), a former American chief justice, said the following: "In civilized life, law floats in a sea of ethics."[5] In other words, a civilized society contains many ethical rules and standards; they vary according to context and generally do not have the status of law. They do, however, underlie the society's laws, which are applicable to everyone and enforceable by the state. Both the law and the myriad ethical rules and standards are rooted in a common value system.

Law and Justice

A Roman statesman once said the following regarding justice: "Let justice be done, though the heavens fall." This view posits that justice must prevail regardless of the consequences. But what is justice? Where does it come from? Are conceptions of justice fixed, or can they change? The answer to these questions depends, of course, on how we define justice (see Box 1.2).

Justice is often associated with criminal law. A person might ask, "Where's the justice?" when a person commits a serious crime and is freed on a technicality or "Where's the justice?" when a person commits murder but only serves jail time. Such questions, often raised during news coverage of criminal trials, reflect the view that our criminal laws place too much emphasis on the rights of criminals and process and that sentencing is generally too lenient. However, theories of justice can transcend criminal law and apply to other areas of the law too.

Justice can be considered in two ways:

1. as an end in itself or
2. as an instrument, or a means to an end.

Definitions of Justice

What I say is that "just" or "right" means nothing but what is in the interest of the stronger party.

Plato (429–347 BCE),
The Republic

Revenge is a kind of wild justice; which the more man's nature runs to, the more ought law to weed it out.

Francis Bacon (1561–1626), "Of Revenge"
from *Essayes or Counsels, Civill and Morall* (1625)

Justice is truth in action.

Benjamin Disraeli (1804–1881),
House of Commons Speech, 1851

Injustice anywhere is a threat to justice everywhere.

Martin Luther King (1929–1968), Letter from Birmingham Jail,
Alabama, 1963

Overcoming poverty is not a gesture of charity. It is an act of justice. It is the protection of a fundamental human right, the right to dignity and a decent life.

Nelson Mandela (1918–2013), Speech at Trafalgar Square in
London, England, 2005

Everyone knows that law is not the same thing as justice.

SM Waddams, *Introduction to the Study of Law*, 8th ed
(Toronto: Carswell, 2016) at 4

---

5   Earl Warren, "Address" (Speech delivered at the Louis Marshall Award Dinner of the Jewish Theological Seminary, Americana Hotel, New York City, 11 November 1962) [unpublished].

Proponents of justice as an end in itself take what is called a **deontological** (from the Greek *deon*, meaning "obligation, duty") approach. This approach is non-consequentialist and rule based; it holds that certain rights and responsibilities are fundamental and universal and that justice consists in upholding them. These standards are objectively good and true and require no analysis of social consequences or outcomes for their justification. They are an end in themselves.

Proponents of justice as a means to an end (an instrument) take what we call the **instrumentalist** approach. A desired social end might be, for example, a safer community or the reduction of poverty. A method of regulation would be a just one, according to this view, if it succeeded in making the community safer or in reducing poverty. This distinction—between deontological and instrumentalist conceptions of justice—offers us a general organizing principle and a context in which to discuss three established and commonly cited models of justice: corrective justice, retributive justice, and distributive justice. And as we will see next, a state's laws will vary according to the model of justice it accepts.

deontological
theories that focus on the inherent rightness or wrongness of behaviour, without regard to the behaviour's consequences or outcomes

instrumentalist
theories that focus on something—for example, justice or the law—as a means to an end

Corrective Justice

The concept of justice most closely attached to the deontological approach—that is, taking justice as an end in itself—is **corrective justice**. Central to the notion of corrective justice is the belief that a person has a moral responsibility for the harm he causes another and that the loss must be rectified or corrected, usually in the form of compensation. (Corrective justice is also known as "rectificatory justice.") Responsibility here is defined by the relationship between the causer and the injured, and there is no regard to consequences beyond the required rectification. The rectification (or correction) itself represents justice.

An early exposition of corrective justice appears in the *Nicomachean Ethics* by Aristotle (384–322 BCE).[6] His theory addresses the imbalance that occurs when one person injures another; corrective justice restores the status quo, which is presumed to be good.

Recently, a Supreme Court of Canada (SCC) judge remarked that private law—and, certainly, tort law (a specific area of private law)—can be "viewed primarily as a mechanism of compensation. Its underlying organizing structure remains grounded in the principle of corrective justice."[7] As the judge's words suggest, corrective justice underlies private law disputes. But it can also apply to criminal cases, where restitutionary orders—based on principles of corrective justice—are possible. For example, a person who physically or mentally injures a victim or damages his property in the course of committing a crime and is convicted of the crime may be ordered, at the time of sentencing, to compensate the victim directly for these losses.[8]

corrective justice
theory of justice according to which (1) a person has a moral responsibility for harm caused to another, and (2) the latter's loss must be rectified or corrected

Retributive Justice

If corrective justice is more relevant to private law disputes, then **retributive justice** relates more to criminal law and to the perceived need for punishment. Does it reflect a *deontological* or an *instrumentalist* approach? Retribution can be viewed either as an end in itself—that is, as a self-evidently appropriate response to morally wrong behaviour—or as the means to socially worthwhile objectives, such as public safety or appeasement. To the extent that one accepts both views, it is a hybrid theory, with both deontological and instrumentalist aspects.

retributive justice
theory of justice based on *lex talionis*, or the law of retaliation

---

6 See Aristotle, *Nicomachean Ethics*, translated by David Ross and revised by JL Ackrill & JO Urmson (Oxford: Oxford University Press, 1998) book V at 4, 8; Jonathan Barnes, *Aristotle: A Very Short Introduction* (Oxford: Oxford University Press, 2000) at 4-5.

7 See LeBel J in *Whiten v Pilot Insurance Co*, 2002 SCC 18 at para 152.

8 See the *Criminal Code*, ss 718, 738.

The Image of Justice

The personification of justice as a woman blindfolded* and holding scales and a sword is based on ancient iconography. Her earliest incarnations were the Egyptian goddesses Maat and Isis. Later, in the classical era, she appeared as the Greek goddess Themis and then as the Roman equivalent of Themis: Justitia.

In the modern context, the personification of justice is often referred to as Lady Justice. Her statues are seen outside courthouses, government buildings, universities, and other buildings where order and fairness are central ideals. The blindfold represents impartiality, her scales signify that she will weigh opposing claims and conflicting evidence, and the sword represents the power she has to enforce her judgments. This icon of justice is associated with the law in general. The statue of Lady Justice atop the dome above the Old Bailey courthouse in London, pictured here, does not include a blindfold. Courthouse pamphlets explain that this is because Lady Justice originally did not wear one. The blindfold did not become standard until the 16th century.

The law of retaliation, or *lex talionis*, is often cited as the guiding principle of retributive justice. We are all familiar with such phrases as "an eye for an eye," "measure for measure," and "let the punishment fit the crime." These expressions are based on the idea that the response should be proportional to the wrong. Retaliation, which is linked to revenge, has always been part of human behaviour. Some of the oldest recorded references to *lex talionis* are in the *Code of Hammurabi*, a collection of Babylonian laws compiled around 1750 BCE.

Although retributive justice is most relevant to criminal law, it can play a role in private law disputes—for example, in tort and breach of contract cases. This doesn't happen often because such disputes rarely involve behaviour worthy of punishment. Yet Canadian courts have awarded punitive damages—that is, damages over and above compensatory damages and designed as a form of punishment—in cases where a defendant's behaviour has been particularly offensive. Such awards have both a moral end-in-itself (deontological) purpose and an instrumentalist purpose, as the SCC has made clear. They "give a defendant his or her just desert (retribution)," but they also "deter the defendant and others from similar misconduct in the future (deterrence)" and "mark the community's collective condemnation (denunciation) of what has happened."[9]

Distributive Justice

distributive justice
theory of justice concerned with appropriate distributions of entitlements, such as wealth and power, in a society

The third form of justice, **distributive justice**, is concerned with the way assets and entitlements are shared among members of a society. In his *Nicomachean Ethics*, Aristotle also described distributive justice. His model of distributive justice provides for the distribution of a state's bounty (property and honours, for example) according to merit.

---

9   *Whiten v Pilot Insurance Co*, *supra* note 7 at para 94.

One of the most significant modern commentators on the subject of distributive justice, and on the subject of justice generally, is John Rawls (1921–2002). In *A Theory of Justice*, he expressed his general conception of justice as follows:

> All social values [or social primary goods]—liberty and opportunity, income and wealth, and the social bases of self-respect—are to be distributed equally unless an unequal distribution of any, or all, of these values is to everyone's advantage.[10]

Injustice, then, according to Rawls, becomes "inequalities that are not for the benefit of all."[11]

Today, debates about distributive justice can arise in the context of, for example, automobile insurance and workers' compensation programs. The debates concern whether and how to *distribute* the cost of injuries. Should all members of a group pay premiums or fees for the sake of the smaller number of members who will suffer injuries? If all members of the group contribute to the fund, then the few unlucky enough to suffer injuries will not have to bear the full weight of medical costs themselves. Outside of this type of context, however, distributive justice plays only a small role in Canadian private law.

Distributive justice is more concerned with public law matters than with private law. For instance, a government initiative may involve raising taxes to pay for new programs to assist a minority community. In other words, the cost of the new program, which would benefit only a portion of the population, would be distributed among all taxpayers.

BOX 1.4

Pierre Trudeau's Just Society

The phrase "just society" was coined by former Canadian prime minister Pierre Elliott Trudeau during his bid to win the 1968 Liberal Party leadership campaign. It has become part of Canada's political terminology.

Trudeau meant the phrase to apply not to any specific policy but to his entire platform. In the years that followed, he applied it to all of his policies: official bilingualism; decriminalizing sexual matters involving consenting adults; and his crowning achievement, the patriation of the Canadian Constitution and the enactment of the *Canadian Charter of Rights and Freedoms*.* Equality was a central theme of the just society.

*   Part I of the *Constitution Act, 1982*, being Schedule B to the *Canada Act 1982* (UK), 1982, c 11.

Law and Religion

In most of the world, there is now a separation between church and state. However, that is a relatively recent phenomenon. In the West, the Christian religion has certainly influenced the law. For example, in one of the most important common law court decisions ever handed down, Lord Atkin formulated his neighbour principle. This principle deals with a person's obligation to take care when engaging in any activity that might affect

---

10   John Rawls, *A Theory of Justice*, revised ed (Cambridge, Mass: Harvard University Press, 1999) at 54.

11   *Ibid.*

other people. In describing this principle, Atkin drew directly from the biblical parable of the Good Samaritan:

> The rule that you are to love your neighbour becomes in law, you must not injure your neighbour; and the lawyer's question, Who is my neighbour? receives a restricted reply. You must take reasonable care to avoid acts or omissions which you can reasonably foresee would be likely to injure your neighbour. Who, then, in law is my neighbour? The answer seems to be—persons who are so closely and directly affected by my act that I ought reasonably to have them in contemplation as being so affected when I am directing my mind to the acts or omissions which are called in question.[12]

Atkin's decision and the principle it expresses continue to shape the law of torts—specifically, the law of negligence—in Canada today. See Chapter 7 under the heading "Negligence."

Our Constitution also reflects the influence of religion. The preamble to the *Canadian Charter of Rights and Freedoms* (often simply referred to as the Charter) reads as follows: "Whereas Canada is founded upon principles that recognize the supremacy of God and the rule of law." This reference to God is slightly paradoxical in the Canadian context; the Charter's guarantee of religious freedom (s 2) in our multicultural society has made references to specific religious influences, such as Atkin's reference to the parable of the Good Samaritan, less acceptable in recent years.

Theories of Law: "Ought" and "Is"

jurisprudence
also known as "philosophy of law" or "science of law"; concerns theories that are used to describe, explain, or criticize the law

Our concern in this section is with **jurisprudence**—the philosophy or science of law—and the theories that compose it. There are many theoretical approaches to the law, and there is some overlap with justice theories. A common way of classifying theories of law is to divide them into two main categories: *analytic* and *normative*. Analytic theories are concerned with what the law *is*, whereas normative theories are concerned with what the law *ought to be*. The two are not mutually exclusive. There are hybrid theories (such as feminist legal theory) and other theories (such as legal realism) that seem to challenge or subvert the distinction between analytic and normative.

Analytic jurisprudence generally concerns critical, explanatory, and value-free assessments of the law. It may involve, for example, examining the internal logic of a system of rules. Sometimes the investigations are more empirical in nature—that is, concerned with experience or observation rather than with theory. The common thread between analytic theories of law is that they do not involve value judgments. They are concerned with what law is, not what it ought to be.

Normative jurisprudence, on the other hand, generally concerns the rightness or wrongness of the law based on various conceptions of justice, fairness, and morality. It involves making value judgments; it is evaluative, not explanatory. Because there are no objective, universally accepted standards of right and wrong, normative legal analysis depends less on logic and empiricism than analytic jurisprudence does.

The following is a brief overview of three well-established fields of jurisprudence: natural law theory, legal positivism, and legal realism.

---

12   *Donoghue v Stevenson*, [1932] AC 562 at 580, [1932] All ER 1 (HL). The case name is also sometimes cited as *M'Alister (or Donoghue) v Stevenson*.

Natural Law Theory

The idea of a higher power or source that guides our behaviour or offers us an ideal standard is likely as old as the first human communities. A person who believes this to be the case—who believes that such external standards exist—believes that human-made (or positive) law is subject or subordinate to this higher or **natural law**.

What is the source of natural law? Is it divine law, virtue, reason, morality, human nature, or some invisible wellspring? How do we come to know it? Do we need a special class of intermediaries to interpret it for us? How do we evaluate the standards that are to guide us? Do we base these standards on the beneficial results they promote, or do we base them on unchangeable notions of what is right, independent of the consequences they produce? Is it sometimes a combination of these? Natural law theorists have offered different answers to these questions.[13]

Aristotle, whom some consider the father of natural law theory, saw natural law as being based on virtue and the golden mean (that is, the idea that everything should be done in moderation). Aristotle developed these ideas in his *Nicomachean Ethics*, along with his theories of justice mentioned above. In the Middle Ages, the Catholic theologian Thomas Aquinas (1225–1274) reworked Aristotle's ideas about natural law into a Christian context. Natural law was associated with the divine wisdom of God, which humans can know and participate in through the power of reason given to us by God. According to Aquinas, when we correctly use our abilities to reason, we will be informed by permanent and immutable natural laws, which, when followed, will ensure the validity of our positive laws.[14]

Hugo Grotius (1583–1645) was a Dutch jurist who contributed to the natural law debate primarily by secularizing it, or removing its religious basis. He believed that natural law would still exist even if God didn't. He grounded natural law in human nature itself, arguing that natural law was discoverable through the use of "right reason," which, to Grotius, is a human faculty rather than a divine one.

Connected to this secularizing shift was the development of social contract theory. This is the theory that human existence in earliest times was not ideal—or, as Thomas Hobbes (1588–1679) wrote in *Leviathan*, it was "nasty, brutish, and short"—and that, to secure our safety and happiness, we surrendered our absolute freedom and agreed to be governed by rulers through a "contract." The English philosopher John Locke (1632–1704) believed that this contract was based on natural law, which he identified with human or natural reason. French philosopher and writer Jean-Jacques Rousseau (1712–1778) had similar ideas (see Box 1.5).

An important modern exponent of natural law was the Harvard law professor Lon Fuller (1902–1978). In *The Morality of Law*, Fuller wrote about the connection between morality and law and described "eight ways to fail to make law."[15] Some of these include failing to publicize laws and make them known to the parties affected by them, enacting rules that contradict one another, and making rules but failing to enforce them.

natural law
source of law that is higher than human-made (or positive) law and with which human-made law must comply in order to be valid

---

13   In this chapter, we have employed a wide definition of natural law, one that includes all definitions of law that are not of human invention. Some writers, from a theological perspective, separate divine law (or God's law) from natural law, resulting in three broad categories of law: divine law, natural law, and human law. Others argue that the only certain and relatively immutable laws are the laws of science. All other laws are human-made, and these are either openly acknowledged as such or attributed to a contrived external source to support their validity.

14   Aquinas believed that there were, in fact, four main types of law—eternal law, divine law, natural law, and human law—all of which are connected in some way to God's will.

15   Lon L Fuller, *The Morality of Law*, revised ed (New Haven, Conn: Yale University Press, 1965) ch 2.

BOX 1.5

Natural Law and the US Declaration of Independence

The works of Locke and Rousseau, among others, provided a philosophical basis for the American Revolution in the late 1700s, in which 13 colonies fought a war to break free from British rule. According to Locke, natural law teaches us that we are all equal and have certain natural rights to life, health, liberty, and possessions. Locke also maintained that no government has the authority to deny its people these rights. If it does, it is placing its subjects in a state of nature, and war is justified.

Rousseau's most famous work is *The Social Contract* (1762). It begins as follows: "Man was born free, yet everywhere he is in chains. One man thinks himself the master of others, but remains more of a slave than they."

The second sentence of the Declaration reads as follows: "We hold these truths to be self-evident, that all men are created equal, that they are endowed by their Creator with certain unalienable Rights, that among these are Life, Liberty and the pursuit of Happiness."

These words constitute the philosophical justification for the American Revolution.

Jean-Jacques Rousseau

Fuller maintained that we need to avoid these pitfalls in order to achieve a legal system that is just and consistent. Unlike earlier natural law thinkers, Fuller did not believe that we discover natural law through external absolutes based on religion or reason. Instead, he believed that law has its own "internal" moral standards (his eight principles of legality), and by following them a state's enactments can truly be characterized as law.[16]

The work of Margaret Mead (1901–1978), an American cultural anthropologist, points to some interesting possibilities concerning natural moral standards—natural laws grounded in human nature that appear across cultures. Her study of human populations revealed common standards of behaviour and common rules relating to such things as justified and unjustified killing, the prohibition of incest, and, in many societies, the right to own private property.[17]

Other writers have suggested looking to various theories of justice and fairness to help define natural law principles. Still, there is no consensus on how to answer the key questions regarding natural law discussed earlier in this section or on how to resolve contradictions between natural law and positive law.

Legal Positivism

legal positivism
theory that the only valid source of law is the principles, rules, and regulations expressly enacted by the institutions or persons within a society that are generally recognized as having the power to enact them

Natural law's main opposition as a legal theory is **legal positivism**. On the scale of "ought" and "is" (that is, normative versus analytic jurisprudence), legal positivism tends more toward the analytic. It evaluates laws and legal systems without, for the most part, placing value judgments on them. As legal theories go, it is a relatively recent development.

16   Fuller's principles of legality are related to procedural fairness (see below under "Rule of Law") and are not moral principles in the ordinary sense. See also above under "Law, Morality, and Ethics."

17   Margaret Mead, "Some Anthropological Considerations Concerning Natural Law (1961)" in Michael DA Freeman, ed, *Lloyd's Introduction to Jurisprudence*, 10th ed (London, UK: Sweet & Maxwell, 2020) 185.

Legal positivism's first real proponent was John Austin (1790–1859), a professor of jurisprudence at the University of London (now University College). He was a utilitarian, believing the goal of legislation to be the greatest happiness of the greatest number, but he was better known for his analytic method and his use of precise terminology to define positivist thinking. His greatest work is *The Province of Jurisprudence Determined*.[18] The core positivist beliefs, according to Austin, are as follows:

1. All commands of the sovereign are valid and enforceable.
2. "Commands" means **positive law**—that is, human-made rules.
3. "The sovereign" refers to the person or agency who receives habitual obedience in a given society.
4. Laws made in accordance with the society's existing formalized and recognized process are valid, regardless of so-called natural law, morality, or any external standard.

positive law
human-made law, as opposed to a higher law (natural law) that transcends persons or institutions

More recently, professors HLA Hart and Joseph Raz (1939–) have continued the positivist tradition. They have made the point that holding positivist beliefs does not prevent the person from either having moral standards or advocating for their legal recognition. However, law and morality are essentially separate spheres, and the validity of the former is not tied to the latter (see above under "Law, Morality, and Ethics").

It is fair to say that the Anglo-Canadian legal tradition has a positivist basis. The principle of parliamentary sovereignty (which we discuss in more detail in Chapter 4) means that laws made in accordance with the recognized process are valid without reference to external standards. The Charter provides for self-imposed standards based on a kind of natural law, but legislators may disregard them in making law (by invoking s 33 of the Charter, the notwithstanding clause; see Chapter 6 under the heading "An Overview of the Charter").

In times of political stability, when governments follow commonly accepted standards and the existing order is acceptable to the majority of people in the society, legal positivism is effective as an underlying theory. It endorses the validity of what *is*. But during times of war or oppressive regimes, people begin to question the validity or fairness of existing laws and to measure them against external standards. According to legal positivism, a bad law properly constituted under a cruel regime is a valid law. To many people, this might seem a shortcoming in the theory.

Legal Realism

Legal realism is a field of jurisprudence that arose in the 20th century. It was largely a response to the emphasis on logic that dominated British positivist theory in the 1800s. The first writers of legal realist theory were American (see Box 1.6), but Scandinavian countries, too, saw a strong theoretical movement in this direction. American and Scandinavian adherents shared the positivist view that law is a human invention. However, they also advocated a more intensely empirical study of the process by which laws are made and applied, and they argued that law is subject to many of the flaws and weaknesses of other human activities.

Several legal realists focus on the judicial process—a single part of the overall legal system—and, specifically, on how judges make their decisions. In theory, the primary role of judges is to make decisions by applying rules to specific fact situations (in other words, the cases appearing before them). Many of us believe, or would like to think, that certainty and objectivity surround this process: in go the facts, and out comes the unerring, inevitable decision.

legal realism
theory, developed in the United States and Scandinavian countries, that encouraged a more thoroughly empirical study of the process by which laws are made and applied

---

18   John Austin, *The Province of Jurisprudence Determined* (London, UK: John Murray, 1832).

BOX 1.6

Legal Realism and Oliver Wendell Holmes (1841–1935)

Oliver Wendell Holmes was born in Boston, Massachusetts, and fought in the American Civil War on the Union side. He studied law at Harvard and practised law for 15 years before becoming, first, a legal editor, then a professor at Harvard Law School, and, finally, a judge of the Supreme Judicial Court of Massachusetts. He was appointed to the United States Supreme Court in 1902 and retired in 1932 at age 90, the oldest judge ever to serve on the Court. He left a legacy of ideas that are still relevant today.

Holmes was an early leading light in a new way of thinking about law. He is noted for many famous pithy sayings, including the following: "The life of the law has not been logic; it has been experience."* With this statement, Holmes was not denying that logic plays an important role in the law; he was affirming his belief that practical experience is a more important factor in the law than pure reason is. Opposed to the doctrine of natural law, he took a pragmatic approach to the study of law and felt it was largely about predicting what courts would decide. He is considered by some to be the father of legal realism in America.

*   Oliver Wendell Holmes, *The Common Law* (Boston: Little, Brown and Company, 1881) at 1.

Many realists say otherwise. They argue that non-legal disciplines, such as history and economics, can help us understand judges' decision-making. Also relevant are the intellectual ability, personality, morality, biases, and circumstances of the judge in question. For instance, what tensions or conflicts is the judge experiencing outside the courtroom in her personal life? How rested and prepared is she for the case? One American jurist, Jerome Frank (1889–1957), remarked that "a judicial decision might be determined by what the judge had for breakfast."[19] It is not surprising that experienced litigators frequently advise their clients to settle and avoid the uncertainty of going to court.

The study of legal realism has waned since the 1980s. It was a theory that pointed out some weaknesses in legal systems, but it did not come up with solutions. Other kinds of legal theories have arisen during this period, but most bear the influence of legal realism's empiricism, pragmatism, and openness to other disciplines.

Other Legal Theories

We have described three important theories of law, but there are many others—too many to describe in detail here. However, a brief mention of some of them will give you an idea of the vast scope of jurisprudential study.

Utilitarianism is an ethical philosophy (mentioned above in connection with John Austin and legal positivism). It originated with Jeremy Bentham (1748–1832) and measures the utility or worth of actions in terms of the overall happiness they generate. It is instrumentalist

---

19   Jerome Frank, *Courts on Trial* (Princeton: Princeton University Press, 1973 [originally published in 1949]) at 208.

(or consequentialist)—taking the law as a means to an end—and underlies any current theory of law that considers the law to be a tool for social change. The "law and economics" movement espouses one such theory; through an economic analysis of law, it measures a law's worth in terms of its capacity to increase social wealth. This theory substitutes wealth for the "happiness" of the utilitarian standard, happiness being difficult to measure.

The **law and society** and **sociology of law** disciplines are related in that they look at law from a broad social, interdisciplinary perspective. The difference between these two theories is that the first identifies most closely with legal studies and the second with sociology. One important issue debated in both is whether laws come about through consensus or through conflict within a society.

Marxist theories of law are based on the writings of Karl Marx (1818–1883), Friedrich Engels (1820–1895), and other advocates of communist policies. Such policies address the distribution of wealth and the class structure within a society. These kinds of legal theories are compatible with distributive justice thinking, which, as we have seen, is also concerned with the distribution of wealth (among other benefits) in a society.

Feminist theories of law cover a wide range of issues and can be seen as an outgrowth of the women's movement in the 1960s and 1970s and as having connections with critical legal studies (described next). Although works on women's rights are not new—for example, the seminal work *A Vindication of the Rights of Woman* (1792) by Mary Wollstonecraft (1759–1797)—feminist jurisprudence arguably did not establish itself until the 1970s. The modern literature in this field is far-reaching and diverse and goes well beyond issues concerning reproductive rights, violence against women, equal pay for equal work, and sex discrimination more generally. Feminist legal theories also examine such areas as how gender roles and women's subordination are perpetuated and concealed by the law's assumptions, language, and structure; how patriarchal interests are supported by the law; and what legal reforms are necessary to improve the position of women in society.

As a theory, **critical legal studies** (also known as "CLS" or "Crit") is an outgrowth of American legal realism. Forged as an independent theory in the late 1970s, it is largely concerned with exposing law as an instrument of the rich and powerful. Its adherents have suggested many legal reforms. Emerging from CLS is **critical race theory** (also known by its acronym, "CRT"), a kindred theory of feminist jurisprudence. The difference between feminist legal theory and critical race theory is that the latter focuses on race-based inequities in place of gender-related issues.

Rule of Law

The term **rule of law** concerns fairness in the administration of the law. Its central tenets are that

1. everyone in a society, regardless of their social or political position, should be treated equally before the law, and
2. power under the law should not be used arbitrarily.

The rule of law is one of the cornerstones of the Canadian legal system and is expressly referred to in the Charter.

Origins

Principles related to the rule of law appear in the legal culture of the Greeks and Romans. Cicero, a famous orator who lived in an era of Roman democracy, is quoted as saying the following: "[We] are servants of the law, that we all may be free."

law and society
kind of legal study that looks at law from a broadly social, interdisciplinary perspective

sociology of law
kind of sociological study that looks at law from a broadly social, interdisciplinary perspective

Marxist theories of law
legal theories, based on the writing of the communist philosopher Karl Marx, that are concerned with the distribution of wealth in a society; related to distributive justice theories

feminist theories of law
theories of law that generally concern the legal, social, and economic rights of and improving opportunities for women

critical legal studies
theory of law largely concerned with exposing law as an instrument of the rich and powerful

critical race theory
theory of law that focuses on race-based inequities; an offshoot of critical legal studies

rule of law
key legal concept whose central tenets are that everyone is equal before the law and that power under the law should not be used arbitrarily

The concept of the rule of law was generally not recognized in the next phase of Western history, the Dark Ages. It resurfaced in the Middle Ages, when King John of England (1167–1216), after enjoying supreme power for much of his reign, was suddenly faced with a revolt by his barons. He capitulated by executing one of the most famous legal documents in the democratic world, the *Magna Carta* (1215). In this document, he agreed to give up some of his power and to recognize some of his barons' liberties. The seeds of the rule of law were planted with the *Magna Carta*. Some of its provisions are still in force today in England and in Canada.

Basic Principles

In the modern era, rule-of-law doctrine was given prominence through the work of AV Dicey (1835–1932), who is widely recognized as one of the fathers of modern English constitutional law. He popularized the phrase "rule of law" in his most influential work, *An Introduction to the Study of the Law of the Constitution* (London, 1885). We may summarize Dicey's three core rule-of-law principles as follows:

1. The law must trump the influence of arbitrary power. It follows from this that no one can be punished except for breach of an established law as determined through an established process before the courts.
2. No one is above the law, whatever his place in society—or, to put it another way, the law applies equally to everyone. Again, recognized judicial process will make the rulings to ensure that this occurs.
3. Personal rights and liberties must be protected by giving every person the ability to apply to the courts for a remedy should any of those rights and liberties be denied.

Dicey's first principle recognizes that the arbitrary application of state power will lead to discontent. Rules must be in place and then enforced according to a set process. Otherwise, punishment for their infringement will not be seen as fair (see Box 1.7).

Adherence to the second principle is a key feature of true democracies; it distinguishes them from autocracies, where rulers have absolute power, and from societies where the law applies to people differently depending on their status. Equal application of the law promotes respect for the legal system.

Dicey's third principle highlights the idea that the courts are instrumental in protecting our rights and liberties. How effective that protection is depends directly on how free our courts are from political interference. (The separation of powers between the legislative, executive, and judicial branches of government is discussed in Part II of this book.)

It has been frequently observed that Dicey's conception of the rule of law relates more to *procedural* fairness than to *substantive* fairness. In other words, it deals with when and how laws are applied (procedural) rather than with the fairness of the laws themselves (substantive). Dicey does not propose any general guidelines for determining whether laws themselves are fair.

Most modern definitions of the rule of law follow Dicey's approach; they leave substantive fairness issues to be dealt with in official bills of rights and human rights documents at both the national and international levels. Modern definitions are generally concerned with elaborating and expanding on the concept of procedural fairness. Although there is no agreed-upon set of principles underlying the rule of law, some examples (beyond Dicey's core principles) include the following:

1. Laws should be clear and prospective (that is, they should not punish past legal actions based on changed, new laws).
2. The judiciary should be independent (that is, able to apply and uphold the law free from any interference or influence).
3. Legal services and access to the courts should be affordable (if they are not, the existence of laws that assist or protect us will be of little use).[20]

BOX 1.7

Roncarelli v Duplessis

The SCC's decision in *Roncarelli v Duplessis** is one of Canada's defining decisions on abuse of power. It illustrates all three of Dicey's rule-of-law principles but in particular highlights how the arbitrary use of discretionary power violates the rule of law.

Roncarelli was a Jehovah's Witness and a successful restaurateur in Montreal. During this period, in the mid-20th century, Quebec was trying to control the distribution of religious literature. A number of Jehovah's Witnesses were arrested for contravening local by-laws that prohibited peddling without a licence. Roncarelli provided bail for many of those arrested. To prevent his further involvement, Maurice Duplessis, who was then the premier and attorney general of Quebec, ordered the province's liquor commissioner to permanently revoke Roncarelli's liquor licence, which had been issued under the *Liquor Act*.[†] Roncarelli sued for damages.

A majority of the SCC found in favour of Roncarelli and ordered Duplessis to pay damages. Justice Rand's judgment, one of two majority judgments, is a classic from our country's highest Court. He reasoned that legislative discretion given to government administrators must be exercised in accordance with the general policies underlying the legislation itself. Extraneous factors such as differing religious beliefs or opposing political views, which are wholly unconnected to the purpose of the legislation (here the regulation of the sale of alcohol in the public interest), must not influence the use of the discretion.

Justice Rand stated the following:

> In public regulation of this sort there is no such thing as absolute and untrammelled "discretion," that is, that action can be taken on any ground or for any reason that can be suggested to the mind of the administrator. ... "Discretion" necessarily implies good

faith in discharging public duty; there is always a perspective within which a statute is intended to operate; and any clear departure from its lines or objects is just as objectionable as fraud or corruption. Could an applicant be refused a permit because he had been born in another province, or because of the colour of his hair? The ordinary language of the legislature cannot be so distorted.[‡]

He also said the following:

> To deny or revoke a permit because a citizen exercises an unchallengeable right totally irrelevant to the sale of liquor in a restaurant is equally beyond the scope of the discretion conferred. ... [W]hat could be more malicious than to punish this licensee for having done what he had an absolute right to do in a matter utterly irrelevant to the *Liquor Act*? Malice in the proper sense is simply acting for a reason and purpose knowingly foreign to the administration, to which was added here the element of intentional punishment by what was virtually vocation outlawry.[§]

Justice Rand intimated that arbitrary power might be exercisable only if there were express statutory language authorizing such an action. He stated the following:

> [N]o legislative Act can, *without express language*, be taken to contemplate an unlimited arbitrary power exercisable for any purpose, however capricious or irrelevant, regardless of the nature or purpose of the statute.[#]

*   [1959] SCR 121, 1959 CanLII 50.

†   *Alcoholic Liquor Act*, RSQ 1941, c 255.

‡   *Supra* note * at 140.

§   *Supra* note * at 141.

Supra note * at 140 (emphasis added).

---

20 Note that these more recent definitions are similar or identical to many of Lon Fuller's principles of legality discussed above under "Natural Law Theory."

Rule of Law in the International Context

Rule of law is not just an English or a Western idea anymore. It has a global influence. The United Nations, established in 1945 and now with 193 member states, has made the rule of law a standing agenda item for its General Assembly since 1992. The Security Council has focused on this issue on a number of occasions, emphasizing the need to adhere to rule-of-law principles in times of conflict.[21]

Canada follows the rule of law, and all member states of the UN profess to do so. A number of organizations collect and summarize data that offer a snapshot of the rule of law around the world on an annual basis. Among them are the World Bank, which measures adherence to the rule of law in over 200 economies as one of its six governance indicators, and the World Justice Project, whose *Rule of Law Index* provides detailed data on 128 countries and jurisdictions.[22]

Divisions of Law

The law can be divided into many different subject areas (see Figure 1.1). However, not all of these areas are discrete and self-contained. For example, insurance law overlaps with contract law (many issues in insurance turn on the interpretation of insurance policies, which are usually based on a contract). Furthermore, some areas of the law are really amalgams, or combinations, of other areas: sports law, for instance, can involve contracts, torts, criminal law, labour law, and even civil liberties. Also, and quite commonly, a single fact situation may give rise to claims in different areas. For example, if one person physically assaults another person, that could lead to a private law tort claim for battery *and* a criminal law charge of assault.

substantive law
law that deals with core rights and obligations

Canada's Constitution—as we will see in Chapters 3 and 4—divides the power to make and regulate the law in the various areas between the federal Parliament and the provincial legislatures. Just as there is overlap between some areas of the law, the jurisdiction over some areas overlaps and is shared by Parliament (federal) and the legislatures (provincial). The area of family law, for example and as we shall see in Chapter 7, is partly regulated by Parliament and partly by the legislatures. Furthermore, there is now a strong movement in Canada to recognize Indigenous law as a parallel system of law in relation to Canadian law generally. (Indigenous law is discussed in more detail in Chapter 2.)

procedural law
law relating to the process by which core rights and obligations are determined and enforced

In the top box of Figure 1.1 is law in general—the whole concept, which includes positive law and natural law (as earlier defined). Figure 1.1 further subdivides positive law according to whether the laws deal with core rights and obligations (**substantive law**) or with the processes for determining and enforcing those rights and obligations (**procedural law**). Running parallel to these two basic types of law are **practice norms**, which influence the law's application when the legal profession is involved (which is frequently the case in more complex legal matters). These norms are not always legally binding, and when they are not, they are not "law" in the strict sense. However, legal professionals' adherence to high standards in practice—whether they are legally enforceable or not—is critical in any system of law that is effective and fair.

practice norms
ethical standards and legal skills that legal practitioners must follow and possess to deliver legal services effectively

domestic law
law of a particular state or society

Note how these three broad categories (that is, substantive law, procedural law, and practice norms) feed into **domestic law** (law of particular states), Indigenous law (law of Indigenous peoples within states), and **public international law (or international law)** and its

public international law (or international law)
law relating primarily to international treaties and customs and to interstate relationships

---

21   See "United Nations and the Rule of Law," online: *United Nations* <http://www.un.org/ruleoflaw>.

22   To view data maps and tables illustrating countries' rankings according to various factors, visit <https://www.worldbank.org>, <https://info.worldbank.org/governance/wgi>, and <https://worldjusticeproject.org>. The interpretation of and adherence to the principles of rule of law vary dramatically between some countries. For example, according to the World Justice Project's *Rule of Law Index 2020*, Denmark ranks first (1) and Venezuela last (128).

branches (law dealing primarily with the treaties, customs, and other legal sources governing interstate relationships). Both domestic law and public international law have substantive and procedural law aspects to them and often require the intercession of the legal profession. How these broad categories feed into Indigenous legal traditions, however, is not as easily defined.

FIGURE 1.1 Divisions of Law

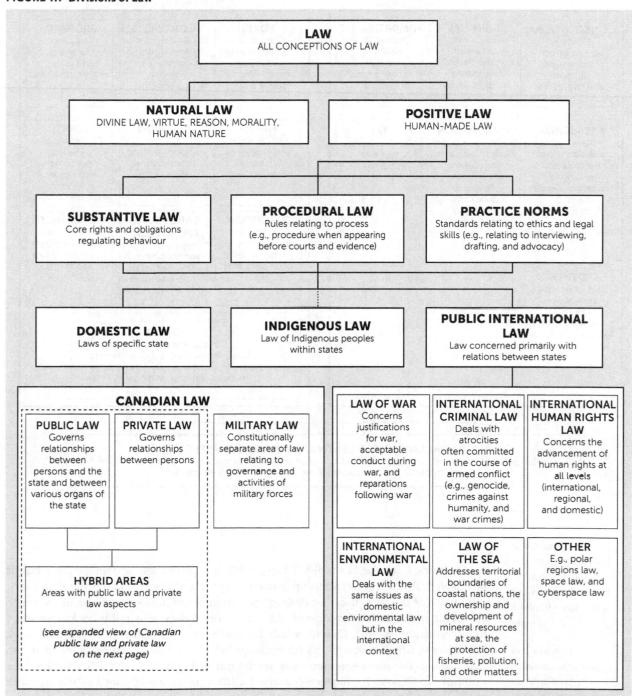

(Figure 1.1 is concluded on the next page.)

FIGURE 1.1 Divisions of Law   (concluded)

PUBLIC LAW Governs relationships between persons and the state and between various organs of the state	**PRIVATE LAW** Governs relationships between persons

CONSTITUTIONAL
Concerns governmental powers and structures and civil liberties

CRIMINAL
Regulates behaviour deemed particularly socially offensive

ADMINISTRATIVE
Deals with the relationship between government agencies and persons

ABORIGINAL
Involves rights, land claims, and other legal issues relating to Indigenous peoples based on Canadian law

IMMIGRATION
Governs immigration into and deportation from Canada (often broadly defined to include matters relating to citizenship)

TAX
Concerns various forms of government taxation

OTHER
E.g., municipal, competition, (antitrust) and public safety

TORTS
Consists of a broad range of civil wrongs not covered by other areas

CONTRACTS
Governs the making and enforcing of binding agreements

PROPERTY
Regulates ownership and use of real, personal, and intellectual property

FAMILY
Defines rights and obligations within family relationships

COMPANY
Relates to corporations and their structures and dealings

EQUITY
Concerns trusts, fiduciary relationships and obligations, and equitable remedies

SUCCESSION
Concerns wills and estates and the transmission of property after death

LABOUR AND EMPLOYMENT
Deals with rights and obligations in unionized and non-unionized work environments

INSURANCE
Pertains to insurable interests, insurance policies, and claims

OTHER
E.g., commercial transactions, secured transactions, real estate transactions, conveyancing, landlord and tenant, professional malpractice, creditors' remedies, and conflict of laws

HYBRID AREAS: PUBLIC LAW AND PRIVATE LAW ASPECTS
E.g., business and consumer, bankruptcy and insolvency, securities, sports, entertainment, elder law, animal law, environmental, natural resources, fisheries, admiralty (or maritime) law

public law
law dealing with the legal relationship between a state and individual members of the state

private law
law that concerns the relationships between persons

Domestic Canadian law is divided into public law, private law, and military law. **Public law** deals with the legal relationship between persons and the state and between the various organs of the state. It can be divided into a number of different areas, many of which are set out in Figure 1.1 and some of which are covered elsewhere in this book: Chapters 4 to 6 (constitutional law), Chapter 9 (administrative law), and Chapter 10 (criminal law). **Private law**, which concerns the relationships between persons, can be subdivided into many areas. The more common ones are set out in Figure 1.1, and a few of these are examined in Chapter 7; Chapter 8 concerns business and consumer law, a hybrid area with public law and private law aspects.

Military law is a special area, a constitutionally separate and largely self-contained system of law regulating the Canadian Forces. It governs the armed forces during times of conflict and in peacetime, at home and abroad.

Finally, note that there are many hybrid areas of law—areas that defy easy classification and that cross broad subdivisions in the law. This is reflected in the boxes linking public law and private law and domestic law and public international law. Note also that military law, although usually classed as a separate area of domestic law, has public law and private law aspects, as well as a public international law aspect.

military law
constitutionally separate and relatively self-contained system of law regulating the Canadian Forces

Legal Terminology

Law is expressed through language. Over the centuries, the language of the law has developed a life of its own. In fact, most students of law feel as if they are learning a whole new language when they begin reading cases and legislation. It's not just that some of the words—particularly the Latin ones—are unfamiliar; it's also the way the words are used and how legal arguments are structured.

HLA Hart referred to a shadow of uncertainty surrounding legal rules. As an example, earlier in this chapter, in our discussion of the structure of rules, we referred to the negligence rule in the context of motor vehicle accidents and noted that the standard of care used to determine negligence was based on the "reasonable motorist." But who is the reasonable motorist? What does this term mean? How well does the reasonable motorist drive? Does it matter if it's dark and raining or if she's rushing to the hospital because her child is sick at the time of the accident? These are the kinds of uncertainties that the language of the law is often unable to avoid. What fills these shadows or grey areas of uncertainty around the legal rules? According to Hart, it is discretion (that is, the discretion of judges when interpreting the law).

Apart from the uncertainty it involves, legal language is very specialized. Its language is so unfamiliar that it may sometimes seem to you that the legal profession has conspired to make the law more difficult than it is. Recently, there has been a reaction against such specialized, deliberately obscure professional language. This has been a positive development for students and legal practitioners, as well as the public. Expressions such as "hereinafter," "aforesaid," "notwithstanding the generality of the foregoing," and "the said party of the first part" are no longer considered impressive.

A plain-language movement in business and law started in the 1970s. This change is often attributed to banks' wishing to simplify their contracts for consumers to prevent unnecessary litigation. The benefits of this measure were soon clear to all, and the plain-language movement has continued to the present day. Nowadays, in most jurisdictions, legislative counsel responsible for drafting legislation are directed to use plain language in writing or rewriting legislation; they are given lists of "difficult" words and told to replace them with clear ones. Newly appointed judges in many jurisdictions are now required to go to "judge school" for training, which includes sessions on how to write clear, structured judgments.

Despite these developments, legal language remains a challenge to new law students. To help you navigate the language of the law, there are resources that you can use alongside your other course materials. These include dictionaries and collections of legal words and phrases. (See the list of dictionary resources under Further Reading at the end of this chapter.) Also, be sure to use the glossaries in this and other law books. Finally, pay close attention to context when reading legal materials; there are many expressions, such as "common law" and "civil law," that have multiple meanings within the law (see Chapter 2). The context in which they are used should help you with the intended meaning.

CHAPTER SUMMARY

Law is not easily or simply defined. We have seen that, at a basic level, it relates to the regulation of human activity by way of rules. The broad categories of rules and their forms are relatively standard, but the content of rules varies greatly. In many societies, especially liberal democracies of the West, the law is distinguished from other types of rules, such as those based on morality, justice, or religion.

There are numerous theories concerning the law and its development. Some of these theories are analytic in nature, describing what the law is. Others are normative in nature, describing what the law ought to be. Some theories have both analytic and normative elements. Many countries, including Canada, have a positivist and an analytic bias.

The concept of rule of law informs the law in most countries around the world, including Canada, although the degree to which its core tenets are adhered to varies. Rule of law concerns fairness in the administration of the law. Equality in the application of the law and balance in the use of power are key principles.

Law has many divisions and subdivisions, particularly within the domestic law category, and many areas of overlap between these divisions. As you continue your legal studies, you will become more familiar with these specific areas, as well as with the legal terminology used to describe them. With that familiarity will come a greater comfort with the whole area of the law.

KEY TERMS

corrective justice, 9
critical legal studies, 17
critical race theory, 17
deontological, 9
distributive justice, 10
domestic law, 20
ethics, 7
feminist theories of law, 17
instrumentalist, 9
jurisprudence, 12

law and society, 17
legal positivism, 14
legal realism, 15
Marxist theories of law, 17
military law, 23
morality, 7
natural law, 13
positive law, 15
practice norms, 20
private law, 22

procedural law, 20
public international law
  (or international law), 20
public law, 22
retributive justice, 9
rule of law, 17
sociology of law, 17
substantive law, 20

FURTHER READING

BOOKS AND ARTICLES

Arlidge, Anthony & Igor Judge, *Magna Carta Uncovered* (Oxford: Hart, 2014).

Black's Law Dictionary, 11th ed (Eagen, Minn: Thomson West, 2019), and the abridged version, *Black's Law Dictionary, Abridged*, 10th ed (Eagen, Minn: Thomson West, 2015).

Culver, Keith C, ed, *Readings in the Philosophy of Law*, 3rd ed (Peterborough, Ont: Broadview Press, 2017).

The Dictionary of Canadian Law, 4th ed (Toronto: Carswell, 2011), and the abridged version, the *Pocket Dictionary of Canadian Law*, 5th ed (Toronto: Carswell, 2011).

Freeman, Michael DA, *Lloyd's Introduction to Jurisprudence*, 10th ed (London, UK: Sweet & Maxwell, 2020).

Fuller, Lon L, "The Case of the Speluncean Explorers" (1949) 62 Harv L Rev 616.

Fuller, Lon L, *The Morality of Law*, revised ed (New Haven, Conn: Yale University Press, 1965).

Harris, Phil, *An Introduction to Law*, 8th ed (Cambridge, UK: Cambridge University Press, 2016) ch 1.

Hart, HLA, *The Concept of Law*, 2nd ed (Oxford: Oxford University Press, 1994).

Holt, James C, *Magna Carta*, 3rd ed (Cambridge, UK: Cambridge University Press, 2015).

Waddams, SM, *Introduction to the Study of Law*, 8th ed (Toronto: Carswell, 2016) chs 1, 3.

WEBSITES

Irwin Law, *Canadian Online Legal Dictionary*: <http://www.irwinlaw.com/cold>.

United Nations and the Rule of Law: <https://www.un.org/ruleoflaw>.

REVIEW QUESTIONS

1. Describe the basic structure(s) of legal rules.

2. What is one way to differentiate morality from ethics?

3. Is a lie ever justified in your opinion? Include in your answer the correct use of the words "deontological" and "instrumentalist."

4. Compare corrective justice with retributive justice, including the areas of law to which they most clearly apply.

5. Briefly describe the relationship between law and religion.

6. Describe natural law in your own words.

7. Describe legal realism in your own words.

8. What is the rule of law, and what are some of its basic principles?

9. What is the difference between substantive law and procedural law?

10. Briefly describe the plain-language movement and its application to legal terminology today.

EXERCISES

1. Choose a definition of law that, in your opinion, has both strengths and weaknesses. Describe the strengths and weaknesses and then rewrite the definition to remove the weaknesses.

2. Locate and read two speeches or articles by or about Pierre Trudeau and his "just society." Next, describe in your own words what you think a just society is.

3. In your view, does the law of retaliation reflect an innate need or a learned response? Provide reasons to support your view.

4. What is the basic difference between analytic and normative theories of law? If you had to write a paper on one or the other, which would you choose and why?

5. Using the United Nations and the Rule of Law website, locate, read, and summarize two UN documents dealing with the rule of law.

2 Common Law, Civil Law, and Indigenous Legal Systems

Introduction 28

Common Law 30

Civil Law 37

Comparison of the Common Law
and Civil Law Systems 41

Harmonizing Common Law and
Civil Law in Canada 43

Indigenous Law 44

Chapter Summary 56

Key Terms 56

Further Reading 57

Review Questions 57

Exercises 58

The Bayeux Tapestry celebrates the events leading to and culminating in the Norman Conquest of England in 1066 by William the Conqueror and dates to the late 11th century. The French-speaking Norman king came from mainland Europe (in what is now the Normandy region of France), where the civil law system was developing and now predominates. William's legal reforms in England led to the establishment of another great legal tradition: the common law system.

LEARNING OUTCOMES

After reading this chapter, you will be able to:

- Describe the common law's origins and defining characteristics.
- Describe the civil law's origins and defining characteristics.
- Understand how the common law and civil law systems compare and their relevance in the Canadian context.

- Recognize some of the measures taken in Canada to harmonize the common law and civil law systems.
- Understand the increasing significance of Indigenous law in Canada and how it may be recognized in the future.

Canadian bijuralism is an integral part of our legal heritage.

Anne McLellan, former minister of justice, quoted in M Brunet, *Out of the Shadows: The Civil Law Tradition in the Department of Justice Canada, 1868–2000* (Ottawa: Queen's Printer, 2000) at ii

Introduction

The variety of legal systems, or traditions, that exists in the world today reflects the diverse and sometimes complex histories of the world's peoples. It is important to be aware of the existence and basic structure of other legal systems besides our own for several reasons:

1. *Multiculturalism.* Canada is a multicultural society made up of people from all around the world. To understand something about the traditions of our fellow Canadians can only be a benefit.

2. *Trade.* International trade is necessary for a healthy economy. Knowing how our trading partners in other countries with different systems of law view legal rights and obligations will improve our business relations.

3. *Globalization.* The world has become a smaller place because of technology. The interconnectedness of all peoples is more apparent now than ever, making it increasingly important for us to understand our "neighbours" in other parts of the world.

There is some debate about how best to classify the different systems of law. At least six categories exist, as follows:

1. common law,
2. civil law,
3. customary law (unofficial, often unwritten, rules that have become conventional or habitual within a society and are accepted as legally binding),
4. religious law (primarily Islamic law or sharia),
5. Indigenous law, and
6. mixed or hybrid systems.[1]

---

1   This classification is based on the work of JuriGlobe, a research group affiliated with the Faculty of Law at the University of Ottawa. However, we have added a new category: Indigenous law. JuriGlobe refers to Indigenous law as an example of customary law, but we have classified it separately because of its importance in the Canadian context. For a global overview of legal systems by continent and for data on individual countries, visit JuriGlobe's website at <http://www.juriglobe.ca/eng>.

Roughly half of the world's nations are monosystems using one of the first four legal systems, whereas the other nations, including Canada, employ a mix of systems. The settlement and colonization of our country by two European nations with different legal traditions, and the presence of Indigenous peoples with their own legal traditions, have resulted in a complex mix of systems in Canada.

Officially, Canada is a **bijural** nation. This means that it has two state-recognized legal systems. All regions in Canada, except Quebec, employ the **common law** system. This reflects our English heritage. Quebec, where roughly one-quarter of our population lives, is bijural; the **civil law** applies in respect of private law matters and the common law in respect of public law matters (primarily federal areas, including criminal law). This reflects our French heritage. Quebec's bijuralism is what makes Canada a bijural nation (see Figure 2.1).

bijural
term describing the operation of two legal systems in one jurisdiction, such as the common law and civil law systems in Canada

common law
system of law, based on the English legal tradition, that relies on precedent rather than on codified rules; may also refer to rules as distinguished from equitable principles, or case law as opposed to legislation

civil law
system of law based on codified rules; may also refer to private law

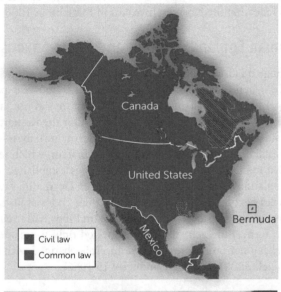

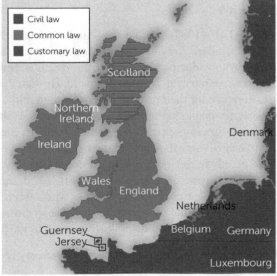

FIGURE 2.1   The Bijural Systems in Canada, the United States, and the United Kingdom
Canada, the United States, and the United Kingdom are often said to have legal systems based on the common law tradition, but that is only partly true. All three places contain areas—Quebec, Louisiana, and Scotland, respectively—in which civil law and common law systems are mixed.

This chapter begins with a look at the first two systems: common law and civil law. Most legal issues in Canada involve one or both of these systems. However, the strength of the recent movement to formally accept Indigenous legal traditions will challenge the status quo, with questions about how best to recognize **Indigenous law** alongside Canada's other two systems. Following the discussion of common law and civil law, there is an introduction to Indigenous law.

Indigenous law
law of Indigenous peoples within states, as distinct from states' laws in relation to them

Common Law

The common law system arose from circumstances unique to England. The system's defining feature is that judges follow precedent. The precedents that are the basis of the system originated with judges who sat in royal courts of justice. These courts were established by early English kings following the Norman invasion of England in 1066.

Law in Pre-Norman England: Romans and Anglo-Saxons

The Roman era in England lasted from 43 CE, when the Romans conquered the island, until the fifth century CE, when they abandoned it. During this 400-year period, the Romans introduced their legal system to Britain. However, this system did not take root in England as it had in continental Europe, and little remained of it after the Roman departure.[2]

Other invaders succeeded the Romans in England. Germanic tribes—the Angles, Saxons, Jutes, and Danes—established the Anglo-Saxon era in Britain, which lasted from the fifth century until the Norman invasion of 1066. These tribes established separate kingdoms across southern England. Each had its own system of Germanic laws based on tribal customs and principles of communal justice. Initially, their codes of justice were not written but were transmitted orally. In time, some Anglo-Saxon kings had their tribes' legal codes compiled in written form. But each tribe's code applied only to its specific territory, and there was no centralized nationwide justice system. This changed with the invasion of the island by the Norman king William the Conqueror in 1066.

Origins of Common Law

feudalism
socio-political system in medieval Europe based on relationships of obligation and allegiance among king, nobles, and subjects, with land given to subordinates in return for loyalty and military support

William the Conqueror (1028–1087), unlike the Anglo-Saxon invaders before him, proceeded to establish a centralized royal kingdom in most of southern England. One way he accomplished this was by introducing a political structure called **feudalism**. Under this system, William claimed ownership of all land on the island. He then distributed large areas of it to favoured nobles in return for their promises of loyalty and military support. The nobles, in turn, granted portions of land to their subjects, known as vassals, in return for their oaths of allegiance. This new socio-political arrangement, with its hierarchical system of obligation and allegiance, helped unify the island under a single monarch. This centralization of authority contributed greatly to the formation of the common law system.

Chancery
department of state established by English monarchs to assist with legal matters and to issue writs

Another way that William gained control over his English domain was to set up a centralized government administration. He and the kings who succeeded him established something called the *curia regis*. This was a group of nobles who advised the king on governing the country. They helped him in the following areas, in particular:

- overseeing departments of state—for example, the **Chancery** for legal matters and the Exchequer for the king's finances;

---

2   George W Keeton, *The Norman Conquest and the Common Law* (London, UK: Ernest Benn, 1966).

- securing royal control throughout the island by issuing royal documents, such as charters, to establish new towns and villages; and

- creating administrative officers, such as sheriffs, who were responsible, within their respective regions of the country, for maintaining the king's powers and privileges.

A further centralizing measure that William introduced was the expansion of the island's legal system through royal courts of justice. These courts were particularly crucial to the emergence of the common law.[3]

Development of a Royal Court System

The Anglo-Norman kings, unlike their Anglo-Saxon predecessors, viewed justice as a royal obligation and believed that, as kings of England, they were responsible for the **king's peace**. This meant that an English king had the right and the duty to preserve public order and to punish anyone who disturbed the well-being of English subjects. A system of criminal law was initiated in the name of the king. In each county, the king appointed justices of the peace to keep order and established a grand jury to seek out suspected wrongdoers and bring them to his judges' attention. Through these measures, which were implemented across most of England, English law began to derive its authority directly from the king.[4]

The royal courts of justice evolved over time. English monarchs such as Henry I (1100–1135) and Henry II (1154–1189) appointed royal judges from the *curia regis* and sent them out on a circuit of the outlying counties, away from the London capital, to preside over the courts. The courts presided over by these travelling judges were known as "assizes." Representing the monarch, these royal judges helped settle local disputes and dealt with local offenders who had contravened the king's peace.

English monarchs set up three separate royal courts of justice—the Court of Common Pleas, the **Court of King's (or Queen's) Bench**, and the Exchequer Court—to decide legal disputes. The Court of Common Pleas decided civil and landholding disputes, the Court of King's (or Queen's) Bench decided criminal matters, and the Exchequer Court decided revenue matters involving the king. The English people favoured these three royal courts. They appreciated the judges' expertise and other features of the courts, including the following:

- their power to summon witnesses;

- their use of juries rather than older modes of trial, such as ordeal or combat (which were physical tests that did not accurately measure the truth of asserted claims);

- their use of written records (which promoted certainty and consistency in decision-making); and

- their power to enforce their judgments.[5]

The Writ System

The royal courts were popular, but they did involve one problematic feature: the writ system of civil procedure. A person—known as the "plaintiff"—who started a civil or non-criminal

king's peace
the ideal peace and well-being of a nation that the English monarch was obliged to uphold and protect

Court of King's (or Queen's) Bench
English court that decided criminal matters

---

3   Raoul C Van Caenegem, *The Birth of the English Common Law* (Cambridge, UK: Cambridge University Press, 1988).

4   William R Cornish, *The Jury* (Harmondsworth, UK: Penguin, 1968).

5   Arthur R Hogue, *Origins of the Common Law* (Bloomington, Ind: Indiana University Press, 1966).

writ
court document,
obtained by a plaintiff,
by which the defendant
was informed that
a particular type
of action had been
started against him

action in these royal courts first had to purchase from the king a specific document called a **writ**. A writ was a written order to a defendant. It came not from the plaintiff but from the king. Affixed with a royal seal, the writ notified a defendant that the plaintiff had a particular complaint or cause of action against him, such as breach of contract, trespass, or assault. It also stated that if the defendant wished to challenge the plaintiff's court action, he must precisely follow the procedures prescribed by the writ.

The problem with this system was that the king could not issue all writs personally; they were too numerous. So the practice arose of having the chancellor, who headed the king's Chancery, issue them instead. Over the course of several centuries, many different writs developed for specific disputes, and each writ had its own formal procedures. The plaintiff's choice of writ became crucial. If plaintiffs chose the wrong writ for their cause of action, later amendment was impossible. At the same time, if no writ was appropriate for the plaintiff's cause of action, then no remedy was available from the royal courts. To overcome these formal, rigid, and increasingly technical pleading rules, litigants began to appeal to the king, who was seen as the fountainhead of justice, to intervene on their behalf.[6] Their appeals were heard by the chancellor, who was the king's representative.

Chancery Separates from Common Law

Court of Chancery
English court, existing
separate from common
law courts, established
to provide equity

Over time, chancellors established a royal court that was separate from the three other royal courts of justice. It was called the **Court of Chancery**, and its purpose was to grant relief on the basis of equitable justice and to adjudicate petitions from plaintiffs appealing outside the writ system. Whereas the other royal courts of justice used the common law, the Court of Chancery created a parallel system of law consisting of its own body of maxims or rules, called **equity**.

equity
discretionary legal deci-
sions offered by judges
in the Court of Chancery,
based on fairness and
providing relief from
the rigid procedures
that had evolved under
common law courts

For example, the common law courts interpreted contracts, particularly contracts involving land, very strictly. If a person who had mortgaged his land (the mortgagor) missed a payment, the mortgagee (or lender) was permitted to exercise his contractual right to take the land in satisfaction. In many cases, this would be unfair, especially if the mortgagor had paid off most of the debt. (The relevant maxim here is "equity abhors a forfeiture.") In such a case, the Court of Chancery could step in and give the mortgagor some extra time (a redemption period) to pay back the lender.

Another special feature of the Court of Chancery was that it could hear disputes informally and quickly, without a jury, and could provide a plaintiff with remedies—for example, specific performance, rectification of a contract, or an injunction—other than monetary damages. These remedies were not available in the three other royal courts.

Judicature Acts

The existence of two completely separate court systems—the royal courts (using common law rules) on the one hand and the Court of Chancery (using equitable rules) on the other—created certain difficulties. These were not resolved until 1873, when the English Parliament passed a series of statutes, the *Judicature Acts*, unifying the courts under one court system. This system was made up of the High Court of Justice (with five specialized divisions) and the Court of Appeal. The system allowed for a further right of appeal to the House of Lords. Both common law and equitable rules could now be administered under one court system. This measure simplified court procedure considerably.

In Canada, each province has its own unified high (or superior) court system with a trial level and an appeal level. These courts—except in Quebec, which employs the civil law system—apply both common law and equitable rules. Generally, the maxim "equity follows the law" governs the relationship between the two sets of rules. This means that the role of

---

6   John H Baker, *An Introduction to English Legal History*, 5th ed (Oxford: Oxford University Press, 2019).

equity is to add to or fill in the gaps left by the common law, based on principles of fairness, but not to change the common law. However, in limited situations where there is a conflict between the two sets of rules, most provincial judicature statutes provide, as do the English *Judicature Acts*, that equity prevails.

Chief Features of Common Law

The distinguishing features of the common law system are the reliance on precedent, the principle of *stare decisis*, and the use of an adversarial process in court.

Use of Precedents

English common law was a product of centuries of evolution. This process began with the development of the royal courts during the medieval period, as described above. The itinerant royal judges, on returning to London from their county assizes, would meet and dine with their fellow judges at the **Inns of Court**. This collegial process promoted respect for and attention to one another's judgments. Court reporting began in 1283, with the Year Books. Two centuries later, the invention of the printing press made it even easier for English judges to critically examine one another's judgments. From there, it was a short distance to the practice of following **precedent**. In other words, a judge would apply an earlier judicial decision to the case before him if the facts and the law were similar.[7]

This practice became institutionalized when royal judges formally accepted the principle known as **stare decisis** ("to stand by decided matters"). According to this principle, cases that are alike should be treated alike. What this meant for English law, practically speaking, was that royal judges on the county circuit would decide cases by following precedents rather than by following local customs. As a result of this practice, one cohesive system of judicial rules and practices common to England arose. This became known as the common law.

PRECEDENT AND STARE DECISIS IN A COURT HIERARCHY

Over time, changes in the English court system affected the operation of *stare decisis*. In the 16th century, the English court structure was eventually reorganized into a hierarchy, with trial courts at the bottom and superior appeal courts at the top. After this, a user of the system was required to enter first through a trial court, where one judge would decide on the matter. Those wanting to dispute the trial judge's decision were then required to appeal the judgment upward, to a higher appeal court at Westminster. At this upper level, a panel of appellate judges (usually three) would hear the trial judgment and decide whether it was correct in law.

The reorganization of the courts affected the principle of *stare decisis*; it was expanded to include the rule that a decision made by a higher appeal court is **binding**. In other words, the higher court's decision must be followed by a lower court in the same judicial hierarchy if the facts and the **ratio** or **ratio decidendi** ("reason for the decision") or principle of law in both cases are substantially similar.

The principle of *stare decisis* is very rational, but it has limitations. In 1966, the House of Lords issued the *Practice Statement*. This was a formal recognition that "too rigid adherence to precedent may lead to injustice in a particular case and also unduly restrict the proper development of the law."[8] It gave the House of Lords the power to overrule itself and to depart from precedent to achieve justice. Since then, most courts in other common

---

Inns of Court
professional associations for lawyers in England and Wales, with supervisory and disciplinary functions over their members and authority to call law students to the bar; the four Inns of Court today are Inner Temple, Middle Temple, Lincoln's Inn, and Gray's Inn

precedent
court decision that, under the doctrine of *stare decisis*, is binding on lower courts in the same jurisdiction

stare decisis
Latin phrase ("to stand by decided matters") referring to the common law principle that a precedent is binding on lower courts in the same jurisdiction

binding
term used to describe a higher court decision that a lower court in the same jurisdiction must follow according to the principle of *stare decisis*

ratio or **ratio decidendi**
Latin phrase ("the reason for the decision") referring to the governing rule in a case or the way it was applied to the facts

---

7   Alan Harding, *The Law Courts of Medieval England* (London, UK: Allen and Unwin, 1973).

8   See *Practice Statement*, [1966] 3 All ER 77 (HL). Prior to 1966, the House of Lords had considered itself bound by its own decisions under the principle of *stare decisis*: see *London Street Tramways Co v London City Council*, [1898] AC 375 (HL). See also Gordon Bale, "Casting Off the Mooring Ropes of Precedent" (1980) 58 Can Bar Rev 255.

law jurisdictions have recognized a similar power to overrule themselves in appropriate circumstances. However, there has to be a good reason for a court to exercise this power. This development has had no effect on lower courts, which continue to be bound by higher court decisions in the same jurisdiction.

Even in the lower courts, the doctrine of precedent is not as absolute as it first appears. For example, lawyers and judges wishing not to follow an apparently binding precedent from a higher appeal court have certain arguments open to them. They might argue, for example, that there are material factual differences between the preceding case and the one under consideration. Such a precedent is said to be **distinguishable**. Other arguments can be made against an apparently binding precedent. You might argue, for example, that a precedent

- has been overruled by an even higher court,
- is no longer applicable because of changed social circumstances,
- was poorly reasoned and has lost its reputation as good law, or
- has been reinterpreted differently by other judges.

distinguishable
term given to a precedent from a higher court that a lower court decides not to follow, usually on the grounds that the facts in the cases differ

Any one of these arguments, if made successfully, could render a precedent non-binding. One English judge wrote the following in this regard: "The common law evolves not merely by breeding new principles but also, when they are fully grown, by burying their ancestors."[9]

Circumstances may arise where there is no binding precedent. In this case, a judge or lawyer may also want to use a precedent from another jurisdiction that is directly on point. Such a precedent, taken from another province or from another common law country, is said to be **persuasive**. Today in Canada, a lawyer trying to "persuade" a judge to examine such a precedent would have to convince her that there was no relevant precedent from the judge's own province or from the Supreme Court of Canada (SCC).

persuasive
describes a precedent that a court is persuaded to give some weight to but is not bound to follow because the precedent is from another jurisdiction or is otherwise not binding

Figure 2.2 shows the flow of precedent downward in the Canadian court system, with the SCC at the top. Each province is considered a separate jurisdiction; decisions from other provinces are therefore not binding but can be persuasive. How persuasive a decision is depends on a number of factors, including the level of the other court, the judge who wrote the decision, the quality of the reasoning, and the date of the decision. The same standard applies to decisions from other countries.

FIGURE 2.2 Flow of Precedent in Canada

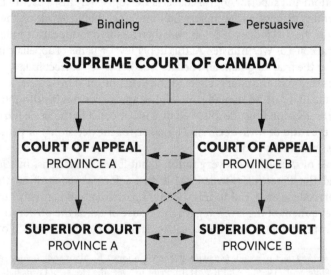

---

9   *Hong Kong Fir Shipping Co Ltd v Kawasaki Kisen Kaisha Ltd*, [1962] 1 All ER 474 at 488, [1962] 2 QB 26 (CA), Lord Diplock.

In Chapter 5, we will look at Canada's court system in more detail, including the federal court system's place in it, as well as how lower courts and administrative tribunals form part of the hierarchy.

DEVELOPING NEW PRECEDENTS

If there is neither a binding precedent applicable to a case nor a persuasive precedent from another jurisdiction, litigants may call on the court to develop a new precedent (see Box 2.1). Under what circumstances would there be no binding precedent? The case might involve, for example, a novel issue, or it might be an old issue in a modern social context.

If a court feels that establishing a new precedent might be too contentious or radical a step, it can leave the matter for elected representatives to address through legislation. If a court is feeling bold or believes that a new precedent would represent a reasonable, incremental change to the common law, it may articulate the new precedent itself.

BOX 2.1

Applying Law Versus Making Law

Where an established rule (from an earlier precedent) seems relevant to a judge's decision in a case, she will *apply* that rule to the facts of the case. In a typical motor vehicle accident case involving liability, for example, the judge's decision will hinge on whether the defendant exercised reasonable care in all the circumstances (the standard-of-care element in a negligence action). Did the defendant breach any of the rules of the road by speeding, by not stopping at a stop sign, or by not yielding at a courtesy corner? Was he impaired? Was he distracted by his cellphone? The judge will apply the reasonable care rule to the specific circumstances of the case and reach a conclusion.

The situation is different in cases where the judge or court is asked to articulate a new rule and opts to do so. The *Donoghue v Stevenson** case (referred to in Chapter 1 and described in more detail in Chapter 7) was famous for a few reasons. First, Lord Atkin proposed something no one had proposed before: that people have a general legal obligation to take care where other people are concerned (the neighbour principle). Second, Lord Atkin narrowed this general principle to fit in a particular context, holding that manufacturers have a specific obligation or duty to ensure that their products are reasonably safe for consumers even though the manufacturer has no contractual relationship with the consumer. By establishing this new precedent, did the court *make* law?

What, precisely, is the role of judges and courts in the common law world? Historically, common law judges were tasked with "finding the law." In other words, they were supposed to determine what the existing law was according to common customs and then apply it to the facts before them. They were

not charged with "making law," which was seen as too activist and not within their bailiwick. If a new law was required, Parliament or the Crown (during the period when the king or queen could make laws) was supposed to step in. But in cases where a matter was pressing, waiting for a legislative response was not always satisfactory. Under these circumstances, judges have sometimes taken the bold step of establishing a new precedent. In an important contract law case where new law was made, Lord Diplock stated that the "common law evolves not merely by breeding new principles but also, when they are fully grown, by burying their ancestors."[†]

Still other judges and commentators have argued that courts always *find* rather than *make* new law. This argument goes as follows: When judges recognize a new rule, they do so in a rational manner, by searching for common threads in existing laws, by furthering established policies, and by effecting incremental change. A process of legal reasoning dictates the result. Those who make this argument are reluctant to acknowledge the courts' power to make law. Their reluctance stems from the historical ideal of how the law was supposed to work. Judges were supposed to apply existing law, not create new laws. A greater creative authority on the part of judges could lead to uncontrolled change and instability.

Whether we characterize the recognition of a new rule as making law or finding it, the crucial element in the process seems to be the quality of the analytical reasoning that generates it.

*   [1932] AC 562 at 580, [1932] All ER 1 (HL).
†   *Hong Kong Fir Shipping Co Ltd v Kawasaki Kisen Kaisha Ltd*, [1962] 1 All ER 474 at 488, [1962] 2 QB 26 (CA).

There are three important factors that a court may take into consideration when establishing a new precedent:

1. the existence of similar cases,
2. the approach taken in other jurisdictions, and
3. policy considerations.

In considering similar cases, the court might see a common thread that connects them all; these cases may reveal a common direction in which the law is moving. Under these circumstances, the new precedent established by the court's decision will simply be a logical extension of the decisions made in these similar cases.

A second factor that courts might consider is the approach that other courts, in other jurisdictions, have taken to the issue at hand. Such comparative analysis has become increasingly important in the last few decades owing to globalization. Increasingly, our courts ask the following question: how have courts elsewhere—in other provinces, other countries, even (on occasion) countries with other legal systems—treated a particular issue? If other jurisdictions have taken a consistent or reasoned approach to a particular problem, our courts might take a similar approach.[10]

Policy is the third factor the courts might consider when deciding whether or not to recognize a new precedent. A court might consider the possibility, for example, that a new rule would benefit society by providing a useful deterrent to some problematic behaviour. On the other hand, the court would shy away from creating a new precedent if it foresaw that the new rule might lead to negative economic consequences or to a flood of cases clogging up the courts (a policy argument known as the "floodgates argument").

Adversarial System

In the common law system, the government appoints judges from among members of the legal profession—lawyers who have practised for a certain number of years. These judges preside over an **adversarial system** of justice. The adversarial system is based on the idea that truth will best be determined when lawyers oppose each other in the courtroom and present their respective cases without interference from the trial judge. Judges can ask questions to seek clarification and can do their own independent research, but the adversarial approach ensures that the primary responsibility for the presentation of cases lies with the opposing litigants and their counsel. At the end of the case, judges render their decisions based on the factual and legal material before them. As noted, this is one other key feature of the common law system.

Sources of Law

Besides judge-made rules, other written laws have at various times been recognized as binding in England. Before 1689, the monarch was able to legislate by decree. This ended with the Glorious Revolution of 1688, when Parliament completely took over the Crown's power to legislate. The English **Bill of Rights (1689)** formally declared that the "pretended" power of the Crown to legislate without the consent of Parliament was illegal.

adversarial system
system, used in common law courts, whereby the primary responsibility for the presentation of cases lies with the opposing litigants and their counsel, not with the judge presiding over the case

Bill of Rights (1689)
English statute that formally ended the power of the Crown to legislate without the consent of Parliament

---

10 For example, in *Whiten v Pilot Insurance Co*, 2002 SCC 18, referred to in Chapter 1 under "Retributive Justice," the SCC looked at how other common law countries (England, Australia, New Zealand, Ireland, and the United States) had dealt with the question of punitive damages before developing a rule for our country.

Since that time, jurisdictions that follow the common law tradition have recognized two primary sources of law:

1. legislation and
2. case law (the decisions of the courts).

The doctrine of parliamentary sovereignty dictates that where there is a conflict between case law and legislation, the latter prevails. In Chapter 4, we examine this doctrine in more detail.

Common Law: A Summary

The distinguishing features of common law, which developed over many centuries of English legal history, are as follows:

- It arose from the English kings' efforts, after the Norman invasion of 1066, to centralize their authority over the island through the use of royal courts of justice with experienced judges who travelled to and held court in the outlying counties. To begin with, these judges applied local customs in deciding their cases.
- Over time, judges of the royal courts of justice began the practice of following one another's precedents to decide cases. They did this when the facts and legal issues of a later case were the same as or similar to those of an earlier case (or precedent).
- Once the courts were organized in a hierarchy, in the 16th century, the requirement to follow precedents became institutionalized in the legal principle of *stare decisis*.
- The court process is based on an adversarial approach, with lawyers opposing each other in the courtroom and presenting their respective cases without interference from the trial judge.
- The legal rules in common law jurisdictions are not set out in one central document or code.
- Judge-made rules are one of two main sources of law. The other is legislation.

Evolving over many centuries, with its own particular legal doctrines, courts, practices, and institutions, the common law system was unique to England and was too strong—too complex and well established—to be overcome by the civil law system used on the European continent. This common law legal system, which English settlers carried with them, was received in Canada as well as in other countries established as English colonies, including the United States, Australia, New Zealand, Jamaica, and Belize.

Civil Law

The civil law system evolved in continental Europe. Under this system, the civil code is the primary source of private law and is more important than judicial decisions. A **civil code**, according to *Black's Law Dictionary*, is a "comprehensive and systematic legislative pronouncement of the whole private, non-commercial law in a legal system of the continental civil law tradition."[11]

civil code
authoritative legislative encoding of a country's private law

The civil law system's methods and techniques of analyzing legal issues are different from those of the common law system. When dealing with private law matters, judges must consult the civil code and decide the cases in accordance with the code's general principles

---

11 *Black's Law Dictionary*, 10th ed, sub verbo "civil code."

and laws. Judicial precedents are used in the civil law system but do not have the same binding nature as they do in the common law system, under the principle of *stare decisis*.

Origins of Civil Law

The most ancient legal code that has survived in its entirety is the *Code of Hammurabi* (see Figure 2.3), mentioned briefly in Chapter 1. Other codes preceded it, such as the *Code of Ur-Nammu*, which dates from around 2050 BCE, but these earlier codes are not complete. The *Code of Hammurabi* was written around 1750 BCE, during the reign of the Babylonian king Hammurabi, in the Akkadian language. Archaeologists unearthed the most famous copy of it in 1901 in Susa (now the modern Iranian town of Shush).

The following are some of the 282 laws from the *Code of Hammurabi*:

FIGURE 2.3   Code of Hammurabi
In a relief on the upper part of this stela, which is 2.25 metres tall, Hammurabi (standing, left) is shown receiving the royal insignia from the god Shamash (seated, at right). The laws are carved into the stone below.

5. If a judge try a case, reach a decision, and present his judgment in writing; if later error shall appear in his decision, and it be through his own fault, then he shall pay twelve times the fine set by him in the case, and he shall be publicly removed from the judge's bench, and never again shall he sit there to render judgment. …

22. If anyone is committing a robbery and is caught, then he shall be put to death. …

59. If any man, without the knowledge of the owner of a garden, fell a tree in a garden he shall pay half a mina in money. …

132. If the "finger is pointed" at a man's wife about another man, but she is not caught sleeping with the other man, she shall jump into the river for her husband. …

196. If a man put out the eye of another man, his eye shall be put out. …

229. If a builder build a house for someone, and does not construct it properly, and the house which he built fall in and kill its owner, then that builder shall be put to death. …

252. If [a man] kill [another] man's slave, he shall pay one-third of a mina. …

282. If a slave say to his master: "You are not my master," if they convict him his master shall cut off his ear. …[12]

The laws in the *Code of Hammurabi* bear little resemblance to those in modern civil law jurisdictions. But any modern civil code, like the ancient Babylonian one, is essentially an authoritative statement of rules regulating conduct in a particular society.

Roman Era

Romans began keeping records of their laws as early as 450 BCE, with their *Law of the Twelve Tables*. This was not a comprehensive statement of all Roman law; it provided definitions of various private rights and obligations.

Rome's first conquests and settlements beyond the Italian peninsula began in the third century BCE. In the centuries that followed, during the time of the late Republic and early

---

12 The complete text is available through the Avalon Project at Yale Law School, online: *The Avalon Project* <http://avalon.law.yale.edu>.

Empire, the Romans expanded across Europe and brought their legal system with them. A common body of laws, developed by Roman legal scholars over many centuries, was imposed on this increasingly vast territory.

In 534 CE, almost 1,000 years after the *Law of the Twelve Tables*, the emperor Justinian produced a comprehensive codification of Roman law in his monumental work **Corpus Juris Civilis**.[13] Also referred to as the *Justinian Code*, it is a compilation of the strongest features and principles of Roman law then in existence.

Justinian's work was an authoritative restatement of Roman legal scholarship and law concerning Roman citizens' private rights and obligations. It addressed, for example, the rights and obligations among family members, the rules about making contracts, and citizens' rights to acquire and dispose of property. The *Justinian Code* included four main parts:

1. the Codex, containing a collection of imperial edicts on private law matters;
2. the Digest, containing Roman jurists' commentary on these laws;
3. the Institutes, providing a textbook portion for Roman law students; and
4. the Novels, detailing new laws applicable to this area.

It was intended as a source of private law for all Roman citizens and as a reference work for Roman legal scholars and for Roman judges deciding cases.

Corpus Juris Civilis comprehensive codification of Roman civil law, compiled by the emperor Justinian (483–565 CE)

Dark Ages

The Roman legal system did not entirely disappear in Europe, as it did in England, with the fall of the Roman Empire in the 5th century CE. The Germanic tribes that succeeded the Romans and settled the southern parts of Europe based many of their tribal customs and traditions on Roman laws.

This was not the case with the Germanic tribes in northern Europe. During the Dark Ages after Rome's collapse, these northern tribes—the Franks, Burgundians, and Visigoths, for example—established diverse regional kingdoms, each with its own customs and its own system of communal justice. Some of the Frankish (or French) kings summoned certain members of their council of noble advisors (the *curia regis*) to form a judicial assembly known as a "*parlement*." A *parlement* compiled written accounts of local tribal customs, called "*coutumes*." During the medieval period, many different French *parlements* developed many different *coutumes*, with the *coutume de Paris* being one of the most important.[14]

French law in the medieval era was not transformed, as English law was, by the centralizing ambitions of a foreign invader. No French king did what William the Conqueror had done in England, creating royal courts that applied a uniform law across the country. French law was changed by a different event: the Renaissance.

The Law in Post-Renaissance Europe

The Dark Ages in Europe gave way to the Renaissance in the late 12th and 13th centuries. During this period, there was a great revival of classical learning; people turned their attention to Greek and Roman art, medicine, literature, philosophy, and theology. A renewed interest in Roman law was part of this revival. Renaissance scholars at Italy's influential University of Bologna developed a special interest in Roman law and its formal codifications, such as the *Justinian Code*. Academics from across Europe who attended this

---

13 Alan Watson, *The Law of the Ancient Romans* (Dallas: Southern Methodist University Press, 1970).
14 René David & Henry P de Vries, *The French Legal System* (New York: Oceana, 1958).

university rediscovered the universal appeal of classical Roman law. They discussed how improved laws, based on the Roman model, could help European society.

Renaissance legal scholars realized that if classical Roman law were to be reapplied across modern Europe, it would need to be updated. Some sought to adapt classical Roman law to the new circumstances in modern Europe. Others felt the need of an entirely new legal system that would address contemporary European concerns related to human rights, justice, morality, order, and security. There was a long-standing debate between those who revered the old Roman law and those who believed that new systems were needed. This debate continued for several centuries. Over time, many European states established their own civil codes of law.[15]

It is also significant that, in the development of the civil law system, legislated codes (and other statutes) were considered the only primary source of law. Judicial decisions were not considered a source of law. Although earlier cases could be consulted for interpretive purposes, they were not considered binding in later cases.

In Canada, France's *Code Civil*, established in 1804 by Napoleon (it is commonly called the *Napoleonic Code*), was very influential. This influence is evident in Quebec's first code (enacted in 1866) and its current code, the **Civil Code of Quebec (Code Civil du Québec)**,[16] which replaced the first one when it came into force in 1994 (see Box 2.2; see also the discussion of Quebec's codes in Chapter 3). The *Napoleonic Code*, like Justinian's *Corpus Juris Civilis*, was designed to be an authoritative and universal statement of private law areas. It also combined the following: (1) the laws and customs based on Roman influences that had remained the basis of law in southern France and (2) the diverse Germanic-based laws and customs of northern France's *coutumes*. Other European countries followed the French lead and established their own civil codes. England was the main exception.[17] The civil law system has been adopted by many countries and is now the most commonly used system worldwide, extending well beyond mainland Europe and its colonial spheres of influence.

Civil Code of Quebec (Code Civil du Québec) Quebec's current civil code, which came into effect on January 1, 1994, and which replaced the *Civil Code of Lower Canada* that had been in force since 1866

BOX 2.2

The Civil Code of Quebec

The *Civil Code of Quebec* became law on January 1, 1994. It was designed to reflect contemporary Quebec society's social realities and modern attitudes to, among other things, marriage, children, human rights, and parental equality rights. The *Civil Code of Quebec* comprises ten books covering private law in Quebec. The topics, by book, are as follows:

1. persons,
2. the family,
3. succession,
4. property,
5. obligations,
6. prior claims and hypothecs [mortgages],
7. evidence,
8. prescription,
9. publication of rights, and
10. private international law.

---

15 John H Merryman & Rogelio Pérez-Perdomo, *The Civil Law Tradition: An Introduction to the Legal Systems of Europe and Latin America*, 3rd ed (Stanford, Cal: Stanford University Press, 2007); and Peter Shears & Graham Stephenson, *James' Introduction to English Law*, 13th ed (Oxford: Oxford University Press, 2005).

16 CQLR, c CCQ-1991.

17 Alan Katz, "France" in *Legal Traditions and Systems: An International Handbook* (New York: Greenwood, 1986) ch 6.

As the foregoing account makes clear, the civil law system has had a long and historical evolution on the European continent. It has been shaped by Roman law more than English common law was. It also differs from the common law system in that judges play a more active role in the judicial process (such as in the questioning of witnesses and marshalling of evidence), in what is referred to as an **inquisitorial system**. Furthermore, the interpretation of civil codes is influenced more by legal scholars than by judges.

inquisitorial system
feature of civil law proceedings whereby trial judges actively assist lawyers in presenting their cases and are free to call and question witnesses and to order investigations into other evidentiary matters; contrasts with the adversarial system used in common law courts

Civil Law: A Summary

The history of the civil law system is much older than that of the common law system. Its antecedents go back thousands of years to when the first attempts to codify laws were made. Some of its key distinguishing features include the following:

- Authoritative law is set out in comprehensive legislative documents called "codes."
- Judicial decisions are not binding, and there is no formal recognition of precedent or the doctrine of *stare decisis*.
- The court process is based on an inquisitorial system.
- Scholarly writing can have significant weight when interpreting civil codes.

The certainty—and, to a degree, the simplicity—of having a central legislated document setting out core principles of the law may explain the importance of this system around the world today.

BOX 2.3

Common Law and Civil Law: Alternate Meanings

As we have seen, some legal expressions have different meanings in different contexts. In addition to referring to legal systems, the terms "common law" and "civil law" can have other meanings too.

The phrase "civil law" is sometimes used as a synonym for "private law"—in other words, laws governing the relationship between persons (as opposed to "public law," which deals with the legal relationship between a state and its individual members). Private law and public law are generally recognized distinctions in both common law and civil law systems (except perhaps in some socialist countries). Therefore, somewhat confusingly, there could be a reference to civil law (where the context means private law) and its application in a common law jurisdiction. Adding to the confusion is the fact that in many civil law countries, their civil codes are primarily concerned with private, or civil, law matters as opposed to public law ones. Criminal law and other areas of public law are frequently dealt with in other "non-code" statutes. However, the key features of civil law systems—such as the inquisitorial approach of judges and the lack of precedent—usually apply to these legislated areas as well.

The phrase "common law," apart from its reference to the legal system that originated in England, can also refer to decisions by courts exercising their common law jurisdiction (used in contradistinction to decisions by courts exercising their equitable jurisdiction) and to case law generally (used in contradistinction to legislation, or enacted laws).

Comparison of the Common Law and Civil Law Systems

Both the civil law system and the common law system strive for certainty, stability, and predictability. Civil law achieves these things through a comprehensive civil code, with laws set out for all to see, understand, and follow. Common law achieves them chiefly by the legal principle of *stare decisis*, with judges following precedents based on the idea that similar cases should be treated in similar ways. Clearly, one of the key differences between the two systems is the different role each assigns to previous judicial decisions. Also, keep in mind that "common law" and "civil law" don't always refer to general systems of law and can have other meanings (see Box 2.3).

Despite this fundamental difference between these two major legal systems, in practice they have much in common. Judges in both systems consult prior decisions and legal scholarship when trying to resolve the issues before them, and in both systems, statutes are a source of law. The biggest challenge for newcomers to a common law jurisdiction is researching and analyzing the stand-alone judge-made rules that apply to their particular case. For newcomers to a civil law jurisdiction, the biggest adjustment tends to come in a litigation context, where judges play a more active role in an inquisitorial system. Table 2.1 summarizes some of the key differences between the civil law and common law systems.

TABLE 2.1   Comparison of Civil Law and Common Law

CHARACTERISTICS	CIVIL LAW SYSTEM	COMMON LAW SYSTEM
Judicial Decisions	*Not Authoritative* • not a primary or authoritative source of law; only legislation (civil code and other statutes) is binding • regard for precedent is informal (however, previous cases may be persuasive, along with academic commentary, as noted below)	*Authoritative* • a primary and authoritative source of law, along with legislation • judges are bound by precedent following the principle of *stare decisis*
Role of Judges in Dispute Resolution Process	*Inquisitorial System* • judges are appointed from a special school for judges in many civil law jurisdictions—prior experience as a lawyer not required • judges conscious of being part of civil service—i.e., representatives of government • courtroom process is based on the idea that judges should actively assist lawyers in presenting their case—truth is best determined this way • judges are free to call and question witnesses and order investigations into other evidentiary matters	*Adversarial System* • judges are appointed from the legal profession, after years of practice as a lawyer or law professor • judges are conscious of being independent of the government that appoints them • courtroom process is based on the idea that truth will best be determined by lawyers presenting their respective cases, unhindered by interference from the trial judge
Academic Commentary	*Important Interpretive Role* • academic commentary is one of the foundations of the civil law system and is called "doctrine" • scholarly texts and articles about the civil code play a significant role overall in helping judges decide cases	*Persuasive* • academic commentary is a type of secondary source and assists in the finding or interpretation of primary sources (judicial decisions and legislation) • texts and articles about the law have varying degrees of persuasiveness in cases in which they are cited, depending on the type of case and the author of the commentary
Juries	Generally not used	Can be used

In the practice of law in common law Canada, it is still important to understand how the civil law system works because it may apply whenever a legal problem involves a connection with Quebec. To resolve social or business issues in our bijural nation, both legal systems are sometimes needed. Another good reason to learn about the civil law system is that, as mentioned above, it is the most common system worldwide. It is used in most of South and Central America, including Mexico, and in Continental Europe, including Russia.[18] Also, many Asian countries (China and Japan, for example) and some Middle Eastern countries employ a civil law system, sometimes in combination with other systems (customary law, religious law, or even common law).

Harmonizing Common Law and Civil Law in Canada

To avoid having a legal divide between the common and civil law systems, the Government of Canada must ensure that federal laws are compatible with the civil law system in Quebec. The following are some examples of government departments, institutions, and other organizations that assist in harmonizing Canada's two legal systems:

- *Federal Department of Justice.* This department was first created in 1868. A civil law section was established in 1952 and a new civil code section in 1993. The department's legislative bijuralism section is concerned with, among other things, developing proposals and programs that will harmonize federal areas of legislative control—which operate under the common law system—with the terms and concepts of Quebec's new civil code, in force as of January 1, 1994.

- *The Supreme Court of Canada.* Canada's highest court is composed of nine judges. By law, under the *Supreme Court Act*, three of these nine judges must come from Quebec.[19] Thus, if a case involving Quebec's civil law comes before the Court, there are French civilian judges on the Court to help decide the appeal based on Quebec's civil law legal system. As well, the choice of who becomes chief justice of Canada has usually alternated between an anglophone and a francophone judge.

- *Law faculties.* Some law faculties—for example, the University of Ottawa and McGill University—offer both civil law and common law degrees. The University of Ottawa and the University of Moncton also offer a common law program in French, and McGill offers a civil law program in English.

- *The Canadian Bar Association.* This national organization, which represents Canada's legal community, has for some time sponsored events and seminars to promote a better understanding of Canada's two different legal systems among civil law and common law lawyers.

In Chapter 3, we examine more specifically how and when the common law and civil law systems were received into the various regions of Canada.

---

18 The legal systems in socialist countries that use the civil law system—such as Russia, China, and North Korea—have some features that distinguish them from most other civil law systems. For example, the role that doctrine (that is, academic commentary) plays in socialist countries varies with the government; authoritarian regimes tend not to permit academic criticism that is political or value based. In such cases, academic commentary on existing laws will be confined to explanation and analysis.

19 RSC 1985, c S-26, s 6.

Indigenous Law

The movement to strengthen Indigenous legal traditions in Canada is stronger now than it has ever been. In its 2015 report, the Truth and Reconciliation Commission of Canada (TRC) recommended the reconciliation of "Aboriginal and Crown constitutional and legal orders to ensure that Aboriginal peoples are full partners in Confederation ... ."[20] Moreover, backed by general public support, the federal and provincial governments have committed to the implementation of the *United Nations Declaration on the Rights of Indigenous Peoples* (UNDRIP), which includes the right to "maintain and strengthen their distinct political, legal, economic, social and cultural institutions ... ."[21] The TRC report and UNDRIP are discussed in more detail below.

This section begins by looking at some basic terminology (Box 2.4) and the colonial setting in which Indigenous peoples find themselves before examining the basic nature of Indigenous legal traditions. It is not possible to cover all the issues involved in such a short introduction, but I hope it will serve as a jumping-off point for further research and reading.[22]

The Colonial Context

The story of our species since it first left Africa around 100,000 years ago has been one of settlement and colonization, of interactions with the environment, and of continued population growth to the point where we now occupy most of the inhabitable space on the planet.

One view is that humans have risen to remarkable heights through our pursuit of knowledge, our creative and artistic accomplishments, and our ability to use science and technology to service our needs and wants. Another view is that we have been a selfish and cruel species that has laid waste to flora and fauna interfering with our settlement and consumption aspirations and that we have perpetrated acts of violence and oppression against our own kind when colonizing already inhabited lands (including, in the distant past, causing the extinction of other species of humans). The evidence supports both views.

All colonizing peoples have oppressed existing populations in some way. The European-Christian wave of colonization that began in the late 1400s stands out; it travelled around the world to Africa, India, Southeast Asia, the Americas, Australia and New Zealand, and beyond. It was not the first colonizing force—and some of the peoples it colonized were colonizers themselves—nor was it the last, but it was the most widespread and had the greatest impact overall.

Although the method of European-Christian colonization varied depending on the colonizing nation and from place to place, the international community as a whole and most individual states now recognize that the effects of this colonization were and continue to be harmful to Indigenous peoples. The same is true of all other examples of colonization.

Aboriginal law
sub-area of Canadian public law involving rights, land claims, and other legal issues concerning Indigenous peoples in Canada

---

20 *Infra* note 28 at 38.

21 *Infra* note 25.

22 I am indebted to experts in this field, upon whose works I have depended in writing this brief overview—in particular, John Borrows but also Gordon Christie, Jim Reynolds, Brenda Gunn, Val Napoleon, Joshua Nichols, Michael Coyle, Pamela Palmater, and others. Note also that in this introduction to Indigenous law, I have focused on peoples within Canada's boundaries, unlike in the sections above on common law and civil law, which examined those traditions beginning with their historical roots outside of Canada.

BOX 2.4

wə x̌iʔ k̓ʷ sqʷel *

Prejudices and ignorance can hide beneath the surface of words, perpetuating a cycle of discrimination and oppression. The word "Indian," for example, was used by the Canadian government to refer to First Nations peoples based on a geographic mistake made by European colonists. It is still used in some contexts, including in legislation (s 91(24) of the *Constitution Act, 1867*[†] assigns legislative power to the federal Parliament over "Indians, and Lands Reserved for the Indians"; the *Indian Act*[‡] is a key statute regulating Indigenous affairs; and s 35 of the *Constitution Act, 1982*[§] recognizes and affirms the rights of Aboriginal peoples, including "Indian" peoples). The word is offensive to some because it is associated with a discriminatory legislative regime and has colonial and other negative connotations.

Our intention in setting out the following short usage guide is to be accurate, respectful, and in line with current terminology. However, we recognize that some Indigenous people may prefer other terms or otherwise disagree with this taxonomy.

When Referring to Persons or Peoples

The term "Indigenous" has become generally accepted in recent years when referring to the first inhabitants of a country, likely in part because of UNDRIP. In this book, we use "Indigenous" inclusively to describe persons and peoples who are First Nations, Inuit, or Métis.

"First Nations" generally refers to the original inhabitants of Canada, who are not Inuit or Métis. They were the first peoples to encounter the European colonists. "Inuit" refers to peoples living in the northern regions of Canada and is the official term used by the federal government. They arrived in Canada more recently than First Nations peoples—crossing the Bering land bridge 4,000 to 8,000 years ago—and are ethnically distinct from First Nations peoples. "Métis" is the term used for persons of mixed Indigenous and European ancestry. Its precise meaning is contentious. When it is not capitalized, it can refer to any community of persons with mixed Indigenous-European heritage, wherever in Canada they are located. When capitalized, it refers more specifically to persons who can trace their ancestry to members of the historic Métis Nation, whose homeland was generally in the western part of Canada. The Métis National

Council and the courts support this definition (see the *Powley* case, summarized below).

We also use "Aboriginal" synonymously with "Indigenous" when it seems appropriate based on context, such as when quoting other sources that use the term or when discussing constitutional rights (because of its use in the *Constitution Act, 1982*).

When Referring to Law

"Indigenous law" (also Indigenous legal traditions or orders) means the law of Indigenous peoples themselves without reference to Canadian law as a determiner of validity. Indigenous legal traditions predate the arrival of Europeans in Canada. **Aboriginal law** refers to a sub-area of Canadian public law that involves the rights, land claims, and other legal issues relating to Indigenous peoples in Canada *as defined by Canadian law*. The TRC report states: "[E]ach Indigenous nation across the country has its own laws and legal traditions. Aboriginal law is the body of law that exists within the Canadian legal system."[#]

---

* This means "Words are Important" in hən̓q̓əmin̓əm̓, the ancestral language of the Musqueam. The Musqueam Language and Culture Department suggests the following pronunciation for **wə x̌iʔ k̓ʷ sqʷel**:

> **wə** is like the English "w." **x̌iʔ** sounds like "tea" if it were spelled "tlea." **k̓ʷ** sounds like the "qu" in "quick"; this is a very quiet sound. **sqʷel** sounds like "quell" but with an "s" in the front.

See <https://www.musqueam.bc.ca/departments/community-services/language> for more information concerning orthography and pronunciation.

† (UK), 30 & 31 Vict, c 3, reprinted in RSC 1985, App II, No 5 (formerly called the *British North America Act, 1867*, or BNA Act).

‡ RSC 1985, c I-5.

§ Schedule B to the *Canada Act 1982* (UK), 1982, c 11.

Truth and Reconciliation Commission of Canada, *Canada's Residential Schools: Reconciliation—The Final Report of the Truth and Reconciliation Commission of Canada* (Montreal and Kingston: McGill-Queen's University Press, 2015) vol 6 at 45, online: <http://www.trc.ca/assets/pdf/Volume_6_Reconciliation_English_Web.pdf>.

International Documents

The *Charter of the United Nations* (UN Charter)[23] states as one of its purposes the development of "respect for the principle of equal rights and self-determination of peoples" (article 1) and includes specific chapters concerning the interests of dependent peoples (chapters XI–XIII).

In 1960, the UN General Assembly passed Resolution 1514, the *Declaration on the Granting of Independence to Colonial Countries and Peoples*.[24] This Declaration reaffirmed the right of all people to self-determination and proclaimed the "necessity of bringing to a speedy and unconditional end [to] colonialism in all its forms and manifestations." Two years later, a special committee on decolonization was established to monitor efforts to decolonize. The Assembly has proclaimed each decade since 1990 as the first, second, and third international decade, respectively, for the eradication of colonialism. According to the UN, since it was established, 80 former colonies have gained their independence.

International efforts to decolonize and a parallel movement to redress wrongs perpetrated against Indigenous peoples led to UNDRIP,[25] which was adopted by the General Assembly in 2007. UNDRIP sets out an international framework for ensuring, for Indigenous peoples, dignity and respect, the enjoyment of all the human rights recognized under the UN Charter, the right of self-determination, the survival of their cultures and languages, the protection of their lands, and related objectives. An important provision concerning Indigenous law, quoted in part above, is article 5:

> *Indigenous peoples have the right to maintain and strengthen their* distinct political, *legal*, economic, social and cultural *institutions*, while retaining their right to participate fully, if they so choose, in the political, economic, social and cultural life of the State. [Emphasis added.]

Precisely how the right to maintain and strengthen Indigenous legal institutions is recognized will determine the role their law plays in relation to state legal systems.

Canadian Responses: Truth and Reconciliation and Implementing UNDRIP

The federal government has acknowledged the negative impact its policies have had on Indigenous peoples. The implementation of the recommendations in the TRC report, which includes a recommendation to implement UNDRIP, is an important step on the road to reconciliation.

TRUTH AND RECONCILIATION

As part of a class-action settlement agreement in 2006 concerning claims of abuse in residential schools,[26] the federal government agreed to fund the TRC. The following is just one example of the abuse, recounted before the TRC was constituted:

> My father was physically tortured by his teachers for speaking Tseshaht: they pushed sewing needles through his tongue, a routine punishment for language offenders
> —Randy Fred[27]

23   26 June 1945, Can TS 1945 No 7.
24   14 December 1960, UNGA Resolution 1514, A/RES/1514(XV).
25   UNHRCOR, 61st session, UN Doc A/RES/61/295 (2007).
26   The Indian Residential Schools Settlement Agreement (IRSSA).
27   Celia Haig-Brown, *Resistance and Renewal: Surviving the Indian Residential School* (Vancouver: Arsenal Pulp Press, 1998) at 16, cited in Kirsten Anker, *Reconciliation in Translation: Indigenous Legal Traditions and Canada's Truth and Reconciliation Commission* (2016) 33.2 Windsor Y B Access Just at 19.

The TRC began its work in 2007 and concluded in 2015 with the publication of its six-volume final report.[28] It made 94 recommendations in the form of "Calls to Action." They are comprehensive, covering all aspects of Indigenous relations; most require working within the existing Canadian legal system, including its constitutional framework.

Some of them are relevant to Indigenous legal traditions and if broadly implemented could require constitutional amendment. For example, Call to Action 45 provides the following:

> 45   We call upon the Government of Canada, on behalf of all Canadians, to jointly develop with Aboriginal peoples a Royal Proclamation of Reconciliation to be issued by the Crown. The proclamation would build on the Royal Proclamation of 1763 and the Treaty of Niagara of 1764, and *reaffirm the nation-to-nation relationship between Aboriginal peoples and the Crown.* The proclamation would include, but not be limited to, the following commitments:
>
> (ii)   Adopt and implement the *United Nations Declaration on the Rights of Indigenous Peoples* as the framework for reconciliation. ...
>
> (iv) *Reconcile Aboriginal and Crown constitutional and legal orders* to ensure that Aboriginal peoples are full partners in Confederation, *including the recognition and integration of Indigenous laws and legal traditions* in negotiation and implementation processes involving Treaties, land claims, and other constructive agreements. ... [Emphasis added.]

Whether a true nation-to-nation relationship is reaffirmed (as it existed at the time of first contact between Indigenous peoples and Europeans), and whether Indigenous laws and legal traditions are recognized and integrated in the contexts mentioned, remains to be seen.[29]

IMPLEMENTING UNDRIP

In 2007, UNDRIP was adopted by a majority of 144 states, with 4 votes against (Australia, Canada, New Zealand, and the United States) and a number of abstentions. Canada's initial objection was based on concerns about conflicts between UNDRIP and existing Canadian laws.

Canada later reversed its position (as did Australia, New Zealand, and the United States). At the end of 2015, Prime Minister Justin Trudeau committed to fully implementing the recommendations in the TRC report, starting with the implementation of UNDRIP. In 2016, federal Minister of Indigenous and Northern Affairs Carolyn Bennett announced: "We intend nothing less than to adopt and implement the Declaration in accordance with the Canadian Constitution. ... By adopting and implementing the Declaration, we are excited that we are breathing life into section 35 [of the *Constitution Act, 1982*] and recognizing it now as a full box of rights for Indigenous peoples in Canada."[30]

---

28 Truth and Reconciliation Commission of Canada, *Final Report of the Truth and Reconciliation Commission of Canada* (Montreal and Kingston: McGill-Queen's University Press, 2015), online: <http://nctr.ca/reports.php>.

29 During the Wet'suwet'en pipeline protests in 2019–2020, the federal and British Columbia governments had to face this issue directly (see below).

30 "Fully Adopting UNDRIP: Minister Bennett's Speech at the United Nations" (11 May 2016), online: *Northern Public Affairs* <http://www.northernpublicaffairs.ca/index/fully-adopting-undrip-minister-bennetts-speech>.

As a first step in the implementation process, all Canadian jurisdictions must enact legislation. Without this legislation, UNDRIP is merely a political commitment.[31] Furthermore, some Indigenous law experts argue that the implementation of UNDRIP, without recognizing the possibility of changes to the existing legal structure, will make a full reconciliation difficult.[32] To reaffirm nation-to-nation status means that constitutional amendment and the cession of some sovereignty to Indigenous peoples might be required.

Nature of Indigenous Law

When the first colonists arrived in Canada from France and England, European-Indigenous interactions were generally peaceful; the relationship was based for the most part on trading. Indigenous peoples had their own cultures and legal traditions, and it probably didn't occur to them that colonization would soon lead to a loss of control over both.

Indigenous legal traditions have a long history (see, for example, Box 2.5) and have not disappeared, despite colonization. To facilitate reconciliation, non-Indigenous people must learn more about these traditions. As a former chief justice of the BC Supreme Court said, "How can we make space within the legal landscape for Indigenous legal orders? The answer depends, at least in part, on an inversion of the question: a crucial part of this process must be to find space for ourselves, as strangers and newcomers, within the Indigenous legal orders themselves."[33]

Indigenous law is difficult to classify because there are hundreds of Indigenous peoples in Canada and no single Indigenous legal tradition. Some writers argue that Indigenous law is custom based, lacks formalized processes, and often has no written record; as such, it is not true "law." This argument assumes that touchstones of validity in one system necessarily determine validity in another. Furthermore, it ignores the recognition that the international community gives to some customary legal systems and the relationship that often exists between Indigenous law and other sources, such as sacred beliefs. It is true that most Indigenous legal traditions have elements that are tied to customary practices. But there is much more to the story than that.

John Borrows, in a number of publications, including a report he prepared for the Law Commission of Canada in 2006,[34] examined Indigenous legal traditions in Canada. I rely heavily on his work in this basic introduction to Indigenous law.

---

31 International documents are not legally binding in domestic legal systems until implemented by local legislation. In 2019, BC became the first jurisdiction in Canada to enact legislation adopting UNDRIP: see the *Declaration on the Rights of Indigenous Peoples Act*, SBC 2019, c 44. The federal government introduced a bill implementing UNDRIP in December 2020; the other provinces and territories still need to introduce and pass similar legislation.

32 See, for example, Joshua Nichols, "We have never been domestic": State Legitimacy and the Indigenous Question" in John Borrows et al, eds, *Braiding Legal Orders: Implementing the United Nations Declaration on the Rights of Indigenous Peoples* (Waterloo, Ont: Centre for International Governance Innovation, 2019) ch 4. Also, Gordon Christie, "Indigenous Legal Orders, Canadian Law and UNDRIP" ch 5 of the same collection.

33 *Ibid*, Hannah Askew, "UNDRIP Implementation, Intercultural Learning and Substantive Engagement with Indigenous Legal Orders" ch 19 at 90, citing Lance Finch, "The Duty to Learn: Taking Account of Indigenous Legal Orders in Practice" (Paper delivered at the Indigenous Legal Orders and the Common Law Conference, Continuing Legal Education Society of British Columbia, Vancouver, November 2012).

34 John Borrows, *Indigenous Legal Traditions in Canada: Report for the Law Commission of Canada* (Ottawa: Law Commission of Canada, 2006). In this report, Borrows surveys the traditions of eight representative peoples: the Mi'kmaq, Hodinohso:ni, Anishinabek, Cree, Métis, Carrier, Nisga'a, and Inuit peoples.

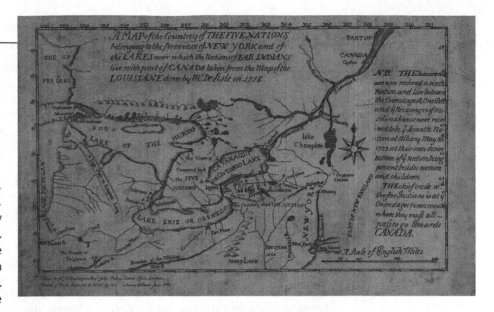

BOX 2.5

Gayanashagowa: Great Binding Law or Great Law of Peace

Canada's Aboriginal peoples … did not write their laws down … but transmitted them orally from generation to generation. This tradition was one of the responsibilities of the elders in each nation's community. Sometimes the tribal laws were transmitted in the form of legends or stories to make them easier to remember and to inspire the listener with respect for the law.

The Iroquois Confederacy, located south of Lake Ontario, was one of the most powerful groups of Aboriginal peoples. Originally it consisted of five nations: the Mohawk, Seneca, Oneida, Onondaga, and Cayuga. The Confederacy was established by two great chiefs, Dekanawida and Hiawatha, around 1142 CE. According to their oral history, it took them 40 years to convince the tribes to form a union bound together by a formal constitution. This constitution was called the *Gayanashagowa*, Iroquois for "great binding law." It provided a system of checks and balances by giving every man and woman in the Confederacy a voice in tribal affairs. The powers of the war chiefs were held in check by those of the peace chiefs. All chiefs were appointed by the clan mothers, who also had the power to remove any chief who did not act in the interests of the people. At some point in the 18th century, the leaders of the Iroquois Confederacy agreed to write down their Great Binding Law. The framers of both the US Constitution and the *Charter of the United Nations* referred to the Iroquois Great Binding Law in drawing up their own legal documents.

Source: Reproduced from George Alexandrowicz et al, *Dimensions of Law: Canadian and International Law in the 21st Century* (Toronto: Emond Montgomery, 2004) at 39-40.

Some Indigenous laws are seen as divine or sacred, based on beliefs about their Creator's intentions for them. For example, the Cree people have an overarching law attributed to the Creator called "*wahkohtowin*," to which all human rules of behaviour must conform. *Wahkohtowin* prescribes a general obligation to act in such a way as to promote positive, healthy relationships with others.[35] Other laws are naturalistic and based on observations of the spirit world and physical environment. The Mi'kmaq, for example, observe their ecological environment and apply rules to human behaviour based on Earth's teachings.[36]

Indigenous laws can also have positivistic or human-made status and are not based on external sources or long-standing customary practice. As Borrows stated:

> Positivistic Indigenous legal traditions are often regarded as being of human origin, and not necessarily connected with any larger system of morality. These traditions can be changed by humans without any external consequences. Positivistic Indigenous laws can be formally proclaimed in feast halls, council houses, wampum readings and

---

35 *Ibid* at 49-50.
36 *Ibid* at 16.

other similar settings. These functions can be carried out by a centralized authority, such as named chiefs, hereditary clan mothers, headmen, sachems and band leaders.[37]

Although many Indigenous legal traditions lack formal processes equivalent to common law and civil systems, it is not accurate to say they are without process. Many have a deliberative aspect and are developed "through councils, circles, and other informal meetings and gatherings."[38] Borrows refers to the deliberative aspect as a source of law, although it could also be seen as a process by which positivistic (or positive) law is made, much like going to court in the common law system (the process and its procedural rules) may result in a decision that becomes binding substantive law.

Custom is a part of common law and civil law legal systems, and of international law.[39] According to JuriGlobe,[40] custom is also the basis for the entire legal system in a few regions of the world: the small nation of Andorra in the Pyrenees and the two Channel Island UK dependencies Guernsey and Jersey.

Indigenous legal traditions also often include customary practices. Two examples serve to illustrate. In the legal tradition of the Carrier people, grandparents who adopt a grandchild are considered to be full parents. This was significant in a case where Canadian law and Carrier law intersected. When Carrier grandparents claimed death benefits under BC legislation as dependent parents, the BC Court of Appeal allowed their claim based on Carrier customary law relating to adoption (there were no statutory or common law impediments to applying Carrier law in the circumstances).[41]

A second example concerns the Métis Law of the Hunt, some of which is codified (rules relating to when they can hunt, working in groups, and punishment for breaking the rules, for example). But the Métis also recognize that customary rules can supplement the codified portion, including rules "involving the respectful killing and use of the animal."[42]

According to Borrows, the five sources just described—divine (or sacred) law, naturalistic (or natural) law, positivistic law, deliberative law, and customary law—form the basis of most Indigenous legal traditions. These traditions are varied and complex, and the mix of sources depends on the tradition in question. However, it is a mistake to assume, as some do, that all Indigenous legal traditions are custom based.[43]

For more discussion and analysis of other aspects of Indigenous law—such as when it is local or "national," how it is recorded and conveyed, theories of responsibility, its systems of dispute resolution, its relationship to Canada's common law and civil traditions (the Carrier law adoption case referred to above is just one example), and international perspectives—I refer you to the work of Borrows and other writers, some of whose publications are listed below under "Further Reading."

---

37 *Ibid* at 7.

38 *Ibid* at 8.

39 Common law and civil law systems are ultimately derived from customary law. Early in the development of common law, the royal courts derived principles from established practices in England, and custom continues to play a role in common law (for example, in modern negligence actions, it is a factor in determining the standard-of-care element). Civil codes are the formalization of established practices. The preamble to the *Civil Code of Quebec* expressly states that the code lays down the society's customary law. Furthermore, Canadian constitutional conventions (or customs) regulate many aspects of governmental behaviour (described in more detail in Chapter 4). Custom is also a recognized source of international law.

40 *Supra* note 1.

41 See *Casimel v Insurance Corp. of British Columbia* (1993), 106 DLR (4th) 720, 1993 CanLII 1258 (BCCA), and the discussion of this case in John Borrows, *Canada's Indigenous Constitution* (Toronto: University of Toronto Press, 2010) at 52. See also the summary of *Powley*, below.

42 Borrows, *supra* note 34 at 53-54.

43 Borrows, *supra* note 34 at 23-24.

Canadian Law and Indigenous Peoples: A Timeline

How did Indigenous law lose its influence after colonization? There are many causes, but one of them was subjecting Indigenous peoples to an imposed order that was not their own. The following is a basic timeline of pre- and post-Confederation colonial laws and events, many of which, until recently, had the effect of pushing Indigenous law into the background. (Some of the points in the timeline are discussed later in the book, when the areas to which they relate arise: for example, when discussing constitutional law in Chapters 3 to 6, property law in Chapter 7, criminal law in Chapter 10, and access to justice in Chapter 12.)

1701–present: Treaties between British colonies (later Canada) and Indigenous peoples. The federal government recognizes 70 **historic treaties** made from 1701 to 1923. After the *Royal Proclamation, 1763*, Indigenous people surrendered large tracts of land in exchange for reserve lands and other benefits. The land surrendered covers much of Canada, but not all. Unceded territory includes large parts of Quebec, most of British Columbia, Atlantic Canada, and some other areas. After the *Calder* case in 1973 (see below), when the SCC first recognized Aboriginal rights to land, the period of **modern treaties** began, leading to the federal government's Comprehensive Land Claims Policy. Since 1975 (and as of this writing), 26 modern treaties dealing with land claims and, in some cases, self-government have been signed.

1763: Royal Proclamation, 1763.[44] King George III reserves to First Nations their lands not already purchased or ceded and, to prevent abuses, requires future purchases and acquisitions to be through the Crown by treaty before the land can be transferred to others. The proclamation has been referred to as the "Indian Magna Carta" (see Box 3.1 in Chapter 3).

1867: Confederation. Section 91(24) of the *Constitution Act, 1867* assigns legislative power to the federal Parliament over "Indians, and Lands Reserved for the Indians" (see also Box 2.4).

1876: Indian Act. This legislation authorizes the federal government to impose governance structures on First Nations peoples, regulate reserve communities, determine Indian status, and generally control the day-to-day affairs of status (that is, registered) Indians, making them wards of the state.

1870s: The first residential schools open. The policy of separating Indigenous children from their families and culture for the purpose of assimilation into Canadian society led to abuse, the effects of which are still felt today.

1887: St Catharines Milling.[45] On appeal from the SCC, the Privy Council refuses to recognize Aboriginal title in relation to unceded land—based on a narrow interpretation of the *Royal Proclamation, 1763*—and decides that Aboriginal lands are held at the pleasure of the Crown.

1951: Amendments to the *Indian Act* remove some discriminatory rules, including bans on customary and sacred practices, the wearing of ceremonial dress off-reserve, and the consumption of alcohol.

1960: First Nations people, who are status Indians under the *Indian Act*, are given the right to vote.

1969: White Paper. Pierre Trudeau sets out a policy initiative proposing the abolition of the *Indian Act* and the assimilation of Indigenous peoples into Canadian society generally. The paper was withdrawn because of a lack of support from the Indigenous community (see Box 3.4 in Chapter 3).

historic treaties
treaties between Indigenous peoples and the Government of Canada made between 1701 and 1923, under the terms of which Indigenous people surrendered large tracts of land in exchange for reserve lands and other benefits

modern treaties
treaties between Indigenous peoples and the Government of Canada made after 1973 when Aboriginal title was recognized

---

44   (UK), reprinted in RSC 1985, App II, No 1.
45   *St Catharines Milling and Lumber Co v R*, (1887), 13 SCR 577, 1887 CanLII 3.

1973: Calder.[46] Nisga'a elders sue the BC government, arguing that title to their lands had never been extinguished by treaty or other means. They lose in the SCC, but in a split decision, the Court recognizes for the first time the possibility of proving Aboriginal title in their unceded lands, calling into question *St Catharines Milling*.

1975: James Bay agreement. Quebec signs an agreement with Cree and Inuit communities, opening the way for new hydro projects (see also Box 3.4).

1982: Constitution Act, 1982, which includes the *Canadian Charter of Rights and Freedoms* (the Charter). Section 35 formally recognizes and affirms Aboriginal rights and treaties, including land claims agreements. Section 25 (part of the Charter) guarantees that Charter rights and freedoms will not be interpreted so as to diminish Aboriginal treaty and other rights, including any rights or freedoms recognized under the *Royal Proclamation, 1763*.

1984: Guerin.[47] The SCC holds for the first time that the federal government has a fiduciary duty to First Nations and that Aboriginal title is *sui generis* or unique.

1985: Amendments to the *Indian Act* restore rights to those who had lost them by living off-reserve and to status women who had lost them by marrying out to non-Aboriginals.

1990: Sparrow.[48] The SCC holds that Aboriginal rights existing in 1982 are protected under section 35 of the *Constitution Act, 1982*. The Court sets out a test, known as the "Sparrow test," for determining whether a right exists (recognizing that rights can evolve over time) and whether an infringement is justified. The decision proceeds on the basis that an established right to fish for food or ceremonial purposes is at stake—not considering that commercial fishing was involved—and focuses on whether the right has been justifiably infringed. Simply put, to extinguish a right requires clear legislation that is measured and reasonable and is backed by a legitimate purpose. Merely regulating the activity is not enough to extinguish the right. There was insufficient evidence before the Court to support a finding of extinguishment, and Sparrow's conviction was overturned.

1996: Van der Peet.[49] The SCC restricts the *Sparrow* definition of Aboriginal rights, holding that the people claiming the right must prove that it is integral to the group's culture and that it *originated prior to contact with Europeans*. Again, fishing rights are at stake, and this time the Court considers the commercial aspect. To prove the right, the Court outlines various criteria, known as the "Van der Peet test." The commercial fishery in this case is held not protected under section 35. Critics of this case point out that the test is difficult to prove and unfairly restrictive (not adequately accounting for cultural change and development over time).[50]

1997: Delgamuukw.[51] The Gitksan and Wet'suwet'en claim control over a large area in northwestern BC. Following *Calder*, the SCC refines the concept of Aboriginal title, deciding that there must be proof the land was integral to the nation's culture *at the time Europeans claimed sovereignty over it*[52] and that occupation of the land was exclusive and continuous. The claim is sent back to the BC Supreme Court for more fact finding and

---

46 *Calder v Attorney-General of British Columbia*, [1973] SCR 313, 1973 CanLII 4.

47 *Guerin v The Queen*, [1984] 2 SCR 335, 1984 CanLII 25.

48 *R v Sparrow*, [1990] 1 SCR 1075, 1990 CanLII 1704.

49 *R v Van der Peet*, [1996] 2 SCR 507, 1996 CanLII 216.

50 See, for example, Gordon Christie, *Canadian Law and Indigenous Self-Determination: A Naturalist Analysis* (Toronto: University of Toronto Press, 2019) at 74-81, and John Borrows, *Freedom & Indigenous Constitutionalism* (Toronto: University of Toronto Press, 2016) at 139-47.

51 *Delgamuukw v British Columbia*, [1997] 3 SCR 1010, 1997 CanLII 302.

52 This is slightly different than the *Van der Peet* contact rule, which apparently applies to other Aboriginal rights besides title. See Jim Reynolds, *Aboriginal Peoples and the Law: A Critical Introduction* (Vancouver: Purich Books, an imprint of UBC Press, 2018) at 92.

allowing for the use of oral history. The SCC also recommends trying to resolve the claim through negotiations (the approach taken). In 2020, significant progress was made in settling the claim (see below and Box 7.7 in Chapter 7).[53]

2000: Nisga'a Treaty. Twenty-seven years after *Calder*, a comprehensive land claims agreement comes into effect and includes a self-government arrangement. It is the first treaty signed by a First Nation covering land in BC since 1899 (see also Box 3.4 and Box 7.7).

2003: Powley.[54] The SCC decides that a father and son charged with illegal hunting are part of a Métis community and their hunting practice was integral to their culture; as such, it is a protected right under section 35 of the *Constitution Act, 1982*. The Court sets out a number of criteria relating to establishing Métis status and Aboriginal rights (such as hunting rights). Concerning the former, a person must self-identify as Métis, have an ancestral connection with a Métis community, and be accepted by the modern community according to its customs and traditions.

2004: Haida.[55] The SCC recognizes the Crown's "duty to consult" with Indigenous peoples pending the negotiation of treaties or litigation to establish Aboriginal rights.[56]

2005: Marshall/Bernard.[57] In two separate cases decided together involving charges against members of the Mi'kmaq nation—one dealing with cutting and removing timber from Crown lands (*Marshall*) and the other concerning unlawful possession of Crown timber (*Bernard*)—the SCC holds that Aboriginal rights do not extend to commercial logging. Although there were ancestral trading activities, which evolved over time and were protected, the commercial logging in this case was not a logical evolution of these practices. The Court also examines the issue of Aboriginal title and, applying *Delgamuukw*, finds that title was not established in this case (see also Box 7.7).

2006: Indian Residential Schools Settlement Agreement (IRSSA; see above).

2014: Tsilhqot'in Nation.[58] The Tsilhqot'in Nation becomes the first Indigenous group without a land claims settlement to prove Aboriginal title in the SCC. The SCC further refines the concept of Aboriginal title and the Crown's duty to consult (see Box 7.7).

2015: The TRC report is issued (see above).

2016: The federal government promises to implement UNDRIP (see above).

2016: Daniels.[59] The SCC decides that Métis and non-status Indians are "Indians" under section 91(24) of the *Constitution Act, 1867*, assigning clear jurisdiction over these groups to the federal Parliament. This led to more discussions concerning rights (including land claims) and access to government services.

---

53 On March 1, 2020, a draft agreement between the federal and provincial governments and Wet'suwet'en hereditary chiefs was reached dealing with the land claim in *Delgamuukw* but, as of writing, had not been finalized. On May 14, 2020, amid COVID-19 restrictions, a memorandum of understanding between the federal and provincial governments and Wet'suwet'en hereditary chiefs dealing with the land claim in *Delgamuukw* and other issues was signed in a virtual ceremony. Both levels of government committed to recognizing Wet'suwet'en rights and title held under their system of governance, with timelines over 12 months for negotiating various details.

54 *R v Powley*, 2003 SCC 43.

55 *Haida Nation v British Columbia (Minister of Forests)*, 2004 SCC 73. See also *Beckman v Little Salmon/ Carmacks First Nation*, 2010 SCC 53.

56 For an analysis of the duty to consult, see Reynolds, *supra* note 52, ch 6.

57 *R v Marshall; R v Bernard*, 2005 SCC 43.

58 *Tsilhqot'in Nation v British Columbia*, 2014 SCC 44. This case is sometimes referred to as the *William* case (or decision) after Roger William, a *Tsilhqot'in* chief and party to the litigation.

59 *Daniels v Canada (Indian Affairs and Northern Development)*, 2016 SCC 12.

2019: The federal government signs self-government agreements with Métis Nations in Alberta, Ontario, and Saskatchewan. The agreements affirm existing rights and set out a plan for the formal legal recognition of Métis governments as Indigenous governments, including their jurisdiction in such areas as citizenship, leadership selection, and government operations.

2019: To facilitate truth and reconciliation, to contribute to the implementation of UNDRIP, and to further other commitments, the federal government passes the *Indigenous Languages Act*[60] and an Indigenous child welfare statute.[61]

2019–2020: Wet'suwet'en hereditary chiefs lead protests against a gas pipeline through their territories. The protests cause significant disruption to rail transportation and port traffic (see below).

2020: The Assembly of First Nations commences a $10 billion class-action lawsuit against the federal government for discrimination in the funding of social services for on-reserve children and families. The action follows a finding by the Canadian Human Rights Tribunal in 2016 of systemic discrimination in the funding of such services.

New Directions for Indigenous Law in Canada

Although the influence of Indigenous law was challenged in the past by colonialism, it never disappeared. Some Aboriginal groups have always applied their own laws in internal matters and in many fields, including family life, land ownership, resource relationships, trade and commerce, and political organization.[62] Since the TRC report and UNDRIP, the importance of Indigenous legal traditions is now more widely acknowledged than ever.

The Wet'suwet'en pipeline protests in 2019–20, in particular, served to focus popular attention on Indigenous law.[63] The protests—in large part attributable to the outstanding land claim in *Delgamuukw*[64] referred to above—quickly expanded across the country, with an unprecedented show of support from other Indigenous and some non-Indigenous groups (see also Chapter 12 under the heading "Law Reform").

As is usually the case in complex disputes, however, there are opposing views. Detractors of the protests, including some members of the Wet'suwet'en people themselves, see positive economic and social gains coming from the pipeline project. The pipeline has been approved

---

60   SC 2019, c 23. The stated purposes of this legislation include supporting, promoting, and funding the use of Indigenous languages. At the time of writing this book, many parts of this Act still needed to be proclaimed in force.

61   *An Act respecting First Nations, Inuit and Métis children, youth and families*, SC 2019, c 24. This legislation affirms the right of Indigenous people to control their own child welfare services and sets out national principles applicable to the provision of these services. The central principle guiding the Act's interpretation and administration is "the best interests of the child" (see also Chapter 7 under "Family Law" concerning the relevance of this principle more generally in connection with child custody and access). At the time of writing this book, this Act was not in force.

62   Borrows, *supra* note 34 at 5-6. See also John Borrows, "Tracking Trajectories: Aboriginal Governance as an Aboriginal Right" (2005) 38 UBC Law Rev 285.

63   The Coastal GasLink pipeline at the centre of the dispute is slated to transport natural gas from Dawson Creek to Kitimat, near the BC coast, where the gas is to be converted to liquefied natural gas and shipped to Asian markets. The protests highlight not only the importance of Indigenous law but also the importance of other issues, such as land stewardship, climate change, and the vulnerability of Canada's resource-based economy. The economic impact of the protests was soon overtaken by the COVID-19 pandemic in 2020 and the recession that followed.

64   *Supra* note 51.

by the federal and provincial governments and all 20 First Nations bands along the pipeline route (including the Wet'suwet'en band).

Despite these approvals, some Wet'suwet'en elders claimed that they have the authority under their law to make decisions about projects of this nature on their land. The elected band council (constituted under the *Indian Act*) believes that it has the authority (following the rules of Canadian Aboriginal law). However this dispute is resolved, it should provide an opportunity to look closely at Indigenous law and its role more generally in Canadian society.

Like all human populations, Indigenous peoples have had their disagreements and violent interactions.[65] Despite this, there are many lessons to be learned from Indigenous legal practices: for instance, as they relate to environmental protection, general codes of conduct, principles of individual and collective responsibility, and methods of decision-making (which tend to be more decentralized and inclusive of the affected parties than is the regular Canadian court system).

An established interconnection between Indigenous law and Canadian law already exists within our current constitutional framework.[66] But to improve and expand that connection, more education is required. Steps in that direction have already started through the incorporation of Indigenous issues training into educational programs generally. In 2018, the University of Victoria launched the world's first Indigenous law program.[67] The hope is that with more training, concrete solutions will follow.

Finally, as we move toward reconciliation, constitutional amendment may also be an option to pursue if we are to "maintain and strengthen" Indigenous legal orders. This could involve creating entrenched areas of jurisdiction for Indigenous peoples. It would also mean questioning basic assumptions that many of us make about Canada's sovereignty, specifically, that it is fixed and invariable.

Canada's sovereignty is accepted by Canadian courts as a political fact and as legally unassailable.[68] However, the British Crown's assertion of sovereignty over lands occupied by Indigenous peoples is not based on some supreme law giving England the right to assume jurisdiction in that way and then transfer control to its colonies.[69] It was really just a political decision made by a colonizing culture.[70]

Sharing jurisdiction with Indigenous peoples, or giving up some sovereignty altogether, is possible if the collective will is there.

---

65   See, for example, John Borrows, "Indigenous Constitutionalism: Pre-existing Legal Genealogies in Canada" in Peter Oliver, Patrick Macklem, and Nathalie Des Rosiers, eds, *The Oxford Handbook of the Canadian Constitution* (Oxford: Oxford University Press, 2017) ch 2 at 13–14.

66   The *Casimel* case, *supra* note 41, and the *Powley* case, referred to above, are just two examples.

67   Students in the four-year program participate in field studies with Indigenous communities across Canada and graduate with a combined Juris Doctor (JD) degree and Juris Indigenarum Doctor (JID) degree. The JD degree is in Canadian common law, and the JID covers Indigenous legal orders. The aim of the combined degree is to build lasting political and legal relationships between Indigenous peoples and Canada: "World's First Indigenous Law Program Launches with Historic and Emotional Ceremony" (22 October 2018), online: *University of Victoria* <https://www.uvic.ca/news/academics/law/2018+jid-program-launch+news>.

68   See, for example, *Sparrow, supra* note 48 at 1103.

69   At most, it is based on common law rules dealing with the reception of English law into "newly" settled lands (see Chapter 3 under the heading "Common Law Rules of Reception of English Law").

70   See the discussion of this issue in Reynolds, *supra* note 52, ch 3.

CHAPTER SUMMARY

In the world today, there are four major legal system groups employed at the state level: common law, civil law, customary law, and religious law. Roughly half of the world's nations are monosystems, using predominantly one of these traditions. The other nations, including Canada, use a mix of traditions. Indigenous law is arguably moving toward status as a fifth discrete system group.

In Canada, the common law and civil law systems frame most areas of regulation. We are officially a bijural nation based on these two systems. The common law system developed in England over many centuries. It was brought to Canada by English settlers and became the legal system in all provinces and territories except for the province of Quebec. The key features of the common law system are the reliance on precedent and the principle of *stare decisis*. Another key feature of this system is the use of an adversarial process in the courtroom, with lawyers opposing each other and presenting their respective cases with (generally speaking) little interference from the trial judge.

The civil law system can be traced to ancient Rome and to societies even more ancient. Where Canada is concerned, the most important civil code is the *Napoleonic Code* of 1804; it strongly influenced Quebec's first code, which came into effect in the 1800s, and its current code, the *Civil Code of Quebec*, enacted in 1994. Codes of this kind play a central

role in the civil law system and are more important than previous judicial decisions. Other distinguishing features of the civil law system are the inquisitorial nature of the decision-making process (with judges playing a much more active role than they do in the common law system) and the importance of academic commentary.

Since the TRC report in 2015 and Canada's commitment in 2016 to implement UNDRIP, Canada is considering how it can recognize Indigenous law as a third legal tradition. The sources of Indigenous law in Canada are varied and include sacred, naturalistic, positivistic, deliberative, and customary sources. These cover the full range of sources that form the basis of the four main systems. Canada's common law and civil law systems are predominantly positivistic, with deliberative processes for creating substantive rules. Indigenous legal traditions go beyond Canada's two official systems and include, more fully, sacred, naturalistic, and customary sources. Recent protests and civil disobedience are focusing the debate about how to incorporate Indigenous law into the Canadian legal framework.

The need for an awareness of all legal systems is greater now than ever. As our world continues to become more interconnected, we find ourselves interacting with people from all parts of the globe, and at home, we are facing the consequences of past wrongs and the call for reconciliation with Indigenous peoples.

KEY TERMS

Aboriginal law, 44

adversarial system, 36

bijural, 29

Bill of Rights (1689), 36

binding, 33

Chancery, 30

civil code, 37

Civil Code of Quebec (Code Civil du Québec), 40

civil law, 29

common law, 29

Corpus Juris Civilis, 39

Court of Chancery, 32

Court of King's (or Queen's) Bench, 31

distinguishable, 34

equity, 32

feudalism, 30

historic treaties, 51

Indigenous law, 30

Inns of Court, 33

inquisitorial system, 41

king's peace, 31

modern treaties, 51

persuasive, 34

precedent, 33

ratio or *ratio decidendi*, 33

stare decisis, 33

writ, 32

FURTHER READING

BOOKS

Baker, John H, *An Introduction to English Legal History*, 5th ed (Oxford: Oxford University Press, 2019).

Borrows, John, *Indigenous Legal Traditions in Canada: Report for the Law Commission of Canada* (Ottawa: Law Commission of Canada, 2006).

Borrows, John, *Canada's Indigenous Constitution* (Toronto: University of Toronto Press, 2010).

Borrows, John et al, eds, *Braiding Legal Orders: Implementing the United Nations Declaration on the Rights of Indigenous Peoples* (Waterloo, Ont: Centre for International Governance Innovation, 2019).

Christie, Gordon, *Canadian Law and Indigenous Self-Determination: A Naturalist Analysis* (Toronto: University of Toronto Press, 2019).

Cross, Rupert & James W Harris, *Precedent in English Law*, 4th ed (Oxford: Clarendon Press, 1991).

David, René & John EC Brierley, *Major Legal Systems in the World Today: An Introduction to the Comparative Study of Law*, 3rd ed (London, UK: Stevens & Sons, 1985).

Flanagan, Tom, Christopher Alcantara & André Le Dressay, *Beyond the Indian Act: Restoring Aboriginal Property Rights* (Montreal and Kingston, Ont: McGill-Queen's University Press, 2010).

Glenn, H Patrick, *Legal Traditions of the World*, 5th ed (Oxford: Oxford University Press, 2014).

Grenon, Aline & Louise Bélanger-Hardy, *Elements of Quebec Civil Law: A Comparison with the Common Law of Canada* (Toronto: Carswell, 2008).

Merryman, John Henry & Rogelio Pérez-Perdomo, *The Civil Law Tradition: An Introduction to the Legal Systems of Europe and Latin America*, 3rd ed (Stanford, Cal: Stanford University Press, 2007).

Reynolds, Jim, *Aboriginal Peoples and the Law: A Critical Introduction* (Vancouver: Purich Books, an imprint of UBC Press, 2018).

Shears, Peter & Graham Stephenson, *James' Introduction to English Law*, 13th ed (Oxford: Oxford University Press, 2005).

Truth and Reconciliation Commission of Canada, *Canada's Residential Schools: Reconciliation – The Final Report of the Truth and Reconciliation Commission of Canada* (Montreal and Kingston: McGill-Queen's University Press, 2015) vol 6, online: <http://www.trc.ca/assets/pdf/Volume_6_Reconciliation_English_Web.pdf>.

WEBSITES

Assembly of First Nations: <https://www.afn.ca/Home>.

Civil Code of Quebec, Annotated: <https://ccq.lexum.com/w/ccq/en>.

Indigenous Bar Association: <https://indigenousbar.ca>.

Indigenous Foundations: <https://indigenousfoundations.arts.ubc.ca/home>.

JuriGlobe: <http://www.juriglobe.ca/eng>.

Yale Law School, The Avalon Project: Documents in Law, History and Diplomacy: <http://avalon.law.yale.edu>.

REVIEW QUESTIONS

1. What is meant by the term "bijural nation"?

2. Why is it important to be aware of legal traditions other than our own? Give at least three reasons.

3. Explain how the common law developed in England.

4. Briefly describe the role of the English Court of Chancery.

5. What is the principle of *stare decisis*? Under what circumstances is a precedent found to be either (a) binding, (b) distinguishable, or (c) persuasive?

6. What are the benefits of the common law system's practice of following precedent?

7. Briefly describe how the civil law system in Europe was indebted to Roman law.

8. What are some of the main features of civil law?

9. What is meant when we say that courts in civil law jurisdictions use an inquisitorial system?

10. What are three differences between the common law and civil law systems?

11. Describe three ways in which Canada has tried to harmonize the common law and civil law legal systems in this country.

12. How does Call to Action 45 in the 2015 TRC report propose to strengthen Indigenous legal traditions in Canada?

13. What are the five main sources of Indigenous law?

14. Given that the Mi'kmaq people had ancestral trading practices, how did the SCC reason to find that commercial logging was not a constitutionally protected right in the *Marshall* and *Bernard* cases in 2005?

EXERCISES

1. When a common law judge recognizes a new precedent, is she *finding* new law or *making* new law? Explain why you think there is—or is not—a difference between these two processes within the common law system.

2. Consider one way in which the civil law is different from the common law and describe a situation where you think that difference might affect the outcome of a case.

3. How is Canadian bijuralism an asset when it comes to Canadians doing business with other countries? In your answer, consider two of Canada's trading partners and their legal systems.

4. Choose an Indigenous nation in Canada and research how it applies its own customary laws.

3 From the Reception of English and French Law into Canada to the Charter

Introduction 60

Common Law Rules of Reception
of English Law 60

Reception of English and French Law into
Canada's Provinces and Territories 63

Prelude to Confederation in 1867 70

Canada Is Born 72

Post-Confederation Problems............ 73

The Movement to Patriate the Constitution
and Adopt a Charter of Rights 77

Patriation and a Revived Constitution ... 82

Chapter Summary 84

Key Terms 84

Further Reading 84

Review Questions 85

Exercises 85

The *Canadian Charter of Rights and Freedoms*, bearing the signature of Pierre Trudeau in the bottom right corner.

LEARNING OUTCOMES

After reading this chapter, you will be able to:

- Describe the general rules governing the reception of law into England's colonies.
- Identify how and when the various regions of Canada received English (or French) law and how and when they joined Confederation.
- Describe the events leading to the enactment of the *British North America Act, 1867* and the nature of the union it created.

- Understand some important post-Confederation issues, such as those relating to the absence of an amending formula in the Constitution and the role of the courts in shaping Canadian federalism.
- Explain the rise of Canadian nationalism and the activism of Indigenous peoples and women with respect to the development of the Constitution and the *Canadian Charter of Rights and Freedoms*.
- Describe the significance of the patriation of the Constitution and the Charter.

> With the advent of the Charter, the principles on which the rights and freedoms of Canadians are based have the status of constitutional law. ... The fundamental principle underlying this dimension of our most basic law is that there are some phases of Canadian life which should normally be beyond the reach of any majority, save by constitutional amendment.
>
> The Hon Brian Dickson, "The Canadian Charter of Rights and Freedoms: Context and Evolution" in Errol Mendes & Stéphane Beaulac, eds, *Canadian Charter of Rights and Freedoms*, 5th ed (Toronto: LexisNexis, 2014) at 3

Introduction

In its early colonial period, Canada's legal history was primarily influenced by English and French traditions. After the First World War, however, it began to travel a uniquely Canadian path. This chapter outlines how and when the various regions of British North America received English common law and, in the case of Quebec, French civil law. It also describes the unification process and some key events leading to Confederation in 1867. Next, the chapter examines some post-Confederation issues, including those related to omissions in our Constitution and the shaping of Canadian federalism. Following this is a consideration of some of the legal and social issues behind the movement to patriate the Constitution and adopt the *Canadian Charter of Rights and Freedoms* (the Charter) in the 1980s. It concludes with an overview of some of the key changes brought about by our new Constitution.

Common Law Rules of Reception of English Law

As we saw in Chapter 2, when the first European settlers from England and France arrived in Canada, they found that it was already occupied by Indigenous peoples, who had their own cultures and legal systems. These settlers arrived mainly in eastern Canada, and after the *Royal Proclamation, 1763*, at least, Indigenous peoples had cause for some hope that further encroachment on their lands would be fair and measured (see Box 3.1). However, European expansion quickly moved westward and northward. Despite the uneasy relationship that developed between the new settlers and Indigenous peoples, colonization was rapid.

BOX 3.1

Royal Proclamation, 1763

The *Royal Proclamation, 1763** was issued by King George III on October 7, 1763, following the Seven Years' War and the *Treaty of Paris, 1763*. Under the terms of the treaty, France surrendered all of its possessions in New France (that is, all of its North American possessions).

The proclamation advanced two important policy objectives from a Canadian perspective. First, it attempted to integrate the French population under British rule, including, apparently, through the application of the common law system (the proclamation was not clear on this point). However, the French resisted, and the English eventually capitulated by enacting the *Quebec Act, 1774*,† which reinstated French civil law (see also below under "Quebec").

Second, the proclamation delineated the boundaries of its existing North American colonies and set in place a structure for acquiring other North American lands that had not already been ceded or otherwise acquired by England. These lands covered territories west of the Appalachian Mountains and north and were "reserved" for the use of "the several Nations or Tribes of Indians" under the "Sovereignty, Protection, and Dominion" of the British Crown. The reservation of these vast territories was disputed by the 13 American colonies (they had plans for western expansion) and contributed to the American War of Independence (1775–1783).

The *Royal Proclamation, 1763* stipulated that future purchases and acquisitions of reserved land were to be through the Crown only. Colonial governments and individuals were enjoined from taking such lands. Only after reserved land had first been ceded to the Crown by treaty could it be transferred to others. Concerning the acquisition of Indigenous lands by individuals, the proclamation provided (in part):

> And whereas great Frauds and Abuses have been committed in the purchasing Lands of the Indians, to the great Prejudice of Our Interests, and to the great Dissatisfaction of the said Indians; in order therefore to prevent such Irregularities for the future, and to the End that the Indians may be convinced of Our

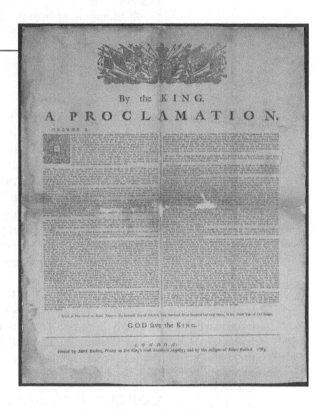

> Justice, … We … strictly enjoin and require, that no private Person do presume to make any Purchase from the said Indians of any Lands reserved to [them] … ; but that if, at any Time, any of the said Indians should be inclined to dispose of the said Lands, that same shall be purchased only for Us, in Our Name, at some publick Meeting or Assembly of the said Indians … .

The proclamation is based on respect for the rights of Indigenous peoples and has been referred to as the "Indian Magna Carta" or "Indian Bill of Rights." It is cited in section 25 of the Charter and is considered by many to be a key source of Aboriginal rights, including Aboriginal title. (See also Chapter 2 under "Canadian Law and Indigenous Peoples: A Timeline.")

* (UK), reprinted in RSC 1985, App II, No 1.

† (UK), 14 Geo III, c 83.

General common law colonization rules determined how English law was received into English colonies.[1] These rules were designed to provide new colonies with a legal structure from the outset and avoid the negative consequences of beginning these colonies in a "legal vacuum." How a particular territory was acquired by England often determined what rule was followed.

A discussion of all of the reception rules is beyond the scope of this text. The following sections describe only the three most relevant to Canada: settlement, conquest or cession, and adoption.

Settlement

When England colonized a territory and sent English subjects there to settle it, that colony received English law then in force, including common law (that is, judge-made rules) and statute law. These became the colony's first laws. This practice prevailed even though the territory was already inhabited; Indigenous legal systems were simply disregarded. Colonial courts in Canada decided that the reception date—that is, the date on which the colony specifically received English laws—would be the same as the date on which a colony first established its own local legislature.

The reception of English law into its colonies as they were settled was subject to some limitations. Only those laws of general application that were suitable, taking into consideration the colonial environment, were received. If a law—whether it was a common law precedent or legislated—was inapplicable in light of the local circumstances, it did not become part of the law of the colony. The laws that were received could be amended or abolished by the colonial legislature at a later date, as required by changing circumstances. The only laws that could not be changed were English **imperial statutes**. These were statutes that the English Parliament enacted specifically for its overseas colonies, over which England reserved ultimate legal control.

imperial statute
law passed by the English Parliament applying specifically to an overseas English colony

Conquest or Cession

If England acquired an overseas colony by conquest (or by transfer or **cession** from another country, pursuant to a treaty), a second common law colonization rule held that laws already existing in the colony continued in force until such time as they were specifically changed by the English government. Provided that no local legislature existed in the colony, English law could be imposed on the colony by the English monarch, exercising his or her prerogative power, or by England's imperial Parliament.

cession
transfer of a colony from one country to another

Adoption

A third way English law could be received into a British colony was by adoption. In this instance, a colony's legislature would pass a reception statute that adopted English law as of a certain date. From that time, English law would be received and in force in the colony. This might occur to clarify any uncertainty surrounding the reception date or to change the laws already in place in the colony.

---

1   See Peter W Hogg, "Reception" in *Constitutional Law of Canada*, 5th ed (Toronto: Carswell, 2007) (loose-leaf updated 2019, release 1) ch 2; JE Cote, "The Reception of English Law" (1977) 15 Alta L Rev 29.

Reception of English and French Law into Canada's Provinces and Territories

The following is an overview of how and when English or French law was received in each Canadian province and territory and the date on which each one joined Confederation. For the five provinces from Quebec east to Newfoundland, English and French laws were introduced by settlement or cession, the first two methods. For the five provinces from Ontario west and the territories, English laws were adopted by reception statutes, the third method. Table 3.1 provides a summary.

Newfoundland and Labrador

Newfoundland was England's first Canadian colony. British fishing fleets—along with others from Spain, France, and Portugal—sailed to the island as early as the 1500s to catch fish on the Grand Banks. In time, some members of the fishing crews began to spend the winter there, cutting wood and preparing for the fishing fleet's return the next spring. Generally speaking, fishing took priority over settlement in this early period.

TABLE 3.1   Reception Dates for Receiving English and French Law and Entering Confederation for Each Canadian Province and Territory

PROVINCE/TERRITORY	RECEPTION OF LAW	ENTERED CONFEDERATION
Alberta	1870	September 1, 1905
British Columbia	1858	July 20, 1871
Manitoba	1870	July 15, 1870
New Brunswick	1758 (or possibly 1660)	July 1, 1867
Newfoundland and Labrador	1832	March 31, 1949
Northwest Territories	1870	July 15, 1870
Nova Scotia	1758	July 1, 1867
Nunavut	1870	April 1, 1999
Ontario	1792	July 1, 1867
Prince Edward Island	1758 (or possibly 1773)	July 1, 1873
Quebec	French civil law restored in 1774	July 1, 1867
Saskatchewan	1870	September 1, 1905
Yukon	1870	June 13, 1898

In 1583, Sir Humphrey Gilbert claimed the island for England, and several British settlements were founded on the island's east coast. Settlers later came under the governance of the admiral of the English naval squadron that arrived each year to guard the fishing fleet. As a result of these developments, the island was considered a settled colony of England. Its first Legislative Assembly was held in St John's in 1832, and this date became the reception date for English law in the colony.[2]

Although Newfoundland was England's first Canadian colony, it was actually the last to join **Confederation** and the last to be admitted to Canada, which occurred on March 31, 1949.

Confederation
coming together of the three British North American colonies of Nova Scotia, New Brunswick, and the Province of Canada (Ontario and Quebec) to form the Dominion of Canada in 1867; the term later included all the provinces and territories that have joined Canada since that date

Nova Scotia

The reception of English law into Nova Scotia was complicated by the fact that this colony was originally part of French Acadia, that part of New France located in Canada's Atlantic region. French colonists first settled this area in the 1600s, and it was under French control until 1713. In that year, under the terms of the *Treaty of Utrecht*, France ceded Acadia to England.

Given that England acquired Nova Scotia by cession, French law ought to have continued there until England changed it. However, things did not proceed according to this common law reception rule. In effect, once England established a colonial administration in Nova Scotia after the *Treaty of Utrecht*, and once Edward Cornwallis set up a seat of government and military base at Halifax in 1749, the colony was treated instead as having been acquired by settlement. The colony convened its first Legislative Assembly in 1758, and this was established as its reception date for English law.

In the next century, Nova Scotia was one of the original three colonies to join Confederation, doing so on July 1, 1867.

Prince Edward Island

The reception of English law into Prince Edward Island was linked to its reception into Nova Scotia. The island was originally settled by France, and, under the *Treaty of Utrecht*, France kept it. However, France ceded the island to England by the *Treaty of Paris, 1763*. Then, by the *Royal Proclamation, 1763*, the island was annexed to Nova Scotia. Shortly afterward, in 1769, the island became a separate colony, and its first elected Assembly was held there in 1773.

As with Nova Scotia, England apparently acquired the island by cession. However, the reception of English law into Prince Edward Island was consistent with the island's being acquired by settlement. The probable date (legal scholars are not all in agreement about this) for receiving English law may not be 1773 (the date of its own first elected Assembly) but 1758 (the date of the first Legislative Assembly in Nova Scotia).[3]

---

2   C English, "From Fishing Schooner to Colony: The Legal Development of Newfoundland, 1791–1832" in LA Knafla & SWS Binnie, eds, *Law, Society, and the State: Essays in Modern Legal History* (Toronto: University of Toronto Press, 1995) 73; J Bannister, *The Rule of the Admirals: Law, Custom, and Naval Government in Newfoundland, 1699–1832* (Toronto: University of Toronto Press, 2003).

3   See Hogg, *supra* note 1, ch 2.5; JD Whyte & WR Lederman, "The Extension of Governmental Institutions and Legal Systems to British North America in the Colonial Period" in WR Lederman, ed, *Continuing Canadian Constitutional Dilemmas* (Toronto: Butterworths, 1981) 70.

Interestingly, although Charlottetown was the location of Canada's first meeting, in 1864, to discuss Confederation (see below), the colony did not enter Confederation for another nine years. It was admitted to Canada on July 1, 1873.

New Brunswick

Like Nova Scotia and Prince Edward Island, New Brunswick was originally settled by French colonists and was also part of French Acadia. Like those colonies, it was ceded or transferred by France to England. Parts of it were ceded in 1713, by the *Treaty of Utrecht*, and the remainder under the *Treaty of Paris, 1763*. In 1763, like Prince Edward Island, New Brunswick was annexed to Nova Scotia. It subsequently (again like Prince Edward Island) separated from Nova Scotia and became a separate colony in 1784.

New Brunswick was also like the other two maritime colonies in that the reception of English law there was deemed to be by settlement and not by cession. However, the actual date for the reception of English law into the colony is unclear. Some legal scholars consider New Brunswick's case to be similar to Prince Edward Island's. In other words, although the province had its first Legislative Assembly in 1786, being previously annexed to Nova Scotia makes Nova Scotia's reception date of 1758 applicable to New Brunswick. Other commentators on this matter, including New Brunswick courts, have held 1660 to be the reception date. According to Peter Hogg, this date was chosen because it was the year in which Charles II was restored to the English throne.[4]

New Brunswick was, like Nova Scotia, one of the three original colonies to join Confederation and was admitted to Canada on July 1, 1867.

Quebec

In contrast to Canada's maritime colonies, Quebec's status as a colony was always clear. England acquired it from France by conquest and later by cession.

French colonists first settled Quebec in the early 1600s, and it thus became a French overseas colony, known as "la Nouvelle-France." As such, the colony received French civil law for its legal system. However, the British general James Wolfe defeated the French general Louis-Joseph de Montcalm at the battle of the Plains of Abraham, also called the Battle of Quebec, near Quebec City in 1759 (see Figure 3.1). Subsequently, France ceded Quebec to England under the terms of the *Treaty of Paris, 1763*. What followed was the *Royal Proclamation, 1763*. Exercising his royal prerogative power, King George III of England declared that Quebec would have English law imposed there in place of French civil law (see also Box 3.1).

This uneasy shift of affairs, with Quebec slated to receive English law, did not last long. The English government was influenced to change things by two early civilian governors there, Murray and Carleton, who were both conciliatory to the French *Canadiens* and who were sensitive to the uncertain state of the legal system in Quebec in the wake of the *Royal Proclamation, 1763*. As a result, the English government passed the *Quebec Act, 1774*, a statute that restored French civil law there. Section 8 of the *Quebec Act* stated that "in all Matters of Controversy, relative to Property and Civil Rights, Resort shall be had to the Laws of Canada, as the Rule for the Decision of the same." This provision restored pre-conquest French civil law to Quebec, although English criminal law was retained there, making 1774 the date for receiving (or restoring) civil law into the province.

---

4 See DG Bell, "A Note on the Reception of English Statutes in New Brunswick" (1979) 28 UNBLJ 195 at 196-200; Hogg, *supra* note 1, ch 2.1 (note 5).

FIGURE 3.1   Battle of the Plains of Abraham
Anglo-American painter Benjamin West famously captured the death of General Wolfe on the Plains of Abraham. The French general, Montcalm, was also killed in the battle, which followed a 3-month siege by the British and lasted only 15 minutes.

One related effect of this Act was also important. At that time, the territory of Quebec extended beyond its current western boundary (the Ottawa River) into what is now southern Ontario. After the American Revolution in 1776, many American settlers, still loyal to England, left their country and re-established themselves in present-day Ontario (at that time part of western Quebec). These United Empire Loyalists soon petitioned the English monarch to have the western part of Quebec, where they had relocated, separated from the older, eastern part. They were successful. In response to their demands, the English government passed the *Constitutional Act, 1791*.[5] This Act separated Quebec into two colonies, called Upper Canada (present-day Ontario) and Lower Canada (present-day Quebec) relative to their geographic location along the Great Lakes–St. Lawrence River watershed.

Quebec continued in this way until the *Union Act, 1840*,[6] by which England once again reunited Lower Canada with Upper Canada into the new Province of Canada (see the discussion below). Under this Act, Quebec was then called Canada East and Ontario was then called Canada West. This united province lasted from 1841, when the *Union Act* took effect, until 1867, when the Province of Canada became one of the original colonies to enter Confederation. At this point, the province was once again divided into Quebec and Ontario. Quebec joined Confederation on July 1, 1867.

The Civil Code of Quebec

During the union period (that is, when Ontario and Quebec composed the Province of Canada), Quebec was undergoing a great economic transition, changing from an agrarian and rural society into a modern one—industrial, capitalist, and urban. The practical demands of this transformation—which involved, for example, the rapid expansion of canals, roads, railways, banks, insurance companies, milling, and lumbering—in combination with an increased influx of British immigration, created the need for a less confusing legal system in the province, especially for commercial law. Uncertainty also arose over which legal

---

5   (UK), 31 Geo III, c 31.

6   (UK), 3 & 4 Vict, c 35.

system—the common law or the civil law system—applied to diverse legal matters needing to be addressed.

The demands for more certainty forced politicians to act. George-Étienne Cartier, Quebec's attorney general, established a three-person Codification Commission in 1857 to revise existing laws in Quebec and consolidate them into a comprehensive civil code. Its efforts resulted in the *Civil Code of Lower Canada*,[7] or *Code civil du Bas Canada*, which took effect in 1866, the year before Confederation. The Code was in force from 1866 until December 31, 1993. By the 1950s, it was increasingly felt that many of the Code's provisions were out of step with modern society in Quebec. As a result, Quebec's Civil Code Revision Office, created in 1955, helped the government reform and modernize the Code. On January 1, 1994, a revised and newly comprehensive *Civil Code of Quebec*,[8] designed to reflect contemporary social realities and modern attitudes, became law (see Box 2.2 in Chapter 2).

The 1866 Code and the 1994 Code have served to protect Quebec law against encroachments by the common law system practised in all other Canadian provinces. Generally speaking, these codes have helped preserve Quebec's separate civil law in predominantly common law North America.[9] (As mentioned in Chapter 2, Quebec is not fully regulated by the civil law system; the common law system pertains to its public law, including criminal law.)

Ontario

As we have noted, present-day Ontario originated when the *Constitutional Act, 1791* divided Quebec and the western part became Upper Canada. However, under section 33, the Act also provided that the laws of Quebec (that is, the civil law) were to continue in force in Upper and Lower Canada until such time as they were changed by the respective assemblies of each new colony.

Quebec retained its civil law unchanged, but Upper Canada did not. At the first Legislative Assembly for Upper Canada, held in Newark (now Niagara-on-the-Lake) in 1792, the first statute passed was a reception act regarding English law. Section III of this Act provided that "in all matters of controversy relative to property and civil rights, resort shall be had to the Laws of England as the rule for the decision of the same." As a result of this Act, the legislature of Upper Canada adopted English law as of 1792. This is recognized as the date for the reception of English laws into the province of Ontario.

Upper Canada continued in this way until the *Union Act, 1840*, when, as noted earlier, the colony was reunited with Lower Canada (Quebec), and the Province of Canada was created. Ontario joined Confederation on July 1, 1867, separating from Quebec at the same time.

Manitoba

At the time Ontario entered Confederation in 1867, the area on its western border, stretching west to the Rocky Mountains, was divided between the Hudson's Bay Company's Rupert's Land and the North-Western Territory (see Figure 3.2).

---

7   (UK), 29 Vict, c 41, (1865).

8   CQLR, c CCQ-1991.

9   B Young, *George-Étienne Cartier: Montreal Bourgeois* (Montreal and Kingston, Ont: McGill-Queen's University Press, 1981); FP Eliadis, "The Legal System in Québec" in GL Gall, ed, *The Canadian Legal System*, 5th ed (Toronto: Thomson, 2004) 263.

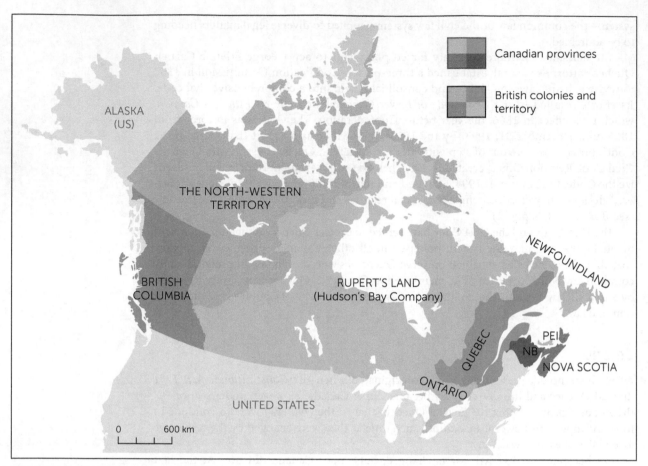

FIGURE 3.2   Dominion of Canada, 1867
Note the vast territory comprising Rupert's Land and the North-Western Territory.

For the newly formed Dominion of Canada, this western area was highly coveted; possession of it was crucial if Canada was to extend its borders "from sea to sea." Canada's first prime minister, John A Macdonald, soon entered into negotiations with the Hudson's Bay Company to purchase its western landholdings with the help of the British government. Terms were reached in 1869, and the area was transferred to Canada in 1870. That same year, the federal Parliament created the province of Manitoba out of part of Rupert's Land and created the Northwest Territories, as this area was renamed, out of the remainder of Rupert's Land and out of the former North-Western Territory. By statute, the reception date for English law into Manitoba was 1870. The actual date for Manitoba's joining Confederation, the fifth province to do so, was July 15, 1870.

Saskatchewan

This province, like Alberta and the three northern Canadian territories, was also created out of the vast Northwest Territories west and north of the province of Manitoba. Saskatchewan joined Confederation on September 1, 1905, and its reception date for English law was 1870 (see Figure 3.3).

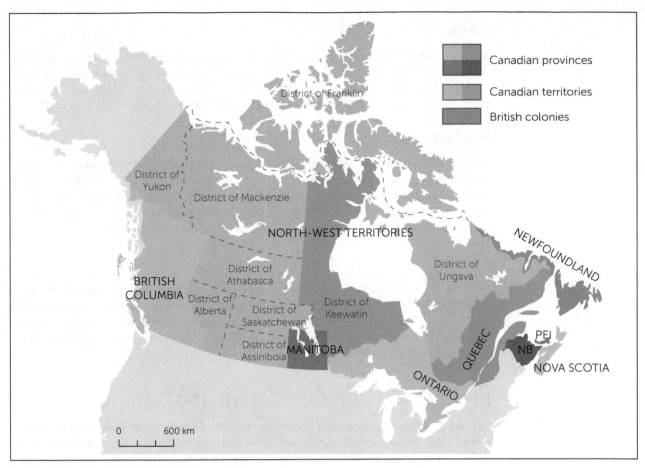

FIGURE 3.3   Map of Canada, 1895
The district boundaries of Saskatchewan, Manitoba, Alberta, and Yukon are shown. Alberta and Saskatchewan had expanded to their northern boundaries by 1905 (into the area marked District of Athabasca), and Manitoba expanded northward in 1912.

Alberta

Like Saskatchewan, this province was created out of the Northwest Territories and joined Confederation at the same time as Saskatchewan, on September 1, 1905. The date of reception for English law there was the same as for Saskatchewan—1870 (see Figure 3.3).

British Columbia

British Columbia was England's Pacific coast colony. Originally, there were two of them: Vancouver Island, created in 1849, and British Columbia on the mainland, created in 1858. When England united these two separate colonies in 1866 and called the new territory British Columbia, the governor declared 1858 (later confirmed by its Legislative Council) as the reception date for English law. British Columbia joined Confederation on July 20, 1871, becoming Canada's sixth province.

Yukon

The gold rush of 1898 was the primary reason for Yukon being created as a separate territory. Mainly as a result of this event, Yukon was created out of the Northwest Territories and became a separate territory on June 13, 1898. The reception date for English law there, as in the three other western provinces created out of the Northwest Territories, was 1870.

Northwest Territories

The Northwest Territories, to the east of Yukon, has retained its original name, which dates from 1870. Its present area is, of course, smaller than it was originally; since 1870, as we have seen, the area has been divided into various other provinces and territories: Alberta, Saskatchewan, Yukon, and, most recently, the territory of Nunavut. The reception date for English law into the Northwest Territories was 1870, the year it originally entered Confederation.

Nunavut

Nunavut is Canada's newest territory. It was officially created out of the eastern half of the Northwest Territories on April 1, 1999, although its boundaries had been established in 1993. The Inuit are the majority population in this territory, and the word "*Nunavut*" means "our land" in Inuktitut, the Inuit language. The date for the reception of English law there, as in the two other arctic territories, is 1870.

Prelude to Confederation in 1867

The idea of uniting some or all of Britain's six separate Canadian colonies—Newfoundland, Nova Scotia, Prince Edward Island, New Brunswick, the Province of Canada (Canada West and Canada East), and British Columbia—began in the early 1800s. The unification movement gained further momentum when, in 1864, politicians from the Atlantic region met at Charlottetown, Prince Edward Island, to discuss the possibility of a maritime union of Britain's Atlantic colonies (see Figure 3.4). They were joined there by politicians from the Province of Canada, led by John A Macdonald and George-Étienne Cartier, who put forward an ambitious plan to unite more of Britain's Canadian colonies. Many of these politicians reconvened to discuss this idea further at two subsequent conferences: one in Quebec City, later that same year, and another in London, England, in 1866.

These conferences led to three of these colonies—Nova Scotia, New Brunswick, and the Province of Canada (Ontario and Quebec)—uniting into the new Dominion of Canada in 1867. They did so under an imperial statute of the British Parliament called the *British North America Act, 1867*[10] (also referred to as the BNA Act and now renamed the *Constitution Act, 1867*). Note that the colonies were called "Provinces" in the preamble to the Act.

Canadian historians and political scientists have examined several key factors leading to Canadian Confederation in 1867 and ascertained important political, military, economic, and imperial forces behind this development.[11] Principal among these were the following:

---

10   (UK), 30 & 31 Vict, c 3, reprinted in RSC 1985, App II, No 5.

11   See PB Waite, *The Life and Times of Confederation, 1864–1867* (Toronto: University of Toronto Press, 1962); R Cook, C Brown & C Berger, eds, *Confederation* (Toronto: University of Toronto Press, 1967); Patrick Malcolmson & Richard Myers, *The Canadian Regime: An Introduction to Parliamentary Government in Canada*, 3rd ed (Peterborough, Ont: Broadview Press, 2005); and Roger Gibbins, *Conflict and Unity: An Introduction to Canadian Political Life*, 3rd ed (Scarborough, Ont: Nelson, 1994).

1. political stalemate in the Province of Canada caused by a number of issues, including the split legal system (the common law in Canada West [Upper Canada] and the civil law in Canada East [Lower Canada]), regional rivalries (Canada West and Canada East were divided on many issues by language, cultural, and religious differences), and the unsettled location of the Legislative Assembly before Queen Victoria chose Ottawa as the capital in 1859;

2. the influence of the United States (including worries about the possibility of an invasion and its westward expansion to the Pacific coast based on an ideology called "manifest destiny"—the belief that the United States "was destined by the will of Heaven to become a country of political and territorial eminence");[12]

3. expansion of railways across British North America;

4. hopes for a larger domestic market for manufactured goods (union could result in a continental economy); and

5. British support and approval for Confederation (Britain was encouraging greater independence for its colonies in British North America for economic reasons).

As mentioned, the last pre-Confederation conference was in London in 1866. Here delegates made final revisions to their union plan, and on March 29, 1867, the British Parliament passed the BNA Act. The Act was proclaimed in force on July 1, 1867, and the newly completed Parliament buildings in Ottawa were set to host Canada's first national government.

FIGURE 3.4   Delegates to the Charlottetown Conference, 1864
The delegates discussed the idea for a union of Britain's separate North American colonies into a new Canadian federal state, which was achieved in 1867.

---

12   Norman A Graebner, "Introduction" in *Manifest Destiny* (Indianapolis, Ind: Bobbs-Merrill, 1968) at xv.

Canada Is Born

federalism
in Canada, the division
of state powers between
the federal Parliament
in Ottawa and the
legislatures of the
provinces and territories

unitary government
form of government
whereby one supreme
authority governs
the whole country

The government structure eventually adopted by the framers of the BNA Act was **federalism**. This was something new to British constitutional history and was different from Britain's own unitary system of government. Federalism was an American, not an English, political idea and was reflected in the BNA Act's division of powers between the new Canadian federal government in Ottawa and the provinces. Interestingly, the federal structure that was the basis of the Iroquois Confederacy predated both the American and the Canadian unions (see Box 2.5 in Chapter 2).

Why did Canadian politicians end up adopting a federal system of government? It was not the first choice of Macdonald, our country's first prime minister. Macdonald desired a **unitary government** like Britain's, whereby all legislative authority would be centred in one governing body for all of Canada. However, he realized that this would not be possible. A unitary government was unacceptable in two quarters: the maritime provinces and Quebec.

The inhabitants of the maritime provinces, although enticed by the prospect of a railway connection to central Canada that would reduce their geographic and economic isolation, feared that a unitary structure would undermine their distinctive political culture. A federal political union would better safeguard their local interests. The same was true for Quebec, which had, in addition, deep-seated cultural and language concerns. Quebec politicians saw the need for a French-controlled provincial government to legislate over areas such as their language, schools, civil law, religion, and political institutions.

Political deadlock in the Province of Canada was, as noted above, a leading underlying factor in the push for a federal union. However, the system that created this political frustration was also, ironically, a key to the future success of Canadian federalism. From 1841 to 1867, the Province of Canada already had an unacknowledged federal form of government. Its civil service and government departments were already dual; they operated in both English and French. It was governed under dual French–English premierships—for example, Baldwin and LaFontaine, Brown and Dorion, and Macdonald and Cartier. For legislation to pass, a double majority of votes was needed—in other words, a majority from representatives of both parts of the province. Although problematic, this political arrangement respected the regional and linguistic rights of the Province of Canada's two entities. As well, the later use of French and English in the province's Legislative Assembly showed that a bilingual Parliament could work in Canada.

John A Macdonald and the New Federal Government

The framers of the BNA Act were aware of American federalism and borrowed some ideas from it. At the same time, however, Macdonald was wary of some negative aspects of American federalism. For one thing, he felt that the American Constitution gave too much power to individual states, at the expense of their federal government in Washington.

Such a perceived weakness in the American system helped convince Macdonald that Canada's new federal government had to be stronger than the provinces. This was reflected in the division of powers between the provinces and the federal government. Macdonald's vision was that

> all the great questions which affect the general interests of the Confederacy as a
> whole, are confided to the Federal Parliament, while the local interests and local laws
> of each section are preserved intact, and entrusted to the care of the local bodies.[13]

---

13   John A Macdonald, "Confederation Debates, Legislative Assembly, Feb 6, 1865" in PB Waite, ed, *The Confederation Debates in the Province of Canada, 1865* (Toronto: McClelland & Stewart, 1963) at 45.

Section 91 of the BNA Act lists a number of matters of national importance under the Parliament of Canada's areas of control, including the following:

- The Regulation of Trade and Commerce (s 91(2));
- The Raising of Money by any Mode or System of Taxation (s 91(3));
- Militia, Military and Naval Service, and Defence (s 91(7));
- Currency and Coinage (s 91(14));
- Indians, and Lands reserved for the Indians (s 91(24)); and
- Criminal Law (s 91(27)).

Section 91 also states that the Parliament of Canada has residual power "to make Laws for the Peace, Order, and good Government of Canada, in relation to all Matters not coming within the Classes of Subjects by this Act assigned exclusively to the Legislatures of the Provinces."

Other sections of the BNA Act assign further powers to the federal Parliament's control. For example, section 24 gives it the exclusive power to appoint senators and section 58 the power to appoint the provinces' lieutenant governors. Section 92(10) gives the Parliament of Canada the power to declare some provincial works "to be for the general Advantage of Canada" and thus to come under federal control. Section 96 authorizes the federal government to appoint judges to the highest courts in each province. Finally, section 101 provides for the Parliament of Canada to establish a "General Court of Appeal for Canada." (The division of powers between Parliament and the provinces is explored in more detail in Chapter 4.)

Post-Confederation Problems

A number of problems emerged following Confederation—principally, those stemming from omissions in the BNA Act and the role the Privy Council played in interpreting the Constitution.

Omissions in the BNA Act

The BNA Act was a crucial development in Canada's political history. However, it later proved problematic in various ways. First, it was an imperial statute of the English Parliament, not of the Canadian Parliament, and lacked a formula enabling Canadians to amend it themselves. "In constitutional and legal terms this was a major blunder," law professor Edward McWhinney noted, "and undoubtedly stemmed from the ignorance of British constitutional lawyers with the problems of written constitutions and the practical necessity of having amendment formulae built in."[14]

The BNA Act's omission of a domestic amending formula was not a problem in 1867. However, it later emerged as a problem in the 1960s and 1970s, when Canadian nationalism became more pronounced. Many Canadians were getting frustrated at being unable to amend the Constitution by themselves, without Britain's approval.

A second problem with the BNA Act over time was that it did not contain an entrenched bill (or charter) of rights for Canadian citizens. In this respect, it differed markedly from the American Constitution, whose first ten amendments are known as the "Bill of Rights." The preamble to the BNA Act stated that Canada's Constitution was to be "similar in Principle to that of the United Kingdom." However, the United Kingdom's Constitution did not have anything similar to the American Constitution's Bill of Rights.

---

14   Edward McWhinney, *Canada and the Constitution, 1979–1982* (Toronto: University of Toronto Press, 1982) at 65.

Britain's Constitution itself came from various sources. Its measures for protecting the civil liberties of English subjects were found, for example, in the 1689 Bill of Rights and written documents such as the *Magna Carta*; they were also based on common law court decisions, customs, political practices, public support for democracy, and remedies such as *habeas corpus*.

The aim of making Canada's Constitution "similar in principle" to England's meant that Canada inherited Britain's varied civil liberties and legal inheritance, which contrasted with the American approach of protecting its citizens' civil rights in one central, entrenched document that could be changed only by a constitutional amendment.

A third problem with the BNA Act, as later events would reveal, was that it was formulated without consulting the first peoples to inhabit the land now called Canada: the Indigenous population of Canada. On the 100th anniversary of Confederation, Chief Dan George of the Tsleil-Waututh Nation, a Coast Salish band in North Vancouver, delivered his "Lament for Confederation" in Vancouver's Empire Stadium, offering a poignant reflection on the meaning of this centenary from a First Nations perspective (see Box 3.2).

BOX 3.2

Chief Dan George, "Lament for Confederation," July 1, 1967

How long have I known you, Oh Canada? A hundred years? Yes, a hundred years. And many, many seelanum more. And today, when you celebrate your hundred years, Oh Canada, I am sad for all the Indian people throughout the land.

For I have known you when your forests were mine; when they gave me my meat and my clothing. I have known you in your streams and rivers where your fish splashed and danced in the sun, where the waters said, "Come, come and eat of my abundance." I have known you in the freedom of the winds. And my spirit, like the winds, once roamed your good lands.

But in the long hundred years since the white man came, I have seen my freedom disappear like the salmon going mysteriously out to sea. The white man's strange customs, which I could not understand, pressed down upon me until I could no longer breathe. When I fought to protect my land and my home, I was called a savage. When I neither understood nor welcomed his way of life, I was called lazy. When I tried to rule my people, I was stripped of my authority.

My nation was ignored in your history textbooks—they were little more important in the history of Canada than the buffalo that ranged the plains. I was ridiculed in your plays and motion pictures, and when I drank your fire-water, I got drunk—very, very drunk. And I forgot.

Oh Canada, how can I celebrate with you this Centenary, this hundred years? Shall I thank you for the reserves that are left to me of my beautiful forests? For the canned fish of my rivers? For the loss of my pride and authority, even among my own people? For the lack of my will to fight back? No! I must forget what's past and gone.

Oh God in Heaven! Give me back the courage of the olden chiefs. Let me wrestle with my surroundings. Let me again, as in the days of old, dominate my environment. Let me humbly accept this new culture and through it rise up and go on.

Oh God! Like the thunderbird of old I shall rise again out of the sea; I shall grab the instruments of the white man's success—his education, his skills—and with these new tools I shall build my race into the proudest segment of your society.

Before I follow the great chiefs that have gone before us, Oh Canada, I shall see these things come to pass. I shall see our young braves and our chiefs sitting in the house of law and government, ruling and being ruled by the knowledge and freedom of our great land.

So shall we shatter the barriers of our isolation. So shall the next hundred years be the greatest in the proud history of our tribes and nations.

Source: "Lament for Confederation, July 1, 1967" from *The Best of Chief Dan George*, © 2004 by Hancock House Publishers Ltd., ISBN 978-088839-544-3, used with permission <www.hancockhouse.com>.

Lastly, although Macdonald thought it "wise and expedient" to empower the Parliament of Canada, under section 101 of the BNA Act, to establish a general court of appeal for Canada, this section did not directly state whether this court would be the final supreme court of appeal for Canada. Nor did the BNA Act indicate who would resolve future disputes likely to arise over the division of powers between the new federal government and the provinces.

Interpreting the Constitution: The Role of the Privy Council

Using section 101 of the BNA Act, the federal government (under the Liberal administration of Prime Minister Alexander Mackenzie) passed the *Supreme Court Act*[15] in 1875. This Act established the Supreme Court of Canada (SCC) as this country's General Court of Appeal for Canada. However, a problem that later emerged with this Court, as indicated above, was that it was not then the final appeal court for Canada. Litigants could still appeal a decision from the SCC to the **Judicial Committee of the Privy Council** (or simply the Privy Council) in London, England. The Privy Council, established in 1833, was then the highest appellate authority for the British Empire. Litigants could even bypass the SCC altogether, taking their appeal from a lower provincial court of appeal directly to the Privy Council.

This was significant for a number of reasons, but perhaps none was more important than the influence this would have on the interpretation of the Constitution. Beginning shortly after Confederation, the courts in Canada would be called upon to decide the precise meaning of the areas of jurisdiction assigned to Parliament under section 91 of the BNA Act and to the provincial legislatures under section 92. Section 91, as already noted, tended to list matters of national importance, and, as we will see in the next chapter, section 92 listed matters of local importance, such as hospitals, municipal institutions, and property and civil rights. A generous or restrictive interpretation of the various areas of jurisdiction could change the balance of power one way or the other.

In addition, Canadian courts would be asked from time to time to decide the constitutionality of legislation based on a division-of-powers argument (see Box 3.3). This is sometimes referred to as **judicial review on federalism grounds**. Today, if one level of government tries to pass legislation in an area assigned to the other level, the courts can strike down the legislation because it offends the Constitution. For instance, if the provinces try to pass legislation that deals with criminal law, an area assigned to Parliament, the legislation

Judicial Committee of the Privy Council highest appeal authority for colonies in the British Empire; exercised final appeal for Canada until 1949

judicial review on federalism grounds process by which a court reviews the constitutionality of legislation based on a division-of-powers analysis, that is, by determining whether one level of government has attempted to enact legislation in an area assigned to the other level under the Constitution

---

15   RSC 1985, c S-26.

could be declared *ultra vires* (that is, outside the jurisdiction of the enacting authority). This power of the courts to strike down legislation was not clearly addressed in the BNA Act and was developed as a necessary implication of having split legislative jurisdiction in a federal system.

The Queen v Chandler (1869), 12 NBR 556 (SC)

This case is widely regarded as the first Canadian case dealing with judicial review on federalism grounds.

In its division of powers between the new federal Parliament and provincial governments, the BNA Act gave the federal Parliament, under section 91(21), exclusive jurisdiction over "Bankruptcy and Insolvency." In 1868, shortly after the Act came into effect, the New Brunswick provincial legislature passed an amendment to its *Insolvent Confined Debtors Act*. This amendment allowed a debtor confined in jail to apply to a county court judge for a discharge. Taking advantage of this amendment, a man named Hazelton, in jail in Saint John for debt, applied to a county court judge (Chandler) to be discharged from his debts.

The issue was whether the New Brunswick government had the power to make a provincial statute concerning insolvency—a legislative area over which the BNA Act gave the federal Parliament exclusive jurisdiction.

Chief Justice Ritchie of New Brunswick held that New Brunswick's 1868 amendment to the *Insolvent Confined Debtors Act*, because it dealt with insolvency, was in "undoubted conflict" with section 91(21) of the BNA Act. His view was that the New Brunswick provincial legislature had "exceeded its powers" with this statute, and he issued an order prohibiting Judge Chandler from proceeding under it.

Source: G Bale, *Chief Justice William Johnstone Ritchie: Responsible Government and Judicial Review* (Ottawa: Carleton University Press, 1991).

For reasons that are not entirely clear, the Privy Council, hearing appeals from Canadian courts, tended to favour an expansive interpretation of provincial powers (particularly the power over property and civil rights, which was interpreted to cover almost all trade within provincial boundaries) and a restrictive interpretation of federal powers (for example, the trade and commerce power was interpreted to cover trade only across provincial or national boundaries). More federal legislation was narrowly interpreted or struck down than was provincial legislation. Arguably, the intent of the drafters of the Constitution was to create a strong federal government, but these decisions by the Privy Council did not favour centralization.

The SCC did not become Canada's final court of appeal until 1949, when appeals to the Privy Council finally ended. Until then, this English body was both the final appeal court for Canadian legal matters generally *and* the final authority when it came to constitutional issues. In other words, the SCC was a subordinate court to the Privy Council. Although some cases with constitutional issues are not appealed (see *The Queen v Chandler* described in Box 3.3, for example), a significant number are. As a result, many of the initial decisions interpreting the BNA Act—decisions that shaped the early evolution of Canadian federalism—came from the Privy Council, not from the SCC. This also meant that the SCC had a difficult beginning developing a distinctive Canadian jurisprudence for this country. (The power of the courts to interpret the Constitution, including striking down legislation, is examined in more detail in Part II.)

The Movement to Patriate the Constitution and Adopt a Charter of Rights

The post-Confederation problems reviewed above were not the only ones causing Canadians to believe that a change in the country's Constitution was needed. A concern among Canadians in the decades after the Second World War was protecting human rights. Many Canadians, aware of wartime atrocities that came to light after the war, worried about the inadequacy of Canada's human rights legislation. They feared that the human rights of individuals—particularly visible minorities coming to Canada in increasing numbers after the war—were inadequately protected against racial, religious, and ethnic discrimination in such areas as housing and employment.

A growing number of civil liberties activists articulated an argument for, and hoped to entrench, a formal bill of rights in Canada's Constitution. They also wanted Canadian courts to have a more active role in protecting civil liberties. They were heartened by the theory of an "implied" bill of rights used by the courts to help protect individuals against misuse of government power (see Chapter 6). However, many realized that, in the end, a concerted federal effort would be needed to achieve their goal. Here they found an ally in then Prime Minister Pierre Trudeau.[16]

Pierre Trudeau and the Quest for a Domestic Amending Formula and Charter of Rights

In his *Memoirs*, Pierre Trudeau noted that one of the main reasons he entered federal politics was the issue of "national unity and the place of Quebec within Canada."[17] During Trudeau's first period as prime minister (1968–1979), Canadian nationalism was on the rise. The 1960s saw the nation adopt a new maple-leaf flag, introduce the Canada Pension Plan, experience a glorious centennial in 1967, and welcome the world at Expo '67. This growing feeling of national pride helped weaken long-standing colonial ties to Britain. A corollary to this national pride was a desire to **patriate** Canada's Constitution from England so that amendments to it could be made by Canadians alone, without needing British approval.

patriate
to remove a nation's legislation or constitution from the control of the mother country and bring it under the control of the nation itself

Trudeau supported the idea of patriation and the idea of securing, through further constitutional reform, a domestic amending formula for Canada's Constitution, although he knew that previous prime ministers who had tried to do this had been unsuccessful. However, he had an added incentive in his pursuit of these goals. Quebec nationalism was rising alongside Canadian nationalism in the 1960s and 1970s and was part of Quebec's "Quiet Revolution." In 1976, Quebec elected its first Parti Québécois government under René Lévesque. In 1980, the party held a referendum on sovereignty association regarding Quebec's future relationship with the rest of Canada. Trudeau, returning as prime minister in 1980 after losing the 1979 election, was determined to oppose Quebec separatists.

Including a charter within his patriation plan and opposing separatism were important to Trudeau. These initiatives would be cornerstones of the "just society" he was trying to achieve in Canada (see also Box 1.4 in Chapter 1). Later, looking back on this period, Trudeau wrote that the Charter expressed his long-held view that "the subject of law must be the individual

---

16   B Dickson, "The Canadian Charter of Rights and Freedoms: Context and Evolution" in Errol Mendes & Stéphane Beaulac, eds, *Canadian Charter of Rights and Freedoms*, 5th ed (Toronto: LexisNexis, 2013) at 3.

17   Pierre Elliott Trudeau, *Memoirs* (Toronto: McClelland & Stewart, 1993) at 228.

human being … [who] has certain basic rights that cannot be taken away by any government."[18] Trudeau also recognized that the Charter would help promote Canadian identity and—since a majority of Canadians favoured the idea of having an entrenched charter of rights—that it would increase public support for his efforts in the patriation process. Strong public support could help him counter provincial opposition to his patriation process, help counter Quebec separatism, and be an instrument of national unity.[19]

When the federalist "no" side defeated the separatist "yes" side in Quebec's 1980 referendum on sovereignty association, Trudeau continued his commitment for a "renewed federalism" and continued to shepherd his patriation plan through to completion. He met with Canada's premiers but found that they continued to add, as the price of their support, their own provincial demands to his undertaking. In response, a seemingly frustrated Trudeau decided to see if he could, as prime minister, patriate the Constitution unilaterally, amending the BNA Act without provincial consent. Although Ontario and New Brunswick supported him, he met strong opposition from the other eight provinces. They argued that such an important change to Canada's constitutional framework also required provincial approval. The question of whether Trudeau could act unilaterally in this regard was put to the SCC. The SCC held that Trudeau's unilateral action to seek a proposed amendment to the BNA Act was legal but that, under the circumstances, a substantial measure of provincial consent was necessary by constitutional convention for Trudeau to proceed further. (See Chapter 4 for a discussion of constitutional conventions.)

Faced with this judgment, in 1981 Trudeau once again met with provincial premiers to try to obtain their consent. At this stage, however, the patriation process was opened up for public input, and two interest groups in particular—Indigenous peoples and women—came forward and pressed their proposals for reforms to members of Parliament. Both groups had been following the patriation process closely and did not want to be excluded from it.

Indigenous Peoples and the Patriation Process

Canada's Indigenous peoples were keenly aware of Trudeau's patriation plan for their own constitutional status and treaty rights. Having had their interests and treaty rights left out of the original BNA Act, they were determined not to be disregarded a second time.

By the mid-20th century, Indigenous peoples had experienced many decades of economic, social, and cultural hardship and suffered serious damage caused by the residential school system. As the Royal Commission on Aboriginal Peoples concluded:

> The relationship between Aboriginal and non-Aboriginal people in Canada has long been troubled and recently has shown signs of slipping into more serious trouble. The relationship can most certainly be mended—indeed, turned from a problem into an asset and one of the country's greatest strengths.
>
> The direction change must take is toward freeing Aboriginal people from domination by and dependence on the institutions and resources of governments. The end of dependence is something Aboriginal and non-Aboriginal people alike profoundly desire. It would be quite unacceptable for First Nations, Inuit and Métis peoples to continue to find their autonomy restricted and constrained in the twenty-first century.

18 *Ibid* at 322.

19 Malcolmson & Myers, *supra* note 11 at 37; Ian Greene, *The Charter of Rights* (Toronto: Lorimer, 1980); Stephen Clarkson & Christina McCall, *Trudeau and Our Times: The Magnificent Obsession* (Toronto: McClelland & Stewart, 1990) vol 1; Michael Mandel, *The Charter of Rights & the Legalization of Politics in Canada*, revised ed (Toronto: Thompson, 1994).

> Yet renewal of the relationship must be done with justice and generosity. History and human decency demand restoration of fair measures of land, resources and power to Aboriginal peoples. On those foundations, self-respect and self-reliance will grow steadily firmer in Aboriginal communities. In their absence, anger and despair will grow steadily deeper—with conflict the likely result.[20]

Indigenous people wanted to improve their situation, a sentiment expressed by Chief Dan George in his "Lament for Confederation," reproduced above (see Box 3.2), and they recognized the importance of organizing themselves politically and developing an infrastructure for activism. It was not easy to accomplish this, however. They faced various difficulties, including poor communication among Indigenous groups (as a result of isolation, vast geographic distances, and language differences); lack of funds for travel and other expenses; hostility from the federal Department of Indian Affairs; and a lack of experience with such mobilization efforts.[21]

Yet Indigenous organizations had slowly begun to form, first at the provincial level and later, in the 1960s, at the national level. They began to inform Canadians about the difficulties Indigenous peoples experienced in trying to preserve their distinctive culture; about the hardships of life on reserves; and about the many problems they experienced in the areas of health, education, and unemployment. They pressured the Canadian government to change its policies toward Indigenous peoples, and their efforts began to meet with some success. For example, the government lifted its ban on the potlatch ceremony, gave all status Indians the right to vote in federal elections, and phased out residential schools. Two events in particular proved critical in bringing Indigenous demands into the public's awareness during Trudeau's constitutional patriation process: the federal government's 1969 white paper on Aboriginal peoples and the SCC's recognition in 1973 of Aboriginal title in a case involving the Nisga'a in British Columbia (see Chapter 2 under "Canadian Law and Indigenous Peoples: A Timeline" and Box 3.4 below).

Having achieved considerable unity and political organization, Indigenous groups became alarmed when it appeared that Trudeau and many of the provincial premiers negotiating patriating the Constitution were once again ignoring them. In 1981, organizations representing the First Nations, Métis, and Inuit people of Canada—the National Indian Brotherhood, the Native Council of Canada, and Inuit *Tapirisat* of Canada, respectively—put pressure on these politicians to allow them to participate in the constitutional amending process. They had long-standing concerns about such issues as land claims, self-government, maintaining their special legal status,[22] and obtaining constitutional recognition from the Crown

---

20   *People to People, Nation to Nation: Highlights from the Report of the Royal Commission on Aboriginal Peoples* (Ottawa: Supply and Services Canada, 1996), online: *Royal Commission on Aboriginal Peoples* <https://www.rcaanc-cirnac.gc.ca/eng/1100100014597/1572547985018>. For additional discussion, refer to John Roberts, Darion Boyington & Shahé S Kazarian, "Current Socio-economic Issues" in *Diversity and First Nations Issues in Canada*, 2nd ed (Toronto: Emond Montgomery, 2012) ch 10. See also the 2015 report of the Truth and Reconciliation Commission of Canada, described in Chapter 2.

21   See Harold Cardinal, *The Unjust Society: The Tragedy of Canada's Indians* (Edmonton: Hurtig, 1969); DE Sanders, "The Indian Lobby" in Keith Banting & Richard Simeon, eds, *And No One Cheered: Federalism, Democracy and the Constitution Act* (Toronto: Methuen, 1983) 301; D Sanders, "Aboriginal Rights in Canada: An Overview" in Olive Patricia Dickason, ed, *The Native Imprint: The Contribution of First Peoples to Canada's Character, vol 2, From 1915* (Athabasca: Athabasca University Educational Enterprises, 1996) 518.

22   "[T]he doctrine of [A]boriginal rights exists ... because of one simple fact: when Europeans arrived in North America, [A]boriginal peoples were already here, living in communities on the land, and participating in distinctive cultures, as they had done for centuries. It is this fact ... above all others, which separates [A]boriginal peoples from all other minority groups in Canadian society and which mandates their special legal ... status" (*R v Van der Peet*, [1996] 2 SCR 507, 1996 CanLII 216 at para 30).

of their Aboriginal and treaty rights. They argued that Indigenous peoples were key stake-holders in Trudeau's constitutional reform process.

Indigenous organizations and their leaders soon realized that they needed to become even more active politically. They began speaking to Canadians with a unified voice, making skillful use of the media, and mobilizing across Canada to put pressure on the government to give more consideration to their interests. They even sent representatives to England to express their concerns before the British Parliament, using their historic treaty relationship with the English Crown. As we've seen, a key document in this relationship is the *Royal Proclamation, 1763* (see Box 3.1).

In the end, the government acceded to pressure from Indigenous peoples to have their rights entrenched in and guaranteed by the new Constitution.

BOX 3.4

The White Paper and Land Claims: Increasing Awareness of Indigenous Issues

In 1969, Prime Minister Trudeau and his minister of Indian affairs, Jean Chrétien, unveiled a white paper that set out the government's new policy for Indigenous peoples. This white paper was issued in response to a government-commissioned report that concluded that Indigenous peoples were Canada's most marginalized and disadvantaged population.* The government proposed measures including repealing the controversial *Indian Act*[†] (the federal legislation that has regulated registered Indians and reserves since 1876 and that was part of the larger government agenda to absorb Indigenous people into mainstream Canadian culture), dissolving the Department of Indian Affairs, eliminating Indian status, converting reserves to private property that could be sold by bands or their members, transferring responsibility for Indigenous affairs to the provinces, and appointing a commissioner to address outstanding land claims, thereby terminating existing treaties over time.

The Indigenous response to the white paper was one of fierce opposition. For one thing, the policy did not take into account the many concerns Indigenous peoples had raised in their consultations with the government prior to the paper's release. As well, although the *Indian Act* severely compromised Indigenous independence, it also secured important rights—namely, reserve lands and a special status within the country. If the *Indian Act* were simply abolished, Indigenous people imagined that whatever legislation replaced it would likely be worse. As well, the government's plan to transfer its responsibility for Indigenous affairs to the provinces was viewed as an effort to evade historic obligations. So angry was

the Indigenous reaction that the government withdrew the white paper shortly after it was issued.

Around the same time, a landmark Supreme Court case involving land claims in British Columbia underscored another key issue. In its 1973 decision *Calder v Attorney-General of British Columbia*,[‡] the SCC affirmed the position of the Nisga'a people of BC that Aboriginal title to land, based on traditional occupancy, survived later European settlement and the Crown's assumption of sovereignty. In recognizing Aboriginal title, the Court weakened the federal and provincial governments' reluctance to negotiate land claims in parts of Canada not covered by existing treaties. In 1975 in Quebec, the Cree and Inuit were successful in securing the James Bay and Northern Quebec Agreement, which compensated Indigenous peoples in that region for Quebec's building of power operations on their land. In 1977, Justice Thomas Berger, who had been appointed to head a royal commission tasked with studying and making recommendations on the effects of a proposed gas pipeline through the Mackenzie Valley, issued a report opposing any construction until Aboriginal land claims in the areas in question had been settled. (See also Chapter 2 under "Canadian Law and Indigenous Peoples: A Timeline" and Box 7.7 in Chapter 7.)

* H Hawthorne, ed, *A Survey of the Contemporary Indians of Canada: Economic, Political, Educational Needs and Policies*, (Ottawa: Information Canada, 1967).

† RSC 1985, c I-5.

‡ [1973] SCR 313, 1973 CanLII 4.

Women and the Patriation Process

Women's groups were also aware of the importance of Trudeau's patriation plan for a new Constitution and were similarly anxious not to be excluded from it. In Canada as elsewhere, women had traditionally been denied many political rights granted to men. They obtained the right to vote long after men: not until 1918 could they vote in federal elections, and not until 1951 could they vote in all provinces and territories. In 1917, the first woman was elected to provincial office, in Alberta, and in 1921, the first woman was elected to the federal Parliament. However, as late as 1929, women were still not considered "persons" eligible to become Canadian senators (see Box 3.5).

BOX 3.5

The Privy Council and the "Persons" Case

Emily Murphy of Edmonton, appointed in 1916 as the first female judge in the British Empire, initiated a drive to become a Canadian senator. However, the federal government believed, based on section 24 of the BNA Act, that she was not a "qualified person" to become a senator. Murphy came up with a strategy. She petitioned the federal government to direct a reference—that is, a formal request for a tribunal's opinion about a certain matter—to the SCC concerning section 24 and the question of whether the phrase "qualified persons" could be interpreted to include female persons. She invited four other women to sign the petition with her.

Prime Minister King accepted their petition. His government then referred the matter to the SCC, which ruled against the "Famous Five," as these women became known. However, King's government agreed to support their appeal to the UK's Judicial Committee of the Privy Council, where Lord Sankey declared that women were "persons" and were eligible to be appointed to the Canadian Senate.

Sources: *Edwards v Canada (AG)*, [1930] AC 124, 1929 CanLII 438 (PC); RJ Sharpe & PI McMahon, *The Persons Case: The Origins and Legacy of the Fight for Legal Personhood* (Toronto: University of Toronto Press, 2007).

Since the end of the 19th century, volunteer women's groups, clubs, and organizations have been advocating for equal rights. In the 1960s and 1970s, the agenda of the women's movement broadened. These decades saw the rise of women's liberation and a greater number of women entering the workforce and pursuing post-secondary education. Many in the women's movement began to lobby governments over concerns such as pay equity; access to good, affordable daycare; violence against women; sexual harassment; reproductive rights; family law reform; pension reform; and education. One of the women's movement's greatest victories during this pre-Charter period came in 1967, when the federal government appointed the Royal Commission on the Status of Women to examine women's concerns in a wide range of equality-related matters, including employment outside the home, child care, affirmative action, and discrimination.[23]

Despite this success, women continued to have major concerns about equality rights in Canada. Some of their dissatisfaction centred on former prime minister John Diefenbaker's *Canadian Bill of* Rights[24] (1960) and its provision in section 1(b) regarding "the right of the individual to equality before the law and the protection of the law." Women were concerned that this section was not worded strongly enough to protect equality rights. Experience had

---

23   See C Hosek, "Women and Constitutional Process" in Banting & Simeon, *supra* note 21, 280;
    P LeClerc, "Women's Issues" in Patrick James & Mark Kasoff, eds, *Canadian Studies in the New Millennium* (Toronto: University of Toronto Press, 2008) 185; Lise Gotell, *The Canadian Women's Movement, Equality Rights, and the Charter* (Ottawa: Canadian Research Institute for the Advancement of Women, 1990).

24   SC 1960, c 44.

shown that, in cases involving women's equality rights, courts tended to interpret this provision narrowly, to the disadvantage of women.

One of these cases was the 1974 *Lavell* case. It involved two Aboriginal women who married non-Aboriginal men and raised the question of whether these women's Indian status ought to be affected by their marriage.[25] If a male status Indian married a non-Aboriginal person, he would not lose his Indian status. However, section 12(1)(b) of the *Indian Act* denied Indian status to an Aboriginal woman who married a non-Aboriginal man. There was obvious inequality here. The issue was whether this section of the *Indian Act*, by discriminating on the basis of sex, violated the equality-before-the-law section (1(b)) of the *Canadian Bill of Rights*. The SCC held that it did not.

In the wake of this and other SCC decisions, and with Trudeau's possible new Charter on the horizon, women from across Canada attended a conference in 1981 to discuss their concerns. Patrice LeClerc summarized these as follows:

> The consensus of the conference was that gender equality rights had to be in the Charter. Specific points were made, especially by the cadre of feminist lawyers: the use of the word "persons," which was familiar in Canadian law after the *Persons* case, should be used throughout. All points in the Charter were to apply equally to male and female persons. It was agreed that equality under the law must be stated as broadly as possible and that as many protections for this as necessary must be written in to cover eventualities. There was an enhanced emphasis on collective rights, on the rights of women as a group.[26]

As noted below, one measure taken by women's groups "to cover eventualities" was to have the framers of the Charter add another specific guarantee of equality rights. This, however, required further vigorous lobbying.

Patriation and a Revived Constitution

Trudeau's patriation efforts culminated in the *Canada Act 1982*,[27] enacted by the UK Parliament on March 29, 1982. Schedule B of the Act included the *Constitution Act, 1982*. The *Canada Act 1982* came into force on March 29 and the *Constitution Act, 1982* some two weeks later. The reason for the delay in the case of the latter statute was that section 58 of the *Constitution Act, 1982* specified that the Act "shall come into force on a day to be fixed by proclamation issued by the Queen or the Governor General under the Great Seal of Canada." In a public ceremony in Ottawa on April 17, 1982, Queen Elizabeth signed the proclamation, bringing it into force. It was the culmination of much hard work by many Canadians.

The *Canada Act 1982* and its Schedule B, the *Constitution Act, 1982*, provided solutions to many of the difficulties the BNA Act had created for Canada. For example, section 2 of the *Canada Act 1982* states the following: "No Act of the Parliament of the United Kingdom passed after the *Constitution Act, 1982* comes into force shall extend to Canada as part of its law." This provision, ending the authority of the English Parliament to legislate for Canada, satisfied this country's growing nationalist impulse. So did part V of the *Constitution Act, 1982*, which sets out the general procedure by which Canadians could amend their own Constitution, without Britain's involvement. In another nod to Canadian nationalism, the *British North America Act,*

---

25 *Canada (AG) v Lavell* [1974] SCR 1349, 1973 CanLII 175. See also *Bliss v Attorney General of Canada (AG)*, [1979] 1 SCR 183, 1978 CanLII 25.

26 LeClerc, *supra* note 23 at 203. See also Sherene Razack, *Canadian Feminism and the Law: The Women's Legal Education and Action Fund and the Pursuit of Equality* (Toronto: Second Story, 1991) at 34.

27 (UK), 1982, c 11.

1867 was renamed the *Constitution Act, 1867*. Part I of the *Constitution Act, 1982* also contains the Charter, which was something else many Canadians keenly wanted.

The Charter guarantees a range of rights and freedoms, including religious freedom, the right to vote, legal rights on arrest, and—some might argue, most importantly—procedural *and* substantive rights of equality. This last right is set out in section 15 of the Charter. The push by women's groups to have gender equality enshrined in the Charter, as discussed above, was a significant contributing factor to the resulting broad-based protection against discrimination that section 15 affords. It goes beyond discrimination on the basis of sex and includes other listed (and analogous unlisted) grounds, such as race, religion, age, and disability. However, to further protect gender equality, section 28 was also included in the Charter. This section makes it clear that not only is there to be equality before and under the law generally (per s 15) but also that Charter rights and freedoms (examined in more detail in Chapter 6) are to be guaranteed equally to male and female persons.

Indigenous groups, as noted above, saw results stemming from their lobbying efforts. Section 25 provides that any Aboriginal and treaty rights already in place, including those recognized by the *Royal Proclamation, 1763* and under land claims agreements, would not be affected by the Charter. Moreover, in part II of the *Constitution Act, 1982*, entitled "Rights of the Aboriginal Peoples of Canada," section 35 formally recognizes and affirms the existing rights of Aboriginal peoples referred to in section 25. In recent years, constitutional protection of Aboriginal rights has led to important land claims agreements and decisions and progress toward the recognition of self-government. (Again, see Chapter 2 under "Canadian Law and Indigenous Peoples: A Timeline.")

In general, the patriation process and the British legislation it generated breathed new life into the Constitution. Our Constitution now provides for formal independence from Great Britain, entrenches our rights and freedoms, and creates a legal structure that will inform Canadian society for many years to come.

A country's constitution and its legal underpinnings play an important role in the determination of the nation's collective identity, and Canada is no exception to this influence. Peter Hogg defines **constitutional law** as follows:

> Constitutional law is the law prescribing the exercise of power by the organs of a State. It explains which organs can exercise legislative power (making new laws), executive power (implementing the laws) and judicial power (adjudicating disputes), and what the limitations on those powers are. In a federal state, the allocation of governmental powers (legislative, executive and judicial) among central and regional (state or provincial) authorities is a basic concern. The rules of federalism are especially significant in Canada because they protect the cultural, linguistic and regional diversity of the nation. Civil liberties are also part of constitutional law, because civil liberties may be created by the rules that limit the exercise of governmental power over individuals. A constitution has been described as "a mirror reflecting the national soul": it must recognize and protect the values of a nation.[28]

constitutional law
law dealing with the distribution of governmental powers under Canada's Constitution

The chapters that follow in Part II describe our constitutional law in more detail. Chapter 4 provides an overview of the key constitutional statutes and describes the processes by which new legislation is enacted; it also explores the responsibility of the executive branch for administering and implementing our laws. Chapter 5 examines judicial power and its role in resolving legal disputes. Finally, Chapter 6 considers how Canadian civil liberties place important limits on private sector behaviour and the power of governments.

---

28   Hogg, *supra* note 1 at 1-1.

CHAPTER SUMMARY

Canada is a bijural nation: Quebec uses the civil law system (in particular for private law matters), and the rest of Canada uses the common law system. Both legal systems have deep roots in this country and have undergone unique developments since the early colonial influences of France and England. Quebec, originally a colony of France, received French civil law, whereas the rest of Canada's provinces and territories were originally English colonies (or later came under England's jurisdiction) and received English common law.

Common law rules of reception dictated how different regions of Canada received English law. These rules varied in part according to how the region came to be an English colony. If colonization came about through settlement, the mother country's laws—both judge-made law and statute law—were received upon settlement, generally agreed to be the date when the colonial legislature first met. If England acquired the territory by conquest (or cession), the region's pre-existing legal system continued until the English monarch or imperial Parliament formally imposed English law there. Alternatively, and regardless of the method of colonization, the colonial legislature could pass a reception statute adopting the laws of England as of a certain date. Each province and territory has a unique history concerning its reception of English (or French) law.

The transformation of a collection of independent colonies into a united Canada was the culmination of a long, difficult reform process. There were strong political, military, and economic reasons for the enactment of the BNA Act, the imperial statute that created our country and federal system of government. However, the BNA Act left certain things unresolved. It lacked, for example, a domestic amending formula and a bill of rights. Its framers disregarded the interests and rights of Indigenous peoples. It did not adequately address the role of the SCC as a final court of appeal or clearly define the power of the courts to review the constitutionality of legislation in disputes regarding the division of powers between the new federal government and the provinces.

As Canadian society became more multicultural and diverse, particularly after the Second World War, various political movements sought to reform the BNA Act. Canadian nationalism became more pronounced in the 1960s, and an initiative arose, led by Prime Minister Pierre Trudeau, to patriate the Constitution from Britain so that Canadians could amend it without recourse to the British Parliament. Along with this initiative, there was a corollary movement to add an entrenched charter of rights to our Constitution. Indigenous peoples mobilized politically to ensure that their special status and treaty rights were protected by the new Constitution, and women lobbied to have the proposed new Charter contain strongly worded equality rights. The result was the passage of the *Canada Act 1982*, which includes the *Constitution Act, 1982* and the Charter. With our revitalized Constitution, we now have legal independence from Britain, the power to amend our Constitution, and the Charter to protect our legal rights and freedoms, together with other reforms, all of which will guide us into the foreseeable future.

KEY TERMS

cession, 62
Confederation, 64
constitutional law, 83
federalism, 72
imperial statute, 62
Judicial Committee of the Privy Council, 75
judicial review on federalism grounds, 75
patriate, 77
unitary government, 72

FURTHER READING

BOOKS

Berger, Thomas R, *A Long and Terrible Shadow: White Values, Native Rights in the Americas, 1492–1992* (Vancouver/Toronto: Douglas & McIntyre, 1991).

Castel, J-G, *The Civil Law System of the Province of Quebec* (Toronto: Butterworths, 1962).

Davenport, Paul & Richard H Leach, eds, *Reshaping Confederation: The 1982 Reform of the Canadian Constitution* (Durham, NC: Duke University Press, 1984).

Frideres, James S & René R Gadacz, *Aboriginal Peoples in Canada*, 9th ed (Toronto: Pearson, 2012).

Girard, P & J Phillips, eds, *Essays in the History of Canadian Law*, vol 3, *Nova Scotia* (Toronto: Osgoode Society/ University of Toronto Press, 1990).

Guth, DeLloyd & W Wesley Pue, eds, *Canada's Legal Inheritances* (Winnipeg: Canadian Legal History Project, Faculty of Law, University of Manitoba, 2001).

James, Patrick & Mark Kasoff, eds, *Canadian Studies in the New Millennium* (Toronto: University of Toronto Press, 2008).

Knafla, LA & J Swainger, eds, *Laws and Societies in the Canadian Prairie West, 1670–1940* (Vancouver: University of British Columbia Press, 2005).

Reesor, Bayard, *The Canadian Constitution in Historical Perspective* (Scarborough, Ont: Prentice Hall, 1992).

Saywell, John T, *The Lawmakers: Judicial Power and the Shaping of Canadian Federalism* (Toronto: University of Toronto Press, 2002).

Sharpe, Robert J & Kent Roach, *The Charter of Rights and Freedoms*, 5th ed (Toronto: Irwin Law, 2013).

Strayer, Barry L, *Canada's Constitutional Revolution* (Edmonton: University of Alberta Press, 2013).

Waite, PB, *The Life and Times of Confederation, 1864-1867* (Toronto: University of Toronto Press, 1962).

WEBSITES

McCord Museum, Montreal Social History Museum: <https://www.musee-mccord.qc.ca/en>.

Osgoode Society for Canadian Legal History: <https://www.osgoodesociety.ca/>.

REVIEW QUESTIONS

1. How did the reception of English law into an overseas colony differ depending on whether England had acquired the colony by settlement or by conquest?

2. List five key factors leading to Confederation.

3. Why did Canadian politicians end up adopting a federal system of government in the BNA Act?

4. List five areas of laws assigned to the federal government under section 91 of the BNA Act.

5. List four problems with the BNA Act that later proved to be problematic in Canada.

6. What difficulties did Indigenous peoples encounter in organizing themselves politically and developing an infrastructure for activism?

7. Explain how sections 15 and 28 of the Charter, respectively, are important for protecting women's equality rights.

EXERCISES

1. What circumstances unique to Canada in our colonial past might have made applying English case law unsuitable here?

2. Consider ways in which having a separate civil law legal system is a benefit to the province of Quebec. Do you think that bijuralism is a good attribute for the nation as a whole? Explain.

3. Why do you think the BNA Act did not originally have a charter of rights in it?

4. Find and read a recent court case that addresses Aboriginal rights. Identify the issue, explain the arguments of each side, and state the court's decision. What implications could this decision have for other Indigenous groups in Canada and for the public?

5. Look at the website for the Women's Legal Education and Action Fund (LEAF) (<https://www.leaf.ca>) and review materials on this public interest group. Why do you think LEAF has been so effective in supporting women's legal rights in Canada?

PART II
Law and the Canadian Constitution

CHAPTER 4 The Legislature and the Executive: The First and Second Branches of Government

CHAPTER 5 The Judiciary: The Third Branch of Government

CHAPTER 6 Civil Liberties

4 The Legislature and the Executive: The First and Second Branches of Government

Introduction 90

Legislative Power 90

Executive Power 109

Chapter Summary 118

Key Terms 119

Further Reading 119

Review Questions 120

Exercises 120

Appendix 4.1: Reading and
Understanding Legislation 120

The Centre, East, and West Blocks of the Parliament buildings in Ottawa were begun in 1859. The original Centre Block was destroyed by fire in 1916 and reopened in 1922. The new design elements reflected the sense of Canadian identity that emerged from the First World War. The Centre Block (pictured from the back looking up from the Ottawa River) closed in 2018 as part of a restoration and modernization project and is not expected to reopen for ten years. During construction, the House of Commons has moved to the West Block and the Senate to the Government Conference Centre (renamed, in 2018, the Senate of Canada Building).

LEARNING OUTCOMES

After reading this chapter, you will be able to:

- Describe the nature of legislative power in Canada and its relationship to the executive branch of government.
- Identify the different types of statute law and the process by which statutes are enacted.
- Explain the nature of subordinate legislation.
- Understand the concept of parliamentary sovereignty.

- Describe the nature of executive power.
- Understand the Canadian system of responsible government.
- Define the key sources of executive power in Canada.
- Describe the basic limits of executive power.

There is no [clear] separation of legislative and executive functions in the Canadian context. The key members of the executive, the prime minister and the Cabinet, must hold seats in Parliament. The government also has the power to control and direct the affairs of the House of Commons. In part, this control is derived from the fact that, in accordance with the principles of responsible government, the government controls a majority of seats in the House of Commons. It can therefore be assured that most of its legislative proposals will be adopted by [Parliament].

Patrick J Monahan, Byron Shaw & Padraic Ryan,
Constitutional Law, 5th ed (Toronto: Irwin Law, 2017) at 102

Introduction

separation-of-powers doctrine
doctrine according to which separate powers are assigned to the legislative, executive, and judicial branches of government

As we noted in the previous chapter, constitutional law is largely concerned with a nation's legislative, executive, and judicial powers. These three powers are sometimes referred to as the three branches or pillars of government. The **separation-of-powers doctrine** deals with the relationship between them. We can summarize this relationship as follows: the legislature makes the law; the executive implements the law; and the judiciary applies and interprets the law.

In this chapter, we look at the first two branches, which, in Canada, despite the separation-of-powers doctrine, are closely connected—a consequence of our system of responsible government. In the next chapter, we consider the judicial branch.

Legislative Power

legislature
representative assembly charged under a constitution with making laws for a particular region or state

The legislative branch is the most powerful of the three branches, with ultimate control over the other two. It operates through a legislative body called a **legislature**. A legislature is a representative assembly charged under a constitution with making laws for a particular region or state. Legislatures go by various names, such as "parliament," "congress," or "legislative assembly." The members are usually elected, but they can be appointed in other ways depending on the political system. Legislatures have a settled number of members or seats. This number may be changed periodically in response to population changes and other factors.

Most legislatures are either **unicameral** or **bicameral**. A unicameral legislature has only one body. A bicameral legislature has two, with lower houses (for example, "House of Commons" or "House of Representatives") and upper houses (for example, "Senate" or "House of Lords"). Canada's Parliament, like the British or United Kingdom (UK) Parliament and the United States (US) Congress, has a bicameral structure. A bicameral legislature may be partly elected and partly appointed, as are the UK and Canadian Parliaments, with their elected House of Commons and their appointed House of Lords and Senate, respectively. Alternatively, both houses of a bicameral legislature can be elected. This is the case with the US Congress: members of both the House of Representatives and the Senate are elected.

In unitary states, such as Britain, legislative power is not constitutionally divided between central and regional authorities (although regions may have revocable power delegated to them); there is just one supreme legislative body. In federal states such as Canada, the US, and Australia, legislative jurisdiction is divided between central and regional authorities. Depending on how many regions the nation contains, its legislative power can be vested in a large number of separate legislative bodies.

Legislation refers to written laws made by legislative assemblies. The following section examines the main form of legislation (statutes), legislative bodies, and the process by which statutes are enacted. The next section briefly considers subordinate legislation, a form of legislation passed under delegated authority granted by enabling statutes, as well as quasi-legislative rules, which—although not legislated—operate analogously. The discussion of legislative power concludes by considering its limits and how the doctrine of parliamentary sovereignty applies in Canada. The last part of this chapter covers executive power.

Statutes

Statutes are the primary form of legislation. In Canada, which is a federal state, the power to make statutes is divided between the federal Parliament and the provincial legislatures. Most Canadian statutes are therefore either federal or provincial statutes.

However, our most important *constitutional* statutes are British. As described in Chapter 3, Canada before 1867 was a collection of separate British colonies. Therefore, our transition to nationhood required the cooperation of the UK Parliament. The principal constitutional statutes, including the *Constitution Act, 1867* itself (formerly called the *British North America Act, 1867*, or BNA Act), were written by and passed at the request of Canadians. But they were British statutes; the UK Parliament had to pass them. It was not until 1982 and the patriation of our Constitution that a Canadian legislative formula or power for amending the Constitution without Britain's involvement existed.

There are four types of statutes, distinguished according to type or jurisdiction:

1. constitutionally entrenched statutes, which are mainly British (or imperial);
2. federal statutes;
3. provincial statutes; and
4. territorial statutes.

We will discuss the four types of statutes in the following sections.

Constitutionally Entrenched Statutes

Canadian constitutional statutes are statutes that concern this country's governmental powers as well as important civil liberties matters. They include federal and provincial

---

unicameral
legislature with one house involved in the passage of legislation

bicameral
legislature with two houses involved in the passage of legislation

legislation
written laws made by legislative assemblies

statutes
primary form of legislation

statutes and statutes from the UK. Many federal and provincial statutes relating to government powers and civil liberties are not entrenched; they can be changed via the usual legislative process.

constitutionally entrenched

describes a statute that falls within the definition of the Constitution of Canada as set out in section 52 of the *Constitution Act, 1982*

Our **constitutionally entrenched** statutes cannot be changed by ordinary federal or provincial legislation. Generally speaking, a statute is entrenched if it requires a special process to change it (see below under "Constitutional Amendments"). Specifically, a statute is constitutionally entrenched if it is part of the Constitution of Canada as set out in section 52 of the *Constitution Act, 1982*. The relevant subsections of section 52 are as follows:

> 52(2) The Constitution of Canada includes
>
> > (a) the *Canada Act 1982*, including this Act [that is, the *Constitution Act, 1982*];
> >
> > (b) the Acts and orders referred to in the schedule; and
> >
> > (c) any amendment to any Act or order referred to in paragraph (a) or (b).
>
> (3) Amendments to the Constitution of Canada shall be made only in accordance with the authority contained in the Constitution of Canada.

This provision tells us that the Constitution of Canada includes not only the *Canada Act 1982* and the *Constitution Act, 1982* (which includes the Charter) but also the 30 statutes and orders listed in the Schedule to the *Constitution Act, 1982* (see Appendix B). These include the *Constitution Act, 1867*; the *Parliament of Canada Act, 1875*;[1] the *Statute of Westminster, 1931*;[2] a number of statutes and orders creating and/or admitting new provinces and territories into Canada; and various amending statutes. The list comprises the main parts of the Constitution of Canada. However, because of the use of the word "includes," it is not exhaustive. The Supreme Court of Canada (SCC) has held that other laws may be included in the Constitution of Canada.

KEY CONSTITUTIONAL STATUTES

Of the various statutes, orders, and other laws that make up our constitution, the following four imperial statutes are the most important:

- *Constitution Act, 1867*;
- *Statute of Westminster, 1931*;
- *Canada Act 1982*; and
- *Constitution Act, 1982*.

As we saw in the last chapter, the *Constitution Act, 1867* created the new country of Canada, which was in the form of a federation, with government power divided between a central authority and the former colonies, now called provinces. The precise nature of the division is described in more detail below (under the "Federal Statutes" and "Provincial Statutes" headings). The *Constitution Act, 1867* also dealt with executive power (described following the discussion of legislative power) and with judicial power (see Chapter 5). Key provisions in the *Constitution Act, 1867* are reproduced in Appendix A.

The *Statute of Westminster, 1931* was another important imperial statute because it repealed an earlier imperial statute, the *Colonial Laws Validity Act, 1865*[3] (which clarified the power of colonies to pass local legislation but also made it clear that colonial statutes could

---

1   RSC 1985, c P-1.

2   (UK), 22 Geo V, c 4.

3   (UK), 28 & 29 Vict, c 63.

not contravene British imperial statutes). The *Statute of Westminster, 1931* took colonial independence one step further: it not only confirmed Canada's legislative autonomy but also recognized Canada's legislative equality with Britain. However, Britain did reserve the power to amend key constitutional statutes, such as the *British North America Act* (now the *Constitution Act, 1867*). This reservation of power was due less to paternalism on Britain's part than to the fact that the federal government and the provinces were unable at the time to agree on a constitutional amending formula. Because of this disagreement, the UK Parliament still had to be involved in Canada's constitutional amendments. Britain was always accepting of Canada's requests for such amendments, however, invariably passing them.

In 1982, with patriation, the final step on the road to legislative independence was achieved. Section 2 of the *Canada Act 1982* declared that the British Parliament no longer had legislative power over Canada. Arguably, however, the most important legacy of the patriation process is the *Constitution Act, 1982* (see Appendix B), which was enacted as Schedule B to the *Canada Act 1982*. The *Constitution Act, 1982* contains the *Canadian Charter of Rights and Freedoms* (part I), addresses Aboriginal rights (part II), and sets out the amending procedures (part V).

Significantly, the *Constitution Act, 1982* also includes section 52(1), the **supremacy clause** (in part VII), which provides the following:

> 52(1) The Constitution of Canada is the supreme law of Canada, and any law that is inconsistent with the provisions of the Constitution is, to the extent of the inconsistency, of no force or effect.

If a federal or provincial statute offends or is inconsistent with the Constitution, section 52(1) states that the law is "of no force or effect." This may seem clear, but precisely what remedial responses are available when dealing with unconstitutional legislation is not always so clear. The courts have interpreted their power to deal with unconstitutional legislation broadly, using section 52(1) and, sometimes, section 24 of the Charter (see Chapter 6). A range of responses are possible, including the following:

1. *striking down* the legislation altogether and declaring it invalid (this is the most extreme response);
2. *severance* of a portion of the legislation (if only part of the statute contravenes the Constitution—for example, a particular section—the court can declare that just that part is invalid and sever it from the rest of the legislation);
3. *reading down* (with this remedy, the courts narrowly interpret the legislation to ensure conformity with the Constitution);
4. *reading in* (this remedy is a little more activist and involves adding language to the legislation to ensure conformity with the Constitution—for example, adding a new class of persons covered by the legislation or adding a new and unlisted ground of discrimination (see Box 6.3 in Chapter 6);
5. a *constitutional exemption* (with this rarely used remedy, so far never used by the SCC, the court does not declare the legislation invalid but finds that it doesn't apply to a particular person or class of persons); and
6. the *temporary suspension* of an order declaring the legislation or part of it invalid (this gives Parliament or the legislature the opportunity to enact new, valid legislation within a set period of time; see Box 10.1 in Chapter 10 as an example).

Prior to patriation, the main ground for challenging the constitutionality of legislation in court was based on a **division-of-powers** argument, where it is argued that one level of

supremacy clause
section 52(1) of the *Constitution Act, 1982*, which provides that the Constitution is the supreme law of Canada and empowers the courts to find that laws that are inconsistent with the Constitution are of no force and effect

division of powers
refers to the divided jurisdiction—between Parliament, on the one hand, and the provinces, on the other hand—to make legislation in a federal state such as Canada

government has tried to pass legislation in an area assigned to the other level (see the discussion of judicial review on federalism grounds in Chapter 3). With the passage of the *Constitution Act, 1982*, another important ground has emerged: challenging the constitutionality of legislation on the basis that it infringes the Charter, sometimes referred to as **judicial review on Charter grounds**, or simply a **Charter challenge** (see Chapter 6 for more on the scope of the Charter).

judicial review on Charter grounds (or Charter challenge) process by which a court reviews the constitutionality of legislation on the basis that it infringes the Charter

CONSTITUTIONAL AMENDMENTS

Amendments to the Constitution require a special process. Section 52(3) states that "[a]mendments to the Constitution of Canada shall be made only in accordance with the authority contained in the Constitution of Canada."

Part V of the *Constitution Act, 1982* sets out the amendment procedures. Typically, an amendment will require the agreement of Parliament and of two-thirds of the provinces, with the support of at least 50 percent of the general population. This is known as the "general procedure" for amendment. The particular requirements are set out in section 38 of the Act. Currently, given the number of Canadian provinces and the way the population is distributed across the country, an amendment following the general procedure would need the support of seven provinces, and one of them would have to be either Ontario or Quebec.

Certain special amendments—for example, involving the use of the English or French language in federal matters and changing the composition of the SCC—require the "unanimous consent" of Parliament and the provinces (s 41). Part V also provides for simpler amendment procedures if the proposed change affects only one or two provinces or the federal government alone. For example, provinces can change their boundaries without the consent or agreement of provinces that are not affected by the change. Only Parliament and the provinces directly affected by the boundary change need agree to it (see Box 4.1).

BOX 4.1

Constitutional Amendments Since Patriation

Since 1982, there have been 11 amendments to the Constitution of Canada using the amending procedures set out in part V of the *Constitution Act, 1982*.

The general procedure pursuant to section 38 requires the consent of two-thirds of the provinces, with at least 50 percent of the population (the so-called 7/50 procedure). One amendment has occurred using this procedure (the *Constitution Amendment Proclamation, 1983**). It followed the constitutional conference mandated by section 37, which considered Aboriginal peoples and their constitutional rights. Aboriginal rights were strengthened through changes to sections 25 and 35, which made it clear that past *and future* rights acquired under land claims agreements were protected. The amendment also ensured that Aboriginal and treaty rights are guaranteed equally to male and female persons.

After the 1983 amendment, there were two significant attempts at constitutional change using the general procedure. One was the Meech Lake Accord of 1987, which aimed to encourage Quebec to endorse the 1982 constitutional changes (Quebec had been the only province not to give its consent when Canada approached England with the patriation proposal in 1982). The Accord included recognition of Quebec as a "distinct society" and gave all provinces the power to veto constitutional amendments. But consensus was never reached, and the Meech Lake Accord was never ratified.

The second attempt at constitutional change using the general procedure was the Charlottetown Accord, negotiated in 1992 by the federal and provincial governments. Proposing changes to the division of legislative powers, it gave the provinces exclusive jurisdiction in several contentious areas where jurisdiction is divided, including natural resources and cultural policy. The Charlottetown proposal also included a social charter that promoted health care, welfare, education, and environmental protection and that formally recognized, by way of the "Canada Clause," certain "Canadian" values, such as equality, diversity, and Quebec's status as a distinct society. The Charlottetown Accord also proposed a number of institutional changes to the SCC, to Parliament, and to the consultation process between the federal, provincial, and territorial governments. Following a national referendum in which the majority voted against the Accord, the Charlottetown Accord was abandoned. It remains to be seen whether we will be able to agree on any broad-based changes in the future as a nation, such as changes modifying the distribution of powers between Parliament and the provinces.

There have been no amendments using the procedure requiring unanimous consent of Parliament and the provinces under section 41. The remaining 10 amendments, made pursuant to sections 43 and 44 and of more limited scope, covered such matters as modifying the method for apportioning seats in the House of Commons, replacing ferry service to Prince Edward Island with the Confederation Bridge (amending Prince Edward Island's constitutional guarantee of "efficient steam service"), education rights within a province, and language rights within a province (in 1993, New Brunswick succeeded in amending the Charter through the addition of a new section—section 16.1—guaranteeing the equal status of the English and French languages in that province).

*   SI/84-102.

Federal Statutes

Federal statutes are enacted by the Parliament of Canada. Because our Parliament is bicameral, there are two houses involved in the making of statutes. At the time of writing, the House of Commons, which is elected, has 338 seats; the Senate, which is appointed, has 105. Constitutional convention dictates that the House of Commons, as an elected body, takes the lead in making new legislation (see Figure 4.1).

FIGURE 4.1 House of Commons
Canada's 338 ridings are represented in the lower house by members of Parliament. The primary colour used (green) is the same colour used in Britain's House of Commons for more than 300 years. The home of the House of Commons in the Centre Block, pictured here, has temporarily moved during renovations.

New statutes can be passed only while Parliament is in session. Each new session commences with a formal state opening at which the governor general (or, occasionally, the British monarch) reads the Speech from the Throne. Each session is formally brought to a close when it is **prorogued**. Most sessions are one to two years in length, sometimes with lengthy adjournments during that time. Under section 4 of the Charter, an election must be

prorogue
to formally close a legislative session

called at least once every five years. This means that, after each election, the governing party has five years in which to advance its legislative agenda through Parliament.

FEDERAL JURISDICTION

The principal sections of the Constitution that give power to Parliament are section 91 (many subject areas), section 94A (old age pensions), and section 95 (agriculture and immigration, although these areas are shared with the provinces). Any new legislation proposed by Parliament must be authorized by a section in the Constitution.

Section 91 is the source of most federal power. It lists 30 specific subject areas over which Parliament has exclusive **jurisdiction**. It also gives the federal government a general power to make laws for the "Peace, Order and good Government of Canada" in areas over which the provinces are not assigned exclusive jurisdiction.

POGG Power

This general power to make laws for the peace, order, and good government of Canada is often referred to as **POGG power**. The POGG power clause in section 91 appears to give Parliament a general "residuary power"—that is, jurisdiction in any area that the Constitution does not explicitly assign to either level of government. In other words, section 91 gives Parliament the power to fill the legislative gaps. This reflects the fact that the framers of the Constitution aimed to build a strong federal authority. In this respect, Canada contrasts with other federations, such as the US and Australia, where the residuary power is given to the regional or state legislatures.

Besides recognizing POGG power as a means to fill legislative gaps in the assigned areas of jurisdiction, the courts have interpreted POGG power as justifying federal laws to regulate matters of national concern (such as marine pollution, aeronautics, and nuclear power) and to deal temporarily with serious emergencies (for example, during times of war, insurrection, extreme economic turbulence, or pandemic).

Specific Areas of Federal Jurisdiction

The list of subject areas in section 91 is extensive. According to this provision's introductory words, Parliament's authority "extends to all Matters coming within the Classes of Subjects" listed. Given that each area listed is a class of subjects and that federal jurisdiction is over all matters within those classes, the federal power to legislate appears to be quite far-reaching. For a full listing of the areas that fall under federal jurisdiction according to section 91 of the *Constitution Act, 1867*, see Table 4.1.

To help determine whether a statute is within a legislature's jurisdiction, the courts try to determine what the "matter" of the law is. The courts are looking for the statute's essence here. Various phrases have been used to refer to a law's essence—for example, its "true meaning," its "true nature and character," and, most often, its "pith and substance."

Determining the statute's pith and substance requires looking at its dominant purpose and effect. If the courts find that the dominant purpose and effect address an appropriate area—that is, an area that falls within the jurisdiction of the legislature that made the statute—the statute will pass the division-of-powers test and will be accepted as constitutional. On the other hand, the new legislation may not pass this test. For example, if a provincial legislature enacts a law whose dominant purpose and effect relate to an interprovincial undertaking (a federal matter), the law will be declared unconstitutional (see Box 4.2).

---

jurisdiction

refers (In the context of legislative power under the Constitution) to the specific subject areas over which the federal Parliament and the provincial legislatures have been assigned authority

POGG power

general residuary power given to Parliament—in other words, the power to fill in the gaps left by the specifically enumerated areas of jurisdiction assigned to the two levels of government

TABLE 4.1 Federal Powers Under Section 91 by Category

CATEGORY	RELATED SUBSECTION(S) OF SECTION 91	NOTES
Taxation, Money, and Public Assets	1A. The Public Debt and Property 3. The Raising of Money by any Mode or System of Taxation 4. The Borrowing of Money on the Public Credit 14. Currency and Coinage 15. Banking, Incorporation of Banks, and the Issue of Paper Money 16. Savings Banks 18. Bills of Exchange and Promissory Notes 19. Interest 20. Legal Tender 21. Bankruptcy and Insolvency	The framers of the *Constitution Act, 1867* saw this category as important. Putting it under Parliament's jurisdiction was a means of creating a strong and effective central government. These powers are supplemented by Part VIII.
Trade and Employment	2. The Regulation of Trade and Commerce 2A. Unemployment Insurance 17. Weights and Measures	The trade and commerce power was interpreted narrowly soon after Confederation by the Privy Council as only applying to interprovincial and international trade and commerce, not intraprovincial trade and commerce, which was held to be a matter within provincial jurisdiction under s 92(13).*
Intellectual Property	22. Patents of Invention and Discovery 23. Copyrights	The law in this area, which involves an intangible form of property without specific geographic context or connection, requires consistent rules across wide-ranging boundaries. It is also affected by international relations and agreements.
First Nations	24. Indians, and Lands reserved for the Indians	The reason for including this area under s 91 was apparently to protect First Nations against European expansion and to have a consistent set of policies across Canada.†
Immigration and Citizenship	25. Naturalization and Aliens	In Canada, as in most countries, immigration and citizenship is primarily a national priority. However, the federal government collaborates with the provinces in establishing goals and policies in this area.
Marriage and Divorce	26. Marriage and Divorce	Family law is also regulated by the provinces, which have some shared jurisdiction with Parliament (e.g., spousal support and child custody) and some exclusive jurisdiction (division of family assets).

(Table 4.1 is concluded on the next page.)

TABLE 4.1   Federal Powers Under Section 91 by Category   concluded

CATEGORY	RELATED SUBSECTION(S) OF SECTION 91	NOTES

Transportation and Communication	13. Ferries between a Province and any British or Foreign Country or between Two Provinces
	
	29. Such Classes of Subjects as are expressly excepted in the Enumeration of the Classes of Subjects by this Act assigned exclusively to the Legislatures of the Provinces
	
	[Section 91(29) must be read together with s 92(10):]
	
	   10. Local Works and Undertakings other than such as are of the following Classes:
	
	   (a) Lines of Steam or other Ships, Railways, Canals, Telegraphs, and other Works and Undertakings connecting the Province with any other or others of the Provinces, or extending beyond the Limits of the Province:
	
	   (b) Lines of Steam Ships between the Province and any British or Foreign Country:
	
	   (c) Such Works as, although wholly situate within the Province, are before or after their Execution declared by the Parliament of Canada to be for the general Advantage of Canada or for the Advantage of Two or more of the Provinces.
		These areas are of national importance.

Water Matters: Coasts, Shipping, and Fishing	9. Beacons, Buoys, Lighthouses, and Sable Island 10. Navigation and Shipping 11. Quarantine and the Establishment and Maintenance of Marine Hospitals 12. Sea Coast and Inland Fisheries	With so much water and coastline, federal jurisdiction was needed for reasons of safety, security, and uniformity.
Criminal Law	27. The Criminal Law, except the Constitution of Courts of Criminal Jurisdiction, but including the Procedure in Criminal Matters 28. The Establishment, Maintenance, and Management of Penitentiaries	Parliament's jurisdiction over criminal law has been used to enact a variety of criminal statutes, including the *Criminal Code* and *Youth Criminal Justice Act*. Not all federations have a national criminal law system. In the US, for instance, criminal law jurisdiction rests with the individual states.
National Defence	7. Militia, Military and Naval Service, and Defence	The need for a national armed services is clear.
Miscellaneous	5. Postal Service 6. The Census and Statistics 8. The fixing of and providing for the Salaries and Allowances of Civil and other Officers of the Government of Canada	National regulation in these areas was thought to be in the country's best interests.

* *Citizens' Insurance Co v Parsons* (1881), 7 App Cas 96 (PC).

† Peter W Hogg, *Constitutional Law of Canada*, 5th ed (Toronto: Carswell, 2007) (loose-leaf updated 2019, release 1) ch 28.1(a).

BOX 4.2

Oil, Politics, and Law: The Bitumen Reference Case

Kinder Morgan, an energy infra-structure company, sought and was granted federal approval to twin an existing pipeline running from Strathcona County near Edmonton to a marine terminal near Vancouver (the Trans Mountain Expansion Project, or TMX). The plan for the new pipeline is that it will carry heavy crude and blended bitumen to the British Columbia (BC) coast, where it will be exported to US and Asian markets. However, despite having approval to proceed, Kinder Morgan decided not to move forward with the project when it became apparent that there were still many challenges and uncertainties ahead. In 2018, for political and economic reasons, the federal Liberal government purchased TMX with the objective of completing the project and re-selling it when it becomes viable.

One of the challenges facing Kinder Morgan was the objection of BC's minority NDP government to the project. With the support of BC's Green Party and environmental and Indigenous groups, the BC government brought a reference case before the BC Court of Appeal to determine whether, under the Constitution, the province had jurisdiction to regulate TMX.*

The stage was set for a division-of-powers argument. Was the pith and substance of the province's legislated approval process part of a general scheme of environmental regulation that only incidentally affected TMX? If so, BC had jurisdiction under section 92(13) or section 92(16). Or was the true nature and character of the approval process an attempt to regulate an interprovincial undertaking, a federal matter covered by section 91(29) and section 92(10)(a)? If that were the case, the legislation was unconstitutional.

The BC Court of Appeal stated (at para 6):

> Given that 'incidental' effects may almost always be expected, and that Canadian courts have in recent decades strongly favoured 'co-operative federalism' over strict compartmentalization of jurisdiction, the

'characterization' process is sometimes difficult. The Supreme Court of Canada has warned that co-operative federalism "cannot override or modify the separation of powers," nor support a finding that an otherwise unconstitutional law is valid.

The Court of Appeal went on to confirm the established position that "environmental protection" is not a separate head of power and that both the provinces and the federal government have authority to regulate the environment if it relates to subject areas within their jurisdiction (for example, the federal government in connection with fisheries or the provinces in connection with local works and undertakings). After considering the legislation in detail, the Court concluded that BC had crossed the line in this case. Even if TMX was not intentionally singled out by the legislation, its potential effect was to stop TMX "in its tracks" (at para 101). This legislation more than incidentally affected the project; its pith and substance was the regulation of a federal undertaking (at para 101). The case was appealed to the SCC, but the appeal was unanimously dismissed for the reasons given by the BC Court of Appeal.†

(Box 4.2 is concluded on the next page.)

Several Indigenous groups made submissions as intervenors, but the BC Court of Appeal did not respond to their arguments to have their legal orders acknowledged as part of the approval process (see also the discussion of the Wet'suwet'en pipeline protests in Chapter 2 under "New Directions for Indigenous Law in Canada"). In a separate but related case in the federal court system, Indigenous groups also challenged TMX on the grounds that the Crown had not adequately consulted with them. The Federal Court of Appeal also unanimously dismissed that case, holding that the federal government had carried out meaningful consultations before finally approving the project.[‡]

*   *Reference re Environmental Management Act (British Columbia)*, 2019 BCCA 181. A reference case is a special case put to the court by the federal or provincial governments on an important legal matter, often relating to the Constitution. References are also discussed in Chapter 5 under the heading "The Supreme Court of Canada."

†   *Reference re Environmental Management Act*, 2020 SCC 1.

‡   *Coldwater First Nation v Canada (Attorney General)*, 2020 FCA 34. Leave to appeal to the SCC was denied, online: <https://scc-csc.ca/case-dossier/info/dock-regi-eng.aspx?cas=39111>.

Progressive Interpretation

As we saw in Chapter 3, some of the early interpretations of section 91 by the Privy Council had the effect of restricting federal power in relation to some subject areas (for example, trade and commerce). In line with this narrow interpretative approach, these Privy Council decisions also suggested that the subject areas listed in section 91 should be viewed as "watertight compartments" and be based on the original understanding of their meaning by the framers of the Constitution (this also applied to the interpretation of s 92 and other sections assigning jurisdiction to one level of government or the other).

However, modern interpretations of the Constitution have found favour with another metaphor, that is, that the Constitution is a "living tree" capable of growth and development.[4] For example, when this issue was confronted in the *Reference re Same-Sex Marriage* case,[5] the SCC held that it was not bound by "frozen concepts" (at para 22). Despite the fact that in 1867 federal power over marriage was thought to apply only to the union between a man and a woman, the Court interpreted the Constitution as able to accommodate the realities of modern life. The Constitution was not frozen in time and based on beliefs over 150 years old. The Court held that Parliament had the jurisdiction to regulate same-sex marriage under section 91(26).[6]

It also follows from this more progressive approach (and the rejection of the watertight compartments idea) that the assigned subject areas in the Constitution will not always be seen as mutually exclusive of one another. For example, some areas of regulation may have aspects that are both federal and provincial (see "Overlapping Jurisdiction," next). Furthermore, even if a legislated area is fully within the jurisdiction of just one level of government, the legislation may incidentally affect an area outside its jurisdiction (the "incidental effects" doctrine). For example, provincial legislation dealing with insurance may validly apply to federally incorporated companies (a federal matter) under this doctrine.

Overlapping Jurisdiction

Determining a law's pith and substance is sometimes complicated by the fact that a law has multiple purposes and effects. A law can relate to more than one jurisdictional area. If the areas overlapping in this way are either all federal areas or all provincial ones, there is no

4   See Peter W Hogg, *Constitutional Law of Canada*, 5th ed (Toronto: Carswell, 2007) (loose-leaf updated 2019, release 1) ch 15.9(f).

5   2004 SCC 79.

6   Note that it is also theoretically possible that the Court could have held that same-sex marriage was covered by the residuary branch of POGG power given that it related to a "new" matter. However, the question of whether newness alone provides a justification for invoking POGG power is not free from controversy.

constitutional problem. However, if the law involves complete overlap between a federal subject area and a provincial one—that is, if it falls fully within the jurisdiction of each—the law is said to have a "double aspect."

A **double-aspect law** can be enacted by either legislative body—Parliament or a provincial legislature. For example, many laws dealing with traffic offences have a double aspect, covered by both the federal criminal law power (s 91(27)) and the provincial power over property and civil rights (s 92(13)) (see Figure 4.2). A law that falls fully within an area that belongs to one level of government but that merely touches on an area belonging to the other is not a true double-aspect law. For these kinds of laws, only the level of government with complete jurisdiction over the area can pass them.

As just noted, either Parliament or the provinces can enact double-aspect laws. But what happens if both levels of government pass laws in a shared jurisdictional area and the laws conflict with one another? To deal with this situation, the courts have developed the **federal paramountcy doctrine**, according to which, in the event of conflict, the federal law prevails over the provincial one.[7]

double-aspect law
law whose subject matter falls within a federal subject area and a provincial one

federal paramountcy doctrine
doctrine according to which, in the event of conflict between a federal law and a provincial law in an area over which both levels of government have jurisdiction, the federal law governs and overrides the provincial one

FIGURE 4.2 Double-Aspect Law

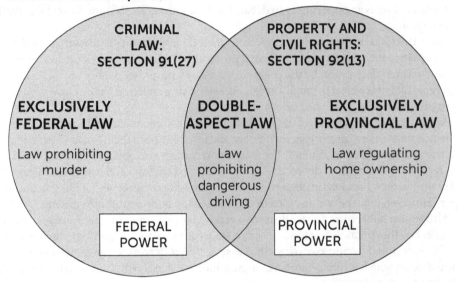

HOW PARLIAMENT MAKES STATUTES

New laws or amendments to old ones are usually a response to a perceived need for regulation in a particular area. They may be preceded by public hearings, commissions, or other forms of study depending on the complexity of the issue addressed by the proposed legislation. The responsibility for drafting proposed legislation falls to legislative counsel employed by Parliament. With Canada's bicameral federal Parliament, both the House of Commons and the Senate are involved in making statutes.

A proposed statute is first introduced as a **bill** either in the House of Commons (as a Commons bill) or in the Senate (as a Senate bill). Most bills are first introduced in the House of Commons; on occasion, however, they are initiated by the Senate. There are two types of bills: public bills and private bills. A **public bill** deals with a matter of public policy and can belong to one of two categories: (1) government bills, which are usually introduced by the

bill
draft version of a proposed new statute

public bill
bill dealing with a matter of public policy

---

7 For a detailed discussion of federal paramountcy, see Hogg, *supra* note 4, ch 16.

responsible minister in the House of Commons (although, on occasion, they are introduced in the Senate), or (2) private members' bills, which are usually introduced by members of the opposition. Most public bills are in the first category.

A **private bill** deals with a private matter (for example, a matter relating to a particular individual, corporation, or charity). Such bills can be introduced by a government, opposition, or a Senate member.

private bill
bill dealing with a private matter that relates, for example, to a particular individual, corporation, or charity

A bill's passage through Parliament, whether it is a public or a private bill, follows a set process. Parliamentary standing orders (which are written rules regulating parliamentary proceedings) provide, among other things, the various procedural stages that all bills must pass through in order to become statutes. A federal bill requires six **readings**, three in the House of Commons and three in the Senate. The process is similar in each house. When a bill is read for the first time, there is no debate, and the purpose is simply to introduce the bill. After the second reading, there is an opportunity to debate the general purpose of the bill but not its detailed provisions. Between the second and third readings in both houses, the bill is referred to a legislative committee for further detailed study, clause by clause, although this process can be expedited in certain situations (for example, if the matter is urgent). The legislative committee may propose amendments, and if it does, these can be debated by the House. The third reading is an opportunity to debate the final form of the bill and to vote on whether to adopt it.

reading
bill's formal presentation to the legislature before it becomes a statute

Once the final reading has been given to the bill, a motion is made for the bill to be given **royal assent**. Royal assent is a formal procedure (which involves either the signing of a special written declaration by the governor general or his or her deputy or a more elaborate ceremonial procession through Parliament) signifying approval by the Crown. After receiving royal assent, the bill becomes a statute.

royal assent
formal approval of a bill by the Queen's representative

Assuming that all six readings and royal assent occur before the end of the session, the newly enacted statute is assigned a chapter number and is published in the *Canada Gazette* Part III and, later, in annual statute volumes. The federal government also publishes electronic versions of its legislation. If a bill does not receive all of the required readings and royal assent before the end of the legislative session (in other words, before the session prorogues), it "dies on the order paper." However, it can be reintroduced in the next session if the opposition consents.

Although a bill becomes a statute once it receives royal assent, the statute may not come into effect at this point. If a statute does not state (or is "silent" regarding) when it comes into force, it does so upon receiving royal assent. The statute may, however, specify some future date on which it comes into force or may indicate that it will come into force on a day to be fixed by **proclamation**.

proclamation
special government order bringing a statute into force

Figure 4.3 summarizes the statutory enactment process.

Provincial Statutes

Provincial statutes are enacted by the provincial legislatures in each of the ten provinces. All provincial legislatures in Canada are elected bodies and are unicameral, with a single house involved in the legislative process.

With each provincial election, there is said to be a new "Parliament" even though the provincial bodies are called "assemblies" or "legislatures." Like federal statutes, provincial statutes can be passed only while the legislature is in session, with sessions lasting one to two years on average but permitted, under section 4 of the Charter, to continue for as many as five years, at which point an election must be called. The Charter also requires that provincial elections be called at least once every five years. Thus, governing parties have as many as five years to advance their legislative agendas.

PROVINCIAL JURISDICTION

The principal sections of the *Constitution Act, 1867* that distribute power to the provincial assemblies are

- section 92 (many subject areas),
- section 92A (natural resources, forestry resources, and electrical energy),
- section 93 (education), and
- section 95 (agriculture and immigration—although the provinces share jurisdiction in these areas with the federal government).

Provincial laws, like federal laws, must be authorized under the Constitution to be valid.

Section 92 is the source of most provincial power. Although the provinces have no general residuary power comparable to federal POGG power, there is a reasonable balance of power between the provincial and federal levels of government. This is because a few areas deemed to be under provincial jurisdiction—for example, property and civil rights and matters of a merely local or private nature—have been broadly interpreted. For a full account of the subject areas listed in section 92, see Table 4.2.

HOW PROVINCIAL LEGISLATURES MAKE STATUTES

The process of making provincial statutes is generally the same in each province. It is very similar to the federal process, with committee review between the second and third readings. Provincial bills, too, can be public or private; the vast majority are public government bills. One important difference between the federal and provincial processes is that provincial bills require only three readings because only one chamber is involved (there is no Senate). Royal assent follows the third reading.

After a bill receives three readings and royal assent, it becomes a statute. It is assigned a chapter number and is later published in print and electronic versions. Regarding when the statute comes into force, the same rules that apply to federal statutes apply to provincial ones. If the statute is silent about when it comes into force, it is effective upon royal assent. Alternatively, it may specify a date upon which it comes into force or leave the date open to be fixed by proclamation.

As with a federal bill, if a provincial bill does not receive all of the required readings and royal assent before the legislative session prorogues, it dies on the order paper. If this happens, a provincial bill (like a federal one) can, with the opposition's consent, be reintroduced in the next session.

FIGURE 4.3 Federal Statutory Enactment Process

1. CANADIAN SOCIETY
Values, beliefs, politics, economics, wealth, capital, income, environmental issues, global events

2. PRE-PARLIAMENTARY RESPONSE
Consensus or conflict (public hearings, commissions, study papers, reports)

3. PARLIAMENTARY RESPONSE

HOUSE OF COMMONS OR SENATE	
1st Reading	• Bill is introduced on a motion • No debates or amendments
2nd Reading	• Bill is debated on its general principles and main features • Still no amendments are permitted
Committee Review	• Bill is referred to committee after second reading • Committee examines proposed legislation, section by section, and can recommend amendments
3rd Reading	• Bill is read again with any recommended changes • Members vote

SENATE OR HOUSE OF COMMONS
For bills that begin in the House of Commons (C-bills, the majority of bills), the process above will be repeated in the Senate. For bills that begin in the Senate (S-bills), the process above will be repeated in the House of Commons. Federal bills, therefore, receive a total of six readings.

GOVERNOR GENERAL	
Royal Assent	• Bill is approved by governor general or representative • Formal ceremony

4. IMPLEMENTATION
- Proclamation (if statute requires)
- Regulations passed pursuant to statute (if required and statute authorizes)

TABLE 4.2   Provincial Powers Under Section 92 by Category

CATEGORY	RELATED SUBSECTION(S) OF SECTION 92	NOTES
Taxation, Money, and Public Assets	2. Direct Taxation within the Province in order to the raising of a Revenue for Provincial Purposes 3. The borrowing of Money on the sole Credit of the Province 5. The Management and Sale of the Public Lands belonging to the Province and of the Timber and Wood thereon 9. Shop, Saloon, Tavern, Auctioneer, and other Licences in order to the raising of a Revenue for Provincial, Local, or Municipal Purposes	The power of the provinces in this area, although more limited than Parliament's, is still significant. It is supplemented by part VIII of the *Constitution Act, 1867*. Forestry and natural resources are also covered by section 92A.
Property and Civil Rights	13. Property and Civil Rights in the Province	This category is a very important one for the provinces and has been interpreted to cover many specific areas, such as intraprovincial trade and commerce (business) (see also (11)), employment, regulation of the professions, contracts, torts, property, family law (see also (12)), civil liberties in the private sector, and many others.
Local Matters	10. Local Works and Undertakings (subject to exceptions listed in the federal table, Table 4.1) 16. Generally all Matters of a merely local or private Nature in the Province	The scope of property and civil rights has relegated these headings to the role of "backup" jurisdiction in many instances.
Health Care	7. The Establishment, Maintenance, and Management of Hospitals, Asylums, Charities, and Eleemosynary Institutions in and for the Province, other than Marine Hospitals	Health care is mainly provincial and comes under a number of different heads of power, including property and civil rights (13), local matters (16), and the power over hospitals ("Establishment, Maintenance, and Management") set out here (7). Parliament has jurisdiction over health matters under POGG power if they become serious enough to have national dimensions or to be classed as an emergency. Parliament also controls health care through substantial payments to the provinces. If a province wants to receive federal funding for health care, it must comply with national standards set out in the *Canada Health Act*.*
"Provincial" Crime and Punishment	6. The Establishment, Maintenance, and Management of Public and Reformatory Prisons in and for the Province 15. The Imposition of Punishment by Fine, Penalty, or Imprisonment for enforcing any Law of the Province made in relation to any Matter coming within any of the Classes of Subjects enumerated in this Section	"True" crime is a federal jurisdiction, but the provinces have the power to proscribe and punish lesser offences, such as traffic and regulatory offences.
Courts	14. The Administration of Justice in the Province, including the Constitution, Maintenance, and Organization of Provincial Courts, both of Civil and of Criminal Jurisdiction, and including Procedure in Civil Matters in those Courts	Each province has jurisdiction generally over its own courts but it is partly a shared jurisdiction (see Chapter 5).
Miscellaneous	4. The Establishment and Tenure of Provincial Offices and the Appointment and Payment of Provincial Officers 8. Municipal Institutions in the Province 11. The Incorporation of Companies with Provincial Objects 12. The Solemnization of Marriage in the Province	At the time of Confederation, regional regulation in these areas was considered most efficient.

* RSC 1985, c C-6.

Territorial Statutes

Territorial statutes are enacted by the legislative assemblies in each of Canada's three territories: Yukon, the Northwest Territories, and Nunavut. All territorial assemblies in Canada are elected bodies and are unicameral, with just one house involved in the legislative process.

After each territorial election there is a new assembly. As with federal and provincial statutes, territorial statutes can be passed only while the assembly is in session. As with Parliament and the provincial legislatures, these sessions may last up to five years, as prescribed by the Charter (ss 4 and 30).

The Yukon assembly is party based, as the provinces and Parliament are, but the Northwest Territories and Nunavut have a consensus style of government. These are the only two jurisdictions in Canada with Aboriginal majorities, and the consensus style reflects the traditional decision-making custom of First Nations and Inuit peoples. In both territories, members of the legislative assembly (MLAs) are elected as independent candidates, and there are no political parties. Unanimity is often achieved, although it is not required for decisions, such as the passage of motions or legislation. A majority vote often suffices.

TERRITORIAL JURISDICTION

The territories do not have an equivalent to section 92 of the *Constitution Act, 1867* assigning them specific areas of legislative jurisdiction. Each territory is under the control of Parliament, and the source of each territory's power is a federal statute that grants provincial-like legislative power to each of them. These statutes are the *Yukon Act*, the *Northwest Territories Act*, and the *Nunavut Act*.[8] They are not constitutionally entrenched and can be legally changed by Parliament at any time, despite legislated and political promises not to do so without first consulting the territories.

The organizational arrangement between Parliament and the territories is one of **devolution**. This refers to a legislative arrangement whereby a central authority grants power to regional authorities that are subordinate to it. The organization of the UK, with subordinate regional elected assemblies in Scotland, Wales, and Northern Ireland, is an example of devolution. Another example is the provinces' delegating authority to municipalities to make by-laws.

devolution
legislative arrangement whereby a central authority grants power to regional authorities that are subordinate to the central authority

Using the legislative powers granted them, the territorial assemblies have passed statutes equivalent to provincial statutes, such as taxation acts, motor vehicle acts, and human rights acts.

With their delegated legislative power (that is not constitutionally protected and can be withdrawn), the territories are legally analogous to municipalities. At the same time, the nature of their power, their geographic size, and their position on the national stage make them politically closer to provinces.

HOW TERRITORIAL LEGISLATURES MAKE STATUTES

The enactment process in the territories is generally modelled on the provincial system. A public or private territorial bill becomes a statute after three readings, with a committee review between the second and third readings, followed by assent. Assent comes from a federal appointee to each territory, called a "commissioner." When it comes to approving a bill, the commissioner's role in the territories is similar to that of the lieutenant governor in the provinces.

With respect to the completion of the process, territorial bills are like provincial or federal ones. A territorial bill must receive assent before the legislative session prorogues or it

---

8   Respectively, SC 2002, c 7; SC 2014, c 2, s 2; and SC 1993, c 28.

dies on the order paper. Assuming that it passes in time, the bill becomes a statute, is assigned a chapter number, and is later published in print and electronic versions. Like other statutes, territorial statutes come into force on assent. Alternatively, a statute may specify a date upon which it comes into force or leave the date open to be fixed by proclamation.

See Table 4.3 for a list of provincial and territorial assemblies.

TABLE 4.3 Provincial and Territorial Legislatures

PROVINCE/TERRITORY	NAME OF ASSEMBLY	MEMBER DESIGNATION*	SEATS
Alberta	Legislative Assembly of Alberta	MLA	83
British Columbia	Legislative Assembly of British Columbia	MLA	85
Manitoba	Legislative Assembly of Manitoba	MLA	57
New Brunswick	Legislative Assembly of New Brunswick	MLA	56
Newfoundland and Labrador	House of Assembly of Newfoundland and Labrador	MHA	48
Northwest Territories	Legislative Assembly of the Northwest Territories	MLA	18
Nova Scotia	Nova Scotia Legislature	MHA	52
Nunavut	Legislative Assembly of Nunavut	MLA	19
Ontario	Legislative Assembly of Ontario	MPP	107
Prince Edward Island	Legislative Assembly of Prince Edward Island	MLA	27
Quebec	National Assembly of Quebec	MNA	125
Saskatchewan	Legislative Assembly of Saskatchewan	MLA	58
Yukon	Yukon Legislative Assembly	MLA	18

* MLA = Member of the Legislative Assembly; MHA = Member of the House of Assembly; MPP = Member of the Provincial Parliament; MNA = Member of the National Assembly

Subordinate Legislation

subordinate (or delegated) legislation
legislation passed pursuant to a statute whereby the principal law-making power has delegated authority to another body to make laws

Primary legislative bodies (in Canada, Parliament or the provincial legislatures) have the power to delegate their powers to subordinate bodies (see Chapter 9 for a more detailed discussion of delegated power). **Subordinate (or delegated) legislation** in Canada is legislation passed pursuant to federal or provincial statutes that authorize the delegation of power to some entity to make subordinate legislation. This kind of legislation is made not by the principal law-making power but by the subordinate body to which the former has delegated authority to make laws.

There are two important limits on the primary legislator's power to delegate:

1. the primary legislator cannot give away its power to legislate completely, and
2. the primary legislator can delegate only powers within its jurisdiction.

Another general constitutional law principle relevant to this area is that of ***delegatus non potest delegare***. This means that the person or body to whom power is delegated cannot subdelegate it.

The main types of subordinate legislation are regulations and municipal by-laws.

Regulations

Regulations are closely related to statutes. They can be made only under the authority of a particular statute and are always associated with that statute. The section of the statute that delegates to another body—usually to the government Cabinet—the power to make regulations is the enabling section. Not all statutes have regulations. Those that do are usually longer, more complex statutes.

Regulations are passed differently from statutes. They are not passed by means of a series of readings, followed by royal assent. To become law, they are simply drafted and approved by the relevant body, filed with a government registrar or clerk (federally, with the clerk of the Privy Council), and then published in the relevant *Gazette* (federally, *Canada Gazette* Part II). Regulations are sometimes republished periodically in bound consolidations, like statutes. Almost all jurisdictions now publish ongoing loose-leaf and electronic versions of their regulations.

Regulations belong to one of two main categories:

1. "ordinary" regulations and
2. rules of practice.

Ordinary regulations are simply referred to as "regulations." They are passed under statutes for the purpose of filling in the details of a statutory regime. Because regulations are much easier to make, amend, or repeal than statutes, they are a more appropriate place to include legislative details (for example, procedural rules or fees) that are changed frequently. For example, the federal *Access to Information Regulations* were passed under the *Access to Information Act*.[9]

Rules of practice set out the procedure or practices to follow when pursuing particular types of claims or when pursuing any kind of claim before particular courts or tribunals. Some examples of federal regulations that are rules of practice include the *Bankruptcy and Insolvency General Rules*, the *Rules of the Supreme Court of Canada*, and the *Federal Court Immigration Rules*.

When dealing with regulations, you should be aware not only of the statute authorizing a particular regulation but of the general regulations statute for the jurisdiction in question. This is a special Act that sets out the precise rules for the making and publishing of regulations. Regulations can be challenged if they fail to follow the procedure set out in the relevant regulations statute or if they exceed the mandate outlined in the enabling section.

Municipal By-Laws

Municipal by-laws are like regulations in that they exist only in relation to a statute. Under section 92 of the *Constitution Act, 1867*, the provinces have power over municipalities. The federal government has likewise given power to the territorial assemblies to regulate municipalities. Municipal by-laws are created pursuant to provincial or territorial statutes and can be thought of as a special type of provincial or territorial regulation. The authorizing

delegatus non potest delegare
principle that a person or body to whom power is delegated cannot subdelegate that power (Latin: "one to whom power is delegated cannot himself further delegate that power")

regulations
form of subordinate legislation passed by a person or body (frequently the government Cabinet) to expand on or fill out a statute's legislative scheme

municipal by-laws
form of subordinate legislation passed by municipalities

---

9 RSC 1985, c A-1.

legislation for these by-laws can be a general municipal statute or a special charter for an individual city.

By-laws cover many topics. Some of the more familiar ones include property taxes, health and safety (for example, no-smoking areas), animals (for example, dog licensing and on-leash areas), structures and property maintenance (for example, clearance of snowy walkways), and business licensing.

Quasi-Legislative Materials

quasi-legislative materials
non-legislated written rules that relate to and affect a legal process

Quasi-legislative materials are non-legislated written rules. Strictly speaking, they are not subordinate legislation or, in fact, legislation at all, and as such they are not legally binding. However, they play an important role in some areas of the law. You must follow, observe, and consider these rules as you do legislated rules. If not, you risk having applications or documents rejected by the relevant authorities, delaying a legal process, or misunderstanding a related piece of legislation. Quasi-legislative materials relate to many different areas of the law. Examples of quasi-legislative materials include government policy statements (for example, policy statements or guidelines issued by tax departments or securities commissions explaining how they interpret certain legislative provisions), court directions (usually in the form of practice directives clarifying legislated procedural rules), and certain kinds of agreements (such as trade arrangements between different governments).

Parliamentary Sovereignty

parliamentary sovereignty
doctrine that Parliament has ultimate and complete power to pass any law

The doctrine of **parliamentary sovereignty** holds that Parliament has total power. It is a doctrine that became entrenched in 17th-century England as parliamentary power superseded that of the Crown. Thus, Parliament, rather than the monarch, became recognized as the country's supreme legislative authority. Parliamentary sovereignty implies at least three principles:

1. Parliament can make or unmake any law;
2. Parliament cannot bind itself against using its power in the future; and
3. a procedurally valid Act of Parliament cannot be questioned by the courts.[10]

In theory, these principles have been transplanted to Canada—part of the English political system we have inherited. In the Canadian context, however, the theory of parliamentary sovereignty is complicated by certain factors.

There are three features of the Canadian system that appear to qualify the notion of Parliament's "total power." First, we are a federation, with legislative power split between two levels of government, the federal and the regional. Second, we have an entrenched Charter (see Chapter 6) that limits the power of our legislators. Third, the power to amend the Constitution lies outside the sole jurisdiction either of Parliament or of the provinces.

Federalism and Parliamentary Power

As we have seen, Canada is a federal state with split jurisdiction. This means that no legislative body in Canada has total power, as the UK Parliament does. However, it is accepted that we have modelled our system on the British one, which means that between the two levels of government (federal and provincial), there is no power vacuum—between them, law-making power exists over *all* subject areas. They have the combined power to enact any law.

---

10 Hogg, *supra* note 4, ch 12.1.

In *Reference re Same-Sex Marriage*,[11] the SCC affirmed this principle. As Hogg summarized:

> The Supreme Court of Canada reaffirmed "the principle of exhaustiveness," which it described as "an essential characteristic of the federal distribution of powers." A "legislative void is precluded." It followed that "legislative competence over same-sex marriage must be vested in either Parliament or the Legislatures," and the most apt home for the matter was s 91(26) [federal].[12]

The conclusion we can draw from this is that, in our federal system, there are no limits on the *combined* power of the federal and provincial legislatures. Parliamentary sovereignty—of a kind—exists.

The Charter and Parliamentary Power

The next challenge to the notion of parliamentary sovereignty in Canada comes from the Charter. As an entrenched statute, it places limits on the powers of Parliament and the provincial and territorial legislatures to pass laws that offend the Charter's guaranteed rights and freedoms. These limits are qualified, however, by the notwithstanding or "override" clause (s 33), which allows legislators to pass legislation that would otherwise infringe many, although not all, of the Charter's provisions (see Chapter 6). To the extent that legislatures can override the Charter, parliamentary sovereignty remains theoretically intact; in practice, this clause is rarely invoked.

Constitutional Amendment and Parliamentary Power

Finally, we must address the fact that the power to amend the Canadian Constitution lies outside the unilateral jurisdiction of either Parliament or the provinces. This also seems to challenge the doctrine of parliamentary sovereignty in the Canadian context. However, this challenge can be resolved as follows: Although it is true that, subject to a few limited exceptions, neither Parliament nor the provinces can amend the Constitution unilaterally, there is no "legislative void" here either. Provided that the two levels of government cooperate according to the legislative process established in part V of the *Constitution Act, 1982*, they can make any amendment to the Constitution, including to the Charter. Although they have yet to exercise this power successfully, it is available to them.

When we consider legislative authority in Canada as a collective of federal and provincial power, we see that the principle of parliamentary sovereignty applies in this country as it does in Britain. The English system has, at least theoretically, been transplanted onto Canadian soil. Of the three branches of government—legislative, executive, and judicial—the legislative branch is supreme. The executive and judicial branches are ultimately subject to its control.

Executive Power

In this section, we explore the second branch of government, the **executive**, which is in charge of implementing or administering our laws. In particular, we examine our system of responsible government, the various sources of executive power, and some of the limits of

executive
branch of government that is responsible for implementing or administering the laws in Canada and whose authority, in this country, is divided between the federal, provincial, and territorial governments

---

11   *Supra* note 5. The Court also held that our Constitution is a living tree capable of growth and is not frozen in time. See earlier discussion under "Progressive Interpretation."

12   Hogg, *supra* note 4, ch 12.2(a).

executive power. In Canada, it is common to refer to the executive branch simply as "the government," although it is, technically, only one of the three branches of government.[13]

Responsible Government

Our system of government evolved in the UK over hundreds of years and is known as **responsible government**. As stated in the quotation at the beginning of the chapter, this system means that there is no clear separation between the legislative and executive branches. The executive branch, although it enjoys the support of the majority in the legislature, controls the legislative branch. Responsible government was formally recognized and named in Great Britain in 1835. In 1848, Nova Scotia became the first colony in the British Empire to adopt the system. In 1867, with Confederation, responsible government became the system for the new country of Canada.

Three main features distinguish the system of responsible government:

1. a dual executive;
2. elected office (that is, members of the political executive must have elected seats in the legislature); and
3. reliance on **convention** (that is, agreed-upon customary practice).

Dual Executive

Peter Hogg described the system of responsible government in the Canadian context as follows:

> In a system of responsible government, there is a "dual executive," consisting of a formal head of state and a political head of state. The *formal* head of state for Canada is the Queen, but she is represented in Canada by the Governor General of Canada and the Lieutenant Governors of the provinces. ... The *political* head of state for Canada is the Prime Minister, who is the leader of the party that commands a majority in the elected House of Commons. In each province, the equivalent of the Prime Minister is the Premier, who is the leader of the party that commands a majority in the elected Legislative Assembly.[14]

The formal head of state and chief executive in Canada, then, is the British monarch—that is, the **Crown**. At the time of Confederation, that was Queen Victoria. Since 1952, it has been Queen Elizabeth II. The Queen "reigns" in Canada through her representatives: the governor general at the federal level and the lieutenant governors at the provincial level. Legally, according to the Constitution, the Queen and her representatives wield executive power in Canada (see Figure 4.4).

As we will see, however, this legal power has passed, by convention, to the Queen's representatives in council—that is, the federal and provincial Cabinets, who hold the real executive power. Most people examining our Constitution for the first time find it confusing that formal executive power, as spelled out in the *Constitution Act, 1867*, is so divorced from political reality and that the Constitution contains no mention of the prime minister of Canada or the provincial premiers.

responsible government
system of government in which the members of the executive branch are drawn from the elected members of the legislative branch and in which their power continues only so long as they enjoy the support of the majority in the legislature

convention
established and traditional "rules" on which our system of responsible government is based and which qualify many of the rules of government set out in constitutional legislation, such as the *Constitution Act, 1867*, but which are not, technically, legally binding

Crown
sovereign (currently the Queen), whose authority in Canada has been formally delegated to the governor general (federally) and to the lieutenant governor (provincially) but is actually exercised by the executive branch of government

---

13   In the US, it is more common to refer to the executive as "the administration," particularly in reference to the federal executive branch.

14   Hogg, *supra* note 4, ch 9.1 (emphasis in original).

FIGURE 4.4

Under the Constitution, Queen Elizabeth II, as the reigning British monarch, is the formal head of the executive government in Canada. Here she is seen meeting with Governor General Julie Payette, her federal representative, in the library at Balmoral Castle in Scotland in 2017.

Elected Office

The second distinctive feature of the Canadian system of responsible government is that the members of the political executive must have elected seats in the legislature. (In rare instances, non-elected members may be appointed to Cabinet, but they are required to seek election within a reasonable time after appointment.) The members of the political executive are "responsible" to the legislature in the sense that they must enjoy the confidence of the majority of the assembly. In turn, the elected members of the assembly must have the support of the people or risk losing their seats in the next election. In the US system, by contrast, the members of the president's Cabinet need not be elected.

The classic model of government from which ours is derived requires a clear separation of powers between the legislative, executive, and judicial branches. However, our system of responsible government, with its (by and large) elected Cabinet, significantly modifies this classic model. In Canada, as mentioned above, the executive exercises significant control over the legislature. However, the executive only maintains this control while it has the support of the majority of the elected assembly. In the US, by contrast, the administration, federally and at the state level, is not part of the legislative branch. If there is a political divide between the two branches—if, for example, the administration is Democratic and the legislative branch is predominantly Republican—the administration will simply have less say in the legislative agenda.

Convention

Perhaps the most surprising aspect of responsible government is that, as Peter Hogg has said, "the rules which govern it are almost entirely 'conventional,' that is to say, they are not to be found in the ordinary legal sources of statute or decided cases."[15] When we say that the rules are "conventional," we mean that they are based on tradition and past practice rather than on principles set out in formal documents. Although there may be political consequences for not following these practices, the SCC has ruled that conventions are not

---

15   Hogg, *supra* note 4, ch 9.3.

legally binding.[16] Again, the US model serves as a contrast to the Canadian system of responsible government. In the US, the national system of government is clearly spelled out in its written Constitution.

It should be noted that, despite the ruling of the SCC, it is the view of some commentators that responsible government does—or at least should—have legal constitutional status in Canada. Their view is based on the preamble clause to the *Constitution Act, 1867*, which states that we have "a Constitution similar in Principle to that of the United Kingdom." They interpret the preamble clause to mean that the rules of responsible government (although they may have been merely conventional in the UK) have become constitutionally entrenched in Canada.

Sources of Executive Power

What are the sources of executive power in Canada? Our constitutional legislation is one source, especially the *Constitution Act, 1867*. But this legislation does not fully define the extent of executive power in the Canadian government. Convention, too, plays an essential role in this area. Also relevant are certain common law and statutory (federal, provincial, and territorial) rules. We examine all of these sources of executive power in this section.

Constitutional Basis

The *Constitution Act, 1867* contains many of the key constitutional provisions dealing with formal executive power in Canada. These provisions include the following: all of part III (ss 9-16), relating to federal executive power, and sections of part V (ss 58-68), concerning provincial executive power.

Peter Hogg summarized these provisions as follows:

> [Section] 9 provides that the "executive government" of Canada is vested in "the Queen"; s. 10 contemplates that the Queen's powers may be exercised by a "Governor General"; and s. 11 establishes a "Queen's Privy Council for Canada" whose function is "to aid and advise in the government of Canada" and whose members are to be appointed and removed by the Governor General. ...
>
> In each province, there is a "Lieutenant Governor" and an "Executive Council" with powers similar to those of the Governor General and Privy Council [ss. 58-68]. The Lieutenant Governors are appointed by the Governor General in Council (s. 58).[17]

governor general Queen's representative in Canada, formally authorized to exercise her powers as head of the executive government in Canada but who, by convention, exercises these powers only on the advice of the prime minister and federal Cabinet

Governor in Council official name for the federal Cabinet

lieutenant governor formal head of the provincial executive government who, by convention, exercises executive power on the advice of the provincial premier and Cabinet

The *Constitution Act, 1867* does not make it expressly clear who is responsible for appointing the **governor general**, but, by implication, it is the reigning British monarch, and this is the practice that is followed. By convention, however, the British monarch appoints the governor general on the advice of the prime minister. Similarly, the Governor General in Council (often shortened to **Governor in Council**), that is, the federal Cabinet, appoints the provincial **lieutenant governors** on the advice of the prime minister.

The governor general and lieutenant governors also play a part in the legislative process. Under sections 17 and 55 of the *Constitution Act, 1867*, the governor general (it could also be the Queen) is required to sign federal bills as a final formal step before they become law. Similarly, the lieutenant governors are required to sign provincial bills into law (s 90). This last step of the legislative process, as described earlier in this chapter, is known as royal

16 See *Reference re a Resolution to amend the Constitution*, [1981] 1 SCR 753, 1981 CanLII 25.
17 Hogg, *supra* note 4, ch 9.3.

assent; it is another example of how the Canadian system of government has modified the separation-of-powers doctrine with respect to the executive and legislative branches.

Conventional Practice

As mentioned, responsible government in Canada is primarily based on convention rather than on principles explicitly set out in the Constitution. Knowing the conventional practice in this area is important because it qualifies—that is, modifies—the rules explicitly set out in the Constitution. The following are some important conventional practices relating to the federal executive:

- *Prime minister.* The political executive is headed by the leader of the political party that controls the majority of Parliament (either by way of an outright party majority or, in the case of a minority government, by way of a coalition with other parties)—namely, the **prime minister**.

- *Cabinet.* Section 11 of the *Constitution Act, 1867* provides that the governor general has the aid and advice of the **Queen's Privy Council for Canada**, referred to more informally as the Privy Council. By convention, the key members of the Privy Council are the Cabinet ministers appointed by the prime minister, with appointments made on a representative basis (with at least one Cabinet minister from each province, if possible). The Cabinet (or Governor in Council) is the part of the Privy Council that, under the direction of the prime minister, has members who currently sit as members of Parliament. There are other members of the Privy Council, including former ministers of government, whose status is nominal rather than practical; they have no real influence. It is extremely rare for the entire Privy Council to meet, and when it does it is usually for ceremonial purposes. As noted above, "Governor General in Council" is generally taken to refer to the federal Cabinet and is often shortened to "Governor in Council." When legislation refers to the Governor General in Council or Governor in Council, it means the federal Cabinet.

- *Political and legislative agenda.* The prime minister takes the lead in setting the government's agenda as well as the composition, organization, and procedures of Cabinet. Cabinet ministers also play a role in policy development, particularly within their portfolios.

- *Ministerial responsibility.* Although the government stands or falls as one, individual ministers are responsible in the sense that they are the executive heads of their portfolios and must take responsibility not only for their own actions but for those of their subordinates within the ministry as well. Ministers are also required to answer to Cabinet and to Parliament for their activities within the Ministry.

- *Confidence convention.* Arguably, the most important convention of all is the **confidence convention**. If the government loses the support of the majority of the elected representatives in the House of Commons, the confidence convention requires the government to resign, and if a new government cannot be formed, it must call an election.

Most of these conventions apply, with certain modifications, to the provinces (see Figure 4.5). The political head provincially is the **premier**. The lieutenant governor—while appointed by the governor general on advice of the prime minister—by convention acts on the advice of the provincial cabinet in most matters. The **Lieutenant Governor in Council**

prime minister
political head of state in Canada who leads the party with control of the majority in the House of Commons

Queen's Privy Council for Canada
formal advisory council of the governor general, the active portion of which is the federal Cabinet

confidence convention
convention requiring the government to resign if it loses the support of the majority of the elected representatives in the House of Commons and, if a new government cannot be formed, to call an election

premier
political head of a provincial or territorial government who leads the party with control of the majority in the Legislative Assembly (in Nunavut, there are no political parties, but the premier must command the support of the majority in the Assembly)

Lieutenant Governor in Council
official name for a provincial Cabinet

is the official name for the provincial Cabinet. The provincial Executive Councils, as they are referred to in part V of the *Constitution Act, 1867*, are made up exclusively of current Cabinet ministers; there are no "outsiders" as there are with the federal Privy Council.

Similar conventions apply in Yukon and the Northwest Territories. Although, as we saw earlier in this chapter, the territories are federal dependencies, their executive governments operate much as the provincial ones do. The federal government appoints a **commissioner** who acts as the formal head of the territorial executive government. The **Commissioner in Executive Council** is the official name for a territorial Cabinet. The system is different in Nunavut, which operates according to a system of consensus democracy, not responsible government, and has no political parties.

The political reality, then, concerning executive power is that it differs significantly from the legal reality spelled out in the Constitution. Does it matter that our administration operates according to a set of rules that are not legally enforceable? Does it matter that those with legal power—namely, the governor general and the lieutenant governors—are expected not to use it except as directed by political leaders? Perhaps not, as long as everyone involved respects and accepts the system. So far, this has been the case in Canada. But there is no guarantee that this will always be the case. Arguably, in times of extreme political uncertainty, rules based on convention are less stable than those enshrined in law.

commissioner
federally appointed official who is the formal head of the territorial executive government

Commissioner in Executive Council
official name for a territorial Cabinet

FIGURE 4.5 Executive and Legislative Government in Canada

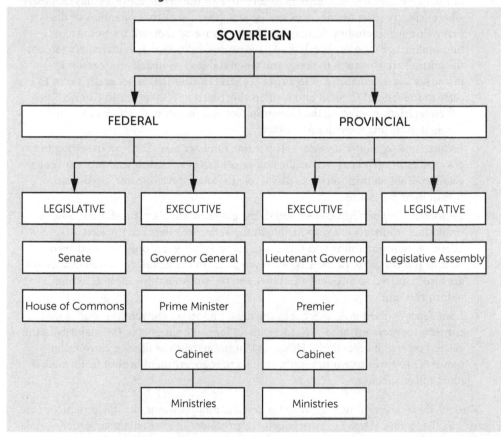

Common Law and Royal Prerogative

The power of the British Crown to legislate by decree or otherwise was limited by the *Magna Carta* (1215) and was finally taken over completely by Parliament when the English Bill of Rights (1689) was passed (see Chapter 2). Similarly, the Crown lost the right to adjudicate disputes, criminal and civil, early in its legal history.

However, the Crown had long exercised *executive* authority. Historically, **royal prerogative** was an important source of this power. It was independent of the courts and Parliament, and the Crown exercised it by issuing various types of orders, such as royal proclamations (which announced executive actions, such as declarations of war, to subjects of the realm)[18] and letters patent (which usually established rights, titles, or offices). Over time, however, the Crown lost this independent power, and today royal prerogative exists only to the extent that the common law allows the Crown to exercise it. In our federal system, it is exercised by the Crown's representatives on the advice of the prime minister and Cabinet or provincially by the premiers and their Cabinets. See Box 4.3 for some examples of royal prerogative today.

royal prerogative powers and privileges given by the common law to the Crown; a source of limited executive power

---

Examples of Prerogative Power

A well-known example of prerogative power is the federal Crown's power to grant mercy in criminal cases. The *Criminal Code* provides that nothing in it "in any manner limits or affects Her Majesty's royal prerogative of mercy" (s 749). Although its exact bounds are not entirely clear, the royal prerogative of mercy (RPM) is considered a far-reaching power that includes all forms of clemency, from free pardons (total expungement of a conviction together with its record) to conditional pardons (expungement, but with the record kept) to the remission or reduction of sentences. The RPM is traditionally associated with the commutation of a death sentence to prison time—an instance of RPM that no longer applies in Canada because we abolished the death penalty in 1976.

Some other areas where prerogative power is exercised, as Hogg has noted, include the following:

- conduct of foreign affairs, including making treaties;
- declarations of war;
- appointment of the prime minister and other ministers;
- issuance of passports; and
- creation of Indian reserves.*

The power to appoint provincial premiers and ministers is an example of the provincial Crown's prerogative power.

* Hogg *supra* note 4, ch 1.9.

Finally, although royal prerogative is usually thought of as authorizing the Crown to act in certain contexts, it has a defensive aspect to it as well. **Crown immunity** is sometimes viewed as part of the law of royal prerogative; it includes immunity from liability as well as any privileges and presumptions that operate in favour of the Crown. Examples include (1) Crown privilege, which is an evidentiary rule that permits the Crown to claim that evidence in a particular case is privileged on the ground that its disclosure would adversely affect some matter of public interest; (2) crown immunity in civil cases, which prevents civil actions against the Crown unless legislation specifically permits it (and, in many situations,

Crown immunity covering term for the various protections afforded the Crown, including Crown privilege, the presumptions of legislation not applying to the Crown, and (formerly) immunity from tortious liability

---

18   See Box 3.1 in Chapter 3 for a discussion of the *Royal Proclamation, 1763*.

legislation does currently permit civil claims against the government); and (3) crown immunity in criminal cases, which protects the Crown from criminal liability (the extent of this protection is unclear, however). It is a complicated area, and a detailed examination of it is beyond the scope of this text.

Statute Law

Despite the historical significance of the common law and royal prerogative, the main source of executive power today is statute law. Federal, provincial, and territorial statutes assign specific executive powers to their respective governments. For example, most ministries or departments have their own statutes that define, among other things, the powers and duties of the responsible minister. The various powers granted to ministers by these statutes include the authority to enter into contracts to facilitate ministry business, to hire and manage staff, and to pursue actions to enforce the liabilities of others.

Other statutes create various extensions of government, over which the executive is assigned control. Examples include (1) the armed forces and the national security service (the Canadian Security Intelligence Service, or CSIS); (2) law enforcement agencies (such as the Royal Canadian Mounted Police, or RCMP, and the Canada Border Services Agency, or CBSA); and (3) administrative boards and tribunals that regulate almost every area of society, from energy to human rights to transportation (see also Chapter 9, which covers administrative law).

These statutes are just a few examples, but they illustrate how, in modern times, most day-to-day executive power is based on legislation that confers executive authority on Cabinets and individual ministers.

Limits of Executive Influence

As noted in the discussion of responsible government, the separation-of-powers doctrine is modified under the Anglo-Canadian system. The modification consists in the fact that, in our system, the executive branch is made up of elected members of the legislature who exert control over the majority of members. The executive in our system therefore controls the legislature with its majority.

It is important to remember, however, that if the executive loses majority control, the reverse becomes true: the legislature controls the executive. Majority control can be lost if a minority government loses the support of its coalition partners or if a party with a majority loses control of its own members. In these situations, the legislature exercises its ultimate control, and the government, by convention, must resign.

Assuming, however, that the executive branch has clear control of the legislature, there are still limits to its power. First, members of the executive cannot overstep the bounds of their appointed executive authority. For example, a minister who has been assigned executive authority in relation to a particular matter pursuant to a statute cannot exercise administrative power in another, unauthorized area.

Second, although the separation of powers between the legislative and executive branches may be murky at times in the Canadian system, the separation between the executive and judicial branches is well established. For example, if a member of the executive attempts to directly influence the outcome of a case before the courts, she does so at the risk of ending her political career. The exact nature and scope of this principle of non-interference, however, are less clear.[19]

Lastly, the executive branch is not permitted to infringe civil liberties unless the law specifically permits it. As just one example, police forces (which act as agents of the executive branch) have various powers to arrest individuals. At common law (and now, by ordinary legislation and the Charter as well), when arresting an individual, the police are required to inform him of the reasons for the arrest. This requirement helps protect the individual against the arbitrary use of power. The failure to give reasons could result in negative legal consequences for the Crown in a related prosecution. (Civil liberties are discussed in detail in Chapter 6.)

---

19 The famous "judges affair" of 1976, which concerned executive interference with the judiciary, highlights some of the uncertainty in this area. In December 1975, a federal Cabinet minister in the Trudeau government, André Ouellet, was cited by Justice Kenneth Mackay of the Quebec Superior Court for contempt when Ouellet criticized him for acquitting three companies that had been charged with price fixing. In the months that followed the citation, other instances of interference with the judicial process—specifically, communications by members of the executive with judges regarding cases that were in the process of being heard—came to light, and in March 1976, material in support of the claims was placed before the House of Commons. In response, Prime Minister Trudeau issued a statement prohibiting members of Cabinet from communicating directly with members of the judiciary concerning any cases they had before them; similar statements were then issued in provincial assemblies. For a detailed account of this affair, see Peter Russell, *The Judiciary in Canada: The Third Branch of Government* (Toronto: McGraw-Hill Ryerson, 1987) at 78-81.

CHAPTER SUMMARY

There are three branches of government in Canada: the legislative branch, the executive branch, and the judicial branch. In our system of responsible government, even though the legislative and executive branches perform separate functions—the legislative branch makes the law, and the executive branch implements it—they strongly influence one another.

The legislative branch is the supreme law-making authority. The doctrine of parliamentary sovereignty holds that our legislatures, collectively, can make or unmake any law. The divided jurisdiction between federal and provincial levels of government can, in theory, be brought together to make law in any area, including changes to the Constitution. Also, some provisions in the Charter can be overridden by the different levels of government on their own, in respect of their laws, through a special procedure. Total legislative power—including the power to amend our Constitution—has only resided in Canada since the patriation of our Constitution in 1982 (before then legislative power was shared in part with the British Parliament).

In our federal union, the power to make legislation is divided more or less equally between Parliament and the provinces. Broadly speaking, Parliament has jurisdiction over matters of national importance, and the provinces have jurisdiction over private law and local matters. Also, Parliament has devolved, or delegated, province-like jurisdictional authority to the territories.

Making statute law in this country follows set procedures, whereby a bill is introduced into the legislative chamber, and after a number of readings, followed by royal assent, it becomes a statute. Also, pursuant to some statutes, authority is delegated to other bodies to make subordinate legislation, such as regulations and municipal by-laws. As well, we are subject to certain non-legislated rules, such as policy statements, issued by various government agencies. Collectively, this growing mass of regulation touches on almost every aspect of our lives.

The executive branch of government is responsible for implementing and enforcing the law. In Canada, the formal head of state is the British monarch, currently Queen Elizabeth II. Her official representative at the federal level is the governor general and, at the provincial level, the lieutenant governors. By convention, her representatives in council, the Governor in Council (the federal Cabinet) and the Lieutenant Governors in Council (the provincial Cabinets), exercise the executive power that is formally vested in her under the Constitution.

Under the classic separation-of-powers doctrine, the executive branch operates independently of the legislative branch. But under the Anglo-Canadian system of responsible government, the executive branch is composed of elected members of the legislature. Federally, the political party that controls the majority of the House of Commons chooses its leader. This leader becomes the prime minister of Canada and, in turn, chooses his or her Cabinet, primarily from the House of Commons. Provincially, the political party that controls the majority of the Legislative Assembly chooses its leader, who becomes the premier of the province and similarly chooses a Cabinet. Executive governments that control a majority of the relevant legislature also control the legislative agenda. However, executive governments that lose the support of the majority of the relevant legislature must resign. In that sense, the prime minister or premier and his or her Cabinets are accountable or "responsible" to the elected assembly.

Executive power comes from a variety of sources: constitutional rules, convention, common law and royal prerogative, and statutory law. Most of our constitutional rules are set out in the *Constitution Act, 1867*, and many of them are followed in form only. The real basis of executive power is political and democratic convention—that is, agreed-upon customary tradition. The federal Cabinet ("the Crown in right of Canada") and the provincial Cabinets ("the Crown in right of the provinces") hold that power as "advisors" to Her Majesty's representatives. The federal Cabinet administers federal law, and the provincial Cabinets administer provincial law.

Royal prerogative, rooted in the common law, is also a source of some executive power. Examples of royal prerogative are the power to conduct foreign affairs and the power to issue passports. Most of the surviving instances of royal prerogative relate to matters within the jurisdiction of the federal Crown. However, the main source of executive power is statute law. Federal and provincial statutes define many of the powers and duties of executive government, such as those concerning the running of everyday ministry business and of administering various government agencies and institutions.

Although executive power is far-reaching, it is subject to limits. Executive governments must act within their appointed authority, must not interfere with judicial proceedings, and must adhere to various standards prescribed by law relating to civil liberties.

KEY TERMS

bicameral, 91

bill, 101

commissioner, 114

Commissioner in Executive
  Council, 114

confidence convention, 113

constitutionally entrenched, 92

convention, 110

Crown, 110

Crown immunity, 115

delegatus non potest delegare, 107

devolution, 105

division of powers, 93

double-aspect law, 101

executive, 109

federal paramountcy doctrine, 101

governor general, 112

Governor in Council, 112

judicial review on Charter grounds
  (or Charter challenge), 94

jurisdiction, 96

legislation, 91

legislative intent, 124

legislature, 90

lieutenant governor, 112

Lieutenant Governor in Council, 113

municipal by-laws, 107

parliamentary sovereignty, 108

POGG power, 96

premier, 113

prime minister, 113

private bill, 102

proclamation, 102

prorogue, 95

public bill, 101

quasi-legislative materials, 108

Queen's Privy Council for Canada, 113

reading, 102

regulations, 107

responsible government, 110

royal assent, 102

royal prerogative, 115

section, 122

separation-of-powers doctrine, 90

statutes, 91

statutory interpretation, 122

subordinate (or delegated)
  legislation, 106

supremacy clause, 93

unicameral, 91

FURTHER READING

BOOKS

Aucoin, Peter, Jennifer Smith & Geoff Dinsdale, *Responsible Government: Clarifying Essentials, Dispelling Myths and Exploring Change* (Ottawa: Canadian Centre for Management Development, 2004), online: <http://publications.gc.ca/collections/Collection/SC94-107-2004E.pdf>.

Bernier, Luc, Keith Brownsey & Michael Howlett, eds, *Executive Styles in Canada: Cabinet Structures and Leadership Practices in Canadian Government* (Toronto: University of Toronto Press, 2005).

Funston, Bernard W & Eugene Meehan, *Canada's Constitutional Law in a Nutshell*, 4th ed (Toronto: Carswell, 2013).

Gifford, Donald J, Kenneth H Gifford & Michael I Jeffery, *How to Understand Statutes and By-Laws* (Toronto: Carswell, 1996).

Heard, Andrew, *Canadian Constitutional Conventions: The Marriage of Law and Politics*, 2nd ed (Don Mills, Ont: Oxford University Press, 2014).

Hogg, Peter W, *Constitutional Law of Canada*, 5th ed (Toronto: Carswell, 2007) (loose-leaf updated 2019, release 1).

McGill Law Journal, *Canadian Guide to Uniform Legal Citation*, 9th ed (Toronto: Carswell, 2018).

Monahan, Patrick J, Byron Shaw & Padraic Ryan, *Constitutional Law*, 5th ed (Toronto: Irwin Law, 2017).

Oliver, Peter, Patrick Macklem & Nathalie Des Rosiers, eds, *The Oxford Handbook of the Canadian Constitution* (Oxford: Oxford University Press, 2017).

Régimbald, Guy & Dwight Newman, *The Law of the Canadian Constitution*, 2nd ed (Toronto: LexisNexis, 2017).

Seidle, F Leslie & Louis Massicotte, eds, *Taking Stock of 150 Years of Responsible Government in Canada* (Ottawa: Canadian Study of Parliament Group, 1999).

Sullivan, Ruth, *Statutory Interpretation*, 3rd ed (Toronto: Irwin Law, 2016).

The Constitutional Law Group, *Canadian Constitutional Law*, 5th ed (Toronto: Emond, 2016).

WEBSITE

Gateway Site for Canadian Legal Databases

Canadian Legal Information Institute (CanLII): <https://www.canlii.org/>.

REVIEW QUESTIONS

1. What are the three branches of government in Canada, and what is the function of each?

2. What does it mean to say that a statute is "constitutionally entrenched"? Name and briefly describe two entrenched statutes under the Canadian Constitution.

3. What is POGG power?

4. What is a double-aspect law? How is conflict between federal and provincial double-aspect laws resolved?

5. What are the two main types of regulations? Briefly explain each.

6. Describe the doctrine of parliamentary sovereignty and its relationship to the separation-of-powers doctrine as applied in Canada.

7. Briefly describe how our system of responsible government modifies the classic separation-of-powers model.

8. Why is it important to read the provisions of the *Constitution Act, 1867* in light of convention? Describe at least three specific situations to support your answer.

9. What is the source of power for most executive authority in Canada today?

10. Name and describe two limits on executive power.

EXERCISES

1. Research the website for the legislative assembly in your province or territory. Find and read all available information about the assembly's location, its members, and the legislative process it follows.

2. Go to the Supreme Court of Canada judgments website (<http://scc-csc.lexum.com>) and type "division of powers" (in quotation marks) in the Decisions search field. Scan through the judgments to find one of interest to you and then read the case to determine how the SCC resolved the argument about which level of government had jurisdiction to enact the challenged legislation.

3. Visit the federal Justice Laws website (<http://laws-lois.justice.gc.ca>). Click the Consolidated Acts link under the Laws sidebar heading. Search through the alphabetical listing of statutes and choose one of interest to you. Locate as many of the structural features of statutes discussed in Appendix 4.1 (for example, the title, preamble, part headings, and different types of sections) as you can.

4. Consider the idea of parliamentary sovereignty in the context of Canadian Confederation and discuss whether you believe that legislative power considered in its totality should be limited (and if so,

how any limits could be imposed). If not, consider whether legislative power is, in practical terms, sufficiently limited or too limited. Provide specific examples and reasons for your opinion.

5. In your opinion, is having a dual executive, with a formal and a political head of state, a good system or a bad system? Support your answer with specific reasons. If you think the system should be changed, indicate how.

6. Although executive (and legislative) power is divided in Canada, there are certain areas—for example, education, the environment, and tourism—in which the federal and provincial/territorial governments cooperate in implementing laws, either because of jurisdictional overlap or because of the availability of federal funding. Choose one such area and research how the federal government and your regional government have together implemented the program that has resulted. Consider, for example, the funding and administrative structures that have been used.

7. Although it is clear that politicians cannot interfere directly with the judicial process, it is less clear whether they can criticize judges and judgments after proceedings have been concluded. Do you believe that politicians should be able to call into question the judicial process in this way? Should it depend on what type of case is involved? In your answer, refer to the separation-of-powers doctrine and provide specific reasons and examples (hypothetical or real) for your position.

APPENDIX 4.1

Reading and Understanding Legislation

When looking at a piece of legislation, knowing a little about its structure and some basic rules of interpretation can enhance your understanding of it. Moreover, knowing how legislation is cited when referred to in legal writing is helpful when trying to locate it in the first place. The following discussion of legislative structure, interpretation, and citation focuses on statute law, but most of it also applies similarly to subordinate legislation.

Structure of Statutes

Canadian statutes have structural components and features that are generally shared regardless of jurisdiction. For example, statutes begin with their titles and chapter numbers (assigned chronologically for the year or session in which they are passed). If the statute is long and complicated, it will often include a table of contents. It may also have a preamble, which is an introductory sentence or two describing the statute's purpose.

section
basic unit of a statute

The basic unit of a statute is a **section**, which is sometimes divided into subsections, paragraphs, subparagraphs, and so on, depending on the level of detail. Special sections to pay particular attention to include the following:

- *definition sections*, which define particular words used in the statute;
- *enabling sections*, which delegate the power to make regulations to a person or body subordinate to the legislature;
- *consequential amendment sections*, which deal with amendments to earlier statutes affected by the subject statute; and
- *commencement (or coming into force) sections*, which can assign specific in-force dates or leave the date open to be set in the future by proclamation. (If there is no commencement section, the statute comes into force on royal assent.)

Sometimes statutes group sections together in parts, usually with headings describing the subject area covered by the sections. Other structural features include marginal notes next to the section, briefly describing the purpose of the section; legislative history notes at the end of the section, describing its history (for example, if it appeared in a previous collection, or revision, of statutes); and schedules, setting out additional information. As well, federal statutes and some provincial statutes are bilingual, published with English and French versions next to each other.

See Figure 4.6 for examples of some of these structural features.

Statutory Interpretation

statutory interpretation
process of interpreting legislation to resolve any ambiguities regarding its meaning or effect

Many statutes contain words and phrases that are ambiguous, despite the best efforts of legislative counsel to make them clear. In these situations, the courts are responsible for resolving the ambiguity. Courts faced with this kind of problem must engage in **statutory interpretation**. To help with this process, the courts have developed common law rules for dealing with interpretation over hundreds of years. More recently, these have been supplemented with various legislated rules (as set out in federal, provincial, and territorial Interpretation Acts).

FIGURE 4.6 Structure of Statutes

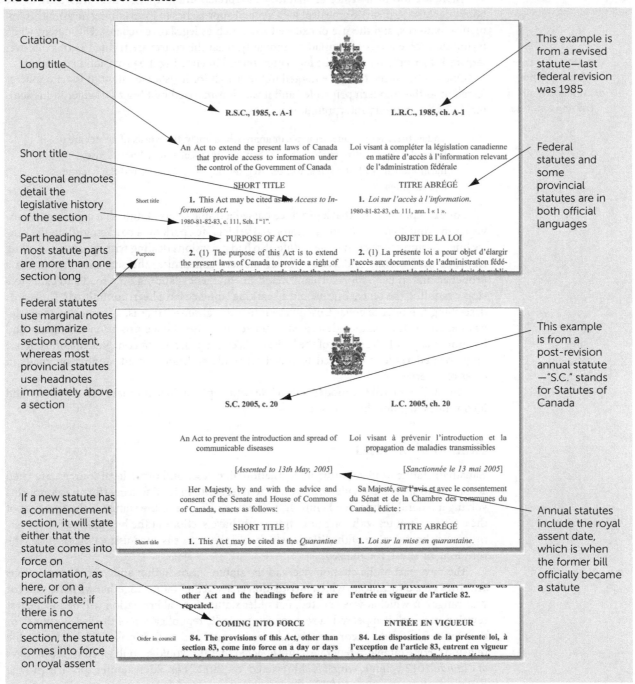

There are too many rules of statutory interpretation to describe here (there are entire books devoted to them). Some deal with general approaches to ascertaining meaning, grammatical patterns, and the use of external aids, such as legislative debates. Ultimately, when trying to resolve issues of legislative ambiguity, what the courts are trying to do is discover **legislative intent**: What did the legislature intend in enacting the provision in question?

legislative intent
legislature's express or implied intent in passing a statute

One central principle has emerged in the search for legislative intent. It is generally referred to as the "modern principle," and it was summarized by Elmer Driedger in his seminal book on statutory interpretation as follows:

> Today, there is only one principle or approach, namely, the words of an Act are to be read in their entire context and in their grammatical and ordinary sense harmoniously with the scheme of the Act, the object of the Act, and the intention of Parliament.[20]

For example, assume that a province passed a traffic safety statute that contained a provision making it an offence for a "motorized vehicle" to "park on a road straddling the centre line." Assume further that the statute also had provisions dealing with speeding, obeying traffic signs, littering, and various other matters concerning the safe use of roads. If a propeller-driven light-sport airplane made an emergency landing on a road and came to a stop straddling the centre line, would a "parking" offence have been committed? The words describing the offence cover this situation in a literal sense (that is, a "motorized vehicle" has parked in the manner described), but, reading the offence provision in context and harmoniously with the object of the legislation, etc., a court might conclude that the offence only covered vehicles designed to travel on roads and not aircraft landing on roads in cases of emergency.

The SCC has cited the modern principle with approval in a number of its decisions, and it continues to guide the courts today.[21]

Citation of Statutes

Canadian statutes and subordinate legislation, like cases and other legal sources, are cited according to specialized rules when they are referred to in legal writing (for an example involving a federal statute, see Figure 4.7). The title or name of the statute is the first part of the citation. Statutes with long titles frequently have sections at the beginning of them setting out a short version of the title, in which case the statute is cited using its short title. The title, long or short, is italicized.

The next part of the citation refers to the statute's jurisdiction and year. Abbreviations are always used to indicate which jurisdiction enacted the statute, together with the year (or year range) in which it was enacted. For older statutes, the abbreviation will be for the last revision in which it appeared (a revision is a periodic republication of the jurisdiction's entire statute collection, incorporating all amendments and corrections as of the date of the revision). For example, a federal statute enacted in 2012 would be published in the *Statutes of Canada* 2012 volume, which is abbreviated "SC 2012." For older statutes appearing in the *Revised Statutes of Canada* 1985—the last and most recent federal revision—the abbreviation is "RSC 1985."

---

20 Elmer A Driedger, *Construction of Statutes* (Toronto: Butterworths, 1974) at 67. Professor Driedger's text continues to be published, but with later editions his name has been dropped. See now Ruth Sullivan, *Sullivan on the Construction of Statutes*, 6th ed (Toronto: LexisNexis, 2014).

21 See, for example, *Celgene Corp v Canada (Attorney General)*, 2011 SCC 1, [2011] 1 SCR 3 at para 21.

After the jurisdiction and year comes the chapter number. As soon as a bill becomes a statute, it is assigned a chapter number (numeric). When statutes are republished in a revision, they are assigned new chapter numbers (sometimes numeric and sometimes alphanumeric) to correspond with their position in the consolidation. The last part of the citation is the *section number*, which is cited only if a particular provision is being referred to; otherwise, the citation ends with the chapter number.

For in-depth coverage of citation protocols, refer to the McGill Law Journal, *Canadian Guide to Uniform Legal Citation*, 9th ed (Toronto: Carswell, 2018). "The McGill Guide," as it is usually referred to, has established itself as the standard reference in this area and is updated every four years.

FIGURE 4.7 Components of Statutory Citation

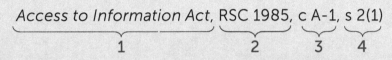

Access to Information Act, RSC 1985, c A-1, s 2(1)

1   2   3   4

1   Title
    The title is italicized, followed by a comma (not italicized) and a space.

2   Jurisdiction and Year
    The jurisdictional reference is abbreviated, followed by a space and the year, followed by a comma and another space. In this example of a federal revised statute, "R" is for revised, "S" is for statutes, and "C" is for Canada. If it were an annual statute, it would be just "SC." Each province and territory has its own abbreviation—for example, "A" for Alberta, "BC" for British Columbia, and "M" for Manitoba. When citing provincial or territorial statutes, "RS" or "S" would precede the relevant jurisdictional abbreviation. The McGill Guide has a comprehensive listing of abbreviations used in legal citations of all types.

3   Chapter
    Chapter is abbreviated to "c." Then comes a space and the numeric or alphanumeric designation ("A-1"), followed by a comma and another space if there is a section reference.

4   Section
    Section is abbreviated to "s." Then comes a space and the number along with any subdivisions, which are placed in parentheses with no spaces in between. Regardless of the particular level or sublevel being referred to, when written as part of a full citation, it always begins with the abbreviation for section, "s." When spoken, the level is noted. For example, at the third level, you would say, "section 2, subsection 1, paragraph b."

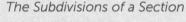

The Subdivisions of a Section

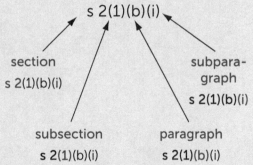

s 2(1)(b)(i)

section
s 2(1)(b)(i)

subsection
s 2(1)(b)(i)

paragraph
s 2(1)(b)(i)

subparagraph
s 2(1)(b)(i)

5 The Judiciary: The Third Branch of Government

Introduction 128

Role of the Judiciary 129

Canadian Courts: Constitutional Basis ... 129

Canadian Courts: Organization
and Function 132

Precedent and Stare Decisis in the
Canadian Court System 144

Judicial Appointments 145

Public Proceedings 149

Judicial Independence 150

Chapter Summary 153

Key Terms 153

Further Reading 153

Review Questions 154

Exercises 155

Appendix 5.1: Reading and
Understanding Case Law 156

The Supreme Court Building in Ottawa, designed by Ernest Cormier, is a national landmark and a symbol of the Canadian justice system.

Courts are the operating rooms of the legal system: theatres where preparation and expertise are brought to bear in critical moments of questioning and arguing, where decisions sometimes have to be made on the fly, where blood sometimes flows—at least metaphorically. … The drama emerges from many points: the evidence of often tragic past events, the emotions of parties and witnesses, the decision-makers' insights into the human condition, and the sense of vindication or outrage that observers experience when the final decision is made. … But underlying all of these and providing the basic plot to the story is the framework upon which our modern courts operate: the adversarial system, which contemplates that a court hearing is generally a contest between two opponents who have come together to do battle with each other over some specific issue, one seeking to blame the other for some form of misdeed in the past.

Jessie J Horner, *Canadian Law and the Canadian Legal System*
(Toronto: Pearson, 2007) at 238

Introduction

The third branch of government is the judiciary. Judges exercise their power by rendering decisions in our country's courts. A **court** is a state-sanctioned forum where disputes between opposing litigants are formally adjudicated. As we will see, the Canadian court system is complex. This is largely because, under the Constitution, the authority over the courts themselves and over the appointment of judges is divided between Parliament and the provinces.

Most courts in Canada are so-called *inferior* courts. ("Inferior" here is not a pejorative term. It refers not to the quality or value of these courts but to their level in the overall hierarchy of the court system.) All such courts are courts of first instance—that is, trial courts—that hear matters for the first time and have a single judge. The provincial inferior courts are the main point of entry for most people when they interact with the justice system. They deal with less serious criminal matters and matters related to traffic, family, and small claims. Inferior courts do not hear appeals.

Other courts in Canada are *superior* courts. Some superior courts are courts of first instance—that is, trial courts. These courts have a general (or inherent) jurisdiction to deal

court
state-sanctioned forum where disputes between opposing litigants are formally adjudicated

with most legal cases but are most often used for important matters such as civil disputes involving large sums of money or serious criminal cases—murder, for example. Other superior courts are appeal courts, which hear appeals from courts of first instance and have more than one judge (and sometimes as many as nine).

It is important for anyone involved with the court system to understand each court's jurisdictional limitations and its place in the overall hierarchy. Such understanding will, for example, guide litigants to the right forum and help them determine routes of appeal.

This chapter begins with a general overview of the Canadian court system. We consider the role of the judiciary and the constitutional basis for the different types of courts in Canada. Then we look more closely at the organization and function of the various courts—the Supreme Court of Canada (SCC), the provincial court systems, the territorial court systems, the federal court systems, and the military courts. We next explain the flow of precedent within the Canadian court system. Then we consider how judges are appointed and discuss the two overarching principles of the Canadian judicial system: the open court principle and the principle of judicial independence.

Role of the Judiciary

A court's judgment or decision is the final outcome of the dispute heard before it. In cases where the court provides reasons for its decision, the record of those reasons becomes part of our law and—depending on the court's position in the hierarchy—may bind later courts under the doctrine of precedent (see Chapter 2, as well as the discussion of precedent and *stare decisis* later in this chapter). Canadian courts make decisions that affect all aspects of our public and private lives.

In the common law provinces (in other words, all provinces except Quebec) and in the territories, judge-made rules play an important if diminishing role in the whole body of the law. Statutes, which are made by legislatures, play an increasing role as the state regulation of society expands. Despite this trend, the judiciary's role is as significant as ever in Canada.

As we saw in Chapter 4, judges add to legislated rules by interpreting statutes. Specifically, they establish the basic meanings of statutory provisions, they determine the jurisdictional validity of statutes, and they decide whether a particular statute offends the *Canadian Charter of Rights and Freedoms*. Once judges have interpreted a statute, the statute will, from that point on, have to be read in light of that interpretation.

On occasion, judges perform a fourth interpretive exercise with respect to statutes: they may be asked to decide if a statute has superseded a common law rule. According to the principle of parliamentary sovereignty, statutes, which are made by legislators, take precedence over judge-made common law rules in the event that they conflict with one another. Sometimes the conflict is clear and may even be expressed (that is, definitely stated rather than implied—for example, where a statute states that "the common law rule concerning XYZ is abolished"). Sometimes, however, the conflict is less clear. Where uncertainty exists, judges may be called upon to rule in this regard.

Canadian Courts: Constitutional Basis

The *Constitution Act, 1867* sets out the power over courts and judicial appointments. The key provisions are the following:

> 92. In each Province the Legislature may exclusively make Laws in relation to Matters coming within the Classes of Subject next hereinafter enumerated; that is to say,...

4. The Establishment and Tenure of Provincial Offices and the Appointment and Payment of Provincial Officers. ...

14. The Administration of Justice in the Province, including *the Constitution, Maintenance, and Organization of Provincial Courts, both of Civil and of Criminal Jurisdiction*, and including Procedure in Civil Matters in those Courts. ...

96. The *Governor General shall appoint the Judges of the Superior, District, and County Courts in each Province*, except those of the Courts of Probate in Nova Scotia and New Brunswick. ...

99.(1) Subject to subsection (2) of this section, the judges of the superior courts shall hold office during good behaviour, but shall be removable by the Governor General on address of the Senate and House of Commons.

(2) A judge of a superior court ... shall cease to hold office upon attaining the age of seventy-five years. ...

101. *The Parliament of Canada may*, notwithstanding anything in this Act, from Time to Time *provide for the Constitution, Maintenance, and Organization of a General Court of Appeal for Canada, and for the Establishment of any additional Courts for the better Administration of the Laws of Canada.*
[Emphasis added.]

Since Confederation, Parliament and the provinces have used their constitutional powers to create three types of court:

1. inferior courts,
2. superior courts, and
3. the Supreme Court of Canada.

They have also used their powers to create a fourth related institution, the administrative tribunal (discussed in Chapter 9).

Inferior Courts

The inferior courts fall into two categories: provincial/territorial and federal.

Provincial and Territorial

inferior courts
provincial and territorial courts whose jurisdiction is limited to the less serious criminal matters, family and youth matters, and small claims disputes; the federal courts martial, part of the military court system, are also inferior courts

The main **inferior courts** are the provincial and territorial ones. Their jurisdiction typically is over the following:

- criminal matters (but not the most serious crimes, such as murder and treason, which go before the provincial superior courts),
- family and youth matters, and
- small claims disputes (note that in Manitoba, Ontario, and Prince Edward Island, small claims court is a division of the provincial superior court).

The provincial inferior courts, as noted above, are constituted under section 92(14) of the *Constitution Act, 1867*, with provincially appointed judges under section 92(4). Parallel provisions exist in the various federal statutes devolving legislative powers to the territories—that is, provisions that set out the power to establish inferior courts and appoint territorial judges.[1] These inferior courts, provincial and territorial, are the workhorses of the court system and are where most Canadians are likely to experience their "day in court." See Box 5.1 concerning terminology when referring to these (and provincial and territorial superior) courts.

Terminology: Provincial and Territorial Courts

The nomenclature applied to the provincial courts, inferior and superior, is inconsistent. For example, provincial superior courts are known variously as Superior Courts, Superior Courts of Justice, Supreme Courts, or Courts of Queen's Bench.

The provincial inferior courts are often simply referred to as the "provincial courts." However, the term "provincial courts" sometimes refers to the provincial superior courts and at other times to all provincially constituted courts, superior and inferior. The context should make the intended meaning clear. There is a similar ambiguity with territorial inferior courts, which are often referred to as the "territorial courts." But this name may also refer to the territorial superior courts or to all of the territorial courts, both superior and inferior. Again, the context should make the reference clear.

Federal

Apart from the provincial inferior courts, there is also a very specialized set of federal inferior courts: the military courts martial. These include the General Court Martial and the Standing Court Martial, and they have jurisdiction over armed forces personnel who commit service offences.

Superior Courts

Like the inferior courts, the superior courts fall into two categories: provincial/territorial and federal.

Provincial and Territorial

The **provincial superior courts**, as noted, are constituted under section 92(14) of the *Constitution Act, 1867*, with their judges appointed federally under section 96 of the Act. Because of this, they are sometimes referred to as **section 96 courts**. Why are the judges in these provincial courts appointed federally? Although these are provincial courts, they can, under section 92(14), hear not only matters falling under provincial legislative power (for example, motor vehicle accident cases) but also some matters falling under federal legislative power (for example, bankruptcy cases). (See Chapter 4 for a discussion of how legislative power is divided under Canada's Constitution.) The fact that the judges in these provincial superior courts are federally appointed ensures balance. Balance is needed because of the power these provincial courts have to adjudicate certain federal matters.

provincial superior courts
provincially constituted courts with inherent jurisdiction to hear all matters (unless taken away by legislation) and with two levels, a trial level and an appeal level; sometimes refers just to the trial level

section 96 courts
provincial superior courts, so called because their judges are federally appointed under section 96 of the *Constitution Act, 1867*

---

1 See the *Yukon Act*, SC 2002, c 7, and the *Northwest Territories Act*, SC 2014, c 2, s 2. Nunavut is an exception, however. It has a unified superior and territorial court called the Nunavut Court of Justice, which has the combined jurisdiction of an inferior and a superior court. It is the only jurisdiction with such an arrangement.

It should also be noted that it would be unconstitutional for the provinces to assign to provincial inferior courts (with provincially appointed judges) matters that historically—at the time of Confederation—were adjudicated by superior courts. Such matters must be heard by section 96 courts, with their federally appointed judges.[2]

The provincial superior courts—that is, section 96 courts—have two levels: a trial level and an appeal level. The provincial courts of appeal are the highest level of court in the provinces.

territorial superior courts
federally constituted superior courts with jurisdiction in the territories

The **territorial superior courts** are very similar, in terms of their function, to the provincial superior courts and likewise have federally appointed judges. They differ, however, in that they are constituted under federal legislation. The source of Parliament's jurisdiction over the territorial courts, superior and inferior, is section 4 of the *Constitution Act, 1871*,[3] an imperial statute that is part of our Constitution.

Federal

federal superior courts (or federal courts)
comprising the Federal Court, the Federal Court of Appeal, the Tax Court of Canada, and the Court Martial Appeal Court

The **federal superior courts** (sometimes just called **federal courts**) are:

- the Federal Court,
- the Federal Court of Appeal,
- the Tax Court of Canada, and
- the Court Martial Appeal Court.

These courts are constituted under federal legislation, with federally appointed judges. Parliament's authority over these courts flows from the second leg of section 101 of the *Constitution Act, 1867*, which gives Parliament the power to create "additional Courts for the better Administration of the Laws of Canada." The term "Laws of Canada" in section 101 has been interpreted as limiting the jurisdiction of these courts to disputes involving federal (as opposed to provincial) laws.

The Federal Court and the Federal Court of Appeal have jurisdiction throughout Canada. The authority of these courts overlaps with that of the provincial superior courts, and this has given rise to a number of jurisdictional disputes. The Tax Court of Canada has jurisdiction throughout Canada, but only in the area of tax law. The jurisdiction of the Court Martial Appeal Court is limited to appeals from the courts martial.

The Supreme Court of Canada

Supreme Court of Canada
Canada's highest court and final court of appeal

The **Supreme Court of Canada** is also a federal superior court. But it has a special status and occupies its own category. Parliament's authority over this court flows from the first leg of section 101, which gives Parliament the power to create a "General Court of Appeal for Canada." The SCC has been Canada's general Court of Appeal since 1875 and its final Court of Appeal since 1949.

Canadian Courts: Organization and Function

Figure 5.1 shows how the three types or categories of courts in Canada are organized. Administrative tribunals sit just below the fourth level. (For more on administrative tribunals, see Chapter 9.)

---

2   See *Toronto (City) v York (Township)*, 1938 CanLII 252, [1938] AC 415 (UKJCPC).

3   (UK), 34 & 35 Vict, c 28.

FIGURE 5.1 Overview of the Canadian Court System

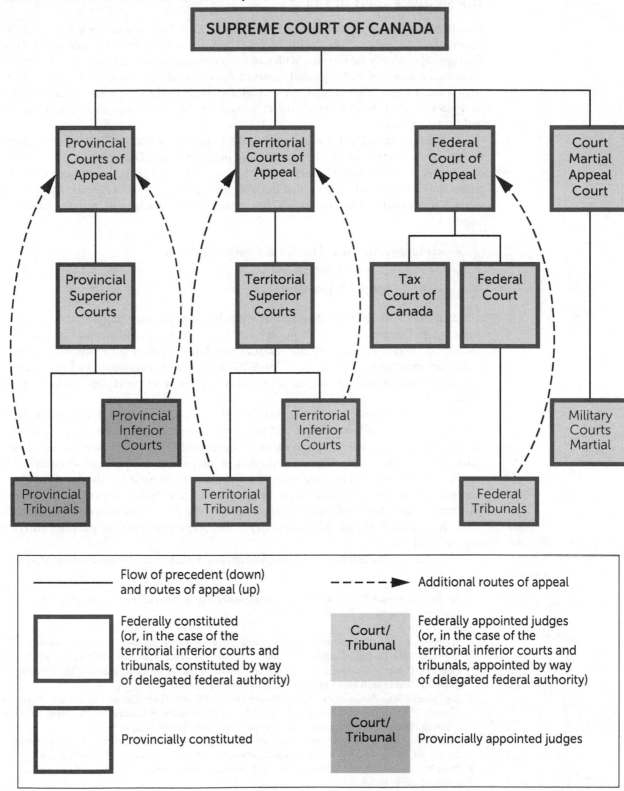

The Supreme Court of Canada

Courts of law existed in the separate British North American colonies before Confederation in 1867. At that time, the English Judicial Committee of the Privy Council was still the final appeal authority for Canada. With Confederation (as we saw in Chapter 3), Canadian statesmen recognized that a general Court of Appeal would be desirable for the country. Such a court was needed to interpret statutes and to decide future constitutional disputes likely to arise over the division of powers between the new federal government in Ottawa and the provinces.[4]

As a result, section 101 was included in the *Constitution Act, 1867*, giving Parliament the power to "provide for the Constitution, Maintenance, and Organization of a General Court of Appeal for Canada." Using this authority, the federal government passed the *Supreme Court Act*[5] in 1875 and created the SCC. As a general Court of Appeal sitting at the top of Canada's judicial system, the SCC has jurisdiction to hear appeals from the following courts:

- all of the provincial and territorial Courts of Appeal,
- the Federal Court of Appeal, and
- the Court Martial Appeal Court.

Until the 1970s, the SCC often heard private law appeals regarding tort, contract, real property, and commercial law disputes.[6] Since the 1980s, its mainstay has been public law appeals involving criminal matters, statutory interpretation questions, and Charter and other constitutional law issues.[7] The SCC also hears appeals from Quebec concerning that province's civil law, as well as appeals from the other provinces concerning the common law.

Historically, Quebec jurists have feared that the common law majority on the SCC would graft common law precepts and techniques onto Quebec's civil law system. This has affected the geographic representation of the court.[8] Originally, two of the court's six judges came from Quebec. The total number of judges was increased to seven in 1927, and in 1949 that number reached nine, where it remains. Section 6 of the *Supreme Court Act* requires that three of these judges be appointed from Quebec. By convention, three are from Ontario, two from the west, and one from the Atlantic provinces.[9] One judge is given the title of chief justice of Canada, and the other eight are called **puisne** ("inferior in rank") judges.

Table 5.1 summarizes the key organizational and jurisdictional aspects of the SCC.

puisne
term applied to describe judges who rank below another judge or judges on the same court—for example, the judges below the chief justice on an appeal court

---

4   See James G Snell & Frederick Vaughan, *The Supreme Court of Canada: History of the Institution* (Toronto: University of Toronto Press, 1985).

5   RSC 1985, c S-26.

6   See Peter McCormick, *Supreme at Last: The Evolution of the Supreme Court of Canada* (Toronto: Lorimer, 2000); Ronald I Cheffins, "The Supreme Court of Canada: The Quiet Court in an Unquiet Country" (1965–66) 4 Osgoode Hall LJ 259; and Peter H Russell, "The Political Role of the Supreme Court of Canada in Its First Century" (1975) 53 Can Bar Rev 576.

7   See Patrick J Monahan, *Politics and the Constitution: The Charter, Federalism and the Supreme Court of Canada* (Toronto: Carswell, 1987); and Peter H Russell, "Introduction: History and Development of the Court in National Society and the Canadian Supreme Court" (1980) 3 Can-USLJ 4.

8   Peter H Russell, *The Supreme Court of Canada as a Bilingual and Bicultural Institution: Documents of the Royal Commission on Bilingualism and Biculturalism* (Ottawa: Queen's Printer, 1969) at 215.

9   Peter W Hogg, *Constitutional Law of Canada*, 5th ed (Toronto: Carswell, 2007) (loose-leaf updated 2019, release 1) ch 8.8.

TABLE 5.1   SCC: Key Facts and Features

Name	Supreme Court of Canada (1875–)
Constitutional Authority	Section 101, *Constitution Act, 1867*
Act	*Supreme Court Act*, RSC 1985, c S-26
Rules	*Rules of the Supreme Court of Canada*
Judges	• 1 chief justice of Canada • 8 puisne judges • Quorum: 5–9 judges
Key Jurisdictional Features	• Hears appeals in criminal and non-criminal cases (if the case concerns a matter of public importance or significant legal question) • Leave to appeal is required in some instances • Hears appeals in criminal cases involving indictable offences where the court of appeal upholds a conviction but with a dissenting opinion • Hears appeals in criminal cases where the court of appeal substitutes a guilty verdict for an acquittal • Hears references

How Cases Come Before the SCC

Cases come before the SCC in one of three ways: (1) leave to appeal, (2) appeal as of right, or (3) on a reference.

LEAVE TO APPEAL

This occurs when a court grants a party leave to appeal her case to the SCC. It is the most common way for non-criminal cases to come before the SCC. In some instances, a provincial Court of Appeal or the Federal Court of Appeal can grant such leave. However, most parties who want to appeal their cases to the SCC must get permission or leave to appeal from the Court itself.

Applicants must file written submissions with the Court. In most cases, these submissions are considered by one of three panels (each composed of three SCC judges) that have been selected by the chief justice of Canada. Either the panel will grant leave or it will not, and it does not provide reasons either way.

Section 40(1) of the *Supreme Court Act* sets out the main criteria the Court considers when deciding whether to grant a party leave to appeal. Under this section, the SCC may grant leave if it is of the opinion that the case involves:

- a matter of public importance,
- a significant legal question, or
- any other matter the Court believes warrants its attention.

Cases involving constitutional issues (including civil liberties) or Aboriginal rights, or important matters dealing with criminal law, administrative law, or private law, stand the greatest chance of success on a leave application. Cases that are purely factual or that involve matters that are specific to a particular province or territory are less likely to succeed.

APPEAL AS OF RIGHT

With certain kinds of criminal cases, there is a right of appeal to the SCC without the need for prior leave. Section 691 of the *Criminal Code* identifies these cases. Circumstances under which an appeal as of right exists for an accused person include the following:

1. The person is convicted of an indictable offence at trial, and the conviction is upheld by the Court of Appeal, but one of the judges dissents on a question of law.
2. The person is acquitted of an indictable offence, but the Court of Appeal sets aside the acquittal and substitutes a guilty verdict.

If there is no prescribed right of appeal under section 691, an accused can still apply for leave to appeal, just as parties in non-criminal cases can. (See the discussion of leave to appeal, above.)

ON A REFERENCE

Section 53 of the *Supreme Court Act* provides a third way for a matter to come before the SCC. Unlike the two preceding ways, this one is not dependent on an existing legal action in a lower court. Under this section, the Governor in Council (the federal Cabinet) may refer important questions of law or fact to the SCC for an advisory opinion. Typically, these questions would concern the constitutionality of a proposed statute or of a course of action the government is considering.

reference
special case in which the executive branch of government refers a question of law to a court of appeal, usually a question concerning the constitutionality of a statute or course of action the government is considering

These questions don't originate only with the federal Cabinet. A provincial Cabinet might direct a **reference** question to its own provincial Court of Appeal. That court's decision regarding the reference question can be appealed as of right (by the provincial Cabinet) to the SCC.[10]

Hearings

Before an appeal is heard, the parties must file with the Supreme Court registrar all of the documents, in both paper and electronic versions, that the Supreme Court judges need in order to prepare for the appeal. These documents include the following:

facta (sing. factum)
written legal arguments to be presented on an appeal

- the trial transcripts;
- the **facta** of all parties, which contain the written legal arguments to be presented on the appeal; and
- a book of authorities containing copies of all precedent cases, statutes, and secondary sources, such as excerpts from books and articles.

The Supreme Court registrar then schedules a date for the hearing of the appeal. At the hearing, the parties may appear before a panel consisting of five, seven, or all nine Supreme Court judges. The chief justice determines the size of the panel, with five judges constituting a quorum—that is, a minimum number of members. The modern practice is generally for all nine judges to hear the appeal.[11]

The Supreme Court judges hear the appeal from a semicircular bench (see Figure 5.2). The chief justice sits in the middle, flanked by the puisne judges, who range outward from

---

10 *Ibid* ch 8.6(b).
11 See McCormick, *supra* note 6; and Bora Laskin, "The Supreme Court of Canada: A Final Court of and for Canadians" (1951) 29 Can Bar Rev 1038 at 1075.

the chief justice in order of seniority. Judges are normally gowned in black silk robes but wear red ones for ceremonial occasions. The courtroom is open to the public. Oral argument is permitted at the appeal hearing, but with strict time limits imposed. Hearings are conducted in either English or French. The judges can (and often do) ask the lawyers questions and can also hear from intervenors—persons or groups who are not parties to the lawsuit but who can participate in the hearing with the Court's permission.

FIGURE 5.2 The nine judges' benches in the main courtroom at the SCC.

Judgments

After the appeal hearing concludes, the judges move directly to a conference room for initial discussion of the case. Although the judges can return from this discussion and give the Court's judgment directly from the bench, the usual practice is to **reserve** their decision. This means that they reserve for themselves a period of time in which to reflect further on the case, to do more research, possibly to review how other common law courts in other countries might have decided a similar matter, and to allow themselves more time to write the reasons for their decision.[12]

reserve
to postpone rendering its decision, after a hearing has concluded, so that the court can carefully prepare the reasons for its judgment

---

12   Michael J Herman, "Law Clerking at the Supreme Court of Canada" (1975) 13 Osgoode Hall LJ 279; Jack Batten, "The Supreme Court of Canada" in *Judges* (Toronto: Macmillan, 1986); Ian Greene et al, *Final Appeal: Decision-Making in Canadian Courts of Appeal* (Toronto: Lorimer, 1998).

In the conference room immediately after the hearing, during the judges' initial discussion of the case (which is presided over by the chief justice), the most junior member appointed to the Court first gives his opinion. The other judges follow, in reverse order of seniority.[13] The main aim of this formalized, private preliminary conference is not just to canvass initial views but also to determine, in a collegial way, who will write the Court's judgment.

Writing a judgment is labour-intensive and time-consuming. Judges often confer with their clerks and develop a draft judgment, which may require further research at the Court's own library. The draft is then circulated among the other panel judges for comments until a consensus is (ideally) reached and a final judgment is completed. The Court's judgment on an appeal is decided by a **majority** and need not be unanimous. Unanimity is preferred, however, because it signals most forcefully the Court's position regarding the appeal, and this kind of clarity is helpful to the legal profession. A judge may also concur (or agree) with the Court's decision and be part of the majority but write different reasons. Another judge may **dissent**, or disagree with the majority, and write the reasons for her dissent. Dissenting judgments may later become influential if shown to be better reasoned than the majority decision.

Once made, the decision is deposited with the Supreme Court registrar, who releases it in both English and French. It is then published in print form in the Supreme Court Reports and online on the Court's website (it will also be reproduced in other report series and in other electronic databases).

majority
refers (in the context of a split decision on appeal) to the group of justices who form the majority and whose decision becomes the decision of the court

dissent
refers (in the context of a split decision on appeal) to the judgment of one or more justices in the minority

Provincial Court Systems

A plaintiff in a civil or non-criminal matter, or an accused in a criminal matter, enters a specific level of the Canadian court system in accordance with pre-established criteria—for example, the monetary amount involved in the plaintiff's civil action or the nature of the accused's criminal charge. Serious criminal charges, such as murder or treason, are tried in a provincial superior trial court, whereas civil claims for smaller amounts involve trials, in most provinces, in small claims divisions of the provincial inferior court.

Most provinces structure their court systems as described earlier in this chapter (see Figure 5.1). In all provinces, there are two levels of superior court: a trial-level superior court and, above it, a provincial Court of Appeal. The chief justice of the latter is usually the chief justice of the province. Beneath the trial-level superior courts are the inferior courts. Cousins to the inferior courts, but beneath them in the overall system of justice, are the many provincial administrative tribunals.

Not all cases can move up the judicial hierarchy from lower-level trial courts to the SCC. Parties must have solid grounds in law to appeal decisions made by a trial judge. Trial cases first must reach the provincial superior Court of Appeal—in other words, the top court in each province—and this court decides whether an appeal is warranted. A case can proceed from the provincial superior Court of Appeal to the SCC only if certain appeal criteria are met, as described above in our discussion of the SCC.

Provincial Superior Courts

The provincial superior courts are historically related to the English royal courts of justice (see Chapter 2) and have inherent jurisdiction over all civil and criminal law disputes in their respective provinces. This absolute jurisdiction is granted by the common law and is

13   Antonio Lamer, "A Brief History of the Court" in *The Supreme Court of Canada and Its Justices, 1875–2000: A Commemorative Book* (Toronto: Dundurn Group, 2000) at 23-25.

limited only where some aspect of it has been exclusively assigned, by clear and constitutionally valid legislation, to another court or tribunal (such as a provincial inferior court).

The provincial superior court's jurisdiction very often overlaps with that of the inferior court. In most provinces, for example, small claims divisions of the inferior court system adjudicate civil claims below a specified dollar value (generally between $10,000 and $50,000 depending on the province). However, the provincial superior court, with its inherent jurisdiction over all civil and criminal disputes in the province, is still authorized to hear such claims.

Why would a plaintiff choose to go to a higher court for resolution of a dispute involving a small amount of money? After all, costs are less and procedures simpler in small claims court. The rationale for going to the provincial superior court, under these circumstances, might be that the higher court's decision will have greater precedential value. For example, the plaintiff might be an insurance company suing to recover moneys it paid out on the basis of a misinterpretation of contract language. If the insurance company is successful, the superior court's decision could subsequently serve as a precedent for similar cases. Each claim might be small, but the cumulative effect could be large, and the insurance company stands to benefit a great deal from the higher court's authoritative decision.

The higher provincial courts are not required to hear all claims brought before them. In certain circumstances, the superior court can transfer such cases to the lower court on its own initiative. For example, if the court's docket were backlogged, or if the matter were insignificant and of concern only to the particular parties, the court could refer the case down.

The superior courts also have an inherent jurisdiction to review the decisions of the inferior courts and administrative tribunals, as well as the right to hear appeals from these courts and tribunals if permitted by their constituting statutes (see Chapter 9). The provincial superior courts' wide-ranging adjudicative power means that they have the largest share of overall judicial power in Canada.

Table 5.2 summarizes the key organizational and jurisdictional aspects of the provincial superior courts.

TABLE 5.2   Provincial Superior Courts: Key Facts and Features

Constitutional Authority	Sections 92(14) and 96, *Constitution Act, 1867*
Key Jurisdictional Features at the Appeal Level	• Is the general court of appeal for the province in both civil and criminal matters • Hears appeals from the provincial superior trial level • Hears some appeals from provincial court decisions • Hears some appeals from provincial administrative tribunal decisions
Key Jurisdictional Features at the Trial Level	• Has inherent jurisdiction in all cases arising in the province • Hears some appeals from provincial court decisions (e.g., from small claims court) • Hears some appeals from provincial administrative tribunal decisions • Hears applications for judicial review of some provincial administrative tribunal decisions

In addition to the general superior court systems (and inferior court systems described below), there are specialized courts that focus on particular types of cases. See "Unified Family Courts" next and Box 5.2 below.

UNIFIED FAMILY COURTS

A number of provinces have modified their court systems in the area of family law. Traditionally, family law disputes are heard in either the provincial inferior or superior courts—or in both depending on the issues. (Constitutional jurisdiction over family law is split between Parliament and the provinces.) Family breakups are emotionally and financially trying enough without the added stress of having to deal with complicated jurisdictional divisions within the court system. To help with this, initiatives in seven provinces—Manitoba, New Brunswick, Newfoundland and Labrador, Nova Scotia, Ontario, Prince Edward Island, and Saskatchewan—have resulted in **unified family courts** (UFCs).

unified family courts
special divisions of the trial level of a provincial superior court with complete jurisdiction over family law matters, including matters that would otherwise be heard in a provincial inferior court

UFCs are special divisions of the trial level of the superior court, and they have complete jurisdiction over family law matters. Judges with special training or expertise oversee these disputes, and the parties are encouraged to use non-adversarial approaches to resolve their claims. The objective is to make the process less onerous. Should the court be called upon to finally adjudicate any issues, there is, at least, only one court involved. The UFCs operate only in select cities and venues within the province, so parties not able or willing to go to these locations must follow the traditional route.

Provincial Inferior Courts

Most provinces have one provincial inferior court with multiple divisions. The following divisions are typical:

- criminal,
- youth (young offender matters),
- traffic,
- family, and
- small claims (civil claims to a maximum ranging from $10,000 to $50,000, as mentioned earlier).[14]

However, the precise structure of these courts varies from province to province. For example, Nova Scotia has multiple provincial courts, as opposed to one umbrella court with multiple divisions. Regardless of the organizational set-up, it is important to understand that these courts are the main point of entry for most people when they interact with the justice system. These courts handle the vast majority of criminal and civil cases in Canada.

Provincial inferior courts are creatures of statute and have no inherent jurisdiction as the provincial superior courts do. In other words, inferior courts can exercise only powers given to them by legislation. (The source of the inherent jurisdiction of the superior courts, as we mentioned above, is the common law.)

Each provincial inferior court or division of an umbrella provincial court must look to its constituting provincial statute to determine the criminal, quasi-criminal, or civil matters over which it has jurisdiction. In the case of jurisdiction over criminal matters, the *Criminal Code* must also be considered; it requires that certain serious offences, such as murder and treason, be tried by a superior court. The provincial inferior courts also have rules of practice governing procedure in all areas over which they have jurisdiction. In civil matters particularly, their court procedures are generally set up to be simpler, faster, and less expensive than those of the superior courts.

---

14   Again, note that although in most provinces small claims courts are part of the inferior court system, in Manitoba, Ontario, and Prince Edward Island, small claims matters are handled by a special branch of the superior court.

As mentioned, the superior courts also have an inherent power to review the provincial inferior courts' decisions. This power is generally confined to reviewing the procedural fairness of the lower court's decision and can be modified by statute. Also, the legislation constituting most provincial inferior courts provides for a general right of appeal to the superior court, which allows the superior court to assess the merits of the lower court's decisions—a much broader power than judicial review. (The basic principles of judicial review and rights of appeal as they apply to administrative decisions are described in Chapter 9. These principles also apply to inferior courts.)

Specialized Courts and Therapeutic Justice

All provinces and territories have now set up specialized courts to deal with offenders where the root cause of their criminal behaviour is connected to societal or other problems and where therapeutic justice is more effective than punishment. For example, offenders struggling with addiction or mental health issues can, in many cases, be helped with treatment. These courts attempt to break the cycle of recidivism, assist with healing, and provide a path to rehabilitation and reintegration into society.

Therapeutic courts are typically part of the inferior court system and work alongside partner agencies to provide, as necessary, mental health services, education and training, and community support. Offenders can apply or be referred to a specialized court, but not everyone is eligible. Assessment guidelines are used to determine whether it is appropriate for a particular offender to proceed outside of the regular court system.

A variety of specialized courts have been created across Canada, and they have different names depending on their function: examples include wellness courts, mental health

Some Indigenous courts may include smudging, a traditional purification ceremony.

courts, drug treatment courts (DTCs), domestic violence courts, and Indigenous courts. DTCs, for example, are usually involved post-conviction (offenders must plead guilty). Using a holistic, collaborative approach, DTCs assess, create, and monitor treatment plans for the offender. Similarly, in most jurisdictions, Indigenous courts are not involved in the trial and only deal with sentencing. Smudging ceremonies and sentencing circles may be used; acknowledgment of the harm caused and reparation, if appropriate, are also part of the process.

See also Chapter 10 under "Criminal Courts."

Territorial Court Systems

Most of what we have said about the provincial court systems applies to the territorial court systems. Perhaps the most significant difference between the two systems is their constitutional basis. As we have seen, the territorial systems are not rooted in a constitutionally entrenched statute, as the provincial ones are, but in federal statutes that can be changed unilaterally by Parliament.[15]

We may assume, however, that this lack of constitutional protection for the territorial court systems is mostly a matter of legal theory. The political and practical difficulties

---

15 *Yukon Act; Northwest Territories Act;* and *Nunavut Act*, SC 1993, c 28.

involved in unilaterally changing them would be significant. In terms of functionality and jurisdiction, the territorial court systems are very similar to the provincial ones.

Territorial Superior Courts

Yukon and the Northwest Territories structure their superior courts as set out in Figure 5.1. There are two superior court levels, with jurisdiction similar to that of the provincial superior courts.

In Yukon, the Court of Appeal of the Yukon Territory is the top court and hears appeals from the Supreme Court of Yukon and the Territorial Court. The Court of Appeal is made up of justices from British Columbia, Yukon, the Northwest Territories, and Nunavut. This Court's small caseload is the reason it does not have a full complement of resident justices. It sits for only one week each year in Whitehorse; at other times, it sits in Vancouver, from which the Court "borrows" some of its judges.

Similarly, the Court of Appeal for the Northwest Territories hears appeals from the Supreme Court of the Northwest Territories and the Territorial Court. It sits regularly in Yellowknife (occasionally, it sits in other territorial locations and in Alberta) and is made up of justices from Alberta, Saskatchewan, and the Northwest Territories.

Nunavut is unique. It has a unified court, the Nunavut Court of Justice, which combines the jurisdiction of an inferior court with the jurisdiction of the trial level of a superior court. It is like a unified family court except that it covers not just family law but all jurisdictional areas. There is a single court for Nunavut because its population is very small—approximately 40,000 people, spread over a region roughly the size of Western Europe. There is a separate Court of Appeal, however. The Court of Appeal of Nunavut sits mainly in the territorial capital, Iqaluit, and is composed of justices from Alberta, Yukon, the Northwest Territories, and Nunavut.

Territorial Inferior Courts

Yukon and the Northwest Territories both have a territorial inferior court (in each territory, simply called the Territorial Court) that is organized along the lines of the provincial inferior courts. The territorial courts are creatures of the territorial assemblies, which exercise provincial-like statutory power under the federal statutes that devolve power to them. Nunavut is an exception to this, as mentioned above.

Federal Court System

As we have seen, the federal court system includes the SCC (discussed above) and four other superior courts: the Federal Court, the Federal Court of Appeal, the Tax Court of Canada, and the Court Martial Appeal Court. The Court Martial Appeal Court and the two military courts martial, which are federal inferior courts, are briefly discussed below under "Military Court System."

Federal Court and Federal Court of Appeal

In 1971, Parliament created the Federal Court of Canada under the *Federal Court Act*.[16] This court replaced the Exchequer Court of Canada. The jurisdiction of the Federal Court of Canada was increased to include not only the matters formerly under the Exchequer

---

16   RSC 1985, c F-7.

Court's jurisdiction—revenue matters, disputes involving the federal government, and other types of claims concerned with copyright, trademarks, and patents—but also (among other things) the review of federal boards and tribunals. The Federal Court of Canada had two divisions: the trial division and the appeal division.

In 2003, the new *Courts Administration Service Act* (CASA)[17] came into force, amending a number of federal statutes involving the administration of justice, including the *Federal Court Act*. The CASA reconstituted the Federal Court of Canada, converting its two divisions (the trial division and the appeal division) into two separate courts: (1) the Federal Court and (2) the Federal Court of Canada. The *Federal Court Act* was renamed the *Federal Courts Act*. One of the main purposes of the new CASA was to "facilitate coordination and cooperation among the Federal Court of Appeal, the Federal Court, the Court Martial Appeal Court and the Tax Court of Canada for the purpose of ensuring the effective and efficient provision of administrative services to those courts."[18]

The Federal Court and Federal Court of Appeal are both itinerant courts, with hearing locations in major cities across Canada. Judges from both courts travel to hear disputes according to a set schedule. The key features of the two courts are summarized in Table 5.3.

TABLE 5.3   Federal Court and Federal Court of Appeal: Key Facts and Features

	FEDERAL COURT	FEDERAL COURT OF APPEAL
Name	Federal Court (1971–)	Federal Court of Appeal (1971–)
Constitutional Authority	Section 101, *Constitution Act, 1867*	Section 101, *Constitution Act, 1867*
Act	*Federal Courts Act*, RSC 1985, c F-7	*Federal Courts Act*, RSC 1985, c F-7
Rules	*Federal Courts Rules* *Federal Courts Citizenship, Immigration and Refugee Protection Rules*	*Federal Courts Rules* *Federal Courts Citizenship, Immigration and Refugee Protection Rules*
Judges	• 1 chief justice of the Federal Court • Numerous itinerant judges and deputy judges • Quorum: 1 judge	• 1 chief justice of the Federal Court of Appeal • 12 puisne judges • Quorum: usually 3–5 judges
Key Jurisdictional Features	• Has *exclusive jurisdiction* in the following areas: (1) reviewing decisions of most federal boards and tribunals, with the exception of those assigned to the Federal Court of Appeal; (2) hearing copyright, trademark, patent, and industrial design matters; hearing citizenship appeals; hearing certain armed forces matters • Has *concurrent jurisdiction* with provincial superior courts in certain disputes (e.g., those involving bills of exchange and promissory notes, aeronautics, and interprovincial works and undertakings) • Has *residuary jurisdiction* to hear matters over which no other court has jurisdiction	• Hears appeals from the Federal Court • Hears appeals from the Tax Court of Canada • Has exclusive jurisdiction to review decisions of certain federal boards and tribunals as specified in the *Federal Courts Act* (e.g., the Canadian Radio-television and Telecommunications Commission, the National Energy Board, and the Copyright Board of Canada)

17 SC 2002, c 8.
18 CASA, s 2.

Tax Court of Canada

The Tax Court of Canada used to be characterized as an inferior court or administrative tribunal but is now considered a superior court. It was created in 1983 pursuant to the *Tax Court of Canada Act*.[19] It has a chief justice and an associate chief justice and numerous puisne judges. Like the Federal Court and Federal Court of Appeal, the Tax Court of Canada is an itinerant court with hearing locations in cities across Canada and regular sittings in those locations.

The Court has jurisdiction to hear appeals from individuals and corporations concerning matters arising out of a number of federal statutes, including the *Income Tax Act*,[20] the *Employment Insurance Act*,[21] the *Excise Tax Act*[22] (GST/HST), the *Canada Pension Plan*,[23] and the *Old Age Security Act*.[24] It is an independent court and not an instrument of the Canada Revenue Agency or other government departments.

Military Court System

Military law is a specialized area and something of which most Canadians who are not in the military have only a vague understanding. Section 91(7) of the *Constitution Act, 1867* gives Parliament jurisdiction over "Militia, Military and Naval Service, and Defence." The *National Defence Act*[25] passed pursuant to this authority is the governing statute for the armed forces. The Office of the Judge Advocate General is responsible for the prosecution and defence functions of the military justice system, which is parallel to but separate from the regular justice system.

As mentioned above, the courts martial (the General Court Martial and Standing Court Martial) are a very specialized set of federal inferior courts with jurisdiction over armed forces personnel who commit service offences. These courts are constituted under the *National Defence Act* and are analogous to the provincial and territorial inferior courts that have jurisdiction over criminal cases. However, unlike the provincial and territorial inferior courts, they also have jurisdiction over serious offences and are vested with the same powers as superior courts. Parliament's constitutional jurisdiction over these courts is based on either section 91(7) or section 101 of the *Constitution Act, 1867*.

The Court Martial Appeal Court hears appeals from the courts martial. It is a superior court and is also constituted under the *National Defence Act*. Parliament's jurisdiction over this court is clearly based on section 101.

Precedent and Stare Decisis in the Canadian Court System

In order to research the law effectively and to assess the binding or persuasive value of earlier decisions properly, you need some familiarity with the hierarchical structure of the courts and their jurisdiction. In Chapter 2, in the section on common law, we described the use of

---

19 RSC 1985, c T-2.
20 RSC 1985, c 1 (5th Supp).
21 SC 1996, c 23.
22 RSC 1985, c E-15.
23 RSC 1985, c C-8.
24 RSC 1985 c O-9.
25 RSC 1985, c N-5.

precedent and the doctrine of *stare decisis*. According to this doctrine, the decision in an earlier court case (a precedent) binds lower-level courts in the same jurisdiction. It does so in cases where the facts and applicable legal principle (sometimes referred to as *ratio deci-dendi*, or simply *ratio*) in the later case are materially similar to those in the earlier one.

What is meant by "jurisdiction" in this context? More specifically, what does it mean in the context of the Canadian court system? Each of the four pathways (or court systems) leading up to the SCC, as shown in Figure 5.1, is considered a separate jurisdiction or jurisdictional grouping. The federal court system is considered a separate jurisdiction, as is the system of courts martial (the military courts). The provincial and territorial court systems are the two other jurisdictional groupings; each province and territory is its own jurisdiction within the general provincial and territorial court pathways. For example, a decision by a court in one province would not bind a court in another province. Precedent flows downward only and only within the jurisdiction in which the decision was made. Decisions of the SCC, however, as Canada's highest court and general Court of Appeal, are binding on all courts across Canada.

Cases from the same level of court within the same jurisdiction aren't, strictly speaking, binding on each other (for example, an earlier decision from the Manitoba Court of Appeal isn't technically binding on a later decision by that same court). But the principle of comity—that is, respect for the decisions of fellow judges at the same level—requires that they be followed unless there is a good reason not to follow them. A judge might choose not to follow an earlier decision if it involved, for example, a missed precedent or a missed statutory provision.

Legal researchers start by looking for *binding* authority from the decisions of higher courts. For example, if researching a matter within the jurisdiction of the provincial superior or inferior court system, they would start by looking for SCC decisions. Then they would look for Court of Appeal decisions from the relevant province, then for decisions of the provincial superior court (trial level). Finally, they would look for decisions from provincial inferior courts and, possibly, from administrative tribunals.

If no binding authority is found—and sometimes even if it is—researchers may find it helpful to search for *persuasive* authority from other jurisdictions. A person researching a matter within the provincial court systems would look at decisions from other provinces or territories, from the federal courts (if there is joint authority over the matter in question), and possibly also from other countries with common law traditions, such as England, Australia, and the United States (generally in that order of preference). The higher the level of court from the other jurisdiction, the more persuasive the decision. Intangibles, such as the reputation of the particular judge who rendered the decision, may also influence the weight given to a particular decision.

As a general rule, the more recent the authority, the better. It should also be noted that decisions that initially appear to be binding or persuasive may seem less so (in other words, they may be "distinguishable") upon careful examination. A precedent may be distinguishable for a variety of reasons (see Chapter 2).

Judicial Appointments

With the exception of SCC judges, there is essentially one appointment process for superior court judges—that is, for provincial and territorial superior court, Federal Court, and Federal Court of Appeal judges. A recently modified process applies to SCC appointments (see the discussion below). All are federally appointed. The provinces and territories each have separate but parallel appointment processes for provincially and territorially appointed judges (that is, judges in the inferior courts). All Canadian judges undergo a period of training when they are first appointed, which includes training through the National Judicial Institute (see Box 5.3).

The National Judicial Institute

Who educates and trains the judges? How confident are you that a judge will really know the law and the context within which a dispute has arisen?

Judges in Canada are appointed from the practising bar and sometimes from the academic world. This means that the usual preparation for a career as a judge is a law practice or an academic position. These experiences don't necessarily give someone a wide experience of the law. New judges often face areas of the law that are relatively unfamiliar to them. For example, a lawyer whose practice has been confined to personal injury disputes may, once she becomes a judge, have to deal with family disputes or criminal law cases.

New judges face two significant challenges. First, they must learn about areas of the law in which they have no previous experience. A second challenge has to do with achieving objectivity. Most lawyers are professional advocates. Lawyers who have spent long careers practising advocacy must, once they become judges, move beyond the advocacy mindset of many years and make themselves sensitive to the circumstances of both parties in a case.

This second requirement is especially challenging. How does a judge fully understand, for example, the social and economic obstacles facing a single mother charged with welfare fraud? How does a judge make sense of the cultural aspects of a case involving a First Nations person charged with hunting out of season? How do judges make themselves sensitive to the social, cultural, and power elements of a case? Where do they obtain the necessary sensitivity training?

In 1988, the National Judicial Institute (NJI) was formed. It is an independent non-profit organization that serves the Canadian judiciary by planning, coordinating, and delivering judicial education concerning the law, the craft of judging, and the social context in which legal disputes arise.

The NJI's mandate is to "engender a high level of social awareness, ethical sensitivity, and pride of excellence within an independent judiciary." For example, new judges are encouraged to attend a four-and-a-half-day seminar that focuses on the craft of judging and the role of judges in the social context. The program includes such topics as:

- judicial independence,
- judicial ethics,
- equality issues in the courtroom,
- Aboriginal law,
- persons with disabilities and the judicial system, and
- introduction to judicial dispute resolution.

The seminars are conducted by experienced judges, legal academics, and other experts.

Canada is widely regarded as having one of the finest judiciaries in the world. The NJI's seminars and workshops, together with training and educational programs from other organizations, play a large part in ensuring that Canada's judiciary lives up to its reputation.

Source: Reproduced from George Alexandrowicz et al, *Dimensions of Law: Canadian and International Law in the 21st Century* (Toronto: Emond Montgomery, 2004) at 54.

Superior Court Judges

In the following sections, we look at the appointment authority, appointment process, and qualifications of superior court judges.

Appointment Authority

The appointment power set out in section 96 of the *Constitution Act, 1867* states that the governor general shall appoint the provincial superior court judges. By constitutional convention, this means that the Governor in Council (that is, the federal Cabinet) makes the appointments.

Section 96 says nothing, however, about the Cabinet's appointing federal superior court judges. In their case, the federal Cabinet's appointment power comes from section 101.

This provision, as we have seen, states that Parliament may from time to time "provide for the Constitution, Maintenance, and Organization of a General Court of Appeal for Canada, and for the Establishment of any additional Courts for the better Administration of the Laws of Canada." This provision has been interpreted as giving the federal Cabinet the executive power to appoint federal superior court judges, including SCC judges. The *Federal Courts Act* and the *Supreme Court Act* have since expressly given the federal Cabinet this power.

The appointment of territorial superior court judges follows the same process as that of provincial superior court judges.

Appointment Process

There are many judicial appointments, and the federal Cabinet cannot be closely involved with all of them. To deal with the volume, a special federal office called the Office of the Commissioner for Federal Judicial Affairs Canada (FJA) was created under the *Judges Act*.[26] Since 1988, the FJA has played a major role in vetting proposed appointments. To assist it in this process, the FJA has overseen the creation of judicial advisory committees in the ten provinces and three territories. Most provinces have one such committee, but Ontario and Quebec, because of their size, have multiple committees (three and two, respectively).

Potential judges now have to apply for the position and go through background checks by the advisory committee. The advisory committee puts forward a list of names, which is then reviewed by the federal minister of justice and the FJA. From this list and following this review, recommendations are made to Cabinet. One of the main purposes in setting up the appointment process this way was to eliminate patronage (that is, appointments based on political connections rather than merit). The advisory committees have members from all corners of the legal profession, so no one person on the committee can dominate the selection process. This diversity inhibits patronage. Patronage may still exist in some degree, but these measures have helped reduce it.

The FJA process is used for all federally appointed superior court judges except SCC judges. In 2016, Prime Minister Justin Trudeau introduced a new appointment procedure for Canada's highest court. Any qualified judge or lawyer can apply to the FJA for appointment to the SCC. The candidate's application will then be reviewed by a seven-member advisory board, which will be free from political influence and will use publicly available assessment criteria. The prime minister will choose a nominee from a short list of three to five applicants. Before the nominee is appointed, Parliament will discuss the selection process, and the nominee will appear before an all-party committee for questioning. The first justice appointed under this new process was Malcolm Rowe (he is also the first judge from Newfoundland and Labrador to sit on the SCC).

By convention, the prime minister decides who will be the chief justice of the SCC. There is also a decades-old tradition, which may have reached the status of a constitutional convention, that the position of chief justice alternates between a francophone justice from Quebec and an anglophone justice from elsewhere in Canada. In 2017, Beverley McLachlin retired (see Box 5.4), and Prime Minister Justin Trudeau appointed Richard Wagner, a civil law lawyer from Quebec who had been appointed to the court in 2012, as her successor.

---

26   RSC 1985, c J-1.

BOX 5.4

The Right Honourable Beverley McLachlin

Beverley McLachlin was born in Alberta and went to law school at the University of Alberta, graduating first in her class. She practised law for six years before joining the Faculty of Law at the University of British Columbia. In 1980, while still a professor, she was appointed to the bench. She quickly rose through the BC courts and in 1989, after four years on the BC Court of Appeal, was appointed to the SCC. In 2000, she was appointed chief justice of Canada by Prime Minister Jean Chrétien.

As chief justice, she strengthened her reputation for fairness and consensus building (more unanimous judgments were issued by the Court under her tenure than ever before). The judgments she authored were respected for their clarity and depth of research; they covered the full range of subject areas, from complex civil matters involving economic loss to pressing constitutional issues involving the Charter.

In December 2017, she retired from the Court as required by section 99(2) of the *Constitution Act, 1867*, which stipulates that a judge of a superior court shall cease to hold office at the age of 75 years. She had been an SCC justice for 28 years and the Court's chief justice for almost 18 years. She was the first woman to hold the position and is the Court's longest-serving chief justice.

Although Beverley McLachlin may have retired from the SCC, she continues to be very active as she moves "into the next chapter of her life."* After her retirement from Canada's top Court, she accepted part-time appointments to the Hong Kong Court of Final Appeal and the Commercial Court of Singapore. She also published a novel, a legal thriller called *Full Disclosure*, and a memoir, *Truth Be Told*.

*   Karen Dickson, "The Rt Hon Beverley McLachlin, PC" (2018) 76:3 Advocate 339 at 344.

Qualifications

To qualify for appointment as a provincial superior court judge, a candidate must:

1. be a barrister or advocate of at least ten years' standing at the bar of any province or
2. have had a total of at least ten years in which the candidate (a) was a barrister or advocate at the bar of any province and then (b) served full-time as a member of a body that performed duties of a judicial nature.[27]

Qualifications for the Federal Court and Federal Court of Appeal are identical, except that a candidate must also be or have been "a judge of a superior, county or district court in Canada."[28]

The required qualifications for SCC judges are the following:

1. prior appointment as a judge of a superior court of a province or
2. being a barrister of at least ten years' standing at the bar of a province.[29]

---

27   *Judges Act*, s 3.
28   *Federal Courts Act*, s 5.3.
29   *Supreme Court Act*, s 5.

Inferior Court Judges

In the following sections, we look at the appointment authority, appointment process, and qualifications for provincial/territorial and federal court judges.

Provincial

APPOINTMENT AUTHORITY AND PROCESS

The constitutional jurisdiction for the appointment of judges to the provincial inferior courts flows from sections 92(4) and (14) of the *Constitution Act, 1867*. Jurisdiction over these appointments belongs to the provincial legislatures. Each provincial legislature has in turn delegated this power, by way of its provincial courts legislation, to the Lieutenant Governor in Council (that is, the provincial Cabinet). The provincial executive branch, therefore, is responsible for appointing judges to this level of court.

The appointment process varies slightly from province to province, but all provinces now have judicial councils created under their respective provincial courts legislation. These provincial councils recruit, screen, and recommend potential candidates for judgeships. Their purpose is to accomplish at the provincial level what the FJA accomplishes at the federal level—that is, to promote quality in judicial appointments and eliminate patronage. The provincial Cabinet still makes the final decision on appointments.

QUALIFICATIONS

The basic qualification for judicial appointment to a provincial inferior court is five years' practice as a lawyer in good standing with the provincial bar or other legal or judicial experience considered satisfactory to the council. The experience requirement, in other words, is half what it is for superior court judges. Close to 50 percent of all Canadian judges are appointed to provincial inferior courts.

Territorial

The appointment process for the territorial inferior courts operates in much the same way as for the provincial ones. Using the power delegated to them by Parliament, the territorial assemblies have passed legislation creating their own territorial courts as well as their own territorial judicial councils—equivalent to the provincial councils—to assist with the appointment process. In Yukon, for example, the statute that accomplishes this is the *Territorial Court Act*.[30]

Federal

The *National Defence Act* sets out the process for appointing judges to the federal courts martial, which are the only federal inferior courts. It gives the power of appointment to the federal Cabinet. However, the FJA process does not apply to these judges. The basic qualification level is ten years' practice as a lawyer at a provincial bar.

Public Proceedings

The **open court principle** is generally taken for granted today in Canada. In the context of criminal charges, it is guaranteed under the Charter, subject to reasonable

open court principle
principle that judicial proceedings should be administered in public

---

30   RSNWT 1988, c T-2.

limits.[31] In Jeremy Bentham's words, publicity is the "security of securities." We expect to be able to observe our justice system at work and to ensure that it is fair.

Courts have not always been open in this way. In England in the 1600s, the Star Chamber abuses highlighted the importance of having open courts. The Star Chamber was a special court set up alongside the well-established common law and equity courts (see Chapter 2). Its jurisdiction was to hear cases considered too important to be handled by the ordinary courts. Its proceedings were secret, and in its final days it became a political instrument used by the Stuart monarchy to punish those who opposed them. After a number of cases of unfair treatment involving prominent political and religious activists, it was abolished by an act of Parliament, the *Habeas Corpus Act* of 1640,[32] just before the English Civil War.

The open court principle has been called "the best security for the pure, impartial, and efficient administration of justice, the best means of winning for it public confidence and respect."[33] What this means is that public proceedings are a check against the injustices that can flourish in private or secret proceedings. Where power is not scrutinized, civil liberties tend to suffer. The English historian Henry Hallam cited public proceedings—the "open administration of justice"—as among the most important safeguards of civil liberty:

> Civil liberty in this kingdom has two direct guarantees; the open administration of justice according to known laws truly interpreted, and fair constructions of evidence; and the right of Parliament, without let or interruption, to inquire into, and obtain redress of, public grievances. Of these, the first is by far most indispensable; nor can the subjects of any State be reckoned to enjoy a real freedom, where this condition is not found both in its judicial institutions and in their constant exercises.[34]

Judicial Independence

judicial independence
principle that judges should be free to make decisions based on the law and free from outside interference

According to the principle of **judicial independence**, judges should be free to make decisions based on the law without threat of negative consequences should their decisions be unpopular. Also, the public needs to see such independence in order to have confidence in the justice system. The idea that the judicial arm of government should be independent of the other branches is related to the rule-of-law doctrine described in Chapter 1 and to the separation-of-powers doctrine that provides a framework for constitutional law (see Chapter 4 under the heading "Limits of Executive Influence").

In Canada, we recognize three main aspects of judicial independence:

1. security of tenure,
2. financial security, and
3. administrative independence.[35]

---

31   See ss 1 and 11(d) of the Charter. Some of the limits that have been recognized include cases involving vulnerable victims (for example, children and individuals who have been sexually abused) and national security issues. In these cases, the court may protect a person's identity from being disclosed or may even close the court to the public altogether.
32   (UK), 16 Car 1 c 10.
33   *Scott v Scott*, [1913] AC 417 at 463 (HL).
34   *Ibid* at 477.
35   Lori Hausegger, Matthew Hennigar & Troy Riddell, "Judicial Process and Alternative Dispute Resolution" in *Canadian Courts: Law, Politics, and Process*, 2nd ed (Toronto: Oxford University Press, 2015) ch 6.

Security of tenure ensures that judges can render decisions without fear of losing their positions if their decisions are not well received. Financial security ensures that any temptation to accept bribes will be minimized. Moreover, administrative independence ensures that the running of the courts is by the judges themselves and not by outside parties who may subject the judges to external biases.

Constitutional protection for the independence of the judiciary comes from a number of sources, most notably the following:

- *The preamble clause to the* Constitution Act, 1867.   The preamble clause provides implied protection by stating that we in Canada have "a Constitution similar in Principle to that of the United Kingdom."[36] Protection is implied because although it exists under the Constitution of the United Kingdom, protection is not expressly referred to in the preamble clause.
- *Section 99 of the* Constitution Act, 1867.   This section provides that superior court judges "hold office during good behaviour" and that they are "removable by the Governor General on address of the Senate and House of Commons." (Security of tenure consists in the fact that they cannot be removed otherwise.)
- *Section 11(d) of the Charter.*   This section provides that any person charged with an offence has the right to a "public hearing by an independent and impartial tribunal."[37] The words "independent" and "impartial" indicate a general standard for the judiciary in Canada.

Judicial independence finds protection as well in various federal, provincial, and territorial statutes.[38] Their provisions recognize judicial independence through salary guarantees and institutional structures. Also, the "good behaviour" tenure provision in section 99 of the *Constitution Act, 1867,* a provision directed at provincial superior court judges, is echoed in provisions directed at federal superior court judges and at provincial and territorial inferior court judges.

Good behaviour tenure means that judges can only be removed from office if their behaviour falls below a certain standard, into what could be termed "bad behaviour." There is no generally accepted common law or statutory definition of bad behaviour or misconduct. Section 65(2) of the federal *Judges Act* sets up the Canadian Judicial Council, which can investigate a superior court judge if he becomes "incapacitated or disabled from the due execution of the office" owing to age or infirmity, misconduct, incompetence, or to "having been placed, by his or her conduct or otherwise, in a position incompatible with the due execution of that office." This provision goes some way toward defining bad behaviour. After an investigation, the Council can recommend that a judge be removed for misconduct. The provinces and territories have constituted similar judicial councils with similar powers in relation to provincially and territorially appointed judges.

---

36 In *Reference re Remuneration of Judges of the Provincial Court (PEI)*, [1997] 3 SCR 3, 1997 CanLII 317, the SCC stated that judicial independence is an unwritten norm, constitutionally entrenched by virtue of the preamble clause to the *Constitution Act, 1867*. Furthermore, this norm is not restricted to superior courts but applies to all courts, including inferior courts.

37 Although this Charter guarantee of an independent tribunal applies only to courts and tribunals exercising criminal jurisdiction, it is clear that judicial independence applies to all courts regardless of the nature of the claim. The protection provided by the preamble clause is not qualified, whereas the Charter guarantee is.

38 Federally, for example, see the *Judges Act*, the *Federal Courts Act*, and the *Supreme Court Act*.

Since Confederation, six attempts have been made to remove superior court judges (including four recommendations for removal from office by the Canadian Judicial Council), but none of these attempts have progressed to the required joint address process set out in section 99(1) of the *Constitution Act, 1867*. The judges in question have so far retired or resigned before that stage. A handful of lower court judges have been removed, however, through less stringent processes.[39]

Judicial independence finds further support in the common law doctrine of judicial immunity (now also legislated in many jurisdictions). This immunity protects judges in courts at all levels from civil liability in lawsuits instigated by dissatisfied litigants or accused persons.

Judicial independence, in all its facets, plays a key role in supporting the freedoms we enjoy in Canadian society.

---

39   Hausegger, Hennigar & Riddell, *supra* note 35 at 187-89.

CHAPTER SUMMARY

The third branch of government, the judiciary, plays an important role in resolving all manner of disputes. Some of these disputes involve private law claims, some involve public law issues, and some involve common law principles. Other disputes deal with statutory interpretation, and still others require answers to important questions concerning the constitutional validity of our laws.

Two overarching principles inform the Canadian judicial system: (1) the open court principle, which requires proceedings to take place in public unless there is a justifiable exception, and (2) the principle of judicial independence. These two principles, when adhered to, help safeguard the rule of law and promote public confidence in our justice system.

Understanding how cases get before the courts requires a basic knowledge of the constitutional basis and structure of our courts. There are three broad categories of courts: (1) inferior courts, (2) superior courts, and (3) the SCC. The jurisdiction to create courts is split between the federal and provincial legislative branches. The power to appoint judges is also a split jurisdiction, between the federal and provincial executive branches. The involvement of both levels of government creates a balance of power in the judicial branch.

The provincial and territorial inferior courts handle most of the cases in the system overall, dealing as they do with the less serious criminal and civil cases (except in Manitoba, Ontario, and Prince Edward Island, where small claims are handled by a division of the superior court). The provincial superior courts have inherent jurisdiction to hear most disputes but are used primarily to resolve more serious claims. The federal courts have a more limited jurisdiction; they hear matters concerned with federal laws, such as intellectual property and taxation disputes. The SCC is the final court of appeal for Canada and generally hears only matters of national importance, whether criminal, civil, or constitutional in nature. Precedent flows downward, from the SCC to the various jurisdictionally separated court systems.

KEY TERMS

appellant, 156

case, 156

case brief, 157

court, 128

decision, 156

defendant, 156

dissent, 138

facta (sing. factum), 136

federal superior courts (or federal courts), 132

inferior courts, 130

judgment, 156

judicial independence, 150

majority, 138

open court principle, 149

plaintiff, 156

provincial superior courts, 131

puisne, 134

reference, 136

reserve, 137

respondent, 156

section 96 courts, 131

style of cause, 157

Supreme Court of Canada, 132

territorial superior courts, 132

unified family courts, 140

FURTHER READING

BOOKS AND ARTICLES

Bushnell, Ian, *The Captive Court: A Study of the Supreme Court of Canada* (Montreal: McGill-Queen's University Press, 1992).

Hausegger, Lori, Matthew Hennigar & Troy Riddell, *Canadian Courts: Law, Politics, and Process*, 2nd ed (Toronto: Oxford University Press, 2015).

Hogg, Peter W, "Courts" and "Supreme Court of Canada" in *Constitutional Law of Canada*, 5th ed (Toronto: Carswell, 2007) (loose-leaf updated 2019, release 1) ch 7-8.

McGill Law Journal, *Canadian Guide to Uniform Legal Citation*, 9th ed (Toronto: Carswell, 2018).

Russell, Peter H, *The Judiciary in Canada: The Third Branch of Government* (Toronto: McGraw-Hill Ryerson, 1987).

WEBSITES

Gateway Site for Canadian Legal Databases

Canadian Legal Information Institute (CanLII): <https://www.canlii.org>.

Federal Courts

Supreme Court of Canada: <https://www.scc-csc.gc.ca>.

Federal Court of Appeal: <https://www.fca-caf.gc.ca>.

Federal Court: <https://www.fct-cf.gc.ca>.

Tax Court of Canada: <https://www.tcc-cci.gc.ca>

Court Martial Appeal Court of Canada: <https://www.cmac-cacm.ca>.

Courts of the Provinces and Territories

Alberta Courts: <https://www.albertacourts.ca>.

British Columbia Courts: <https://www.bccourts.ca>.

Manitoba Courts: <http://www.manitobacourts.mb.ca>.

New Brunswick Courts: <https://www.courtsnb-coursnb.ca/content/cour/en.html>.

Newfoundland and Labrador Courts: <https://court.nl.ca>.

Northwest Territories Courts: <https://www.nwtcourts.ca>.

Nova Scotia Courts: <https://www.courts.ns.ca>.

Nunavut Courts: <http://www.nunavutcourts.ca>.

Ontario Courts: <https://www.ontariocourts.ca>.

Prince Edward Island Courts: <https://www.courts.pe.ca>.

Quebec Courts: <http://www.tribunaux.qc.ca/mjq_en/index.html>.

Saskatchewan Courts: <https://sasklawcourts.ca>.

Yukon Courts: <https://yukoncourts.ca>.

Legal Abbreviations

Cardiff Index to Legal Abbreviations: <http://www.legalabbrevs.cardiff.ac.uk>.

REVIEW QUESTIONS

1. Explain how the role of the judiciary is still significant despite the prevalence today of legislated rules as a means of regulating society.

2. Explain why the provincial superior courts, which are constituted under section 92 of the *Constitution Act, 1867*, are sometimes referred to as "section 96 courts."

3. What are the main criteria the SCC considers when deciding whether to grant leave to a party to appeal to the Court?

4. How does the source of the jurisdiction of provincial and territorial inferior courts to hear cases differ from that of their superior court relatives?

5. Name three types of cases over which the Federal Court of Appeal has jurisdiction.

6. Describe the flow of precedent in the Canadian court system.

7. Describe the role of the Office of the Commissioner for Federal Judicial Affairs Canada (FJA) in the appointment process of superior court judges.

8. How does the National Judicial Institute (NJI) help prepare new judges for the transition from lawyer to adjudicator?

9. Explain the purpose of the open court principle and name two exceptions to it.

10. What are the three main facets of judicial independence?

11. What is the *ratio decidendi* (or *ratio*) of a case?

EXERCISES

1. Using Figure 5.1 as a reference point, research the website for the courts in your province or territory and chart the four levels of the court system using the correct names for the courts at all levels.

2. Using the website for the courts in your province or territory, determine who are the three most recent appointees to the trial level of the superior court. Read their biographical information and prepare a short opinion concerning each, focused on the following question: Do you think political patronage or professional competence was the primary factor in his or her appointment?

3. Search the SCC's judgments database (<https://scc-csc.lexum.com/scc-csc/en/nav.do>) and locate a 2011 decision that involves the open court principle.

4. Locate the statute for your province or territory that constitutes the provincial/territorial court. Review the provisions in the statute dealing with judicial independence and then prepare a reasoned argument as to why, in your opinion, these provisions adequately or inadequately support judicial independence.

APPENDIX 5.1

Reading and Understanding Case Law

When confronted with a judgment of the courts, knowing a little about how judgments are reported and how to summarize or "brief" cases can help you understand its significance. If you don't have the judgment before you, knowing how cases are cited can help you find it in the first place. The following is a brief introduction to the analysis of case law, beginning with a preliminary point concerning terminology.

Terminology: Terms for Parties and Reasons

A record of a court's decision normally begins with the names of the parties on opposite sides of the legal dispute. In civil disputes, the individual, corporation, or other entity who initiates the lawsuit is called the **plaintiff**. The plaintiff's name is listed first. The abbreviation *v* (meaning "versus") separates the plaintiff's name from that of the individual, corporation, or other entity being sued, who is called the **defendant**. In criminal cases, there is no plaintiff. The government initiates cases in the name of the Queen. For this reason, almost all Canadian criminal cases begin with *R*. This is an abbreviation for *regina* (or *rex*), which is the Latin word for queen (or king). It is followed by *v* and the name of the defendant or accused.

On an appeal, the individual, corporation, or other entity who lost at trial and who initiates an appeal to a higher court is called the **appellant**. The other party is called the **respondent**. In such instances, the name of the appellant is generally placed first, followed by *v* and then the name of the respondent. There are other terms used to refer to the parties, but these are the most common ones.

Concerning terms for the court's decision itself, the words **judgment**, **decision**, and **case** are sometimes used interchangeably to refer to the entire set of reasons the court provides to explain how it has resolved a dispute. It is in this sense that we use these words here. In the court file for the matter in question, this set of reasons is usually one of the last documents in the paper or electronic folder.

Unfortunately, the words "judgment," "decision," and "case" have alternate meanings, and it is important to pay close attention to the context in which they appear. Both "judgment" and "decision," for example, can simply refer to the disposition or outcome of the case, as in "judgment for the plaintiff." The word "case" is similarly prone to ambiguity. To the parties and the court, it can mean the entire proceedings before the court. To the lawyer, paralegals, and others who worked on the file, it can mean the whole process, starting with the client interview and proceeding through to trial, then to the appeal (if there is one), and then to the final judgment of the court. Again, context should help you determine the sense in which the words are used.

Law Reports

Many cases are reported in print volumes (referred to variously as law reports, case reports, report series, reporters, etc.) or their online equivalents. The editors don't simply reproduce the judgment from the court file, however. They add features to help the reader understand the decision, such as summaries of the decision, called "headnotes," and lists of cases and statutes referred to in the judgment.

---

plaintiff
individual, corporation, or other entity who initiates a non-criminal lawsuit

defendant
individual, corporation, or other entity who defends a non-criminal lawsuit initiated by the plaintiff

appellant
individual, corporation, or other entity who lost at trial and who initiates an appeal to a higher court

respondent
individual, corporation, or other entity who won at trial and is responding to the appellant on an appeal to a higher court

judgment
final outcome or disposition of the dispute heard before the court or, when the court provides reasons for its judgment, the entire set of reasons

decision
depending on context, refers to the outcome or disposition of a case, to the holding in the case, or (where the court provides them) to the entire set of reasons the court gives for its judgment

case
depending on context, refers to the reasons for judgment (where the court provides them), to the court process more generally, or to the entire dispute from beginning to end

Note also that even if a case is "unreported" (that is, it hasn't been independently published), it is still possible to locate the full text of the judgment in various places, such as in the court's registry file for the matter in question, the court's online judgment database (many courts have such databases now), or a third-party database that provides access to unreported judgments (CanLII, for example—see under "Further Reading" at the end of this chapter). Locating an unreported judgment in this way means that you will generally only have the text of the judgment at your disposal, however, and not the value-added features that come with reported cases.

Briefing Cases

An effective technique for learning how to analyze legal problems is not just to read court decisions. Going one step further by summarizing or briefing judgments can help intensify the learning process. A **case brief** follows a defined pattern, with the constituent parts of the court's judgment summarized in a set order (key parts include the legal issues and the governing rules). The brief also provides a concise, easy-to-remember overview of the case.

There is no one way to brief a case, and different names may be used for constituent parts of the summary. It is important that you understand what you are summarizing and how it relates to the overall process of reaching a reasoned legal decision.

case brief
summary of a case, with the constituent parts of the court's reasons for judgment arranged in a set order

Citation of Cases

As we have seen, formal references to legal sources, including legislation and case law, follow specialized citation rules (see Appendix 4.1). For example, when referring to a case, its **style of cause** (or case name) is italicized; its neutral citation appears next, if it has one (a neutral citation is a special form of court-sanctioned citation); and, following that, other citation information may be set out, all following accepted protocols for abbreviations and other elements. For in-depth coverage, refer to the McGill Guide.

Following is an example of a neutral citation:

style of cause
name of the case or title of the proceeding, consisting of the names of the parties to the dispute

Kerr v Baranow, 2011 SCC 10 at paras 12-15
  1   2   3 4   5

The components in this neutral citation are as follows:

1 **Style of cause**
   The style of cause is the name of the case or title of the proceeding, and it consists of the names of the parties to the dispute. It is italicized, with a *v* (no period) separating the parties, followed by a comma (not italicized).

2 **Year of the decision**

3 **Unique jurisdiction and court abbreviation**
   In this example, the abbreviation is for the Supreme Court of Canada (SCC).

4 **Decision number**
   The decision number is followed by a space if a pinpoint reference follows, as it does here.

5 **Pinpoint**
   Where a particular passage from the judgment is being quoted, individual or multiple paragraph numbers are preceded by "para" or "paras," respectively, or the symbol "¶" can be used in place of either.

Following the neutral citation, a reference to the law report may be included:

Kerr v Baranow, 2011 SCC 10 at paras 12-15, [2011] 1 SCR 269.

In this case, the year of publication, shown in square brackets, is the same as the year of the decision: 2011 (sometimes it is later). The volume number ("1") for that year's volumes appears next, followed by the law report abbreviation ("SCR," which is the abbreviation for Supreme Court Reports), and, finally, the page number on which the decision begins ("269").

By 2010, all Canadian courts had implemented the neutral citation system, with some starting as early as 1998. For earlier cases, the citation may be only to law reports.

6 Civil Liberties

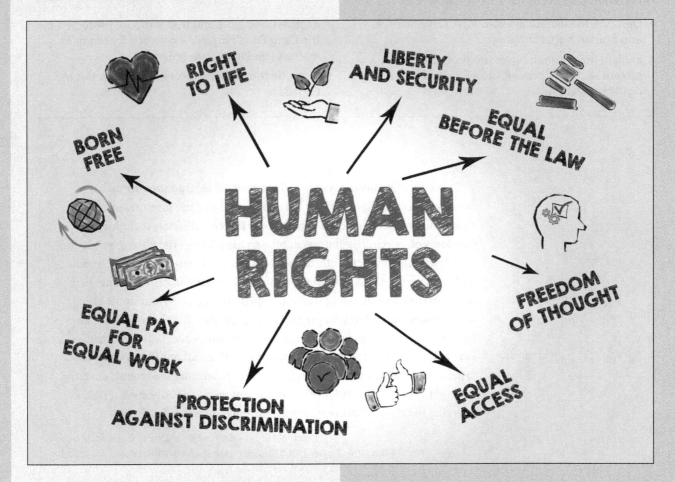

Introduction 160

The Evolution of Civil Liberties in Canada .. 161

Protection of Civil Liberties in
the Private Sector 163

Protection of Civil Liberties When
Governments Are Involved: The Charter ... 167

The Future of Civil Liberties in Canada ... 176

Chapter Summary 178

Key Terms 178

Further Reading 178

Review Questions 179

Exercises 180

After reading this chapter, you will be able to:

- Describe the historical evolution of civil liberties and human rights in Canada.
- Explain how human rights are protected in the private sector by provincial and federal human rights legislation.

- Explain how rights and freedoms are protected by the *Canadian Charter of Rights and Freedoms* in matters involving governments.
- Describe the possible future of civil liberties in Canada.

Civil liberties encompass a broad range of values that support the freedom and dignity of the individual, and that are given recognition in various ways by Canadian law. The political civil liberties include the freedoms of speech, religion, assembly and association; the right to vote and be a candidate for elected office; and the freedom to enter and leave Canada and to move from one province to another. Legal civil liberties include the freedom from search, seizure, arrest, imprisonment, cruel and unusual punishment and unfair trial procedures. Egalitarian civil liberties include equality of access to accommodation, employment, education and other benefits, implying, at least, an absence of racial, sexual or other illegitimate criteria of discrimination. Particular to Canada are language rights, covering the right to use the English or the French language; and educational rights, covering the rights of denominational (or separate) schools.

Peter W Hogg, *Constitutional Law of Canada*, 5th ed
(Toronto: Carswell, 2007) (loose-leaf updated 2019, release 1) ch 34.1

Introduction

In Canada, there is a distinction between the terms "civil rights" and "civil liberties." Section 92(13) of the *Constitution Act, 1867* gives provinces jurisdiction over "Property and Civil Rights in the Province." When the Act was drafted, it was understood that the term "civil rights" referred to private law rights between individuals in areas such as torts, contracts, and property.[1]

civil liberties
rights and freedoms
protected by the Charter
and other sources

The term **civil liberties** has a different meaning and is generally interchangeable with "human rights." As our chapter's opening quotation from Peter Hogg suggests, civil liberties reflect values related to the freedom and dignity of all individuals in their dealings with government, such as in politics (for example, when voting or running for office) and when

---

1   Peter W Hogg, *Constitutional Law of Canada,* 5th ed (Toronto: Carswell, 2007) (loose-leaf updated 2019, release 1) ch 21.3. Note, however, that despite this formal distinction in Canada, "civil rights" is sometimes also used here to mean "civil liberties." The context should make the intended meaning clear.

interacting with the justice system, as well as in areas associated with the private sector, such as accommodation and employment. Human rights legislation in Canada—at the provincial, territorial, and federal levels—supports these values, perhaps most importantly through the prevention of discrimination.

This chapter begins by tracing the historical evolution of civil liberties in Canada, from their origins in England to their eventual inclusion in our regional and federal human rights acts and in our Charter. Next, we explain how these human rights acts protect rights and freedoms in the private sector. Following this is an overview of the Charter, which provides a similar kind of protection when governments are involved. We conclude with a look at possible future directions for civil liberties in Canada.

The Evolution of Civil Liberties in Canada

Civil liberties in Canada eventually gained legislative protection because of four main factors:

1. growing dissatisfaction in Canada, after the Second World War, with having only an "implied" bill of rights;
2. the influence of the civil rights movement in the United States;
3. dissatisfaction with the *Canadian Bill of Rights* (1960); and
4. the advent of the *Canadian Charter of Rights and Freedoms* in 1982.

Canada's implied bill of rights is based on the *Constitution Act, 1867*, which states in its preamble that Canada is to have "a Constitution similar in Principle to that of the United Kingdom." These words reflect the drafters' intention that, among other features of England's Constitution, its historical legacy of civil liberties and the rules that were developed to safeguard them were also included in our Constitution. Some examples of the civil liberties and safeguards that Canada has derived from England include a respect for the rule of law and due process, or fairness, in criminal matters, which includes legal rights upon arrest, the presumption of innocence, and the right to an open and fair trial. Many of these "liberties" can be traced to the *Magna Carta* (1215) (see also Chapter 1). In addition to these legal rights, certain political civil rights developed that stemmed from England's system of government. Among these were the rights to freedom of speech, freedom of religion, freedom of the press, and peaceful assembly. These rights were only implied, however, and many commentators felt that Canada needed a clearly worded and constitutionally entrenched document to give them legitimacy.

With respect to the second factor, the implied bill of rights does not adequately address all civil liberties matters—for example, discrimination. The 1950s and 1960s were important decades for the civil rights movement in the United States. In the landmark 1954 US Supreme Court case of *Brown v Board of Education*,[2] the Court outlawed racial segregation of blacks and whites in public schools. The 1950s also saw the mobilization of activist organizations such as the National Association for the Advancement of Colored People (NAACP). Inspired by Dr Martin Luther King Jr, black Americans began to engage in protest marches, boycotts, and sit-ins, particularly in the American South, with the aim of ending segregation in public places such as transit systems, lunch counters, and voting

---

2   347 US 438 (Kansas 1954).

FIGURE 6.1 In 1964, when Martin Luther King Jr (1929–1968) became the youngest man to receive the Nobel Peace Prize, he contributed all of the prize money to the civil rights movement.

districts. Such actions in America, as well as civil rights movements abroad—for example, the movement to end apartheid in South Africa—further influenced civil rights activists in Canada to seek anti-discrimination legislation here.

Among Canadians strongly influenced by these civil rights movements in the United States and elsewhere was Prime Minister John Diefenbaker. In 1960, his government enacted the *Canadian Bill of Rights*, which included the right to "equality before the law." However, the legislation had its weaknesses. It was a federal statute and not constitutionally entrenched, and it didn't apply to the provinces. As well, it also presented some interpretive problems, and in several cases pertaining to equality before the law using the Bill of Rights, the Supreme Court of Canada (SCC) was reluctant to use it to invalidate federal legislation that raised issues concerning equality between men and women.

Finally, however, after a number of years, Prime Minister Pierre Trudeau's efforts to patriate Canada's Constitution and add a charter of rights came to fruition (see Chapter 3). Fundamental rights became legitimized in Canada. On April 17, 1982, Queen Elizabeth proclaimed the *Constitution Act, 1982* in force, and the *Canadian Charter of Rights and Freedoms* was officially entrenched in Canada's Constitution.

The Charter has become the central instrument for the protection of civil liberties in Canada, but it is important to recognize that it only applies to governments, which are generally involved in public sector activities (such as making, implementing, and enforcing laws). For protection in the private sector, other legislation is needed. Figure 6.2 summarizes the key areas of protection and the legislation that applies. The next two sections describe the relevant legislation in the private sector context and when governments are involved.

FIGURE 6.2 Protection of Human Rights in Canada

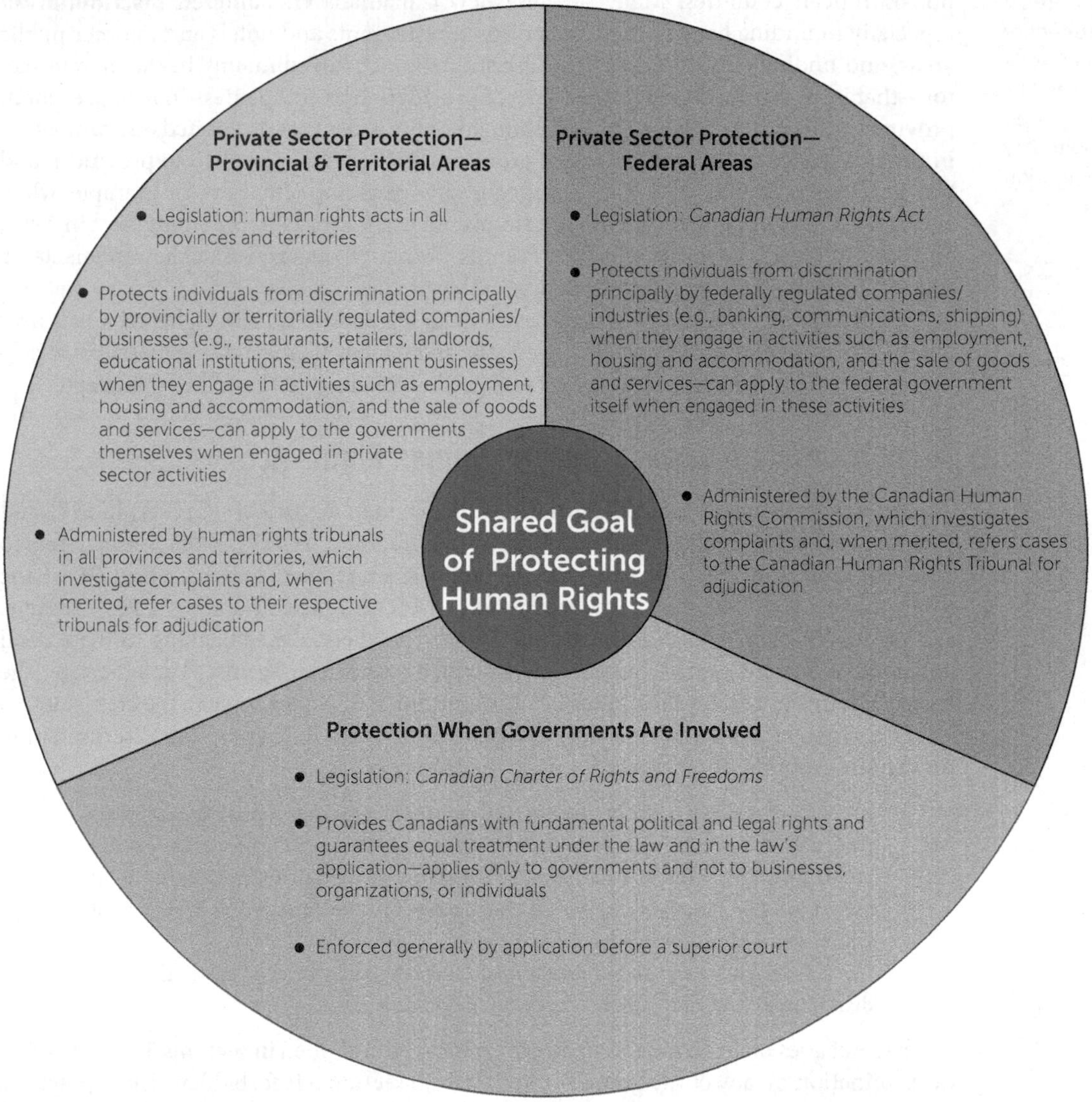

**Private Sector Protection—
Provincial & Territorial Areas**

- Legislation: human rights acts in all provinces and territories

- Protects individuals from discrimination principally by provincially or territorially regulated companies/businesses (e.g., restaurants, retailers, landlords, educational institutions, entertainment businesses) when they engage in activities such as employment, housing and accommodation, and the sale of goods and services—can apply to the governments themselves when engaged in private sector activities

- Administered by human rights tribunals in all provinces and territories, which investigate complaints and, when merited, refer cases to their respective tribunals for adjudication

**Private Sector Protection—
Federal Areas**

- Legislation: *Canadian Human Rights Act*

- Protects individuals from discrimination principally by federally regulated companies/industries (e.g., banking, communications, shipping) when they engage in activities such as employment, housing and accommodation, and the sale of goods and services—can apply to the federal government itself when engaged in these activities

- Administered by the Canadian Human Rights Commission, which investigates complaints and, when merited, refers cases to the Canadian Human Rights Tribunal for adjudication

Shared Goal of Protecting Human Rights

Protection When Governments Are Involved

- Legislation: *Canadian Charter of Rights and Freedoms*

- Provides Canadians with fundamental political and legal rights and guarantees equal treatment under the law and in the law's application—applies only to governments and not to businesses, organizations, or individuals

- Enforced generally by application before a superior court

Protection of Civil Liberties in the Private Sector

In the private sector, human rights legislation is mainly concerned with preventing discrimination. Egalitarian rights issues can arise in many contexts, including employment, housing and accommodation, and the provision of goods and services. These activities may be regulated regionally (by the provinces and territories) or nationally (by the federal government). Different legislation applies depending on the jurisdiction under which the activity falls.

Provincial and Territorial Legislation

Canada's provinces introduced **human rights** legislation in this country before the federal government did. By the middle of the 20th century, Canada was starting to undergo demographic changes because of a growing influx of visible-minority immigrants from

human rights
rights that respect the dignity and worth of an individual

discrimination
prejudicial treatment of people on the ground of race, age, sex, disability, or other recognized ground; prohibited by human rights legislation

non-European countries. Many of these new Canadians encountered **discrimination**, especially in finding housing, getting service in restaurants and hotels and in other public areas, and finding employment.[3] This discrimination occurred mainly in the private sector—that is, by landlords, employers, service providers, and companies. To help prevent it, provinces and territories began to enact human rights codes that prohibited discrimination in the private sector on certain defined grounds. The codes also applied to provincial and territorial governments when they engaged in private sector activities (for example, when acting as landlords or employers). Ontario passed the *Racial Discrimination Act*[4] in 1944, and, due in large part to the efforts of Premier Tommy Douglas, Saskatchewan enacted a Bill of Rights in 1947—the first legislation of this kind in Canada.

Today, all provinces and territories have similar legislation. Human rights tribunals hear complaints involving discrimination, investigate and remedy them, and take measures to help prevent discrimination from occurring (see "Further Reading" at the end of this chapter).

Federal Legislation: The Canadian Human Rights Act

The federal government passed its own *Canadian Human Rights Act*[5] (CHRA) in 1977 and established the Canadian Human Rights Commission (CHRC) one year later to administer it. The Act applies to private sector matters that, under section 91 of the *Constitution Act, 1867*, come under federal jurisdiction (see Chapter 4). For example, section 91(15) of the *Constitution Act, 1867* gives jurisdiction over banking to the federal government. Accordingly, if a human rights complaint were made against a bank manager, the federal CHRA, not one of the provincial human rights acts, would apply to the complaint.

Like provincial and territorial human rights statutes, the CHRA prohibits discrimination on various grounds. These grounds are set out in section 3:

> 3(1) For all purposes of this Act, the prohibited grounds of discrimination are race, national or ethnic origin, colour, religion, age, sex, sexual orientation, gender identity or expression, marital status, family status, genetic characteristics, disability and conviction for an offence for which a pardon has been granted or in respect of which a record suspension has been ordered.
>
> (2) Where the ground of discrimination is pregnancy or child-birth, the discrimination shall be deemed to be on the ground of sex.

The Act goes on to define certain specific practices described in sections 5 to 14.1 where discrimination on any of the grounds referred to in section 3 is forbidden. These practices occur most often in the private sector and include the provision of goods and services, real estate dealings (commercial or residential), employment, and harassment. Concerning harassment (s 14), there have been an increasing number of cases recently, particularly in the employment context. Although harassment can take many forms, section 14(2) makes it clear that "sexual harassment shall ... be deemed to be harassment on a prohibited ground of discrimination." And as with provincial and territorial governments in areas under their jurisdiction, if the federal government engages in any of these activities (for example, employment) and discriminates against someone on a prohibited ground while doing so, it is subject to the Act (s 66).

---

3 See, for example, George Tanaka, "Wartime Toronto and Japanese Canadians" (1984) 6 Polyphony 240; and Constance Backhouse, *Colour-Coded: A Legal History of Racism in Canada, 1900–1950* (Toronto: University of Toronto Press, 1999).

4 SO 1944, c 51.

5 RSC 1985, c H-6.

FIGURE 6.3 Prime Minister Justin Trudeau marches in the 2019 Pride Parade in Vancouver, British Columbia. In 2016, Trudeau became the first prime minister to march in a Pride Parade, showing the government's support for the LGBTQ2+ community.

The grounds of "gender identity or expression" and "genetic characteristics" were added to the CHRA by Parliament in 2017 to protect individuals from discrimination because of their gender characteristics (for example, being transgendered) or genetic information (for example, because of a genetic predisposition to a certain disease). According to the CHRC, in 2019, 58 percent of all complaints were employment related. The most cited ground of discrimination overall was disability (52 percent of the total complaints received, with more than half of these concerning mental health), and the second most cited ground was national or ethnic origin (27 percent of the total).[6]

Indigenous People and the Canadian Human Rights Act

The original version of the CHRA included section 67, which stated: "Nothing in this Act affects any provision of the *Indian Act* or any provision made under or pursuant to that Act." Effectively, this prevented anyone from filing a complaint with the CHRC about a decision that was made or an action that was taken by the federal government, a band council, or a related agency, such as a school board, pursuant to or under the *Indian Act*.[7] Although the CHRA protected Canadians and First Nations persons living or working off-reserve from

---

6 "Stand Together: The Canadian Human Rights Commission's 2019 Annual Report to Parliament" (Ottawa: CHRC, 2020), online: *Canadian Human Rights Commission* <http://chrcreport.ca/assets/pdf/chrc_ar_2019-eng.pdf>.

7 RSC 1985, c I-5.

discrimination by an employer or a service provider, First Nations persons living or working on a reserve were unable to file complaints with the CHRC. In other words, they did not have full access to human rights protection.

In 2008, section 67 was repealed, and since then Indigenous people have been able to file complaints against the federal government; as of 2011, they have also been able to file complaints against First Nations governments and federally regulated Indigenous organizations. The majority of the complaints against the federal government following the repeal cite national or ethnic origin, family status, or race as the grounds for discrimination and relate to issues including Indian registration pursuant to the *Indian Act*; funding for child and family services, special education, and programs for individuals with disabilities and their families; and other issues, including consultation issues.[8] Complaints against First Nations governments primarily cite family status and national or ethnic origin as grounds for discrimination and relate to the provision of services, retaliatory action, and employment.[9]

In 2016, the Canadian Human Rights Tribunal (CHRT), the judicial arm of the CHRC, ruled that the federal government had discriminated against First Nations children by underfunding the on-reserve child welfare system and creating an incentive to remove them from their families.[10] In 2019, following up on its 2016 decision, the CHRT ordered the government to pay children and parents (or grandparents) who had been affected by the discrimination since 2006 up to a maximum of $40,000 each. In 2020, the Assembly of First Nations commenced a $10 billion class-action lawsuit against the government, claiming that the scope of the CHRT decision should be expanded to include children and families discriminated against between the years 1991 and 2005. (See also Chapter 2 under "Canadian Law and Indigenous Peoples: A Timeline.")

Exceptions

A number of exceptions are built into human rights acts. For example, under the CHRA, there are certain defined exceptions in which a "discriminatory practice" cannot be applied to an employer's actions. A key one is where a **bona fide occupational requirement** for a job is involved. This means that a job requirement exists for a legitimate reason and cannot be removed without undue hardship for the employer. Section 15(1)(a) states:

> 15(1) It is not a discriminatory practice if
>   (a) any refusal, exclusion, expulsion, suspension, limitation, specification
> or preference in relation to any employment is established by an employer to be
> based on a *bona fide* occupational requirement.

One example of this could be where an employer specified that all employees must wear a hard hat on the company's construction site. If an employee's religion prevents him from wearing head apparel, would the company be discriminating against him on religious

bona fide occupational requirement
in the context of employment, a bona fide (Latin for "in good faith") requirement is one that exists for a legitimate reason—for example, safety—and that cannot be removed without undue hardship on the employer

---

8   Aboriginal Affairs and Northern Development Canada, "Report to Parliament on the Five-Year Review of the Repeal of Section 67 of the Canadian Human Rights Act" (Gatineau, Que.: September 2014), online: <http://publications.gc.ca/pub?id=9.699842&sl=0>.

9   *Ibid*

10   *First Nations Child and Family Caring Society of Canada v Attorney General of Canada (for the Minister of Indian and Northern Affairs Canada)*, 2016 CHRT 2. See also the National Film Board's full-length documentary on the Tribunal and this historic decision, called *We Can't Make the Same Mistake Twice*, online: <https://www.nfb.ca/film/we_can_t_make_the_same_mistake_twice>.

grounds by requiring him to wear a hard hat—or is the requirement a bona fide occupational requirement to ensure worker safety?

Other exceptions in which discrimination of a kind is permitted by the CHRA are **affirmative action** programs, under section 16(1). These are special government or business initiatives to help certain identifiable groups who have experienced discrimination in the past—for example, women, Indigenous persons, visible minorities, and persons with disabilities—achieve equality with others. Section 16(1) states:

> 16(1) It is not a discriminatory practice for a person to adopt or carry out a special program, plan or arrangement designed to prevent disadvantages that are likely to be suffered by, or to eliminate or reduce disadvantages that are suffered by, any group of individuals when those disadvantages would be based on or related to the prohibited grounds of discrimination, by improving opportunities respecting goods, services, facilities, accommodation or employment in relation to that group.

In the context of employment, this means that an employer may pass over one applicant and choose another on the basis of an affirmative action program (that is, a program designed to improve opportunities for the group to which the successful applicant belongs), and the unsuccessful applicant will have no grounds for a complaint of discrimination.

Provincial and territorial human rights acts include similar exceptions.

affirmative action
policy, particularly in relation to education or employment, intended to assist groups who have suffered past discrimination

Protection of Civil Liberties When Governments Are Involved: The Charter

As we have seen, the arrival of the Charter was a significant milestone in the history of civil liberties in this country. The Charter entrenches many of the rights, freedoms, and protections we inherited from England and adds new ones. It clearly sets them out in a formal document and allows for change in the future, if necessary, following a constitutional amendment procedure.

The Charter applies to governments and their relationship to others—which "others" depends on the particular right or freedom.[11] Although it generally applies to public sector activities, such as law-making and law enforcement, it can apply to the private sector in limited situations. For example, if government is directly involved in private sector activities (as employer or landlord, for example), the Charter will apply (see below under "Sections 32 and 33: Application of the Charter"). The Charter can also apply indirectly through challenges to the constitutionality of legislation regulating private sector activities (see Box 6.3).

An Overview of the Charter

The following is a brief examination of Charter provisions. See Appendix B for the full text of these provisions.

---

11 The Charter uses different words—such as "citizen," "individual," "person," or "everyone"—when describing the various rights and freedoms. Who exactly is protected by, or receives the benefit of, a particular Charter provision depends on the word used. "Citizen" means a Canadian citizen, "individual" means a human being as opposed to a corporate entity (and not necessarily a citizen), and "person" generally includes both human beings and corporate entities. Words such as "everyone" and "anyone" are also generally inclusive.

Section 1: Guarantee of Rights and Freedoms

Section 1 of the Charter guarantees the rights and freedoms it sets out but also states that they are not absolute. They are subject to "reasonable limits prescribed by law as can be demonstrably justified in a free and democratic society."

One of the most important early Charter cases for the SCC, *R v Oakes*,[12] concerned the test for determining whether a law that infringes the Charter can be justified under section 1. Normally, a law that is inconsistent with the Constitution runs the risk of being struck down pursuant to the supremacy clause, section 52 of the *Constitution Act, 1982*. However, if the law is a reasonable limit on a right, it can be saved under section 1. Today, the courts still apply the two-part test set out in the *Oakes* case when making this determination. Briefly stated, for a Charter infringement that is "prescribed by law" to be saved under section 1, the law must:

1. serve an important social objective (one that is "pressing and substantial") and
2. use proportionate means to reach that objective (the measures must be clearly connected to the objective, the law must impair individual rights as little as possible, and the social benefits of the law must outweigh the negative effects on those whose rights are affected by the law).

For example, we have laws that prohibit a person from threatening to kill someone; from making, distributing, or possessing child pornography; and from inciting hatred against an identifiable group. Could a person charged with one of these offences argue that the law infringed her "freedom of thought, belief, opinion and expression" under section 2 of the Charter? The answer is "yes" (it is up to the accused to prove the infringement), but the government could successfully argue that the infringement is justified under section 1 (it is up to the government to prove the infringement is a "reasonable limit").

For further discussion of the *Oakes* case and a schematic of the section 1 analysis, see Box 6.1 and Figure 6.4.

Section 2: Fundamental Freedoms

Section 2 of the Charter lists four fundamental freedoms: freedom of conscience and religion; freedom of thought, belief, opinion, and expression; freedom of peaceful assembly; and freedom of association. See Box 6.2 for a discussion of freedom of religion.[13]

These freedoms were established in English constitutional history and are essential to the functioning of our democracy in Canada. For example, our right to criticize government action or policy on television or in a newspaper, without fear of reprisal, or to peacefully protest against government actions, is fundamental to our parliamentary system of government and free and democratic society. However, there are limits to these freedoms, as we just saw. Hate speech, for instance, is not a protected form of expression.[14]

---

12 [1986] 1 SCR 103, 1986 CanLII 46.

13 See also *R v Big M Drug Mart Ltd*, [1985] 1 SCR 295, 1985 CanLII 69, an early Charter case in which the SCC struck down the federal *Lord's Day Act*, RSC 1970, c L-13, which required stores to shut down on Sundays to allow for religious observance.

14 See *R v Keegstra*, [1990] 3 SCR 697, 1990 CanLII 24, involving an Alberta high school teacher who was charged with promoting hatred against a racial group (Jews) contrary to the *Criminal Code*. A majority of the SCC took a broad view of freedom of expression, concluding that the *Criminal Code* provision was an infringement of freedom of expression. The Court followed an earlier SCC decision—*Irwin Toy Ltd v Quebec (Attorney General)*, [1989] 1 SCR 927, 1989 CanLII 87—and held that non-violent expression is protected if it conveys meaning regardless of the content of the message. However, following the *Oakes* test (see above under "Section 1: Guarantee of Rights and Freedoms"), the *Criminal Code* provision was found to be a reasonable limit on that freedom and justified.

BOX 6.1

Section 1: The "Reasonable Limits" Clause and the Oakes Test

In 1982, David Oakes was found with a small quantity of narcotics and charged with unlawful possession of a narcotic for the purpose of trafficking, an offence under section 4(2) of the *Narcotic Control Act*.* At the time, section 8 of the Act stated: "[I]f the court finds that the accused was in possession of the narcotic he shall be given an opportunity of establishing that he was not in possession for the purpose of trafficking." The constitutionality of this provision, which placed a reverse onus on the defendant by requiring him to prove he did not intend to traffic, was challenged by Oakes on the grounds that it infringed his right under section 11(d) of the Charter to be presumed innocent until proven guilty.

The case eventually made its way up to the SCC.† The SCC noted that Canadian Charter jurisprudence accords a high degree of protection to the presumption of innocence and that section 11(d) had been infringed. The Court then had to determine whether, in light of this, the infringement was justified by section 1 of the Charter. In other words, was section 8 of the *Narcotic Control Act* and its reverse onus a "reasonable limit" on Mr Oakes's right to be presumed innocent under section 11(d) of the Charter? Under section 1, it had to first be established that the limit was "prescribed by law." This was easy to show; the reverse-onus requirement was set out in section 8 of the *Narcotic Control Act*. Next, it had to be shown that the infringement was a "reasonable limit ... demonstrably justified in a free and democratic society." The Court developed a general two-part test, now known as the *Oakes* test, to determine whether a law that infringes the Charter is a reasonable limit on one's Charter rights. The onus is on the Crown to show on a balance of probabilities (or preponderance of probability) that the limit is reasonable by proving (1) that it relates to an important social objective and (2) that it is a proportionate response to the problem. Specifically, the Crown must prove the following:

1. *Important social objective ("pressing and substantial" concern)*
   The government's objective in creating the law must be shown to be "of sufficient importance" to warrant overriding a Charter right. The standard for this part of the test is high but is often met by the government in Charter cases. In the words of the SCC, for an objective

to qualify as sufficiently important, it must relate "to concerns which are *pressing and substantial* in a free and democratic society" (at para 69; emphasis added).
2. *Proportionality*
   If the objective is found to be sufficiently important, the government must then show that the means used are a reasonable and fair way to achieve its legislative objective. To make this determination, a court considers three components or criteria, all of which must be satisfied in the circumstances:
   i. *Rational connection:* The measures that impair the Charter right must be designed to achieve the government's objective; in other words, the measures must be "rationally connected" to the objective. They must not be "arbitrary, unfair, or based on irrational considerations" (at para 70).
   ii. *Minimal impairment:* If a rational connection exists, the court will then examine the degree to which the measures impair the right or freedom. The right should be impaired "as little as possible" (at para 70), and if it is possible to impair a right to a lesser degree and still achieve the objective, the government must do so in drafting its legislation. Many arguments put forward by governments in defending legislation fail this part of the test.
   iii. *Proportionate effect:* The effects of the measures that limit the right or freedom must be proportionate to the objective identified in the first part of the test. In other words, this third part of the test weighs the benefit to society as a result of the law's being in place with the negative effects on those whose rights the law impairs. The greater the impairment of the right, the more important the objective must be.

Applying the test to section 8 of the *Narcotic Control Act*, the Court held that the social objective involved was "pressing and substantial" and that the first part of the "reasonable limits" determination was satisfied. Controlling drug trafficking is a sufficiently important social objective to justify a violation of Charter rights. However, the provision failed to pass the proportionality test. Specifically, the first component of the test was not satisfied because the Court found that there was no rational connection between the reverse-onus requirement and the objective of controlling trafficking. At para 78, Chief Justice Dickson stated:

* RSC 1970, c N-1. See now the *Controlled Drugs and Substances Act*, SC 1996, c 19.

† *Supra* note 12.

[I]t would be irrational to infer that a person had an intent to traffic on the basis of his possession of a very small quantity of narcotics. The presumption required under s. 8 of the *Narcotic Control Act* is overinclusive and could lead to results in certain cases which would defy both rationality and fairness. In light of the seriousness of the offence in question, which carries with it the possibility of imprisonment for life, I am further convinced that the first component of the proportionality test has not been satisfied by the Crown.

As a result of its analysis, the SCC found that section 8 of the *Narcotic Control Act*, which infringed the Charter, could not be saved under section 1 and was therefore of no force or effect.

FIGURE 6.4 Section 1 Analysis: The *Oakes* Test

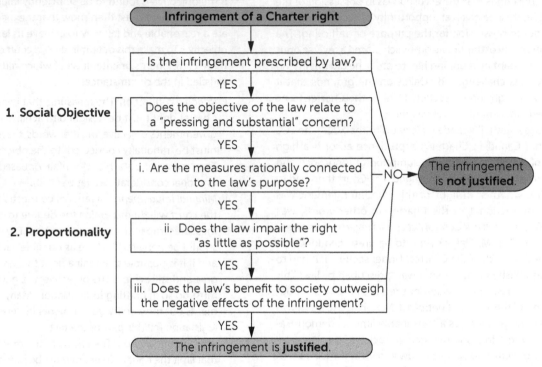

Sections 3-5: Democratic Rights

Sections 3-5 of the Charter further allow our democratic system of government to function by giving every citizen of Canada the right to vote and by limiting the duration of legislatures (no longer than five years, with the possibility of extensions in certain circumstances, such as war) and ensuring an annual sitting of our legislative bodies.

Canadian women have had the right to vote for over 100 years and Indigenous peoples for over 60 years. The Charter now constitutionally protects this basic right for all citizens. In 2002, section 3 of the Charter was used successfully to give prison inmates the right to vote.[15] In 2019, the SCC held that Canadian citizens living abroad for more than five years could not be denied the right to vote.[16]

---

15   *Sauvé v Canada (Chief Electoral Officer)*, 2002 SCC 68.
16   *Frank v Canada (Attorney General)*, 2019 SCC 1.

BOX 6.2

Freedom of Religion and Development Within Indigenous Territory

In *Ktunaxa Nation v British Columbia (Forests, Lands and Natural Resource Operations)*,* the SCC had to consider freedom of religion in the context of the development of a glacier sightseeing and ski resort in southeastern British Columbia, the Jumbo Glacier Resort. With respect to the Crown's duty to consult concerning development within disputed territory (where Aboriginal title had not been proven), a majority of the Court held that the Crown had satisfied this obligation under section 35 of the *Constitution Act, 1982*. (See also Box 7.7 on Aboriginal title in Chapter 7.)

However, the Ktunaxa Nation also claimed that the proposed resort lay in an important sacred area called Qat'muk, which is the grizzly bear's spiritual home, and that the development would drive the Grizzly Bear Spirit from its home. This, they argued, would interfere with their freedom of religion under section 2(a) of the Charter. At para 68, the Court held that to establish this infringement, a claimant must demonstrate

> (1) that he or she sincerely believes in a practice or belief that has a nexus with religion, and (2) that the impugned state conduct interferes, in a manner that is non-trivial or not insubstantial, with his or her ability to act in accordance with that practice or belief ... .

The majority found that the second part of the test was not met. At para 71, they stated that the state's duty is to protect everyone's "freedom to hold [his or her] beliefs and to manifest them in worship and practice or by teaching and dissemination" but "not to protect the object of beliefs, such as

* 2017 SCC 54.

Jumbo Glacier, Lake of the Hanging Glacier protected area, and Glacier Dome in British Columbia.

Grizzly Bear Spirit." In short, they held that the Charter "protects the freedom to worship, but does not protect the spiritual focal point of worship." Indigenous spiritual beliefs would not forestall development in this case.

Some have argued that this decision diminishes the sphere of protection that this particular Charter freedom provides. It also raises questions about when the interference with a sacred place affects the right to worship and how to prove that it does. If an object of belief is central to the belief itself, what kind of interference with the object will also be characterized as an interference with the freedom to worship?

Despite their loss in the SCC, the Ktunaxa Nation continued its efforts to protect the area from development by pursuing a buy-out plan. In 2020, it reached an agreement with the developers to purchase their tenures (with funding support from the federal government and private foundations) and turn the land into a First Nations protected area.

Section 6: Mobility Rights

Section 6 of the Charter makes it clear that Canadians living in one part of the country can move to another province and obtain work there. For example, many people living in the maritime provinces work in the oil sands of Alberta. Generally speaking, a province cannot enact laws preventing citizens from other provinces (or from the territories) from setting up residence or working there. One exception to this, however, is where a province with a low rate of employment enacts laws to help its current residents who are socially or economically disadvantaged (and this prejudices out-of-province citizens).

Sections 7-14: Legal Rights

Sections 7-14 of the Charter set out important safeguards for everyone who enters the Canadian criminal justice system. They ensure that fairness is an essential part of our system.

Section 7 is a complex provision that provides significant protection for everyone encountering the Canadian criminal justice system.[17] It states that everyone has the "right to life, liberty and security of the person" and that an individual cannot be deprived of these things unless the "principles of fundamental justice" have been followed. In simple terms, this means that one's basic liberties, including both physical and psychological freedoms, cannot be taken away without both procedural *and* substantive fairness. For example, procedural unfairness could occur if a person were forced to speak or give evidence against himself (an accused person has the right to remain silent), whereas substantive unfairness could occur if a defendant were convicted of a crime for actions only, without the requirement of a guilty mind, or *mens rea* (see Chapter 10).[18]

Section 8 protects against "unreasonable search or seizure." Section 9 covers the "right not to be arbitrarily detained or imprisoned." Section 10 concerns rights on arrest and detention (the right to be given reasons for the arrest or detention, the right to retain counsel, and the right to have the validity of the detention determined by way of *habeas corpus*).

---

17 A detailed examination is beyond the scope of this text. For a full examination of s 7, see Peter W Hogg, "The Brilliant Career of Section 7 of the Charter" (2012) 58 SCLR (2d) 195.

18 There have been many cases involving s 7. *Morgentaler* (1988), *Carter* (2015), and *Truchon* (2019) are important examples. In these cases, *Criminal Code* provisions were held to infringe s 7, and the infringements were not justified under s 1. In *R v Morgentaler*, [1988] 1 SCR 30, 1988 CanLII 90, the SCC struck down Canada's abortion law, which at the time prohibited abortions unless a woman's life or health was endangered, as determined by a "therapeutic abortion committee" of an "accredited or approved hospital." A majority of the Court held that the law caused a risk to health, infringing the right to security of the person, and did so without fundamental justice (there were problems with the requirement of approval by a committee, including the risk of delays). Since *Morgentaler*, there have been no legal barriers to accessing abortions in Canada, one of the few countries in the world without any restrictions. *Carter* and *Truchon* are related cases. In *Carter v Canada (Attorney General)*, 2015 SCC 5, the SCC declared Canada's laws prohibiting medically assisted suicide to be in violation of s 7 and unconstitutional. Following *Carter*, Parliament passed a new law allowing medical assistance in dying (MAID) but with conditions, including the requirement that natural death had to be "reasonably foreseeable." In *Truchon v Attorney General of Canada*, 2019 QCCS 3792 (CanLII), one of the court challenges to this new law, the Superior Court of Quebec declared that the requirement of reasonably foreseeable death was contrary to s 7. It infringed the plaintiffs' rights to life, liberty, and security of the person and was inconsistent with fundamental justice because it was overbroad and disproportionate compared to the measure's purpose (which was to protect vulnerable persons who might be induced to end their lives in a moment of weakness by preventing errors when assessing requests for MAID). The Court went on to find that the provision also violated s 15 of the Charter. In 2020, in the wake of *Truchon*, the federal government introduced legislation amending its MAID laws and removing the requirement that natural death be reasonably foreseeable: Bill C-7, *An Act to amend the Criminal Code (medical assistance in dying)*, 1st Sess, 43rd Parl, 2020. As of July 2020, this amendment had not been passed into law.

Section 11 sets out the rights of individuals who are charged with an offence (and includes the presumption of innocence), whereas section 12 safeguards against cruel and unusual treatment or punishment. Section 13 protects witnesses against self-incrimination, providing that "[a] witness who testifies in any proceedings has the right not to have any incriminating evidence so given used to incriminate that witness in any other proceedings, except in a prosecution for perjury or for the giving of contradictory evidence." Finally, section 14 guarantees the right to an interpreter.

In a sense, sections 8-14 are specific examples of the broad protection afforded by section 7. Indeed, it is possible for one government law or action to infringe both section 7 and one of these other sections.

Section 15: Equality Rights

Section 15(1) of the Charter concerns equality rights. As noted in Chapter 3, in the lead-up to the Charter's enactment, concerns were expressed about the limited scope of Diefenbaker's 1960 *Canadian Bill of Rights*. One specific concern related to its phrasing of equality rights, referring as it does to "equality before the law and the protection of the law." The language in section 15(1) is stronger: it refers to the individual's equality "before *and under the law*" and grants every individual the "right to the equal protection *and equal benefit of the law*" (emphasis added). Clearly, this wording refers to equality not only when it comes to procedural protection (process issues) but also substantive protection (the content or substance of the laws themselves). Benefits, as well, must be equally distributed.

The Charter's equality rights apply with reference to prohibited grounds of discrimination.[19] Specifically, section 15(1) guarantees these rights without discrimination based on "race, national or ethnic origin, colour, religion, sex, age, or mental or physical disability." However, the SCC has held that the listed grounds are not exhaustive and that discrimination must not occur on "analogous" grounds either.[20] So far, only three analogous grounds have been recognized: citizenship, marital status, and sexual orientation (see Box 6.3).

Section 15(1) has limits, however. It does not protect against discrimination based on grounds that are not listed or grounds that are not analogous to listed grounds (examples

---

19 Women have lobbied forcefully for gender equality, but other groups (for example, seniors and Canadians with mental and physical disabilities) have also applied concerted pressure on governments for recognition.

20 *Andrews v Law Society of British Columbia*, [1989] 1 SCR 143, 1989 CanLII 2, was the first SCC decision to make this determination. Andrews was a British lawyer wanting to practise law in British Columbia. He was denied admission to the bar because he was not a Canadian citizen, as required by BC legislation. Andrews argued that his rights under s 15 had been infringed. Although citizenship is not specifically listed as a protected ground, the SCC concluded that it was an analogous ground and therefore also protected. The majority held that Andrews had been discriminated against, and the law was not saved by s 1. Of particular interest was the majority's analysis of the meaning of "discrimination" in s 15. For example, does it mean different treatment when compared to others generally or different treatment when compared to those who are similarly situated? The majority adopted a middle ground, requiring different treatment compared to others based on a listed or analogous characteristic *where this treatment causes a disadvantage* (by imposing a burden or denying a benefit).

BOX 6.3

Sexual Orientation: An Analogous Prohibited Ground

Delwin Vriend worked for a Christian college in Alberta. When the college found out that Vriend was homosexual, it terminated his employment. Vriend complained about this to the Alberta Human Rights Commission. The commission said it could not intervene on Vriend's behalf because Alberta's *Individual's Rights Protection Act** (IRPA) did not have "sexual orientation" as a prohibited ground of discrimination.

The case was appealed to the SCC. The issue the Court had to decide was whether Alberta's IRPA violated the Charter by not including sexual orientation as a prohibited ground of discrimination. Justice Cory stated that sexual orientation was a "personal characteristic which has been found to be analogous to the grounds enumerated in s. 15."[†] However, rather than strike down the Alberta Act, the Court instead made it comply with the Charter. Sexual orientation was "read into" Alberta's IRPA—in other words, added by analogy to the Act's prohibited grounds of protection. Justice Iacobucci stated the following: "I conclude that reading sexual orientation into the impugned provisions of the IRPA is the most appropriate way of remedying this under inclusive legislation."[‡]

This case also illustrates how the Charter can indirectly affect private sector rights. Vriend did not have a claim directly against his employer for discrimination based on the Charter, but he had a claim against the Alberta government because its human rights legislation was discriminatory and violated the Charter. Once the IRPA was brought into compliance with the Charter, Vriend would have a private sector claim based on the IRPA.

Delwin Vriend (right) and his partner, Andrew Gagnon, at the Supreme Court in 1997.

* RSA 1980, c I-2.

† *Vriend v Alberta*, [1998] 1 SCR 493, 1998 CanLII 816 at para 107. Sexual orientation was first recognized by the SCC as a protected analogous ground in *Egan v Canada*, [1995] 2 SCR 513, 1995 CanLII 98, a case involving entitlement to spousal benefits under Canada's old age security legislation.

‡ *Ibid* at para 179.

---

of non-protected grounds include employment status and poverty). Furthermore, there is always the possibility that a particular discriminatory law could be justified as a reasonable limit under section 1. Lastly, section 15(2) expressly permits affirmative action programs and allows discrimination against individuals in order to help certain disadvantaged groups by giving them special consideration.

Sections 16-23: Official Languages of Canada and Minority-Language Educational Rights

These sections of the Charter include a number of language provisions that are important for our country. Section 16(1) provides, for example, that "English and French are the official languages of Canada and have equality of status and equal rights and privileges as to their use in all institutions of the Parliament and government of Canada." They also provide that Canadians have the right to communicate and receive bilingual services in either English or French when dealing with any institution of the federal government. Section 23 also covers minority-language educational rights for citizens of Canada.

Section 24: Enforcement

We have seen that the supremacy clause (s 52(1) of the *Constitution Act, 1982*) provides for various forms of remedial relief in the event that a law is found to be unconstitutional, including because it violates the Charter. The two subsections of section 24 provide some additional forms of relief specifically in connection with Charter violations.

Section 24(1) provides for a wide range of remedies based on what the court considers "appropriate and just in the circumstances." For example, using this provision, courts can grant "defensive" remedies to prevent the continuation of an illegal state of affairs (for example, a court may dismiss a charge, quash a search warrant, or declare a law invalid, which is also a possible remedy under the supremacy clause). The courts may also grant "affirmative" remedies (for example, by ordering the return of property that has been seized or by awarding damages to a person whose Charter rights have been infringed).

Section 24(2) is narrower in scope and provides for the exclusion of illegally obtained evidence if its admission in the proceedings would "bring the administration of justice into disrepute." To make this determination, the courts apply a three-part test, considering the seriousness of the Charter infringement, its impact on the accused, and society's interest in having reliable evidence admitted in criminal cases.[21]

Sections 25-31: General

As mentioned in Chapter 3, section 25 ensures that existing Aboriginal and treaty rights will not be affected by the Charter. Section 35, which is in part II of the *Constitution Act, 1982* and not part of the Charter, formally recognizes and affirms the existing rights of Aboriginal peoples referred to in section 25.

Section 26 states that the Charter guarantees of rights and freedoms do not preclude the existence of other rights, such as may exist as part of the "implied" bill of rights, for example. Section 27 provides that the Charter must be interpreted in a way that is consistent with our multicultural heritage. Section 28, again as noted in Chapter 3, further protects gender equality (beyond the protection afforded by s 15) by ensuring that the Charter rights and freedoms themselves are guaranteed equally to male and female persons.

Sections 29-31 cover some miscellaneous matters.

Sections 32 and 33: Application of the Charter

Section 32 states that the Charter applies to the federal, provincial, and territorial governments in respect of all matters within their respective jurisdictions or spheres of authority. These include the laws within their jurisdiction (legislation and common law) and their

---

21 See the leading case of *R v Grant*, 2009 SCC 32, [2009] 2 SCR 353, on this test (where a firearm was illegally obtained by the police but was not excluded as evidence) and *R v Fearon*, 2014 SCC 77 (where text messages and photos on an illegally obtained cellphone also were not excluded).

administrative actions (which can include, for example, the conduct of police operating on behalf of government).

As we have seen, the Charter does not apply directly to private sector disputes involving only individuals or corporations—for example, to disputes between you and your neighbour, your landlord, or your employer or to how you are treated in a restaurant or a department store. Such situations, however, may be covered by federal, provincial, or territorial human rights legislation. Note that in situations where the government is involved in private sector activities (for example, as an employer or landlord), the Charter will apply, as well as any relevant human rights legislation.

Section 33 is commonly referred to as the "notwithstanding" or "override" clause. It allows the federal Parliament or provincial legislatures to pass legislation that may operate even though it may infringe certain sections of the Charter—specifically, section 2 or sections 7-15. To do so, however, the government must expressly declare in the Act that it is to operate "notwithstanding" those sections. The declaration lasts only for five years, but it can be renewed. Section 33 cannot be used to override voting rights under section 3 or Aboriginal rights under section 25.

Governments rarely exercise their power under section 33 because of the political consequences of openly stating that the Charter is being ignored when enacting a particular law. So far, the most noteworthy examples have involved Quebec.[22] The first example was in 1988 when the Quebec government used section 33 to protect its language law, the *Charter of the French Language* (also referred to as Bill 101). Earlier that year, the SCC had found that some of the provisions in this legislation contravened the Charter.[23] Following this case, the language law was re-enacted, and section 33 was invoked to shield it from further Charter challenges for five years. In 1993, the language law was amended so that it no longer contravened the Charter; the use of the notwithstanding clause was no longer necessary.

The second example was in 2019, when Quebec invoked the notwithstanding clause in passing *An Act respecting the laicity of the State* (commonly referred to as Bill 21), legislation that prevents public servants in positions of authority or who are participating in public functions from wearing religious symbols.[24]

The Future of Civil Liberties in Canada

Civil liberties around the world have evolved differently and at different paces. However, across all cultures, they evolve over time and with changing social values. In Canada, we have seen a dramatic growth in the recognition of civil liberties from the time of Tommy Douglas's Bill of Rights (1947) to the Charter (1982) and to the changes occurring today.

Canada's legislatures will continue to play a key role in this area. As new rights are identified, there will be calls for new legislation. For example, in connection with transgender rights,

---

22 Other provinces have invoked the notwithstanding clause, but, for various reasons, none of these legislative initiatives have come into force. For example, Alberta passed legislation in 2000 banning same-sex marriage (but the legislation was unconstitutional on division-of-powers grounds and therefore *ultra vires*), and Saskatchewan passed legislation in 2018 concerning the funding of Catholic schools (but as of writing, this statute has not been proclaimed).

23 See *Ford v Quebec (Attorney General)*, [1988] 2 SCR 712, 1988 CanLII 19.

24 SQ 2019, c 12. The legislation is seen by some as unfairly targeting Muslims, in particular Muslim women who wear clothing that covers the face, such as niqabs and burkas. Other religious minorities are also affected.

governments have responded with changes to human rights legislation to expressly list gender identity as a prohibited ground of discrimination.[25]

Similarly, our courts—particularly the SCC—will continue their work in the development of civil liberties. For example, the implied bill of rights may be expanded. More significantly, however, the Charter will be used as an instrument of growth. Confronted with new situations, the courts will develop new interpretations and new tests (or modify old ones) for the broad phrases in the Charter—phrases such as "reasonable limits," "freedom of conscience," "fundamental justice," "unreasonable delay," and "appropriate and just," among others. New grounds of discrimination will be recognized, and new remedies will be fashioned to respond to novel forms of infringement. Furthermore, parallel work will occur as the courts interpret similar language in federal, provincial, and territorial human rights legislation.

We live in an era of rapid social change. With respect to civil liberties, Canada seems well equipped, legally and culturally, to respond positively.

---

25 As of 2017, the federal government (see discussion of the CHRA above) and all provinces and territories had amended their human rights legislation to include this ground. One of the consequences of gender identity protection is that provinces and territories are increasingly allowing for the issuance (or reissuance) of birth certificates, health cards, and other government documents that are gender neutral—that is, without a female or male designation. This may be important to individuals who are intersex or who do not self-identify as male or female. In 2017, British Columbia issued its first gender-neutral health card, with a "U" marker, and in 2018, Ontario issued its first non-binary birth certificate, with an "X" marker. As of 2017, Canadian passports can be issued, when requested, without a male or female gender designation (with an "X" marker). Before the issuance of gender-neutral documents, it was (and still is) possible to change one's designation from male to female or female to male. Initially, proof of gender reassignment surgery was required, but this requirement has been removed in most Canadian jurisdictions.

CHAPTER SUMMARY

Civil liberties in Canada evolved over many years and gained legislative protection as a result of various factors, such as dissatisfaction with our implied bills of rights, the US civil rights movement, weaknesses in the *Canadian Bill of Rights* (1960), and the patriation of the Constitution, which included the Charter.

In Canada, we distinguish between civil liberties in the private sector and civil liberties where governments are involved (based on their actions or laws under their jurisdiction). The former concerns the private sphere—in other words, relations between (for example) landlords and tenants, employers and employees, or customers and service providers. Various provincial and territorial human rights statutes and codes—and, at the federal level, the 1977 *Canadian Human Rights Act*—provide protection against such discrimination, subject to certain limits, in the private sector. Sections 91 and 92 of the *Constitution Act, 1867* set out the

different jurisdictional areas and are used to determine whether a particular private sector civil liberties matter falls under federal or provincial jurisdiction.

Civil liberties where governments are involved are primarily regulated by the Charter, which constitutionally entrenches and guarantees a number of rights and freedoms, such as the fundamental freedoms of conscience, expression, and association; various democratic rights, including the right to vote; mobility rights; legal rights, including the right to "life, liberty and the security of the person"; equality rights; and language rights. As in the case of private sector protection, Charter rights are also not absolute; most notably, they are subject to "reasonable limits" under section 1.

Civil liberties in Canada continue to evolve in response to social change, through new legislation and the work of courts in interpreting and developing the rights and freedoms Canadians currently enjoy.

KEY TERMS

affirmative action, 167

bona fide occupational requirement, 166

civil liberties, 160

discrimination, 164

human rights, 163

FURTHER READING

BOOKS AND ARTICLES

Corbett, SM, *Canadian Human Rights Law and Commentary* (Toronto: LexisNexis, 2007).

Greenspan, Edward L, John B Laskin & Melanie Dunn, eds, *Canadian Charter of Rights Annotated* (Toronto: Canada Law Book, 2009) (loose-leaf).

Hogg, Peter W. "Civil Liberties" in *Constitutional Law of Canada*, 5th ed (Toronto: Carswell, 2007) (loose-leaf updated 2019, release 1) pt III, ch 34-57.

Mendes, Errol & Stéphane Beaulac, eds, *Canadian Charter of Rights and Freedoms*, 5th ed (Toronto: LexisNexis, 2013).

Sharpe, Robert J & Kent Roach, *The Charter of Rights and Freedoms*, 6th ed (Toronto: Irwin Law, 2017).

LEGISLATION

Canada

Canadian Bill of Rights, SC 1960, c 44, reprinted in RSC 1985, App III: <https://laws.justice.gc.ca/eng/acts/C-12.3/index.html>.

Canadian Human Rights Act, RSC 1985, c H-6: <https://laws.justice.gc.ca/eng/acts/H-6/index.html>.

Alberta

Alberta Human Rights Act, RSA 2000, c A-25.5: <https://www.qp.alberta.ca/documents/Acts/A25P5.pdf>.

British Columbia

Human Rights Code, RSBC 1996, c 210: <https://www.bclaws.ca/civix/document/id/complete/statreg/00_96210_01>.

Manitoba

The Human Rights Code, CCSM c H175: <http://web2.gov.mb.ca/laws/statutes/ccsm/h175e.php>.

New Brunswick

Human Rights Act, RSNB 2011, c 171: <http://laws.gnb.ca/en/showdoc/cs/2011-c.171>.

Newfoundland and Labrador

Human Rights Act, 2010, SNL 2010, c H-13.1: <http://assembly.nl.ca/Legislation/sr/statutes/h13-1.htm>.

Northwest Territories

Human Rights Act, SNWT 2002, c 18: <https://www.justice.gov.nt.ca/en/files/legislation/human-rights/human-rights.a.pdf>.

Nova Scotia

Human Rights Act, RSNS 1989, c 214: <https://nslegislature.ca/sites/default/files/legc/statutes/human%20rights.pdf>.

Nunavut

Human Rights Act, SNu 2003, c 12: <https://www.nhrt.ca/files/NHR_Act_Eng.pdf>.

Ontario

Human Rights Code, RSO 1990, c H.19: <http://www.ohrc.on.ca/en/ontario-human-rights-code>.

Prince Edward Island

Human Rights Act, RSPEI 1988, c H-12: <https://www.princeedwardisland.ca/sites/default/files/legislation/H-12%20-Human%20Rights%20Act.pdf>.

Quebec

Charter of Human Rights and Freedoms, CQLR, c C-12: <http://legisquebec.gouv.qc.ca/en/showdoc/cs/c-12>.

Saskatchewan

The Saskatchewan Human Rights Code, 2018, SS 2018, c S-24.2: <https://saskatchewanhumanrights.ca/wp-content/uploads/2020/03/Code2018.pdf>.

Yukon

Human Rights Act, RSY 2002, c 116: <http://www.gov.yk.ca/legislation/acts/huri.pdf.>

REVIEW QUESTIONS

1. What is the distinction between "civil rights" and "civil liberties" in the Canadian context?
2. In Canada, what were four main factors in the development of legislative protection for civil rights?
3. What is the basis of Canada's "implied" bill of rights?
4. Why did Diefenbaker's 1960 Bill of Rights prove disappointing?
5. What is a bona fide occupational requirement? What do you think would be a bona fide occupational requirement for a firefighter?
6. If an employee were fired from her job at Canadian Tire, would the Charter or a provincial human rights act apply? Explain.
7. If a human rights complaint were brought against a bank manager, what human rights act would apply: federal or provincial? Give reasons.

EXERCISES

1. Weigh the pros and cons of affirmative action programs. Do you approve or disapprove of them? Explain.

2. Assume that you are an employer concerned with prohibiting harassment in your workplace. You are determined to be proactive in preventing occurrences of it. List three steps you might implement in this regard.

3. Locate the human rights code for your province or territory online. Compare your provincial or territorial code's prohibited grounds of discrimination with those in section 15 of the Charter.

4. Research Bill 21 (*An Act respecting the laicity of the State*, SQ 2019, c 12), a controversial bill that was passed into law by the Quebec government in 2019. Explain whether or not this statute, in your view, contravenes the freedoms of religion and expression guaranteed by section 2 of the Charter. Assuming that it does, discuss whether or not the law is justified as a reasonable limit on these freedoms under section 1 of the Charter.

5. Discuss what you think might in time become a new prohibited ground of discrimination under section 15 of the Charter.

PART III
Key Subject Areas in Law

CHAPTER 7 Private Law Survey: Tort, Contract, Property, and Family Law

CHAPTER 8 Business and Consumer Law

CHAPTER 9 Administrative Law

CHAPTER 10 Criminal Law

7 Private Law Survey: Tort, Contract, Property, and Family Law

Introduction 184

Constitutional Basis of Private Law 185

Burden of Proof and Standard of
Proof in Private Law Claims 185

Tort Law 186

Contract Law 197

Property Law 207

Family Law 216

Chapter Summary 224

Key Terms 225

Further Reading 225

Review Questions 225

Exercises................................... 226

After reading this chapter, you will be able to:

- Describe the nature of private law and its relationship to other areas of the law.
- Explain the constitutional basis of private law.
- Define the burden and standard of proof in private law claims.
- Discuss the scope of tort law, its main categories and subcategories, defences to tort liability, and the remedies available to victims of torts.
- Understand the importance of contractual arrangements, how contracts are formed, important types of contracts and contract terms, excuses for non-performance, and remedies for breach of contract.

- Identify the different types of property (real, personal, and intellectual), forms of property ownership, rights and obligations connected to property ownership, security interests, and registration systems.
- Explain the law relating to marriage, marriage breakdown and divorce, common law relationships, and the rights and obligations of family members, including those relating to children.

P rivate law is a pervasive phenomenon of our social life, a silent but ubiquitous participant in our most common transactions. It regulates the property we own and use, the injuries we inflict or avoid inflicting, the contracts we make or break. It is the public repository of our most deeply embedded intuitions about justice and personal responsibility.

Ernest J Weinrib, *The Idea of Private Law*, revised ed
(Oxford: Oxford University Press, 2012) at 1

Introduction

In Chapter 1, we described the divisions of law in broad terms. In Part III of this text, we examine some key domestic law subjects. Private law, which governs the relationships between persons, is a large subcategory of domestic law and is the focus of this chapter. Public law, another significant subcategory of domestic law, governs the relationship between persons and the state and between the various organs of the state; public law topics are the focus of Chapters 9 and 10. (Note that constitutional law, which we covered in Part II, is also part of public law.) Business and consumer law, the subject of Chapter 8, has both private law and public law aspects to it.[1]

---

1   There are a number of subject areas that we are not able to cover in this book. Some of these include public international law, certain public domestic law areas (such as tax, immigration, and municipal law), various private law topics (including insurance, succession, creditors' remedies, and the civil law approach to private law in Quebec), and military law. See Figure 1.1 for a comprehensive listing of the divisions and areas of the law. Keep in mind, as we alluded to in Chapter 1, that dividing the law into separate subject areas is somewhat artificial, although it is a useful learning tool. We speak of specific areas of law, but the reality is that many legal problems overlap subject areas, and some areas themselves overlap each other.

This chapter surveys four important areas of private law (from a Canadian common law perspective): torts, contracts, property law, and family law.

Constitutional Basis of Private Law

Most private law falls under the jurisdiction of the provincial and territorial legislatures. This is because the provinces have jurisdiction over "Property and Civil Rights" under section 92(13) of the *Constitution Act, 1867*. The territories have a similar jurisdiction delegated to them by special federal legislation. As we noted in Chapter 6, the term "civil rights" in this context means "private law rights" in areas such as torts, contracts, and property. However, there are areas of private law where Parliament's role is more significant. For example, under sections 91(22) and 91(23) of the *Constitution Act, 1867*, intellectual property is regulated federally.

In some areas, jurisdiction is more complex because it is split between the provinces and the federal government. For example, in the area of family law, section 91(26) of the *Constitution Act, 1867* gives Parliament jurisdiction over "Marriage and Divorce" (that is, the substantive requirements of a valid marriage and grounds for divorce), and section 92(12) assigns power to the provinces over "Solemnization of Marriage" (that is, the procedure or manner in which marriages must take place). The provinces also have jurisdiction over division of family assets when relationships break down and over the adoption of children and child protection (based on their power over "Property and Civil Rights," noted above, and also "Matters of a merely local or private Nature," assigned by section 92(16)). Support obligations and child custody matters are areas of shared jurisdiction. Family law is not the only area where jurisdiction is split; labour and employment law, business and consumer law, creditors' remedies, and entertainment law are other examples.

Burden of Proof and Standard of Proof in Private Law Claims

Private (or civil) law disputes are like most other disputes in that the party making a claim has the burden of proving it. Therefore, the plaintiff (or defendant on a counterclaim) generally has the burden of proving the allegations supporting the cause of action. In a few situations, however, a presumption in favour of the claimant reverses the burden and requires the person defending to prove that something did *not* happen (see below in connection with the "trespass" torts for an example).

Private (or civil) law disputes can involve significant amounts of money and may have life-changing consequences for the litigants. However, being involved in a private law dispute is generally considered less of a social concern than being involved in a public law dispute (particularly a criminal matter). A criminal conviction, as we will see, has a moral stigma attached to it and can result in a loss of freedom (if the person found guilty is sentenced to a period of incarceration). This difference between private law and criminal law cases is reflected in the different standards of proof in these two types of cases. In civil claims, parties only need to prove their allegations on a balance of probabilities (that is, prove that they are more likely to be true than not). In criminal cases, on the other hand, the prosecution must adduce evidence proving that the person charged has committed the crime beyond a reasonable doubt (which requires a high degree of certainty). (See Chapter 10 for more on the burden of proof and standard of proof in criminal cases.)

Tort Law

Tort law is an area of private law that deals with certain types of wrongful conduct and the remedies available to those affected by that conduct. It covers a wide range of behaviours and is primarily concerned with providing a means of compensation (see Chapter 1 under the heading "Corrective Justice"). However, depending on the conduct in question, it can serve other purposes, such as deterrence and punishment. A **tort**, therefore, is a type of civil wrong for which the person wronged can obtain damages or some other remedy (the English word "tort" derives from the Latin *tortum*, meaning "something twisted" or "something crooked"). A **civil wrong** is a wrong defined by private law, which covers the relationships between persons.

Tort law is often seen as a "residuary" category within private law—in other words, a catch-all or miscellaneous category that includes all of those civil wrongs that are not covered by other areas of private law, such as contract law, property law, family law, or equity.

Modern tort law can be divided into four categories, based on the type of fault involved:

1. intentional torts,
2. negligence,
3. strict liability torts, and
4. a miscellaneous group of torts, with unique principles of liability.

These four categories, along with some of the more commonly litigated torts in each, are described below (space restrictions prevent a discussion of all torts).

Intentional Torts

The defendant's intentional behaviour characterizes intentional torts. The defendant's behaviour is intentional where she intended to bring about the consequences of her actions or at least knew they were likely to result. The intentional nature of the conduct makes these torts the most serious ones. In fact, many of the torts in this category are also crimes for which the defendant could be found criminally responsible.[2] These torts typically involve interferences with persons, their property, or purely economic interests.

Interferences with Persons or Property

With respect to interferences with persons or their property, the more common torts are trespass to person, trespass to land, and trespass to goods (or trespass to chattels).

Trespass-to-person actions are usually referred to by their more specific sub-tort names: assault, battery, and false imprisonment. **Assault** is a kind of psychological tort; it

---

tort
type of civil wrong for which damages can be obtained by the person wronged

civil wrong
wrong that occurs in the context of relationships between persons and is addressed by one of the areas of private law

trespass to person
intentional tort encompassing three subcategories of tort: assault, battery, and false imprisonment

assault
psychological tort involving one person's apprehension of harmful physical contact from another person

---

2   There have been many famous cases in Canada with both a criminal and a civil component—for example, cases involving on-ice violence in hockey, such as the Todd Bertuzzi and Steve Moore case (criminal assault and related civil action, which ended up settling out of court), and the Colonel Russell Williams case (murders, sexual assaults, and related civil actions). Usually, the criminal proceedings are completed first, before any civil actions move forward. This can be an advantage to the victim: if there is a conviction in the criminal case, the underlying facts can be taken as proven in the civil case. Even if there is an acquittal in the criminal case, most civil cases still proceed because the standard of proof the plaintiff must meet in such cases (balance of probabilities) is more easily met than the standard of proof that must be met in criminal ones (beyond a reasonable doubt).

does not require physical contact. If the plaintiff is threatened and believes that harmful physical contact from the defendant may occur (that is, apprehends harmful contact), and if the defendant has the means to carry out the threat in the near future, an assault has occurred. For example, threatening to hit, shoot, stab, or sexually interfere with someone is an assault if the victim believes the threat will soon materialize, even if the assailant stops short of physical contact.

Battery requires that harmful or offensive physical contact occur. Many trespass-to-person claims have both an assault and a battery component. For example, if a threat creates an apprehension of harm and then the threatened physical contact occurs, there has been an assault prior to contact and a battery once it occurs. Note also that, in criminal law, there is no distinction between assault and battery; both actions are covered by the crime of assault.[3]

battery
tort requiring actual occurrence of harmful or offensive physical contact

False imprisonment occurs when one person totally restrains the movement of another person. The defining element here is the presence of an enclosed boundary around the person being restrained so that there is no reasonable means of escape. The boundary can be physical (for example, a locked jail cell) or psychological (for example, someone with a gun telling another person not to move). This tort is sometimes referred to as "false arrest" in cases where a police officer or security guard is the person being sued. But false imprisonment and false arrest are, legally speaking, the same action. In both cases, the word "false" is a bit misleading. The plaintiff is not required to prove that his imprisonment was "false" (that is, unjustified), only that he was imprisoned. Once that is established, the onus is on the defendant to establish that the imprisonment was authorized. If the defendant is a police officer, this authority usually comes from a statutory power of arrest.

false imprisonment
tort whereby one person totally restrains the movement of another person

Trespass to land involves the physical intrusion by one person onto land occupied by another. This may take the form of a person entering another's land, or it may involve a person propelling an object onto another person's land. There are also criteria related to height and depth when determining whether trespass has occurred. Intruding on another person's airspace—that is, the space above that person's piece of land—up to a reasonably usable height (for example, by an overhanging sign) may qualify as a trespass. So may the intrusion on another person's subsoil down to a reasonably usable depth—for example, in a case where one person, to secure a structure on her own land, has inserted anchor rods into the plaintiff's land.

trespass to land
tort involving the physical intrusion by one person onto land occupied by another

Trespass to goods (or **trespass to chattels**) is a tort whereby one person intentionally interferes with another's possession of movable property, such as a motor vehicle (for example, by moving it).

These "trespass" torts all involve forms of direct interference, such as hitting, walking on, or moving. Actual damage is not a required element of these torts, although without actual damage any monetary award is likely to be small. In Canada, once the plaintiff proves the direct interference in question, fault on the part of the defendant is presumed, and it is up to the defendant to prove that he didn't intend the consequences (and that he wasn't otherwise at fault—for example, by being careless).

trespass to goods (or trespass to chattels)
tort whereby one person intentionally interferes with another's rightful possession of movable property

---

3 Wrongful sexual conduct is criminal conduct and may be prosecuted as a sexual assault under the *Criminal Code* (in other words, in the sphere of public law), but there are also a number of potential tort claims based on sexual wrongdoing. Such actions, however, are not based on a stand-alone tort; there is no tort known as "sexual wrongdoing." Rather, these actions are founded on established torts, such as assault, battery (often referred to in this context as "sexual battery"), or intentional infliction of nervous shock.

There are a number of other torts involving interferences with persons and property that do not necessarily involve direct interference. Common among these other torts are invasion of privacy (covering all manner of intrusions, such as surveillance, eavesdropping, and publishing private communications)[4] and intentional infliction of nervous shock, which involves the intentional infliction of mental suffering by one person on another (like assault, there is a psychological component to this tort, but it is extremely difficult to prove, requiring proof of socially offensive conduct by the defendant resulting in serious psychological injury to the plaintiff).

Interferences with Economic Interests

Common in this category are torts arising in business contexts. For example, the tort of deceit occurs when the defendant intentionally misleads the plaintiff into taking a course of action that results in damage to the plaintiff (such as might happen when the plaintiff invests in a doomed venture based on false information provided by the defendant, who knows the information is false).[5] Another example, passing off, occurs where the defendant "trades on" the plaintiff's superior goods or services (for example, by producing inferior, "knock-off" products that the defendant passes off as having been produced by the plaintiff, resulting in damage to the plaintiff through loss of market share and consumer goodwill).

Defences to Intentional Torts

There are many defences to intentional torts. The defences argued most frequently—consent, self-defence, and legal authority—typically arise in the context of intentional interferences with persons or property. *Consent* occurs where a claimant agrees to the interference in question. For example, inviting someone onto your land would negate your trespass-to-land claim. Consent can be given *expressly* (for example, in a written release) or *implicitly* (for example, by voluntarily participating in the activity). Consent issues often arise in cases involving medical procedures and sporting injuries.

Self-defence applies if the defendant can show that she committed the tort, such as assault or battery, to protect herself. Two important requirements in this case are that the defendant (1) honestly and reasonably believed that she was going to be attacked and (2) responded in a way that was reasonable in the circumstances. *Legal authority*, as a justification for committing a tort, is not one cohesive defence but a collection of defences based on various statutory rules, each of which allows for intentional interferences with persons or property in specified circumstances. The legislation generally provides that (1) there must be reasonable grounds for the interference (for example, because a crime was being or was about to be

---

4   Invasion of privacy and related claims are relatively new and developing common law torts. For example, in 2012, the Ontario Court of Appeal recognized a tort of intrusion upon seclusion, finding the defendant liable when she used her position at a bank to repeatedly look at the banking records of her spouse's ex-wife (*Jones v Tsige*, 2012 ONCA 32). This decision was followed in 2016 by the Ontario Superior Court of Justice when it found a defendant liable who had posted a sexually explicit video of his ex-girlfriend on a pornography website without her consent (*Doe 464533 v ND*, 2016 ONSC 541). Some provinces—British Columbia, Manitoba, Newfoundland and Labrador, and Saskatchewan—have bypassed the common law by enacting legislation clearly making invasion of privacy a tort: see *Privacy Act*, RSBC 1996, c 373; *The Privacy Act*, RSM 1987, c P125; *Privacy Act*, RSNL 1990, c P-22; and *The Privacy Act*, RSS 1978, c P-24.

5   Deceit claims are not confined to business contexts or even economic loss situations, however. For example, deliberately misleading a neighbour about how to use dangerous equipment could support a deceit claim if personal injury resulted.

committed), and (2) any force used must be reasonable (for example, a "punch" to temporarily disable a drunken aggressor as opposed to lethal force).

See also Box 7.1 for a discussion of lack of capacity to commit torts.

BOX 7.1

Capacity to Commit a Tort

"Lack of capacity" is sometimes raised as a defence in the case of intentional torts, usually on behalf of infants (that is, people under the age of majority) or mentally incompetent adults. Technically, capacity is a required element in all of the intentional torts. However, it is presumed that the defendant had the capacity to commit the tort in question unless the defendant challenges this presumption. There is no fixed age when children begin to be held responsible for intentionally inflicted injury; it depends on the intelligence and cognitive ability of the child in question. For both children and mentally incompetent adults, the key question is whether they have the mental ability to understand and appreciate the nature and consequences of their actions. If they do, then they have the capacity to be sued. A four-year-old child could potentially be held tortiously responsible for his actions. A similar approach to capacity applies to all areas of tort law, not just the intentional torts. See also the discussion of vicarious liability below under the heading "Strict Liability Torts" and in particular note 13 concerning the responsibility of parents for their children's tortious behaviour.

Negligence

The largest area of tort law is the law of negligence. It applies to almost every type of human activity, including motor vehicle accidents (the most commonly litigated area), excessive contact situations in sports, the manufacture of defective products, substandard construction, professional malpractice, careless words when giving advice (or negligent misrepresentation), and careless inspections of buildings and maintenance of highways by governments. It covers actions or *misfeasance* (for example, driving through a red light) and failing to act or *nonfeasance* (for example, failing to wear a seat belt) and provides compensation for many forms of injury, from personal and psychological injury to property damage to financial loss. Unlike intentional tortious behaviour, which is made up of numerous individual torts with their own names and special rules, the tort of negligence has one set of rules, developed by the courts, covering most instances of carelessly inflicted injury.

The word **negligence** can have at least two legal meanings. In its broadest sense, negligence refers to the tort itself, meaning the entire cause of action or claim in negligence, including all of its constituent elements (see below). In its narrowest sense, it refers to just one element in the claim, the standard of care—or, more specifically, to breach of the standard of care (a defendant who falls below the required standard of care for the activity in question is said to be "negligent," or careless in a legal sense).

negligence
area of tort law that addresses harm caused by carelessness, not intentional harm

Elements of a Negligence Claim

The elements of a basic negligence claim have been variously named, described, and numbered. There is still no consensus on terminology, although the courts in Canada today generally refer to the following five elements: (1) duty, (2) standard of care and breach, (3) factual causation, (4) legal causation, and (5) damages.

DUTY

In order for the law of negligence to apply, the law must first recognize that the defendant has an obligation or duty to take care to avoid injuring the plaintiff given the relationship between the parties and the activity in question.

Today, we take for granted the idea that we have a general obligation to be careful if others may be affected by our conduct, but it was not always this way. In the 1800s and early 1900s, the common law only recognized duties to be careful in limited circumstances, such as when the parties had a contractual relationship imposing such a duty. In 1932, in the famous case of *Donoghue v Stevenson*,[6] the House of Lords recognized for the first time that a manufacturer could owe a duty to a consumer, even though there was no contractual connection between them. Lord Atkin, who wrote one of the majority judgments in the case, also posited that the duty net could be cast wider to cover anyone who was a "neighbour," that is, any person whom the defendant could reasonably foresee would be affected by her acts or omissions.[7] However, it would be almost 50 years before the House of Lords would recognize Lord Atkin's neighbour principle generally, qualified, however, by the idea that policy considerations would play a role in the recognition of new duties (see *Anns v Merton London Borough Council*).[8]

In Canada, we have adopted and refined the neighbour principle.[9] If a plaintiff is trying to establish a new duty and a similar one has been recognized in the past, a court may simply extend the existing duty incrementally without referencing policy concerns. However, if the situation is unprecedented, the court will engage in a detailed two-stage analysis to determine whether to recognize a new duty (based on the *Anns* case). At the first stage, the court considers the "reasonable foreseeability of harm" arising from the defendant's conduct and the "proximity," or closeness, of the relationship between the parties. In examining proximity, the court looks at the nature of the relationship (in light of factors such as expectations, representations, and any property involved) to determine whether it would be just and fair, as a matter of broad policy, to impose a duty. If the harm is reasonably foreseeable, and the relationship is sufficiently close, then a *prima facie* ("at first sight") duty of care will arise. At the second stage, assuming that a *prima facie* duty of care has been established, the court considers any residual policy considerations supporting or militating against the recognition of such a new duty (for example, the new duty might have a deterrent effect on others and reduce accidents, or it might lead to indeterminate liability costs for defendants). If the policy considerations against the recognition of a new duty are of sufficient weight, the court will not extend the duty concept, and the plaintiff's claim will be denied.

See Box 7.2 for an example involving an alleged duty of care owed by a mother to her child for injuries caused to the child while the mother was pregnant.

---

6   [1932] AC 562 at 580, [1932] All ER 1 (HL).

7   See also the discussion of the neighbour principle in Chapter 1 under the heading "Law and Religion."

8   (1977), [1978] AC 728, [1977] 2 All ER 492 (HL). For a documentary about *Donoghue v Stevenson* and its significance—written by Mr Justice Martin Taylor and funded in part by the Law Foundation of British Columbia and the Law Foundation of Ontario—see *The Paisley Snail* (1995): <https://www .youtube.com/watch?v=ogm1URzhTjA>.

9   See, for example, *Cooper v Hobart*, 2001 SCC 79, and *Rankin (Rankin's Garage & Sales) v JJ*, 2018 SCC 19.

BOX 7.2

Does a Mother Owe a Duty to Her Unborn Child?

In *Dobson (Litigation Guardian of) v Dobson*,* the Supreme Court of Canada (SCC) dealt with a case involving a pregnant woman who was driving her vehicle carelessly when it collided with another vehicle. Her child was born with permanent mental and physical disabilities as a result of the prenatal injuries sustained in the accident.

There was no precedent for this, and the Court had to decide for the first time whether a mother owes a duty to her child with respect to her behaviour while pregnant. The Court had to consider the law's role in regulating the lifestyle choices of pregnant women. It was clear that injury is foreseeable if a pregnant woman drives without care and attention and that the relationship between mother and child is a close one. However, after weighing various policy considerations—in particular, the concern over imposing additional burdens on pregnant women and the possible psychological consequences

of liability for a new mother and the family—the Court concluded that imposing a duty on women in these circumstances was not appropriate.

Note that the child was suing his mother (through a representative) because she was covered by insurance. The insurance money would have been used to offset the extra expenses his disability brought to his upbringing. Courts do not generally consider the existence of insurance in making their decisions about liability.

*   [1999] 2 SCR 753, 1999 CanLII 698.

STANDARD OF CARE AND BREACH

Assuming that there is a duty, the question then arises as to whether the defendant has acted in accordance with that duty. This is the most frequently disputed element in negligence cases. Ordinarily, the test for standard of care is based on the following question: How would a reasonable person have acted in the circumstances? However, the test is modified for certain defendants (for example, professionals—whether doctors, lawyers, or engineers—are held to the same standard as reasonable professionals in the same field with the same specialization, and children are required to act as would other children of similar age, intelligence, and experience). To determine whether a defendant has fallen below this "reasonableness" standard, the court will consider all of the circumstances of the case, including factors such as the risk of injury inherent in the activity, the social benefits flowing from the activity, the extent to which others have acted similarly, and the existence of legislative rules governing the activity and whether they have been followed or ignored.

For example, in one famous case, the court had to consider whether a municipality was liable for injuries caused to one of its firefighters when a jack in the back of a fire truck rolled onto the firefighter while the truck was responding to a fire. The jack was needed for the fire but couldn't be properly secured on this particular truck, which was the only one available at the time. In weighing the risk of injury by deploying the truck with an improperly secured jack against the benefit of saving "life and limb" in responding to the fire, the court concluded that in all of the circumstances, the standard of care had not been breached (see *Watt v Hertfordshire County Council*).[10]

---

10   [1954] 2 All ER 368, [1954] 1 WLR 835 (CA).

FACTUAL CAUSATION

Often simply referred to as "causation," this element concerns whether the defendant's negligent conduct has caused the loss. Two tests are commonly used here: (1) the "but for" test, which asks whether there would have been no loss but for—that is, in the absence of—the defendant's conduct (or, framed another way, whether the defendant's conduct was necessary for the loss to occur), and (2) the "material contribution" test, which asks whether the defendant's conduct materially contributed to the loss (this test openly recognizes that there may be other contributing causes).

LEGAL CAUSATION

Because negligence liability concerns carelessness rather than intentional wrongdoing, the law places a limit on the extent of the defendant's liability, even when he has clearly caused the loss. For defendants to be liable, there must be a sufficiently close connection between their conduct and the loss. The question here is whether the defendant's conduct was a "proximate cause" of the loss; it concerns the conduct's remoteness—or, more precisely, lack of remoteness—as a causal factor in the loss. The test used to limit liability is the "reasonable foreseeability" test; a defendant is only responsible for losses that are a reasonably foreseeable consequence of his behaviour.

In 2008, the SCC had to decide whether a supplier of bottled water was responsible for a serious psychological illness suffered by a consumer who witnessed a dead fly in an unopened bottle of water. The SCC held that all of the elements of the negligence cause of action were met on these facts except legal causation. The injury in this case was too remote to be compensable; it was not reasonably foreseeable that a person of ordinary fortitude would suffer serious injury from seeing a dead fly in a bottle of water (see *Mustapha v Culligan of Canada Ltd*).[11]

DAMAGES

The plaintiff has to show that she has suffered, or will suffer, a loss or injury that the court recognizes as worthy of compensation, such as personal injury, serious psychological injury, property damage, or financial loss (for example, loss of earnings, cost of care, or investment loss). "Ordinary" inconvenience, stress, or aggravation resulting from a careless defendant's behaviour is not compensable.

Defences to a Negligence Claim

The three main defences to a claim of negligence are (1) contributory negligence, (2) consent, and (3) illegality. The onus is on the defendant to raise and prove these defences.

Contributory negligence applies in a case where the plaintiff has negligently contributed to his own losses. It is not a complete defence, however; where the court finds contributory negligence, it will apportion liability between the plaintiff and the defendant. Where it is not clear that one party is more at fault than the other (or others, if there are multiple defendants), the court will apportion liability equally. All provinces and Yukon have enacted legislation setting rules regarding apportionment of liability under this defence.

Consent and illegality are complete defences. This means that, if the court finds these defences applicable to the case, the plaintiff recovers nothing. *Consent* applies if, prior to engaging in the activity that led to injury (for example, skiing), the plaintiff consented to the

---

11   2008 SCC 27.

physical risks associated with it and expressly or implicitly agreed to give up the right to sue the defendant in the event of injury. Releases and exclusion clauses on the backs of tickets can be used as evidence of such an agreement. The defence of *illegality* has been severely restricted by the SCC recently. It may now only be used in very limited situations—for example, in a case where the plaintiff is trying to use the negligence action to avoid a criminal penalty (this might occur if the plaintiff was sentenced to pay a fine and sued the defendant, an accomplice in the crime, to help pay for the fine).

occupiers' liability
liability of occupiers of land for injuries that visitors sustain while on the occupiers' property

---

BOX 7.3

Occupiers' Liability: A Tort Related to Negligence

An area of liability closely related to negligence but with its own set of rules is **occupiers' liability**. It concerns the liability of occupiers of land for injuries that visitors (that is, entrants) sustain while on the property. At common law, the occupier's duty or obligation varies according to the type, or category, of entrant. For example, an occupier only has a duty to act with "common humanity" with respect to trespassers (an occupier would not be required generally to make her property safe for trespassers, but she would still not be permitted to set traps to seriously harm someone cutting across her front yard). On the other hand, if someone has been invited onto your property or is paying to be there, the duty increases considerably.

In most provinces, legislation has modified the common law concerning occupiers' liability, simplifying the rules. This legislation has abolished the formal categories of entrants and imposed one general statutory duty that can be adjusted to cover different circumstances. Typically, the new statutory duty requires occupiers to ensure that entrants and their property are reasonably safe "in all the circumstances of the case." Given that the duty is to take reasonable care in the circumstances, the level of care will vary depending on whether the visitor is a violent intruder, a friend over for dinner, or a customer at a store. (Saskatchewan, Newfoundland and Labrador, and the territories still apply the common law in this area, and New Brunswick has no specialized occupiers' liability rules and relies, for the most part, on basic negligence liability to regulate occupiers' liability disputes.)

The same defences apply to occupiers' liability (at common law and under legislation) as to negligence generally.

Strict Liability Torts

As we have seen, much of tort law is focused on the fault of the defendant. For intentional torts, the defendant must have intended to bring about the consequences of his actions. With the tort of negligence, it is necessary to prove that the defendant's conduct fell below a reasonable standard of care. However, some forms of tort liability are not based on either intention or negligence. Under certain conditions, a defendant can be held responsible even if the consequences of her tortious actions were not intended and even if she was not negligent. Such actions are known as **strict liability torts**. Strict liability torts in Canada most often involve the following three activities: (1) the use of dangerous substances, (2) the ownership of animals, and (3) the use of agents (vicarious liability).

Strict liability involving dangerous substances is based on the so-called "rule in *Rylands v Fletcher*."[12] The rule here is that a person who brings a dangerous substance onto his property (or uses a substance that is not ordinarily dangerous in a dangerous way) is answerable for the damage it causes if it should escape. The property owner's strict

strict liability tort
tort for which the defendant is held responsible even if the damaging action was neither intentional nor a result of negligence

---

12   (1868), LR 3 HL 330.

liability under *Rylands v Fletcher* is subject to two conditions: (1) the substance brought onto the defendant's land must escape to a neighbouring property and cause property damage or personal injury there, and (2) the use of the substance must be a non-natural use—meaning that it is unusual, extraordinary, or unsuitable and that it increases the risk of danger to others. For example, if a person brought explosives onto her residential property and they exploded, causing damage to her neighbour, she would be strictly liable for her neighbour's losses. Possible defences to *Rylands v Fletcher* claims include that the plaintiff consented to the use of the substance by the neighbour and that the escape was caused by an "act of God" (an unforeseeable natural disaster, such as a violent storm).

Strict liability principles can also apply to owners of animals. Unlike dangerous substances, strict liability for damage caused by animals, whether they are wild or domestic, is generally not predicated on their escape from the defendant's property. Wild animals (for example, bears, lions, chimpanzees, and alligators) are always presumed to be dangerous, and their owners are strictly liable for the damage they cause. When domestic animals cause injury or damage, liability is strict only if (1) the animal had previously manifested a vicious or mischievous propensity to cause injury of a particular type and (2) the owner knew of this propensity. For example, a dog owner who knows his dog has attacked other people before would be strictly liable for future attacks. Consent can be a defence, however, such as where the plaintiff entered the defendant's property without permission and despite a "Beware of Dog" sign.

vicarious liability
the strict liability of one party for the fault of another due to the special relationship between them (typically, an employer–employee relationship)

The last main type of strict liability tort is the kind involving **vicarious liability**, and it is an important one. Vicarious liability involves the liability of one party for the fault of another due to the special relationship between them. A relationship of this kind exists, for example, between a car owner and the people who drive the owner's car with her permission. When such people commit a tort in the course of driving the owner's car, the owner is generally held vicariously responsible under provincial and territorial motor vehicle legislation. With respect to employment relationships, employers will be vicariously liable based on the common law if the person committing the tort truly is an employee (that is, if an employer–employee relationship, as opposed to a business–contractor relationship, exists) and the tort is committed while the employee is working (employers are not responsible for torts committed by their employees on the employees' own time).[13]

Miscellaneous Torts

Two important torts that do not fit neatly into the three categories discussed above (intentional torts, negligence torts, and strict liability torts) are nuisance and defamation. These torts have their own special rules. Arguably, they could both be considered forms of strict liability torts because the focus in assessing them, as with strict liability torts, is on the effect of the defendant's actions on others, not on whether the defendant intentionally or negligently brought about the damaging consequences.

---

13 Note that parents are generally not vicariously liable for torts committed by their children. Parents can be found primarily responsible in negligence, however, if a person is injured as a result of the parents' failure to properly supervise their children. A few provinces (for example, British Columbia, Manitoba, and Ontario) have enacted legislation making it easier to hold parents responsible for their children's actions in certain situations.

Nuisance

In law, **nuisance** can be one of two kinds: public nuisance or private nuisance. A **public nuisance** occurs when a public interest is interfered with, such as when a highway is obstructed or a river is polluted through the defendant's actions. Generally, it is up to the government to seek redress for public nuisances; private citizens can sue for public nuisances only if they have suffered "special" damage that distinguishes them from the public at large.

A **private nuisance** occurs when the defendant has interfered with a person's reasonable use and enjoyment of his land. Trespass and/or physical damage may be involved—for example, where the defendant neighbour's felled tree lands on the plaintiff's house. But neither trespass nor physical injury is required. Interferences may involve foul odours or loud noises.

Possible defences to both public and private nuisances include consent to the activity causing the nuisance by the plaintiff and legislative authority (municipalities, for example, are protected by legislation in most provinces and territories from being sued in nuisance by citizens for damages caused by blocked storm drains and sewers).

Defamation

Defamation is concerned with published allegations of impropriety (for example, wrongdoing, misconduct, corruption) that injure a person's reputation. The word "published," in this context, simply means "communicated to others"; it doesn't necessarily mean that these allegations have appeared in print (see Box 7.4 and the question of whether hyperlinking is publishing). The rules relating to defamation attempt to balance individual rights with broader rights relating to free speech and access to information. The two main types of defamation are **libel** and **slander**. Libel deals with defamatory language that is written—for example, in a newspaper article or a book, whether in print or online. Slander deals with oral communications and other transitory kinds of communications (for example, looks or gestures). The common law considers libel a more serious form of defamation than slander; it doesn't require proof of damage for libel, but it does, in most cases, for slander.[14]

A number of defences can be raised in defamation actions. "Truth" is a defence and is also referred to as "justification." However, simply believing the information is true, or repeating what others have said, is not enough; the information must, in fact, be true (that is why, especially for publishers, it is important that sources be checked). Other defences include privilege and responsible journalism. These defences apply even if the statements are untrue. "Privilege" can apply in a variety of situations: for example, statements by high-ranking government officials made in the course of official duties are always protected, and statements by defendants trying to protect their own interests or those of third parties are also protected (provided that no malice is involved). "Responsible journalism" (more accurately named "responsible communication on matters of public interest") is available as a defence to any person who reports responsibly (by diligently trying to verify sources) on matters of public interest, which can include anything that invites public attention, affects public welfare, or concerns matters of notoriety or controversy.

---

14 The distinction between libel and slander has been abolished in some provinces—Alberta, Manitoba, New Brunswick, Newfoundland and Labrador, Nova Scotia, and Prince Edward Island—and in the territories. In these jurisdictions, libel and slander are treated equally, and damage is presumed or not required to support an action for either.

nuisance
in law, either public or private nuisance

public nuisance
occurs when a public interest is interfered with—for example, when a highway is obstructed or a river is polluted through the defendant's actions

private nuisance
tort that involves one person's using her property in such a way as to substantially interfere with another person's enjoyment or use of his property, but without any actual trespass occurring

defamation
tort involving allegations of impropriety that injure a person's reputation

libel
kind of defamation that involves defamatory language in writing, such as in a newspaper article or book, whether in print or online

slander
kind of defamation transmitted via oral or other transitory forms of communication

BOX 7.4

Hyperlinking and Defamation

In *Crookes v Newton,** new information practices ran up against old law. The SCC had to determine whether placing a link to a defamatory article on a website was the same as reproducing the article on the website. In other words, was the website owner liable for defamation? Newspapers and other publishers are responsible for checking the accuracy of the information they publish and print. Are website owners similarly responsible if they provide a hyperlink to defamatory material?

The plaintiff, Crookes, owned a business and commenced a number of lawsuits against various persons, including Newton, who he felt had defamed him. Crookes claimed to be the victim of a smear campaign. Newton owned a website that contained commentary on political matters, including free speech, and that included a hyperlink to another site that allegedly contained information that was defamatory of Crookes.

The narrow issue in this case was whether hyperlinking is publishing. A majority of the SCC concluded that it was not. They concluded that placing the burden of defamation lawsuits on website owners who had done no more than link to other sites that were defamatory would unduly restrict the free flow of information on the Internet. There was nothing on Newton's site itself that was defamatory. A site's providing a link to a second site is not the same thing as the first site's publishing that information itself, and the victim of defamation can always go after the owner of the site that contains the defamatory words.

*   2011 SCC 47.

Tort Remedies

Among the remedies available to victims of torts are (1) damages, (2) injunctions, and (3) extrajudicial remedies.

The remedy claimed most often is damages. Damages can be classified in different ways. One approach is to classify them according to the purpose the award serves. Based on this approach, the two most important types of damages are compensatory damages and punitive damages.

Compensatory damages compensate the plaintiff for proven and recognized types of losses. Sometimes the losses are easy to quantify—for example, where there have been out-of-pocket expenses necessitated by the tort, and receipts can be entered into evidence (these are often referred to as "special damages"). In other cases, the calculation is less exact—for example, where the court is attempting to compensate the plaintiff for pain and suffering or for future lost earnings (these are called "general damages").

Punitive damages are granted in situations where the court wishes to punish the defendant for socially objectionable behaviour. Such damage awards are, in a sense, a windfall to the plaintiff because they are over and above any amount needed for compensation. Usually, intentional torts result in this kind of award. In extreme cases of negligence and defamation, however, punitive damages have been awarded.

After damages, the next most important remedy for tort victims is the injunction. Injunctive relief is most commonly prohibitory (that is, it takes the form of an order to stop doing something—for example, to stop making loud noises or foul smells). Nuisance claims, more than any other, include requests for injunctions.

Finally, extrajudicial remedies may be an option. However, they are rare and available only in limited circumstances. Two examples of extrajudicial remedies are *abatement of nuisance* and *recapture of goods*. The abatement remedy allows the claimant to bring an end to the nuisance herself, without waiting to go to court. For example, this remedy could allow a claimant to cut down a branch from a neighbour's tree if the branch is overhanging the claimant's property. The remedy of recapture allows an aggrieved person to recover goods that have been wrongfully removed or withheld provided that the person acts reasonably in doing so (and without violence or breaking and entering). The exact limits of these remedies are not clear, and they should only be exercised with caution, if possible after seeking legal advice.

Contract Law

Contract law is a special area of the law. It empowers us to enter into agreements with others and to create legal relationships based on our own set of rules. For the most part, we are free to choose these rules. This makes contract law different from many other areas of the law—for example, torts and criminal law—where the rules are imposed upon us by the common law or by legislation.

Freedom of contract has its limits, however. These limits have to do with accepted community standards. For example, many types of contracts or contractual terms are subject to judge-made or statutory rules dealing with illegality, human rights, employment standards, business practices, and consumer protection. These contracts or terms will be unenforceable if they do not follow those rules.

Pervasiveness of Contracts

Contracts are everywhere. Most of us enter into multiple contractual arrangements every day, without realizing it. We enter into contracts when we purchase gasoline for our vehicles (contract with a gasoline retailer), take public transit or hire a taxi (common-carrier contracts), or purchase food for immediate consumption (contract with a fast-food business). Then there are our contracts for non-food items (for example, clothing); for personal services (for example, haircuts) and home services (for example, cable and Internet access); and for entertainment (for example, movie rentals or tickets to sporting events). The list is long.

Even when we're not making new contracts, we're living by the terms of old ones: meeting our continuing service obligations (for example, making monthly payments on a gym membership) and requiring that the goods we purchase meet the contractual terms concerning their fitness for their stated purpose. If your new condominium begins to leak soon after you purchase it, you may have a claim in contract against the developer who sold it to you. If your smoke alarm fails to sound during a fire, you may have a contract claim against the home supply store that sold it to you. These are just a few examples.

Elements of a Valid Contract

As with the tort of negligence, there is no firmly established list of or nomenclature for the elements of a valid contract, at least beyond the first three. There is, however, some degree of consensus that up to six elements may be required: (1) offer, (2) acceptance, (3) consideration, (4) certainty of terms, (5) intention to contract, and, in some cases, (6) formal requirements. Figure 7.1 summarizes the components of an enforceable contract. As in tort law, capacity (here, capacity to contract) is a required element but is presumed unless the defendant raises the issue. Because it is presumed, it is not usually listed as an element, and a lack of capacity is treated as a type of defence (see "Excuses That Protect Weaker Parties" later in this section).

FIGURE 7.1   **Summary of Contract Elements**

1 + 2	+	3	+	4	+	5	+	6
A mutual agreement—offer and acceptance		Consideration—the exchange of something of value		Certainty—important terms expressed with sufficient clarity		Intention to contract—parties intend to create a legal relationship		Compliance with formalities—required for certain kinds of contracts

Offer

An offer is a statement by one person (offeror) to another (offeree) indicating a willingness to commit to a binding arrangement. If a reasonable person would think—considering what was said and done and the surrounding circumstances—that the offeror intended to be bound by the terms of the proposal should it be accepted, then a court would conclude that an offer has been made. Precise words are not required, and for most contracts, offers can be made either orally; in writing (for example, by letter or brochure, by posting a reward notice, or by means of a newspaper advertisement); electronically (for example, by email, by fax, or on a website); by conduct with no words at all (for example, by gesture or by providing a service); or through a combination of these methods.

Offers can be revoked (taken back) at any time prior to acceptance.

Acceptance

Acceptance is the signification by the offeree of his willingness to enter into an agreement with the offeror. The test for whether an acceptance has been made is whether the offeree has absolutely and unequivocally agreed with the terms of the offer. If there is any change to the material terms of the offer (in the offeree's response), such as when a counteroffer is made, this "kills" the original offer. In this situation, for a contract to be formed, the parties must continue negotiating until one party's offer is fully and clearly accepted by the other. As with offers, precise words are not required for an acceptance to be valid, and for most contracts, acceptances can be communicated orally, in writing, electronically, or by the offeree's conduct.

Generally, acceptance must be communicated to the offeror before it is binding. However, this is not always required. For example, if it is reasonable to use regular mail to accept an offer, acceptance may be binding as soon as a letter is mailed. Or, if the offeror requests performance of a stipulated service or action as a means of acceptance—such as when offering payment for a home improvement service—then the contract may be binding as soon as performance is complete (whether or not the offeror knows about it). After acceptance, a contract is formed (assuming that all other elements are present), and the parties are bound; at this point, it is too late for the parties to withdraw.

Consideration

At common law, contracts require an exchange, or a bargain. Consideration is something of value given by one party (for example, a purchaser who agrees to pay for land) in return for the promise or obligation of the other party (for example, a seller who has promised to sell the land). Consideration is crucial to making the contract binding.

A contractual promise must be supported by a requested consideration coming from the other party (promisee), which is a benefit to the promisor (for example, a promise to sell something could be supported by payment or a reciprocal promise to pay) and/or a loss to the promisee (using the same example, the loss of the purchase moneys by the purchaser/promisee to obtain what is being sold). However, if one party promises to "sell" something for nothing (or close to nothing, such as selling a $1,000,000 house for $10), the promise would not be contractually enforceable. The promisor would not be receiving any real benefit from the promisee in exchange for the promise, and neither would the promisee be suffering any real loss. In this situation, the promise to sell is not supported by consideration.

Certainty of Terms

If important terms—for example, those relating to the price or nature of the property or service in question—are so vaguely expressed or uncertain in the contract that the court cannot ascribe any reasonable meaning to them, then the contract will be struck down as void on the grounds of uncertainty. The same applies if important terms are omitted altogether or if they are left open to be negotiated at a later date. However, if the uncertainty relates to less important terms—such as times and places of delivery—the court will usually imply terms based on what is reasonable in the circumstances, and the contract will still be binding.

Intention to Contract

For a contract to be valid, the parties must intend to be legally bound by the terms of their arrangement.

In commercial settings, it is presumed that the parties did intend a legally binding relationship. This presumption can be rebutted by clear language to the contrary if the parties want the arrangement to be in "honour" only and not binding.

In family and social settings, it is presumed that the parties did *not* intend a legally binding relationship. (This presumption, too, can be rebutted by clear language to the contrary.) This presumption does not apply in the case of marriage contracts and separation agreements, where the intention is always to bind.

Formal Requirements

All provinces and territories have legislation requiring certain kinds of contracts, such as land contracts or specific types of consumer contracts (for example, direct sales contracts—contracts entered into away from a seller's regular place of business), to be in writing and to contain certain information. The legislation in this area can be complicated and must be read carefully to determine the precise requirements, any exceptions, and the consequences of failing to meet specific requirements.

Duties of Good Faith and Honesty

Our economic system favours open competition and freedom of contract. Adhering to these principles, it is argued, promotes a healthy economy. A consequence of this approach has been that although parties are subject to the terms of their bargain, they have not, as a general rule, been subject to duties of good faith and honesty in their dealings with each other, either during negotiations or contract performance.

This was only a general rule, however, and there were and continue to be exceptions (for example, if the parties are in a fiduciary relationship,[15] they will be subject to duties of good faith and honesty). In many cases, however, the dishonest behaviour in question does not fall within an exception, with the result that the aggrieved party has no remedy.

In 2014, in *Bhasin v Hrynew*,[16] the SCC decided that this was no longer acceptable. The plaintiff in *Bhasin* was an investment dealer who had a contract with a financial corporation, Can-Am, to sell its educational savings plans (ESPs). Can-Am misled Bhasin in a number of respects concerning its plans to renew Bhasin's dealership contract. In the end, his contract was not renewed, and he lost his business selling Can-Am's ESPs. He was forced to take less profitable work elsewhere. The SCC held that the time had come to recognize a general organizing principle in contract law based on good faith and specifically to require parties to be honest with one other. The Court found that Can-Am had breached the newly recognized duty of honest performance, and Bhasin was awarded damages.

It has been suggested that this decision will have a significant impact on business practices. Time will tell if this is true and how exactly a broadly enforceable requirement of honesty will change behaviour. At a minimum, parties will not be able to deliberately mislead each other. Canada is not the first country to adopt such a principle in business dealings (although it is the first whose top court has led the way). The United States, Australia, and New Zealand also recognize a similar approach.

Individually Negotiated Contracts and Standard Form Contracts

Contracts can be structured in different ways and come in different forms. For example, most contracts can be oral, written (hard copy), or electronic (see Box 7.5). Two important types of contract are those that are individually negotiated and those that are based on a standard form.[17]

Individually negotiated contracts are tailored to the specific circumstances of a situation. They are time-consuming to draft and tend to be used when the transaction is specialized or unique (for example, a contract for the development of a new sports arena or for the creation of a work of art).

Standard form contracts, on the other hand, tend to be used for predictable, uniform, common transactions—situations where individual negotiation would be impractical. Examples of standard form contracts include the tickets you receive when using public transit or going to movies. More complex transactions—such as banking, insurance, real estate purchases, and car rental agreements—can also involve standard form contracts. Most written contracts are standard form contracts.

---

15 A fiduciary relationship is based on trust and confidence. When the law recognizes that such a relationship exists between the parties, it requires the fiduciary—that is, the party with whom trust has been placed—to act in the best interests of the party placing that trust. General obligations of honesty and good faith between the parties are also imposed. Examples of fiduciary relationships include trustees and beneficiaries, principals and agents, lawyers and clients, and guardians and wards.

16 2014 SCC 71.

17 There are many other contract structures and forms, but an examination of them all is beyond the scope of this introduction.

Electronic Contracts and E-Commerce

Contracts can be formed by means of electronic media. As mentioned, offers and acceptances can be made electronically through, for example, faxes, emails, text messages, website forms, or combinations of these methods. Virtually any contract, regardless of its subject matter, can be electronic (subject to a few exceptions, such as real estate contracts).

All Canadian jurisdictions have legislation providing that contracts may be made by electronic means and that clicking on computer icons, touching computer screens, and even speaking to computers are effective means of communicating contractual intentions.* This legislation is modelled on a law for electronic transactions adopted in 1996 by the United Nations Commission on International Trade Law (UNCITRAL), supplemented by further work on the law by the Uniform Law Conference of Canada, a body dedicated to the harmonization of provincial and territorial laws (and federal laws where appropriate).

Various terms are gaining acceptance to describe the precise method by which e-contracts are entered into, such as "shrink-wrap," "click-wrap," and "browse-wrap" agreements:

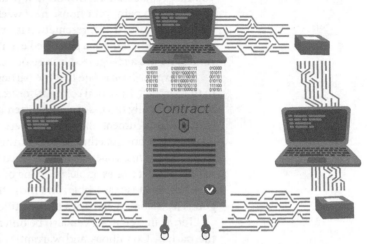

- A *shrink-wrap agreement* usually relates to software and gets its name from the fact that some software is sold in a box enclosed in shrink wrap. But when the software is loaded, often from a CD or DVD, a further agreement presents itself on the computer, this time between the software creator and the user as opposed to the retailer and the user. Such agreements are usually licences restricting the user's ability to copy the software.
- A *click-wrap agreement* refers to a purchase contract made over the Internet, including but not restricted to software purchases. It gets its name from the fact that the user of the website is required to read an online contract and click an "I agree" icon or something similar.
- A *browse-wrap agreement*, like a click-wrap agreement, refers to Internet purchases. It is distinguished by the fact that the user indicates assent or agreement simply by using the product after having been made aware of the product's terms of use.†

E-commerce is responsible for a larger percentage of overall consumer sales each year and by some estimates now accounts for 50 percent of such sales. Moreover, decisions about 80 percent of all purchases, whether or not they are made online, are influenced by online research. M-commerce, which refers to purchases using mobile communication devices such as cellphones, although still a relatively small segment of total e-commerce, has been identified as a rapidly growing area.

* For example, see Ontario's *Electronic Commerce Act, 2000*, SO 2000, c 17, and British Columbia's *Electronic Transactions Act*, SBC 2001, c 10.

† For a discussion of these kinds of agreements, see *Century 21 Canada Limited Partnership v Rogers Communications Inc*, 2011 BCSC 1196.

Contract Terms and Terminology

There are many different types or categories of contract terms. Some of the more significant ones are (1) representations and promises, (2) express and implied terms, (3) conditions and warranties, (4) conditions precedent, and (5) exclusion clauses. The specific content of these various types of terms will vary from contract to contract.

Terms in contracts can be simple *representations* of fact (for example, "This car I'm selling you has 100,000 kilometres on it"), or they can be in the form of *promises* (for example, "I promise to paint your house next week"). With respect to liability, there is no difference between the two. If a representation is untrue, the party who made it can be sued for breach of contract. Similarly, if a promised event does not come to pass, the promisor will be liable (unless he has a recognized excuse or defence).

An *express term* is one that the parties have put their minds to and deliberately included in the contract. In an oral contract, for example, an express term is something that the parties have specifically discussed. In a written contract, an express term will be spelled out in the text of the document. *Implied terms* are terms that the parties have not expressed in their contract but are nonetheless part of the deal. There are various subcategories of implied terms, but the main ones are those implied because they are necessary to give "business efficacy" to the contract (for example, implying omitted details concerning times or places of delivery based on what is reasonable) and those that are required by law (for example, where sale of goods legislation mandates a form of title assurance on the part of the seller).

Terms in a contract can also be differentiated according to their level of importance to the parties. Conditions and warranties are two such terms. A *condition*, in this context, means an important contract term—for example, payment of the purchase price or delivery of the promised goods. A *warranty* is a less significant term, such as one relating to the inclusion of some inexpensive furnishings in the sale of a building. The available remedies vary according to the type of term involved. All that an innocent party can recover for a breach of warranty is damages (see below under the heading "Contract Remedies"). But in the event that a condition is not met, the innocent party can not only sue for damages but can also terminate the contract if she so chooses.

A *condition precedent* is a special kind of term that delays the performance of a contract (or, in some cases, the formation of the contract in the first place) until a defined event occurs. A "subject to financing" clause in a home purchase contract is an example of a condition precedent; until financing is obtained by the purchaser, the contract will not move forward. If no financing is obtained by the set deadline, the contract simply fizzles out before it begins. An agreement with a condition precedent is a "contingent" agreement.

Exclusion clauses can be found in all kinds of contracts but are often associated with standard form contracts. They typically limit the liability of one of the parties either to a fixed dollar amount or—for certain types of breaches—altogether. For example, a ski-hill ticket may limit the liability of the resort operator for any injuries the patron sustains while on the ski hill, even if these injuries are caused by the operator's negligence in grooming or marking the runs.[18] Exclusion clauses are important, particularly for businesses, because they allow the parties to the contract to manage their risks and insure accordingly.

Many different words are used to describe contract terms in a general sense—words such as "term," "clause," "representation," "provision," "stipulation," and "rider." Sometimes, however, these words can have other, more specific meanings, and close attention to context

---

18   There are other types of clauses that are related to exclusion clauses, such as forum selection clauses, choice of law clauses, and arbitration clauses. Instead of limiting liability, these clauses limit the manner in which one party may pursue a claim against the other; they are often used by large corporations providing a product or a service. A *forum selection clause* determines where disputes will be heard. A *choice of law clause* requires that the law from a particular jurisdiction be used to resolve claims under the contract. Often forum selection and choice of law clauses are combined and require customers residing in other jurisdictions to come to the seller's jurisdiction to pursue their claims. *Arbitration clauses* provide that disputes between the parties must be pursued using an arbitrator (an impartial third party). Resolution through arbitration is generally faster and less expensive than the regular court process. Arbitration and other forms of alternative dispute resolution are described in Chapter 12.

is required. For example, the words "warranty" and "condition" can refer to contract terms generically, but they can also have a more technical meaning, referring to the level of importance of a term, as just described (and "warranty" can refer as well to a guarantee of quality or performance—for example, by a manufacturer).

Excuses for Non-Performance of Contracts

After a contract has been entered into, problems may occur, information may come to light, or new circumstances may arise that make the agreement unfair or even impossible to fulfill as originally made. With contracts, we talk not of "defences" but of "excuses" for not having to perform our contractual obligations. In a sense, the right of an innocent party to walk away from a contract without liability is a type of remedy (remedies against a guilty party are examined below). The more common excuses are described next.

Serious Breach of Contract

As noted above, terms can be classified according to their relative importance to the parties. Obligations concerning payment and delivery of the subject matter of the contract, for example, are usually interpreted to be conditions of further performance. If a condition is breached, the innocent party will have the option of lawfully repudiating (or terminating) the contract and of being relieved of the obligation of further performance on his part.

Misrepresentation

During the course of negotiations, one party may falsely represent a fact relating to the contract—for example, stating that a house for sale has just had a new roof put on it when, in fact, it hasn't. Even if the representation has not been made a term of the contract, it can still be legally significant. A false statement of this nature is called a **misrepresentation**, and if it is material—that is, significant enough to induce a reasonable person to enter into a contract she otherwise would not have—then it may provide an excuse for terminating the contract. In cases of misrepresentation, the contract can be set aside using a special equitable remedy called "rescission." This remedy allows the court to order the return of money and property acquired under the contract and to make other adjustments in the interest of fairness. Rescission is also available to remedy other defects in the formation of the contract.

misrepresentation
false representation made during contract negotiations

Mistake and Frustration

Mistake and frustration are also excuses for not performing. The law of *mistake* in contractual settings is complex and not always consistently applied by the courts. Two relatively clear instances of mistake occur (1) where the parties are confused about the terms they have agreed to (for example, where the terminology used in the contract is ambiguous and capable of multiple meanings) and (2) where both parties have made a mistaken assumption about some fundamental or essential matter underlying the contract (for example, in a construction contract where the parties assumed that the land was zoned for the project in question when it wasn't). In both situations, once the mistake is discovered, it may provide an excuse for discontinuing further performance.

Frustration, as an excuse for non-performance of a contract, is similar to the mistaken assumption excuse, but the timing involved is different. In the case of mistake, the problem exists at the time of the contract. With frustration, the problem develops after the contract has been entered into and during performance, and it comes about because of a change in circumstances. The changed circumstances must be significant enough to make continued performance impossible or at least to change the fundamental nature of the agreement. Consider the zoning example again. If a construction contract is based on existing zoning, and the municipality, during performance, changes the zoning rules so as to make it impossible to complete the contract, the contract may become frustrated, thereby excusing the parties from further performance. Another example involves the COVID-19 pandemic. Hundreds of thousands of contracts in Canada (and around the world) became frustrated because of illness and state-enforced physical distancing rules. The question of who is responsible for any losses incurred up to the point when a contract becomes frustrated is not always clear under the law and varies somewhat across jurisdictions in Canada (the applicable common law and legislative rules can be complicated).

Excuses That Protect Weaker Parties

Some excuses for non-performance of a contract are intended to protect weaker parties. The main excuses of this type are duress, undue influence, unconscionability, and incapacity.

Duress applies when one of the parties entered into the agreement against his will. It is a common law doctrine and does not apply unless the will of the victim is taken away. If someone holds a gun to your head to make you sign a contract, the agreement can be set aside. Generally, there has to be a threat of physical violence for duress to apply.

Undue influence can be thought of as "duress light." Undue influence is an equitable doctrine, meaning that it was developed by courts exercising their equitable jurisdiction. It qualifies as an excuse for non-performance of a contract when one party has unfairly pressured another (weaker) party to enter into the contract; unfair pressure will be presumed in the case of certain "special relationships," such as doctor–patient or lawyer–client relationships. This influence may fall short of depriving the weaker party of her will.

Unconscionability, like undue influence, is an equitable doctrine; it applies where there is a power imbalance between the two parties. The difference is that unconscionability doesn't necessarily involve the application of actual or presumed pressure. As an excuse for non-performance of a contract, it applies when one party takes advantage of another. To establish it, two elements are required: (1) inequality of bargaining power (such as might exist between a younger, mentally fit person and a seriously ill or mentally incompetent older relative) and (2) an unfair bargain (meaning that the stronger party obtains property or some other benefit for less than its fair market value by taking advantage of the weaker party).

Incapacity may also be raised as an excuse by weaker parties. Technically, capacity to contract is a required element of a valid contract. In contract law as in tort law, capacity is presumed; the onus is on the party seeking to escape responsibility to prove a lack of capacity (see Box 7.1). Almost every person has the capacity to contract; the two main exceptions today are infants and individuals who are mentally incompetent. An infant is someone under the age of majority (fixed by legislation in all provinces and territories at either 18 or 19). However, although they lack capacity generally, infants have a limited capacity to enter into certain kinds of contracts, such as contracts for necessities (such as food and clothing) and for student loans. Incapacity based on mental incompetence applies where one party's mental incapacity prevents him from appreciating the nature of the contract in question (the incapacity may be permanent, because of a mental disability, or temporary, usually because of impairment by drugs or alcohol). Apparently, although the case law is uncertain in this respect, one party's mental incompetence qualifies as an excuse for his non-performance only if the other party is aware of it.

Illegality

Finally, contracts that are contrary to public policy at common law or are illegal under legislation may be unenforceable. In such cases, the parties have an excuse for not adhering to the agreed-to terms. For example, contracts to commit criminal or tortious acts are contrary to public policy and are not enforceable; parties may, in fact, face criminal charges for such agreements.

Contracts with restraint-of-trade provisions generate the most litigation on the grounds of illegality. Non-competition arrangements in contracts of employment often include these kinds of provisions, whose purpose is to prevent employees from competing against their former employers. Restraint-of-trade provisions are also included in contracts for the sale of businesses; they are intended to prevent former business owners (the sellers) from competing with the purchasers. The courts will strike down such provisions and sometimes the whole contract if the restraint-of-trade provision is unreasonably restrictive, especially with respect to its duration and the geographic area it is supposed to cover.

Other kinds of contracts that may prove unenforceable owing to illegality include contracts for unregulated medical services, surrogacy contracts, contracts with a sexual services component, and gaming and wagering contracts (these kinds of contracts are generally illegal under insurance legislation, although specific exceptions apply to government-sanctioned gambling).

Contract Remedies

Remedies are available for breach of contract, misrepresentations, and other problems connected to contractual formation or performance. Rights of non-performance for an innocent party were discussed above. The main remedies that may be pursued against a defendant[19] are damages, specific performance, and injunctive relief.

Damages

As in tort law, the most important remedy in contract law is damages. Contract damages are classified differently, however. The three main categories in contract law are (1) expectation damages, (2) reliance damages, and (3) restitution damages. Punitive damages may also be available, but only in unusual cases.

Expectation damages attempt to place the innocent party in the position she would have been in if the contract had been performed as promised and all of the contractual representations were true. This method of assessing damages is the standard method used to calculate damages in contract disputes. Expectation damages typically claimed include out-of-pocket expenses to correct defective performance (for example, where construction work is shoddy and has to be fixed) and loss of profits (for example, where a commodity was not delivered, and the purchaser was unable to resell it for a profit as planned).

Expectation damages sometimes have alternate names depending on what they represent or how they are calculated. For example, out-of-pocket expenses can also be called "special damages" because they have already been incurred and are certain. The term "general damages" can be used to describe the value of a lost expectation that is not specifically quantifiable,

expectation damages remedy for contract disputes that attempts to place the innocent party in the position she would have been in if the contract had been performed as promised and all of the contractual representations had been true

---

19   Generally, only parties to a contract acquire rights or incur obligations under it. This is known as the "privity rule." Privity of contract—that is, being a party to it—is generally required to maintain an action for damages or other remedy. Some exceptions apply, however, in the case of "third-party beneficiaries." A third-party beneficiary is someone mentioned in the contract who benefits in some way from it.

such as the enjoyment the plaintiff hoped to experience on a vacation (where a vacation planner failed to deliver as promised). "Liquidated damages," which are another type of expectation claim, refer to damages that the parties have calculated in advance. They can only be claimed, however, where the parties have put a clause in the contract setting out what the damages are to be and where the amount represents a genuine pre-estimate of the loss expected to be suffered in the event of breach. Liquidated damages clauses can save the parties the trouble of arguing about what the damages are if the contract is broken.

Reliance and restitution damages can be claimed as alternatives to expectation damages in cases where there is no expectation of loss or it can't be proved. **Reliance damages** are intended to cover expenses incurred in preparing for contractual obligations (for example, the cost of special materials purchased by a building contractor that become wasted when the other party cancels the contract). **Restitution damages** generally cover moneys—deposits and part payments, for example—that the innocent party paid over to the other party. By recovering such expenses and moneys paid, the innocent party at least breaks even and doesn't suffer a loss as a result of the other party's breach.

A party may be able to claim punitive damages in addition to either expectation, reliance, or restitution damages. As in tort claims, punitive damages are designed to punish the defendant for socially objectionable behaviour (however, this is difficult to show in most breach of contract situations). Again, they represent a windfall to the plaintiff because they are over and above what is needed for compensation.

Lastly, mitigation of damages, causation, and remoteness of damages issues can arise in some contract damage claims. Innocent parties to a breach of contract have an obligation to take reasonable steps to mitigate (or minimize) their losses. For example, a business that is losing profits because a supplier fails to deliver contracted goods may be required to find replacement goods if it would be reasonable to do so—losses that can be reasonably prevented cannot be recovered. And similarly to negligence claims (see above), plaintiffs in contract claims must show that the breach of contract caused the loss (satisfying the but for test) and that the damages are not too remote (satisfying the reasonable foreseeability test).

Specific Performance and Injunctions

Specific performance is an equitable remedy ordering the party in breach to perform his obligations as promised by transferring the property or—more rarely—by performing the service agreed to. The rights of third parties can be significant in this context. For example, the court would not order a party to transfer a residence if that party's ex-spouse were still living on the property.

When courts grant injunctions in contract claims, it is usually to prevent a party from ignoring a contractual provision intended to prevent that party from engaging in certain behaviour, such as selling competing products or stealing customers.

reliance damages
remedy for contract disputes that compensates the innocent party for expenses he incurred preparing for the performance of contractual obligations

restitution damages
remedy for contract disputes that compensates the innocent party for moneys usually paid over to the other party (deposits and part payments, for example)

specific performance
remedy for contract disputes whereby the court orders the party in breach to perform his obligations as promised

BOX 7.6

Damages for Wrongful Dismissal: A Special Case

Generally speaking, the measurement of expectation losses in breach of contract cases is "open." In other words, there is no fixed formula for calculating the damages. However, in wrongful dismissal cases, the courts have developed a unique approach.

This special approach applies specifically to open-ended employment contracts, which cover most employment arrangements. An open-ended employment contract is one that is not for a fixed term or based on a collective agreement negotiated on behalf of the employee by a union (labour legislation tightly regulates collective agreements). Employees covered by open-ended employment contracts can be let go immediately for cause (for stealing or serious insubordination, for example). This is not surprising. More surprising is that employees covered by these kinds of contracts can also be dismissed at any time without cause and for almost any reason or even for no reason.* The only difference is that, if an employee is dismissed without cause, the employer must give the employee reasonable notice or salary in lieu. Open-ended employment contracts include an implied term at common law that employers must provide reasonable notice or equivalent pay in the case of without-cause dismissals. The common law "formula" for calculating reasonable notice† factors includes such things as length of service, type of employment, the employee's age, and availability of similar employment.

Employment standards legislation, federally and in the provinces and territories, also applies in this area and sets minimum notice periods for employees dismissed without cause; they work out to roughly one week of notice for every year of service. However, the common law assessment is almost always more generous—the more responsibility and seniority an employee has, the longer the required notice will be—and can be as much as one month (or more) of notice per year of service, far in excess of the statutory minimums.

The legislation doesn't prevent the employee from pursuing a claim at common law, and, in the event of a dispute, a dismissed employee will most often choose the common law remedy over (or in addition to) the legislation. For example, in a recent Ontario Court of Appeal decision, *Love v Acuity Investment Management Inc*,‡ a 50-year-old senior vice-president with only two and a half years' service, who had been dismissed without cause or notice, was awarded nine months' salary. The statutory minimum was just two weeks.

There is one important qualification to an employee's right to pursue this common law remedy, however. It applies when an employee expressly agrees, when hired, to limit notice entitlement upon dismissal. Generally, in this situation, the employee is restricted to the termination rights, if any, as agreed. The employee would still be able to pursue a statutory notice claim, however, as this right cannot be taken away by such an express term in an employment contract.

---

* There are a few exceptions, however. Dismissing an employee for discriminatory reasons, for example, is prohibited by human rights legislation, federally and in all provinces and territories.

† See, for example, *Bardal v Globe & Mail Ltd*, 1960 CanLII 294, 24 DLR (2d) 140 at 145 (Ont H Ct J), and *Honda Canada Inc v Keays*, 2008 SCC 39.

‡ 2011 ONCA 130.

Property Law

Property law regulates the ownership and use of property. Three types of property are examined here: (1) real property, (2) personal property, and (3) intellectual property.

Real Property

Real property (or **real estate**) refers to land and anything attached to land, such as buildings. A house, for example, is not owned separately from the land on which it is located; the owner of the land owns the house too. He also owns the natural resources beneath the land unless they belong to the Crown by virtue of the original grant or according to legislation (the Crown owns the natural resources in most areas of Canada). Furthermore, the owner of land owns and controls the airspace above the land to a reasonable height unless that ownership and control have been taken away by legislation.

In most of Canada, the law relating to real property is based on concepts of ownership that evolved in Norman England 1,000 years ago. After the Norman conquest in 1066, William I (William the Conqueror) became the owner of all land in England, and he gradually imposed a feudal system on the country. He did this by dividing England into parcels of land over which—except for the portions he kept for himself—his barons were given rights. However, the barons' control over their lands was conditional on their giving the King continued

real property (or real estate)
land and anything attached to the land, such as buildings and resources

support (fealty) and military service. In other words, these feudal lords were not absolute owners but tenants of a kind. They, in turn, assigned subtenancy rights to subordinates of their own in exchange for loyalty and service.

In countries such as Canada, where the British Crown remains the formal head of state, the feudal era has left a legacy—namely, the notion that the Crown owns all the land and that landowners below this station are, in a sense, tenants who hold a lesser interest or estate in the land (see below). This applies in Quebec, too, although there are slight legal and terminological differences owing to the influence of the French civil law tradition (mortgages, for example, are called "hypothecs" in Quebec). See Box 7.7 concerning Aboriginal title, a unique form of land ownership in Canada that is protected under the Constitution.

BOX 7.7

Aboriginal Title

For a complete picture of land ownership in Canada, we must take into account Aboriginal title. Aboriginal rights, including Aboriginal title, are constitutionally recognized and protected under section 35 of the *Constitution Act, 1982* (see Chapter 3). As defined by court decisions, some Aboriginal rights, such as the right to hunt and fish, are not based upon exclusive occupancy of the land. In contrast, Aboriginal title (although associated with traditional uses) is based on exclusive occupancy. Claims to land and resources by Aboriginal peoples began to occur with increasing frequency in the 20th century (see also Chapter 2 under "Canadian Law and Indigenous Peoples: A Timeline" and Box 3.4).

When Europeans first settled and occupied Canada, their encounters with First Nations peoples were not governed by a legal protocol. After the Seven Years' War, King George III issued the *Royal Proclamation, 1763*,* claiming territory in North America for Great Britain. Part of the proclamation dealt with relations with First Nations and included a general proscription against purchasing or otherwise acquiring land from them; only the Crown could do this. The proclamation is a key instrument in the history of Aboriginal title (see also Box 3.1). Today, it is generally accepted that Aboriginal title can be extinguished only through surrender of lands to the Crown by treaty or, since 1982 and the constitutional protection of Aboriginal rights, by constitutional amendment (from the time of Confederation until 1982, title could be extinguished by ordinary federal legislation).

Historically, many treaties were entered into and land was surrendered to the Crown. Not all of these treaties were clear or fair, however, and in many instances the two sides have interpreted them differently. Disputes still arise concerning their interpretation. Most of Canada is covered by these old treaties, but not all of it; for example, in parts of Quebec,

Labrador, and the territories and in almost all of British Columbia, no treaties were entered into, and the land was never formally surrendered to the Crown. With respect to claims to land that has not been formally surrendered, the two main mechanisms by which claims are established are (1) court challenge or (2) participation in a land claims process leading to a treaty.

In several important cases—*Calder v Attorney-General of British Columbia*,[†] *Guerin v The Queen*,[‡] *Delgamuukw v British Columbia*,[§] *R v Marshall*; *R v Bernard*,[#] and *Tsilhqot'in Nation v British Columbia***—the SCC has examined the concept of Aboriginal title more closely. In general terms, the Court has recognized that Aboriginal title is *sui generis* (that is, in its own class or unique) and is not based on "traditional real property rules." It is also, as noted, included within the broader conception of Aboriginal rights and is constitutionally protected. The following key principles have emerged concerning Aboriginal title:

1. Aboriginal title derives from the exclusive occupation of land, and that occupation must have existed at the time the Crown asserted sovereignty over the land. There can be breaks in the continuity of the occupation provided that a substantial connection to the land has been maintained. Furthermore, concerning the sufficiency of the occupation, title is not confined to specific settlement sites and includes areas over which effective control has been exercised when hunting and fishing, etc.

2. Although the occupation of the land is determined by reference to particular uses (or activities) that create an attachment to the land, those uses can change over time provided that they are not inconsistent with the uses that form the basis of the attachment.

3. It is a communal title that inheres in a particular group in relation to a particular area. Aboriginal title does not recognize rights of individual ownership in parcels of land the way the common law does, for example.
4. Aboriginal lands are inalienable except to the Crown. For third parties to acquire Aboriginal lands, the lands must first be surrendered to the Crown and then transferred to the third parties.
5. Prior to the establishment of Aboriginal title in disputed lands, governments have a duty to consult in good faith about proposed uses and, if appropriate, make accommodations (this duty is based on the honour of the Crown, which is a type of fairness obligation arising because of the Crown's assertion of sovereignty over Aboriginal peoples and control of their lands). For a recent case involving the Trans Mountain Expansion Project, or TMX, where the duty to consult was found not to have been breached, see *Coldwater First Nation v Canada (Attorney General)*†† (see also Box 4.2).
6. Once established, Aboriginal title includes the right to manage and control the land in question together with its economic benefits and resources. In exercising this stewardship, however, Aboriginal groups must not impair the rights of future generations over the land (for example, by clearcutting land and destroying traditional hunting habitats). Governments retain a limited jurisdiction over the land if justifiable (resource development and possibly pipeline construction could be justified if a "compelling and substantial government objective" is reconcilable with Aboriginal rights). (See, in particular, *Tsilhqot'in Nation*.)

Not all Indigenous peoples agree that these principles are accurate markers of their title, and some believe they are still rooted in non-Aboriginal ideas of land ownership. Concerning the requirement of traditional occupancy, this has often been difficult to establish; the *Tsilhqot'in Nation* case in 2014 is the first case where a specific claim of Aboriginal title has been proven and recognized by the SCC. The recognition of Aboriginal title continues to inform the modern treaty process, however, and most modern claims to Aboriginal lands are being asserted through a formalized land claims negotiation process (for example, the BC treaty process or the comprehensive claims process). Prior to *Tsilhqot'in Nation*, the greatest success in establishing rights to and control over land by Aboriginal peoples had come through such processes (for example, the Nisga'a Treaty entered into with the federal government in 2000). Recently, stalled negotiations to settle the land claim in *Delgamuukw* were given an impetus to proceed because of the Wet'suwet'en pipeline protests. In May 2020, the federal and provincial governments signed a memorandum of understanding with Wet'suwet'en hereditary chiefs and committed to recognizing Wet'suwet'en rights and title (see also Chapter 2 under "New Directions for Indigenous Law in Canada").

* (UK), reprinted in RSC 1985, App II, No 1.
† [1973] SCR 313, 1973 CanLII 4.
‡ [1984] 2 SCR 335, 1984 CanLII 25.
§ [1997] 3 SCR 1010, 1997 CanLII 302.
\# 2005 SCC 43.
** 2014 SCC 44.
†† 2020 FCA 34.

Interests in Land and Types of Ownership

When we use the term "interest" in the context of real property, we mean any right, claim, or privilege that an individual has in relation to the property. In theory, the Queen is the ultimate owner of all land in Canada. In reality, the executive authority here in Canada—that is, the federal and provincial governments, which we refer to as "the Crown"—holds the underlying title to all of the land. Practically speaking, that underlying ownership only manifests itself if a person dies intestate—that is, without having made a will—and has no relatives who can inherit the land on an intestacy. The land, in that case, will revert back to the Crown and become "government" property. The technical phrase in this situation is that the Crown will take the land "by escheat."

The Crown's underlying title to the land makes all other forms of ownership in Canada conditional and subordinate. These subordinate interests in the land come in many types. The most common ones are fee simple, leases, and mortgages. Interests in land can be owned by one person or co-owned with others. Also, the ownership can be legal or equitable. These interests and types of ownership are described next.

FEE SIMPLE OWNERSHIP

Owning land in fee simple is the closest a person can come to absolute ownership in Canada. The bundle of rights attached to the estate in fee simple gives the owner more power and flexibility to deal with the land than any other form of ownership. The **fee simple** owner has the right to possess the land and to build on it. She also has full power to transfer the estate to others while she is alive (a process known as "inter vivos transfer") and to transfer the property in a will once she dies (a process known as "testamentary transfer"). Should the owner die intestate, the property will pass to her relatives according to statutory intestacy rules. The fee simple owner also has the right to carve less permanent estates, such as leases, out of the fee simple whole. When these lesser estates expire, they revert back to the fee simple owner, making her estate whole again.

LEASEHOLD INTERESTS

Leasehold interests are distinguishable from freehold interests. Freehold interests are a form of ownership that does not involve an obligation to pay rent. Fee simple ownership is a type of freehold estate. **Leasehold interests**, on the other hand, imply an obligation to pay rent.

When an owner leases his property to someone, he creates a landlord–tenant relationship. The owner is the landlord, or "lessor," and the renter is the tenant, or "lessee." A leasehold interest can be residential (renting a place to live) or commercial (renting a place to do business). It can also be in one of two main forms: fixed term or periodic. A fixed term tenancy is for a defined period of time (one year or two years, for example), after which it automatically comes to an end. There may or may not be a right of renewal. A periodic tenancy (for example, week to week or month to month) automatically renews itself at the end of each period unless either party gives notice.

The lease, a type of contract, determines many of the rights and obligations of the parties under the tenancy. Residential tenancies, however, are regulated by provincial and territorial legislation, and residential lease agreements must comply with the legislation in matters relating to rents, repairs, notice obligations, compliance with health and safety regulations, etc. Commercial tenancies are also regulated but to a lesser degree, allowing the parties greater freedom to determine their respective rights and responsibilities under the lease.

MORTGAGES

Charges and encumbrances against real property secure debts or provide limited rights to the property. Interests in this category include rights of way, options to purchase, restrictive covenants, builders' liens, agreements for sale, and mortgages. A **mortgage**, the most common type of charge or encumbrance, secures a debt owed by the landowner.

Traditionally, a mortgage involved transferring the landowner's title to the land to the lender. The lender would hold this title as security against the loan, with a promise to transfer title back to the owner once the latter had repaid the mortgage loan in full. If the owner/borrower (the mortgagor) missed a payment or otherwise went into default, the lender (the mortgagee, often a bank) was entitled to keep the land unconditionally. However, in equity, the mortgagor was given a period of time to come up with the balance—in other words, a redemption period (see the discussion of the Court of Chancery in Chapter 2). The owner's right to redeem his property came to be known as the mortgagor's "equity of redemption"; it was valued at the worth of the property minus the amount of the mortgage debt still owing. Hence, we now refer to a property owner's "equity" in the property, which refers to the net market value of his unencumbered interest in the property.

After a mortgagor went into default, the mortgagee would have to bring proceedings to "foreclose" the mortgagor's right to redeem the property. These proceedings were called "foreclosure proceedings." If the redemption period expired without the mortgagor's coming up with the balance owing, the mortgagee could take absolute title to the property.

In many jurisdictions today, mortgages have been simplified by legislation and no longer involve the actual transfer of title to the creditor. In other respects, they operate the same way as before. Mortgagors are still given redemption periods, and mortgagees are still required to bring foreclosure proceedings if they wish to take over the property.

CO-OWNERSHIP

It is possible for more than one person to own an interest in land, and the interest most commonly co-owned is the fee simple. All co-owners of possessory interests such as the fee simple have equal rights of possession and use of the property.

The two principal forms of co-ownership of possessory interests are joint tenancy and tenancy in common. The main features of a **joint tenancy** are the unity of interest (all owners must own equal percentage shares) and the right of survivorship (which means that on the death of one co-owner, the remaining co-owner(s) automatically inherit the deceased owner's share; the last remaining co-owner becomes the sole owner). Joint tenants are not allowed to leave their share in a will because of the right of survivorship. They can, however, transfer their interest during their lifetime, but if they do, it has the effect of converting the joint tenancy into a tenancy in common.

A **tenancy in common** is similar to a joint tenancy insofar as possession is equally shared. However, tenants in common can own different percentage interests in the property, and there is no right of survivorship with this kind of ownership. Tenants in common can leave their interests in their wills or transfer them to others while they are alive without destroying the tenancy in common.

Another special form of co-ownership exists when a "strata lot" (that is, a condominium or townhouse) is purchased. Ownership of a strata unit combines individual ownership with shared or common ownership. The individual ownership relates to the actual unit. The shared ownership relates to common areas such as hallways, elevators, foyers, and exercise rooms. This form of co-ownership is relatively recent (first introduced in Australia in the 1960s) and is purely a creation of legislation; it requires a strata corporation to manage the property and the passage of by-laws to set the rules for this form of community living.

LEGAL AND EQUITABLE TITLE

A unique aspect of property ownership is the idea of "legal" and "equitable" ownership. This evolved out of the split jurisdiction between the royal courts and the Court of Chancery (see Chapter 2).

Title to estates in land can be split between a legal owner, called a "trustee," and a beneficial owner, sometimes called an "equitable owner." The legal owner's name will appear on any title documents, usually with an indication that the land is held "in trust" (or words to that effect), but this person (the trustee) will have to own and manage the property for the benefit of the equitable owner. The trustee may be required to ensure that the land and any buildings on it are cared for adequately and that any rents or profits are kept for or passed on to the beneficial owner. This split form of ownership is most common in connection with land, but it can apply to all forms of property, not just real property.

Split ownership of this kind is not recognized in Quebec, where ownership of property is "exclusive"; the civil law does not recognize a split between legal and equitable title.

joint tenancy
form of co-ownership that features the right of survivorship as well as the "four unities" of *possession* (each co-owner has an equal right to possess the entire property), *interest* (each co-owner has an identical interest in the property), *time* (the co-owners receive their interests at the same time), and *title* (the co-owners receive their interests under the same instrument, such as a will)

tenancy in common
form of co-ownership that does not involve the four unities or the right of survivorship, meaning that a co-owner can transfer his interest to others during his lifetime or leave it to others in his will

Rights and Obligations Attached to Land Ownership

In addition to the basic rights and obligations described above, there are other important rights and obligations attached to land ownership, such as those relating to support, use of water resources, and land use generally.

A property owner is entitled to rely on the physical support that a neighbour's property provides to his or her own property. This obligation between neighbours is reciprocal, and it becomes a matter of legal significance when, for example, one party is having her property excavated as part of a construction project. Excavation on or close to the property line may cause the neighbour's soil to subside and thereby cause damage to his buildings. In this situation, the property owner who is doing such work must ensure that adequate steps are taken to shore up the neighbouring property. Otherwise, she may face a damage claim. Liability in this case is strict, and negligence or intent to cause damage does not have to be established.

Properties next to lakes or rivers may have something called "riparian rights" attached to them. Riparian rights include the right to make reasonable use of the water for activities such as swimming, fishing, and boating and even the right to divert some of the water for drinking, washing, and irrigation. However, these rights are qualified by the obligation not to interfere unfairly with the riparian rights of others. A property owner would not be meeting this obligation, for example, if he diverted so much river water to irrigate his fields that the flow downstream was compromised or if the discharge of effluent from his agricultural concern made the water unsafe for others to use.

Every jurisdiction has particular legislation relating to support and to the use of water. Property owners must carefully consider these rules when working close to their property lines or exercising their riparian rights.

Generally speaking, property ownership comes with many responsibilities and restrictions concerning use. The federal, provincial, and municipal (or local) governments all regulate it. Property owners must be aware of the relevant restrictions, which concern such matters as type of use (for example, single-family, multi-family, or commercial use), allowable construction, rentals, cutting down trees, and pollution.

Systems of Land Registration: Deed Registry and Land Titles

deed
formal document showing ownership of property

The common law procedure for transferring land, which evolved centuries ago, relied entirely on deeds. **Deeds** are formal documents showing evidence of ownership. They have always involved a certain amount of risk. After successive transfers and generations of owners, there was always the possibility that mistakes would be made, frauds committed, or deeds missed when tracing the line of ownership.

To increase the certainty related to property ownership, registration systems were devised. Two main systems emerged, both used in Canada today: (1) the deed registration system and (2) the Torrens system. The deed registration system uses the traditional idea of transfer by deed. But it provides some certainty by requiring deeds to be registered, and it creates a deed repository to help with the tracing process.

Torrens system (or land titles system)
system for registering property ownership that eliminates the transfer of title by deeds and replaces them with statutory transfer forms, meaning that the title is guaranteed (or indefeasible)

The **Torrens system** (or **land titles system**) is named after Robert Torrens, the Australian who first devised and implemented the system in 1858. The Torrens system and systems modelled on it eliminate the transfer of title by deeds, replacing them with statutory transfer forms. Title for all land within the jurisdiction must be registered, and anyone purchasing property can rely on the state of the register. Registered title is indefeasible, which means that the legislation essentially guarantees that "what you see is what you get" when you look at the registry entries for a particular piece of property. The true owner's name will appear on title, and any charges relating to the property—for example, mortgages or liens—must be registered against the title to be effective. An assurance fund, set up under the legislation, is there to protect any innocent parties in the event that a fraud is perpetrated and someone gets on the title improperly. In 1870, British Columbia became the first jurisdiction in North America to adopt the Torrens system.

In Canada, deed registration systems are used in the maritime provinces. Quebec uses a similar system. Deed registration systems had been used in Ontario since the 1700s, but recently Ontario has almost entirely converted to a land titles system. The four western provinces use the land titles system. The uncertainty over true title is less common than it used to be but still exists to some extent in jurisdictions using deed registration systems. There is a much greater demand for "title insurance" in these jurisdictions than there is in jurisdictions using the "newer" land titles system.

Personal Property

Personal property includes not only tangible, movable objects, such as computers and cars, but also intangible interests, such as corporate securities. We have seen that there are many kinds of estates or interests in real property. The case is different with personal property, ownership in which is usually absolute. However, liens and charges can be placed against personal property to secure debts, and tangible objects (goods) can be leased (for example, cars). Personal property can also be held in trust so that ownership is divided between a trustee (the legal owner) and a beneficiary (the equitable owner).

personal property
tangible, movable objects as well as intangible interests, such as shares in a company

The sale of personal property is regulated by legislation in most situations. Some of that legislation—dealing with sales of goods, consumer protection, and business transactions, for example—is discussed in Chapter 8.

Tangible Personal Property

Tangible, movable objects—such as furniture, equipment, and cars—are sometimes referred to as **chattels**. Interests in them are referred to as "corporeal interests." There are a few well-known expressions concerning physical possession and ownership. One of these is "possession is nine-tenths of the law"; the other is "finders, keepers; losers, weepers." The principle expressed here—the idea that physically possessing property is somehow proof of ownership—is not necessarily accurate, however. Possession may be evidence of ownership, but it is not conclusive. If it were, this would be very good news for thieves. All evidence of ownership needs to be considered, including any bills of sale or agreements of sale relating to the property.

chattels
tangible, movable objects such as furniture, equipment, and cars

Intangible Interests

Intangible interests are sometimes called "incorporeal interests." The classic examples of these interests are corporate securities (for example, shares and bonds), as already noted. A chose (pronounced "shows") in action is another example of an intangible personal property right. A chose in action is the right to sue someone for an unpaid debt or other liability. For example, if a business owner had the right to sue a customer for property delivered but not paid for, the business owner could transfer that right, or chose in action, to a collection agency. In this situation, the collection agency often "purchases" the debt from the business owner at a discount.

Special legislative rules sometimes apply to the transfer of such interests, including notice requirements (for example, effectively assigning or transferring a debt or chose in action may require notice to the debtor depending on the type of debt).

Personal Property Security Legislation

Whenever a creditor (such as a seller or a lender) is owed money that is secured by personal property the debtor controls, there is a risk that the debtor will sell the personal property or further encumber it. This can lead to complex disputes over priority between the creditor and innocent third parties who dealt with the debtor in good faith, believing the property was not subject to any competing interests.

personal property security
creditor's security based on the debtor's personal property

Personal property security legislation provides for the registration of a creditor's interest in personal property that the debtor controls or possesses. This enables others to check the state of the property in question before entering into dealings with the debtor. The common expression for this kind of background search is "checking for liens."

In the 1970s, Ontario adopted a new personal property security regime with the enactment of the *Personal Property Security Act*.[20] Since then, all common law provinces and the territories have adopted similar legislation by the same name. Quebec, too, has legislation based on civil law principles that protect creditors through a system of registration. These statutes are complicated. Among their key features are the following:

1. coverage of almost all forms of personal property, both tangible and intangible;
2. provisions that protect a creditor with respect to the debtor's personal property;
3. a special interest called a "purchase money security interest," or PMSI, which can be granted to a lender who enables a debtor to acquire goods (for example, where a finance company lends money to a purchaser of a motor vehicle at the point of purchase);
4. the protection of creditors through the registration of their security interests; and
5. the creation of a system of priorities and "superpriorities," which starts from the principle that priority is given to creditors whose security interests in a debtor's property are registered earliest.

All provinces and territories have registries that can be checked electronically for security interests against personal property. If a check reveals no charge against the property, prospective creditors or lenders can be confident that when they register their security it will take priority over the securities of others who register later. For example, if a bank lends money to a client and registers the first security interest in the client's personal property, the bank knows that when the property is sold it will have first priority over the sale proceeds, which it can apply to the loan if it is not repaid by the client. If a second lender is approached by the client for another loan, the second lender will be able to see the bank's previous registered security interest. This will help the second lender decide whether loaning the client more money is too risky. The value of the property and the total value of the two loans will be important considerations.

Intellectual Property

intellectual property
property derived from the intellect or mind—works of art, inventions, and designs

Intellectual property (IP) has gained prominence in recent years; it refers to property derived from the intellect or mind—for example, works of art, musical creations, books, inventions, and designs. It is an intangible form of property but is usually classed separately from other forms of intangible personal property, such as securities.

---

20   RSO 1970, c 344.

As noted under "Constitutional Basis of Private Law" at the beginning of this chapter, IP is federally regulated. National standards make sense for this form of property, the precise location of which can be difficult to determine. Also, the federal government is best equipped to negotiate international agreements in this area. IP is increasingly traded—some would say stolen—across national boundaries, becoming part of the intellectual "human" commons. Federal regulators are better able to respond effectively to international changes and pressures than local regulators would be.

The Canadian Intellectual Property Office (CIPO) is the central registry for Canadian IP. International cooperation and agreements have led to the creation of the World Intellectual Property Organization (WIPO), which is an agency of the United Nations. Its headquarters are in Geneva, Switzerland. Registration with WIPO can assist with the protection of IP rights on the international stage.

Table 7.1 summarizes four key areas of IP and their associated federal statutes.

TABLE 7.1   Types of Intellectual Property

CATEGORY	DESCRIPTION	SOURCE
Copyright	Copyright refers to the right to copy, which only belongs to the copyright owner, who is usually the creator of the work or a person assigned ownership by the creator. Copyright exists as soon as the work is created and does not need to be registered to be enforceable. However, registration with CIPO provides evidence of ownership that can be used in court. Copyright protection lasts for the life of the creator plus 50 years and applies in respect of original dramatic, musical, artistic, and literary works (including computer programs) and performances, communication signals, and sound recordings.	*Copyright Act*, RSC 1985, c C-42
Industrial Design	An industrial design is a design used in making an object by hand, tool, or machine. Industrial designs can be protected for up to ten years if registered with CIPO. Without registration, a person cannot claim ownership of the design and thereby prevent others from using it to make articles. To qualify for registration, the design must be an original design with unique visual features that is used to make objects (e.g., a unique design for an ordinary object, such as a chair).	*Industrial Design Act*, RSC 1985, c I-9
Patents	A patent is a right that the government grants to an inventor to prevent others from using his or her invention. Patent holders are protected for up to 20 years after the patent application is filed with the Patent Office, which is part of CIPO. If the patent has not been filed, the inventor has no protection. Patents cover only the following: new inventions (which can be processes, machines, or compositions of matter), new improvements in an existing invention, and inventions that satisfy the three basic criteria of novelty, utility, and ingenuity.	*Patent Act*, RSC 1985, c P-4
Trademarks	A trademark distinguishes the goods or services of a person, a business, or an organization from those of others in the marketplace. Trademark registration provides evidence of ownership, but, as with copyrights, it is not conclusive. A registered trademark gives its holder an exclusive right to use the trademark throughout Canada for 15 years, and it is renewable after that. A trademark, to be registrable, must be a word, symbol, or design (alone or in combination) used to distinguish goods or services.	*Trademarks Act*, RSC 1985, c T-13

Family Law

Family law, the last area of private law we consider in this chapter, is concerned primarily with marriage, marriage breakdown and divorce, common law relationships, and the rights and obligations of family members (including those relating to children). Family law is a fundamental part of the private law of any country and is influenced by religion more than any other area. In Canada, however, the separation of religion and state means that our laws, rather than religious rules, guide us legally in family matters. For example, religious marriage ceremonies are not by themselves "official"; a legal marriage requires that a civil procedure (such as obtaining a licence) occur as well. Family law also includes matters such as adoption, child welfare, and support of parents, but space limitations prevent an examination of these issues.

Under our Constitution, jurisdiction over family matters is split between the federal and provincial governments (see "Constitutional Basis of Private Law" at the beginning of this chapter).

Marriage

essential validity
concerns a person's
capacity to marry
and the substantive
requirements of a
valid marriage

formal validity
concerns the formalities
or ceremonial require-
ments of a marriage

Canadian law recognizes a difference between the essential validity and the formal validity of a marriage. **Essential validity** concerns a person's capacity to marry and the substantive requirements of a valid marriage. Questions of this kind are under federal jurisdiction. **Formal validity** refers to the formalities or ceremonial requirements of a marriage, and these matters come under provincial jurisdiction.

Essential Validity

Despite the federal government's power to regulate essential validity, there is no comprehensive legislation setting out the rules. There are just two statutes dealing with specific aspects of a person's capacity to marry (the *Civil Marriage Act*[21] and the *Marriage (Prohibited Degrees) Act*,[22] discussed below). In this area, courts have relied heavily on common law rules, which are strongly influenced by English canon (or church) law, which, in turn, relies on the Christian Bible and other sources, such as the Anglican *Book of Common Prayer*. It is an area where religious rules have clearly shaped the law, as mentioned above.

A marriage that has essential validity must meet the following six requirements:

1. two persons must be involved;
2. both parties must have the ability to consummate the marriage;
3. there must not be too close a degree of consanguinity or affinity between the two parties (for example, the marriage of a brother and a sister is not valid);
4. the parties involved must be unmarried;
5. both parties must have given consent; and
6. both parties must be old enough to marry.

After a marriage ceremony, if it becomes apparent that one or more of these requirements has not been met, the union can be set aside or annulled. Depending on which requirement is not satisfied and on the exact nature of the problem, the marriage will be either void from the beginning (regardless of whether it is challenged), referred to as being void *ab initio*, or voidable (that is, it will be set aside only if challenged; otherwise, it will stand). The rules about the void/voidable distinction and about which party can challenge the validity of the marriage are complicated and not always clearly or consistently applied.

---

21   SC 2005, c 33.

22   SC 1990, c 46.

TWO PERSONS

This requirement used to be the common law opposite-sex rule. But in 2005, after a number of constitutional court challenges to this requirement, Parliament passed the *Civil Marriage Act*. Section 2 of this Act provides that "marriage, for civil purposes, is the lawful union of two persons to the exclusion of all others," and section 4 provides that "a marriage is not void or voidable by reason only that the spouses are of the same sex."

In Canada, then, same-sex marriages are now recognized. What used to be the "opposite-sex" element of essential validity can be restated as the "two individuals" (or "two persons") requirement. The requirement that marriages be a union of two people clearly also concerns the number of individuals involved. It means that polygamous marriages, for example—marriages involving more than two persons—are not legally recognized. In fact, polygamy is an offence under the *Criminal Code* (s 293). Some religious and other groups have challenged the constitutional validity of limiting marriage to just two people and of specifically criminalizing polygamy (see Box 7.8).

BOX 7.8

Polygamy and Canadian Law

The town of Bountiful, in southeastern British Columbia, is the home of a fundamentalist Mormon community that believes in polygamy. Its population is around 1,000. The first member of this Mormon group bought property there in 1946, and most of the town's residents today have descended from just six men.

In the wake of media attention and a police investigation into allegations of abuse involving Bountiful's young women and underage girls, a special prosecutor was appointed to decide whether criminal charges should be laid. He concluded that there was little evidence of sexual abuse and exploitation in the community and recommended instead that a reference question be placed before the court concerning the constitutionality of the rarely used section of the *Criminal Code* dealing with polygamy, section 293.*

In a 335-page decision handed down by the chief justice of the BC Supreme Court in November 2011, the Court concluded that although section 293 of the *Criminal Code* infringed the constitutional right to religious freedom (under s 2 of the Charter) and to fundamental justice (under s 7 of the Charter), a criminal prohibition against polygamy was a "reasonable limit" on that freedom under section 1 of the Charter, which states that the rights and freedoms are subject "to such reasonable limits prescribed by law as can be demonstrably justified in a free and democratic society." The Court found section 293's prohibition against polygamy justified because of the demonstrable "harm to women, to children, to society and to the institution of monogamous marriage" caused by the practice (at para 5). In other words, the harms associated with polygamy outweigh any claims to religious freedom.

Children running back to class after a recess at Mormon Hills school in the polygamous community of Bountiful, BC in 2008.

The decision was not appealed, and it set the stage for prosecution under section 293. In 2014, charges of polygamy were laid against two men from Bountiful, Winston Blackmore and James Oler. In 2017, they were both convicted, and in 2018, they were sentenced to house arrest (six months and three months, respectively) along with community service work. These are the first polygamy convictions in Canada in over a century (there have only been two others, one in 1899 and one in 1906). In a related prosecution, in 2019, James Oler was found guilty of transporting a child (his 15-year-old daughter) to the US in 2004 to be married to an older member of an affiliated religious group, contrary to s 273.3(1)(b) of the *Criminal Code*. He was sentenced to one year in jail.[†]

* *Reference re Section 293 of the Criminal Code of Canada*, 2011 BCSC 1588.

† *R v Oler*, 2019 BCSC 784 (conviction) and 2019 BCSC 1453 (sentencing).

ABILITY TO CONSUMMATE

For a marriage to be valid, both parties must have the ability to consummate it. The common law test for the consummation of an opposite-sex marriage is whether both parties are capable of having sexual intercourse at the outset of the marriage.[23] If one or both parties are impotent (that is, incapable of consummation) due to some incurable physical or mental disability, then the marriage may be annulled. Curable defects must be remedied and will not support an **annulment**. Note also that sterility—the inability to have children—is not the same thing as impotence and will also not support an annulment.

annulment
the legal cancellation or invalidation of a marriage

If a spouse is capable of consummating the marriage but simply refuses, or has a curable defect but refuses to fix it, the other party will not be able to obtain an annulment.

A marriage only needs to be consummated once for the consummation requirement to be satisfied. Once consummated, the marriage is always consummated. A lack of capacity or impotence that develops later is not grounds for annulment.

DEGREE OF CONSANGUINITY OR AFFINITY

consanguinity
a blood relationship between relatives

affinity
the relationship that a person has to the blood relatives of his or her spouse

Consanguinity refers to a blood relationship between relatives (that is, the relationship of people who descend from the same ancestor), and **affinity** refers to the relationship that a person has to the blood relatives of his or her spouse. Early in its development, the common law, adopting canon law rules, prohibited a wide range of relatives from marrying. The prohibited degrees of consanguinity and affinity extended up to and included the third degree of relationship. This means that third cousins and those lineally above and below them were prohibited from marrying. Later, these rules were relaxed—a gradual relaxation at common law over time.

In 1990, federal legislation was passed that clarified and simplified the rules. The *Marriage (Prohibited Degrees) Act* states that marriage between relatives is generally permissible unless they are lineal relatives (parents, grandparents, children, grandchildren), directly up or down, or brothers or sisters (or half-brothers and half-sisters), including by adoption.[24] Section 2 provides as follows:

> 2(1) Subject to subsection (2), persons related by consanguinity, affinity or adoption are not prohibited from marrying each other by reason only of their relationship.
>
> (2) No person shall marry another person if they are related lineally, or as brother or sister or half-brother or half-sister, including by adoption.

First cousins are permissible marriage partners in Canada, and nephews and nieces may marry their aunts and uncles.

UNMARRIED

Being married to one person, even if separated and apart from that person, is a bar to marrying a second person. Marrying one person while still married to another is bigamy and an offence under the *Criminal Code* (ss 290-91).

If one of the parties to a proposed marriage was previously married, the officiant or minister at the new marriage will need documentary evidence to prove that the previous marriage ended, either by annulment, divorce, or the death of the other spouse.

---

23   So far, the courts have not defined the consummation requirements for gay and lesbian couples.

24   SC 1990, c 46.

CONSENT

Both parties must consent to marry, freely and voluntarily. If one party consents to a marriage but lacks the capacity to understand the nature of its duties and responsibilities, the consent is invalid. This lack of capacity may be temporary—a matter of impairment due to drugs or alcohol—or it may be the effect of a permanent mental disability.

When one party enters a marriage under duress, compelled by fear of harm to herself or to a third person, the marriage will not be considered consensual and will not be valid. The expression "shotgun wedding" is based on this idea.

Fraud or mistake can invalidate apparent consent. However, the misunderstanding must concern the nature of the ceremony or the identity of one of the parties. One party's misrepresentation of his wealth or status, for example, will not invalidate the other party's consent—although it might support a tort claim for deceit.

Finally, sham marriages that people enter into for immigration or other purposes, with no intention of living as a married couple, are considered not to involve real consent and are therefore invalid.

AGE

The common law age requirements for marriage are 12 for females and 14 for males. No federal legislation has changed these minimums. They are somewhat incongruous, for the following reason: depending on the exact ages and age differences between two young people getting married, the act of consummation necessary to validate the marriage could amount to a sexual offence under the *Criminal Code* (ss 150-53).

However, the issue of sexual offences in the context of marriages between infants (that is, people under the age of majority) has not been a problem in Canada. This is because the *Criminal Code* recognizes close-in-age and marriage defences starting at ages 12 and 14, respectively. Also, not many infants are able to obtain the necessary consents or approvals to get married in the first place. That is because provincial and territorial legislation requires parental (or guardian) consent to the solemnization of a marriage between young people under the age of majority. Infants under the age of 16 generally cannot be married even with the consent of parents or guardians. In very limited situations, however, courts are authorized under the legislation to order the solemnization of a marriage involving a person under 16. The usual test is that the marriage must be "in the interests of the parties." In making its decision, a court could consider such factors as cultural expectations or the pregnancy of one of the parties. Such marriages are rarely authorized, however.[25]

Formal Validity

The provinces and territories have jurisdiction over solemnization procedures or formalities that must occur for a marriage to be valid. The provincial and territorial marriage acts set the requirements, which typically include the following:

1. a marriage licence (some jurisdictions, such as Ontario, allow the **banns of marriage**—the public announcement in church of an impending marriage—to be used in place of licences);

2. a public marriage ceremony (religious or civil) before at least two witnesses;

banns of marriage
the public announcement in church of an Impending marriage

---

25 Given that age is a matter of essential validity, there is at least an argument that these provincial and territorial age minimums are unconstitutional because they are higher than the ages set by the common law (in an area of federal jurisdiction). However, Canadian social norms today support barriers to marriage between youths, so it is unlikely that any challenges will occur.

3. a presiding official (religious or civil) who is authorized under the legislation to perform marriage ceremonies; and
4. registration of the marriage with the vital statistics office for the province or territory in question.

Basic Rights and Responsibilities in Marriage

During the marriage, the parties to the marriage have basic rights and obligations to each other and to their children.

At common law, and now as set out in provincial and territorial family law legislation, spouses are expected to financially support each other. The level of support is usually based on a test of what is reasonable in the circumstances, with regard to such things as the role of each spouse in the family, express or implied agreements on the matter, caregiving obligations for any children, and economic status.

Similarly, spouses within a marriage have an obligation to do what is reasonable and necessary to maintain and support their children, including providing for their education.

Matrimonial Property

Historically, the common law viewed marriage as creating a "unity of personality." This idea can be traced to the Christian belief that, upon marriage, the couple became one. What this meant in a patriarchal society, practically speaking, was that, upon marrying, the wife came under the husband's control. The husband assumed control over everything related to the family, including family property (even property that the wife brought into the marriage).

Manitoba was the first province, in 1871, to pass legislation enabling a woman to hold property in her own name and to control it free of her husband's influence and debts. Separate legislation was later passed in Manitoba to ensure that women's earnings during marriage were their own. By the early 1900s, most other provinces had followed suit, with similar legislation.[26] Legislation has since given women in Canada the same power as men to own and control property in their own right during marriage. In other words, the *unity* of personality concept has been replaced by a *separation* of personality concept.

Marriage Breakdown and Divorce

Marriage breakdown is usually a gradual process that begins while the parties are still together and moves next to separation and then divorce, although some parties may choose to stay separated without divorce. On marriage breakdown, support and other obligations are triggered under provincial legislation whether or not there is a divorce.

Individuals in the midst of family breakdown are facing significant life decisions and are usually more emotionally fragile than are people involved in other kinds of legal conflicts. Dealing with individuals in such situations requires sensitivity from family law professionals. The special nature of disputes in this area is the reason that lawmakers in almost every Canadian jurisdiction have introduced unique measures for their resolution. These measures typically include:

- encouraging or requiring the parties to use alternative dispute resolution mechanisms (for example, collaborative law or negotiation-based approaches) before resorting to the courts and
- creating unified family courts to simplify the process should the courts be needed (see Chapter 5).

---

26 For examples of current legislation, see the following: *The Married Women's Property Act*, CCSM c M70; *Married Women's Property Act*, RSNWT (Nu) 1988, c M-5; and *Family Law Act*, RSO 1990, c F.3, s 64.

Grounds for Divorce

Divorce in Canada is federally regulated, and the governing statute is the *Divorce Act*. When it was first passed in 1968, the *Divorce Act* simplified the rules of divorce and introduced the idea of "no-fault" divorce.

For couples who want to formally end their relationship, there is just one ground of divorce under the *Divorce Act*—namely, marriage breakdown. Marriage breakdown can be established in one of three ways:

1. living separate and apart for one year (the no-fault basis),
2. adultery by the other party, or
3. physical or mental cruelty by the other spouse "of such a kind as to render intolerable the continued cohabitation of the spouses."[27]

The vast majority of divorces in Canada proceed under the first ground, with the couple first living separate and apart for one year. It is not necessary to go to court to get a divorce decree if the parties consent to the order. It can simply be filed in the appropriate court registry.

Spousal and Child Support

As mentioned, support obligations exist prior to marriage breakdown under provincial and territorial legislation. However, they are most often disputed on marriage breakdown. Sometimes different terms are used to describe the obligations. "Maintenance" and "alimony" are synonyms for payments one spouse makes to another once marriage breakdown has occurred whether or not there has been divorce. The word "support" is more general and can refer to pre- and post-breakdown obligations and apply to both spousal and child payment obligations.

The parties can agree between themselves, by way of a separation agreement, who will support whom and for how long and what the payments will be, or they can go to court and have a judge make the determination for them. If they settle out of court, they may still file a consent order along with the agreement in court, which will make the settlement easier to enforce and can be adjusted if circumstances change.

Support orders, consent or otherwise, are made under provincial and territorial family law legislation until the parties proceed to divorce. If the parties proceed to divorce, support orders are made under the federal *Divorce Act*.

There are federal guidelines for spousal and child support obligations. In practice, these federal guidelines are followed in negotiated settlements involving legal professionals, as well as in court-ordered resolutions, and they are followed regardless of whether the support orders are made under provincial/territorial legislation or under the federal *Divorce Act*. Support orders can be changed at a later date if there is a significant change in circumstances.

Children: Custody and Access

When spouses who are separating have children, the main issue concerning the children is whether there will be joint custody or sole custody for one parent with (or without) access rights for the non-custodial parent.

As with support, if there is no divorce, any non-negotiated resolution will have to be made under provincial or territorial family law legislation. If there is a divorce, any custody and access orders will be under the *Divorce Act*. Regardless of which route is taken, the test for determining custody and access rights is essentially the same under all legislation, and that is to determine what is in the "best interests of the child" in light of all of the circumstances.

---

27 RSC 1985, c 3 (2nd Supp), s 8.

Division of Family Assets

The provinces and territories have exclusive jurisdiction over the division of matrimonial property upon the breakdown of marriage. When the marriage collapses, family law legislation in all jurisdictions triggers rights to share in the marital possessions.

The legislation defines what constitutes family property, and the definitions vary depending on the province or territory. Typically, houses, pensions, retirement savings plans (RSPs), and bank accounts are included, whereas business assets are excluded. Inheritances are sometimes included and sometimes excluded depending on the circumstances.

In general, this legislation creates a presumption that family assets should be split 50/50 between the parties. However, the court has the power to reapportion the division—that is, to split the assets otherwise than 50/50—in cases where an even split would be unfair or unconscionable. In choosing to reapportion, the court will consider various factors—for example, the length of the marriage, how much property each spouse brought into the marriage, the extent of each party's personal debts, and the economic self-sufficiency of each spouse. Marriage agreements and separation agreements that provide for a split other than 50/50 will also be considered by the courts but are not conclusive. The courts may choose to disregard such agreements.

Common Law Marriages and Marriage-Like Relationships

When two people live together in an intimate, marriage-like relationship but without going through the solemnization procedures required for a formally valid marriage (see above under "Formal Validity"), they may take on some of the rights and obligations of a married couple. There are various names for such relationships—for example, common law marriages (or common law relationships), domestic partnerships, and civil unions.

The precise meaning of "common law marriage" is not free from controversy.[28] In our discussion here, we adopt a broad definition and take it to include any marriage-like relationship or "non-traditional" marriage, in the sense of a conjugal union between two individuals where the requirements of formal validity have not been met.[29]

Legislation in each province and territory dealing with general family law matters and financial issues (for example, taxes, pensions, and income supplements) defines when a non-traditional marriage will attract rights and obligations. The federal government does this too in its financial legislation.

In general, couples, including same-sex couples, living together in a marriage-like relationship for two years will take on some of the same rights and obligations as couples in formally valid marriages. However, the applicable legislation must be read carefully. For example, under federal tax legislation, two people qualify as a common law couple if they cohabit in a conjugal relationship for just one year or have a child together, triggering many of the same tax rules as if they were formally married. In Ontario, on the other hand, support obligations apply only to couples who have been together for three years or who have a child in common.

Assuming that a couple satisfies the relevant legislative definition of common law marriage (or other term used for a marriage-like relationship), the rights and obligations

---

28 It can be confusing, too, because often it is legislation, not the common law, that defines what is meant by common law marriage in a particular context.

29 Note that some foreign marriages and domestic Indigenous marriages that would be characterized as non-traditional under Canadian law may nonetheless be recognized as valid marriages in Canada. The interplay between foreign and Indigenous laws relating to family matters and Canadian law is a complicated area, and we just mention it briefly here.

concerning spousal support and government financial matters will generally be the same as if their marriage was formally valid. Quebec is an exception and does not recognize support obligations between partners in common law relationships. Support obligations apply only to Quebec couples who are lawfully married or who are in a special type of civil union, not found elsewhere in Canada, that involves certain ceremonial formalities and a registration process similar to the process used for marriages.

Child support obligations are the same for common law couples as for married couples because they are based on parenthood, not marriage.

One area where a significant difference exists between common law marriages and formally valid marriages has to do with the division of family property in the event of breakup. Most provinces and territories require couples to be lawfully married before the presumption of a 50/50 split will apply.[30] This means that a person living in a common law relationship whose partner owns most or all of the family property will be at risk of receiving little or no property if the couple breaks up.

Where no division-of-property rights exist, the main way common law partners can protect themselves in the event of breakup is through a cohabitation agreement—in other words, an agreement between unmarried couples that deals with property rights. They may also insist on co-ownership of family property—for example, owning the matrimonial home as joint tenants or tenants in common. It is possible that if a common law spouse who is not on title has contributed in some way to the acquisition of property owned by the other spouse, a trust argument could be made that the contributing spouse is entitled to a share of the property. Such arguments are complicated and can be expensive to litigate. Generally, they are a last resort.

---

30 So far, only British Columbia (*Family Law Act*, SBC 2011, c 25), Saskatchewan (*The Family Property Act*, SS 1997, c F-6.3), Manitoba (*Family Property Act*, RSM 1987, c M45), the Northwest Territories (*Family Law Act*, SNWT (Nu) 1997, c 18), and Nunavut (which adopts the Northwest Territories legislation in this area) have extended division-of-property rights to common law couples.

CHAPTER SUMMARY

Private law is concerned primarily with the regulation of relationships between persons. Canada's Constitution assigns jurisdiction over private law, for the most part, to the provinces. However, some areas rest with Parliament (for example, intellectual property), and for a few (such as family law), jurisdiction is split between the provinces and the federal government. Private law disputes are resolved, like most other disputes, by assigning the burden of proof to the plaintiff or person asserting the claim. The standard of proof is *balance of probabilities*, which is less than the criminal standard, *beyond a reasonable doubt*. Four key private law areas are torts, contracts, property law, and family law.

Tort law covers a wide and diverse range of civil wrongs not covered by other areas of private law. Tort claims can be classified according to whether they involve intentional or negligent wrongdoing or are based on strict liability principles. Classic examples of intentional torts are assault and battery. Torts involving negligence include many situations, from car accidents to professional malpractice. Strict liability torts deal with relatively few situations, such as using dangerous substances, owning dangerous animals, and vicarious liability. A few miscellaneous torts, such as nuisance and defamation, are more difficult to classify but are similar to strict liability torts insofar as they are focused on the effects of behaviour rather than fault associated with it.

Contract law is one of the few areas of law where parties can create their own rules and define the terms of their own relationship. Contracts apply to many aspects of our daily routines. The main elements of contract formation are offer, acceptance, and consideration (the parties' reciprocal exchange of something of value). Contract disputes often centre on the interpretation of terms and on whether excuses are available for non-performance of the contract. Excuses for one party's non-performance might be, for example, misrepresentations by the other party during negotiations or mistakes made about the nature of the contract agreed to. Breach of contract occurs where one party fails to live up to the terms of the agreement. The most common remedies in contract disputes are damages to compensate the innocent party for her lost expectation or a court order forcing the party in breach to specifically perform his obligations.

Property has been a source of power in Western society since ancient times. The laws concerning the ownership and use of real property, or land, are among our oldest. In Canada, absolute ownership of land can only rest with the Crown, and the closest a person (who is not Queen or King) can come to absolute ownership is with the fee simple estate. Fee simple ownership allows an owner full power to dispose of her land as she wishes during her life and upon her death. Various lesser estates and charges against property come with specific rights and obligations and with more limited powers of control. Co-ownership of property is possible, as is the separation of legal (right to control) and equitable (right to benefits) ownership. Interests in land can be registered, either in a deed registry or a land titles system, depending on the province or territory in which the land is located; registration provides a measure of security of ownership. Property law also regulates the ownership and use of personal property, which includes tangible goods as well as some intangible interests, such as corporate securities. Ownership rules for personal property are generally simpler than for land. Personal property security legislation, in force in all provinces and territories, governs the process by which one party uses another's personal property as security, usually for a debt owing. Finally, the law also regulates intellectual property (that is, property that is created through intellectual effort). IP has become a more important form of property in recent years and is regulated exclusively at the federal level. The principal forms of IP protection relate to copyright, industrial designs, patents, and trademarks.

Family law governs marriage, marriage breakdown and divorce, common law relationships, and related matters (including those involving children and family assets). Certain aspects of family law—for example, the substantive requirements of a valid marriage and divorce—are federally regulated. Other aspects, such as the formal and ceremonial requirements of a marriage and the division of family assets on marriage breakdown, are under provincial jurisdiction. New laws concerning same-sex marriage and permissible degrees of consanguinity (blood relation) and affinity have expanded the range of marriageable couples. When marriages end, most couples get divorced, and most divorces in Canada are based on the no-fault, one-year separation rule set out in the federal *Divorce Act*. Issues relating to support and care of children become important on the breakdown of marriage. Spousal support focuses on what is reasonable for both parties in the circumstances. Child support and custody and access determinations are based on what is in the best interests of the child. Division-of-property rules, which are regulated by the provinces and territories, favour a 50/50 split of family property unless good reasons exist to adjust this division—a process known as reapportionment. The law treats common law relationships similarly to traditional marriages, except (in most jurisdictions) when it comes to division of property upon the breakup of the relationship; in such cases, ownership of property must be proved in the usual way.

KEY TERMS

affinity, 218

annulment, 218

assault, 186

banns of marriage, 219

battery, 187

chattels, 213

civil wrong, 186

consanguinity, 218

deed, 212

defamation, 195

essential validity, 216

expectation damages, 205

false imprisonment, 187

fee simple, 210

formal validity, 216

intellectual property, 214

joint tenancy, 211

leasehold interest, 210

libel, 195

misrepresentation, 203

mortgage, 210

negligence, 189

nuisance, 195

occupiers' liability, 193

personal property, 213

personal property security, 214

private nuisance, 195

public nuisance, 195

real property (or real estate), 207

reliance damages, 206

restitution damages, 206

slander, 195

specific performance, 206

strict liability tort, 193

tenancy in common, 211

Torrens system (or land titles system), 212

tort, 186

trespass to goods (or trespass to chattels), 187

trespass to land, 187

trespass to person, 186

vicarious liability, 194

FURTHER READING

BOOKS

Duxbury, Robert, *Nutshells Contract Law*, 10th ed (London, UK: Sweet & Maxwell, 2015).

Fridman, GHL, *An Introduction to the Law of Torts*, 3rd ed (Markham, Ont: LexisNexis, 2012).

Hovius, Berend, Mary-Jo Maur & Nicholas Bala, *Family Law: Text, Cases, Materials and Notes*, 9th ed (Toronto: Thomson Reuters, 2017).

Kurtz, JoAnn, *Family Law: Practice and Procedure*, 5th ed (Toronto: Emond, 2018).

Linden, Allen M & Bruce Feldthusen, *Canadian Tort Law*, 10th ed (Markham, Ont: LexisNexis, 2015).

MacLean, Carolyn A et al, *Contract and Tort Law for Paralegals*, 2nd ed (Toronto: Emond, 2018).

McCallum, Margaret & Alan M Sinclair, *An Introduction to Real Property Law*, 7th ed (Toronto: LexisNexis, 2017).

McCamus, John D, *The Law of Contracts*, 2nd ed (Toronto: Irwin Law, 2012).

Waddams, Stephen M, *The Law of Contracts*, 7th ed (Toronto: Canada Law Book, 2017).

Ziff, Bruce, *Principles of Property Law*, 6th ed (Toronto: Carswell, 2014).

WEBSITES

Canadian Intellectual Property Office (CIPO): <http://www.ic.gc.ca/eic/site/cipointernet-internetopic.nsf/eng/Home>.

World Intellectual Property Organization: <https://www.wipo.int/portal/en/index.html>.

REVIEW QUESTIONS

1. List three intentional torts.

2. Identify the most common defences to intentional torts and explain these defences.

3. List the elements of a negligence claim.

4. Of the three main defences to negligence liability, which one allows for the apportionment of liability between the parties?

5. Explain the law relating to defamation and describe the varieties of this tort.

6. List the elements of a valid contract.

7. Explain the concept of an implied term in a contract.

8. What are standard form contracts, and what kinds of transactions are they appropriate for? Provide an example.

9. What are the distinguishing features of the fee simple estate?

10. Explain how mortgages work and describe how the modern concept of a mortgage differs from the traditional concept.

11. What is the difference between joint tenancy and tenancy in common?

12. What is the purpose of registration systems for property ownership, and what are the registry systems currently used in Canada?

13. What are the six basic requirements of essential validity for marriage?

14. What is the difference between the annulment of a marriage and a divorce?

15. Upon marriage breakdown, what is the main test for determining custody and access rights concerning children?

EXERCISES

1. Consent is a common defence to the intentional torts. In the case of *Norberg v Wynrib*, [1992] 2 SCR 226, a young woman had sex with an elderly doctor in order to get prescription painkillers. Locate and read La Forest J's judgment in the *Norberg* case and answer the following questions:

   a. Why was the defence of consent not applicable on these facts?

   b. On the basis of what tort was the doctor found liable?

   c. Why do you agree or disagree with this decision?

2. First, refer to the summary of the duty principles for negligence. Then:

   a. Locate and read the SCC case of *Childs v Desormeaux*, 2006 SCC 18, in which the SCC had to decide whether a social host owed a duty of care to third parties injured by an intoxicated guest. Describe the reasoning of the Court in reaching its decision that, generally, no such duty exists.

   b. Consider the following problem. A psychiatrist has a patient who says he's going to kill his wife. The psychiatrist tells no one, and the patient does attempt to murder his wife. Although his attempt fails, the attack causes her serious injury. She now wants to sue the psychiatrist for not warning her. Assume that no duty to warn a potential victim of

a patient has ever been imposed on a doctor. Prepare an argument explaining why you think such a duty should, or should not, be recognized.

3. Imagine that you have started a new job and only have two weeks' vacation time in your first year. As the end of this year approaches, you start to look forward to your first chance to relax and unwind since you started the job. You have just ended a relationship, and you book a holiday to a Caribbean island through a local tour operator, who promises luxurious five-star accommodations at a small boutique hotel that caters to "singles." The owner is described as a charming person who speaks fluent English, and you are told there will be beach parties, snorkelling and scuba diving in crystal-clear waters, local entertainment, and a lot of other singles to meet. When you arrive, you find a decrepit, run-down hotel. The owner is bad-tempered and speaks almost no English (the only language you speak). Two couples and an older single person are already there, but they all leave after a few days. You are by yourself, and no one else comes. There is no equipment for snorkelling or scuba diving on the premises, although there is an inflatable inner tube to use. There is no entertainment (except when the owner's cousin drops by to play "Auld Lang Syne" on the steel drums for five minutes), the food is bad, and there are bugs in your room. Finally, you decide to book an early

flight home, thoroughly disappointed and extremely depressed by the experience. You now have to wait another year for a holiday. Assume that you paid $2,500 for this vacation. Based on the types of damages available for breach of contract, how do you think your damages should be assessed? See *Jarvis v Swan Tours*, [1973] 1 QB 233 (Eng CA).

4. A general principle that underlies Canadian contract law is freedom of contract, meaning that parties generally have the freedom to enter into binding agreements according to the terms they choose. Based on the overview of contract law in this chapter, detail three scenarios where the law would impose limits on that freedom and explain which specific rule imposes the limit in each case.

5. Locate the statute that regulates residential tenancies in your province or territory and review the provisions dealing with termination. For a month-to-month tenancy, name three no-fault reasons that will support a decision by a landlord to end the lease and describe the specific notice requirements.

6. You have just written a script for an animated film that you believe has the potential to be Disney's next big hit. You want to send it around for others to read and critique but are concerned about its being plagiarized. Go to the CIPO website listed under "Further Reading" and review the information about copyrights. What steps must be taken to register your original script? Once registered, does CIPO guarantee protection for your work? Explain.

7. In your opinion, should couples who choose not to get married but who live in a committed, marriage-like relationship be treated the same way as married couples when it comes to division of family assets? Provide reasons for your answer.

8 Business and Consumer Law

Introduction 230

Business Structures 231

Business Transactions 237

Builders and Repairers: Security for
Services Performed 238

Product Sales and Consumer
Protection Legislation 238

Advertising Standards 244

Chapter Summary 246

Key Terms 246

Further Reading 247

Review Questions 247

Exercises 247

After reading this chapter, you will be able to:

- Describe the most common business structures in Canada—sole proprietorships, partnerships, and corporations—and the advantages and disadvantages of each.

- Describe the basic nature of business transactions, payment methods, and collection options.

- Recognize the circumstances that give rise to builders' and repairers' liens.

- Understand the importance of sale of goods acts in Canada.

- Explain how consumers are protected under the federal *Competition Act*.

- Define the role of the federal *Food and Drugs Act* and the *Canada Consumer Product Safety Act* in protecting the health and safety of Canadian consumers.

- Identify selected areas covered by provincial consumer protection legislation.

- Describe how the Canadian advertising industry attempts to protect consumers.

Modern technology has placed at the disposal of the Canadian consumer a bewildering variety of highly complex products, consumable and non-consumable, many of which were unknown before the war. The notion of the consumer bargaining from a position of equal strength has become a fiction in any but the most attenuated sense.

JS Ziegel, "The Future of Canadian Consumerism" in
MH Ogilvie, ed, *Consumer Law: Cases and Materials*,
3rd ed (Toronto: Captus Press, 2007) at 2

Introduction

Choosing a business structure is one of the first decisions entrepreneurs make when planning a new business venture or developing an existing one. The most common ways of structuring a business—working alone and unincorporated, or with others in partnership, or behind the veil of a corporation—all have advantages and disadvantages. The nature of the business, the need for capital to grow it, and the risks involved in running the business are factors that will influence the choice of structure.

Regardless of the business structure chosen, all businesses must enter into business transactions; in almost all cases, these are based on contracts with customers that will determine the rights and obligations of the parties. Decisions about payment options, whether or not to offer credit or to take security for payment, and collection methods in the event of non-payment will be an important part of these transactions. And particular businesses, such as those involved in the building or repairing trades, need to consider whether any special rights apply to them.

Furthermore, all businesses need to be aware of legislation, both federal and provincial, regulating the sale of products or services. Both levels of government have enacted legislation that sets standards and defines rights and responsibilities with regard to these products and services.

This chapter considers all of these issues and examines some basic rules under provincial sale of goods acts; the significance of certain federal consumer protection legislation (specifically, the *Competition Act*,[1] the *Food and Drugs Act*,[2] and the *Canada Consumer Product Safety Act*[3]); and how changes in the marketplace have led to increased protection of consumers at the provincial level. Lastly, it considers a code of standards administered by Advertising Standards Canada designed to protect consumers.

Business Structures

In Canada, the three most common business structures are sole proprietorships, partnerships, and corporations.

Sole Proprietorships

The simplest form of business structure in Canada is the **sole proprietorship**. The business, in this case, is owned and operated by one person—the sole proprietor. For example, a sole proprietorship might be a neighbourhood dog-grooming business, a street vendor, or a business selling products on the Internet. With sole proprietorships, besides the owner there are generally few (if any) employees, and it is not unusual for the business to be based in the sole proprietor's home; however, depending on the size and type of business (and this applies regardless of how the business is structured), it could be in a retail store, a warehouse, or an office building or even be a mobile business. Legal requirements for starting up a sole proprietorship are minimal but still must be followed.

Depending on particular laws in each province, a sole proprietor may conduct her business under her own personal name. If the sole proprietor chooses to do otherwise—if she wishes to give her business a name different from her own name—she may (depending again on the province) be required to register that different name with the provincial government. There may be further restrictions in this regard. In Saskatchewan, for example, section 8(1) of *The Business Names Registration Act*[4] states that no business name shall be registered if, in the opinion of the registrar, it is the same as or similar to an existing corporation's name and would likely cause confusion or if the name suggests or implies a connection with the Crown, the government, a political party, a professional association, or a university.[5]

With a sole proprietorship, there are federal and provincial laws and taxes that may also apply to its operation. There is the federal goods and services tax (GST), provincial sales tax (PST), and, in some provinces, including Ontario and the Atlantic provinces, a combined harmonized sales tax (HST) that is collected by the Canada Revenue Agency, which then remits a portion back to the participating provinces. Municipal by-laws may also apply to

sole proprietorship
business that is owned and operated by an individual and that is not a legal entity separate from the owner

---

1 RSC 1985, c C-34.

2 RSC 1985, c F-27.

3 SC 2010, c 21.

4 Being c B-11 of *The Revised Statutes of Saskatchewan, 1978* (effective February 26, 1979) as amended by the *Statutes of Saskatchewan*, 1980-81, c 3 and 21; 1986-87-88, c 40; 2006, c 14; 2010, c B-12; 2012, c 21; 2013, c O-4.2; 2015, c 21; and 2018, c 42.

5 RSS 1978, c B-11.

facets of the business, such as land use, zoning, parking, noise, and the location of advertising signs. Business permits and other licences may also be needed—for example, for electricians—depending on the type of business. Indeed, all of the business structures reviewed in this part are subject to taxes and other obligations under federal, provincial, and municipal laws.

Advantages and Disadvantages

A sole proprietorship is relatively easy to start up and operate. Income from the business is considered taxable income for the sole proprietor, but an income tax deduction based on a percentage of the costs of operating the business at home may be available.

The main disadvantage of a sole proprietorship is that it is not a separate legal business structure apart from its owner. Sole proprietors are legally liable for all of the business's debts and obligations. Such business debts may also put the sole proprietor's personal assets at risk.

Partnerships

Business owners may choose to change their business structure as their circumstances change. For example, a sole proprietor might wish to expand his home-based dog-grooming business. In order to raise capital to rent a storefront office and buy more equipment, he might convert his business into a partnership with a co-owner. This partnership structure could reduce business costs per person and increase business opportunities; the partners could share costs and work together to attract new customers.

A partnership exists whenever two or more persons carry on business together with a view to profit; collectively, they are referred to as a "firm." Most partnerships are based in part on a partnership agreement, which defines their rights and obligations. However, partnership agreements are subject to any rules mandated by legislation, such as those relating to limiting liability in connection with the conduct of the business. Also, partners who are involved in the management of the business owe each other a **fiduciary duty**, which requires them to act in good faith (that is, to act honestly and for the common benefit of the partners) and to share profits and opportunities. They are also required to act carefully and reasonably in their partnership dealings.

fiduciary duty
in the context of a partnership, the responsibility to act carefully and reasonably in the best interest of the firm

The three types of partnerships available in Canada are:

1. general partnerships,
2. limited partnerships, and
3. limited liability partnerships.

general partnership
business structure in which two or more persons carry on business in common with a view to profit

A **general partnership** is the most common form of partnership. It exists when all of the partners manage the business together and share profits, as well as debts and obligations. All provinces and territories have partnership legislation, which sets out certain rules characterizing general partnerships.[6] Most importantly, partners are each other's agents (meaning that each is authorized to act on behalf of the others), and each partner is jointly and severally liable for the conduct of the business while she is a partner in it. This means that every partner is fully liable for all debts and liabilities of the firm (although an individual partner who is found liable for a partnership debt or other liability has a right to seek contribution from the other partners).

---

6   See, for example, the *Partnerships Act*, RSO 1990, c P.5; *Partnership Act*, RSA 2000, c P-3; and *Partnership Act*, RSBC 1996, c 348.

The main difference between a **limited partnership** and a general partnership is that, in a limited partnership, not all partners participate in the management of the business: a limited partnership consists of one or more *general* partners and one or more *limited* partners. The general partners are the ones who operate the partnership and are liable for any partnership liabilities. A limited partner, on the other hand, contributes money or property to the partnership but does not operate the partnership or take part in managing its business. The limited partner has the right to a share in the partnership profits but, unlike the general partners, is not liable for any partnership obligations. The liability of limited partners is restricted to only the value of money and other property they have contributed to the partnership. Specific rules dealing with the creation of limited partnerships and the liability of limited partners are regionally legislated.[7]

The **limited liability partnership** (LLP) is a special form of partnership that, for the most part, is restricted to certain professionals, such as lawyers and accountants. It allows such professionals to limit their liability for the consequences of professional malpractice to their own conduct. In other words, they may not be held responsible for the malpractice of their partners. LLPs are available across Canada—for lawyers and accountants in all provinces except Prince Edward Island and in the Northwest Territories.[8]

See Table 8.1 for a comparison of the three types of partnerships.

Advantages and Disadvantages

Concerning *general partnerships*, the main advantage is that, like sole proprietorships, they can be established with minimal expense. A general partnership can reduce business costs on an individual basis and increase business opportunities through the pooling of resources. A major disadvantage of this business structure is that, as mentioned, the individual partners are jointly and severally liable for the actions of the business (in other words, every partner is liable with the other partners for any debts or liabilities incurred by the firm). This liability places the partners' personal assets at risk of a creditor suing to collect money owing to it by the partnership.

An advantage of the *limited partnership* is that it enables the partners to raise the funds required by attracting new investors. These investors can share in the partnership profits while limiting the risks involved in their investment to only the money or property they have contributed. Not all investors in a partnership want to assume all of its risks. One difficulty involved in a limited partnership is that the distinction between general and limited partners can become blurred. A limited partner who takes part in managing and controlling the partnership risks losing her limited partner status under the

---

limited partnership
partnership structure involving at least one general partner, who operates the partnership and is liable for any partnership debts, and at least one limited partner, who invests in the partnership but does not operate it or take part in managing its business and is not personally liable for its debts and obligations

limited liability partnership
partnership structure used by certain professions in Canada (accountants and lawyers, for the most part) whereby partners are not liable for the professional negligence of other partners

---

7 These rules appear either in general partnerships legislation or in special limited partnerships acts, such as Ontario's *Limited Partnerships Act*, RSO 1990, c L.16. Under Ontario's legislation, a limited partnership is formed when a declaration is filed with the provincial government.

8 The governing legislation in each jurisdiction where LLPs are permitted sets out the rules for their creation and the attendant rights and responsibilities attaching to this business structure. In Ontario, for example, the legislation regulating lawyers allows them to carry on their business using the LLP business structure, and the province's *Partnerships Act* (RSO 1990, c P.5) provides that an LLP is formed when two or more persons sign a written agreement that designates their partnership as an LLP and states that the *Partnerships Act* governs the agreement. Under this Act (ss 44.1-44.3), the firm name of the LLP must be registered under Ontario's *Business Names Act* (RSO 1990, c B.17), and the firm name must also contain the words "limited liability partnership" or the abbreviation "LLP" as the last words or letters of the firm name. At the time of writing, British Columbia is the only province that allows LLPs for professions other than law and accounting and for businesses generally.

TABLE 8.1 Comparison of the Three Types of Partnerships

	GENERAL PARTNERSHIP	LIMITED PARTNERSHIP	LIMITED LIABILITY PARTNERSHIP
Typical Example	Two friends go into business together; they share capital costs, debts, work, profit, and liability.	A sole proprietor needs capital and finds investors who become limited partners; they provide capital, share debts, and are entitled to profit, but they do not work in the business and have limited liability. The sole proprietor becomes a general partner.	A group of accountants form a partnership; they share capital costs, debts, work, and profit; and they are not liable for each other's professional negligence.
Liability	All partners are jointly and severally liable for each other's debts and negligence, including professional negligence. Liability is unlimited.	At least one general partner must be fully liable for the debts of the firm and any negligence of the other partners. Liability of general partners is limitless. Limited liability partners are liable for the debts of the firm and any negligence of the other partners only to the extent provided in the partnership agreement (usually to the extent of their capital investment).	Some or all partners may be limited liability partners, who are liable only for the general debts of the firm and not for the professional negligence of the other partners.
Decision-Making and Profit Taking	Partners often make decisions and share profit equally. A partnership agreement may provide that some partners have more decision-making power and are entitled to more profit (usually because of a larger initial investment) than others.	Limited partners have no decision-making powers. If they become involved in business decisions, they risk losing their limited liability status. Limited partners are entitled to profit according to the terms of the partnership agreement.	Limited liability partners may have decision-making powers and are entitled to profit according to the terms of the partnership agreement.

Source: Tamra Alexander & Pat Papadeas, *Canadian Business Law*, 3rd ed (Toronto: Emond, 2018) at 225-26.

governing legislation and being held liable as a general partner for any debts or liabilities of the business.

The main advantage of the *limited liability partnership* is that one partner is not liable for the professional malpractice of the other partner(s), although the partner himself will be responsible for his own malpractice (he cannot hide behind limited liability protection with respect to his own conduct). One limitation on this business structure is that, even where it is recognized, it is generally not available to all professions or businesses.

Corporations

Two main concerns for those operating a sole proprietorship or a partnership are (1) raising new money for the business and (2), as noted, being personally liable for the business's debts and obligations.

A **corporation** is a legal entity separate from those who create it.[9] Because it is independent from its owners (the shareholders) and those who manage it (the directors and officers or their appointees), these individuals are in most cases not personally and legally liable for the company's debts and obligations. However, in exceptional cases, the court does have the power to find that they are personally responsible. For example, in a process known as "piercing" (or "lifting") "the corporate veil," a court may ignore the separate legal status of the corporation and find that the individuals running the corporation are personally liable for its debts.[10] Also, directors and officers can be liable for up to six months of unpaid wages under employment legislation, and under pension, tax, and other legislation they may be liable for remittances not deducted or passed on as required.[11] In more extreme cases, when a corporation has committed regulatory or criminal offences, the individuals controlling the corporation can be found criminally responsible and be punished accordingly[12] (see also Box 8.1).

Aside from any concerns about future liabilities, when first incorporating a company, one must consider who will provide the initial investment and be its shareholders and who will be its directors and officers. Often in the initial stages of a corporation's existence, the owners, or shareholders, will also be the directors and officers—its first managers.

It is also necessary to consider where the head office will be located and whether to incorporate federally or provincially. Incorporating under the federal *Canada Business Corporations Act*[13] ensures a right to carry on business anywhere in Canada and provides increased name protection. If a company plans to carry on business locally, however, incorporation under the relevant provincial or territorial statute is common. These companies can still carry on business in other provinces and territories if they wish provided that they

corporation
company or group of people authorized by statute to act as a single entity (legally a person) and recognized as such in law

---

9   The independent legal status of corporations, or the Salomon principle, was firmly established in the late 1800s (in *Salomon v Salomon & Co Ltd*, [1896] UKHL 1, [1897] AC 22) and is now enshrined in all Canadian corporate legislation.

10   This is a complex area, but, in general terms, if a corporation's resources are being expropriated for personal use, or the corporation is otherwise being used as a shield for fraudulent or improper conduct, then the principals may be personally liable. See, for example, *Shoppers Drug Mart Inc v 6470360 Canada Inc (Energyshop Consulting Inc/Powerhouse Energy Management Inc)*, 2014 ONCA 85.

11   See, for example, the *Canada Pension Plan*, RSC 1985, c C-8, s 21.1, and the *Employment Insurance Act*, SC 1996, c 23, s 83.

12   Under the *Criminal Code*, for example, corporate principals may be criminally responsible in cases involving negligence, securities manipulation, fraud, and other conduct. An important subarea of negligence concerns industrial accidents and failures to take reasonable care for worker safety. In these cases, principals may be charged under s 217.1 and the corporation itself under s 22.1 as a party to the offence (this is the case even if a responsible senior officer cannot be identified or is not convicted). These provisions are part of what is known as the Westray amendment to the *Criminal Code*, so named after the Westray mining disaster in Nova Scotia in 1992 that killed 26 workers. In *R v Metron Construction Corporation*, 2013 ONCA 541, the Westray amendment was in issue. The case involved a construction accident in Toronto, in which four workers fell to their deaths as a result of faulty scaffolding. Metron Construction pleaded guilty under s 22.1 and was fined $750,000. In related proceedings, the sole director of Metron was fined $112,500 under provincial health and safety legislation, and the project manager was convicted under s 217.1 and sentenced to 3½ years in prison, the first individual to be convicted and imprisoned under this section (see *R v Kazenelson*, 2018 ONCA 77). In 2019, in another important case relating to personal and corporate criminal liability—this one involving bribery of foreign officials—SNC-Lavalin pleaded guilty to fraud under s 380 of the *Criminal Code* (and was fined $280 million, the highest fine, so far, for such an offence), and one of its senior officers was convicted by a jury of fraud and other offences (and was sentenced in 2020 to 8½ years in prison: see *R c Bebawi*, 2020 QCCS 22).

13   RSC 1985, c C-44.

register as required in those jurisdictions. (Federal companies have to register in jurisdictions in which they do business too, but the process is simpler.)

A corporation is created when its incorporators file with the appropriate government office a document known either as (depending on the province) letters patent, memorandum of association, or—in the case of federal incorporation—articles of incorporation. These are standard form documents containing certain information the government requires, such as the company name, the location of its head office, the names and addresses of its first directors, and the number and types of company shares.

In addition, the application for incorporation must also include a NUANS (Newly Updated Automated Name Search) report. This report confirms that the government names database has been searched and that there are no existing corporations already using the proposed name. If the name is similar to that of an existing corporation, and the similarity is likely to cause confusion, the proposed new name may not be accepted. If the name proves problematic in this way and the incorporators want to get their new company up and running quickly, a company can be created using a number instead of a name. Once all of the required paperwork is submitted and the submission fee is paid, the company comes into existence.

Corporations have the ability to raise capital by issuing and selling shares to the public, something not possible for a sole proprietor or partnership. Deciding whether to offer shares to the public, thereby creating a *public company*, or limiting the number of shareholders and operating as a *private company*, is one of many important matters to review with legal advisors when structuring or expanding a company. Public companies, whose shares can be sold on stock exchanges, are much more heavily regulated than private companies. Securities regulation is a very complex and detailed area of the law.

Advantages and Disadvantages

One legal advantage of corporations as a business structure is that the owners and directors of a company are not personally liable for its debts and obligations (subject to the exceptions noted above). Another advantage, for public companies, is that the corporation can sell shares to raise new capital. Disadvantages for public companies include the cost and complexity of running them because of the detailed securities regulations that apply and the increased costs associated with those regulations.

BOX 8.1

Application of Charter Protections and Criminal Law to Corporations

What other implications flow from the special legal status of corporations? What treatment do corporations receive under statutes—such as the *Canadian Charter of Rights and Freedoms* or the *Criminal Code*—that were primarily designed to apply to people? Generally, whether the special legal status of corporations entitles them to the protections of the Charter depends on the type of right or freedom under consideration. For example, freedom of expression has been interpreted as extending to corporations in the case of *Irwin Toy Ltd v Quebec (Attorney General)*,* but the right to equality and the freedom of religion have been restricted to human beings.

Does criminal law apply to corporations? A corporation cannot be sent to jail for criminal acts, but governments are more and more willing to create criminal offences (such as environmental offences) for which corporations can be found guilty and punished through substantial fines. In some cases, the directors of a corporation can be jailed for serious criminal offences perpetrated by the corporation.

* [1989] 1 SCR 927, 1989 CanLII 87.

Source: Tamra Alexander & Pat Papadeas, *Canadian Business Law*, 3rd ed (Toronto: Emond, 2018) at 235-36.

Business Transactions

No matter what form of business structure one chooses, the successful operation of the business itself will depend on selling something—property, the use of property, services, or some combination of these things—to somebody (the customer or client) at a profit. Sales can be business to business or business to consumer, and the main vehicle used for accomplishing such sales is the contract. Contracts are used to define the rights and obligations of the parties in business transactions and, frequently, to place limits on the potential liability of the selling party (see Chapter 7 for a discussion of contract law generally).

There are numerous types of business transactions, and many have generated their own specialized standard form contracts (and some their own areas of law, such as real estate transactions and insurance). Furthermore, the transactions can be local or can cross regional or national boundaries. Cross-boundary transactions introduce new levels of complexity because of the possible application of laws from jurisdictions other than the seller's.

Payment options for sellers include cash, cheque (and other negotiable instruments—see Box 8.2), credit card (which can be linked to smartphones and companies such as PayPal that facilitate online payments), debit card (allowing payment directly from the customer's bank account), wire transfer (bank to bank), and letter of credit (which can be used when a purchaser of goods resides in another jurisdiction and usually comes in the form of a guarantee from the purchaser's bank promising to release funds to the seller as soon as the bank receives proof of shipment of the goods). New methods of payment will continue to evolve as technology changes and adapts.

> **negotiable instrument**
> document that promises the payment of a specific amount of money to the payee, on demand or at a set time, and that can be transferred to a third party

---

BOX 8.2

Negotiable Instruments

A **negotiable instrument** is a document that promises the payment of a specific amount of money to a person, on demand or at a set time, and that can be transferred to a third party. Negotiable instruments are portable and easier to use when large sums of money are involved (a single page can represent the entire amount and be simply carried from one place to another) and can minimize the risk of theft because only the named payee (or another person if the instrument is endorsed) can cash them. They can be used as a method of payment for most types of business transactions. In Canada, they are regulated under the *Bills of Exchange Act** and come in three forms: cheques, promissory notes, and bills of exchange.

A *cheque* involves three parties: the payer (the person making payment and who has an account at a financial institution), the drawee (the financial institution), and the payee (the person to whom the financial institution is directed to make payment). A cheque is payable on demand on or after the date on the cheque. However, a bank is required to honour the cheque only if there are sufficient funds in the payer's account. The payee can transfer the cheque by endorsing it—that is, by signing the back of the cheque. If the cheque is simply endorsed without naming another person as payee (this is called "endorsement in blank"), the cheque can be passed on multiple times to other bearers, until it is eventually presented to the bank for payment. If the cheque is endorsed and stated to be payable to a specific person (called a "restrictive endorsement"), only that person named can cash it; it cannot be passed on again.

A *promissory note* involves only two parties and is simply a promise by one person (the maker) to pay another person (a creditor) a specified amount according to the terms set out in the note (for example, the time of payment, interest charges, etc.). The maker must sign the note before it is enforceable. The creditor can endorse the note if she chooses and give it to another person, who becomes the holder and who has the same rights to enforce the note as the original creditor.

Bills of exchange can operate either like cheques or like promissory notes depending on how they are structured. They are used infrequently today because of the popularity of cheques and promissory notes and because they are more complex and require more formalities when making them.

*   RSC 1985, c B-4.

When sellers sell on credit, and when the consumer or business debt is connected to personal property, the sellers can protect themselves by registering various security interests against the property (see Chapter 7 for a discussion of personal property security legislation).

More generally, in the event of non-payment, creditors have a large arsenal of techniques to help them collect their debts, including pre-judgment garnishment of bank accounts, post-judgment garnishment of wages, seizures and sales of personal property, and the registration of judgments against real property. In all cases, however, collections rules tend to be interpreted strictly, and the requirements of the relevant legislation must be followed carefully.

Builders and Repairers: Security for Services Performed

The business of builders and repairers comprises a large part of the service industry. It includes building construction and renovation work and storage of and repairs to (and other work related to) personal property (including motor vehicles, boats, aircraft, and other tangible property). In this section, we briefly examine some of the remedies available to builders and repairers when they are not paid for their work.

With respect to construction and renovation work done on real property, an unpaid contractor can pursue the civil remedy of damages for breach of contract. This is time-consuming and costly and comes with the uncertainty associated with litigation generally. One well-established method of securing payment in these circumstances is the **builders' (or construction) lien**. An unpaid contractor has a lien for the amount owed for work done on the landowner's property, and this lien can be registered against the property. All provinces and territories have legislation detailing matters such as timelines for filing claims of liens against property, procedures for removal of liens after payment, and court-ordered sales of the land in the event of non-payment.[14]

With respect to unpaid work in relation to personal property (storage and repair work, etc.), all provinces and territories have legislation setting out rules for establishing liens against the property in question. For example, Ontario's *Repair and Storage Liens Act*[15] (RSLA) provides that "a repairer has a lien against an article that the repairer has repaired for an amount equal to [the amount agreed upon or if there was no agreed amount the fair value of the repair], and the repairer may retain possession of the article until the amount is paid."[16] A similar lien exists with regard to unpaid storage costs. Furthermore, these liens exist whether or not the contractor remains in possession of the property. The legislation allows for the registration of the lien in the personal property security registry of the relevant jurisdiction (see Chapter 7).

builders' (or construction) lien
charge against land that builders use to secure amounts owed them for work done on landowners' property

Product Sales and Consumer Protection Legislation

A business that sells products and services to the public today must comply with legislation covering a variety of issues relating to contract terms and product or service standards and

---

14   See, for example, the *Construction Act*, RSO 1990, c C.30; *Builders' Lien Act*, RSNS 1989, c 277; and *Mechanics' Lien Act*, RSNL 1990, c M-3.

15   RSO 1990, c R.25.

16   RSLA, s 3.

safety. In the past, there was a much more lenient approach to the marketplace generally. Two phrases that are indicative of this approach are *laissez-faire* and *caveat emptor*. *Laissez-faire* (French: literally, "let do or make") refers to the economic philosophy that the marketplace should be free from constraints by government and that businesses should be free to profit from their ventures subject only to the contracts they negotiate with others. *Caveat emptor* (Latin: "buyer beware") refers to the idea that purchasers must take the property they purchase "as is." It is up to them to protect themselves by inspecting and testing the property before purchasing it or by negotiating terms with respect to quality and to cover the risks of future defects.

The marketplace has changed significantly in the last 150 years and has become more complex. Businesses used to be smaller and have a closer connection with the communities where they sold their products or services. Many commercial operations today have grown into national or international enterprises, with few local allegiances. Moreover, many products now are mass-produced and technologically advanced, and it is difficult to inspect them before they are purchased, either because they are sealed (or their packaging is sealed) or because they are purchased online or from catalogues. Also, sellers often require purchasers to agree to standard form contracts, limiting their ability to negotiate favourable terms.

As Jacob Ziegel observed (see the quotation at the beginning of this chapter), "[t]he notion of the consumer bargaining from a position of equal strength has become a fiction in any but the most attenuated sense." The response of legislators to a changing marketplace and changing values has been varied and complex. In this section, we briefly examine (1) sale of goods legislation and its impact on product sales contracts, (2) federal legislation specifically enacted to protect consumers, and (3) provincial and territorial legislative responses to consumer protection.

Sale of Goods Acts

The English *Sale of Goods Act*[17] was enacted in 1893. It was the first attempt to codify laws about buying and selling goods and to add some basic safeguards respecting the rights of buyers and sellers. All common law provinces and territories in Canada have passed similar acts based on this English statute. These acts modernize sale of goods law for the benefit of purchasers. In doing so, they help counter the traditional harshness of *caveat emptor*. One instance of this modernization is the introduction of some conditions implied into every contract of sale. We will use British Columbia's *Sale of Goods Act*[18] as an example in discussing these implied conditions.

Five major implied conditions listed in BC's *Sale of Goods Act* are the following:

1. *Seller's title and right to sell.*   There is an implied condition under section 16 of the Act that a seller has a right to sell or lease the goods.
2. *Sale by description.*   If goods are sold by description, there is an implied condition under section 17 that the goods correspond with that description.
3. *Fitness for purpose.*   If a buyer expressly or by implication indicates to a seller her particular purpose requiring a product and is relying on the seller's skill or judgment, and the seller is in the business of selling that product, then there is, under section 18(a) of the Act, an implied condition that the goods sold are reasonably fit for the purpose for which the product was bought.

---

17   (UK), 1893, 56 & 57 Vict, c 71.

18   RSBC 1996, c 410.

4. *Goods of merchantable quality.* If goods are bought by description from a seller who deals in goods of that description, there is an implied condition, under section 18(b) of the Act, that the goods are of merchantable quality—that is, fit to be used for the ordinary purposes for which products of its kind are manufactured and sold.

5. *Sale by sample.* If goods are sold by sample, there is an implied condition under section 19 of the Act that the goods in bulk correspond to that sample in type and quality.

Although this legislation protects consumers to a degree, as these five implied conditions illustrate, it is important to note that sale of goods acts are primarily about contractual rights and responsibilities generally and not consumer protection per se. These codified rules apply to all sale of goods transactions, whether they are between businesses (for example, one commercial enterprise selling machinery to another), between private individuals (such as a sale of goods at a garage sale), or between businesses and consumers (for example, a retail business selling clothing to a customer).

Federal Consumer Protection Legislation

Although provincial sale of goods acts assist purchasers by imposing implied conditions—along with additional safeguards—on sale transactions, these statutes do not cover all areas affecting consumers who buy an item for their own personal use. Increasingly, both the federal and provincial/territorial governments have enacted numerous other pieces of legislation more comprehensive in scope than sale of goods acts to help protect consumers from changing marketplace concerns, such as:

- anti-competitive and dishonest business tactics,
- false and misleading advertising,
- deceptive marketing practices, and
- products that may jeopardize the safety of consumers.

Three examples of this additional federal legislation are discussed below.

The Competition Act

The *Competition Act*[19] is the principal federal statute regulating trade and commerce with respect to conspiracies, trade practices, and mergers that affect competition. It is the oldest competition (or antitrust) statute in the Western world and was first enacted in 1889. Its purpose, as set out in section 1.1, is "to maintain and encourage competition in Canada in order to promote the efficiency and adaptability of the Canadian economy."

The Act authorizes the federal government to take action against those who it alleges violate its provisions, either through criminal proceedings or by administrative review. The commissioner of competition is responsible for the administration and enforcement of this Act.

Criminal matters relating to competition include such things as price-fixing (agreements fixing prices among competitors), bid-rigging (agreements restricting open bidding processes), interferences with professional sports (for example, by unreasonably limiting opportunities to participate in professional sports or to negotiate contracts with clubs in professional leagues), and operating pyramid schemes (multi-level marketing plans that depend for profits on the recruitment of others who pay to participate). These kinds of

---

19   RSC 1985, c C-34.

offences are prosecuted in the criminal courts and, if the offending party is convicted, can result in fines or imprisonment.

Certain less serious market behaviours are classed as reviewable conduct and are not considered criminal matters; they are subject to administrative review by the Competition Bureau, the Competition Tribunal, or the courts. Reviewable conduct includes such things as deceptive market practices (for example, misleading misrepresentations about product performance, bait-and-switch selling, or sale above the advertised price practices) and mergers that substantially lessen competition in a trade or industry (see Box 8.3 for an example). Administrative penalties for engaging in reviewable conduct are not as serious as criminal penalties and include orders to stop the offending practice or to publish notices informing consumers about the conduct and administrative monetary penalties (which, for corporations, can be as high as $15 million).

BOX 8.3

Media Monopoly

Because of their significance as vehicles for airing diverse points of view, the news media are businesses in which healthy competition is extremely important. Although the case described below is a case that merely concerned an advertising supplement, it has wider implications.

In *Canada (Director of Investigation and Research) v Southam Inc*,* the defendant corporation, a media giant, purchased two BC newspapers, the *North Shore News* and the *Real Estate Weekly*. The *North Shore News*, a profitable and widely read newspaper, contained a weekly real estate supplement. Before the defendant corporation purchased the papers, this supplement and the *Real Estate Weekly* were the only two real estate advertising papers distributed on the North Shore.

The Competition Tribunal's director of investigation and research brought an application asking the tribunal to order that the corporation sell one or the other of the two papers, alleging that the defendant's ownership of both papers eliminated competition in the real estate market in the area. The defendant proposed, as an alternative remedy, that the *North Shore News* begin to carry, as an insert, an independent real estate supplement referred to as "HOMES."

The tribunal found that the corporation's ownership of both the *Real Estate Weekly* and the *North Shore News* eliminated competition in the real estate advertising sales market in the region. It was unconvinced that an independent HOMES supplement would be as attractive to advertisers or as financially viable as the existing *North Shore News* supplement (which, at the time of the merger, was slightly outperforming the *Real Estate Weekly*). The tribunal also believed that it lacked the power to make the order the defendant requested.

The tribunal ordered the corporation to sell either the *North Shore News* or the *Real Estate Weekly* to restore competition in the marketplace.

*   1991 CanLII 1702 (Comp Trib).

Source: Margaret Buchan et al, *Canadian Business Law*, 2nd ed (Toronto: Emond Montgomery, 2012) at 182.

The Food and Drugs Act

Canada's *Food and Drugs Act*[20] is another key piece of federal legislation protecting consumers. It aims to protect the health and safety of Canadians in connection with the sale of food, drugs, cosmetics, and medical devices manufactured and sold in Canada. The Act prohibits sellers from selling the following:

- food that is unfit for human consumption, is deceptively labelled or packaged, or was manufactured or stored in unsanitary conditions (manufacturers are similarly prohibited from engaging in such practices) (ss 4, 5, and 7);

---

20   RSC 1985, c F-27.

- drugs that were manufactured or stored in unsanitary conditions (a similar prohibition applies to manufacturers), that are adulterated, or that are deceptively labelled or packaged (ss 8, 9, and 11);
- cosmetics that contain injurious substances or were manufactured or stored in unsanitary conditions (a similar prohibition applies to manufacturers) (ss 16 and 18); and
- medical devices that may cause injury when used as directed (and any person who is involved with labelling or packaging such products can be liable if the labelling or packaging is misleading) (ss 19 and 20).

The Canada Consumer Product Safety Act

In 2011, the *Canada Consumer Product Safety Act*[21] (CCPSA) came into force, bringing Canada's consumer protection laws in line with the new realities of international manufacturing and the marketplace and responding to the desire of consumers for more information about the products they use. The Act is administered by Health Canada.

The purpose of the CCPSA, as set out in section 3, is to protect the public by addressing or preventing dangers to human health or safety that are posed by consumer products in Canada, including imported products. The Act applies to consumer products that individuals may use for non-commercial purposes—such as domestic, recreational, and sports purposes—as well as to their parts, accessories, and packaging. A wide range of products is thus covered, from children's toys to household products and sporting goods, to name a few. The Act does not apply to goods that are governed by other specific legislation, such as food, cosmetics, medical devices, natural health products, drugs, and vehicles.

Sections 7(a) and 8(a) of the CCPSA contain what is known as the general prohibition. Section 7(a) prohibits manufacturers and importers from manufacturing, importing, advertising, or selling consumer products that constitute a danger to human health or safety, and section 8(a) prohibits anyone from advertising or selling a consumer product they know is a danger to human health or safety. Under the Act, the minister of health has the authority to order a manufacturer, an importer, or a seller to recall any product that the minister believes is a danger to human health or safety. Industry is expected to undertake recalls voluntarily when necessary.

Other key provisions of the Act include the following:

- Industry must provide Health Canada and suppliers of products with information related to safety incidents or product defects that could result in death or harmful health effects.
- Packaging, labelling, and advertising must not mislead or deceive consumers as to the safety of a product.
- Certain records must be kept by manufacturers, importers, advertisers, vendors, and testers of consumer products in order to make it possible to trace unsafe products back to their source.
- Manufacturers or importers may be required to provide or obtain information about their products (including studies) so that Health Canada can verify that a product is in compliance with the requirements of the CCPSA.

---

21 SC 2010, c 21.

Provincial and Territorial Areas of Consumer Protection

The federal government is not alone in protecting consumers. The provinces and territories are also involved in this area and have enacted legislation specifically focused on the protection of consumers. Typically, this legislation defines a consumer as someone who has entered into a transaction "for personal, family or household purposes" and excludes from its application business or commercial transactions. This is different from sale of goods acts, which apply generally to all transactions. In other respects, however, consumer protection legislation is broader than sale of goods acts because it applies to sales of goods *and* services and, in some jurisdictions, even to the sale of real property.

One example of this legislation is Ontario's *Consumer Protection Act, 2002*,[22] which applies to all Ontario consumer transactions. For example, it covers consumer rights and warranties, credit agreements, leasing, and procedures for consumer remedies. The Act lists a number of "unfair practices," such as making a "false, misleading or deceptive representation" (s 14(1)) or pressuring a consumer to renegotiate a transaction by keeping custody or control of their goods (s 16). As well, the Act contains additional rights and obligations for some specific consumer agreements, such as those involving time shares, personal development services, and Internet agreements.

As illustrated in Box 8.4, businesses that are aware of serious defects in their products but fail to take swift action to resolve them may have punitive damages awarded against them by the courts.

Another specific area the Act covers is motor vehicle repairs, a major concern for all consumers who drive. Part VI of the Act helps protect drivers against inflated bills for car repairs. Among its provisions are the following:

- No repairer shall charge consumers for any work or repairs without first giving them an estimate (s 56(1)).
- A repairer cannot charge a fee for giving the estimate unless the consumer is told in advance that a fee will be charged (s 57(1)).
- Repairers cannot charge for any work or repairs unless the work and repairs have been authorized by the consumer (s 58(1)).
- A repairer shall be deemed to warrant all new and reconditioned parts and labour for a minimum of 90 days or 5,000 kilometres, whichever comes first (s 63(1)).

BOX 8.4

Punitive Damages for Failure to Protect Consumers

In the Supreme Court of Canada (SCC) case *Prebushewski v Dodge City Auto (1984) Ltd*,* the consumer bought a new Dodge Ram half-tonne truck from a dealership. She and her husband drove the truck without incident for 16 months until, one day, the husband's employer noticed a fire outside the office. The husband ran outside to discover the truck in flames. It was completely destroyed.

Both the dealer and the manufacturer denied liability, referring the consumer and her husband to their insurer.

After some investigation, it was determined that the fire was caused by a defect in the daytime running light system. A representative of the manufacturer eventually testified that the manufacturer had known of this defect for several years without issuing a recall.

The trial court found a breach of a statutory warranty under the Saskatchewan *Consumer Protection Act*.† In addition to ordering regular damages of about $40,000, the trial judge ordered exemplary (punitive) damages of $25,000

22 SO 2002, c 30, Schedule A.

against the manufacturer and dealer. The manufacturer and dealer appealed to the Court of Appeal and were successful in having the exemplary damage award struck out. The consumer appealed to the SCC.

The SCC restored the order of exemplary damages, finding that the consumer protection legislation had increased the accessibility of exemplary damages (under common law, it is very difficult to win damages of this kind). (The Ontario *Consumer Protection Act, 2002* also permits awards of exemplary damages under s 18(11).)

* 2005 SCC 28.

† SS 1996, c C-30.1.

Source: Reproduced from Margaret Buchan et al, *Canadian Business Law*, 2nd ed (Toronto: Emond Montgomery, 2012) at 172.

Advertising Standards

To supplement federal and provincial consumer legislation, major stakeholders in the advertising and marketing industries have formed industry associations that also help protect consumers. These associations have established self-regulating and industry-approved codes of standards and policy guidelines. Advertising Standards Canada (ASC), created in 1957, is one such body; it administers the *Canadian Code of Advertising Standards*,[23] first published in 1963. The Code is widely endorsed by Canadian advertisers and sets out standards for advertising that is truthful, fair, and accurate in the following areas:

1. accuracy and clarity;
2. disguised advertising techniques;
3. price claims;
4. bait and switch;
5. guarantees;
6. comparative advertising;
7. testimonials;
8. professional or scientific claims;
9. imitation;
10. safety;
11. superstition and fears;
12. advertising to children;
13. advertising to minors; and
14. unacceptable depictions and portrayals of behaviours that are discriminatory, violent, demeaning, or otherwise offensive.

In administering the Code, ASC has set up Standards Councils (Councils), which are composed of senior advertising industry and public representatives who volunteer their time to adjudicate complaints under the Code by consumers, special interest groups, and businesses involved in trade disputes. A Council rendering a decision in a particular case determines whether any of the standards in the 14 areas above—each one described more fully in a separate clause in the Code—have been infringed. As part of its commitment to a transparent consumer complaint process, ASC compiles reports of the complaints it

---

23   Online: <https://adstandards.ca/code/the-code-online>.

receives and the Council decision on each one. The reports are listed by year on ASC's website. The following are some examples of Council decisions:[24]

- In 2009, an advertisement in a Punjabi-language newspaper in Ontario assured readers that, through black magic, the advertiser could eliminate all of their personal worries, fulfill all of their desires, remove all of the obstacles in the way of their marrying a loved one, and eliminate their lottery problems and business worries. The ad stated that results were 100 percent guaranteed. Council found that the ad exploited superstitions and played upon fears to mislead consumers, contrary to clause 11 (concerning superstition and fears).

- In 2010, a manufacturer in the food/supermarkets industry in Quebec released a commercial in which a man shown in a deserted area was suddenly surrounded by a group of people who hit him repeatedly until he fell to his knees on the ground. Council considered a complaint that the commercial encouraged violence and found that, despite its humorous elements, the scenario did seem to condone violence, contrary to clause 14(b) (concerning unacceptable depictions and portrayals of violence).

- In 2013, a popular Canadian clothing retailer advertised that all fall merchandise was being offered at a discount of 20 to 50 percent off the regular price. The complainant alleged that the discount was less than 20 percent off on many items. Council found that the ad contained a misleading savings claim contrary to clauses 1(a) and 3(a) (concerning accuracy and deceptive pricing), and the advertiser agreed that the ad should have stated that only select items were being offered at 20 to 50 percent off.

- In 2019, an online video promoting an air carrier's "kids' club" showed a family vacation from a child's perspective. The commercial included a scene of passengers on an aircraft with more spacious seating and legroom than were provided. The scene was one second long, and the total duration of the commercial was 15 seconds. Council, in discussing false and misleading representations by businesses, referred to the SCC case of *Richard v Time Inc*[25] for the proposition that the general impression created by an advertisement should be considered from the perspective of a naïve consumer in a hurry. Despite the fact that the scene was of short duration and the advertiser made no specific claims about seating, Council found that the commercial implied that the advertiser's aircrafts featured spacious legroom, and that was the general impression conveyed; as such, it contained misleading representations and contravened clause 1(a) (concerning accuracy).

ASC updates the Code regularly to ensure that it keeps pace with consumer and societal expectations. ASC reporting and the Code are instrumental in ensuring truth in advertising in Canada.

---

24 Advertising Standards Canada, "Ad Complaints Reporting," online: <https://adstandards.ca/complaints/complaints-reporting>.

25 2012 SCC 8.

CHAPTER SUMMARY

There are many ways to carry on a business in Canada. The three most common business structures are the sole proprietorship, the partnership, and the corporation. Each one has its advantages and disadvantages. Sole proprietorships are relatively easy and inexpensive to set up and operate, but they are not a separate legal structure from their owners, who are liable for all debts and obligations that their businesses may incur and whose personal assets are thus put at risk.

There are several kinds of partnership structure, each with advantages and disadvantages. The *general partnership* structure is the standard one. It offers the advantage of being relatively inexpensive to create and provides the business with a collegial environment, an extended pool of capital based on cost-sharing, and a group of members whose connections may help the business attract new clients. Its main disadvantage is that each partner is personally liable for all of the firm's debts and liabilities, which may put the partners' personal assets at risk. A *limited partnership* has one or more general partners and one or more limited partners. A limited partner contributes money and property and shares in partnership profits but is not liable for the partnership's obligations unless she takes part in managing the partnership. A *limited liability partnership*, if it meets certain criteria, has one key advantage: one partner is not liable for the professional negligence of the other partner(s).

A corporation is a legal entity separate from those who create it. The owners and directors are not personally liable for the company's debts and obligations, but the incorporation process can be expensive, and running a corporation can be a complicated undertaking.

All businesses engage in business transactions of various types with a view to profit. Contracts, which are frequently specialized for particular businesses, are important tools for determining rights and obligations and allocating risks. Payment methods are varied, but negotiable instruments (in particular, cheques and promissory notes) are important because they are portable, transferable, and safe. Businesses that are owed money and have rights against property have an option to register liens and other security interests to enforce their debts. In the event of non-payment, all businesses have a number of collections options, including garnishment of bank accounts and wages.

If a business is selling goods to other businesses or to consumers, sale of goods acts apply. These acts codify laws about buying and selling goods and add some basic safeguards respecting the rights of buyers and sellers. Particularly significant are the implied conditions and warranties relating to the seller's title and right to sell the goods, the correspondence of the goods with their description, and the fitness of the goods for their intended purpose.

Legislation protecting consumers has greatly expanded in recent times. Both the federal and provincial governments have enacted consumer protection statutes that are wider in scope than sale of goods acts. The federal *Competition Act* and *Food and Drugs Act*, for example, ensure that consumers have competitive prices and product choices, as well as laws protecting their health and safety respecting food, drugs, cosmetics, and medical devices manufactured and sold in Canada. Provincial consumer protection legislation, such as Ontario's *Consumer Protection Act, 2002*, protects consumers in a variety of other areas, including motor vehicle repairs. Advertising standards also aim to protect consumers by ensuring that advertising is truthful, fair, and accurate.

KEY TERMS

builders' (or construction) lien, 238

corporation, 235

fiduciary duty, 232

general partnership, 232

limited liability partnership, 233

limited partnership, 233

negotiable instrument, 237

sole proprietorship, 231

FURTHER READING

BOOKS

Alexander, Tamra & Pat Papadeas, *Canadian Business Law*, 3rd ed (Toronto: Emond, 2018).

DuPlessis, Dorothy et al, *Canadian Business and the Law*, 6th ed (Toronto: Nelson, 2017).

Ogilvie, Margaret, ed, *Consumer Law: Cases and Materials*, 3rd ed (Toronto: Captus Press, 2007).

Pritchard, Brenda & Susan Vogt, *Advertising and Marketing Law in Canada*, 5th ed (Toronto: LexisNexis, 2015).

Waddams, SM, *Products Liability*, 5th ed (Toronto: Carswell, 2011).

Weir, D Jan & Fran Smyth, *Critical Concepts of Canadian Business Law*, 6th ed (Toronto: Pearson, 2014).

Yates, Richard A, Teresa Bereznicki-Korol & Trevor Clarke, *Business Law in Canada*, 11th ed (Toronto: Pearson, 2016).

WEBSITES

Advertising Standards Canada: <https://adstandards.ca>.

Competition Bureau Canada: <https://www.competitionbureau.gc.ca/eic/site/cb-bc.nsf/eng/home>.

Cosmetics Alliance Canada: <https://www.cosmeticsalliance.ca>.

Health Canada: <https://www.hc-sc.gc.ca>.

Innovation, Science and Economic Development Canada: <http://www.ic.gc.ca/Intro.html>.

REVIEW QUESTIONS

1. List two advantages of a sole proprietorship.

2. Explain the meaning of the term "fiduciary duty."

3. What is the advantage of a limited partnership for an investor?

4. What must be included in the name of a limited liability partnership?

5. List two main advantages to be gained by incorporating a company.

6. How can a contractor who performs work on real property—for example, a renovation—protect herself in the event of non-payment?

7. List five implied conditions of sale under provincial sale of goods acts.

8. What are two ways the marketplace today causes difficulties for consumers who want to know more about a product before they buy it?

9. List four areas covered by the federal *Food and Drugs Act*.

EXERCISES

1. Four architects decide to form a general partnership and to work out of one office suite. List three advantages these architects could gain from such an arrangement and some potential problems that could arise from their partnership.

2. Why is the law providing ever more legislative protections for consumers? Is it a trend that you expect to continue? Why or why not?

3. Section 3(1) of the *Food and Drugs Act* states that "no person shall advertise any food, drug, cosmetic or device to the general public as a treatment, preventative or cure for any of the diseases, disorders or abnormal physical states referred to in Schedule A." Look at Schedule A to this Act and discuss conditions that you think ought or ought not to be included on the list.

9 Administrative Law

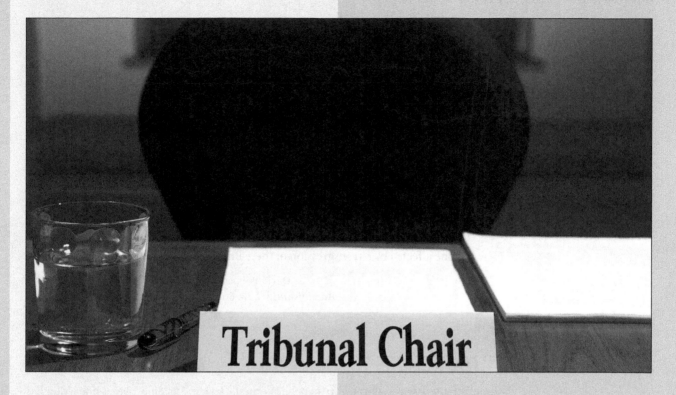

Tribunal Chair

Introduction 250

The Role of Administrative
Agencies in Society 251

The Constitutional Basis of
Administrative Agencies 252

Delegated Power and Functions
of Administrative Agencies 253

The Public's Interaction with
Administrative Bodies 258

Challenging Administrative Decisions 259

Chapter Summary 267

Key Terms 267

Further Reading 268

Review Questions 268

Exercises 268

Administrative law deals with the legal limitations on the actions of governmental officials, and with the remedies which are available to anyone affected by a transgression of these limitations.

David P Jones & Anne S de Villars, *Principles of Administrative Law*, 6th ed (Toronto: Carswell, 2014) at 3

Introduction

Administrative law is a subcategory of public domestic law, and its objective, as one writer has stated, "is to regulate the relationships between the government and governed—the population."[1] Although criminal law is often highlighted when considering a person's relationship to the state, for the average person, administrative law is more important because it concerns how we interact with and are regulated by governments in many areas of everyday life.

Such interaction and regulation influence our lives from beginning to end and help define our place in society. For example, medical boards regulate the practices by which we are brought into the world. School boards determine what we learn. New Canadians interact with the Immigration and Refugee Board of Canada when it applies immigration laws to them. When we build our homes, building codes and municipal inspectors control our choices. The decisions of energy boards and utility commissions affect the price we pay for energy and fuel to keep ourselves warm. If an issue arises involving our employment, labour relations boards, workers' compensation boards, and human rights tribunals may be called upon to resolve our disputes. The Canadian Radio-television and Telecommunications Commission (CRTC) determines what we can watch for entertainment and the rates we pay to communicate with one another. The food we eat and drugs we ingest, the investments we make, the privacy we enjoy (or don't)—in fact, almost all aspects of our lives—are regulated to varying degrees through the instrument of administrative law.[2]

---

1 Guy Régimbald, *Canadian Administrative Law*, 2nd ed (Toronto: LexisNexis, 2015) at 1.

2 See also Sara Blake, *Administrative Law in Canada*, 6th ed (Toronto: LexisNexis, 2017) at 3 and *Newfoundland Telephone Co v Newfoundland (Board of Commissioners of Public Utilities)*, [1992] 1 SCR 623 at 634-35, 89 DLR (4th) 28.

However, the influence of administrative law, although inescapable, has its limits. The mass of regulation permeating modern societies, although connected to administrative law, is also separate from it in a sense. Complaints we may have with the amount or quality of government regulation (most of it in the form of subordinate legislation, as described in Chapter 4) are more political than legal in nature. Administrative law is not so much about the *value* of our regulation as it is about the *manner* in which this regulation is imposed on us. Put another way, "[i]t is more concerned with *the process for making a decision* than with the result."[3]

In this chapter, we examine the role of regulatory bodies in society. We consider the constitutional framework in which they operate and important limitations on their power connected to the delegatory relationship they have with governments. The structure and functions of administrative agencies are also examined, along with a consideration of the principal methods and grounds for challenging their decisions and the types of remedies that may be claimed when seeking relief.

To see how administrative law is situated overall as an area of law in Canada, review Figure 1.1 on page 21.

The Role of Administrative Agencies in Society

Governments and elected officials cannot participate directly in all aspects of the implementation of our laws. This is due to both the *quantity* of regulation applicable to most activities involving the public and the *complexity* of this regulation. To fulfill their obligation to administer the law, governments delegate many of their responsibilities to administrative agencies. **Administrative agencies** are regulatory bodies created under various federal, provincial, and territorial statutes. Their purpose is to administer the legislative schemes set out in these enabling statutes and their regulations. The word "agency" in this context simply means any person, institution, body, board, or tribunal that has been assigned governance powers under legislation.[4]

Delegating tasks to administrative agencies offers a number of advantages for both governments and the public. First, it speeds things up. Having more decision-makers on the ground enables the government to respond more quickly and efficiently to the needs of the public. A second advantage is specialization; agency officials are usually appointed on the basis of their familiarity with the area of regulation. Such expertise produces better decisions, which can, in turn, enhance the credibility of government.

As indicated, the reach of administrative agencies is extensive. They include not only traditional government entities—such as licensing bodies, securities commissions, and labour boards—but also hospitals, universities, self-regulating professions, and certain trade associations that have been delegated regulatory authority under legislation.

administrative agency
government bodies created under various federal, provincial, and territorial statutes with the purpose of administering particular statutory regimes

---

3   Blake, *ibid* at 4 (emphasis added).

4   Administrative agencies are referred to in various ways. Generically speaking, they are known as "bodies," "entities," or "agencies." Their actual names or titles commonly include, if not the word "agency," one of the following terms: "board," "commission," "council," "institution," "office," "organization," "service," or "tribunal." Generally, an agency's name tells us little about its particular delegated function. There is one exception to this. An administrative body that is referred to as a "tribunal" usually performs quasi-judicial functions (discussed in more detail below).

To appreciate their influence, it is important to understand:

- how these delegated entities are structured;
- the ways in which they interact with "the governed";
- the extent of their jurisdiction—that is, the types of activities they can engage in and the types of decisions they can make; and
- the means by which their actions and decisions can be challenged.

The following sections explore these issues in more detail.

The Constitutional Basis of Administrative Agencies

How do we determine whether the constitutional authority to create an administrative agency comes from the federal government or from the provincial government? We look to the *Constitution Act, 1867*, which tells us which level of government has jurisdiction over the subject matter of the agency's enabling statute. To take one example, section 91(23) of the *Constitution Act, 1867* gives the federal government jurisdiction over copyrights. Thus empowered, the federal government has enacted legislation creating the Copyright Board of Canada, a federal administrative tribunal that makes decisions about copyright.

The provinces have jurisdiction over other areas. Section 92(8) of the *Constitution Act, 1867*, for example, gives the provinces power over "Municipal Institutions." With this power, the provinces have enacted legislation under which cities, towns, and other municipal organizations are created. The territories have a parallel jurisdiction assigned to them.

There are several constitutional provisions that are specifically relevant to administrative law. For example, the federal government's power to appoint and to pay delegated officials to sit on administrative agencies is specifically reinforced under section 91(8) of the *Constitution Act, 1867*. The provincial government's power in this regard is spelled out in section 92(4).

Constitutional Limitations on Administrative Tribunals

As explained below, administrative agencies may be assigned different functions. Sometimes they are given the power to resolve disputes and exercise court-like (or quasi-judicial) functions. For example, a labour board may hear a dispute between an employer and a union about the right to picket. When court-like functions are assigned to an agency in this way, it is acting like a tribunal. One significant constitutional limitation on a government's ability to delegate court-like powers to administrative agencies is that the agency thus created must not be too close in operation to a section 96 court—that is, a provincial superior court (see Chapter 5).

If the constitutionality of an administrative agency's powers is challenged in court on the basis of this limitation, the court has to make a determination, based on three questions:

1. whether the subject matter of the dispute is one that had been historically assigned (that is, by common law at the time of Confederation) to superior courts;
2. whether the tribunal is exercising a judicial function by applying recognized rules in an impartial manner to resolve disputes; and
3. whether the judicial function is part of a wider institutional framework or whether, as with a section 96 court, the adjudicative role is its sole or primary function.

If the tribunal is exercising a power similar to that of a traditional superior court and is resolving disputes as a court does (that is, applying recognized rules), it may still be acceptable as an administrative agency if the decision-making aspect of its jurisdiction is merely part of what it does.

If the tribunal resembles a provincial superior court in all three ways, then it will be deemed to be a section 96 court and will be required, like other superior courts, to have federally appointed judges. Without federally appointed judges, the agency will be declared unconstitutional. This is a problem for provincial boards (and provincial inferior courts) that have been delegated too much power and too many responsibilities.

The requirement that only federally appointed judges can hear matters at the superior court level can be problematic for federal administrative tribunals as well as for provincial ones. It is not uncommon for some panellists on administrative tribunals to be lay appointees without formal legal training. Their qualifications and the process by which they are appointed are not necessarily the same as those for superior court judges.

Delegated Power and Functions of Administrative Agencies

Administrative agencies can exercise only power that has been delegated to them by the federal government or by provincial (or territorial) governments. They are charged with administering the legislative regime set out in the legislation that created (or enabled) them.

The government functions that can be delegated to these agencies reflect the three branches of government itself:

1. *legislative* functions (for example, passing by-laws or rules of procedure for appearing before a tribunal),
2. *administrative* or executive functions (for example, issuing business licences), and
3. *quasi-judicial* functions (for example, rendering decisions in labour disputes, as noted above).

A single administrative body may exercise more than one function. When an administrative action or decision is challenged, the available remedies vary according to function. For example, there are fewer opportunities to challenge legislative actions than administrative ones. (Challenging administrative decisions is discussed later in this section.)

With most administrative agencies, a single level of government—federal or provincial (or territorial)—creates an agency and delegates to it all of the power it needs (basic delegation). But it is sometimes the case, depending on the area of regulation for which the agency is responsible, that an agency will require powers from more than one level of government.

Under the Constitution, *cross-delegation*—that is, the process whereby one level of government delegates power directly to the other level—is not permitted.[5] However, the Supreme Court of Canada (SCC) has recognized that *interdelegation*, whereby one level of government creates an agency and the agency subsequently receives some of its power from the other level of government, *is* permissible.[6] For example, a provincial agency that normally licenses trade within the province (intraprovincial trade) may wish to license a

---

5 *Attorney General of Nova Scotia v Attorney General of Canada*, [1951] SCR 31, [1950] SCJ No 32 (QL).

6 *Coughlin v The Ontario Highway Transport Board*, [1968] SCR 569, 1968 CanLII 2.

business to do some trade outside the province (interprovincial trade). Interprovincial trade, however, is under federal jurisdiction. In this case, the federal government could delegate some power to that provincial agency. A final type of delegation arrangement is *subdelegation* (or redelegation), whereby an agency attempts to further delegate some of the power it has already received. Subdelegation is generally not permitted unless the enabling legislation authorizes it. This is the *delegatus non potest delegare* principle described in Chapter 4 in connection with subordinate legislation. For example, municipalities—which themselves exercise delegated power—are not able to delegate the power to make by-laws to a subordinate body they create, such as a planning committee. Figure 9.1 illustrates these delegation principles.

Administrative agencies, regardless of the delegation arrangement they involve or the particular functions they have been delegated, operate as part of the executive branch of government and are controlled by it, with the legislative branch authorizing the executive branch's power in this regard.

Legislative Functions

Administrative agencies fulfill legislative functions in two main areas: (1) municipal institutions making by-laws and (2) quasi-judicial tribunals creating rules of procedure.

In the case of municipalities, the delegation of legislative authority to administrative agencies works in the following way. The provincial or territorial legislation that provides for the incorporation of local governments delegates to these governments the power to pass by-laws. These by-laws concern a wide range of municipal matters, including the following:

- taxes for schools and utilities,
- zoning requirements, and
- city planning and land use.

The provincial or territorial legislation sets out procedures for passing by-laws, and these procedures usually parallel those for enacting primary legislation (see Chapter 4). As with primary legislation, for example, the enacting of by-laws usually requires three readings and the opportunity for public input.

Administrative tribunals with quasi-judicial powers can also fulfill legislative functions insofar as they are frequently empowered to make their own rules governing how they hold hearings and how they resolve disputes.

Administrative Functions

Many executive or administrative functions are commonly delegated to administrative bodies. The issuing of licences and permits is one such function. In Canada, licences are required for numerous activities. Some common examples include driver's licences, fishing and hunting licences, business licences, liquor licences, broadcasting licences, special event permits, building permits, and pollution permits. All of these licences and permits require applications to administrative agencies.

FIGURE 9.1   Basic Rules of Delegation

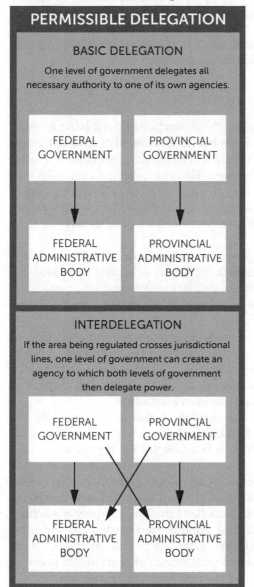

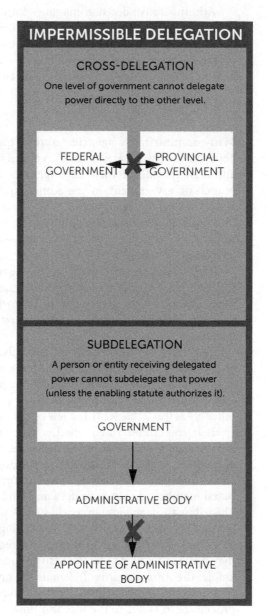

Administrative agencies perform many other functions in their decision-making capacity. Among these functions are the following:

- ordering expropriations of property,
- authorizing adoptions,
- issuing discipline orders (in the case of administrative bodies that regulate trades or professions),
- granting passports,
- making dispensations or deportation orders in immigration cases, and
- granting pardons.

Administrative decision-making—for example, dealing with applications of various kinds or deciding who will be granted a licence and who will not—involves an element of discretion. The enabling legislation will offer guidelines about the exercise of delegated power. In the end, however, an official in an administrative agency has considerable discretion regarding his or her decisions. This can lead to abuse of power.

Quasi-Judicial Functions

Many administrative agencies exercise quasi-judicial functions by resolving disputes between opposing parties. In this capacity, these bodies are **administrative tribunals**, although, like all administrative agencies, they are still considered part of the executive branch of government. When administrative agencies are acting in a court-like capacity, they can be thought of as cousins to the inferior courts. (As we have discussed, one important constitutional limitation relating to such tribunals is that they cannot too closely resemble section 96 courts—that is, provincial superior courts—in their operation.)

The difference between administrative tribunals and inferior courts is that the former function more quickly and less formally than the latter. This is in keeping with their relatively limited jurisdiction in comparison with the courts' jurisdiction. (See Figure 5.1 in Chapter 5 for the position of administrative tribunals in the overall Canadian court system.)

Generally speaking, administrative tribunals reduce the pressure on an overburdened court system and, in some areas, help alleviate concerns about access to justice. Human rights tribunals play an integral role in the protection of civil liberties in the private sector (see Chapter 6). In Canada, tribunals play an important role in adjudicating disputes in other areas too. Table 9.1 lists a few of the many Canadian tribunals.

It is sometimes asked whether judicial independence—that is, the principle that judges should be free to make decisions based on the law, without threat of negative consequences should their decisions be unpopular (see Chapter 5)—applies to administrative tribunals. The answer varies according to the tribunal. Generally speaking, tribunal members do not have the same kind of salary and tenure protection as judges do. The tribunal's enabling statute will specify what protections, if any, have been afforded the tribunal's members. Apart from the enabling statutes, there are also—in some jurisdictions in Canada—certain "general" statutes regulating administrative tribunals, and these may provide for some form of institutional independence. In British Columbia, for example, the *Administrative Tribunals Act* gives administrative tribunals in that province "the power to control [their] own processes and [to] make rules respecting practice and procedure to facilitate the just and timely resolution of the matters before [them]."[7] It is necessary to review these statutes to determine a tribunal's degree of judicial independence.

administrative tribunal
administrative agency that fulfills quasi-judicial functions as part of its mandate

---

7   SBC 2004, c 45, s 11. See also Alberta's *Administrative Procedures and Jurisdiction Act*, RSA 2000, c A-3, and Ontario's *Statutory Powers Procedure Act*, RSO 1990, c C-22.

TABLE 9.1   Administrative Tribunals by Subject and Jurisdiction

SUBJECT	JURISDICTION	ADMINISTRATIVE TRIBUNALS
Access to Information	British Columbia	Information and Privacy Commissioner
	Ontario	Information and Privacy Commissioner
Aeronautics	Federal	Transportation Appeal Tribunal of Canada
Corporate, Commercial Law	Federal	Competition Tribunal
	British Columbia	British Columbia Securities Commission, BC Financial Services Tribunal, Liquor and Cannabis Regulation Branch
	Ontario	Ontario Securities Commission
Energy	Federal	Canada Energy Regulator
	Alberta	Alberta Energy Regulator
	British Columbia	British Columbia Utilities Commission
	Ontario	Ontario Energy Board
Environmental Law	Alberta	Environmental Appeals Board
	Ontario	Environmental Review Tribunal
Forestry Law	British Columbia	British Columbia Forest Practices Board
Human Rights	Federal	Canadian Human Rights Tribunal
	British Columbia	BC Human Rights Tribunal
	Nova Scotia	Nova Scotia Human Rights Commission
	Ontario	Human Rights Tribunal of Ontario
Immigration	Federal	Immigration and Refugee Board of Canada
Intellectual Property	Federal	Copyright Board of Canada, Patent Appeal Board, Trademarks Opposition Board
Labour and Employment Law	Federal	Canada Industrial Relations Board, Federal Public Sector Labour Relations and Employment Board, Umpires under the *Employment Insurance Act**
	Alberta	Appeals Commission for Alberta Workers' Compensation
	British Columbia	Labour Relations Board, Employment Standards Tribunal, WorkSafeBC
	Manitoba	Manitoba Labour Board
	Ontario	Workplace Safety and Insurance Appeals Tribunal
Telecommunications	Federal	Canadian Radio-television and Telecommunications Commission
Trade	Federal	Canadian International Trade Tribunal
Transportation	Federal	Canadian Transportation Agency

* SC 1996, c 23.

The Public's Interaction with Administrative Bodies

Most interactions between the public and administrative agencies occur in connection with the latter's exercise of administrative or quasi-judicial functions. But legislative functions can involve the public, too. For example, when local governments are proposing new by-laws that affect the public interest, the legislative process may allow for public hearings and a chance for a broad consideration of competing views before the by-laws are passed.

Generally speaking, there are two sets of rules for the public to be aware of when dealing with administrative bodies: substantive rules and procedural rules.

Substantive Rules

Substantive rules are the public's fundamental rights and obligations with respect to an administrative regime. For the most part, these rules will be found in the relevant legislation. For example, if a person were applying for a broadcasting licence from the CRTC, the substantive rules of which the applicant needs to be aware—for example, Canadian-content restrictions and the various media delivery limitations—are located in the *Canadian Radio-television and Telecommunications Commission Act*,[8] the *Broadcasting Act*,[9] and a few other statutes, along with the regulations passed pursuant to them. The substantive rules will also include any CRTC and judicial interpretations of the legislation.

Occasionally, substantive rules may be found in the common law as well, such as in the area of civil liberties (for example, the right of free speech).

A review of all of the relevant substantive rules is the first step in dealing successfully with administrative agencies.

Procedural Rules

Many administrative agencies have established their own rules of practice and procedure that members of the public must follow in order to move forward with applications and hearings. These rules concern such things as what documents need to be filed with the agency, who else needs to receive copies, what the timelines are, and whether legal representation is allowed. Generally, the procedural rules for administrative agencies are less formal or rigid than those for court proceedings.

When trying to determine what the procedural rules are, one begins by checking the enabling legislation and then proceeding to the administrative agency itself. Checking agency websites and contacting agency personnel are generally the best ways to obtain information about procedural rules.

In addition to considering the legislated rules that are in place for a particular administrative agency, one must also consider common law rules. Common law rules concerning procedural fairness and natural justice in relation to administrative bodies are well established (see below). They must be followed unless they have been abrogated by the legislation.

---

8 RSC 1985, c C-22.

9 SC 1991, c 11.

Challenging Administrative Decisions

A party negatively affected by an administrative decision (or action) may wish to challenge it. There are various means of doing so. The following discussion primarily concerns decisions involving administrative and quasi-judicial functions.

Internal Means of Challenge

As a first step, a party wishing to contest an administrative decision should exhaust all internal means of challenge. The agency structure may have mechanisms providing for this. Once these options have been exhausted, it may be necessary to consider intervention by the courts.

Challenging in the Courts

There are two ways in which an administrative decision can be challenged in the courts: on **appeal** or by judicial review (note that the term "judicial review" in this context refers to the review of the decisions of administrative bodies and is not the same as judicial review of provincial and federal legislation on constitutional grounds, as discussed in Chapters 3 and 4).

The process of appealing an administrative decision is generally similar to the process of appealing a court decision. The difference has to do with the scope of the appeal and the remedies available. When a court decision is appealed, the court engages in a full substantive reconsideration of the merits of the decision, corrects any errors that were made, and makes orders as it normally would. With an administrative decision, the scope of the appeal and the available remedies are always subject to the enabling legislation. Generally speaking, *any right to appeal exists only if legislation—usually the enabling legislation for the administrative body in question—expressly provides for it.* There is no inherent common law right to appeal an administrative decision. Where the enabling legislation does provide for such a right, the person contesting the administrative decision must go this route before mounting a challenge by the other possible means—namely, judicial review.

Judicial review, as a means of challenging an administrative decision, is a final option. Sara Blake has made this point as follows:

> Application to the court for review of a decision of an inferior tribunal should be made only as a last resort. Parties should take advantage of internal procedures available to a tribunal to correct its errors and of rights of appeal granted by statute. These other ways of correcting tribunal errors tend to be more satisfactory especially as an application for judicial review may be dismissed for failure to pursue other processes. Only when those routes are unavailable, or have been tried without success, should parties resort to judicial review.[10]

Judicial review of an administrative decision tends to be more limited in scope than proceeding by way of an appeal (when such a right is granted by statute). Substantive reviews are possible, but the applicable standard of review may be more restrictive than on appeal (as described below). And when it comes to procedural reviews, the courts are confined to reviewing the process by which decisions have been reached.

appeal (of decisions by administrative bodies) process whereby a court is authorized by legislation to hear an appeal of an administrative decision, which is generally less restrictive than the judicial review process

judicial review (of decisions by administrative bodies) process by which a superior court can review the decision of an administrative body or inferior court on two main grounds: substantive review (review of the merits of the decision) and procedural review (review of the process followed in making the decision)

10   Blake, *supra* note 2 at 193.

Jurisdiction of Superior Courts to Review

The provincial superior courts have an inherent common law power to oversee and review the decisions of both inferior courts and administrative boards and tribunals. This jurisdiction has been modified by legislation. The *Federal Courts Act*[11] assigns exclusive jurisdiction to review federal tribunals to the Federal Court and to the Federal Court of Appeal.

Sections 18 and 18.1 of the *Federal Courts Act* combine to give the Federal Court exclusive power to review federal agencies in general. The exceptions are set out in section 28 of the Act; it gives the Federal Court of Appeal exclusive jurisdiction to review the decisions of certain federal agencies, which are specifically identified. Section 28 provides in part that:

> 28(1) The Federal Court of Appeal has jurisdiction to hear and determine applications for judicial review made in respect of any of the following federal boards, commissions or other tribunals:
>
> (a) the Board of Arbitration established by the *Canada Agricultural Products Act*;
>
> (b) the Review Tribunal established by the *Canada Agricultural Products Act*;
>
> (b.1) the Conflict of Interest and Ethics Commissioner appointed under section 81 of the *Parliament of Canada Act*;
>
> (c) the Canadian Radio-television and Telecommunications Commission established by the *Canadian Radio-television and Telecommunications Commission Act*; ...
>
> (e) the Canadian International Trade Tribunal established by the *Canadian International Trade Tribunal Act*;
>
> (f) the National Energy Board established by the *National Energy Board Act*. ...

Section 28 goes on to list other tribunals over which the Federal Court of Appeal has the power of review. These include the following:

- the Canada Industrial Relations Board,
- the Federal Public Sector Labour Relations and Employment Board,
- the Copyright Board,
- the Canadian Transportation Agency,
- the Competition Tribunal,
- the Public Servants Disclosure Protection Tribunal, and
- the Specific Claims Tribunal.

To summarize, the *Federal Courts Act* gives the Federal Court of Appeal exclusive jurisdiction over certain federal agencies and the Federal Court exclusive jurisdiction over all of the others. The provincial superior courts, based on what remains of their inherent common law jurisdiction, have exclusive jurisdiction over provincial agencies but have no general power of review over federal ones. Review of territorial tribunal decisions is assigned by federal legislation to the territorial superior courts.

---

11 RSC 1985, c F-7.

Privative Clauses

A privative clause is a statutory provision that attempts to restrict or prevent altogether the judicial review of an administrative agency's decision. Legislatures sometimes include such provisions because they want a particular administrative process to be final. There can be a variety of reasons for their wanting this finality—for example, the special expertise of the tribunal officials may make judicial review of their decisions especially difficult.

The specific terms of the statutory provision may be relevant in determining the limits of judicial review. However, judicial review is always a possibility, whatever the legislation says. Even where a privative clause states that the administrative agency's decision is "final and conclusive" or states that the tribunal has "exclusive jurisdiction" in the matter, or states—even more strongly—that judicial review is prohibited, the court still has the jurisdiction to review. Any attempt by a legislature to enact a privative clause so strong as to exclude review in all cases—even in a case, for example, where a tribunal has exceeded its jurisdiction—would likely be declared unconstitutional.

This is not to say that the privative clause has no function. The strength of the privative clause may be one of the factors the court will consider in determining how much deference it will pay to the administrative decision (see below under "Substantive Review"). In the end, however, the courts always have the right to review an administrative agency's decision. Let's say—to use an extreme example—that a labour board rendered a decision ordering a union official to burn down a production facility to pressure an employer into settling a contract dispute. In such a case, even a privative clause clearly prohibiting judicial review under any circumstances would not prevent a court from reviewing the board's decision.

Grounds for Review

There are two broad grounds upon which to review administrative decisions: (1) substantive review and (2) procedural review. These grounds are distinct, but in a given case both may be argued (for example, see Box 9.1).

Substantive Review

Substantive review refers to a review that looks at the merits of a decision by examining the legal and sometimes the factual bases of the decision-maker's analysis. When conducting a review of this kind, the courts first have to decide what **standard of review** is applicable. The standard of review defines the level of deference the court pays to the administrative body. In 2008, in *Dunsmuir v New Brunswick*,[12] the SCC simplified the standard-of-review analysis, stating that there are only two standards of review: (1) correctness and (2) reasonableness. However, in the years following this decision, there was uncertainty about exactly when the two standards would apply and what was involved in assessing each standard. In 2019, in a trilogy of cases (the *Vavilov-Bell-NFL* trilogy, or the "administrative law trilogy"),[13] the SCC revisited its decision in *Dunsmuir* and provided further clarity.[14] In all

substantive review
review of an administrative decision's merits that considers both the legal and factual bases of the tribunal's analysis

standard of review
defines the level of deference the court pays to the tribunal when conducting a judicial review

---

12 2008 SCC 9.

13 *Canada (Minister of Citizenship and Immigration) v Vavilov*, 2019 SCC 65, and *Bell Canada v Canada (Attorney General)*, 2019 SCC 66 (this case was a double appeal involving both Bell Canada and the National Football League [NFL]).

14 For the SCC's summary of the new approach based on the trilogy, see online: <https://www.scc-csc .ca/case-dossier/cb/2019/37748-37896-37897-eng.aspx>.

cases now, the default position is the reasonableness standard, and the correctness or other standard will arise only in two situations:

1. where the legislation specifies a different standard, either because:
    a. it expressly sets out a different standard of review, in which case that standard must be followed; or
    b. it provides a right of appeal to the court, in which case the court applies the "appellate" standard (when dealing with questions of law this means the correctness standard)—technically, the court is not engaged in judicial review on an appeal (see above under "Challenging in the Courts" and the difference between an appeal and judicial review); and
2. where a rule of law issue is involved, in which case the correctness standard will be applied—in this context, a rule of law issue means a question relating to the Constitution, a matter of importance to the legal system as a whole, or the jurisdictional boundaries between two or more administrative bodies (see also Chapter 1 under "Rule of Law").[15]

In the Bell and NFL cases, two of the three cases in the trilogy, the applicable standard was the correctness standard because the relevant legislation provided a right of appeal and questions of law were involved. These cases arose out of a decision by the CRTC to exempt the Super Bowl from the general rule that when programs are simultaneously broadcast on Canadian and US networks, the US commercials are blocked and Canadian ones are substituted in their place (a requirement also known as "simsub"). The CRTC made this decision in response to public demand to see the US Super Bowl commercials, but it meant that fewer people would watch Canadian network coverage of the Super Bowl. The case eventually reached the SCC, which interpreted the relevant legislation. The Court found that the CRTC had acted beyond its powers in making a special exemption from simsub rules for the Super Bowl. The CRTC decision was, therefore, not correct, and the Court overturned it.[16]

In cases where neither of the two situations described above apply, the court must apply the reasonableness standard, which means that the court must pay deference to the administrative decision-maker. It doesn't matter whether the court agrees with the decision or thinks it's correct. As long as the decision is reasonable, the court must allow the decision to stand. In reviewing the reasonableness of the decision, the focus is on the reasoning process and whether it justifies the outcome. Some of the factors the court will consider in determining reasonableness include:

- the internal coherence of the reasoning;
- the tenability of the outcome given the relevant legal and factual constraints;
- the decision-maker's regard for precedent;

---

15 Because these two situations are relatively limited in scope, it means that the majority of cases involving substantive review will be based on the reasonableness standard. For example, it used to be the case that when a board or tribunal was alleged to have exceeded its jurisdiction under its enabling legislation (which would therefore make its decision *ultra vires*), the correctness standard would apply. Moving forward, however, these types of cases will, as a rule, be decided according to the reasonableness standard (unless a jurisdictional boundaries issue or other exceptional situation, as noted above, is also applicable).

16 For a more detailed summary by the SCC of its decision in these two cases, see online: <https://www.scc-csc.ca/case-dossier/cb/2019/37896-37897-eng.aspx>.

- whether the modern principle of statutory interpretation has been followed (for more about the modern principle, see Appendix 4.1 to Chapter 4 under "Statutory Interpretation");
- appropriate consideration of the submissions of the parties; and
- the decision-maker's regard for the potential harm to individuals affected by the decision.[17]

When the decision is held to be unreasonable, then the court will, as a general rule, send the matter back to the administrative body for reconsideration.

In *Vavilov*, the other case in the trilogy, the registrar of citizenship made a determination revoking Vavilov's citizenship after it came to light that Vavilov's parents were Russian spies. Vavilov, who was born in Canada and was unaware that his parents were spies, sought a review of the registrar's decision. The case was appealed up to the SCC. The Court applied the reasonableness standard because neither of the two exceptions applied; it concluded that the reasoning of the registrar was unreasonable on a number of grounds, including questionable statutory interpretation, a failure to address certain submissions, and a lack of regard for the potential harm to Vavilov. Interestingly, after its finding, the Court decided not to send the case back to the registrar for reconsideration, as it indicated would be the usual case. The decision was "quashed" (see below under "Remedies on Review," including Box 9.2), and Vavilov was declared to be a Canadian citizen.[18]

The administrative law trilogy has simplified the analytical framework for substantive judicial review and clarified when the different standards of review will apply and what the relevant considerations are in assessing them. This should result in efficiencies in almost all areas of government regulation.

SUBSTANTIVE REVIEW INVOLVING INDIGENOUS ISSUES

Indigenous issues can arise in a variety of administrative law contexts, including any situation where Aboriginal and treaty rights under section 35 of the *Constitution Act, 1982*—for example, hunting or fishing rights or claims to land and resources, which are generally the most contentious—are affected by a board or tribunal decision.

In *Haida Nation v British Columbia (Minister of Forests)*,[19] the SCC recognized that the Crown has a duty to consult with Indigenous peoples pending the negotiation of treaties or litigation to establish Aboriginal rights (see also Chapter 2 under "Canadian Law and Indigenous Peoples: A Timeline" and Box 7.7 in Chapter 7). The duty to consult is based on the "honour of the Crown" and is constitutionally mandated under section 35. On the facts of this case, the SCC held that the BC government had breached this duty by failing to

---

17 Concerning privative clauses (see above), the Court in *Vavilov* did not expressly discuss them as factors in determining the level of deference to be paid to the decision-maker or in assessing the reasonableness of the decision. In fact, the Court suggested that such clauses would have "no independent or additional function in identifying the standard of review" (at para 49). This may signal another departure in approach from previous cases, where such clauses were considered in measuring the level of deference. The legal basis for not factoring in an express directive from a legislature to restrict the scope of judicial review is not entirely clear unless the right of judicial review of all administrative decisions is considered to be constitutionally protected, and any attempt to limit that right is unconstitutional.

18 For a more detailed summary of *Vavilov* by the SCC, see online: <https://www.scc-csc.ca/case -dossier/cb/2019/37748-eng.aspx>.

19 2004 SCC 73.

consult with the Haida people when it granted a tree farm licence to a forestry company on the lands of Haida Gwaii off the BC coast, over which the Haida claimed title.

In *Taku River Tlingit First Nation v British Columbia (Project Assessment Director)*,[20] a companion case to *Haida*, a dispute arose over a decision by the BC government to allow a mining company to reopen an old mine in northwestern BC. The Taku River Tlingit First Nation (TRTFN) had participated in an environmental review process concerning the mine and objected to the mining company's plan to build a logging road in an area over which they claimed title (a claim, like the Haida's, that has still not been proven or settled). They petitioned the court to quash the project-approval decision. On appeal to the SCC, the Court affirmed the existence of a duty to consult, which, the SCC explained, varies with the circumstances, such as the strength of the claim and the potential impact the approved project or other activity would have on the claim. In this case, the claim was strong, and the potential for negative consequences resulting from the road was high. However, the Court concluded that the TRTFN had participated fully in the administrative approval process under BC's *Environmental Assessment Act*,[21] and the final approval contained measures addressing the TRTFN's concerns. The duty to consult had been fulfilled, and there were no grounds upon which to quash the approval decision on review.

In *Vavilov*, the SCC provided further clarification about the applicable standard of review in cases involving Aboriginal rights, which were placed in the category of rule of law issues. The Court stated:

> [55] *Questions regarding* the division of powers between Parliament and the provinces, the relationship between the legislature and the other branches of the state, *the scope of Aboriginal and treaty rights under s 35 of the* Constitution Act, 1982, and other constitutional matters *require* a final and determinate answer from the courts. Therefore, *the standard of correctness* must continue *to be applied* in reviewing such questions … .[22]

Vavilov makes it clear that courts reviewing administrative decisions involving Indigenous issues will not have to pay deference to the decision-maker. The standard is correctness, and the court can make the final determination in the case. This will arguably provide an added measure of protection to Indigenous peoples, who will always have the right to fully question the legality of administrative decisions affecting their rights.

Procedural Review

Arguments concerning process or procedure generate the most litigation. Even if there are no substantive issues surrounding a decision, there may still be procedural grounds for review.

At common law, administrative officials are required to adhere to standards of **fairness**, also referred to as **procedural fairness** or **natural justice**, when making decisions that affect a person's interests. Natural justice dictates that certain rights will be accorded to persons engaged with an administrative process, regardless of whether the process involved is administrative or quasi-judicial. Some of these rights include the following:

- the right to notice (in other words, the right to know what the opposing case is),

fairness (also procedural fairness or natural justice) principle that fairness requires that certain "rights" be accorded to persons engaged with an administrative process, such as the right to notice, the right to be heard and to respond, the right to representation, and the right to an adjudicator who is free from bias or an appearance of bias

---

20 2004 SCC 74.

21 RSBC 1996, c 119 [see now the *Environmental Assessment Act*, SBC 2018, c 51].

22 *Vavilov, supra* note 13 (emphasis added).

- the right to be heard and to respond,
- the right to representation,
- the right to cross-examine,
- the right to reasons, and

BOX 9.1

Procedural Fairness and Substantive Review in an Immigration Case

In 1992, Mavis Baker was ordered to be deported to Jamaica. She came to Canada in 1981 as a visitor but never received permanent resident status. When her visitor's visa expired, she stayed in Canada and worked illegally as a live-in domestic worker. During her time in Canada, she had four children, all Canadian citizens. She also suffered from mental illness, for which she was receiving treatment.

The deportation order required her to apply for permanent residency status from outside Canada. She argued that she should be exempted from this requirement on humanitarian and compassionate grounds as provided for in the *Immigration Act*;* the order would cause her to be separated from her children, and treatment for her mental condition might not be available in Jamaica.

The senior immigration officer handling her file gave her the opportunity to make written submissions but not to appear in person and make oral submissions. She argued that this infringed her right to procedural fairness. Her case eventually made it to the SCC.[†] The SCC held that procedural fairness was a flexible and variable concept. She had been given the opportunity to respond fully and completely in writing, and this was sufficient in the circumstances. The Court also

held that the documentation provided in support of the reasons for the decision was sufficient. However, in reviewing the notes of the immigration officer, the Court concluded that he may have been influenced by evidence that was not before him (including the fact that she was a single mother with a mental illness); a reasonable person, said the Court, would conclude that he was biased.

Although the SCC held that the decision was procedurally unfair because there was a reasonable apprehension of bias, the Court continued with a substantive review of the decision based on the reasonableness standard. The Court held that the immigration officer, in exercising his discretion, had failed to follow the intent of the legislation by ignoring the impact his decision would have on Baker and her children. The order was overturned on the basis that it was unreasonable. Baker was therefore successful on both procedural and substantive grounds for review.

* RSC 1985, c I-2, s 114(2). Note that the *Immigration Act* was replaced in 2001 by the *Immigration and Refugee Protection Act*, SC 2001, c 27.

† *Baker v Canada (Minister of Citizenship and Immigration)*, [1999] 2 SCR 817, 1999 CanLII 699.

- the right to an adjudicator who is free from bias or an appearance of bias.

The degree of fairness and the number of these rights that natural justice requires in a particular case will vary according to a number of factors, including the following:

1. the nature of the decision to be made by the administrative body,
2. the relationship existing between that body and the individual, and
3. the effect of that decision on the individual's rights.

Legislation may also dictate that certain procedural standards be adhered to in a given situation. Generally, the more significant the decision's impact, the more procedural safeguards that will be required.[23] For example, a decision that resulted in a person losing her

---

23   See *Knight v Indian Head School Division No 19*, [1990] 1 SCR 653, 1990 CanLII 138, the leading case in Canada on procedural fairness.

job or means of livelihood would trigger more procedural protection than a decision denying a person the right to light fireworks in her backyard on her birthday.

Remedies on Review

prerogative writs
special common law remedies for administrative infractions

A number of special common law remedies are available to those who have suffered as a result of substantive or procedural errors made by administrative bodies. These remedies, called **prerogative writs**, are granted following an application to the superior courts. There are various kinds of prerogative writs (see Box 9.2). Historically, subjects would apply to the Crown, which could issue these writs as part of the monarch's royal prerogative power (see Chapter 4). Control over these writs has long since passed into the hands of the courts.

In addition to prerogative writs, the courts also have the power to grant injunctive relief (that is, order someone to do something), as well as declaratory relief (that is, simply declare what the legal position is). Most provinces and territories have now enacted legislation simplifying the procedure for applying for prerogative writs and for these other remedies. At one time, a separate application was required for each prerogative writ. Ontario and British Columbia have the simplest application procedure. In these provinces, one statutory application for judicial review serves as an application for all available remedies (except damages).[24]

Note, as well, that besides any available remedies on review (or on appeal), a person challenging an administrative decision may also have a private law claim depending on the

---

BOX 9.2

Prerogative Writs

The main prerogative writs are the following:

- Writ of *certiorari*: In the context of Canadian judicial review proceedings, this kind of writ is used to "quash" or overturn an administrative body's decision in cases where there have been substantive errors, abuse of discretion, or procedural unfairness.
- Writ of prohibition: This writ is an order, issued by the superior court, requiring the administrative body not to proceed with a planned action.
- Writ of *mandamus*: This writ is the reverse of a writ of prohibition. It is an order by the superior court requiring the administrative body to proceed with an action it wouldn't have proceeded with otherwise (for example,

the court might order the administrative body to issue a permit).

- Writ of *quo warranto*: With this remedy, a public official is ordered to give up his office because he has not been validly appointed. Such an order would, of course, prevent the official from making any official decisions.
- Writ of *habeas corpus*: This most ancient of the prerogative writs is mentioned in the *Magna Carta* of 1215. It concerns the lawfulness of an individual's detention by government authorities. Today, it is most significant in connection with the detention of immigrants (by immigration officials), of prisoners (by prison officials), of children (by child protection agencies), and of the mentally disabled (by mental health facilities).

---

circumstances.[25]

---

24   See the *Judicial Review Procedure Act*, RSBC 1996, c 241, and *Judicial Review Procedure Act*, RSO 1990, c J.1.

25   Sometimes it is possible to sue agencies in negligence if they have been careless in carrying out their duties under legislation. A number of cases involving negligent inspections have resulted in successful claims for damages. For example, see *Just v British Columbia*, [1989] 2 SCR 1228, 1989 CanLII 16. If a government official abuses his discretionary power, damages in tort based on a claim of "abuse of power" may be recoverable.

CHAPTER SUMMARY

Administrative law is an important area of public domestic law that affects individuals and businesses in various contexts. Because of the degree and complexity of regulation in developed societies today, it is necessary for governments to delegate many governmental tasks to specialized agencies. Administrative law is concerned with the governance structures of these agencies and the limitations on their powers in their dealings with the objects of their power: the governed.

Some limits on the power of administrative agencies are based on the Constitution—specifically, rules relating to the delegation of power. For example, if the federal government sets up an administrative agency under federal legislation, as a general rule only matters over which Parliament has jurisdiction under the Constitution can be delegated to the agency (interdelegation is an exception to this, allowing the provinces to delegate some power to federal agencies). A similar approach applies to provincial boards. Another important limitation relates to the power of governments to set up tribunals exercising court-like functions. Administrative tribunals whose sole or primary function is to exercise powers that were traditionally assigned to section 96 courts must have federally appointed judges.

Regulatory agencies are created under specific statutes— federal, provincial, or territorial—that determine their structure and outline many of the rules governing their interactions with the public. Their functions range from making rules and regulations to administering the law and adjudicating disputes.

The public can challenge administrative decisions in various ways. The exact methods depend on the particular agency, its functions, and the legislation involved. A statutory right of appeal, if available, is the most effective method. When such a right of appeal exists, the scope of the appeal and the available remedies are determined by and subject to the enabling legislation.

If there is no statutory right of appeal, the decision can be challenged through judicial review. Judicial review of regulatory decisions is based on one of two broad grounds: (1) substantive review of the merits of the decision and (2) procedural review, which concerns the process by which the decision was reached. When a court engages in a substantive review, two main standards of review are possible: (1) correctness and (2) reasonableness. When applying the correctness standard, the court can substitute its own view as to the correctness of the law. However, the correctness standard only applies in limited situations, such as where a rule of law issue is involved (for example, when dealing with questions about the scope of Aboriginal rights under the Constitution). The default standard is the reasonableness standard, which requires the court to pay deference to the administrative decision-maker. In assessing the reasonableness of a decision, the court considers various factors, such as the internal coherence of the decision, whether the modern principle of statutory interpretation has been followed, and the decision-maker's regard for the potential harm to individuals affected by the decision.

When a court engages in a procedural review, the court considers whether rights relating to the fairness of the process have been accorded to the person affected by the administrative decision. Such rights include the right to be heard, the right to reasons, and the right to a decision made without bias. The degree of fairness and number of rights involved in a particular case vary according to the nature of the decision, any legislative requirements, and other factors.

Key remedies on review include the writs of *certiorari* (used to quash or overturn an administrative body's unlawful decision), *mandamus* (which orders an administrative body to proceed with an action it wouldn't have proceeded with otherwise, such as issuing a permit), and *habeas corpus* (which concerns the lawfulness of an individual's detention by government authorities, such as in immigration or child protection cases).

KEY TERMS

administrative agency, 251

administrative tribunal, 256

appeal (of decisions by administrative bodies), 259

fairness (also procedural fairness or natural justice), 264

judicial review (of decisions by administrative bodies), 259

prerogative writs, 266

standard of review, 261

substantive review, 261

FURTHER READING

BOOKS

Blake, Sara, *Administrative Law in Canada*, 6th ed (Toronto: LexisNexis, 2017).

Jones, David P & Anne S de Villars, *Principles of Administrative Law*, 6th ed (Toronto: Carswell, 2014).

Mullan, David J, *Administrative Law* (Toronto: Irwin Law, 2001).

Régimbald, Guy, *Canadian Administrative Law*, 2nd ed (Toronto: LexisNexis, 2015).

Swaigen, John & Jasteena Dhillon, *Administrative Law: Principles and Advocacy*, 3rd ed (Toronto: Emond, 2016).

WEBSITE

Research Guide for Canadian Administrative Boards and Tribunal Decisions: <https://guides.library.ubc.ca/cases/can>.

REVIEW QUESTIONS

1. What three factors do the courts consider in determining whether an administrative tribunal is too close in operation to a section 96 court?

2. What does "interdelegation" refer to in relation to an administrative body's power?

3. Name and briefly describe the three general types of functions or powers that are delegated to administrative agencies.

4. Explain the difference between substantive and procedural rules as they relate to dealings with administrative agencies.

5. Which court has exclusive jurisdiction to review Copyright Board of Canada decisions?

6. Describe the remedy sought with the prerogative writ of *quo warranto*.

EXERCISES

1. On the website listed under "Further Reading," click "Canada" and then "Administrative Boards and Tribunals Decisions"; next, select a board or tribunal (human rights, labour, or employment standards, for example) and then choose a decision listed in the database. Read the decision and prepare a short summary of it.

2. In your own words, explain why the standards of review applicable to the judicial review of administrative decisions are generally more limiting than a full appeal of such decisions would be.

3. Locate and read the decision in *Canada (Minister of Citizenship and Immigration) v Vavilov*, 2019 SCC 65. Prepare a short commentary explaining why you agree or disagree with the Court's reasons that the registrar of citizenship's decision to cancel Vavilov's certificate of citizenship was unreasonable.

10 Criminal Law

Introduction 270

Sources of Canadian Criminal Law 271

True Crimes Versus Quasi-Criminal
Offences 273

Basic Principles of Criminal Law 275

Organization and Classification
of Criminal Code Offences 276

Police Investigation of Crime 279

Prosecution of Crime and the Duty
to Disclose 283

The Criminal Trial Process 285

Youth Criminal Justice Act 294

Indigenous Peoples and the Criminal
Justice System 295

Chapter Summary 299

Key Terms 299

Further Reading 299

Review Questions 300

Exercises 300

LEARNING OUTCOMES

After reading this chapter, you will be able to:

- Understand the division of responsibility between federal and provincial governments regarding criminal justice in Canada.
- Describe the sources of Canadian criminal law.
- Explain how criminal offences are classified and how offenders are prosecuted under Canada's *Criminal Code*.
- Define police powers to investigate crime.

- Understand constitutional safeguards in the *Canadian Charter of Rights and Freedoms* applicable to criminal justice in Canada.
- Describe procedures for conducting a criminal trial and the principles that apply to the sentencing of offenders.
- Discuss the application of the *Youth Criminal Justice Act* to young offenders and its key provisions.
- Understand Indigenous perspectives on criminal justice.

F or the ordinary person one of the most interesting and fascinating topics of discussion is that of law and order. … To many people, the term "criminal law" simply refers to society's prohibitions against acts that threaten its very existence—acts such as murder, assault, and theft. In the same vein, "crime" simply means the breaking of these laws, and the "criminal" is the person who has broken them. Criminal law, then, may be seen as one form of social control—a term encompassing all kinds of pressure upon individuals to do what is customarily considered the right thing in a given society.

> David Perrier, "An Introduction to Criminal Law" in Joel E Pink &
> David Perrier, eds, *From Crime to Punishment: An Introduction
> to the Criminal Law System*, 8th ed (Toronto: Carswell, 2014) at 1

Introduction

In addition to providing a continuous source of news headlines and heated political debates, the criminal justice system is a critical component of Canadian society. Unlike private law matters, in which private citizens take legal action against one another, criminal law concerns the state itself: criminal offences are seen as transgressions against society as a whole and are prosecuted by lawyers known as **Crown attorneys**, Crown prosecutors, or Crown counsel,[1] so named because they represent the official head of government in Canada, the reigning British (and Canadian) monarch.[2]

Crown attorney
lawyer, also known as a Crown prosecutor or Crown counsel, who is an agent of the attorney general and who represents the Crown in court, particularly in criminal matters

---

1 "Crown attorney" is the most commonly used term in Canada. However, "Crown prosecutor" is the preferred term in Alberta, Saskatchewan, and New Brunswick and "Crown counsel" in British Columbia.

2 This is reflected in the style of cause of criminal cases, which generally begin with the letter "R," standing for *regina* or *rex*, the Latin words for "queen" and "king." See also Appendix 5.1 to Chapter 5 under the "Terminology: Terms for Parties and Reasons" heading.

Canada's criminal justice system works to determine whether or not persons charged with criminal offences are guilty according to the law and, if they are, what measures should be taken to punish, deter, and/or rehabilitate them and to protect the rest of society from further harm. Our criminal justice system is jurisdictionally complex. Substantive criminal law and the procedures involved in the system—namely, police investigation of a crime, bringing the accused to court, trying the accused, and sentencing accused persons who are found guilty—are carried out within a constitutional framework that involves both the federal and provincial governments. Since the advent of the *Canadian Charter of Rights and Freedoms*, constitutional safeguards protect an accused person's rights throughout the criminal process.

This chapter presents an overview of the criminal justice system in Canada. We examine criminal law in relation to the division of federal and provincial powers under the Constitution, explain the classification of offences, and outline how a criminal offence is investigated by police, including a review of the Charter rights of persons who are detained or arrested and the limits on police powers of search and seizure. We consider criminal pre-trial matters and the conduct of a criminal trial, as well as sentencing. Lastly, we briefly examine the correctional system in Canada, the *Youth Criminal Justice Act* (YCJA),[3] and the relationship between Indigenous peoples and the Canadian criminal justice system.

Figure 10.1 illustrates both the larger context of Canada's criminal justice system and the individual elements of which it is composed.

Sources of Canadian Criminal Law

When Canada became a nation in 1867, we adopted a Constitution that assigned jurisdiction over criminal law and criminal procedure to the federal Parliament. In the debates leading up to Confederation in 1867, John A Macdonald stated that "[i]t is one of the defects in the United States system, that each separate state has or may have a criminal code of its own—that what may be a capital offence in one state, may be a venial offence, punishable slightly, in another."[4]

Macdonald believed this potential for variance among state criminal codes produced confusion and argued that criminal law in Canada should be assigned to the general (that is, federal) government so that it would be the same throughout the country. Under our Constitution, said Macdonald:

> [W]e shall have one body of criminal law, based on the criminal law of England, and operating equally throughout British America, so that a British American, belonging to what province he may, or going to any other part of the Confederation, knows what his rights are in that respect, and what his punishment will be if an offender against the criminal laws of the land.[5]

Macdonald's view carried, and section 91(27) of the *Constitution Act, 1867* gave the Parliament of Canada exclusive jurisdiction over criminal law and procedure in criminal matters. This means that criminal law and criminal procedure are national in scope. They apply throughout Canada.

---

3   SC 2002, c 1.

4   Quoted in PB Waite, ed, *The Confederation Debates in the Province of Canada, 1865* (Toronto: McClelland & Stewart, 1963) at 46.

5   *Ibid* at 46.

FIGURE 10.1 Overview of Canada's Criminal Justice System

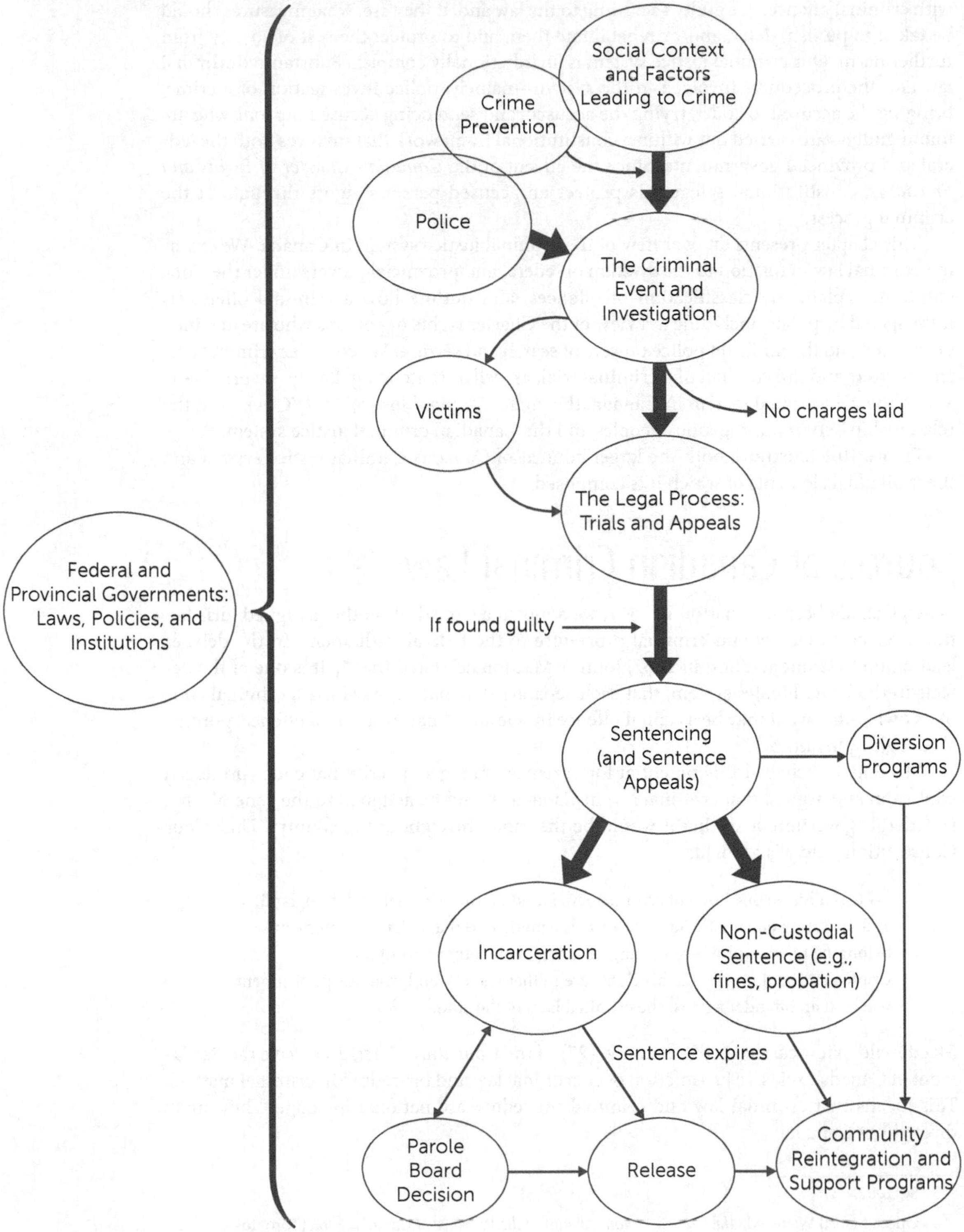

Source: Karla O'Regan & Susan Reid, *Thinking About Criminal Justice in Canada*, 2nd ed (Toronto: Edmond, 2017) at xxii.

Two major sources of criminal law in Canada today are statute law and common law. Originally, criminal law in Canada was largely judge-made law, as it was in England; there was no central criminal law statute. Our *Criminal Code* was enacted in 1892, and today it is the main source of Canadian criminal law. Since its inception, it has been extensively amended. The Code is a lengthy and complex statute that defines and classifies criminal offences and describes the procedures for prosecuting them. It also provides directions for sentencing. The Code is composed of 28 parts, each concerned with a specific subject area.

Besides the Code, there are other important federal statutes that relate to the criminal law field, including:

- the *Canada Evidence Act*,[6]
- the *Controlled Drugs and Substances Act* (CDSA),[7] and
- the *Youth Criminal Justice Act*.

The *Canada Evidence Act* covers witnesses and evidence law. Section 2 in part I, for example, provides that part I applies to "all criminal proceedings and to all civil proceedings and other matters whatever respecting which Parliament has jurisdiction."

The CDSA regulates certain kinds of dangerous drugs and narcotics in Canada, called "controlled substances." Search, seizure, and detention are covered in part II of the Act, which concerns enforcement, whereas part III covers the disposal of controlled substances.

The YCJA is a federal statute that deals with young persons who commit crimes in this country. It came into force on April 1, 2003, replacing the *Young Offenders Act*.[8] The YCJA applies to young persons who are between the ages of 12 and 17 when they commit a criminal offence. The Act outlines procedures for trying young persons separately from adult offenders, in youth justice courts. We will look at youth justice later in this chapter.

The common law, too, continues to be another important source of our criminal law, mainly in connection with defences (all offences are now legislated). There is also a considerable amount of case law interpreting the *Criminal Code* and other criminal law statutes. For this reason, many lawyers practising criminal law in Canada use annotated and easy-to-carry versions of the Code and related statutes. These all-in-one books are usually updated annually and include relevant case law together with the legislation. A well-known annotated version is *Martin's Annual Criminal Code*, and a useful small companion book is *Martin's Pocket Criminal Code*, both published by Thomson Reuters.[9]

True Crimes Versus Quasi-Criminal Offences

"True" crimes are offences over which the federal government has jurisdiction pursuant to its power under section 91(27) of the *Constitution Act, 1867*. These federal crimes are typically serious in nature and are often thought of as being inherently wrong. They generally have a *mens rea*, or guilty mind, element (see below under the heading "The Elements of a Criminal Offence"). In addition to penalties that can be severe, being convicted of a crime carries with it a criminal record and a social stigma. Treason, terrorism, firearms offences,

---

6   RSC 1985, c C-5.

7   SC 1996, c 19.

8   RSC 1985, c Y-1.

9   *Martin's Annual Criminal Code*, 2021 ed (Toronto: Canada Law Book, 2020); *Martin's Pocket Criminal Code*, 2021 ed (Toronto: Canada Law Book, 2020).

sexual assault, murder, robbery, and arson—all dealt with in the *Criminal Code*—are just a few examples of criminal offences.

Quasi-criminal offences, on the other hand, are less serious offences and do not fall under the federal criminal law power. They are sometimes referred to as "regulatory offences" and deal with the regulation of conduct in the public interest. They may have a *mens rea* component but are more frequently *strict liability offences* (that is, offences without a mental element and where an accused can argue as a defence that she exercised due diligence in trying to avoid committing the offence—for example, pollution offences) or *absolute liability offences* (offences based solely on the commission of the proscribed act—such as driving over the speed limit—and without a mental element or possible defence of due diligence).

Quasi-criminal offences can be federal, provincial, territorial, or municipal, but most of these offences are creatures of provincial legislation (provincial quasi-criminal offences are often simply referred to as "provincial offences"). Section 92(15) of the *Constitution Act, 1867* states that the provinces have jurisdiction over "[t]he Imposition of Punishment by Fine, Penalty, or Imprisonment for enforcing any Law of the Province made in relation to any Matter coming within any of the Classes of Subjects enumerated in this Section." The territories have an analogous power to create quasi-criminal offences in relation to the areas over which they have legislative jurisdiction (as devolved to them by the federal Parliament). Municipalities (or local governments) have a similar power delegated to them by the provinces. And the federal government can always pass legislation creating quasi-criminal offences under a power other than its criminal law power. (See Chapter 4 for a discussion of the areas or subjects over which Parliament, the provinces, and territories have legislative jurisdiction.)

There are a vast number of quasi-criminal, or regulatory, offences in Canada, including:

- motor vehicle offences, such as careless driving and parking offences (for example, under Ontario's *Highway Traffic Act*[10]);
- offences related to the selling or supplying of liquor (for example, under New Brunswick's *Liquor Control Act*[11]);
- offences related to workplace safety covering a range of violations, such as an employer's failure to provide a safe work environment or to immediately report accidents causing critical injury or death (for example, under BC's *Workers Compensation Act*[12]);
- pollution offences covering land, air, or water (for example, under the federal *Fisheries Act*[13]); and
- offences relating to the sale and distribution of securities (for example, under Yukon's *Securities Act*[14]).

Quasi-criminal offences are prosecuted according to the procedures set out in the relevant act—for example, provincial offences in Ontario are prosecuted under the *Provincial Offences Act*.[15] Punishment for these types of offences is usually a fine (although it can involve

quasi-criminal offences

less serious offences, such as pollution or traffic offences, that do not fall under the federal criminal law power; they may be passed by all levels of government but are frequently created under provincial legislation

10 RSO 1990, c H.8.

11 RSNB 1973, c L-10.

12 RSBC 1996, c 492.

13 RSC 1985, c F-14.

14 SY 2007, c 16.

15 RSO 1990, c P.33.

imprisonment) and may also include other penalties, such as demerit points on a convicted person's driver's licence or the loss of the licence itself. Because quasi-criminal offences are not true criminal offences, they do not result in a criminal record.

Basic Principles of Criminal Law

Because the consequences of being convicted of a criminal offence are so serious and can result in individuals being deprived of their liberty, the Crown attorney's burden in proving that an accused committed a crime is very high. In this section, we will look at *what* the Crown must prove and *how* it must prove it.

The Elements of a Criminal Offence

Criminal offences in Canada are set out in the *Criminal Code* and several other statutes. We saw in Chapter 8, for example, that price-fixing agreements in relation to competition are a crime under the *Competition Act*.[16] Generally speaking, criminal offences are composed of an objective physical element, known as the ***actus reus***, or "guilty act," and a subjective mental element, known as ***mens rea***, or "guilty mind."

In committing the guilty act component of an offence, an individual must engage in a proscribed action, conduct, or behaviour. In addition, the *actus reus* may involve the accused being found in particular circumstances; failing to act when required to do so by a legal duty; or causing particular consequences. An important feature of the *actus reus* is that, for criminal consequences to apply, it must be carried out consciously and voluntarily. Some defences go to these factors—for example, duress (see the discussion of defences later in this chapter).

For a person to be found guilty of a criminal offence, not only must he commit a criminal act, he must also do so with a guilty mind as required by the particular criminal offence. This can mean different things depending on the offence but can include, for some offences, intending to bring about the consequences of the criminal act (sometimes referred to as specific intent) and, for other offences, just intending to engage in the act without intending any specific consequences (general intent). For example, section 265(1)(a) of the *Criminal Code* states that a person commits an assault when "without the consent of another person, he applies force intentionally to that other person, directly or indirectly." Force can be applied to another person in a variety of ways: intentionally in a fight or during a robbery or unintentionally in a crowded public area due to factors beyond the person's control. Although some of these acts are blameworthy and could attract criminal consequences, others might not.

Burden of Proof and Standard of Proof

A key principle of our criminal justice system that has existed for centuries is the presumption of innocence. This common law safeguard is now a Charter legal right: section 11(d) states that any person charged with an offence has the right "to be presumed innocent until proven guilty according to law in a fair and public hearing by an independent and impartial tribunal." In addition, section 6(1)(a) of the *Criminal Code* prescribes that a person shall be deemed not to be guilty until she is convicted or discharged of the offence. In other words, the state has the burden or the onus of proof to establish its case, and an accused is presumed innocent until proven guilty in court.

actus reus
"guilty act" or objective physical part of a criminal offence

mens rea
"guilty mind" or subjective mental element of a criminal offence (such as, depending on the offence, intending to bring about the consequences of one's actions or simply intending to perform the *actus reus*)

---

16 RSC 1985, c C-34.

In contrast to civil matters, which require proof on a balance of probabilities, the criminal standard of proof is a much higher standard of proof "beyond a reasonable doubt." This means that the Crown must also prove all of the elements of the offence beyond a reasonable doubt for the accused to be found guilty. If the defence is able to raise a reasonable doubt in the minds of the judge or jury as to whether the accused committed the offence, the accused must be found not guilty.

Organization and Classification of Criminal Code Offences

In this section, we look first at how criminal offences are organized in the *Criminal Code* and then review its three categories of offences. These are:

1. summary conviction offences,
2. indictable offences, and
3. hybrid offences.

How an offence is classified largely determines, for example, the scope of investigatory powers granted to the police, the terms of the accused's pretrial release, how the offence is prosecuted, which court hears the matter, which punishments can apply on a conviction, and the process for an appeal.[17]

Organization of Criminal Code Offences

The *Criminal Code* organizes specific offences into general subject matter categories, as follows:

- Part II covers offences against public order—for example, treason, sedition, unlawful assemblies and riots, duels, piracy, and offences against air or maritime safety.
- Part II.1 covers terrorism.
- Part III covers offences involving firearms and other weapons.
- Part IV covers offences against the administration of law and justice, including corruption and disobedience, and misleading justice.
- Part V covers sexual offences, public morals, and disorderly conduct.
- Part VI covers invasion of privacy.
- Part VII covers disorderly houses, gaming, and betting.
- Part VIII covers offences against the person and reputation—for example, criminal negligence, homicide, murder, suicide, assault, kidnapping, defamatory libel, and hate propaganda.

---

17 Richard Barnhorst & Sherrie Barnhorst, *Criminal Law and the Canadian Criminal Code*, 6th ed (Toronto: McGraw-Hill Ryerson, 2013); Kent Roach, *Criminal Law*, 7th ed (Toronto: Irwin Law, 2018); Nora Rock & Valerie Hoag, *Foundations of Criminal and Civil Law in Canada*, 3rd ed (Toronto: Emond Montgomery, 2011); Mary Ann Kelly, "Criminal Procedure" in Laurence Olivo, ed, *Introduction to Law in Canada*, Ont ed (Toronto: Captus Press, 1995–2009) at 245; Joel E Pink & David C Perrier, eds, *From Crime to Punishment*, 9th ed (Toronto: Carswell, 2020); Michael Gulycz & Mary Ann Kelly, *Criminal Law for Legal Professionals*, 2nd ed (Toronto: Emond, 2018).

- Part IX covers property offences—for example, theft, robbery, breaking and entering, and forgery.
- Part X covers fraudulent transactions relating to contracts and trade.
- Part XI covers wilful and forbidden acts in respect of certain property, including mischief and arson.
- Part XII covers offences relating to currency, and part XII.2 covers proceeds of crime.
- Part XIII covers attempts, conspiracies, and accessories.

Canadian criminal laws (and our laws generally) are a reflection of Canadian values and beliefs and change as our society changes. Since 1985, the rights and freedoms in the Charter have provided a basis and framework for many of these changes. There is and will continue to be debate and analysis regarding the type of behaviour that should be criminalized. In 2014, new prostitution laws were enacted after the existing ones were found to be in violation of section 7 of the Charter (see Box 10.1 and also Chapter 6 under "An Overview of the Charter" for more information about s 7). In 2018, after years of debate, Canada became just the second country in the world (after Uruguay) to fully legalize the recreational use of cannabis.[18] In 2019, animal protection laws were expanded by criminalizing certain forms of animal cruelty.[19] In 2020, Parliament introduced a bill changing the law relating to medical assistance in dying (MAID) by removing the "foreseeability of death" requirement.[20] Also in 2020, Parliament proposed new legislation protecting LGBTQ2+ rights by banning certain aspects of conversion therapy and other harmful practices that attempt to change a person's sexual orientation or gender identity.[21] These are just a few examples of some recent changes.

Summary Conviction Offences

Summary conviction offences are the least serious offences in the *Criminal Code* and are dealt with under part XXVII. Such offences include, for example, making an indecent telephone call and public nudity. Trials for summary conviction offences are held before a provincial court judge; no jury is permitted, and there is no preliminary hearing. **Limitation periods** apply to summary offences; in general, summary offence charges must be laid within six months from the time the offence was committed.

summary conviction offence
least serious type of offence in the *Criminal Code* (for example, trespassing or disturbing the peace), tried only in provincial court and subject to the lightest sentences

limitation period
period in which a legal action must be taken or the ability to do so is lost

---

18 The *Cannabis Act*, SC 2018, c 16, which brought about this change, required amendments to the CDSA, the *Criminal Code*, and other legislation. The regulation of cannabis is multifaceted and extends well beyond the legalization of its recreational use. For example, the provinces, territories, and municipalities set their own rules concerning sale and distribution (and these rules vary from region to region); the *Cannabis Act* imposes different licensing requirements for cultivation, processing, and sale for medical purposes and testing and research; and the *Cannabis Act* also sets conditions for advertising, promotion, and packaging (such as prohibiting advertising directed at minors). Beyond these matters, cannabis law concerns workplace issues, Indigenous jurisdiction over cannabis, the existence of intellectual property protection for cannabis "products," the impact of our new laws on immigration and international affairs, and a number of other issues.

19 See *Ending the Captivity of Whales and Dolphins Act*, SC 2019, c 11 (the so-called "Free Willy" law banning the keeping of cetaceans in captivity), and *An Act to amend the Criminal Code (bestiality and animal fighting)*, SC 2019, c 17 (which broadens the law in the two areas indicated).

20 Bill C-7, *An Act to amend the Criminal Code (medical assistance in dying)*, 1st Sess, 43rd Parl, 2020. For more on the Charter challenge leading to this proposed change, see Chapter 6 and the discussion of s 7 under "An Overview of the Charter."

21 Bill C-8, *An Act to amend the Criminal Code (conversion therapy)*, 1st Sess, 43rd Parl, 2020.

BOX 10.1

Canada's Prostitution Laws: Unconstitutional

In 2010, three Ontario sex workers challenged the constitutionality of Canada's prostitution laws in the Ontario Superior Court, and their case eventually made its way to the Supreme Court of Canada (SCC).* The women argued that certain provisions in the *Criminal Code* needlessly endangered them, violating their right to security of the person under section 7 of the Charter. The provisions in question were:

1. section 210, which prevented sex workers from working in a "bawdy house" (fixed indoor location) and limited them instead to street prostitution or outcalls (that is, meeting clients in different locations);
2. section 212(1)(j), which criminalized "living on the avails" of prostitution and made it illegal for sex workers to hire drivers, security, and so on to protect themselves against some of the risks inherent in prostitution under the regime in force at the time; and
3. section 213(1)(c), which prohibited communicating in public for the purposes of prostitution, effectively making it illegal for sex workers to negotiate terms related to their activities with clients.

In December 2013, the SCC delivered its landmark ruling on the prostitution provisions in the Code. Setting out the issue before the court, Chief Justice McLachlin stated that the appeals and cross-appeal were not about whether prostitution should be legal or not but "about whether the laws Parliament has enacted on how prostitution may be carried out pass constitutional muster."[†] In a unanimous 9-0 ruling, the Court declared that the sections in question were inconsistent with the Charter and therefore void. In the words of Chief Justice McLachlin:

> The prohibitions at issue do not merely impose conditions on how prostitutes operate. They go a critical step further, by imposing *dangerous* conditions on prostitution; they prevent people engaged in a risky—but legal—activity from taking steps to protect themselves from the risks.[‡]
> [Emphasis in original.]

The bawdy-house and communication offences[§] had as their main purpose the control of nuisances, but the Court held that the outright ban against keeping a bawdy house or communicating in public for the purpose of prostitution was a grossly disproportionate response in pursuing this objective (in many cases, these activities would not create a nuisance); furthermore, the outright ban made prostitution more dangerous because it took away opportunities for sex workers to increase their safety. Concerning the offence of "living on the avails,"[#] although the control of exploitive relationships was its objective, the Court held that, as worded, it was an overbroad response because it also punished those who were not in exploitive relationships, including those who could increase the safety of sex workers, such as drivers and bodyguards. All three provisions were therefore held to be contrary to section 7 of the Charter.

Although the Court declared the challenged provisions invalid, it acknowledged Parliament's right to impose limits on how prostitution may be conducted and noted that its regulation is a "complex and delicate matter." With regard to all of the interests at stake, the Court decided to suspend the declaration of invalidity for one year to give Parliament the opportunity to redraft Canada's prostitution laws.

In 2014, the Conservative government passed the *Protection of Communities and Exploited Persons Act* (PCEPA),** which included amendments to the *Criminal Code* and created new offences related to prostitution. There are provisions dealing with communicating and advertising for sexual purposes and profiting from another person's sex work. It is also now an offence to purchase sexual services, although the sale of sexual services by sex workers is not criminalized.

Section 45.1 of the PCEPA requires a committee of the House of Commons to prepare a comprehensive review of its provisions within five years (by 2019) and to report its finding to the Speaker of the House within one year of the review (by 2020). At their convention in 2018, the Liberal Party passed a resolution calling for the decriminalization of prostitution and overturning of Canada's PCEPA. As of July 2020, the Parliamentary review and report were still outstanding, and the Liberal government had not acted on the 2018 resolution.

Sex workers and legal experts argue that current laws do the opposite of what was intended and continue to put sex workers at an increased risk of harm because of the criminalization of almost every aspect of their jobs. Whether the new prostitution laws will withstand a Charter challenge remains to be seen.

* *Canada (Attorney General) v Bedford*, 2013 SCC 72.

† *Ibid* at para 2.

‡ *Ibid* at para 60.

§ *Criminal Code*, ss 210 and 213(1)(c).

Ibid, s 212(1)(j).

** SC 2014, c 25.

If convicted of a summary conviction offence, a person is liable, under section 787(1) of the Code, to "a fine of not more than five thousand dollars or to a term of imprisonment not exceeding six months or to both." The maximum penalty for a number of offences, known as "super summary conviction offences," exceeds the general penalty. For example, the offences of assault with a weapon and sexual assault both carry a maximum summary conviction sentence of 18 months.

Indictable Offences

Indictable offences are the most serious offences in the *Criminal Code*, and the procedure by which they are prosecuted is more involved than the process for summary conviction offences. Limitation periods do not apply to indictable offences, and a person can be charged at any time. Being convicted of them also brings more severe penalties, to a maximum of life imprisonment. The seriousness of an indictable offence determines what court has jurisdiction to hear it. One of the most serious indictable offences is murder, along with some others listed under section 469 of the Code, such as treason and piracy. These offences must be tried before a judge and a jury in a province's **superior court of criminal jurisdiction**[22] unless both the accused and the attorney general consent to a trial before a superior court judge alone under section 473 of the Code. The least serious types of indictable offences are those listed in section 553 of the Code—for example, theft (other than theft of cattle), obtaining money or property by false pretenses, and failure to comply with a probation order. These offences are under the absolute jurisdiction of a provincial court judge, without a jury.

If charged with an indictable offence not listed in either section 469 or section 553, an accused may choose or elect his mode of trial. The accused can choose to be tried before either a provincial court judge alone, a superior court of justice judge alone, or a superior court of justice judge with a jury. Section 536 of the Code outlines the election procedure.

indictable offence most serious type of offence in the *Criminal Code* (for example, murder), carrying the most serious sentences

superior court of criminal jurisdiction highest court in each province and territory to hear criminal matters, sometimes with a jury, its designation varying by province and territory

Hybrid Offences

A **hybrid offence** is also called a "dual procedure offence or a Crown election offence." This means that the Crown attorney has the option of choosing whether to prosecute it as a summary conviction offence or as an indictable offence. The offence of assault causing bodily harm is an example of a hybrid offence; the procedure and potential penalties are different depending on whether the Crown decides to proceed by indictment or summarily. Factors that will affect the Crown's decision include the accused's previous criminal record, the specific circumstances involved, and the time since the offence (limitation period). A hybrid offence is deemed to be an indictable offence by default unless the Crown attorney chooses to prosecute it as a summary offence.

hybrid offence dual procedure offence, meaning that the Crown attorney has the option of choosing whether to prosecute it as a summary conviction offence or an indictable offence

Police Investigation of Crime

When a crime is committed and this fact becomes known to authorities in the criminal justice system, the first step is an investigation by the police. The police gather evidence and attempt to determine who is responsible for the offence; they may then arrest and

---

22   Section 2 of the *Criminal Code* provides the names of the superior court of criminal jurisdiction in each province and territory. For example, in Nova Scotia, British Columbia, and Newfoundland and Labrador, the superior court of criminal jurisdiction is the Supreme Court or the Court of Appeal, whereas in Ontario, it is the Court of Appeal or the Superior Court of Justice, and in Nunavut, it is the Nunavut Court of Justice.

charge (or recommend charges against) the person or persons they believe to be responsible.

There are three levels of police forces in Canada: federal, provincial, and municipal. The federal police force is the Royal Canadian Mounted Police (RCMP). Not all provinces and territories have their own provincial/territorial police forces, and in such cases the RCMP is responsible for policing in that province or territory. At the municipal level, many local governments have their own police forces; the majority of police officers in Canada are members of municipal police forces.

Police do not have unlimited powers to investigate crime. The *Criminal Code*, the common law, and the Charter all place limits on the investigatory powers of police and safeguard the rights of individuals with whom police interact. Failure on the part of police to abide by the law in this regard may result in evidence against an accused being excluded in a criminal trial. As described in Chapter 6, section 24(2) of the Charter requires courts to exclude evidence whose admission "would bring the administration of justice into disrepute" when an application is made under section 24(1).

In the following sections, we will look more closely at the law related to the detention and arrest of persons suspected of committing crimes and the law governing the search and seizure of evidence by police.

Detention and Arrest

arrest
detaining or holding
a person by legal
authority

The Charter sets out further legal requirements with which police must comply whenever they are dealing with persons whom they detain or **arrest**. For example, section 10 of the Charter states:

> 10. Everyone has the right on arrest or detention
>   (a) to be informed promptly of the reasons therefor;
>   (b) to retain and instruct counsel without delay and to be informed of that right; and
>   (c) to have the validity of the detention determined by way of *habeas corpus* and to be released if the detention is not lawful.

With respect to reasons, section 29(2)(b) of the *Criminal Code* states that it is the duty of everyone who arrests a person to give notice to that person of the reason for the arrest; the common law requires this too. Sections 7 and 11(c) of the Charter provide an accused person with the right to remain silent while being questioned by police and during her trial.

If an accused decides to waive his right to silence and give a statement, the court must determine whether it was given *voluntarily before the statement can be admissible against the accused*; this is usually established in a *voir dire*, or a trial within a trial. The common law confessions rule aims to prevent wrongful convictions by requiring the Crown to prove that any statement made by an accused person to a person in authority was given voluntarily for the statement to be admissible against the accused (see Box 10.2).

Search and Seizure

Police investigation can involve searching people and places, as well as seizing physical evidence that is related to the crime. The Charter places limits on the ability of police to search for and seize evidence. Section 8 states that everyone "has the right to be secure against unreasonable search or seizure," and court decisions have determined what constitutes a

BOX 10.2

Voluntariness and *Oickle*

In *R v Oickle*,* the SCC noted that false confessions are "rarely the product of proper police techniques"† and stated that, if a confession is produced in certain situations or under certain circumstances, the voluntariness of the confession is difficult to determine. Judges must look carefully at all of the circumstances surrounding a confession and how it was obtained and consider the degree to which the following four factors were present:

1. threats or promises (for example, the promise of preferential treatment or the threat of physical violence/torture);
2. an atmosphere of oppression (contributing actions include prolonged interrogations, fabricated evidence, and disregard for the dignity/well-being of the accused);
3. an operating mind (the accused must have the cognitive ability to understand what is being said to her, what she is saying, and the consequences of saying it to police; the presence of an operating mind may be affected by shock, intoxication, the presence of a mental disorder, etc.); and

4. police trickery (unacceptable trickery is determined by the "community shock test"—for example, an officer pretending to be a chaplain and extracting a confession).

The first three factors are connected with the voluntariness of a statement; depending on the context in which the statement was made, the presence of just one of these three factors to a sufficient degree, or a combination of all three, may be enough to render the statement involuntary. The presence of the fourth factor to a sufficient degree may be enough to exclude a statement on the basis of the fact that the actions of the police reflect negatively on the justice system and have the potential to bring the administration of justice into disrepute.

* 2000 SCC 38.

† *Ibid* at para 45.

Source: Reproduced from Kerry Watkins, Gail Anderson & Vincenzo Rondinelli, *Evidence and Investigation: From the Crime Scene to the Courtroom* (Toronto: Emond Montgomery, 2012) at 300.

---

reasonable or an unreasonable search. For a search to be considered reasonable, it must meet the following test, as stated by the SCC in *R v Collins*:[23]

1. it must be authorized by law;
2. the law itself must be reasonable (that is, the law that authorizes the search); and
3. the search must be conducted in a reasonable manner.

Section 487(5) of the *Criminal Code* authorizes a justice to issue a police officer a **search warrant**, which provides police with the legal authority to conduct a search. Once authorized to conduct a search, the police must then, as noted in *Collins* and following section 8 of the Charter, conduct the search in a reasonable manner. This normally requires them to have the search warrant with them and show it if asked; use reasonable force when executing the warrant; request voluntary admittance before making a forcible entry; and search premises only during the daytime unless the search warrant authorizes execution at night.[24]

There are a limited number of exceptions to the general rule requiring police to obtain a warrant before conducting a search and seizure. For example, section 487.11 of the Code permits a peace officer to conduct a search without a warrant "if the conditions for obtaining

search warrant
warrant, issued by a justice of the peace or a provincial court judge, authorizing police to conduct a search

---

23   [1987] 1 SCR 265, 1987 CanLII 84. See also Gulycz & Kelly, *supra* note 17 at 142.

24   Kelly, "Criminal Procedure," *supra* note 17 at 252-54.

a warrant exist but by reason of exigent circumstances it would be impracticable to obtain a warrant."[25]

Other Aspects of Police Investigation

Some criminal investigations are relatively simple and are completed within hours or days after the crime has been committed. Others are more complex and can take weeks or months to conclude. In extreme cases, criminal investigations can take years, cost millions of dollars, and require coordination with other law enforcement agencies.

Methods of evidence gathering depend on the crime in question. Common techniques include interviewing victims and witnesses, reviewing any CCTV footage or other forms of electronic surveillance, and employing various methods of crime scene investigation (such as the analysis of fingerprint and DNA evidence). Investigations can also involve the review of documentary evidence, the use of outside expert reports, following money trails, geographic profiling (that is, using the location of related crimes to find the offender's residence), and other techniques. Recently, the overt or, more commonly, veiled use of racial profiling by police forces when investigating criminal activity has generated calls for reform around the world (see Box 10.3).

BOX 10.3

Racism and the Police

On May 25, 2020, in Minneapolis, Minnesota, George Floyd, a 46-year-old African American man, died after being handcuffed and pinned to the ground by a police officer whose knee was on his neck. Floyd said repeatedly, "I can't breathe," but the police officer continued to apply pressure. The initial police account of the incident—which had started as a response to a call from a store about a "forgery in progress"— was significantly different from the video evidence that came to light. Demonstrations and protests started in Minneapolis the day after Floyd's death (later ruled a homicide) and quickly spread across the United States and to other countries around the world, including Canada.

The officer who had knelt on Floyd's neck was fired and eventually charged with murder. Three other officers involved in the arrest were also fired and charged with aiding and abetting the homicide. Other incidents of the excessive use of force by the police in the US, Canada, and other countries were widely reported in the months following Floyd's death. The Black Lives Matter movement was energized, and calls to eliminate systemic racism in policing grew stronger. There were also calls to "defund the police" (that is, reallocate part of policing budgets to other social initiatives).

In Canada, reported incidents of police profiling, targeting, and the use of excessive force have involved persons of many different ethnicities, but a disproportionate number have involved Indigenous people. In response to the protests, Prime Minister Justin Trudeau promised to take strong action to address systemic racism in policing, particularly in relation to Indigenous people.* The head of the RCMP, Commissioner Brenda Lucki, also acknowledged that Canada's national police force has a history of racism involving Indigenous and other groups and that change is required.†

Definitions of "systemic racism" vary with the source and the institution, organization, or body in question. They often include references to the interplay between cultural attitudes,

---

25   For a detailed discussion of police investigatory powers, see Kerry Watkins, Gail Anderson & Vincenzo Rondinelli, *Evidence and Investigation: From the Crime Scene to the Courtroom* (Toronto: Emond Montgomery, 2012) ch 6, and Gulycz & Kelly, *supra* note 17 at 142-54.

laws, policies and practices, and institutional norms that disadvantage members of a particular race. In policing, an institutional directive to target a racial group—such as a requirement that police officers perform regular street checks of Indigenous persons—would satisfy almost all definitions, but clear examples of racism such as this rarely exist in modern policing. However, hidden or veiled racism does exist and, by its nature, is more difficult to identify and deal with. For example, is racist behaviour by a few members of a police force systemic racism? How widely does such behaviour need to be known within the force?

The approach of some political leaders and heads of police agencies has been to sidestep definitional debates and to accept the existence of systemic racism. This is arguably the best approach. The challenge for lawmakers and police forces in the coming years is to put in place specific reforms and training initiatives so that racialized communities will no longer be profiled, targeted, or subjected to unreasonable levels of force.

* Kristy Kirkup, "Trudeau Said Indigenous People Disproportionately Targeted by Police, Vows Reforms," *Globe and Mail* (18 June 2020), online: <https://www.theglobeandmail.com/politics/article-trudeau-concedes-indigenous-people-disproportionately-targeted-by>.

† Graham Slaughter, "Lucki Acknowledges Systemic Racism in RCMP," *CTV News* (12 June 2020), online: <https://www.ctvnews.ca/canada/lucki-acknowledges-systemic-racism-in-rcmp-1.4982165>.

After an investigation is completed and it looks as if the evidence is strong enough to support a conviction, the police will prepare a report and send it to the Crown for review. Either the police or the Crown may lay the charges,[26] but it is the Crown who decides whether or not to proceed with them, as described next.

Prosecution of Crime and the Duty to Disclose

The jurisdiction to prosecute criminal offences in Canada is split between the provincial and federal governments. The provincial Crown prosecutes most *Criminal Code* offences (which covers the majority of prosecutions overall), and the federal Crown prosecutes most offences under other federal criminal legislation, such as the CDSA and the *Competition Act*.[27] After the police deliver their report to the relevant Crown office, it is reviewed and the decision is made whether or not to prosecute. The Crown's decision is based on whether there is a likelihood of obtaining a conviction *and* whether the prosecution would serve the public interest. In assessing the public interest, various factors are considered, such as the nature of the offence and its impact on the community, the level of culpability of the accused, the consequences to the victim, and the likely sentencing outcome. When Indigenous offenders and communities are involved, the Crown must also consider the possibility that a prosecution would further contribute to existing trauma and victimization caused by historical and systemic factors (see also below under "Sentencing" and "Indigenous Peoples and the Criminal Justice System").

Both the provincial and federal governments have delegated the responsibility for the prosecution of crimes to independent Crown agencies or offices: in the provinces, agencies

---

26 There are some differences in practice concerning the laying of charges depending on the jurisdiction. For example, in most provinces it's common for the police to lay charges, but in BC a charge approval system is used, and the Crown is primarily responsible for laying charges. If a charge is improperly laid but later dropped, it can still have a negative impact on an accused (for example, it can cause reputational damage and become an obstacle when applying for travel documents).

27 In the territories, the federal Crown also prosecutes *Criminal Code* offences.

such as the BC Prosecution Service, Manitoba Prosecution Service, Nova Scotia Public Prosecution Service, and Crown attorney offices in Ontario and, federally, the Public Prosecution Service of Canada (PPSC), a national prosecuting authority. These agencies report to the attorneys general for their respective governments.

Attorneys general oversee the criminal justice system and occupy a special position in government. Prosecutions in Canada are based on the principle of prosecutorial discretion (or independence), that is, that prosecutorial decisions will be free from political interference.[28] The SCC has held that this principle is constitutionally entrenched and that a decision to prosecute is not reviewable (except in rare cases where there has been an abuse of process, such as would occur if a prosecutor was motivated by bad faith or malice).[29] Although Crown attorneys ultimately work for the Crown, more immediately they work for their particular prosecution service or office. Final responsibility for prosecutorial decisions rests with the head of their agency—for example, in the PPSC, this means the director of public prosecutions—and the responsible attorney general.

Once the Crown decides to prosecute, and prior to the criminal trial, the Crown has a legal duty to provide the accused with all relevant information in its possession that relates to the investigation (in the absence of any legal restrictions) so that the accused can better understand and prepare a defence to the charge(s) against him—in other words, make "full answer and defence." This duty, known as the **duty of disclosure**, exists at common law and is guaranteed by section 7 of the Charter. In the SCC case of *R v Stinchcombe*,[30] the Court framed the duty as follows:

duty of disclosure
Crown's mandatory disclosure to the accused, before the trial, of the evidence against him

> [T]here is a general duty on the part of the Crown to disclose all materials it proposes to use at trial and especially all evidence which may assist the accused even if the Crown does not propose to adduce it.[31]

The Court also explained the proper use to which the information gathered by the Crown should be put:

> The fruits of the investigation which are in its possession are not the property of the Crown for use in securing a conviction but the property of the public to be used to ensure that justice is done.[32]

---

28   In 2019, the issue of prosecutorial discretion was highlighted by a conflict within the Liberal government that became known as the "SNC-Lavalin affair." Prime Minister Trudeau and others in the Liberal government were alleged to have pressured then attorney general of Canada, Jody Wilson-Raybould, to interfere with a prosecutorial decision by the PPSC to proceed with criminal charges against SNC-Lavalin based on its activities in Libya. Trudeau wanted the charges to be dropped in favour of a deferred prosecution agreement (DPA). This would still result in penalties but avoid a criminal prosecution, and SNC-Lavalin would be allowed to continue bidding on government contracts. Wilson-Raybould refused to pursue a DPA. She later resigned from Cabinet, and the Liberal caucus eventually expelled her from the party. After an investigation, Canada's ethics commissioner found that Trudeau had been in a conflict of interest concerning lobbying efforts by SNC-Lavalin to have its charges dropped in favour of a DPA. However, the commissioner did not find that Trudeau had interfered with prosecutorial discretion; this was partially due to a lack of evidence. SNC-Lavalin did eventually face charges and pleaded guilty. See also Chapter 8 under "Corporations" for more detail concerning these charges.

29   See, for example, *Miazga v Kvello Estate*, 2009 SCC 51 at para 46, and *Krieger v Law Society of Alberta*, 2002 SCC 65 at para 30.

30   [1991] 3 SCR 326, 1991 CanLII 45.

31   *Ibid* at 338, adopting as correct law this statement from McEachern CJBC in *R v C (MH)* (1988), 46 CCC (3d) 142, 1988 CanLII 3283 (BCCA).

32   *Supra* note 31 at 333.

The Crown's duty of disclosure places a corollary duty on police to disclose the "fruits of the investigation" to the Crown and to ensure that the evidence they collect is not contaminated, lost, or destroyed and that the chain of continuity is not broken (that is, it must be possible to account for the whereabouts of any piece of physical evidence from the time of its collection to the time it is entered as an exhibit in the trial record).

The Criminal Trial Process

In this section, we examine the criminal courts, pretrial procedures, the trial itself, defences, and sentencing.

Criminal Courts

Although our federal Parliament has sole jurisdiction over criminal law and criminal procedure, section 92(14) of the *Constitution Act, 1867* gives the provinces jurisdiction over "[t]he Administration of Justice in the Province, including the Constitution, Maintenance, and Organization of Provincial Courts, both of Civil and of Criminal Jurisdiction." This means that most criminal cases are heard in provincial (or territorial) inferior courts, or criminal divisions of them, and in provincial (or territorial) superior courts. Inferior courts hear the vast majority of these cases, but superior courts have exclusive jurisdiction over certain serious crimes, such as murder, treason, and piracy. Some serious crimes (including attempted murder, manslaughter, and sexual assault) can be heard in either inferior or superior courts.

The Federal Court, constituted under section 101 of the *Constitution Act, 1867*, has limited criminal jurisdiction. For example, it has non-exclusive jurisdiction (that is, shared jurisdiction with the provincial courts) over trade and commerce offences under the *Competition Act* (see discussion in Chapter 8) and jurisdiction to hear certain matters in connection with terrorism offences under the *Criminal Code* (for example, dealing with the forfeiture of property).

Appeals from decisions of any of these courts of original jurisdiction can make their way through the court system to the SCC. See Figure 5.1 and the descriptions of these courts in Chapter 5.

In addition to the courts just mentioned, a number of specialized courts have been created outside of the regular court system. They deal with particular types of offences and offender classes. These courts set specific eligibility requirements. Sometimes they offer diversion programs allowing an offender to avoid prosecution, subject to conditions such as submitting to treatment and regular reporting or making restitution for damage caused. Often they require a guilty plea and then focus on sentencing options. Also, they regularly work with other organizations, for example, legal aid, community outreach, and mental health societies. The aim of these courts is to achieve better long-term outcomes for offenders and for society as a whole (see also Box 5.2 in Chapter 5 and under "Sentencing" below). The main types of specialized courts are as follows:

- *Mental health courts.* Mental health courts (MHCs) have been created in most provinces and territories, but not all,[33] and are a response to the growing number of accused appearing before the courts who are suffering from mental disorders (the first MHC opened in Toronto in 1998). Process options include diversion,

---

33 BC and Prince Edward Island have yet to establish MHCs.

guilty pleas, sentencing, and sometimes NCRMD pleas (NCRMD or just NCR means "not criminally responsible on account of mental disorder" and refers to a plea made under s 16 of the *Criminal Code*). MHCs all operate under similar principles. They are non-adversarial and available to individuals who are suffering from mental illness and have been charged with non-violent criminal offences. Ideally, arrested persons who meet the eligibility criteria will be sent to an MHC, where they will be seen by psychiatrists, legal aid counsel, and social workers; they will then have a fitness hearing and a bail hearing. The goals of these courts are to heal and "to expedite case processing, create effective interactions between the mental health and criminal justice system, increase access to mental health services, reduce recidivism, improve public safety and reduce the length of confinement in jails for mentally disordered offenders."[34]

- *Drug treatment courts.* There are six drug treatment courts (DTCs) operating across Canada: in Toronto (since 1998); Vancouver (since 2001); Edmonton (since 2005); and Winnipeg, Ottawa, and Regina (since 2006).[35] Participation is open to non-violent offenders with addictions who have been charged with possession or trafficking of small quantities of drugs such as crack, cocaine, and heroin; minor property crimes; or prostitution. Offenders must plead guilty prior to the commencement of a DTC treatment program. On the successful completion of the program, participants are eligible for a reduced sentence such as a suspended sentence with a period of probation. The aim of DTCs is to reduce the amount of crime committed due to substance abuse by a combination of court-monitored treatment and community support for offenders; the larger aim is to reduce, for Canadian law enforcement and legal and corrections systems, the costs stemming from addiction. Participation in the courts is voluntary, but participants are required to appear in court regularly, attend counselling sessions, receive medical attention as needed (for example, methadone treatment), and undergo random drug tests.

- *Domestic violence courts.* Almost all provinces and territories have created domestic violence courts (DVCs) with slightly different names depending on the region (for example, Integrated Domestic Violence Court in Ontario, Family Violence Intervention Court in Newfoundland and Labrador, and Domestic Violence Treatment Option Court in Yukon).[36] They deal primarily with criminal cases that involve allegations of domestic abuse but sometimes will integrate family law issues (other than divorce, division of property, and child protection). DVC programs aim to facilitate the prosecution of charges (but sometimes allow for diversion away from prosecution in less serious cases), provide early intervention and better support to victims, and increase offender accountability. As with other specialized courts, DVCs do not operate in isolation. They collaborate with the police, Crown attorneys, community agencies, victim/

---

34 Edward F Ormston, "Mental Health Court in Ontario" (2005) 2:8 Visions: BC's Mental Health & Addictions Journal 31.

35 See "Drug Treatment Court Funding Program," online: *Department of Justice Canada* <https://www.justice.gc.ca/eng/fund-fina/gov-gouv/dtc-ttt.html>; and "6.1 Drug Treatment Courts, Public Prosecution Service of Canada Deskbook," online: *Public Prosecution Service of Canada* <https://www.ppsc-sppc.gc.ca/eng/pub/fpsd-sfpg/fps-sfp/tpd/p6/ch01.html>.

36 For more discussion of Canadian responses to domestic violence by region, including the creation of DVCs, see "Programming Responses for Intimate Partner Violence," online: *Department of Justice Canada* <https://www.justice.gc.ca/eng/rp-pr/jr/ipv-vpi/toc-tdm.html>.

witness assistance program staff, and others who try to make the safety and needs of victims of domestic violence and their children a priority.

- *Indigenous courts.*   Indigenous courts (sometimes also called Gladue courts) have been established in most provinces and all of the territories.[37] They hear criminal matters involving Indigenous persons but generally don't try cases and are only involved in sentencing. They incorporate Indigenous cultural traditions and ideas about justice and follow the sentencing guidelines set by the SCC in *R v Gladue*[38] (see below under "Sentencing"). Saskatchewan's Cree Court is a unique example of one of these courts; it is a circuit court and holds its hearings in whole or in part in Cree, the Indigenous language of the region. Like regular courts, Indigenous courts include a judge, duty counsel, and Crown and defence lawyers, but most of the individuals involved are trained in the issues pertinent to the offenders who appear before them. Caseworkers prepare reports on offenders' life circumstances, which are used to determine an appropriate sentence. Partnerships often exist between the Indigenous courts and non-governmental organizations to ensure that *Gladue*-type information is systematically incorporated into sentencing procedures.

Pretrial Procedures

A number of procedures occur prior to a criminal trial.[39] Once the police have finished investigating a crime and have gathered and assessed their evidence, they may lay a criminal charge against a suspect. They must also ensure that the accused person comes before a court. Part XVI of the *Criminal Code* sets out several ways police may do this.

First, if the offence is an indictable type mentioned in section 553 (the least serious indictable offences), a hybrid offence, or a summary conviction offence, the police officer may issue an **appearance notice** to the accused person. The appearance notice is a document given to a person, usually at the scene of the offence, requiring that person to come to court on a certain date and time to answer to a charge. The accused must sign the appearance notice and then may leave. Having issued an appearance notice, the police officer must then swear an information before a justice that the accused person has committed an offence. The officer must do this as soon as practicable, before the date and time prescribed in the appearance notice for the accused's future court appearance.

Second, sometimes the accused will be brought to court by a **summons**. To start this process, the police officer goes before a justice and swears an information that there are reasonable grounds to believe an accused has committed an offence. If the justice is satisfied that an arrest warrant is not necessary, a summons is issued, following the requirements set out in section 509 of the *Criminal Code*. The summons requires the accused to attend court on a certain date and time to answer to the charge. It is served personally on the accused.

The third way of bringing an accused before the court is for a justice to issue a warrant for the person's arrest, directing the police to take the accused into custody and bring her

appearance notice document given to a person, usually at the scene of the crime, requiring that person to come to court on a certain date and time to answer to a charge

summons document served personally on an accused person requiring her to be in court at a certain date and time

---

37 Some provinces (Manitoba and Quebec, for example) only use the regular court system for cases involving Indigenous offenders, together with Indigenous court workers as necessary. For an overview of Indigenous courts in Canada, see "Spotlight on *Gladue*: Challenges, Experiences, and Possibilities in Canada's Criminal Justice System," online: *Department of Justice Canada* <https://www.justice.gc.ca/eng/rp-pr/jr/gladue/p4.html#sec1>.

38 [1999] 1 SCR 688, 1999 CanLII 679.

39 For more information on pretrial procedures, see Gulycz & Kelly, *supra* note 17, ch 17.

to court. As always, police actions in compelling the accused to appear in court are subject to the rights everyone has under the Charter.

Generally, a considerable amount of time elapses between the date an accused is charged with an offence and the date the actual trial takes place. Note that section 11(b) of the Charter states that any person charged with an offence has the right "to be tried within a reasonable time." Given that an accused's trial may be some time in the future, the *Criminal Code* outlines procedures by which a police officer, a justice of the peace, or a judge may release an accused prior to his trial. Here, again, the Charter applies. Section 11(e) states that any person charged with an offence has the right "not to be denied reasonable bail without just cause."

Pretrial release of the accused, often called "bail," is formally known in the *Criminal Code* as **judicial interim release**. If the accused is still in custody, the pretrial release of that person is determined at a bail hearing. The bail hearing follows different procedures depending on the seriousness of the charge. For less serious offences—that is, for offences not listed in section 469—the accused must be taken before a justice for her bail hearing within 24 hours of arrest and detention.

At this regular bail hearing, the Crown attorney has the onus to show cause why the accused should not be released or should be released with certain conditions attached. If the Crown does not show cause, the justice must release the accused on an **undertaking** without conditions or "with such conditions as the justice directs" (the conditions that may be applied are set out in section 515(2) of the *Criminal Code*). However, the onus is not always on the Crown. There are a number of situations, set out in section 515(6) of the Code, in which the onus is on the accused to show why he should not be detained in custody prior to the trial. Such a reverse onus could happen if, for example, the accused were charged with an indictable offence while already out on bail for another indictable offence.

For an accused charged with a more serious section 469 indictable offence (for example, murder or treason), more stringent considerations apply. The accused must apply for a bail hearing before a judge in a superior court of criminal jurisdiction, under section 522 of the *Criminal Code*. In this case, due to the seriousness of the offence, the accused has the onus to show cause why her detention is not justified. If the judge is not persuaded, the accused will be detained until her trial.

Before the trial begins, the accused and his lawyer have a number of important matters to consider, including the following:

- Obtaining disclosure of all of the Crown's relevant evidence against the accused. Such disclosure is required by common law, as per *Stinchcombe*, as well as the Charter.
- Having a pretrial hearing conference, as set out in section 625.1 of the *Criminal Code*. Such conferences are mandatory for jury trials.
- Discussing how to **plead** to the offence. Under section 606 of the *Criminal Code*, permitted pleas are either guilty or not guilty or one of the special pleas authorized under section 607 of the Code. These are:
  - *autrefois acquit* (available when the person charged has been previously acquitted with respect to the charge),
  - *autrefois convict* (available when the person charged has been previously convicted with respect to the charge), and
  - pardon (the offence and the penalty are forgiven, usually by a head of state or Parliament).
- Considering whether a **plea bargain** should be negotiated with the Crown. A plea bargain comes about when the Crown attorney and the defence counsel negotiate

judicial interim release
formal name for bail; the release of an accused prior to her trial

undertaking (by an accused)
promise by an accused to the court, usually to appear back in court at a certain date and time

plead
to answer to a criminal charge in ways permitted by the *Criminal Code*

plea bargain
agreement between the Crown and the defence on how the accused will plead in court and on the sentence he will receive

an agreement on matters such as how the accused will plead to the offence and what sentence the Crown will ask for in court if the accused pleads guilty. For example, the accused may plead guilty to a lesser offence and receive a reduced sentence.

- Electing the mode of trial. This consideration is relevant if the accused is charged with an indictable offence that is not listed in either section 469 or section 553 of the *Criminal Code*. The options are trial by a judge of the superior court of justice with a jury, trial by a judge of the superior court of justice without a jury, and trial by a provincial court judge without a jury.

- Considering (in a case where the accused chooses to have the trial in the superior court) whether to have a **preliminary inquiry**. The procedure for a preliminary inquiry is described in part XVIII of the *Criminal Code*. It is conducted before a provincial court judge, who determines whether there is sufficient evidence to require the accused to stand trial for the offence.

- Deciding whether the accused will testify at his own trial. (There is no requirement that the accused do so.) This right is also protected under section 11(c) of the Charter.

The Trial

In Canada, trials are open to the public. If the trial is in a provincial court, the charging document describing the offence(s) with which the accused is charged is called an **information**. If the trial is in superior court, the charging document describing the offence(s) is called an **indictment** (although some indictable offences, which require indictments, can proceed in provincial court). The nature of a criminal trial is complex, and various sections of the *Criminal Code* outline how the trial proceeds. The trial itself starts with the **arraignment**, whereby the charge is read to the accused in open court, and the accused is asked how she wishes to plead. If the accused pleads guilty to the offence, the Crown will read a summary of the facts to the judge, and the defence will admit to them. If the trial judge agrees, he finds the accused guilty and enters a **conviction**. The accused will then be sentenced (see the discussion below).

If the accused pleads not guilty to the offence, the Crown attorney presents its case first. The Crown then attempts to prove its case with evidence against the accused. Evidence may take a number of forms, including oral evidence (spoken evidence given by a witness under affirmation or oath), physical evidence (actual objects, such as DNA, photographs, or a weapon), and documentary evidence (any documents produced mechanically or by hand, such as medical records or transcripts).

In general, all relevant evidence is admissible unless a statutory or common law rule excludes it. For example, evidence may be deemed unreliable under the common law hearsay rule and excluded as a result (hearsay is an out-of-court statement by a person not before the court that is being used to prove the truth of what is asserted in the statement and is being related to the court by someone else). Or evidence may have been acquired in contravention of the Charter (for example, by way of an illegal seizure) and may be excluded under section 24(2) (see the discussion of section 24 of the Charter in Chapter 6). There are many other evidentiary rules under which relevant evidence may be excluded because the evidence is unreliable or because admitting it would be unfair (including rules relating to character evidence, privileged communications, and the competence and compellability of witnesses).

As mentioned, the Crown must prove all of the elements of the offence beyond a reasonable doubt. Following the Crown's own examination-in-chief of their witness, the

preliminary inquiry
hearing before a provincial court judge to determine whether the Crown has sufficient evidence for the accused to stand trial for the offence

information
written document, used in provincial court, describing the offences with which the accused is charged

indictment
written document, used in superior court, describing the offences with which the accused is charged

arraignment
procedure by which the charge is read to the accused in open court and the accused is asked how she wishes to plead

conviction
judge or jury's finding an accused person guilty of an offence

defence counsel may conduct a cross-examination, which the Crown may then follow with a re-examination. The judge may also question the witness, and then the next witness may be called. After the Crown has finished calling all of its witnesses and presenting all of its evidence, the Crown closes its case. If the defence believes the Crown has not provided any evidence on an essential element of the offence, the defence may make a motion to the trial judge for a directed verdict of acquittal. If the motion is allowed, the accused will be acquitted; if it is dismissed, the trial will continue, with the defence then opening its case and calling its evidence. At this stage of the trial, the defence conducts the examination-in-chief of its own witnesses; the Crown then cross-examines the witnesses, and the defence re-examines them. As stated, the accused is not obligated to testify at her own trial.

A number of defences are set out in the *Criminal Code*. (These are discussed briefly in the following section.) When the defence has finished presenting all of its evidence, it closes its case. The Crown and the defence then both make closing submissions to the judge. If the trial is before a judge alone, the judge decides if the accused is guilty or not guilty. If the trial is before a judge and a jury, the judge reviews the evidence and each side's case for the jury and instructs or charges them on how to apply the law to the facts of the case in order to reach their decision. The jury then retires to a jury room to deliberate and determine a **verdict** of guilty or not guilty. Jurors do not need to give reasons for their verdict, but their verdict must be unanimous. If they find the accused guilty, the trial judge imposes the sentence (see the discussion below).

verdict
finding of a jury on the matter before it—for example, whether the accused is guilty or not guilty

Defences

Prior to the enactment of the *Criminal Code*, defences to criminal offences were based on the common law. Today, they are found in the Code and, by section 8(3), at common law. The following are some examples of defences:[40]

- *Self-defence.*   The defence of self-defence is set out in section 34 of the *Criminal Code*. It states that a person is not guilty of an offence if (a) he believes on reasonable grounds that force is being used against him or another person or that a threat of force is being made against him or another person; (b) the act that constitutes the offence is committed for the purpose of defending or protecting himself or the other person from that use or threat of force; and (c) the act committed is reasonable in the circumstances. In determining whether the act committed is "reasonable in the circumstances," the court will consider factors including but not limited to the nature of the force or threat; the extent to which the use of force was imminent and whether there were other means available to respond to the potential use of force; whether any party to the incident used or threatened to use a weapon; and the size, age, gender, and physical capabilities of the parties to the incident.

- *Consent.*   To rely on the defence of consent, the accused must prove that the alleged victim freely consented to the acts carried out by the accused. Assault is an offence to which the defence of consent may apply—for example, in sporting matches involving physical contact. Certain offences exclude the defence of consent—for example, the infliction of death.

- *Provocation.*   This defence is available only where the accused is charged with murder. It is a partial defence, which, if established, does not result in the acquittal

---

40   For more information on defences, see Gulycz & Kelly, *supra* note 17, ch 10.

of the accused but rather in the accused being convicted of the lesser offence of manslaughter. The provocation may take various forms (such as words or gestures), but the result must be that the accused suddenly lost self-control and did not have time to take into account the consequences of her actions.

- *Duress.* The defence of duress exists at common law and in section 17 of the *Criminal Code*. It is a complex defence when the accused was compelled to commit a criminal offence as a result of threats of immediate death or bodily harm from a person present when the offence was committed. Section 17 does not apply to some specific offences, such as murder, sexual assault, or robbery.

- *Mental disorder.* Section 16 of the *Criminal Code* states that no person is criminally responsible for a criminal act or omission made "while suffering from a mental disorder that rendered the person incapable of appreciating the nature and quality of the act or omission or of knowing that it was wrong." Furthermore, the presence of such a disorder must be proved on a balance of probabilities. When raising an NCRMD defence, the burden of proof rests with the accused to show that he was suffering from a mental disorder that exempts him from criminal responsibility within the meaning of section 16. See also the discussion of MHCs above.

- *Intoxication.* The intoxication defence is a common law defence, but it has been modified by the *Criminal Code*. Canadian law recognizes three levels of intoxication: (1) mild (which generally will not provide a defence), (2) advanced (which may provide a defence to certain kinds of *mens rea* offences—those where specific intent is required—if the accused is unable to form the necessary intent),[41] and (3) extreme (which provides a limited defence when the level of intoxication is so extreme that it prevents the accused from forming a general intent, in effect preventing her from acting voluntarily and nullifying the *actus reus* element).[42] Concerning extreme intoxication, it is limited to non-violent crimes. This is because in 1995 section 33.1 was added to the *Criminal Code* banning self-induced extreme intoxication as a defence to violent crimes. Section 33.1 was enacted because of a ruling in 1994 that allowed the extreme intoxication defence in a case of a sexual assault.[43] However, in 2020, the Ontario Court of Appeal declared section 33.1 to be unconstitutional because it violates sections 7 and 11(d) of the Charter.[44] Until the question of section 33.1's constitutionality is resolved by the SCC, technically, there will be two laws in Canada concerning the defence of extreme intoxication. In Ontario, the defence will be broadly available, and, in the rest of Canada, it will be much more limited, and section 33.1 will continue to apply.

Other defences include necessity, automatism, mistake of fact, and mistake of law.

Sentencing

A **sentence** is the punishment imposed by a trial judge on someone found guilty of a criminal offence. The sentence aims to protect society, as well as to punish the offender and deter

sentence
punishment the judge imposes on a person convicted of a criminal offence

---

41 As noted earlier, specific intent offences require the accused to intend to bring about the consequences of her actions. Murder and robbery are examples of specific intent offences. See *R v Tatton*, 2015 SCC 33, for an explanation of the difference between specific intent and general intent offences.

42 See *R v Daley*, 2007 SCC 53, for an analysis of these three types of intoxication.

43 *R v Daviault*, [1994] 3 SCR 63, 1994 CanLII 61.

44 *R v Sullivan*, 2020 ONCA 333. The *Sullivan* decision has been appealed to the SCC.

others from committing crimes. Sentencing is dealt with in part XXIII of the *Criminal Code*.[45] The purpose and objectives are set out in section 718 as follows:

> 718. The fundamental purpose of sentencing is to protect society and to contribute, along with crime prevention initiatives, to respect for the law and the maintenance of a just, peaceful and safe society by imposing just sanctions that have one or more of the following objectives:
>
> (a) to denounce unlawful conduct and the harm done to victims or to the community that is caused by unlawful conduct;
>
> (b) to deter the offender and other persons from committing offences;
>
> (c) to separate offenders from society, where necessary;
>
> (d) to assist in rehabilitating offenders;
>
> (e) to provide reparations for harm done to victims or to the community; and
>
> (f) to promote a sense of responsibility in offenders, and acknowledgment of the harm done to victims or to the community.

The fundamental principle of sentencing is expressed in section 718.1 of the *Criminal Code*, which states: "A sentence must be proportionate to the gravity of the offence and the degree of responsibility of the offender." In determining the appropriate sentence, section 718.2 provides other sentencing principles. For example, section 718.2(b) states that a sentence "should be similar to sentences imposed on similar offenders for similar offences committed in similar circumstances," whereas section 718.2(c) states that "where consecutive sentences are imposed, the combined sentence should not be unduly long or harsh."

Note that there is a particular sentencing principle in the *Criminal Code* that applies specifically to Indigenous offenders, whose overrepresentation has been called "one of the most documented trends in the Canadian criminal justice system."[46] Section 718.2(e) states that "all available sanctions, other than imprisonment, that are reasonable in the circumstances and consistent with the harm done to the victims or to the community should be considered for *all* offenders, *with particular attention to the circumstances of [A]boriginal offenders*" (emphasis added). This principle, which was added to the Code in 1996, represents, among other things, an attempt to redress Indigenous overrepresentation in the criminal justice system. In the seminal case *R v Gladue*,[47] the SCC first articulated the rules and principles applicable to this section when imposing sentences on Indigenous offenders. Particular background factors that judges must consider are the following:

> (A) The unique systemic or background factors which may have played a part in bringing the particular [A]boriginal offender before the courts; and
>
> (B) The types of sentencing procedures and sanctions which may be appropriate in the circumstances for the offender because of his or her particular [A]boriginal heritage or connection.[48]

---

45 A detailed description of sentencing is outside the scope of this text. Interested readers should consult Gulycz & Kelly, *supra* note 17, ch 20.

46 Brian R Pfefferle, "Gladue Sentencing: Uneasy Answers to the Hard Problem of Aboriginal Over-Incarceration" (2009) 32:2 Man LJ 113.

47 *Supra* note 38. The case involved an Indigenous woman from British Columbia, Jamie Tanis Gladue, who pleaded guilty to manslaughter for killing her common law husband. For more information on the case and *Gladue* rights, see Jay Istvanffy's *Gladue Primer* under Further Reading at the end of this chapter.

48 *R v Gladue, supra* note 38 at para 66.

The Court elaborated on these further, as follows:

> The background factors which figure prominently in the causation of crime by [A]boriginal offenders are by now well known. Years of dislocation and economic development have translated, for many [A]boriginal peoples, into low incomes, high unemployment, lack of opportunities and options, lack or irrelevance of education, substance abuse, loneliness, and community fragmentation. These and other factors contribute to a higher incidence of crime and incarceration.[49]

The Court also noted some differences between traditional Indigenous sentencing ideals and those of Canada's criminal justice system, highlighting their importance to the analysis:

> A significant problem experienced by [A]boriginal people who come into contact with the criminal justice system is that the traditional sentencing ideals of deterrence, separation, and denunciation are often far removed from the understanding of sentencing held by these offenders and their community. … [M]ost traditional [A]boriginal conceptions of sentencing place a *primary* emphasis upon the ideals of restorative justice. This tradition is extremely important to the analysis under s. 718.2(e).[50]

Unfortunately, more than a decade after the precedent-setting *Gladue* decision, the SCC observed that—according to statistics and due in part to "a fundamental misunderstanding and misapplication of both s. 718.2(e) and this Court's decision in *Gladue*"—section 718.2(e) has not had a "discernible impact" on Indigenous overrepresentation in the criminal justice system to date.[51] However, more recently, positive change is becoming apparent. The "establishment of courts specializing in Indigenous matters is considered one of the most direct and representative implementations of Gladue principles," and there is evidence that outcomes of Indigenous offenders are being improved as a result of these courts.[52] See also the discussion of Indigenous courts above.

Under section 718.2, a judge must also consider possible aggravating circumstances before imposing a sentence. An **aggravating circumstance** is any circumstance related to the offence or the offender that increases the seriousness of the offence and that may result in an increased sentence. Section 718.2(a) sets out a number of circumstances that may be considered aggravating—for example, evidence that the offence was motivated by bias, prejudice, or hate based on a prohibited ground of discrimination; that the offender abused someone under the age of 18; that the offender, in committing the offence, abused a position of trust or authority in relation to the victim; and that the offence was a terrorism offence. A **mitigating circumstance** is any circumstance associated with the offence or the offender that decreases the seriousness of the offence and that may result in a reduced sentence. Although section 718.2 does not provide examples, some could include whether the offender cooperated with police, the offender's age and absence of a criminal record, whether the offender showed remorse, or whether the offender committed the offence as a result of having been provoked.

aggravating circumstance factor in the case that causes the judge to impose a harsher sentence on the convicted person than he or she would otherwise

mitigating circumstance factor in the case that causes the judge to impose a milder sentence on the convicted person than he or she would otherwise

49   *Ibid* at para 67.

50   *Ibid* at para 70 (emphasis in original).

51   *R v Ipeelee*, 2012 SCC 13 at para 63.

52   Department of Justice, "Spotlight on *Gladue*," *supra* note 37.

BOX 10.4

Sentencing and Canada's Correctional System

In Canada, correctional jurisdiction is divided between the provinces/territories and the federal government. Adults who receive a custodial sentence of less than two years serve their sentence in a provincial or territorial correctional facility operated by the province/territory under relevant provincial/territorial legislation; in Ontario, for example, corrections are administered under the *Ministry of Correctional Services Act**by the Ontario Ministry of Community Safety and Correctional Services. Adults who receive a custodial sentence of two years or more serve their sentence in federal institutions, referred to as penitentiaries, which are operated by the Correctional Service of Canada (CSC) under the *Corrections and Conditional Release Act.*[†]

Depending on the assessment and classification of a particular offender by correctional officials, the offender may serve his sentence in a maximum, medium, or minimum security facility or in a multi-level institution. Offenders may be released once their entire sentence has been served or by parole granted prior to completion of the sentence by either the Parole Board of Canada or various provincial/territorial parole boards established by some provinces/territories for inmates serving time in provincial/territorial correctional facilities. In addition to the provincial/territorial and federal correctional systems, the third correctional system in Canada is the youth criminal justice system for young persons (see the discussion under the heading "Youth Criminal Justice Act").

Another way in which someone convicted of an offence can serve a sentence in the community and remain out of custody is through a suspended sentence and probation. Under section 731(1)(a) of the *Criminal Code*, provided that no minimum punishment is prescribed by law, a judge can, having regard to the offender's age and character, the nature of the offence, and the circumstances surrounding it, suspend the sentence and release the offender on probation. This order prescribes certain mandatory conditions and permits the court to prescribe "additional conditions" listed in section 732.1(3). If, however, the offender fails or refuses to comply with the order without a reasonable excuse, she may be charged with an additional offence of breach of probation under section 733.1 of the Code.

* RSO 1990, c M.22.

† SC 1992, c 20.

---

pre-sentence report
report, prepared by a probation officer, that provides information about the background and character of the offender to assist a judge in sentencing

To help them decide on an appropriate sentence, particularly in the case of a first-time offender, judges may also request a **pre-sentence report**, prepared by a probation officer, to learn more about the background and character of the offender. In addition to the pre-sentence report, the victim and relatives of the victim may prepare and file a victim impact statement describing the impact the crime has had on their lives. At the sentencing hearing, both the Crown and defence counsel have an opportunity to make submissions; they may also make a joint submission. Possible sentences include an absolute or a conditional discharge, a fine, a suspended sentence and probation, or imprisonment (see Box 10.4). If either the Crown or the accused person decides to appeal, part XXI of the *Criminal Code* governs appeals for indictable offences, whereas part XXVII governs appeals for summary conviction offences.[53]

Youth Criminal Justice Act

In Canada today, young people who commit criminal offences set out in the *Criminal Code* are treated differently from adults. Young persons 12 years of age or older but less than 18 years of age do not have their offence dealt with in adult criminal court but rather are

---

53 For more information on appeals, see Gulycz & Kelly, *supra* note 17, ch 21.

tried in a youth justice court established under the provisions of the YCJA, which came into force in 2003.

The YCJA has a declaration of principle in section 3 that contains the policy in Canada for dealing with young persons. The Act is structured to process young persons charged with *Criminal Code* offences from their first contact with police through to (if applicable) their trial and sentence with this policy in mind. Special procedures aim to ensure the fair treatment of young persons and the protection of their rights.

Among the Act's features is the use of extrajudicial measures, requiring a police officer to consider, for example, giving a warning to a young person or making a referral to a community program before starting judicial proceedings (s 6); giving young persons the right to retain and instruct counsel without delay at any stage of the proceedings (s 25); requiring parental notice of their child's arrest (s 26); and provisions relating to the sentencing, custody, and supervision of young persons in parts 4 and 5 of the Act. The sentencing principles in section 38(1) state that

> [t]he purpose of sentencing under section 42 (youth sentences) is to hold a young person accountable for an offence through the imposition of just sanctions that have meaningful consequences for the young person and that promote his or her rehabilitation and reintegration into society, thereby contributing to the long-term protection of the public.

Sentences may include a judicial reprimand, a fine, compensation or restitution, or a community service order. Custody and supervision orders are also possible.

Youth sentences are generally less severe than adult sentences, but in some cases the Crown can apply to the court to have the youth sentenced as an adult. An adult sentence may be appropriate where the youth is convicted of a serious violent crime (such as murder, manslaughter, or aggravated sexual assault) or where the offence is part of a pattern of violent offences. Youths receiving adult sentences serve their sentences in youth facilities; however, if they turn 20 in a youth facility, they may be transferred to an adult facility (ss 64-81).

Indigenous Peoples and the Criminal Justice System

In recent decades, the overrepresentation of Indigenous peoples in Canada's criminal justice system, especially corrections, has reached alarming proportions.[54] The Office of the Correctional Investigator now estimates that the incarceration rate for Indigenous adults is as much as ten times higher than for non-Indigenous adults. As of 2013, although Indigenous peoples made up only approximately 4 percent of Canada's population, they accounted for over 23 percent of the federal inmate population.[55]

A range of studies, task forces, royal commissions, conferences, and inquiries have highlighted the adverse impact of the enforcement and administration of criminal law on Indigenous peoples and put forth suggestions for intervention. The Office of the

---

54   For a detailed discussion, see Darion Boyington et al, "Indigenous People and the Criminal Justice System" in *Diversity and Indigenous Peoples in Canada*, 3rd ed (Toronto: Emond, 2017) ch 11.

55   "Aboriginal Offenders—A Critical Situation" (Backgrounder) (16 September 2013), online: *Office of the Correctional Investigator* <http://www.oci-bec.gc.ca/cnt/rpt/oth-aut/oth-aut20121022info-eng.aspx>.

Correctional Investigator noted recently that, compared to non-Indigenous inmates, Indigenous inmates are:

- classified as higher risk and higher need in areas such as community reintegration, family supports, and unemployment;
- released later in their sentences, with most leaving prison at the statutory release or warrant expiry date;
- overrepresented in segregation and maximum security populations;
- disproportionately involved in self-injury and use-of-force interventions while incarcerated; and
- more likely to return to prison on revocation of parole for administrative reasons rather than criminal violations.[56]

In addition to the background factors described by the SCC in *Gladue*, the fundamental differences between Euro-Canadian and traditional Indigenous notions of justice have been suggested as another factor contributing to the higher incidence of Indigenous crime and incarceration (see Table 10.1). Manitoba Justice Murray Sinclair, who served as the chair of the Truth and Reconciliation Commission (TRC), explained:

> The starting point is a difficult one for people raised with the liberal ideals of "civil rights" and "equality"; it requires one to accept the possibility that being Aboriginal and being non-Aboriginal involve being different. It requires one to come to terms with the concept that the Aboriginal Peoples of North America, for the most part, hold world views and life philosophies fundamentally different from those of the dominant Euro-Canadian society, and that these … are so fundamentally different as to be inherently in conflict. …
>
> There are areas of thought and belief that are substantially shared by both Aboriginal and non-Aboriginal peoples. Nevertheless, the differences are broad enough and general enough to make many Euro-Canadian institutions incompatible with the moral and ethical value systems and approaches of Aboriginal Canadians.[57]

The modern instruments of criminal justice—jails, police officers, and courts—were unknown to Indigenous peoples prior to European contact. Mediation was used to resolve disputes and restore the offender to a harmonious relationship with the rest of the community, through the acceptance of responsibility and through making the necessary amends, both to the victim and the larger community. All community members, and Elders in particular, played an important role.[58]

Given all that has occurred over the past few hundred years, however, as Mary Ellen Turpel suggests in the Royal Commission on Aboriginal Peoples report on justice issues, it would be fruitless to attempt simply to return to pre-colonial ways:

> Can the pre-colonial regime ever be reconstructed? My own view is no, not except as a relic of the past. It cannot be resurrected because we have all been touched by

---

56 *Ibid.*

57 Murray Sinclair, "Aboriginal Peoples, Justice and the Law" in Richard Gosse, James Youngblood Henderson & Roger Carter, eds, *Continuing Poundmaker and Riel's Quest: Presentations Made at a Conference on Aboriginal Peoples and Justice* (Saskatoon: Purich, 1994) 173 at 175-76.

58 Boyington et al, *supra* note 54 at 332-33. These were the broad principles of Indigenous justice. Different moral codes, religious beliefs, and life philosophies existed among different Indigenous peoples.

TABLE 10.1 Comparison of Canadian and Indigenous Approaches to Justice

CANADIAN JUSTICE	INDIGENOUS JUSTICE
Society based on the rights of the individual and the pursuit of personal wealth and property	Society based on the rights of the community and communal sharing of wealth and property
Laws made by legislative assemblies and courts	Laws based on custom, sacred and naturalistic beliefs, as well as deliberative tribal or band processes
Christianity providing a moral basis for legal authority	Indigenous sacred beliefs informing behavioural norms
Criminality seen as damaging the relationship between the individual and the state	Criminality seen as damaging the relationship between individuals and communities
Laws enforced by state-sanctioned mechanisms (police forces, courts, and detention facilities)	Laws often applied with the participation of victims, families, and community representatives
Punishment and incarceration used to control criminal behaviour	Collaborative decision-making and expulsion from the community used to control the peace

imperialism and colonialism, and there is no simplistic escape to some pre-colonial history except a rhetorical one. In my view, we [Aboriginal people] need to regain control over criminal justice, indeed all justice matters, but in a thoroughly post-colonial fashion. ... One cannot erase the history of colonialism, but we must, as an imperative, undo it in a contemporary context. ... We have to accept that there are profound social and economic problems in Aboriginal communities today that never existed pre-colonization and even in the first few hundred years of interaction. Problems of alcohol and solvent abuse, family violence and sexual abuse, and youth crime—these are indications of a fundamental breakdown in the social order in Aboriginal communities of a magnitude never known before. A reform dialogue or proposals in the criminal justice field have to come to grips with this contemporary reality and not just retreat into a pre-colonial situation.[59]

The Royal Commission on Aboriginal Peoples recommended that the federal, provincial, and territorial governments "recognize the right of Aboriginal nations to establish and administer their own systems of justice,"[60] and others, such as Manitoba's Aboriginal Justice Implementation Commission, have recommended an autonomous Indigenous justice system to address the failure of the current criminal justice system for Indigenous peoples. Other possibilities include "Indigenizing" the current criminal justice system through increased Indigenous representation among police officers, lawyers, judges, and correctional officers; creating autonomous Indigenous agencies to work within the existing system; and

---

59 Royal Commission on Aboriginal Peoples, *Bridging the Cultural Divide: A Report on Aboriginal People and Criminal Justice in Canada* (Ottawa: Supply and Services Canada, 1996) at 65-66.

60 *Ibid* at 312.

the continued implementation of the CSC strategic plan for Indigenous corrections, which aims to provide culturally appropriate programming and services in custody facilities.[61]

In its 2015 report, the TRC acknowledged the profound and crippling effect that colonialism and discriminatory federal policies (concerning the residential school system, funding of Indigenous programs, and other matters) have had on Indigenous peoples. The TRC described the challenge of reconciliation:

> Canada has a long history of colonialism in relation to Aboriginal peoples. This history and its policies of cultural genocide and assimilation have left deep scars on the lives of many Aboriginal people, on Aboriginal communities, as well as on Canadian society, and have deeply damaged the relationship between Aboriginal and non-Aboriginal peoples. It took a long time for that damage to be done ... and it will take us a long time to fix it. But the process has already begun. [It] began in the 1980s with church apologies for their treatment of Aboriginal peoples and disrespect of their cultures. It continued with the findings of the Royal Commission on Aboriginal Peoples, along with court recognition of the validity of the Survivors' stories. It culminated in the Indian Residential Schools Settlement Agreement and the prime minister of Canada's apology in Parliament in June 2008. ... Reconciliation is in the best interests of all of Canada. It is needed not only to resolve the ongoing conflicts between Aboriginal peoples and institutions of the country but to remove a stain from Canada's past so that it can maintain its claim to be a leader in the protection of human rights among the nations of the world. Canada's historical development, as well as the view held strongly by some that the history of this development is accurately portrayed as beneficent raises significant barriers to reconciliation in the twenty-first century.[62]

In recent years, the TRC report and its Calls to Action, federal and provincial promises to implement the *United Nations Declaration on the Rights of Indigenous Peoples* (UNDRIP), increased use of Indigenous courts, more funding for Indigenous children and families, and movement on outstanding land claims are all positive developments. However, many bridges still need to be built to cross the cultural divide between mainstream and Indigenous concepts of law and justice and to address the underlying causes of Indigenous overrepresentation in the criminal justice system. (See also Chapter 2 and the section on Indigenous law for an examination of colonialism, the TRC and UNDRIP, and a timeline of Canadian laws and policies affecting Indigenous peoples.)

---

61 Boyington, *supra* note 54 at 336-37.

62 *Canada's Residential Schools: Reconciliation—The Final Report of the Truth and Reconciliation Commission of Canada* (Montreal and Kingston: McGill-Queen's University Press, 2015) vol 6 at 20, online: <http://www.trc.ca/assets/pdf/Volume_6_Reconciliation_English_Web.pdf>.

CHAPTER SUMMARY

Canada's *Constitution Act, 1867* gives the Parliament of Canada exclusive jurisdiction over criminal law and procedure in criminal matters. Pursuant to this power, the federal government enacted a *Criminal Code* in 1892, which, since then, has been the primary source of Canadian criminal law. The Code contains key principles of our criminal law. It organizes specific offences into general subject matter categories and classifies offences into three categories: summary, indictable, and hybrid. It also contains law relating to the criminal trial process, defences, sentencing, and appeals.

In addition to the *Criminal Code*, other federal statutes and the Charter play an important role in this area. As well, decisions of the courts—especially SCC decisions interpreting criminal law statutes and the Charter—are an integral part of our criminal law.

The larger field of criminal justice also involves policing, corrections, and youth justice. Police investigation of crime may lead police to charge an individual with a criminal offence. If, after their trial, individuals are found guilty, then, depending on their offence, they may be sentenced to incarceration in either a provincial or a federal correctional institution. In Canada today, young persons who commit criminal offences are treated differently than adults and are tried separately in a youth justice court.

The problem of higher rates of incarceration of Indigenous peoples and their negative interactions with the Canadian criminal justice system more generally is being addressed by governments. Acknowledgment of the harmful effects of colonialism and racist laws and policies, the creation of Indigenous courts, and an increased willingness to negotiate self-government arrangements are a few steps being taken, but more work still needs to be done to repair the damaged relationship between Indigenous peoples and the rest of Canadian society.

KEY TERMS

actus reus, 275

aggravating circumstance, 293

appearance notice, 287

arraignment, 289

arrest, 280

conviction, 289

Crown attorney, 270

duty of disclosure, 284

hybrid offence, 279

indictable offence, 279

indictment, 289

information, 289

judicial interim release, 288

limitation period, 277

mens rea, 275

mitigating circumstance, 293

plea bargain, 288

plead, 288

preliminary inquiry, 289

pre-sentence report, 294

quasi-criminal offences, 274

search warrant, 281

sentence, 291

summary conviction offence, 277

summons, 287

superior court of criminal jurisdiction, 279

undertaking (by an accused), 288

verdict, 290

FURTHER READING

BOOKS

Atkinson, Paul, *The Canadian Justice System: An Overview*, 4th ed (Toronto: LexisNexis, 2017).

Barnhorst, Richard & Sherrie Barnhorst, *Criminal Law and the Canadian Criminal Code*, 6th ed (Toronto: McGraw-Hill Ryerson, 2013).

Bell, Sandra J, *Young Offenders and Youth Justice: A Century After the Fact*, 5th ed (Toronto: Nelson, 2014).

Gulycz, Michael & Mary Ann Kelly, *Criminal Law for Legal Professionals*, 3rd ed (Toronto: Emond, 2021).

Hamilton, AC, *A Feather Not a Gavel: Working Towards Aboriginal Justice* (Winnipeg: Great Plains, 2001).

Hennessy, P, *Canada's Big House: The Dark History of the Kingston Penitentiary* (Toronto: Dundurn, 1999).

Ismaili, Karim, Jane B Sprott & Kim Varma, eds, *Canadian Criminal Justice Policy: Contemporary Perspectives* (Toronto: Oxford University Press, 2012).

Istvanffy, Jay, *Gladue Primer* (Vancouver: Legal Services Society, BC, 2011), online: <https://pubsdb.lss.bc.ca/pdfs/pubs/Gladue-Primer-eng.pdf>.

O'Regan, Karla & Susan Reid, *Thinking About Criminal Justice in Canada*, 2nd ed (Toronto: Emond, 2017).

Pink, Joel E & David C Perrier, eds, *From Crime to Punishment*, 9th ed (Toronto: Carswell, 2020).

Roach, Kent, *Criminal Law*, 7th ed (Toronto: Irwin Law, 2018).

Stuart, Don, *Canadian Criminal Law: A Treatise*, 7th ed (Toronto: Carswell, 2014).

Watkins, Kerry et al, *Evidence and Investigation: From the Crime Scene to the Courtroom*, 2nd ed (Toronto: Emond, 2019).

REVIEW QUESTIONS

1. What did John A Macdonald dislike about the American system of criminal law, and how did he prevent it from happening in Canada?

2. List four federal statutes that are sources of Canadian criminal law.

3. List and describe the two elements of a criminal offence in the *Criminal Code*.

4. Explain the criminal standard of proof "beyond a reasonable doubt." To whom does this standard apply?

5. What are the three classifications of criminal offences under the *Criminal Code*?

6. Why is disclosure so important to an accused person?

7. What is an aggravating circumstance? Give three examples.

8. List five important matters for an accused to consider before the trial begins.

EXERCISES

1. Do you think a specialized court such as Ontario's Integrated Domestic Violence Court is a good idea? Why or why not?

2. Locate and read the SCC decision in *Bedford* (see Box 10.1). Next, locate and review the provisions in the *Protection of Communities and Exploited Persons Act*, SC 2014, c 25, amending Canada's prostitution laws. Do you think the provisions alleviate the concerns expressed by the SCC in connection with the old laws—particularly those relating to the safety of sex workers? Give reasons for your answer.

3. Examine the first paragraph in the preamble to the *Youth Criminal Justice Act*. What do you think are the "developmental challenges and the needs of young persons"? What members of society are best placed to guide young persons into adulthood and why?

4. In recent decades, changes to the way Canada's criminal justice system deals with Indigenous people accused and convicted of crimes have sought to improve treatment and outcomes for Indigenous offenders. What do you think of these solutions and their potential for reform? Depending on your answer, should Indigenous people have jurisdiction to operate their own criminal justice system? Defend your answer.

PART IV
Working with the Law

CHAPTER 11 The Practice of Law: Careers, Education, and Ethics

CHAPTER 12 Access to Justice and Law Reform

11 The Practice of Law: Careers, Education, and Ethics

Introduction 304

Origins and Development of the
Legal Profession 305

Legal Practitioners in Canada Today 305

Ethics and the Practice of Law 313

Chapter Summary 326

Key Terms 327

Further Reading 327

Review Questions 328

Exercises 328

After reading this chapter, you will be able to:

- Understand the origins and development of the legal profession.
- Describe the practice of law in Canada today and the various practitioner classes.
- Discuss the educational requirements for legal professionals.
- Describe the nature and purpose of legal ethics.
- Recognize the codes of conduct and the ethical obligations imposed on judges, lawyers, paralegals, notaries, and other legal practitioners.

- Define professionalism and integrity in the legal profession.
- Understand the specific duties imposed on lawyers, including those owed to the state, the court, the profession, the public, and the client.
- Describe the regulatory framework for monitoring ethical behaviour in the legal profession and the process for disciplining ethical breaches.

I ntegrity without knowledge is weak and useless, and knowledge without integrity is dangerous and dreadful.

Samuel Johnson (1709–1784) from *Rasselas*, ch 41

Introduction

The legal profession is an essential part of the Canadian system of law. Lawyers are prominent in public life, and they play a significant role in our three branches of government. Judges in the judicial branch are appointed from the legal profession. Numerous members of our legislatures, including Parliament, have been and are lawyers. In the executive branch, many prime ministers, premiers, and Cabinet ministers also have been and are lawyers. Lawyers also play a key role in the civil service, formulating government policies, drafting new legislation, and serving on various administrative boards and tribunals.

This chapter begins by looking at the historical development of the legal profession. Next, it examines the main players in the practice of law in Canada today; in addition to lawyers and judges, these include paralegals, law clerks, legal assistants, notaries, immigration consultants, and others. We also consider the educational requirements of legal professionals, focusing on common law lawyers and those with whom they work. The chapter concludes with an examination of the ethical rules guiding judges, lawyers, paralegals, and others. We look at the nature of legal ethics, codes of conduct, professionalism and integrity, specific duties as they apply to lawyers (including duties to the state, the court, the profession, the public, and the client), and disciplinary consequences of ethical breaches.

Origins and Development of the Legal Profession

In Western society, the legal profession can be traced to ancient Greece, where the use of orators to argue legal points developed. These skilled speakers were not formally recognized as belonging to a legal profession. Athenian law, for example, forbade the charging of fees for such work. (Public advocates, appointed to prosecute important criminal cases, were, however, paid a small fee.[1])

The situation was similar for many years in ancient Rome, where orators or advocates would plead cases for others without remuneration. Over time, Rome saw the emergence of a class of legal specialists, called "jurisprudents," who had a recognized expertise in the law, acquired through study.[2] Like the unpaid orators before them, however, they were amateurs and also worked for free. It was not until the reign of Emperor Claudius (41–54 CE) that the practice of law was "professionalized," and legal representatives in Roman society could charge fees for their services up to a maximum of 10,000 sesterces (approximately $5,000 in today's currency).[3]

With the fall of the Western Roman Empire and the onset of the Dark Ages, the legal profession essentially disappeared. The church became the dominant force, and ecclesiastical or canon law provided the basis of social regulation. However, in the Middle Ages and with the rise of civil government, a separate legal profession re-emerged. Initially, these legal practitioners were thought of narrowly as canonists—that is, experts in ecclesiastical law. But by the 1200s, throughout Europe and in England, paid jurists again established themselves as part of the state's regulatory structure.

The early history of the English legal profession is complicated due to the wide variety of practitioner classes. There were many kinds, or classes, of lawyers, each with its own set of responsibilities. This complexity diminished over time, until two main types of lawyers remained: barristers and solicitors. This distinction between barristers (that is, litigators) and solicitors (who generally do not litigate but restrict their practice to giving advice and preparing legal documentation) is still observed in England today, although it is less pronounced than it once was.

In Canada, by comparison, the profession has always been simpler in this regard; Canadian lawyers can practise as both barristers and solicitors. That said, most lawyers in Canada specialize either in pleading cases before courts and tribunals (barrister work) or in representing and serving clients in non-litigious matters (solicitor work).

Legal Practitioners in Canada Today

Lawyers and judges are the primary actors in the legal profession, but, in the modern era, other professionals, such as paralegals and notaries, have joined lawyers in delivering legal

---

1   Robert J Bonner, *Lawyers and Litigants in Ancient Athens: The Genesis of the Legal Profession* (New York: Benjamin Blom, 1927) at 201.

2   John A Crook, *Legal Advocacy in the Roman World* (London: Duckworth, 1995) at 40.

3   *Ibid* at 129-30.

services to the public. The main kinds of legal practitioners working in Canada today, as well as their educational requirements, are described next.

Judges and Other Adjudicators

Judges are usually senior lawyers who have been appointed to the bench after many years of successful and distinguished practice. They can also be lawyers who have made their careers in academia or politics. Legislative rules set minimums for required years of experience before a lawyer can become a judge, along with frameworks for the appointment process. There are some differences depending on the court involved and whether the appointments are federal or provincial.

See Chapter 5 for a detailed discussion of judicial qualifications and appointments. The specialized education that judges receive upon their appointment to the bench is described in Box 5.4.

Justices of the peace (JPs) are judicial officers affiliated with the provincial courts. They perform a variety of functions related to the administration of justice, including the adjudication of minor criminal or quasi-criminal matters. JPs play an important role in rural communities far from the regular courts. Although not all jurisdictions require JPs to be lawyers, a record of community involvement and some post-secondary education is generally a condition of appointment.

Administrative tribunals resolve disputes in a multitude of areas. Adjudicators appointed to such tribunals are often lawyers, although in some instances they may not be. Appointment qualifications and processes depend on the board and jurisdiction involved (see Chapter 9).

Increasingly, disputes are being resolved outside of formal adjudicative processes. Alternative dispute resolution (ADR), examined in Chapter 12, deals with the resolution of disputes primarily through negotiation, mediation, or arbitration. ADR is used in various contexts, including business disputes and family matters. Third parties participating in ADR processes often have legal training.

Lawyers

Lawyers can perform almost all forms of legal work. For example, they can advise clients on legal matters, draft legal documents, and prepare for and represent clients at hearings before courts and tribunals. Legislation in every province and territory has empowered law societies to regulate their members and to set standards of practice for the profession. All lawyers must be members of the **law society** for their jurisdiction in order to practise law. The names of these law societies vary. For example, the law society in Nova Scotia is known as the Barristers' Society; in Ontario, it is called the Law Society of Ontario (LSO). In Quebec, the law society has two divisions: the *Barreau du Québec* and the *Chambre des notaires du Québec*.

Law societies are responsible for, among other things, establishing qualifications to be called to the bar (that is, to be a member of the law society), monitoring professional competence and providing continuing education, and handling public complaints about lawyers and disciplining lawyers in cases of malpractice. Law societies are composed of a small executive group of elected lawyers known in most jurisdictions as **benchers** and may also have some government-appointed non-lawyers known as "lay benchers." One of the benchers, called the president or treasurer, acts as the head. All of the benchers meet in

law society
governing body of lawyers in a province or territory

benchers
lawyers (and some non-lawyers) who are responsible for administering and governing a provincial or territorial law society

convocation and form committees—the discipline committee, for example. The profession is, therefore, essentially self-regulated.[4]

The business structures and settings in which lawyers work are varied. Lawyers can practise law independently as sole practitioners with general or specialized practices (such as personal injury or criminal law), in firms of all sizes (see the discussion of partnerships in Chapter 8), in corporate legal departments, or with government departments and agencies. They can also work with regulatory bodies, for unions, for non-profit societies (for example, civil liberties associations and legal aid societies [described in Chapter 12]), and for other organizations, including international bodies such as the United Nations.

In the last century, with the growth and increased sophistication of our economy and regulatory frameworks, some law firms saw a corresponding growth in terms of both size and breadth of expertise. Larger firms today might have departments specializing in corporate law and securities, taxation, insurance, labour and employment, administrative and regulatory law, real property, personal injury law, family, succession, and other areas, allowing them to service all or most of their clients' legal needs. Some firms have become so large through mergers and alliances that they have national, North American, and even international reach; these megafirms hope to improve efficiencies and better serve large commercial and international clients. Other firms have expanded their practices through collaborations with non-legal professionals such as accountants, financial services professionals, health care professionals, engineers, and architects (such collaborations are commonly referred to as "multidisciplinary practices," or MDPs).

Educational Requirements

Historically, in Canada, there was debate over rival methods for teaching law. Some members of the legal community believed that traditional English vocational methods for training lawyers should be followed. These methods were based on an apprenticeship model whereby law students served "under **articles**" and obtained practical experience and direct knowledge of the law by working with and under the supervision of a practising lawyer. This training could also be supplemented with law society lectures. On the other side of the legal education debate were those who favoured the idea of formal university training at a recognized law school, where professors (rather than practising lawyers) taught the law. The debate was resolved in favour of the current model, which combines academic coursework with articling requirements.[5]

articles
apprenticeship under a practising lawyer

Prospective lawyers in common law provinces must now generally meet the following educational requirements:

- an undergraduate bachelor's degree with a high grade-point average (although many applicants have more advanced degrees, such as master's degrees, and some law schools may take incoming students with a minimum of two years at a university);
- a high score on the Law School Admission Test (LSAT);

4　Some commentators question whether the legal profession in Canada should continue to be self-regulated. There is a global trend away from self-regulation toward co-regulation, in which a separate body comprising both lawyers and non-lawyers provides regulatory oversight, such as in the United Kingdom and Australia; see Laurel S Terry, "Trends in Global and Canadian Lawyer Regulation" (2013) 76 Sask L Rev 145 at 152.

5　William H Hurlburt, *The Self-Regulation of the Legal Profession in Canada and in England and Wales* (Calgary and Edmonton: Law Society of Alberta/Alberta Law Reform Institute, 2000) at 69-78.

- three years of full-time study at law school completing a bachelor of laws (LLB) degree or today the more commonly awarded (and equivalent) juris doctor (JD) degree (in 2018, the University of Victoria launched a unique Indigenous law program, graduates of which receive both a JD degree and juris indigenarum doctor (JID) degree; see also Chapter 2 under "New Directions for Indigenous Law in Canada");
- a period of articling as determined by their province's law society; and
- completion of a bar admission course, consisting of a series of lectures and examinations established by a province's law society.

called to the bar
formal ceremony whereby a law student becomes entitled to practise law

Once all of these educational and placement requirements are met, law students are then **called to the bar**, a formal ceremony whereby they are admitted to the law society of their province and may begin to practise law. In Canada, once a person is qualified to practise law, the professional designation most commonly used to describe the person is simply "lawyer"; more formally, "barrister and solicitor" is also used.[6] In the United States, "attorney" or "attorney-at-law" is a common designation, particularly when referring to lawyers who represent clients in court.

Paralegals

In most jurisdictions in North America, other than Ontario, the term "paralegal" refers to a person who is qualified by education and experience to perform specifically delegated substantive and procedural legal work while working *under the supervision of a lawyer*. Paralegals can work in all of the same legal settings that lawyers can. They are not formally regulated or certified under legislative authority, and the stature they enjoy comes from the specific education they have received and the experience they have gained through their employment in the legal field. In Ontario, a person referred to as a paralegal in other Canadian jurisdictions and in the United States would be referred to as a "law clerk" (see below).

In most jurisdictions, then, paralegals can provide the same legal services as lawyers can (and at a reduced cost to the client or employer), subject to the limitations set out in the legislation regulating the legal profession generally and law society rules. Their work typically includes the following:

- file management;
- interviewing clients and witnesses;
- drafting pleadings, contracts, wills, and conveyancing and corporate records documents;
- legal research; and
- assisting with trials.

---

6   Additional terms are used to refer to lawyers when appearing in court, and these vary depending on the nature of the case and the court. For example, "Crown attorney" is a common term to describe a lawyer prosecuting a criminal case on behalf of the Crown (see Chapter 10). Also, "counsel" is used in some provinces to describe lawyers generally when they appear as legal representatives in their courts. Last, "solicitor of record" is sometimes used in court documents to refer to a lawyer or law firm representing a person in a matter (of which the litigation is a part), as distinct from the lawyer appearing before the court to argue the case; for example, a law firm could be referred to as the solicitor of record and the lawyer making the arguments before the court as counsel or in some other way.

Paralegals are typically restricted from doing the following:

- giving legal advice directly to clients,
- providing undertakings to third parties, and
- appearing in courts and tribunals by themselves, as advocates.

These restrictions are not rigid, however, and may not apply if the relevant rules of practice and rules of procedure before particular courts and tribunals permit the activities described.

Paralegals in Ontario

In Ontario, the term "paralegal" refers to a person with a unique classification. In that province alone, paralegals are permitted to practise independently of lawyers. In most common law jurisdictions in Canada, lawyers have long had a virtual monopoly over the practice of law. Historically, Ontario was the one jurisdiction where lawyers did not have this kind of monopoly. The Ontario legislation used to define specific areas of practice that were reserved for lawyers and left all other areas unregulated. One consequence of this was the emergence of an unregulated "paralegal" profession. In 2007, however, the legislative framework in Ontario changed. Lawyers in Ontario, as in other jurisdictions, are now given a virtual monopoly over the practice of law except in certain broad areas where paralegals, who are now regulated, are allowed to practise.

Paralegals in Ontario, then, licensed by the LSO, are authorized to provide certain legal services independently of lawyers—that is, the work need not be delegated—within the limits set out in the relevant legislation and the LSO rules (by-laws). Work that licensed paralegals in Ontario can perform independently of lawyers includes the following:

- representing clients in Small Claims Court, in the Ontario Court of Justice in respect of provincial offences, on summary conviction offences where the maximum penalty does not exceed six months' imprisonment, and before administrative tribunals;
- giving legal advice concerning rights and responsibilities in connection with the subject matter of a proceeding;
- drafting court documents for use in a proceeding; and
- negotiating on behalf of a client who is a party to a proceeding.[7]

Educational Requirements

As described, paralegals outside of Ontario cannot practise independently and are not formally regulated or obliged to fulfill specific educational requirements in order to practise. Increasingly, however, employers are making formal training a condition of employment for the paralegals they employ. In addition, voluntary industry associations may set educational or experiential standards as conditions of membership.[8]

---

7 For a history of the legal profession in Ontario and the process, beginning in 2007, that led to the regulation of paralegals in that province, see S Patricia Knight, "Paralegal Governance in Ontario" in *Ethics and Professional Practice for Paralegals*, 4th ed (Toronto: Emond, 2018) ch 1. See also the Law Society of Ontario, online: <https://lso.ca/home>.

8 See, for example, the Canadian Association of Paralegals (CAP), the Alberta Association of Professional Paralegals (AAPP), and the BC Paralegal Association (BCPA).

Most paralegals today are graduates of specialized certificate or diploma programs offered by colleges or universities. These programs may be offered part-time or full-time and onsite or online; admission requirements vary as well, with some programs requiring work or post-secondary educational experience and others allowing admission directly from high school. Some academic institutions also now offer four-year degree programs in paralegal education.[9]

In Ontario, as noted, paralegals may practise independently, representing clients in connection with certain kinds of offences and regulatory matters. They are licensed by the LSO and, as a condition of licensure, must graduate from an accredited paralegal program and pass a licensing exam. Other law societies are considering adopting a similar approach for paralegals in their jurisdictions.

Law Clerks

In most jurisdictions, the term "law clerk" refers to a person who assists judges or tribunal adjudicators. Frequently, law clerks are recent graduates of law school who are working and who, depending on the jurisdiction, may be able to use this experience in partial or full completion of their articling training. A law clerk's work can involve legal research, preparing draft judgments, and other work assisting the court or tribunal. Law clerks are sometimes also referred to as "judicial clerks."

As law firms with strong connections to Ontario establish practices in other regions of Canada, the term "law clerk" may be used at those firms in the sense in which it is used in Ontario, as described next.

Law Clerks in Ontario

In Ontario, the term "law clerk" refers to an employee who works under the supervision of a lawyer, primarily providing assistance with basic administrative and legal matters. Legal tasks tend to focus more on practice and procedural matters than substantive legal work (such as legal research and preparing legal arguments) but can involve the latter depending on the level of delegation by the lawyer.

Outside Ontario, a law clerk would generally be referred to as a paralegal, or a person working in a hybrid role as a legal assistant (see the next section).

EDUCATIONAL REQUIREMENTS

Like paralegals outside of Ontario, law clerks in Ontario cannot practise independently and are not formally regulated. The Institute of Law Clerks of Ontario (ILCO) is a voluntary organization that sets standards for membership, including educational requirements. Student members must be enrolled in an ILCO-approved Ontario law clerk program. Other membership categories are based on employment in the field and having passed an ILCO examination.

Legal Administrative Assistants and Legal Assistants

Legal administrative assistants are administrative assistants trained to work in the field of law. Typically, they work as assistants to lawyers but can also work with paralegals, notaries, and other legal professionals. Their duties often include answering calls, responding to

---

9   For example, Humber College in Ontario and Capilano University in British Columbia.

emails, scheduling appointments, and taking notes at meetings. They can assist with the preparation of all types of legal documents, including letters, litigation-related materials, contracts, wills, conveyancing documents, and corporate and securities documentation. They also work with paper and electronic filing systems, both internally (that is, belonging to their employers) and externally (such as with court and other government registries).

Job titles can be confusing in this area. Legal administrative assistants used to be called "legal secretaries." Paralegals used to be called "legal assistants" in many jurisdictions, although not in Ontario; the term "legal assistant" can also refer to a hybrid position, somewhere in between a paralegal (outside of Ontario) and a legal administrative assistant. Increasingly, however, legal administrative assistants are being called "legal assistants."

Educational Requirements

Like law clerks in Ontario, legal assistants and legal administrative assistants are similarly unregulated. However, as a condition of employment, most employers require them to have a certificate or diploma designed for legal support staff from a public or private post-secondary institution.

Notaries

Notaries (or notaries public) provide certain types of legal services that could be classed as "solicitor" work. Examples of typical notarial work include the following:

- witnessing affidavits (used as evidence in court proceedings) and statutory declarations (generally used for purposes other than court proceedings, such as for name changes and lost passport declarations);
- preparing contracts;
- preparing real estate documentation (for example, transfers, mortgages, easements, and rezoning applications);
- estate planning;
- assisting with passport documentation; and
- preparing powers of attorney and representation agreements.

In most jurisdictions, lawyers are automatically (or on application can become) notaries. Non-lawyers can also apply to be notaries, and, after meeting defined criteria (which vary from region to region), they can be appointed by the government (generally by the attorney general or the minister of justice of the province or territory in which they reside or by the Crown on their advice). Some jurisdictions, including Alberta and Ontario, require non-lawyer notaries to be affiliated with a specific organization that regularly requires notarized documents. Other jurisdictions, such as British Columbia, allow notaries to practise independently.

Notaries in Quebec are not the same as in other parts of Canada. Civil law notaries in Quebec are, in fact, lawyers and are required to have a civil law degree; their practice is roughly equivalent to a solicitor's practice in common law jurisdictions.

Educational Requirements

As mentioned, when lawyers are called to the bar, they qualify automatically as, or on application can become, notaries. In most jurisdictions, non-lawyers can become notaries after following an application process, which may or may not involve specific educational requirements. British Columbia, which allows notaries to practise independently, has the strictest educational requirements in Canada; prospective notaries must first complete a designated master's degree in legal studies.

Other Law-Related Positions

A legal education opens many doors, and legal professionals can and do change careers or take on additional roles. There are also many career possibilities and positions with a legal connection that are open to individuals from outside the legal profession who qualify and undertake the necessary training. For example, a prospective patent agent could have a background in engineering or science and could train for the position without any previous legal experience. A lawyer, however, could also qualify as a patent agent and add that role to his intellectual property (IP) practice. In some instances—for example, commissioners for taking affidavits—lawyers, notaries, and certain government officials automatically qualify for the role.

The following are some positions and career areas with a legal connection (some may be pursued as full-time occupations in their own right, whereas others may be taken on part-time, supplementing other legal or non-legal positions):

- *Commissioners for taking affidavits.*   Sometimes referred to as "commissioners of oaths," these professionals, whose scope of practice is limited, can administer oaths and witness affidavits and statutory declarations, usually in the context of other work, such as corporate business or government regulation.
- *Court administrators* (such as a court clerk, reporter, or trial coordinator).
- *Court agents.*   In some provinces, courts permit lay practitioners, known as "court agents," to appear before them as advocates for individuals who would otherwise go unrepresented due to the unavailability of trained professionals.
- *Corporate compliance officers* (corporate officers charged with ensuring compliance with regulatory requirements and internal policies and procedures).
- *Human resources and office management* (involving employee services and control of office systems at a law firm or other organization).
- *Immigration consultants.*   These federally regulated professionals, who are permitted to practise independently, provide advice on immigration matters, such as permanent residence applications, temporary residence and visa applications, and refugee claims.
- *Insurance* (including work as a claims adjuster, a broker, or an insurance agent).
- *Law librarians* (for example, with courthouse, law school, law firm, or government libraries).
- *Legal education* (for example, teaching in legal studies programs).
- *Legal publishing* (for example, legal editors, legal software developers, or technical writers).
- *Legal recruiters* (employment specialists who recruit for law firms and other organizations).
- *Marriage commissioners* or other government appointees authorized to perform civil marriage ceremonies (titles and qualifications vary according to region).
- *Patent and trademark agents.*   These are federally regulated IP professionals who are permitted to practise independently and who can assist with the registration of patents and trademarks and other related matters.

- *Private investigation* (involving investigative work collecting evidence, often for lawyers in business, insurance, family, or criminal matters).
- *Policing and corrections* (including work as RCMP officers, provincial and municipal police officers, and probation and parole officers).

Educational Requirements

The educational requirements for other legal professionals vary. They depend on whether the profession is regulated and on the employment market. For example, immigration consultants are federally licensed through Immigration, Refugees and Citizenship Canada and must take an accredited practitioner program and pass examinations (the Immigration Consultants of Canada Regulatory Council [ICCRC] is the designated regulator for immigration consultants). Patent and trademark agents, who are federally licensed through the Canadian Intellectual Property Office (CIPO), are similarly required to pass licensure examinations before they can practise.

Some professionals must meet certain educational standards, not because they are mandated by legislation but because of industry expectations or requirements. For example, law librarians generally must have a library sciences degree, police officers and corrections workers are usually required to have post-secondary education and to complete agency-specific training, and law teachers usually must have a legal education (such as a law degree or paralegal credential; law schools typically require advanced law degrees, such as an LLM or LLD degree).

Ethics and the Practice of Law

In Chapter 1, we compared law to other rules, or norms, including moral and ethical obligations. We noted that although there is no generally accepted distinction between morality and ethics, the two terms can have slightly different connotations. For example, ethical norms can be associated with specific social contexts, such as acceptable standards of behaviour within certain professions. The purpose of this section is to provide an overview of the ethics of the legal profession.

Ethical standards and the practice of law have long been closely connected, despite popular characterizations to the contrary. These standards were reflected in the oaths that lawyers were required to swear before civil and ecclesiastical courts throughout Europe, after the legal profession's re-emergence in the Middle Ages. They were incorporated into England's first *Statute of Westminster*,[10] enacted in 1275, which made it an offence to perpetrate a fraud before the court. And they are defined in the codes and rules that govern the profession today.

Legal ethics go beyond the rules proscribing civil wrongs or criminal behaviour generally, which apply to everyone. Holding legal professionals to high ethical standards is necessary in order to protect the public. Legal professionals exercise considerable power. They have expertise in the workings of the state and often have access to personal and financial information that could be damaging to their clients and others if misused or disclosed.

The ethical rules that apply to judges, lawyers, paralegals, notaries, and other legal professionals are described next. See Further Reading for links to a selection of these ethical codes of conduct.

legal ethics
rules of conduct that govern the legal profession, the primary purpose of which is to protect clients, the public, and the administration of justice

---

10   Also known as *Statute of Westminster, The First*, 1275 (UK), 3 Edw I.

Judges

As described in Chapter 5, the judiciary is the third branch of government in Canada, and the independence of judges is constitutionally protected. Judicial tenure, which allows judges to render decisions without fear of losing their jobs if their decisions are not well received, is based on the judges' maintaining a standard of "good behaviour"—a standard that is rarely breached.

Complementing the idea of tenure based on good behaviour is the expectation that judges maintain high ethical standards. The Canadian Judicial Council, a federal body created under the *Judges Act*[11] in 1971, has a mandate to (among other things) improve quality and promote accountability in courts with federally appointed judges, which includes all superior courts. To that end, the Council has published a document entitled *Ethical Principles for Judges*.[12] Its stated purpose is to provide "ethical guidance" for judges, but the Council is careful to note that the principles are advisory in nature and do not constitute a list of prohibited behaviours or set standards for judicial misconduct. Otherwise, these guidelines could be interpreted as a form of interference with the principle of judicial independence.

Under these guidelines, federally appointed judges are encouraged to conduct themselves with integrity, be diligent in the performance of their judicial duties, ensure equality before the law, and be impartial. Similar ethical obligations and guidelines apply to provincial and territorial inferior court judges and to other adjudicators.

Complaints about the conduct of federally appointed judges are handled by the Council, which will investigate in appropriate cases and make recommendations.[13] However, under the Constitution, only Parliament can formally remove superior court judges, and this has never happened (see Chapter 5). Comparable disciplinary processes, but with greater remedial flexibility, including possible removal, apply to provincial and territorial

---

11 RSC 1985, c J-1.

12 This document is currently under review, and a draft version is available online: <https://cjc-ccm.ca/sites/default/files/documents/2019/EPJ%20-%20PDJ%202019-11-20.pdf>.

13 Until recently, there had been only four attempts (since Confederation) to remove superior court judges, but in 2017, the Canadian Judicial Council recommended the removal of two judges in separate investigations. In the case of Justice Michel Girouard, a Quebec superior court judge, the Council found that Girouard had misled its inquiry into his purchase and use of cocaine in 2010 just before he was appointed to the bench. His conduct, the Council concluded, demonstrated a lack of integrity that prevented him from discharging his duties as a judge. Girouard applied for judicial review of the findings of the Council, but in 2019 the Federal Court concluded that the Council was justified in its recommendation that he be removed and dismissed his application: *Girouard v Canada (Attorney General)*, 2019 FC 1282. In separate proceedings, the Council argued that its decisions were immune from judicial review but lost that argument: *Canada (Judicial Council) v Girouard*, 2019 FCA 148. At the time of writing, Girouard has not resigned and continues to collect his salary of over $320,000 per year and have the legal expenses connected to his challenges paid for by the government. In the second case, involving Justice Robin Camp, the Council concluded that Camp made inappropriate comments to an alleged rape victim, including asking her why she didn't keep her "knees together." His comments were made in 2014 during a sexual assault trial when he was an Alberta provincial court judge. The review of his conduct, however, didn't begin until over a year later, by which time he had been elevated to the federal court. Camp resigned shortly after the Council recommended his removal.

inferior court judges and other adjudicators. Judges and adjudicators may retire or resign before the process reaches the point of removal.[14]

Lawyers

The most developed and specifically defined rules and guidelines for ethical behaviour in the legal profession—and possibly across all professions—are those that apply to lawyers.

Written codes of conduct for lawyers are a relatively recent development in common law jurisdictions. In the past, there was some statute law and case law defining inappropriate conduct in the practice of law. But the profession initially resisted adopting anything more comprehensive than that. The common assumption seems to have been that the legal profession was, after all, an ancient, noble, and learned profession; it went without saying that honour and integrity governed its practice. This notion persisted until the 19th century.

Codes of Conduct

In the late 1800s, the governing bodies for lawyers in common law jurisdictions began developing written **codes of conduct** to guide their members. Generally speaking, these codes are not directly enforceable by court action. The profession itself, through law societies, takes disciplinary action against its members who breach the codes of conduct.

codes of conduct
written sets of rules regulating the ethical behaviour of professionals

The Canadian Bar Association (CBA) is a federal organization, membership in which is voluntary for lawyers in some provinces but mandatory in others. It developed and adopted its first code of conduct in 1920—Canada's first code for lawyers. The Canons of Legal Ethics (CBA Canons), as they were called, borrowed in part from the Canons of Professional Ethics, adopted in 1908 by the American Bar Association. The CBA Canons were revised and replaced in 1974 with the Code of Professional Conduct. This latter Code has been revised a number of times, most recently in 2009, but is being discontinued in favour of the FLSC Model Code referred to below.

Almost every law society in Canada has passed its own code of conduct, similar to the CBA Code if not identical to it. (Prince Edward Island, the Northwest Territories, and Nunavut have simply adopted the CBA Code.)

In 2009, the Federation of Law Societies of Canada (FLSC), working with the law societies from all Canadian provinces and territories, adopted the Model Code of Professional Conduct (FLSC Model Code). It is drawn in part from the CBA Code. Membership in provincial/territorial law societies is mandatory for lawyers practising in a particular jurisdiction, as is following the law society's particular code. One of the consequences of living in a federal state is a multiplicity of rules. Uniformity is valuable in this context, however— hence the move to create the FLSC Model Code of Professional Conduct (see Box 11.1). The Model Code has now been adopted, in whole or in part, by all law societies in Canada except the *Chambre des notaires* in Quebec.[15]

---

14   As noted in Chapter 5, only a handful of lower court judges have ever been removed. And, as with superior court judges, findings of misconduct are uncommon. For example, in Ontario, since 2000, there have been just three findings of misconduct by the Ontario Judicial Council. In 2004, a provincial court judge was reprimanded for indiscreet comments she had made about an accused and her family. In the same year, the Council found a judge guilty of misconduct for inappropriately touching a female staff member; the judge resigned before a penalty was imposed. And in 2007, the Council officially warned a judge after he altered court transcripts to remove objectionable comments he had made. See Michael McKiernan, "Judging the Judges" (2012) 26:2 Can Lawyer 32 at 36.

15   See "Implementation of the Model Code," online: *Federation of Law Societies of Canada* <https://flsc.ca/resources/implementation-of-the-model-code>.

BOX 11.1

The FLSC Model Code of Professional Conduct

The preface to the FLSC Model Code emphasizes the importance of legal ethics in relation to the public interest. It includes the following provision:

> Rules of conduct should assist, not hinder, lawyers in providing legal services to the public in a way that ensures the public interest is protected. This calls for a framework based on ethical principles that, at the highest level, are immutable, and a profession that dedicates itself to practise according to the standards of competence, honesty and loyalty.

The seven chapters of the FLSC Model Code are as follows:

- Chapter 1: Interpretation and Definitions
- Chapter 2: Standards of the Legal Profession
- Chapter 3: Relationship to Clients
- Chapter 4: Marketing of Legal Services
- Chapter 5: Relationship to the Administration of Justice
- Chapter 6: Relationship to Students, Employees, and Others
- Chapter 7: Relationship to the Society and Other Lawyers*

* For more information about the Model Code, including its full text, see <https://flsc.ca/national-initiatives/model-code-of-professional-conduct>.

Professionalism and Integrity

Underlying all of the more specific ethical obligations imposed on lawyers is the general obligation to act honourably, in good faith, and with integrity when dealing with others.

The preface to the CBA Code stated the following:

> The essence of professional responsibility is that the lawyer must act at all times *uberrimae fidei*, meaning with utmost good faith to the court, to the client, to other lawyers, and to members of the public.

Chapter I of the CBA Code, entitled "Integrity," stated the following:

> The lawyer must discharge with integrity all duties owed to clients, the court or tribunal or other members of the profession and the public.

Rule 2.1 of chapter 2 of the FLSC Model Code, also entitled "Integrity," provides as follows:

> 2.1-1 A lawyer has a duty to carry on the practice of law and discharge all responsibilities to clients, tribunals, the public and other members of the profession honourably and with integrity.
>
> 2.1-2 A lawyer has a duty to uphold the standards and reputation of the legal profession and to assist in the advancement of its goals, organizations and institutions.

The commentary following these provisions states that integrity is the "fundamental quality of any person who seeks to practise as a member of the legal profession." The commentary goes on to state that although dishonourable conduct in a lawyer's private life can be so serious as to call into question the lawyer's professional integrity, law societies will not, generally speaking, be concerned with a lawyer's purely private activities (see Box 11.2).

Ethical Duties

Lawyers owe ethical obligations to the state, the court (and others when engaged in an advocacy role), the profession, the public, and their clients.

BOX 11.2

A Question of Integrity

Ryan was a lawyer hired by clients to pursue a possible wrongful dismissal claim against their employer. For over six years, he did nothing to further their claim. In response to their inquiries about the progress of the claim, he "spun an elaborate web of deceit." He told them that others were responsible for the delays, including other members of the bar; that discoveries had been cancelled; that he was pursuing a contempt motion against the defendants for failing to appear; and that a new precedent would require them to start the entire process over again. He even went so far as to forge a decision of the Court of Appeal. Finally, he admitted to his clients that he had done nothing and that all of his excuses were lies.

His clients filed a complaint with the Law Society of New Brunswick. Ryan was "apologetic and contrite and admitted his fault." In his defence, he argued that he was suffering from physical and emotional problems after separating from his wife and that he was abusing alcohol and taking medication for panic attacks. Ryan had been disciplined twice before for failing to carry out services for his clients. The decision of the Discipline Committee was that Ryan should be disbarred. They reasoned that, given all of the circumstances, his "unethical behaviour" was very serious and that "his honesty, trustworthiness, and fitness as a lawyer were irreparably compromised." When the case finally made it to the Supreme Court of Canada (SCC), the decision of the Discipline Committee was affirmed.*

Do you think that Ryan's excuses for failing to pursue his client's claim mitigate the lack of integrity demonstrated by his lies and by the forged court document? Was his lack of integrity so serious as to justify disbarment?

* *Law Society of New Brunswick v Ryan*, 2003 SCC 20.

DUTY TO THE STATE

The old CBA Canons and some older provincial codes provided that a "lawyer owes a duty to the State, to maintain its integrity and its law." The notions of "duty to the state" and "integrity" are flexible ones, changing with the times. The modern codes do not expressly refer to a duty to the state, but they do cite an obligation to "encourage public respect for and try to improve the administration of justice."[16]

It might seem common sense that lawyers must not break the law or promote its breach. That is the ideal, of course, but the reality is bound to be different. Numerous practising lawyers have broken the law. Their offences have ranged from impaired driving, to possession of narcotics, to theft, to violent crimes. The disciplinary consequences have varied depending on the circumstances, from reprimands, to fines, to disbarment. There is a difference, of course, between, on the one hand, breaking the law or advocating that it should be broken and, on the other hand, using legal means to argue that the law should be changed or challenged. Unjust or unconstitutional laws can be questioned by appropriate methods, such as court challenges or fighting for political or legislative change.

Advising or assisting in the violation of the law—aiding and abetting—can be illegal in itself. Just as breaking the law directly will attract disciplinary consequences, so, too, will advising or assisting in the violation of the law.

DUTY TO THE COURT AND THE ETHICS OF ADVOCACY

Lawyers are "officers of the court" in Canada, a status now confirmed by legislation in most provinces and territories.[17] As officers of the court, lawyers are subject to the summary

---

16 See CBA Code, ch XIII and FLSC Model Code, ch 5, r 5.6-1. See also Mark M Orkin, *Legal Ethics*, 2nd ed (Toronto: Canada Law Book, 2011) ch 2 ("Duty to the State").

17 See, for example, *Legal Profession Act*, RSA 2000, c L-8, s 102(2); *Legal Profession Act*, SBC 1998, c 9, s 14(2); *Legal Profession Act*, RSNWT (Nu) 1988, c L-2, s 64; and *Law Society Act*, RSO 1990, c L.8, s 29.

jurisdiction of the court and can be held liable for civil or criminal contempt for misconduct.

A lawyer's duty to the court entails a number of obligations, as stipulated in the modern codes. Some of these obligations include:

- acting with *courtesy and respect* when appearing before the court;
- *not abusing the process* by bringing proceedings that may be technically legal but are motivated by malice on the part of a client and are brought solely to injure the other party;
- *not misleading the court* by using false evidence or withholding binding authority; and
- *not publicly criticizing the court.*

These obligations apply equally to lawyers appearing before administrative tribunals and working in other dispute resolution contexts. Their purpose is to foster respect and confidence in our system of justice.

The ethics of advocacy overlap with lawyers' duty to the court but are distinguishable in one way. Although the duty to the court focuses on responsibilities that affect the court process, the ethics of advocacy are more concerned with lawyers' need to balance their obligations to the court with their obligations to others. For example, when does a lawyer's obligation to act with courtesy and respect toward the court conflict with his "duty to the client to raise fearlessly every issue, advance every argument, and ask every question, however distasteful, that the lawyer thinks will help the client's case"?[18] Simultaneously maintaining proper courtroom etiquette and pursuing justice for a client can be difficult in some situations, such as when an aggressive cross-examination of a witness is required.

Other ethical problems can arise when a lawyer is in an advocacy role involving certain types of clients or cases. For example, when defending a client in a criminal matter, knowing that her client is guilty can limit the lawyer's defence strategies, and when representing a parent in a custody matter, knowing that the best interests of the child will not be served by the client's position can restrict the approach the lawyer will take. These are just a few of the ethical challenges that lawyers in advocacy situations may face. For another example, see Box 11.3.

DUTIES TO THE PROFESSION AND TO THE GENERAL PUBLIC

Along with the duties they owe to the state and to the court, lawyers owe duties to their governing bodies, to other legal professionals, and to members of the public. These obligations are reflected in various provisions in the CBA Code and the FLSC Model Code.

Concerning duties to their governing bodies (that is, the law societies), lawyers are required to communicate effectively with the law society, including responding promptly when contacted by the law society. Lawyers must also report malpractice by other lawyers, particularly when it involves serious matters, such as misappropriation of client funds or criminal activity related to the lawyer's practice. Reporting such conduct is important because of the potentially serious consequences to clients and to the public if it is left unchecked.

Lawyers must also act courteously, fairly, and in good faith in their dealings with other legal professionals, their clients, and the public. The rationale for this is that the legal profession plays an important role in society, and the actions of its representatives must therefore reflect positively on the system of justice they serve. Among the more important specific obligations flowing from these general obligations are those relating to undertakings and advertising.

---

18 See the commentary following FLSC Model Code, ch 5, r 5.1-1.

BOX 11.3

What Would You Do?

Assume that you are a lawyer. The client you are representing in a case is a young child who has been seriously and permanently disabled by the negligence of a doctor—the defendant in the case. The claim is centred on the cost of future care for the child. At the time your firm was retained, the child was in an expensive facility that cares 24 hours a day for patients with your client's type of disability.

You win a favourable award at trial, an award that will cover the cost of the care facility for the rest of the child's life. The case is appealed. During argument on appeal, a judge asks you if the child is still in the facility. You answer truthfully that, as far as you are aware, the child is still in the facility. On a break in the proceedings, you contact the parents of the child,

who tell you that they couldn't stand being apart from their child, he is now back at home with them, and they are caring for him at a much reduced cost.

What would you do? When the proceedings resume, will you inform the court of this new information, knowing that it could affect the quantum (that is, amount) of the award for your client's future care?

Now assume that you are a paralegal assisting the lawyer in this case and that you phone the parents during the break and become aware of this new information. Do you tell the lawyer—your employer? What if you tell the lawyer and he fails to pass this information on to the court? What do you do then?

An **undertaking** in this context is usually a clear statement of intention by one lawyer to another lawyer made to facilitate a legal transaction, such as promising not to release funds to her client until a particular condition has been met. Any lawyer who fails to live up to an undertaking has committed a serious ethical breach and will be liable for professional misconduct.

With respect to advertising legal services, advertising is acceptable if it meets certain criteria—that is, if it is not misleading or untruthful, if it meets a public need, and if it is carried out with integrity.[19]

DUTY TO THE CLIENT

Of all of their ethical obligations, the duty to the client is the one that concerns most lawyers in their day-to-day practice. Lawyers have a general right to refuse to take on a particular client or case if they don't want to.[20] But once a lawyer takes on a client, a special relationship is created.

The relationship between lawyer and client is based on contract, but it is a special kind of contractual relationship. It is one of confidence and one that has attached to it certain **fiduciary obligations** that require the lawyer to be open and honest, to be loyal, and to treat the client with good faith. The contractual relationship also involves an implied term that the lawyer must be competent and must exercise reasonable care in the delivery of the agreed-upon services.

As well as having contractual obligations, lawyers are subject to a duty in negligence. In other words, a lawyer can be liable for his negligent performance of services and for his careless words if the client's reliance on them results in damage to the client. In such a case, the degree of the lawyer's liability depends on the closeness of the lawyer–client relationship and on the "neighbour principle"—that is, every person's obligation to take reasonable care

undertaking (by a lawyer) clear statement of intention by a lawyer that is reasonably relied on by another person (often another lawyer) and amounting to a solemn promise that must be kept or the lawyer giving the undertaking will be liable for misconduct

fiduciary obligations trust-like obligations, such as loyalty and good faith, that apply in certain contexts, including lawyer–client dealings

---

19 See CBA Code, ch XIV (and the 2009 supplement, "Guidelines for Ethical Marketing Practices Using New Information Technologies") and FLSC Model Code, ch 4, r 4.2.

20 The right to refuse a client is subject to a few exceptions. For example, lawyers can't refuse a client assigned to them by the court and must not refuse a client on discriminatory grounds.

to avoid acts or omissions that might injure his or her neighbour. (For more in-depth discussion of this principle and of torts generally, see Chapter 7.)

In addition to these contractual and tortious obligations, lawyers have related ethical duties, the most important of which are duties of competence, confidence, and loyalty. What distinguishes these ethical duties from most others is that they coincide with legal or fiduciary obligations in contract and tort, as described above. Clients can clearly sue for their breach. For example, if a lawyer represents a purchaser in a real estate transaction and stands to profit from the sale because of her relationship with the seller, she has to disclose this conflict of interest to her client—the purchaser. If she fails to do so, she will be in breach of not only her ethical obligations to her client but also her contractual and fiduciary obligations and can be sued.[21]

In the following sections, we examine the duties that lawyers owe to their clients: competence, confidentiality, and loyalty.

Duty of Competence

duty of competence
lawyer's obligation to provide services that meet the standard of a reasonably skilled lawyer

Lawyers have an obligation to provide services competently. The **duty of competence** does not require the lawyer to meet a standard of perfection, but it does require him to meet the standard of a reasonably skilled lawyer. If a matter is outside a lawyer's competence, the lawyer has a number of options: he may decline to act, he may request permission to bring in skilled co-counsel, or he may seek extra time to become competent in the matter (as long as this does not involve added risk or expense for the client).

Duty of Confidentiality

Lawyers have an obligation not to divulge information concerning a client's affairs that is acquired in the course of the "professional relationship" unless they are authorized to do so by the client. However, information acquired in informal settings, outside of a professional relationship, is not protected.

duty of confidentiality
lawyer's obligation not to divulge information concerning a client's affairs that has been acquired in the course of the professional relationship unless the client authorizes the lawyer to divulge this information

The rationale for this **duty of confidentiality** is that it is required for the proper administration of justice. If clients had no assurance of the full confidentiality of their communications, many would only partially disclose relevant information to their lawyers, and this would hinder the lawyer's ability to provide appropriate and effective legal services.

This duty of confidentiality applies to all information concerning a client, subject to a few exceptions. One notable exception is a case where the lawyer reasonably believes, on the basis of information disclosed by the client, that there is an imminent risk of serious harm to someone. Also, although the codes are silent on this point, we may assume that the duty of confidentiality doesn't apply to "criminal communications"—in other words, to communications that are criminal in themselves (for example, a threat of physical harm to the lawyer or to her employees) or to communications made with a view to furthering a criminal scheme.[22]

The duty of confidentiality survives the professional relationship. The lawyer cannot subsequently use information about the client for personal benefit or for the benefit of others. This duty also applies to the lawyer's colleagues (for example, articling students and other lawyers) and staff (for example, paralegals, legal administrative assistants, and human resources personnel).

---

21 Lawyers are permitted to structure their law practices so as to limit liability for ordinary operational risks (see the discussion of limited liability partnerships [LLPs] and corporations in Chapter 8). However, legislation prevents lawyers from using LLPs or the corporate shield to avoid personal liability for failing to satisfy contractual, tortious, or other private law obligations. See, for example, *Legal Profession Act*, SBC 1998, c 9, s 84; *Legal Profession Act*, CCSM c L107, s 36(1); *Legal Profession Act*, SNS 2004, c 28, s 23(1); and *Law Society Act*, RSO 1990, c L.8, s 61.0.5(1).

22 Alice Woolley, *Understanding Lawyers' Ethics in Canada*, 2nd ed (Toronto: LexisNexis, 2016) at 183.

The duty of confidentiality is distinguishable from the related rule concerning **lawyer–client privilege**, also known as solicitor–client privilege. The latter is a rule of evidence and is slightly narrower in application than the duty of confidentiality. Lawyer–client privilege applies to confidential information that meets the following two criteria:

1. it is connected to the giving or receiving of legal advice, and
2. it is in the form of a communication between lawyer and client.

The duty of confidentiality applies to all client information regardless of whether it is connected with legal advice and regardless of the source of the information. The difference between the duty of confidentiality and lawyer–client privilege is not important to most clients. What is not covered by the privilege is covered by the duty.

Duty of Loyalty: Avoiding Conflicts of Interest

A lawyer's **duty of loyalty** applies to both conflicts of interest between clients and conflicts of interest between the lawyer and his client.

Lawyers must avoid conflicts of interest between clients so that one client's interests are not advanced at the expense of another client's interests. For example, lawyers cannot represent two clients who are opposing each other in a dispute or who are on opposite sides of certain kinds of transactions (such as a real estate purchase or sale of a business). Advancing one client's interest in these situations may come at the expense of the other client's interest. Where the conflict of interest is minimal, however, a lawyer might be permitted to represent both clients. In order to do so, and as a general rule, both parties must be informed of the conflict and give their consent.

Conflicts of interest between clients are especially a problem for large law firms that have many lawyers and many clients (with the rise of megafirms and multinational mergers, clients of one firm could number in the thousands). Difficulties in this regard also arise from the fact that lawyers are very mobile, often moving from one firm to another. For example, a lawyer may work for a period of time in a firm that represents a client on one side of a dispute. Then, subsequently, this lawyer may leave that firm and go to work for the firm that represents the other party in the dispute. Law firms are required to be diligent in this regard and to have systems in place to ensure that any conflicts are discovered and dealt with appropriately.

With respect to former clients, the SCC has recognized that, even without client disclosure and consent, it might be possible for members of a law firm to represent a client in a dispute despite the fact that another member of the firm has formerly represented the other party (a former client) and has confidential information that could be used against that former client. In order for this to happen, the members of the law firm representing the client must not have received any confidential information about the other side from the colleague who formerly represented the other side, and the firm must have measures in place to ensure that this cannot happen (such measures preventing the disclosure of confidential information are sometimes called **cones of silence**; the expression "Chinese wall" is also used, referring to the Great Wall of China and an institutional barrier to the sharing of confidential information).

Concerning current clients, the SCC has set out a **bright line rule** that provides that a lawyer cannot represent two current clients whose interests are directly adverse to each other unless both clients consent after receiving full disclosure from the lawyer. It is not only the individual lawyer who is subject to this rule but the lawyer's firm as well.[23]

---

23   For recent applications of the bright line rule, see *Strother v 3464920 Canada Inc*, 2007 SCC 24; *Wallace v Canadian Pacific Railway*, 2011 SKCA 108; and *Canadian National Railway Co v McKercher LLP*, 2013 SCC 39.

lawyer–client privilege
lawyer's obligation not to divulge confidential information concerning a client's affairs that has been communicated to the lawyer by the client and is connected to the giving or receiving of legal advice

duty of loyalty
lawyer's obligation to avoid conflicts of interest between clients and between lawyer and client

cones of silence
institutional mechanisms used by law firms to secure confidential information so that lawyers working at the same law firm are prevented from accessing information that could prejudice a former client; sometimes also called Chinese walls

bright line rule
strict rule that a lawyer or law firm cannot represent two current clients whose interests are directly adverse to each other unless both clients consent after receiving full disclosure from the lawyer

Concerning conflicts of interest between lawyers and clients, they must be avoided for the obvious reason that the lawyer might be tempted to advance her own interests at the expense of the client's interests. This kind of conflict can arise not only where a lawyer (or an associate or a relative of the lawyer) has direct business dealings with a client but also where the dealings are with others and might prejudice the client's interests.

Lawyers who are faced with such a conflict must decline to enter into the transaction or must obtain the client's consent after full disclosure (and, preferably, after the client has received independent legal advice). A lawyer who proceeds with the transaction after disclosure and consent should also ensure that doing so is fair and reasonable in the circumstances.

Other Obligations

Other ethical obligations lawyers owe their clients are the obligations:

1. to maintain client property entrusted to the lawyer,[24]
2. not to withdraw services without good cause, and
3. to avoid close personal or sexual relationships with clients.

These other ethical obligations may or may not coincide with legal or fiduciary obligations in contract or tort. For example, the second and third obligations listed will not in most cases. The possibility of a laywer facing civil liability for breaching them is unlikely, although he may face discipline for professional misconduct. Regarding the last obligation— to avoid close personal or sexual relationships with clients—there is no absolute rule in this regard where lawyers are concerned.[25] However, there is a risk that such relationships may affect the lawyer's ability to act with integrity and good faith, to maintain confidences, and to avoid conflicts of interest. (See FLSC Model Code and the commentary following ch 3, r 3.4-2.) Codes of ethics for some other professions, particularly in the medical field, are more strict in this area and absolutely ban sexual relationships.

Disciplinary Proceedings

As mentioned, law societies and their discipline committees are charged with disciplining lawyers in cases of malpractice. The governing legislation or the law society rules will determine the composition of the committee (which is typically made up of benchers, non-elected lawyers, and at least one non-lawyer). The legislation or rules will also set out thresholds that will trigger disciplinary action. These thresholds are usually defined as conduct that amounts to:

1. professional misconduct,
2. conduct unbecoming a lawyer,
3. professional incompetence, or
4. breach of the governing legislation itself.

---

24 Typically, this will involve money held by the lawyer in a trust account. See CBA Code, ch VIII and commentaries and FLSC Model Code, ch 3, r 3.5 and commentaries.

25 In the United States, the situation is divided. Approximately one-third of state law societies have a strict "no sex with clients" ethics rule, whereas the others have no such rule. California's law society, the largest in the United States, adopted a complete sex ban in 2017, with limited exceptions (such as when the sexual relationship between the lawyer and the client preceded the professional relationship).

Lawyers' misconduct generally comes to the attention of the discipline committee through complaints from the public, from other lawyers, or from the courts. Occasionally, the committee is alerted by media reports or by a lawyer admitting her own misconduct. To qualify as misconduct, the lawyer's actions must have breached the profession's ethical code of conduct. In some cases, these actions may amount to more than professional misconduct: they may amount to civil or criminal wrongdoing.

After an investigation and a hearing (if the process moves to that stage), the discipline committee will determine whether the lawyer's action qualifies as misconduct on one of the grounds identified above. If the committee concludes that discipline is appropriate, a number of sanctions are possible. These include one or more of the following: reprimands, fines, practice conditions, suspension, retraining, and disbarment. Misconduct that is isolated and not on the serious end of the scale might only result in a reprimand (for example, a lack of civility in dealing with a particular client or lawyer), whereas misconduct that is far-reaching and has serious consequences will often result in disbarment (see, for example, the *Ryan* case, described in Box 11.2).

Figure 11.1 shows how complaints are typically processed. The majority of complaints turn out to be unsubstantiated and are closed.

FIGURE 11.1 General Complaint Process for Malpractice by Lawyers

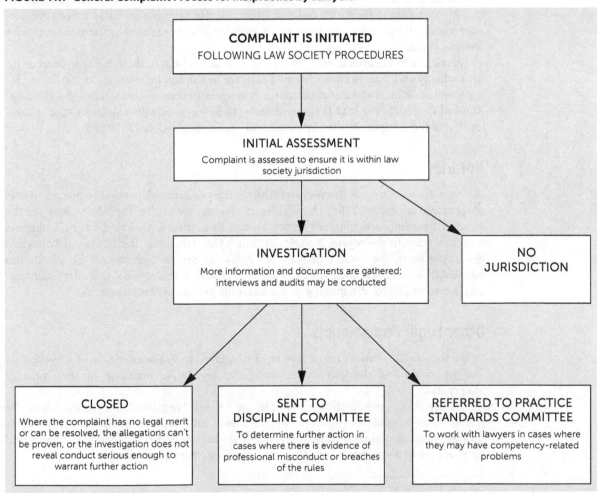

Paralegals, Law Clerks (Ontario), and Legal Assistants

Law society rules and ethical codes address the relationship between lawyers and their employees, including paralegals, Ontario law clerks, and others (including legal assistants, legal administrative assistants, and articling students). For example, rule 6.1-1 of chapter 6 of the FLSC Model Code provides as follows:

> 6.1-1 A lawyer has complete professional responsibility for all business entrusted to him or her and must directly supervise staff and assistants to whom the lawyer delegates particular tasks and functions.

By implication, therefore, lawyers' ethical obligations with respect to their work apply to the employees to whom they delegate that work. Lawyers have complete professional responsibility for all business entrusted to them, so their employees' ethical lapses could subject the supervising lawyers to discipline. It is the lawyers' responsibility to ensure that their employees are aware of the high ethical standards that must guide them in their work. Employees who fall below those standards will likely suffer employment consequences, including being let go from their positions in cases of serious breaches.

Employees of lawyers may also belong to voluntary associations—for example, Ontario law clerks and the ILCO, Alberta paralegals and the AAPP, and BC paralegals and the BCPA—that publish their own codes of ethics. Membership in these associations requires adherence to these codes, which mirror in short form some of the obligations set out in the lawyers' codes.

Paralegals in Ontario, because of their special status (that is, their ability to practise independently and their licensure by the LSO), are in a different position. In 2007, the LSO approved an ethical code of conduct for paralegals practising in Ontario: the Paralegal Rules of Conduct. The LSO is responsible for handling complaints against Ontario paralegals and for disciplinary decisions concerning their professional misconduct.

Notaries

For notaries who are non-lawyers and who do not practise independently, but practise as government appointees, the ethical rules of conduct governing their behaviour are the same as those imposed on public servants generally in their jurisdiction. British Columbia is an exception in this regard. Notaries in British Columbia have their own legislation and governing body, the Society of Notaries Public of British Columbia.[26] This body has adopted its own ethical code, the Principles for Ethical & Professional Conduct Guideline, and is responsible for disciplining its members for professional misconduct.

Other Legal Professionals

Other legal professionals may or may not be required to follow specific codes of conduct and be subject to disciplinary action under legislative mandate in the event of malpractice.

Immigration consultants, for example, are formally regulated. They must follow the ICCRC's ethical guidelines as set out in its Codes of Ethics and are subject to discipline for professional misconduct. Similarly, patent and trademark agents are federally licensed and must adhere to a specific code of ethics or face disciplinary proceedings.

---

26 See the *Notaries Act*, RSBC 1996, c 334.

Some legal positions are more limited in scope—for example, marriage commissioners and commissioners for taking affidavits—and there are no separate ethical codes of conduct applicable to them. They may be bound to general codes connected to their status as government appointees or other sources of employment.

Although there are no separate codes applicable to court agents, they are nonetheless held to a high standard of behaviour. In British Columbia, for example, the legislation provides that the court has the right to refuse audience to a court agent and "has the same control over an unprofessional person practising in the court or before the justice as the court or justice would have over a qualified practitioner practising in there."[27]

Others working in law-related careers, such as insurance and policing, will have governing bodies, codes of ethics, and disciplinary processes specific to their professions.

---

27   *Court Agent Act*, RSBC 1996, c 76, s 2.

CHAPTER SUMMARY

The practice of law has changed dramatically in the last 100 years, from a profession made up largely of sole practitioners and small partnerships to one that includes more large law firms, some megafirms, and MDPs. The legal landscape has also changed, through the introduction of new practitioner classes, such as paralegals, law clerks, and notaries, among others.

Legal education in Canada has evolved too. Lawyers are no longer trained according to the old English apprenticeship model, in which law students were taught by a practising lawyer while serving under articles. Instead, in the common law provinces today, they are educated through a combination of academic coursework with articling requirements. Education requirements for paralegals have changed significantly too. Whereas, previously, no formal education was required, most paralegals today are graduates of a college diploma program or a degree program in paralegal studies. In Ontario, paralegals must satisfy defined educational standards as a condition of licensure with the LSO. Other legal professionals are similarly required to meet certain educational standards because of either market demand or regulatory requirements.

In every province and territory, law societies composed of elected lawyers regulate and supervise the practice of law. Their functions include administering a code of conduct for lawyers, handling public complaints, providing continuing legal education, and disciplining lawyers. Other legal professionals may also have regulatory bodies governing their particular area of practice.

A range of opportunities exist for lawyers outside of the traditional law firm, including work at all levels of government; in community legal aid clinics; as in-house counsel for companies; and with administrative agencies and tribunals, public interest advocacy organizations, and legal publishers. Paralegals and other legal professionals also enjoy flexibility in career options because of their training; possibilities include work in court administration, private investigation, legal research, legal publishing, policing, insurance, and human resources.

High ethical standards have always been expected of the legal profession. An effective system of justice needs such high standards, which help protect the public. Historically, these high standards were taken for granted, at least within the profession itself. In the modern era, codes of conduct are the main ethical guides for lawyers and other legal professionals. For lawyers in particular, these codes define various duties, including their duties to the state (or administration of justice), to the courts, to the profession and public, and to clients.

Integrity and good faith underlie the notion of professional responsibility. A lawyer's duty to the state involves, at the very least, his upholding the law and not advising or assisting in its violation. A lawyer's duty to the court involves showing courtesy and respect, respecting the established process, and not misleading the court or unfairly criticizing judges. The ethics of advocacy, which overlap with the duty to the court, often involve balancing obligations to the client with obligations to others. Lawyers sometimes find it difficult to pursue a client's case resolutely, as they are obliged to do, while maintaining courtesy to the courts and witnesses.

Lawyers' duties to the profession include providing prompt and accurate communications to the law society and reporting malpractice. Duties that lawyers owe to others are courtesy and good faith. Lawyers observe these duties through the absolute reliability of their undertakings and through professionalism in advertising. The lawyer's ethical duty to the client has three main aspects: (1) providing competent services, (2) keeping client information confidential, and (3) avoiding conflicts of interest between clients and between lawyer and client. Frequently, breaches of ethics in this area will also involve civil liability based on contractual, fiduciary, or tortious duties.

Law societies are responsible for disciplining lawyers. Discipline committees treat complaints against lawyers seriously and investigate these complaints. A finding of professional misconduct and conduct unbecoming a lawyer, based on breaches of ethical and other duties, can result in fines, suspension, or disbarment, among other sanctions. Lawyers are also responsible for the ethical lapses of their employees, including paralegals and legal assistants; depending on the nature and severity, such lapses will have employment consequences for the employee. Other legal professionals who are regulated—such as paralegals in Ontario, notaries in British Columbia, and immigration consultants—will be subject to disciplinary sanctions for ethical breaches by the regulatory bodies that govern their profession.

KEY TERMS

articles, 307

benchers, 306

bright line rule, 321

called to the bar, 308

codes of conduct, 315

cones of silence, 321

duty of competence, 320

duty of confidentiality, 320

duty of loyalty, 321

fiduciary obligations, 319

law society, 306

lawyer–client privilege, 321

legal ethics, 313

undertaking (by a lawyer), 319

FURTHER READING

BOOKS

Backhouse, Constance & W Wesley Pue, eds, *The Promise and Perils of Law: Lawyers in Canadian History* (Toronto: Irwin Law, 2009).

Brockman, Joan, *Gender in the Legal Profession: Fitting or Breaking the Mould* (Vancouver: University of British Columbia Press, 2001).

Collis, Diana & Cynthia Forget, *Working in a Legal Environment*, 2nd ed (Toronto: Emond Montgomery, 2011).

Graham, Randal NM, *Legal Ethics: Theories, Cases, and Professional Regulation*, 3rd ed (Toronto: Emond Montgomery, 2014).

Hutchinson, Allan, *Legal Ethics and Professional Responsibility*, 2nd ed (Toronto: Irwin Law, 2006).

Knight, S Patricia, *Ethics and Professional Practice for Paralegals*, 4th ed (Toronto: Emond, 2018).

MacKenzie, Gavin, *Lawyers and Ethics: Professional Responsibility and Discipline*, 6th ed (Toronto: Carswell, 2018) (loose-leaf updated 2018, release 3).

MacNair, M Deborah, *Conflicts of Interest: Principles for the Legal Profession* (Toronto: Canada Law Book, 2005) (loose-leaf updated 2018, release 31).

Orkin, Mark M, *Legal Ethics*, 2nd ed (Toronto: Canada Law Book, 2011).

Sheehy, Elizabeth & Sheila McIntyre, eds, *Calling for Change: Women, Law, and the Legal Profession* (Ottawa: University of Ottawa Press, 2006).

Woolley, Alice et al, *Lawyers' Ethics and Professional Regulation*, 3rd ed (Toronto: LexisNexis, 2017).

WEBSITES

Provincial Law Society Websites

Alberta: <https://www.lawsociety.ab.ca>

British Columbia: <https://www.lawsociety.bc.ca>

Manitoba: <https://lawsociety.mb.ca>

New Brunswick: <https://lawsociety-barreau.nb.ca>

Newfoundland and Labrador: <https://lsnl.ca>

Northwest Territories: <https://www.lawsociety.nt.ca>

Nova Scotia: <https://nsbs.org>

Nunavut: <https://www.lawsociety.nu.ca>

Ontario: <https://lso.ca/home>

Prince Edward Island: <http://lawsocietypei.ca>

Quebec: <https://www.barreau.qc.ca>

Saskatchewan: <https://www.lawsociety.sk.ca>

Yukon: <https://lawsocietyyukon.com>

Codes of Conduct

Judges

Canadian Judicial Council, Ethical Principles for Judges: <https://cjc-ccm.ca/cmslib/general/news_pub_judicialconduct_Principles_en.pdf>

Lawyers

FLSC Model Code, Model Code of Professional Conduct, Federation of Law Societies of Canada: <https://flsc.ca/national-initiatives/model-code-of-professional-conduct>

Notaries

Society of Notaries Public of BC, Principles for Ethical & Professional Conduct Guideline: <https://www.snpbc.ca/wp-content/uploads/2020/07/Code-of-Ethical-Professional-Conduct.pdf>

Immigration Consultants

Immigration Consultants of Canada Regulatory Council (ICCRC), Codes of Ethics: <https://iccrc-crcic.ca/rules-obligations/code-of-business-conduct-ethics>.

Paralegals and Law Clerks

Alberta Association of Professional Paralegals (AAPP), Code of Ethics: <https://www.alberta-paralegal.com/code-of-ethics>

BC Paralegal Association (BCPA), Code of Ethics: <https://www.bcparalegalassociation.com/cpages/code-of-ethics>

Institute of Law Clerks of Ontario (ILCO), Code of Ethics: <https://www.ilco.on.ca/about/our-code-of-ethics>

Law Society of Ontario (LSO), Paralegal Rules of Conduct: <https://lso.ca/about-lso/legislation-rules/paralegal-rules-of-conduct>

Patent and Trademark Agents

Intellectual Property Institute of Canada, Code of Ethics: <https://ipic.ca> (search for Code of Ethics)

REVIEW QUESTIONS

1. In Canada, is there a clear divide between lawyers who are barristers (litigators) and lawyers who are solicitors? Explain.

2. Describe the main practice settings for lawyers.

3. List three responsibilities of provincial and territorial law societies.

4. Explain the role of paralegals in your province.

5. Besides judges, lawyers, and paralegals, name four other types of legal professionals or law-related careers in Canada.

6. In Canada's common law provinces today, what educational requirements must a prospective lawyer meet?

7. Briefly define legal ethics.

8. Name two ethical codes of conduct for Canadian lawyers that are national in scope.

9. In the practice of law, what core ethical principle underlies professional responsibility?

10. Describe three specific obligations involved in a lawyer's duty to the court.

11. What is an undertaking by a lawyer?

12. Explain the difference between a lawyer's duty of confidentiality and lawyer–client privilege.

13. What are "cones of silence"?

EXERCISES

1. Visit the website for your province's law society. Comment on how effectively the website provides information concerning how to find a lawyer practising in an area of the law of interest to you.

2. Do you believe that lawyers should be self-governed by their own professional body or be regulated directly by their provincial government? Discuss.

3. Imagine a Canadian justice system in which legal professionals are no longer held to any particular ethical standards and the legal profession is treated like any other business. Using specific arguments and examples, describe how you think these altered expectations and standards would change the Canadian justice system as we know it.

4. A lawyer has recently received a judgment in a court action in which a piece of real property was sold. The court ordered that the proceeds of the sale be paid out by the lawyer to various parties, in specified amounts. A paralegal (or a law clerk, in Ontario), working under the supervision of the lawyer, was delegated the task of arranging payment to the various parties. By mistake, the paralegal neglected to pay one of the parties. When the party contacted the lawyer's firm, the paralegal was asked to deal with the inquiry. He realized his mistake but refused to admit what had happened. It was not until the supervising lawyer reviewed the whole affair that the mistake was discovered and the money paid out as required.

   Name and describe at least two specific ethical rules that have been breached here.

5. Research the law society website for your province or territory and locate the record of disciplinary hearings. Find cases involving lawyers who have been cited for professional misconduct that involved criminal activity (for example, impaired driving, possession of illegal drugs, domestic violence, or fraud). From among these cases, choose one that interests you and describe which ethical obligations were violated in the case.

12 Access to Justice and Law Reform

Introduction 332

Access to Legal Services 333

Courts and Alternative Dispute
Resolution Mechanisms 336

Public Access to Legal Information 338

Government Measures to
Enhance Access to Justice 339

Law Reform 343

Chapter Summary 347

Key Terms 347

Further Reading 347

Review Questions 348

Exercises 348

Protesters block traffic in support of Wet'suwet'en hereditary chiefs attempting to prevent construction of a natural gas pipeline on their traditional territories (Vancouver, 2020).

After reading this chapter, you will be able to:

- Describe what lawyers in Canada have accomplished to provide affordable legal services to the public.
- Explain how alternative dispute resolution mechanisms function in comparison with courts.

- Discuss important steps taken to make the law and legal knowledge more accessible to the public.
- Identify key law reform initiatives that governments have introduced.
- Explain how public interest groups and their legal strategies influence law reform.

We are fortunate to live in a country with a robust justice system buttressed by an independent judiciary. Yet access to justice in Canada remains a serious problem that imperils the public's confidence in the justice system. … While progress has been made, there is still much to do. Rules and processes are still more complicated than they should be, causing unnecessary delays. Financial barriers continue to thwart access to justice. The low level of funding for legal aid leads litigants to appear in courtrooms without the support of counsel, placing unfair burdens on courts, the litigants, the bar and, ultimately, the public purse. And finally, some may hold attitudes of mistrust or fear toward the justice system, refusing to engage with it or acknowledge its legitimacy.

The Right Honourable Beverley McLachlin, PC,
Chief Justice of Canada, *Remarks to the Council of the Canadian Bar Association at the Canadian Legal Conference*
(Ottawa: Canadian Bar Association, 11 August 2016)

Introduction

As described in earlier chapters, Canadian law has seen many changes since colonial times, when French civil law and English common law were first received into this country. For example, with Confederation in 1867 came significant changes to our legal system, and with our country's growth and development came parallel changes in our laws.

We have seen how a heightened awareness of human rights in the aftermath of the Second World War, in combination with the influence of the American civil rights movement in the 1950s and 1960s, helped motivate the provinces and territories to introduce human rights codes. These forces joined with others to bring about the patriation of our Constitution and passage of the *Canadian Charter of Rights and Freedoms* in 1982 (see Chapter 6). We have also seen a movement for greater consumer protection in today's marketplace (see Chapter 8).

This chapter looks at elements of the multifaceted access-to-justice movement and discusses some modern law reform initiatives undertaken by governments, lawyers, courts, and the public that are helping change (and improve) Canadian law.

Access to Legal Services

A general legal trend in Canada, beginning prior to the Second World War, has been toward increased access to legal services for *all* Canadians, regardless of their socio-economic level or their status as a minority or person with a disability. A number of developments in the criminal justice system and the legal profession illustrate this trend.

Legal Aid Plans

It has been an increasing concern of lawyers and the public in Canada that lower-income and otherwise disadvantaged individuals have better access to legal services. A movement based on this concern began in the decades before the Second World War and continued to grow after the war. Lawyers in Ontario and lawyers belonging to the national Canadian Bar Association began to acknowledge a social responsibility as a group regarding the legal needs of *all* Canadians, especially those who could not afford to pay for the services of a lawyer.[1] Lawyers also became aware that the legal needs of indigent persons were different from those of wealthier clients capable of paying lawyers' fees. People living on a lower income—including those living on a pension or social assistance—were more likely to need legal help with matters such as rental accommodation, welfare, employment assistance, discrimination, debt, workers' compensation, education expenses, and accessing government services in general.[2] Increasingly conscious of the barriers faced by lower-income Canadians, lawyers all across Canada began working with their respective law societies and provincial governments to effect change. Their efforts resulted in formalized, publicly funded **legal aid** programs that began in the 1960s.

Today, legal aid services for designated matters, criminal and non-criminal, are provided to lower-income Canadians across Canada either free of charge or for a modest fee. Legal aid plans vary from province to province. Generally speaking, they help those in need in the following ways:

legal aid
government funding of lawyers who provide legal assistance to persons with low income

- Lawyers in private practice can do legal aid work based on a judicare, or fee-for-service, delivery system. The process works in the following way: a person who needs legal help attends his local legal aid office, which determines whether he is qualified to receive legal aid on the basis of his particular legal need and a financial means test. If qualified, this person takes a legal aid certificate to a lawyer of his choice who is on a legal aid panel. The lawyer then performs the legal work and bills for it in accordance with the rates set by the legal aid tariff. The lawyer is paid by legal aid, not by the client.

---

1 Mary P Reilly, "The Origins and Development of Legal Aid in Ontario" (1988) 8 Windsor YB Access Just 81; N Larsen, "Legal Aid in Manitoba" in C Harvey, ed, *The Law Society of Manitoba, 1877-1977* (Winnipeg: Peguis, 1977) at 158.

2 James E Lockyer, QC, "The Roles and Responsibilities of the Legal Profession in Furthering Access to Justice" (1992) 12 Windsor YB Access Just 356; I Cotler & H Marx, eds, *The Law and the Poor in Canada* (Montreal: Black Rose Books, 1977).

- Many people coming to court for the first time do so without legal representation, and many lack an understanding of the courtroom process. Legal aid plans help these individuals by directing them to a lawyer known as "duty counsel," who typically can help with criminal, immigration, or family law matters (exact eligibility rules vary depending on the province or territory). Duty counsel lawyers in criminal court might, for example, speak to the judge on an individual's behalf and arrange an adjournment so that the accused can apply for legal aid.

- Legal aid plans in some jurisdictions have also established community legal clinics. These are an alternative form of delivering legal services. Their salaried staff—lawyers and community legal workers—help low-income Canadians with legal matters concerning such areas as landlord and tenant obligations, social welfare assistance, job search, immigration, debt collection, and human rights.[3] In Ontario, for example, specialty legal clinics help Canadians from ethnically diverse communities, as well as people with disabilities, with their unique needs. These legal clinics also tend to have offices that are easily accessible.

In addition to provincial legal aid plans, other measures that lawyers in Canada have taken to help make this country's justice system less costly and more accessible to the public are as follows:[4]

- offering pro bono legal services,
- increasing the use of paralegals,
- offering prepaid legal services plans, and
- producing legal scholarship on access-to-justice matters.

Pro Bono Legal Services

Many lawyers may not be involved with legal aid work but may still want to help lower-income Canadians, charities, and disadvantaged persons with their legal needs. These lawyers can choose to offer assistance to the public **pro bono**, or without charge (from the Latin *pro bono publico*, meaning "for the public good"). They can do this, for example, by:

pro bono
term applied to legal work that lawyers do at no charge to help the public (from the Latin *pro bono publico*: "for the public good")

- providing justice education in high schools and participating in school "law days";
- providing legal talks at neighbourhood community centres on selected topics, such as making a will;
- helping people on social assistance; or
- giving free legal advice to new immigrants to Canada.

Pro bono organizations have been established in many provinces (see Box 12.1).

---

3   Mary Jane Mossman, "Community Legal Clinics in Ontario" (1983) 3 Windsor YB Access Just 375.

4   See Roderick A Macdonald, "Access to Justice in Canada Today: Scope, Scale and Ambitions" in Julia Bass, WA Bogart & Frederick Zemans, eds, *Access to Justice for a New Century: The Way Forward* (Toronto: Law Society of Upper Canada, 2004) at 19.

BOX 12.1

Pro Bono Ontario

Pro Bono Ontario (PBO) is a charity founded in 2001 to bridge the justice gap between lawyers who want to give back and the many Ontarians who can't afford legal services and have a legal problem not covered by government funding. PBO creates and manages volunteer programs that connect these lawyers with low-income Ontarians—either directly or in partnership with charitable organizations working in the local community. Through this work, PBO has emerged as the legal profession's primary volunteer response to unmet legal needs. In 2019, PBO served almost 30,000 clients who had nowhere else to turn. The demand for PBO's services increases each year.

Programs for the Public

PBO manages a variety of programs in-house and provides strategic guidance to several others that are managed externally. PBO's in-house programs focus on:

- helping families address health-harming legal problems;
- helping low-income litigants who are unrepresented;
- providing province-wide help to Ontarians with everyday legal problems through its Free Legal Advice Hotline (the hotline was launched in 2017, the first such service in Canada);
- protecting students and child refugees; and
- strengthening non-profits, start-ups, and the arts.

"Wherever possible, we embed our free legal services in front-line environments like courthouses, schools and hospitals—places frequented by people with legal problems they can't afford to address." This means that many individuals dealing with legal problems on their own have access to legal help at the very time and place they need it.

Source: Pro Bono Ontario, online: <https://www.probonoontario.org>.

Increased Use of Paralegals

Legal services are becoming increasingly expensive. Another way that lawyers in law firms have sought to reduce expenses and make their legal services more affordable to the public is by using more paralegals.[5] Lawyers can assign work that they would otherwise do to paralegals, billing for this work at a lower rate and passing the cost savings on to their clients.

As discussed in Chapter 11, paralegals are not lawyers, but they are trained to do procedural and substantive legal work under the supervision of a lawyer (in Ontario, such paraprofessionals are called "law clerks"). Many paralegals nowadays are responsible for work that, previously, would have been done by lawyers. Moreover, paralegals in Ontario have a special status allowing them to represent clients in some lower-level courts and before administrative bodies (Ontario paralegals are formally regulated by the Law Society of Ontario). Other jurisdictions are considering moving in the direction of the Ontario model as they try to improve access to justice. Implementing the necessary changes will depend on rules set by provincial or territorial legislation for the jurisdiction in question, by the relevant courts and tribunals, and by the province's or territory's law society. In British Columbia, for example, "designated paralegals" may be given increased responsibilities when dealing with clients; however, they still work under the supervision of a lawyer.

Prepaid Legal Services Plans

Another new delivery method for legal services—and a model that is particularly attractive to middle-income Canadians—is a prepaid legal services benefits plan. Such plans arose in

---

5   Frederick H Zemans, "The Non-Lawyer as a Means of Providing Legal Services" in Robert G Evans & Michael J Trebilcock, eds, *Lawyers and the Consumer Interest: Regulating the Market for Legal Services* (Toronto: Butterworths, 1982) at 263.

Canada in the 1980s, under the leadership of the Canadian Auto Workers. Members of this union make individual contributions to the plan, which helps pay for a lawyer who does prescribed legal services under the plan for members at a reasonable cost.[6]

Legal Scholarship

Canada's legal community includes many legal academics who support law reform. They write books and articles on this subject, and such scholarship can be influential in effecting changes in the law. The *Windsor Yearbook of Access to Justice* is an example of a specialized law journal that publishes learned articles in this area.

Courts and Alternative Dispute Resolution Mechanisms

The traditional adjudicative process of resolving legal disputes in courts has come under increasing criticism in Canada. Many people worry about the cost of a lawyer. Long trial delays, complex legal procedures, lack of privacy, unfamiliar legal terminology and rules of evidence, and an expensive appeal process are further concerns about the court process held by many middle-income Canadians. Many are also intimidated by the adversarial system used in civil court, whereby one side tries to win outright, with the loser paying the winner's costs.

As a result, a growing number of people are favouring **alternative dispute resolution (ADR)** mechanisms instead of courts. There are three main ADR mechanisms: (1) negotiation, (2) mediation, and (3) arbitration.

alternative dispute resolution (ADR)
process used instead of a court trial to help settle a dispute

Negotiation

Negotiation is the simplest method of resolving disputes and is conducted by the parties themselves (either directly or using representatives). Both sides talk to each other, usually informally, to determine the possibility of finding a mutually acceptable solution to their dispute. Because both sides must agree to the settlement for it to be binding, both parties need to cooperate, be flexible, and be willing to compromise for a negotiation to be successful.

negotiation
dispute resolution process whereby the parties talk to each other directly and seek a mutually acceptable solution to their problem

Mediation

Mediation takes negotiation one step further. A neutral and impartial third party, called a mediator, assists the parties in their efforts to resolve their dispute. It may be a dispute, for example, between two neighbours over pets in the backyard. Or it could involve a dispute between two tenants over loud noise, between spouses going through a marriage breakdown and dealing with financial arrangements and custody matters, or between business partners (for example, a franchisor and franchisee) arguing about their contractual obligations. The mediator, who is chosen by the parties beforehand, helps both sides find a

mediation
dispute resolution process whereby the parties try to reach a settlement with the assistance of a third party

---

6   C Wydrzynski, K Hildebrandt & D Blonde, "The CAW Prepaid Legal Services Plan: A Case Study of an Alternative Funding and Delivery Method for Legal Services" (1990) 10 Windsor YB Access Just 22 at 72.

solution to their problem. This person does not necessarily have to be a lawyer. The mediator's role is to keep both sides talking, clarify issues, help uncover sources behind the conflict, and suggest compromises and solutions that both sides can accept. The mediator meets often with both sides, individually as well as together, and can do so at their own homes. Sessions are confidential and informal, and they may be flexible in terms of timing. For example, the meetings might take place in the evenings or on weekends. However, as with negotiation, a mediator can only *recommend* a solution, which is not binding on the parties unless both sides agree to it.

When we compare the traditional court process of resolving disputes with this alternative approach, we can see why many people are attracted to mediation. In the court system, the parties cannot pick their judge. The judge will not come to the parties' home or meet with them on weekends—nor will a judge meet with one side in the absence of the other. In the traditional court system, the judge's decision must be obeyed, even if one side does not like it, and the costs for legal representation there can be expensive.

With respect to certain kinds of disputes, however, legislation may make mediation mandatory. Examples of these kinds of disputes include family law conflicts, small claims actions, and various administrative tribunal matters. Although in these situations the mediator's recommendations are still not binding, the parties may have less flexibility in terms of the choice of the mediator (for example, a judge or tribunal adjudicator may be assigned to the parties) and the time and place of the mediation.

Arbitration

In the case of **arbitration**, as with mediation, the parties consent beforehand to the appointment of an impartial third party, here called an arbitrator, to help resolve their dispute. They also agree to assume the costs involved. However, unlike mediation, the parties can also decide beforehand to accept binding or non-binding arbitration. In binding arbitration, the decision of the arbitrator must be followed. In non-binding arbitration, the arbitrator's decision is only advisory. The parties may submit to an arbitration arrangement by way of an arbitration agreement reached after a dispute arises or in advance of the dispute pursuant to an arbitration clause in an existing contract between the parties.

The advantages of using arbitration are the following:

- the parties can pick their own arbitrator, often someone with experience in the area;
- sessions can be informal and confidential; and
- the process can proceed at the parties' own pace.

One difficulty with arbitration is that the process can become quite legalistic and formal, particularly if the arbitrator is a lawyer and both sides are represented by a lawyer as well.[7]

As with mediation, and as an exception to the generally consensual nature of ADR, legislation may make arbitration compulsory in certain contexts, such as for some labour disputes and residential tenancy matters.

Table 12.1 shows a comparison of the three main forms of ADR with litigation.

arbitration
dispute resolution process whereby the parties agree beforehand on an arbitrator to assist them and on whether the arbitrator's decision will be advisory or binding

---

7   Cheryl Picard et al, *The Art and Science of Mediation* (Toronto: Emond Montgomery, 2004); EG Tannis, *Alternative Dispute Resolution That Works* (Toronto: Captus Press, 1989); W Estey, "Who Needs Courts?" (1981) 1 Windsor YB Access Just 263.

TABLE 12.1   Comparison of the Three Main Forms of ADR with Litigation

	NEGOTIATION	MEDIATION	ARBITRATION	LITIGATION
Third-Party Intervention	No	Yes	Yes	Yes
Choice of Third Party	n/a	Usually parties select on agreement	Usually parties select on agreement	No, assigned by court
Role of Third Party	n/a	Helps facilitate a settlement	Assesses evidence and arguments and makes binding or non-binding decision	Assesses evidence and arguments and makes binding decision
Decision Outcome	Not binding	Not binding	Usually binding	Binding on parties
Confidentiality	Yes, private	Yes, private	Usually private but may be public	No, public court process
Participation of Parties	Voluntary	Usually voluntary	Usually voluntary	Coercive
Style of Participation of Parties	Collaborative	Collaborative	Adversarial	Adversarial
Process and Rules of Procedure	Informal, flexible	Informal, flexible	More formal, somewhat flexible	Formal, inflexible

Public Access to Legal Information

Even if ADR mechanisms become more widely used, courts are still central to the administration of justice and are not likely to be replaced anytime soon. Canadians who are unable to afford a lawyer or who do not qualify for legal aid face some difficult problems when going to court. Among their most pressing concerns are how and where they can obtain legal information about:

- how the formal legal system works,
- what the law is concerning their legal matter, and
- what their rights are in court.

Many such people have to be self-reliant and find answers to these questions on their own. For this reason, they want the law demystified and technology to help them gain knowledge about the law.

This topic—public access to legal information—was examined by professor Martin Friedland in a ground-breaking 1975 study he conducted for the Law Reform Commission of Canada.[8] Friedland noted that many people did not know where to go for accurate and complete legal information and had trouble using and understanding legal materials such as cases, statutes, and regulations. He identified four ways of providing the public with better access to law:

1. improving the clarity of existing legal materials;
2. doing more to educate the public about law;

---

8   ML Friedland, *Access to the Law: A Study Conducted for the Law Reform Commission of Canada* (Toronto: Carswell/Methuen, 1975).

3. improving the quality of legal information that intermediary facilities, such as community information centres and public libraries, provide to the public; and

4. developing a new reference source, such as an encyclopedia of law for non-lawyers, that could be regularly updated and made available in public libraries, schools, and government offices.

Many technological measures for improving public access to legal information have been taken since Friedland's 1975 study. These measures include, for example, telephone access to legal information providers such as the Legal Information Society of Nova Scotia; a lawyer referral service administered by provincial law societies; dial-a-law programs for taped legal information; online legal research websites such as that created by the Canadian Legal Information Institute (CanLII); and having federal, provincial, and territorial governments place government statutes, regulations, and other legal information online on official government websites.[9]

Government Measures to Enhance Access to Justice

The access-to-justice movement has influenced federal and provincial governments to make further reforms that increase public access to government institutions and benefits. Some of these reforms include making changes to court processes, providing better access to government information, creating public advocacy offices, and improving access to justice for Indigenous persons.

Improving Court Processes

Reforms that make court procedures simpler, faster, more affordable, and easier to understand are changes for the better. A lack of resources is sometimes an obstacle to making these changes, but efforts are being made. The following are some modifications to court processes designed to improve accessibility and outcomes:

- encouraging the use of collaborative law models, particularly in the resolution of family law matters—collaborative law tries to minimize the adversarial aspect of a dispute and avoid the courts altogether through negotiation and settlement (a form of ADR), which benefits both the parties and the court system itself (through a reduction of caseloads);
- creating unified family courts, where family matters, which are under the jurisdiction of both the federal and the provincial governments, are heard in one convenient place (see also Chapter 5 under "Unified Family Courts");
- raising the monetary limits of small claims courts (where procedures are simpler and more suitable for non-lawyers) so that matters need not go to a higher court where self-representation is more difficult—current small claims limits range from $10,000 to $50,000 (see Chapter 5 under "Provincial Court Systems");

---

9   T Gregory Kane & Edward R Myers, "The Role of Self-Help in the Provision of Legal Services" in Evans & Trebilcock, *supra* note 5 at 439.

- creating specialized courts, such as mental health, drug treatment, domestic violence, and Indigenous courts, which aim to achieve better long-term outcomes for some types of offenders and for society as a whole (see the discussion of criminal courts in Chapter 10);
- implementing case management systems, where a designated court official, such as a judge or master, is responsible for supervising the flow of cases going through the courts so that delays are minimized; and
- establishing administrative bodies to address areas of law that are more efficiently dealt with outside the court process. (See the discussion of administrative agencies in Chapter 9.)

Increasing Access to Government Information

Public access to government records is another area related to access to justice. In the 1960s, a determined campaign began in Canada for greater public access to information contained in government records. Influenced by a similar movement in the United States and led by lawyers, academics, the press, and some members of Parliament, proponents argued that increased access would make governments more accountable to the public.

Today, access-to-information legislation exists at the provincial, territorial, and federal levels. The Supreme Court of Canada (SCC) has characterized the overarching purpose of this legislation as facilitating democracy in two related ways: "It helps to ensure first, that citizens have the information required to participate meaningfully in the democratic process, and secondly, that politicians and bureaucrats remain accountable to the citizenry."[10] Note that although this passage is from the dissenting judgment, the majority expressly agreed with the dissent in its general approach to the interpretation of the legislation—the disagreement related to the specific application of the legislation to the facts. The federal *Access to Information Act*[11] came into effect in July 1983, making Canada one of the first countries in the world to protect this right. The Act gives Canadian citizens and permanent residents the right to access information contained in government records. Section 2(1) sets out the three principles that underpin the Act:

1. government information should be available to the public,
2. necessary exceptions to the right of access should be limited and specific, and
3. decisions on the disclosure of government information should be reviewed independently of government.

Since this Act was first passed, requests for information have steadily increased. For the 2018–19 reporting period, 123,421 requests were received, up from 106,255 in the 2017–18 reporting period. The federal agency generating the most requests in 2018–19 was Immigration, Refugees and Citizenship Canada (66.8 percent of the total), followed by the Canada Border Services Agency (6.2 percent).

Creating Public Advocacy Offices

In addition to information acts, in many provinces the office of the ombudsman has helped improve access to justice for Canadians by drawing public attention and scrutiny to

---

10   *Dagg v Canada (Minister of Finance)*, [1997] 2 SCR 403, 1997 CanLII 358 at para 61.

11   RSC 1985, c A-1.

problems people have with the government—for example, government waste or inaction. The ombudsman (called an "ombudsperson" in certain provinces, such as British Columbia) is an official with powers to investigate alleged government abuses or maladministration at the request of citizens. The ombudsman acts independently of the legislature and reports to it. Alberta was the first province to introduce this office, in 1967, and other provinces and territories have followed suit. The ombudsman does not have unlimited jurisdiction to investigate maladministration in all government departments, ministries, agencies, and institutions. It is also an office whose powers vary from province to province. In all cases, the ombudsperson's services are provided free of charge (see Box 12.2).

Improving Access to Justice for Indigenous Peoples

Existing treaty rights and section 35 of the *Constitution Act, 1982* are the basis of the relationship between Indigenous peoples and Canadian governments, but change is needed. The federal and provincial governments have committed to renewing this relationship, and, as we saw in Chapters 2 and 10, government promises to implement the *United Nations Declaration on the Rights of Indigenous Peoples* (UNDRIP) are an important part of this renewal. UNDRIP includes provisions relating to access to justice. For example, Article 40 provides:

> Indigenous peoples have the right to access to and prompt decision through just and fair procedures for the resolution of conflicts and disputes with States or other parties, as well as to effective remedies for all infringements of their individual and collective rights. Such a decision shall give due consideration to the customs, traditions, rules and legal systems of the indigenous peoples concerned and international human rights.

In addition, Article 13(2) requires states to ensure that Indigenous peoples can be understood in legal proceedings, "where necessary through the provision of interpretation or by other appropriate means."

In the 2015 report of the Truth and Reconciliation Commission (TRC), Calls to Action 50 to 52 (headed "Equity for Aboriginal People in the Legal System") concern access to justice. Call to Action 50, in particular, provides:

> In keeping with the *United Nations Declaration on the Rights of Indigenous Peoples*, we call upon the federal government, in collaboration with Aboriginal organizations, to fund the establishment of Indigenous law institutes for the development, use, and understanding of Indigenous laws and access to justice in accordance with the unique cultures of Aboriginal peoples in Canada.[12]

Both UNDRIP and the TRC report underscore the importance of integrating Indigenous legal traditions into new approaches to dealing with access to justice problems. Education and funding will also be key elements. Some of the steps already taken to improve access to justice for Indigenous peoples include:

- *the use of Indigenous courts*—as discussed in Chapter 10 under "Criminal Courts," Indigenous courts can improve outcomes for Indigenous offenders;

---

12 *Canada's Residential Schools: Reconciliation—The Final Report of the Truth and Reconciliation Commission of Canada* (Montreal and Kingston: McGill-Queen's University Press, 2015) vol 6 at 231, online: <http://www.trc.ca/assets/pdf/Volume_6_Reconciliation_English_Web.pdf>.

BOX 12.2

What Kinds of Matters Can an Ombudsperson Help Resolve?

A provincial or territorial ombudsperson may help resolve a range of problems or misunderstandings, subject to certain exceptions. Ombudspersons oversee provincial or territorial ministries; Crown corporations; and administrative tribunals, agencies, boards, and commissions—for example, in Ontario, the Ministry of Indigenous Affairs, the Ministry of the Attorney General, the Ministry of the Solicitor General, the Liquor Control Board of Ontario, and the Ministry of Government and Consumer Services. They may deal with thousands of complaints each year. Ombudspersons *cannot* investigate matters between individuals and private companies, individuals and other individuals (for example, judges, doctors, or lawyers), or individuals and the federal government.

The case summaries below illustrate just a few of the many situations an ombudsperson may help resolve.

BC Ombudsperson Case Summary
Jolene, Jolene

Having carefully inputted all the information online, Jolene was surprised to see her daughter's birth certificate arrive with a glaring error: "Jolene" was repeated twice as the mother's name.

When Jolene contacted Vital Statistics to correct the error, she was told to pay the $71 fee for the correction of online registration user errors. Jolene grudgingly paid the fee and happily received a correct birth certificate for her newborn.

Still, Jolene did not like paying for someone else's mistake and wanted a refund. Vital Statistics declined to investigate or refund the fee. Unhappy with this response, Jolene came to us.

We agreed to investigate, concerned that Vital Statistics might have dismissed Jolene's request for a refund without first taking reasonable steps to identify the source of the error on her daughter's birth certificate.

Vital Statistics' electronic files showed that the mistake was indeed not Jolene's fault. Because of our investigation, Vital Statistics agreed to amend its internal procedures. Now, when a customer calls about an error on their baby's birth

certificate, Vital Statistics will review the customer's file to determine the cause—before deciding whether to request a fee. Vital Statistics also agreed to provide a refund to Jolene and a letter of apology.[*]

Ontario Ombudsperson Case Summaries
Hits the Spot

When a woman hit a pothole on a county road that damaged her vehicle, she tried to seek reimbursement. The county told her it was the Ministry of Transportation's jurisdiction, but the Ministry told her the opposite. After our staff contacted both levels of government, Ministry officials determined it was indeed in their jurisdiction, and the woman was compensated the more than $1,100 it cost to repair her vehicle.[†]

Just Missed the Mark

A mother of three who was enrolled in a combined college and university nursing program was not allowed to progress to the university portion of the program because her grade in a college course was 1.5 percent below the required threshold. She appealed the mark but complained to us that the college's appeal decision did not address an in-course evaluation that had a major impact on her grade. Our Office referred her to the college's ombudsman, who was able to help her get a new evaluation by a different professor. This resulted in a high enough grade to allow her to enrol in the university portion of the program.[‡]

---

[*]   "Jolene, Jolene" (2015), online: *Office of the Ombudsperson, Province of British Columbia* <https://bcombudsperson.ca/case_summary/jolene-jolene>.

[†]   "Hits the Spot" (26 June 2018), online: *Ombudsman Ontario* <https://www.ombudsman.on.ca/resources/reports-and-case-summaries/selected-cases/2018/hits-the-spot>.

[‡]   "Just Missed the Mark" (26 June 2018), online: *Ombudsman Ontario* <https://www.ombudsman.on.ca/resources/reports-and-case-summaries/selected-cases/2018/just-missed-the-mark-en>.

- *the establishment of the federal Indigenous Justice Program*—this program "supports Indigenous community-based justice programs that offer alternatives to mainstream justice processes in appropriate circumstances" and is designed to help Indigenous communities assume greater responsibility for "the administration of justice in their communities; to reflect and include Indigenous values within the justice system; and, to contribute to a decrease in the rate of victimization, crime and incarceration among Indigenous people in communities … ."[13]
- *the Attorney General of Canada's Directive on Civil Litigation Involving Indigenous Peoples*—the central objective of this directive is to promote negotiation and settlement in connection with civil litigation regarding section 35 of the *Constitution Act, 1982;*[14] and
- *the transfer or devolution of power by way of self-government agreements*—for example, the 2019 agreements between the federal government and Métis Nations in Alberta, Ontario, and Saskatchewan include the recognition of Métis jurisdiction in such areas as citizenship, leadership selection, and government operations and provide a framework for further negotiations to promote reconciliation (see also Chapter 2 under "Canadian Law and Indigenous Peoples: A Timeline").

Reaching a long-term and satisfactory solution to Indigenous access-to-justice issues will no doubt take some time and involve an array of measures. Besides the steps just mentioned, other measures could range from the creation of adequately supported and funded Indigenous legal aid programs to changing the system of regulation under the *Indian Act*[15] (including the structure of band governance).

Law Reform

Both the federal and provincial governments, as well as citizens working alone or in organized groups, can try to change laws. Law reform may be initiated by law reform commissions, public inquiries, political demonstrations, lobbying by national organizations, or public interest groups appearing as interveners before the SCC.

Law Reform Commissions

Law reform commissions are independent bodies set up by either the provincial or the federal government to study selected areas of law and recommend ways to improve, modernize, and reform them. Members of the commission publish reports recommending how

---

13   See "Indigenous Justice Program," online: *Department of Justice Canada* <https://www.justice.gc.ca/eng/fund-fina/acf-fca/ajs-sja/index.html>.

14   See "The Attorney General of Canada's Directive on Civil Litigation Involving Indigenous Peoples," online: *Department of Justice Canada* <https://www.justice.gc.ca/eng/csj-sjc/ijr-dja/dclip-dlcpa/litigation-litiges.html>. This directive is detailed and sets out 20 litigation guidelines that government counsel must follow when involved in Indigenous litigation. Included in the guidelines is a mandate to consider Indigenous legal traditions or other traditional Indigenous approaches when pursuing a resolution to civil disputes.

15   RSC 1985, c I-5.

laws in that area could be improved. (Martin Friedland's 1975 report on access to justice, mentioned above, was one of these reports.) Although the government is not bound to accept and implement all (or any) of the commission's recommendations, its reports are considered important contributions to legal scholarship and can be cited in courts.

The Law Reform Commission of Canada, which existed from 1971 to 1993 and again from 1997 to 2006 (as the Law Commission of Canada), was set up to make recommendations regarding areas of law under federal jurisdiction—for example, criminal law and criminal procedure. It also considered bijural aspects regarding our law, which, as we have seen, use both the common law and civil law legal systems.

At the provincial level, most of Canada's provinces have established provincial law reform commissions at one time or another (although most have now ceased operation as a result of funding cuts). Law reform commissions recommend measures to improve and reform laws under provincial jurisdiction, such as the administration of justice in a province. They generally operate with a small number of lawyers, academics, and judges on their board of governors and utilize research staff to conduct research into areas considered in need of reform. This scholarly analysis of the law found in background and discussion papers, and in final reports published by commissions, provides an excellent source of well-researched information about many areas of law.

Canada-wide, the Federation of Law Reform Agencies of Canada is also involved in promoting cooperation between Canada's law reform agencies on the broad topic of law reform. As well, the Uniform Law Conference of Canada, in existence since 1918, works to improve harmony between laws of the provinces and territories across Canada.

Public Inquiries

Public inquiries into matters of national and public concern, formerly known as royal commissions, have played an important role in the development of law and policy in Canada. They may be tasked with finding facts and reporting on those facts, with making recommendations aimed at developing public policy, or with a combination of these two functions.[16] Either the federal government or a provincial government may call an inquiry; legislation provides the executive with the authority to appoint a commission and provides the commission with the authority it needs to carry out its mandate.[17]

Fact-finding inquiries (and inquiries that combine fact-finding and policy recommendations) are often established in response to an event, such as a high-profile scandal or a tragedy, that negatively affects the public's trust in or perception of public institutions—for example, miscarriages of justice such as wrongful convictions, suspicious deaths in hospitals, and tainted water scandals. The goal of such inquiries is often to address failings and restore the public's confidence in the system. High-profile inquiries include the Air India Inquiry into the terrorist bombing of Air India Flight 182, the Braidwood inquiry into the tasering death of Robert Dziekański, and the Missing Women Commission of Inquiry into the disappearance of women from Vancouver's Downtown Eastside.

Inquiries with a focus on policy analyze issues and make recommendations for policies in the future. For example, an inquiry conducted by Justice Emmett Hall in the 1960s was

---

16   Hon Associate Chief Justice Dennis R O'Connor & Freya Kristjanson, "Some Observations on Public Inquiries" (Canadian Institute for the Administration of Justice, Annual Conference, 10 October 2007, Halifax), online: <https://www.ontariocourts.ca/coa/en/ps/speeches/publicinquiries.htm>.

17   The federal legislation is the *Inquiries Act*, RSC 1985, c I-11; an example of provincial legislation is Ontario's *Public Inquiries Act, 2009*, SO 2009, c 33, Schedule 6.

instrumental in the creation of the national Medicare system, and the *Official Languages Act*[18]—which was passed in 1969 and declares French and English to be the official languages of Canada and requires all federal institutions to provide their services in both languages—was one of the most important legacies of the Royal Commission on Bilingualism and Biculturalism.

Political Demonstrations

People upset with a particular government law or policy and who also want laws reformed have traditionally participated in public protest marches and political demonstrations, which might end up before a city hall, before a provincial legislature, or on Parliament Hill in Ottawa. The widespread use of social media today has made it easier for people to organize and coordinate such events. The problem with demonstrations as a political tactic is that not all Canadians support them, and they can also attract negative publicity depending on the tactics used. Another disadvantage is that they tend to be one-off events, with momentum and publicity often subsiding at their conclusion. As well, the government may not support the change requested.

Protests can be effective, however. The recent Wet'suwet'en pipeline protests in 2019–20 (see Chapter 2 under "New Directions for Indigenous Law in Canada") and the protests against racism in 2020 (see Box 10.3 in Chapter 10) went beyond the "local" incidents that started them and took on national and international dimensions. Both had widespread public support and resulted in government action.[19] The Wet'suwet'en protests, which temporarily halted portions of the Canadian economy, led to a framework agreement on a land claims dispute that had languished for nearly 25 years. In Canada, the racism protests led to commitments by governments and police forces to make changes to end systemic racism.

National Organizations and Lobbying

Many professional and occupational groups across Canada have established national organizations that meet annually to discuss issues important to their members. Examples of such national organizations are:

- the Canadian Bar Association,
- the Assembly of First Nations, and
- the Canadian Labour Congress.

These associations also try to influence governments to introduce law reforms or policies that favour their group's interests. Many of these national organizations have full-time staff and offices in provincial capitals or in Ottawa. They submit briefs to the government and meet with members of Parliament and with key bureaucrats in the civil service to further their association's goals. Many also seek to influence government action by **lobbying**. Lobbying is an organized effort to influence legislators and bureaucrats with respect to laws and government policies. For example, lobbying can be done to obtain material benefits

lobbying
organized effort to influence legislators on behalf of a particular interest

---

18 RSC 1985, c 31 (4th Supp).

19 The world in 2020 was in the midst of the COVID-19 pandemic, and Canadian governments (along with governments in other countries) were responding on a massive scale to the economic fallout, including widespread unemployment. This may have contributed to a willingness to respond more effectively to these protests, as part of structural change that was more wide-ranging.

from the government, such as favourable tax breaks, research grants, subsidies, or government supply contracts. Lobbying may not result in as high a public profile as demonstrating in the streets. It is perhaps more effective, however; lobby groups can retain a law firm or the services of skilled public relations professionals and former politicians who have direct knowledge of the political process and previous familiarity with the legislators.[20]

Public Interest Groups as Interveners

intervener
party, other than the original parties to a court proceeding, who does not have a substantial and direct interest in the proceeding but has interests and perspectives helpful to the judicial determination and whose input is accepted by the court

Another way public interest groups can try to influence and change Canadian law or government policy is to participate as **interveners** in cases before the SCC[21] (see also Chapter 5). If granted intervener status, which is given at the court's discretion, an interest group may be entitled to give further evidence to supplement the record or be authorized to present an oral argument at the hearing.[22] They have to demonstrate sufficient interest in the court case, have submissions that are useful and different from the other parties' submissions, and be a credible organization. Examples of public interest groups that have participated as interveners in this way are LEAF (the Women's Legal Education and Action Fund) and the Canadian Civil Liberties Association. The SCC is now increasingly receptive to hearing from public interest interveners; the judges on the Court realize that many matters facing them are complex and that their decisions will have far-reaching implications for Canadian law. An interest group may influence the Court to take a broader perspective on a matter under consideration and increase its awareness of the issues, or change, it is intervening to support.

---

20 Rand Dyck, *Canadian Politics: Critical Approaches* (Toronto: Nelson, 2012) at 425; Keith Archer et al, *Parameters of Power: Canada's Political Institutions*, 3rd ed (Toronto: Nelson, 2002).

21 See Sharon Lavine, "Advocating Values: Public Interest Intervention in Charter Litigation" (1993) 2 NJCL 27; Ian Brodie, *Friends of the Court: The Privileging of Interest Group Litigants in Canada* (Albany, NY: State University of New York Press, 2002).

22 Under the Rules of the Supreme Court of Canada (SOR/2002-156), a Motion for Intervention is rule 55. Adding, Substituting and Removing Parties is rule 18. See also Ian Brodie, "Lobbying the Supreme Court" in H Mellon & M Westmacott, eds, *Political Dispute and Judicial Review: Assessing the Work of the Supreme Court of Canada* (Toronto: Nelson, 2000) at 195.

CHAPTER SUMMARY

The issue of access to justice has become increasingly important to Canadians as court costs rise, court delays increase, and court processes challenge many low- and middle-income Canadians. A key problem is the affordability of legal services; legal aid plans, pro bono services, and the increased use of paralegals are some of the ways in which the public can overcome cost barriers. A multi-faceted reform movement exploring ADR mechanisms, such as mediation and arbitration, is also gaining acceptance. The benefits of these alternative forms of dispute resolution are many. They offer reduced court costs, less time in court, and more personal control over the process. Other benefits of ADR are confidentiality and the opportunity for the parties to craft solutions they feel are best suited to their disputes.

Canadian law has changed over time in response to broad shifts in our society. As a result, many people today want or need to access legal information on their own and want this legal information to be understandable. Access to legal materials has improved in recent decades, particularly through online sites. Also, government measures to reduce access-to-justice difficulties have included improving court processes, creating public advocacy offices, and improving access to justice for Indigenous peoples.

Concerning specific initiatives to reform the law, law reform commissions and institutes have researched various areas of the law and made recommendations for improvement (and some of these recommendations have been implemented through legislative change). Sometimes individual Canadians try to change the law on their own, whereas others pursue collective action. Such action can take a variety of forms, including political demonstrations, national organizations, lobbying, and applying to participate as interveners in court cases.

KEY TERMS

alternative dispute resolution (ADR), 336

arbitration, 337

intervener, 346

legal aid, 333

lobbying, 345

mediation, 336

negotiation, 336

pro bono, 334

FURTHER READING

BOOKS

Brodie, Ian, *Friends of the Court: The Privileging of Interest Group Litigants in Canada* (Albany, NY: State University of New York, 2002).

Hanycz, Colleen M, Trevor CW Farrow & Frederick H Zemans, *The Theory and Practice of Representative Negotiation* (Toronto: Emond Montgomery, 2008).

Jhappen, Radha ed, *Women's Legal Strategies in Canada* (Toronto: University of Toronto Press, 2002).

Rowat, Donald Cameron ed, *The Making of the Federal Access Act: A Case Study of Policy-Making in Canada* (Ottawa: Carleton University, 1985).

Trebilcock, Michael, Anthony J Duggan & Lorne Sossin, *Middle Income Access to Justice* (Toronto: University of Toronto Press, 2012).

Young, Margot et al, eds, *Poverty: Rights, Social Citizenship, and Legal Activism* (Vancouver: University of British Columbia Press, 2007).

Zubick, Jennifer & Samantha Callow, *ADR for Legal Professionals* (Toronto: Emond, 2017).

JOURNALS AND ARTICLES

Morton, FL & Avril Allen, "Feminists and the Courts: Measuring Success in Interest Group Litigation in Canada" (2001) 34 Can J Poli Sci 55.

Windsor Yearbook of Access to Justice (Windsor, Ont: University of Windsor Faculty of Law), online: <https://www.uwindsor.ca/law/wyaj>.

REVIEW QUESTIONS

1. How do legal aid plans help lower-income people in need of legal services? List three main ways.

2. List three measures that lawyers in Canada have taken to increase access to justice for disadvantaged Canadians.

3. List five common criticisms of the traditional court process of resolving disputes.

4. What is the main difference between negotiation and mediation?

5. How does arbitration differ from mediation?

6. When two parties are using arbitration to resolve their disputes, what can they decide beforehand regarding the arbitrator's decision?

7. What four measures did Martin Friedland propose for improving Canadians' access to legal information?

8. List three measures the government has taken to increase the Canadian public's access to justice.

EXERCISES

1. Do you think enough is being done in this country to increase access to justice for lower-income and disadvantaged Canadians? Explain. Suggest another measure that you think might be introduced.

2. Look up the legal term *in forma pauperis*. Would the Canadian legal system be improved by lawyers adopting this concept? Why or why not?

3. Using the Internet, look up the website for the Canadian Federation of Students. List and discuss ways that this association tries to help post-secondary students.

4. Describe the qualities you think a good mediator would possess. Give reasons for your choices.

Appendixes

APPENDIX A Constitution Act, 1867

APPENDIX B Constitution Act, 1982

Note: To view the complete versions of the *Constitution Act, 1867* and the *Constitution Act, 1982*, with full explanatory footnotes, visit the "For Students" tab at <https://emond.ca/ILC2.html>.

A Constitution Act, 1867

30 & 31 Victoria, c 3 (UK)

TABLE OF CONTENTS

1	I. PRELIMINARY	96	VII. JUDICATURE
3	II. UNION	102	VIII. REVENUES; DEBTS; ASSETS; TAXATION
9	III. EXECUTIVE POWER	127	IX. MISCELLANEOUS PROVISIONS
17	IV. LEGISLATIVE POWER	127	General
21	The Senate	134	Ontario and Quebec
37	The House of Commons	145	X. INTERCOLONIAL RAILWAY
53	Money Votes; Royal Assent	146	XI. ADMISSION OF OTHER COLONIES
58	V. PROVINCIAL CONSTITUTIONS		THE FIRST SCHEDULE
58	Executive Power		THE SECOND SCHEDULE
69	Legislative Power		THE THIRD SCHEDULE
69	1. Ontario		THE FOURTH SCHEDULE
71	2. Quebec		THE FIFTH SCHEDULE
81	3. Ontario and Quebec		THE SIXTH SCHEDULE
88	4. Nova Scotia and New Brunswick		
89	5. Ontario, Quebec, and Nova Scotia		
90	6. The Four Provinces		
91	VI. DISTRIBUTION OF LEGISLATIVE POWERS		
91	Powers of the Parliament		
92	Exclusive Powers of Provincial Legislatures		
92A	Non-Renewable Natural Resources, Forestry Resources and Electrical Energy		
93	Education		
94	Uniformity of Laws in Ontario, Nova Scotia, and New Brunswick		
94A	Old Age Pensions		
95	Agriculture and Immigration		

An Act for the Union of Canada, Nova Scotia, and New Brunswick, and the Government thereof; and for Purposes connected therewith

(29th March 1867)

WHEREAS the Provinces of Canada, Nova Scotia, and New Brunswick have expressed their Desire to be federally united into One Dominion under the Crown of the United Kingdom of Great Britain and Ireland, with a Constitution similar in Principle to that of the United Kingdom:

And whereas such a Union would conduce to the Welfare of the Provinces and promote the Interests of the British Empire:

And whereas on the Establishment of the Union by Authority of Parliament it is expedient, not only that the Constitution of the Legislative Authority in the Dominion be provided for, but also that the Nature of the Executive Government therein be declared:

And whereas it is expedient that Provision be made for the eventual Admission into the Union of other Parts of British North America:

I. PRELIMINARY

Short title

1. This Act may be cited as the *Constitution Act, 1867*.

2. Repealed.

II. UNION

Declaration of Union

3. It shall be lawful for the Queen, by and with the Advice of Her Majesty's Most Honourable Privy Council, to declare by Proclamation that, on and after a Day therein appointed, not being more than Six Months after the passing of this Act, the Provinces of Canada, Nova Scotia, and New Brunswick shall form and be One Dominion under the Name of Canada; and on and after that Day those Three Provinces shall form and be One Dominion under that Name accordingly.

Construction of subsequent Provisions of Act

4. Unless it is otherwise expressed or implied, the Name Canada shall be taken to mean Canada as constituted under this Act.

Four Provinces

5. Canada shall be divided into Four Provinces, named Ontario, Quebec, Nova Scotia, and New Brunswick.

Provinces of Ontario and Quebec

6. The Parts of the Province of Canada (as it exists at the passing of this Act) which formerly constituted respectively the Provinces of Upper Canada and Lower Canada shall be deemed to be severed, and shall form Two separate Provinces. The Part which formerly constituted the Province of Upper Canada shall constitute the Province of Ontario; and the Part which formerly constituted the Province of Lower Canada shall constitute the Province of Quebec.

Provinces of Nova Scotia and New Brunswick

7. The Provinces of Nova Scotia and New Brunswick shall have the same Limits as at the passing of this Act.

Decennial Census

8. In the general Census of the Population of Canada which is hereby required to be taken in the Year One thousand eight hundred and seventy-one, and in every Tenth Year thereafter, the respective Populations of the Four Provinces shall be distinguished.

III. EXECUTIVE POWER

Declaration of Executive Power in the Queen

9. The Executive Government and Authority of and over Canada is hereby declared to continue and be vested in the Queen.

Application of Provisions referring to Governor General

10. The Provisions of this Act referring to the Governor General extend and apply to the Governor General for the Time being of Canada, or other the Chief Executive Officer or Administrator for the Time being carrying on the Government of Canada on behalf and in the Name of the Queen, by whatever Title he is designated.

Constitution of Privy Council for Canada

11. There shall be a Council to aid and advise in the Government of Canada, to be styled the Queen's Privy Council for Canada; and the Persons who are to be Members of that Council shall be from Time to Time chosen and summoned by the Governor General and sworn in as Privy Councillors, and Members thereof may be from Time to Time removed by the Governor General.

All Powers under Acts to be exercised by Governor General with Advice of Privy Council, or alone

12. All Powers, Authorities, and Functions which under any Act of the Parliament of Great Britain, or of the Parliament of the United Kingdom of Great Britain and Ireland, or of the

Legislature of Upper Canada, Lower Canada, Canada, Nova Scotia, or New Brunswick, are at the Union vested in or exerciseable by the respective Governors or Lieutenant Governors of those Provinces, with the Advice, or with the Advice and Consent, of the respective Executive Councils thereof, or in conjunction with those Councils, or with any Number of Members thereof, or by those Governors or Lieutenant Governors individually, shall, as far as the same continue in existence and capable of being exercised after the Union in relation to the Government of Canada, be vested in and exerciseable by the Governor General, with the Advice or with the Advice and Consent of or in conjunction with the Queen's Privy Council for Canada, or any Members thereof, or by the Governor General individually, as the Case requires, subject nevertheless (except with respect to such as exist under Acts of the Parliament of Great Britain or of the Parliament of the United Kingdom of Great Britain and Ireland) to be abolished or altered by the Parliament of Canada.

Application of Provisions referring to Governor General in Council

13. The Provisions of this Act referring to the Governor General in Council shall be construed as referring to the Governor General acting by and with the Advice of the Queen's Privy Council for Canada.

Power to Her Majesty to authorize Governor General to appoint Deputies

14. It shall be lawful for the Queen, if Her Majesty thinks fit, to authorize the Governor General from Time to Time to appoint any Person or any Persons jointly or severally to be his Deputy or Deputies within any Part or Parts of Canada, and in that Capacity to exercise during the Pleasure of the Governor General such of the Powers, Authorities, and Functions of the Governor General as the Governor General deems it necessary or expedient to assign to him or them, subject to any Limitations or Directions expressed or given by the Queen; but the Appointment of such a Deputy or Deputies shall not affect the Exercise by the Governor General himself of any Power, Authority, or Function.

Command of Armed Forces to continue to be vested in the Queen

15. The Command-in-Chief of the Land and Naval Militia, and of all Naval and Military Forces, of and in Canada, is hereby declared to continue and be vested in the Queen.

Seat of Government of Canada

16. Until the Queen otherwise directs, the Seat of Government of Canada shall be Ottawa.

IV. LEGISLATIVE POWER

Constitution of Parliament of Canada

17. There shall be One Parliament for Canada, consisting of the Queen, an Upper House styled the Senate, and the House of Commons.

Privileges, etc., of Houses

18. The privileges, immunities, and powers to be held, enjoyed, and exercised by the Senate and by the House of Commons, and by the members thereof respectively, shall be such as are from time to time defined by Act of the Parliament of Canada, but so that any Act of the Parliament of Canada defining such privileges, immunities, and powers shall not confer any privileges, immunities, or powers exceeding those at the passing of such Act held, enjoyed, and exercised by the Commons House of Parliament of the United Kingdom of Great Britain and Ireland, and by the members thereof.

First Session of the Parliament of Canada

19. The Parliament of Canada shall be called together not later than Six Months after the Union.

20. Repealed.

THE SENATE

Number of Senators

21. The Senate shall, subject to the Provisions of this Act, consist of One Hundred and five Members, who shall be styled Senators.

Representation of Provinces in Senate

22. In relation to the Constitution of the Senate Canada shall be deemed to consist of Four Divisions:

1. Ontario;
2. Quebec;
3. The Maritime Provinces, Nova Scotia and New Brunswick, and Prince Edward Island;
4. The Western Provinces of Manitoba, British Columbia, Saskatchewan, and Alberta;

which Four Divisions shall (subject to the Provisions of this Act) be equally represented in the Senate as follows: Ontario by twenty-four senators; Quebec by twenty-four senators; the Maritime Provinces and Prince Edward Island by twenty-four senators, ten thereof representing Nova Scotia, ten thereof representing New Brunswick, and four thereof representing Prince Edward Island; the Western Provinces by twenty-four senators, six thereof representing Manitoba, six thereof representing British Columbia, six thereof representing Saskatchewan, and six thereof representing Alberta; Newfoundland shall be entitled to be represented in the Senate by six members; the Yukon Territory, the Northwest Territories and Nunavut shall be entitled to be represented in the Senate by one member each.

In the Case of Quebec each of the Twenty-four Senators representing that Province shall be appointed for One of the Twenty-four Electoral Divisions of Lower Canada specified in Schedule A. to Chapter One of the Consolidated Statutes of Canada.

Qualifications of Senator

23. The Qualifications of a Senator shall be as follows:

(1) He shall be of the full age of Thirty Years;

(2) He shall be either a natural-born Subject of the Queen, or a Subject of the Queen naturalized by an Act of the Parliament of Great Britain, or of the Parliament of the United Kingdom of Great Britain and Ireland, or of the Legislature of One of the Provinces of Upper Canada, Lower Canada, Canada, Nova Scotia, or New Brunswick, before the Union, or of the Parliament of Canada after the Union;

(3) He shall be legally or equitably seised as of Freehold for his own Use and Benefit of Lands or Tenements held in Free and Common Socage, or seised or possessed for his own Use and Benefit of Lands or Tenements held in Franc-alleu or in Roture, within the Province for which he is appointed, of the Value of Four thousand Dollars, over and above all Rents, Dues, Debts, Charges, Mortgages, and Incumbrances due or payable out of or charged on or affecting the same;

(4) His Real and Personal Property shall be together worth Four thousand Dollars over and above his Debts and Liabilities;

(5) He shall be resident in the Province for which he is appointed;

(6) In the Case of Quebec he shall have his Real Property Qualification in the Electoral Division for which he is appointed, or shall be resident in that Division.

Summons of Senator

24. The Governor General shall from Time to Time, in the Queen's Name, by Instrument under the Great Seal of Canada, summon qualified Persons to the Senate; and, subject to the Provisions of this Act, every Person so summoned shall become and be a Member of the Senate and a Senator.

25. Repealed.

Addition of Senators in certain cases

26. If at any Time on the Recommendation of the Governor General the Queen thinks fit to direct that Four or Eight Members be added to the Senate, the Governor General may by Summons to Four or Eight qualified Persons (as the Case may be), representing equally the Four Divisions of Canada, add to the Senate accordingly.

Reduction of Senate to normal Number

27. In case of such Addition being at any Time made, the Governor General shall not summon any Person to the Senate, except on a further like Direction by the Queen on the like Recommendation, to represent one of the Four Divisions until such Division is represented by Twenty-four Senators and no more.

Maximum Number of Senators

28. The Number of Senators shall not at any Time exceed One Hundred and thirteen.

Tenure of Place in Senate

29(1) Subject to subsection (2), a Senator shall, subject to the provisions of this Act, hold his place in the Senate for life.

Retirement upon attaining age of seventy-five years

(2) A Senator who is summoned to the Senate after the coming into force of this subsection shall, subject to this Act, hold his place in the Senate until he attains the age of seventy-five years.

[Sections 30–36 omitted.]

THE HOUSE OF COMMONS

Constitution of House of Commons in Canada

37. The House of Commons shall, subject to the Provisions of this Act, consist of three hundred and eight members of whom one hundred and six shall be elected for Ontario, seventy-five for Quebec, eleven for Nova Scotia, ten for New Brunswick, fourteen for Manitoba, thirty-six for British Columbia, four for Prince Edward Island, twenty-eight for Alberta, fourteen for Saskatchewan, seven for Newfoundland, one for the Yukon Territory, one for the Northwest Territories and one for Nunavut.

Summoning of House of Commons

38. The Governor General shall from Time to Time, in the Queen's Name, by Instrument under the Great Seal of Canada, summon and call together the House of Commons.

Senators not to sit in House of Commons

39. A Senator shall not be capable of being elected or of sitting or voting as a Member of the House of Commons.

[Sections 40–49 omitted.]

Duration of House of Commons

50. Every House of Commons shall continue for Five Years from the Day of the Return of the Writs for choosing the House (subject to be sooner dissolved by the Governor General), and no longer.

[Section 51 omitted.]

Constitution of House of Commons

51A. Notwithstanding anything in this Act a province shall always be entitled to a number of members in the House of Commons not less than the number of senators representing such province.

Increase of Number of House of Commons

52. The Number of Members of the House of Commons may be from Time to Time increased by the Parliament of Canada, provided the proportionate Representation of the Provinces prescribed by this Act is not thereby disturbed.

MONEY VOTES; ROYAL ASSENT

Appropriation and Tax Bills

53. Bills for appropriating any Part of the Public Revenue, or for imposing any Tax or Impost, shall originate in the House of Commons.

Recommendation of Money Votes

54. It shall not be lawful for the House of Commons to adopt or pass any Vote, Resolution, Address, or Bill for the Appropriation of any Part of the Public Revenue, or of any Tax or Impost, to any Purpose that has not been first recommended to that House by Message of the Governor General in the Session in which such Vote, Resolution, Address, or Bill is proposed.

Royal Assent to Bills, etc.

55. Where a Bill passed by the Houses of the Parliament is presented to the Governor General for the Queen's Assent, he shall declare, according to his Discretion, but subject to the Provisions of this Act and to Her Majesty's Instructions, either that he assents thereto in the Queen's Name, or that he withholds the Queen's Assent, or that he reserves the Bill for the Signification of the Queen's Pleasure.

Disallowance by Order in Council of Act assented to by Governor General

56. Where the Governor General assents to a Bill in the Queen's Name, he shall by the first convenient Opportunity send an authentic Copy of the Act to One of Her Majesty's Principal Secretaries of State, and if the Queen in Council within Two Years after Receipt thereof by the Secretary of State thinks fit to disallow the Act, such Disallowance (with a Certificate of the Secretary of State of the Day on which the Act was received by him) being signified by the Governor General, by Speech or Message to each of the Houses of the Parliament or by Proclamation, shall annul the Act from and after the Day of such Signification.

Signification of Queen's Pleasure on Bill reserved

57. A Bill reserved for the Signification of the Queen's Pleasure shall not have any Force unless and until, within Two Years from the Day on which it was presented to the Governor General for the Queen's Assent, the Governor General signifies, by Speech or Message to each of the Houses of the Parliament or by Proclamation, that it has received the Assent of the Queen in Council.

An Entry of every such Speech, Message, or Proclamation shall be made in the Journal of each House, and a Duplicate thereof duly attested shall be delivered to the proper Officer to be kept among the Records of Canada.

V. PROVINCIAL CONSTITUTIONS

EXECUTIVE POWER

Appointment of Lieutenant Governors of Provinces

58. For each Province there shall be an Officer, styled the Lieutenant Governor, appointed by the Governor General in Council by Instrument under the Great Seal of Canada.

Tenure of Office of Lieutenant Governor

59. A Lieutenant Governor shall hold Office during the Pleasure of the Governor General; but any Lieutenant Governor appointed after the Commencement of the First Session of the Parliament of Canada shall not be removeable within Five Years from his Appointment, except for Cause assigned, which shall be communicated to him in Writing within One Month after the Order for his Removal is made, and shall be communicated by Message to the Senate and to the House of Commons within One Week thereafter if the Parliament is then sitting, and if not then within One Week after the Commencement of the next Session of the Parliament.

Salaries of Lieutenant Governors

60. The Salaries of the Lieutenant Governors shall be fixed and provided by the Parliament of Canada.

Oaths, etc., of Lieutenant Governor

61. Every Lieutenant Governor shall, before assuming the Duties of his Office, make and subscribe before the Governor General or some Person authorized by him Oaths of Allegiance and Office similar to those taken by the Governor General.

Application of Provisions referring to Lieutenant Governor

62. The Provisions of this Act referring to the Lieutenant Governor extend and apply to the Lieutenant Governor for the Time being of each Province, or other the Chief Executive Officer or Administrator for the Time being carrying on the Government of the Province, by whatever Title he is designated.

Appointment of Executive Officers for Ontario and Quebec

63. The Executive Council of Ontario and of Quebec shall be composed of such Persons as the Lieutenant Governor from Time to Time thinks fit, and in the first instance of the following Officers, namely,—the Attorney General, the Secretary and Registrar of the Province, the Treasurer of the Province, the Commissioner of Crown Lands, and the Commissioner of Agriculture and Public Works, with in Quebec the Speaker of the Legislative Council and the Solicitor General.

Executive Government of Nova Scotia and New Brunswick

64. The Constitution of the Executive Authority in each of the Provinces of Nova Scotia and New Brunswick shall, subject to the Provisions of this Act, continue as it exists at the Union until altered under the Authority of this Act.

Powers to be exercised by Lieutenant Governor of Ontario or Quebec with Advice, or alone

65. All Powers, Authorities, and Functions which under any Act of the Parliament of Great Britain, or of the Parliament of the United Kingdom of Great Britain and Ireland, or of the Legislature of Upper Canada, Lower Canada, or Canada, were or are before or at the Union vested in or exerciseable by the respective Governors or Lieutenant Governors of those Provinces, with the Advice or with the Advice and Consent of the respective Executive Councils thereof, or in conjunction with those Councils, or with any Number of Members thereof, or by those Governors or Lieutenant Governors individually, shall, as far as the same are capable of being exercised after the Union in relation to the Government of Ontario and Quebec respectively, be vested in and shall or may be exercised by the Lieutenant Governor of Ontario and Quebec respectively, with the Advice or with the Advice and Consent of or in conjunction with the respective Executive Councils, or any Members thereof, or by the Lieutenant Governor individually, as the Case requires, subject nevertheless (except with respect to such as exist under Acts of the Parliament of Great Britain, or of the Parliament of the United Kingdom of Great Britain and Ireland,) to be abolished or altered by the respective Legislatures of Ontario and Quebec.

Application of Provisions referring to Lieutenant Governor in Council

66. The Provisions of this Act referring to the Lieutenant Governor in Council shall be construed as referring to the Lieutenant Governor of the Province acting by and with the Advice of the Executive Council thereof.

Administration in Absence, etc., of Lieutenant Governor

67. The Governor General in Council may from Time to Time appoint an Administrator to execute the Office and Functions of Lieutenant Governor during his Absence, Illness, or other Inability.

Seats of Provincial Governments

68. Unless and until the Executive Government of any Province otherwise directs with respect to that Province, the Seats of Government of the Provinces shall be as follows, namely,—of Ontario, the City of Toronto; of Quebec, the City of Quebec; of Nova Scotia, the City of Halifax; and of New Brunswick, the City of Fredericton.

LEGISLATIVE POWER

1. Ontario

Legislature for Ontario

69. There shall be a Legislature for Ontario consisting of the Lieutenant Governor and of One House, styled the Legislative Assembly of Ontario.

[Section 70 omitted.]

2. Quebec

Legislature for Quebec

71. There shall be a Legislature for Quebec consisting of the Lieutenant Governor and of Two Houses, styled the Legislative Council of Quebec and the Legislative Assembly of Quebec.

[Sections 72–80 omitted.]

3. Ontario and Quebec

[Sections 81–85 omitted.]

Yearly Session of Legislature

86. There shall be a Session of the Legislature of Ontario and of that of Quebec once at least in every Year, so that Twelve Months shall not intervene between the last Sitting of the Legislature in each Province in one Session and its first Sitting in the next Session.

[Section 87 omitted.]

4. Nova Scotia and New Brunswick

Constitutions of Legislatures of Nova Scotia and New Brunswick

88. The Constitution of the Legislature of each of the Provinces of Nova Scotia and New Brunswick shall, subject to the Provisions of this Act, continue as it exists at the Union until altered under the Authority of this Act.

5. Ontario, Quebec, and Nova Scotia

89. Repealed.

6. The Four Provinces

Application to Legislatures of Provisions respecting Money Votes, etc.

90. The following Provisions of this Act respecting the Parliament of Canada, namely,—the Provisions relating to Appropriation and Tax Bills, the Recommendation of Money Votes, the Assent to Bills, the Disallowance of Acts, and the Signification of Pleasure on Bills reserved,—shall extend and apply to the Legislatures of the several Provinces as if those Provisions were here re-enacted and made applicable in Terms to the respective Provinces and the Legislatures thereof, with the Substitution of the Lieutenant Governor of the Province for the Governor General, of the Governor General for the Queen and for a Secretary of State, of One Year for Two Years, and of the Province for Canada.

VI. DISTRIBUTION OF LEGISLATIVE POWERS

POWERS OF THE PARLIAMENT

Legislative Authority of Parliament of Canada

91. It shall be lawful for the Queen, by and with the Advice and Consent of the Senate and House of Commons, to make Laws for the Peace, Order, and good Government of Canada, in relation to all Matters not coming within the Classes of Subjects by this Act assigned exclusively to the Legislatures of the Provinces; and for greater Certainty, but not so as to restrict the Generality of the foregoing Terms of this Section, it is hereby declared that (notwithstanding anything in this Act) the exclusive Legislative Authority of the Parliament of Canada extends to all Matters coming within the Classes of Subjects next hereinafter enumerated; that is to say,

1. Repealed.
1A. The Public Debt and Property.
2. The Regulation of Trade and Commerce.
2A. Unemployment insurance.
3. The raising of Money by any Mode or System of Taxation.
4. The borrowing of Money on the Public Credit.
5. Postal Service.
6. The Census and Statistics.
7. Militia, Military and Naval Service, and Defence.
8. The fixing of and providing for the Salaries and Allowances of Civil and other Officers of the Government of Canada.
9. Beacons, Buoys, Lighthouses, and Sable Island.
10. Navigation and Shipping.
11. Quarantine and the Establishment and Maintenance of Marine Hospitals.
12. Sea Coast and Inland Fisheries.
13. Ferries between a Province and any British or Foreign Country or between Two Provinces.
14. Currency and Coinage.
15. Banking, Incorporation of Banks, and the Issue of Paper Money.
16. Savings Banks.
17. Weights and Measures.
18. Bills of Exchange and Promissory Notes.
19. Interest.
20. Legal Tender.
21. Bankruptcy and Insolvency.
22. Patents of Invention and Discovery.
23. Copyrights.
24. Indians, and Lands reserved for the Indians.
25. Naturalization and Aliens.
26. Marriage and Divorce.

27. The Criminal Law, except the Constitution of Courts of Criminal Jurisdiction, but including the Procedure in Criminal Matters.

28. The Establishment, Maintenance, and Management of Penitentiaries.

29. Such Classes of Subjects as are expressly excepted in the Enumeration of the Classes of Subjects by this Act assigned exclusively to the Legislatures of the Provinces.

And any Matter coming within any of the Classes of Subjects enumerated in this Section shall not be deemed to come within the Class of Matters of a local or private Nature comprised in the Enumeration of the Classes of Subjects by this Act assigned exclusively to the Legislatures of the Provinces.

EXCLUSIVE POWERS OF PROVINCIAL LEGISLATURES

Subjects of exclusive Provincial Legislation

92. In each Province the Legislature may exclusively make Laws in relation to Matters coming within the Classes of Subjects next hereinafter enumerated; that is to say,

1. Repealed.

2. Direct Taxation within the Province in order to the raising of a Revenue for Provincial Purposes.

3. The borrowing of Money on the sole Credit of the Province.

4. The Establishment and Tenure of Provincial Offices and the Appointment and Payment of Provincial Officers.

5. The Management and Sale of the Public Lands belonging to the Province and of the Timber and Wood thereon.

6. The Establishment, Maintenance, and Management of Public and Reformatory Prisons in and for the Province.

7. The Establishment, Maintenance, and Management of Hospitals, Asylums, Charities, and Eleemosynary Institutions in and for the Province, other than Marine Hospitals.

8. Municipal Institutions in the Province.

9. Shop, Saloon, Tavern, Auctioneer, and other Licences in order to the raising of a Revenue for Provincial, Local, or Municipal Purposes.

10. Local Works and Undertakings other than such as are of the following Classes:
    (a) Lines of Steam or other Ships, Railways, Canals, Telegraphs, and other Works and Undertakings connecting the Province with any other or others of the Provinces, or extending beyond the Limits of the Province:
    (b) Lines of Steam Ships between the Province and any British or Foreign Country:
    (c) Such Works as, although wholly situate within the Province, are before or after their Execution declared by the Parliament of Canada to be for the general Advantage of Canada or for the Advantage of Two or more of the Provinces.

11. The Incorporation of Companies with Provincial Objects.

12. The Solemnization of Marriage in the Province.

13. Property and Civil Rights in the Province.

14. The Administration of Justice in the Province, including the Constitution, Maintenance, and Organization of Provincial Courts, both of Civil and of Criminal Jurisdiction, and including Procedure in Civil Matters in those Courts.

15. The Imposition of Punishment by Fine, Penalty, or Imprisonment for enforcing any Law of the Province made in relation to any Matter coming within any of the Classes of Subjects enumerated in this Section.

16. Generally all Matters of a merely local or private Nature in the Province.

NON-RENEWABLE NATURAL RESOURCES, FORESTRY RESOURCES AND ELECTRICAL ENERGY

Laws respecting non-renewable natural resources, forestry resources and electrical energy

92A(1) In each province, the legislature may exclusively make laws in relation to

(a) exploration for non-renewable natural resources in the province;

(b) development, conservation and management of non-renewable natural resources and forestry resources in the province, including laws in relation to the rate of primary production therefrom; and

(c) development, conservation and management of sites and facilities in the province for the generation and production of electrical energy.

Export from provinces of resources

(2) In each province, the legislature may make laws in relation to the export from the province to another part of Canada of the primary production from non-renewable natural resources and forestry resources in the province and the production from facilities in the province for the generation of electrical energy, but such laws may not authorize or provide for discrimination in prices or in supplies exported to another part of Canada.

Authority of Parliament

(3) Nothing in subsection (2) derogates from the authority of Parliament to enact laws in relation to the matters referred to in that subsection and, where such a law of Parliament and a law of a province conflict, the law of Parliament prevails to the extent of the conflict.

Taxation of resources

(4) In each province, the legislature may make laws in relation to the raising of money by any mode or system of taxation in respect of

(*a*) non-renewable natural resources and forestry resources in the province and the primary production therefrom, and

(*b*) sites and facilities in the province for the generation of electrical energy and the production therefrom, whether or not such production is exported in whole or in part from the province, but such laws may not authorize or provide for taxation that differentiates between production exported to another part of Canada and production not exported from the province.

"Primary production"

(5) The expression "primary production" has the meaning assigned by the Sixth Schedule.

Existing powers or rights

(6) Nothing in subsections (1) to (5) derogates from any powers or rights that a legislature or government of a province had immediately before the coming into force of this section.

EDUCATION

Legislation respecting Education

93. In and for each Province the Legislature may exclusively make Laws in relation to Education, subject and according to the following Provisions:

(1) Nothing in any such Law shall prejudicially affect any Right or Privilege with respect to Denominational Schools which any Class of Persons have by Law in the Province at the Union;

(2) All the Powers, Privileges, and Duties at the Union by Law conferred and imposed in Upper Canada on the Separate Schools and School Trustees of the Queen's Roman Catholic Subjects shall be and the same are hereby extended to the Dissentient Schools of the Queen's Protestant and Roman Catholic Subjects in Quebec;

(3) Where in any Province a System of Separate or Dissentient Schools exists by Law at the Union or is thereafter established by the Legislature of the Province, an Appeal shall lie to the Governor General in Council from any Act or Decision of any Provincial Authority affecting any Right or Privilege of the Protestant or Roman Catholic Minority of the Queen's Subjects in relation to Education;

(4) In case any such Provincial Law as from Time to Time seems to the Governor General in Council requisite for the due Execution of the Provisions of this Section is not made, or in case any Decision of the Governor General in Council on any Appeal under this Section is not duly executed by the proper Provincial Authority in that Behalf, then and in every such Case, and as far only as the Circumstances of each Case require, the Parliament of Canada may make remedial Laws for the due Execution of the Provisions of this Section and of any Decision of the Governor General in Council under this Section.

Quebec

93A. Paragraphs (1) to (4) of section 93 do not apply to Quebec.

UNIFORMITY OF LAWS IN ONTARIO, NOVA SCOTIA, AND NEW BRUNSWICK

Legislation for Uniformity of Laws in Three Provinces

94. Notwithstanding anything in this Act, the Parliament of Canada may make Provision for the Uniformity of all or any of the Laws relative to Property and Civil Rights in Ontario, Nova Scotia, and New Brunswick, and of the Procedure of all or any of the Courts in those Three Provinces, and from and after the passing of any Act in that Behalf the Power of the Parliament of Canada to make Laws in relation to any Matter comprised in any such Act shall, notwithstanding anything in this Act, be unrestricted; but any Act of the Parliament of Canada making Provision for such Uniformity shall not have effect in any Province unless and until it is adopted and enacted as Law by the Legislature thereof.

OLD AGE PENSIONS

Legislation respecting old age pensions and supplementary benefits

94A. The Parliament of Canada may make laws in relation to old age pensions and supplementary benefits, including survivors' and disability benefits irrespective of age, but no such law shall affect the operation of any law present or future of a provincial legislature in relation to any such matter.

AGRICULTURE AND IMMIGRATION

Concurrent Powers of Legislation respecting Agriculture, etc.

95. In each Province the Legislature may make Laws in relation to Agriculture in the Province, and to Immigration into the Province; and it is hereby declared that the Parliament of Canada may from Time to Time make Laws in relation to Agriculture in all or any of the Provinces, and to Immigration into all or any of the Provinces; and any Law of the Legislature of a Province relative to Agriculture or to Immigration shall have effect in and for the Province as long and as far only as it is not repugnant to any Act of the Parliament of Canada.

VII. JUDICATURE

Appointment of Judges

96. The Governor General shall appoint the Judges of the Superior, District, and County Courts in each Province, except those of the Courts of Probate in Nova Scotia and New Brunswick.

Selection of Judges in Ontario, etc.

97. Until the Laws relative to Property and Civil Rights in Ontario, Nova Scotia, and New Brunswick, and the Procedure of the Courts in those Provinces, are made uniform, the Judges of the Courts of those Provinces appointed by the Governor General shall be selected from the respective Bars of those Provinces.

Selection of Judges in Quebec

98. The Judges of the Courts of Quebec shall be selected from the Bar of that Province.

Tenure of office of Judges

99(1) Subject to subsection (2) of this section, the judges of the superior courts shall hold office during good behaviour, but shall be removable by the Governor General on address of the Senate and House of Commons.

Termination at age 75

(2) A judge of a superior court, whether appointed before or after the coming into force of this section, shall cease to hold office upon attaining the age of seventy-five years, or upon the coming into force of this section if at that time he has already attained that age.

Salaries, etc., of Judges

100. The Salaries, Allowances, and Pensions of the Judges of the Superior, District, and County Courts (except the Courts of Probate in Nova Scotia and New Brunswick), and of the Admiralty Courts in Cases where the Judges thereof are for the Time being paid by Salary, shall be fixed and provided by the Parliament of Canada.

General Court of Appeal, etc.

101. The Parliament of Canada may, notwithstanding anything in this Act, from Time to Time provide for the Constitution, Maintenance, and Organization of a General Court of Appeal for Canada, and for the Establishment of any additional Courts for the better Administration of the Laws of Canada.

VIII. REVENUES; DEBTS; ASSETS; TAXATION

[Sections 102–104 omitted.]

Salary of Governor General

105. Unless altered by the Parliament of Canada, the Salary of the Governor General shall be Ten thousand Pounds Sterling Money of the United Kingdom of Great Britain and Ireland, payable out of the Consolidated Revenue Fund of Canada, and the same shall form the Third Charge thereon.

[Sections 106–107 omitted.]

Transfer of Property in Schedule

108. The Public Works and Property of each Province, enumerated in the Third Schedule to this Act, shall be the Property of Canada.

Property in Lands, Mines, etc.

109. All Lands, Mines, Minerals, and Royalties belonging to the several Provinces of Canada, Nova Scotia, and New Brunswick at the Union, and all Sums then due or payable for such Lands, Mines, Minerals, or Royalties, shall belong to the several Provinces of Ontario, Quebec, Nova Scotia, and New Brunswick in which the same are situate or arise, subject to any Trusts existing in respect thereof, and to any Interest other than that of the Province in the same.

[Sections 110–116 omitted.]

Provincial Public Property

117. The several Provinces shall retain all their respective Public Property not otherwise disposed of in this Act, subject to the Right of Canada to assume any Lands or Public

Property required for Fortifications or for the Defence of the Country.

[Sections 118–120 omitted.]

Canadian Manufactures, etc.

121. All Articles of the Growth, Produce, or Manufacture of any one of the Provinces shall, from and after the Union, be admitted free into each of the other Provinces.

Continuance of Customs and Excise Laws

122. The Customs and Excise Laws of each Province shall, subject to the Provisions of this Act, continue in force until altered by the Parliament of Canada.

[Sections 123–124 omitted.]

Exemption of Public Lands, etc.

125. No Lands or Property belonging to Canada or any Province shall be liable to Taxation.

[Section 126 omitted.]

IX. MISCELLANEOUS PROVISIONS

GENERAL

127. Repealed.

Oath of Allegiance, etc.

128. Every Member of the Senate or House of Commons of Canada shall before taking his Seat therein take and subscribe before the Governor General or some Person authorized by him, and every Member of a Legislative Council or Legislative Assembly of any Province shall before taking his Seat therein take and subscribe before the Lieutenant Governor of the Province or some Person authorized by him, the Oath of Allegiance contained in the Fifth Schedule to this Act; and every Member of the Senate of Canada and every Member of the Legislative Council of Quebec shall also, before taking his Seat therein, take and subscribe before the Governor General, or some Person authorized by him, the Declaration of Qualification contained in the same Schedule.

Continuance of existing Laws, Courts, Officers, etc.

129. Except as otherwise provided by this Act, all Laws in force in Canada, Nova Scotia, or New Brunswick at the Union, and all Courts of Civil and Criminal Jurisdiction, and all legal Commissions, Powers, and Authorities, and all Officers, Judicial, Administrative, and Ministerial, existing therein at the Union, shall continue in Ontario, Quebec, Nova Scotia, and New Brunswick respectively, as if the Union had not been made; subject nevertheless (except with respect to such as are enacted by or exist under Acts of the Parliament of Great Britain or of the Parliament of the United Kingdom of Great Britain and Ireland,) to be repealed, abolished, or altered by the Parliament of Canada, or by the Legislature of the respective Province, according to the Authority of the Parliament or of that Legislature under this Act.

[Sections 130–131 omitted.]

Treaty Obligations

132. The Parliament and Government of Canada shall have all Powers necessary or proper for performing the Obligations of Canada or of any Province thereof, as Part of the British Empire, towards Foreign Countries, arising under Treaties between the Empire and such Foreign Countries.

Use of English and French Languages

133. Either the English or the French Language may be used by any Person in the Debates of the Houses of the Parliament of Canada and of the Houses of the Legislature of Quebec; and both those Languages shall be used in the respective Records and Journals of those Houses; and either of those Languages may be used by any Person or in any Pleading or Process in or issuing from any Court of Canada established under this Act, and in or from all or any of the Courts of Quebec.

The Acts of the Parliament of Canada and of the Legislature of Quebec shall be printed and published in both those Languages.

[Sections 134–144 omitted.]

[Part X omitted.]

XI. ADMISSION OF OTHER COLONIES

Power to admit Newfoundland, etc., into the Union

146. It shall be lawful for the Queen, by and with the Advice of Her Majesty's Most Honourable Privy Council, on Addresses from the Houses of the Parliament of Canada, and from the Houses of the respective Legislatures of the Colonies or Provinces of Newfoundland, Prince Edward Island, and British Columbia, to admit those Colonies or Provinces, or any of them, into the Union, and on Address from the Houses of the Parliament of Canada to admit Rupert's Land and the North-western Territory, or either of them, into the Union, on such Terms and Conditions in each Case as are in the Addresses expressed and as the Queen thinks fit to approve, subject to the Provisions of this Act; and the Provisions of any Order in Council in that Behalf shall have effect as if they had been enacted by the Parliament of the United Kingdom of Great Britain and Ireland.

[Section 147 omitted.]

[The First and Second Schedules omitted.]

THE THIRD SCHEDULE

PROVINCIAL PUBLIC WORKS AND PROPERTY TO BE THE PROPERTY OF CANADA

1. Canals, with Lands and Water Power connected therewith.
2. Public Harbours.
3. Lighthouses and Piers, and Sable Island.
4. Steamboats, Dredges, and public Vessels.
5. Rivers and Lake Improvements.
6. Railways and Railway Stocks, Mortgages, and other Debts due by Railway Companies.
7. Military Roads.
8. Custom Houses, Post Offices, and all other Public Buildings, except such as the Government of Canada appropriate for the Use of the Provincial Legislatures and Governments.
9. Property transferred by the Imperial Government, and known as Ordnance Property.
10. Armouries, Drill Sheds, Military Clothing, and Munitions of War, and Lands set apart for general Public Purposes.

[The Fourth Schedule omitted.]

THE FIFTH SCHEDULE

OATH OF ALLEGIANCE

I *A.B.* do swear, That I will be faithful and bear true Allegiance to Her Majesty Queen Victoria.

Note.—The Name of the King or Queen of the United Kingdom of Great Britain and Ireland for the Time being is to be substituted from Time to Time, with proper Terms of Reference thereto.

Declaration of Qualification

I *A.B.* do declare and testify, That I am by Law duly qualified to be appointed a Member of the Senate of Canada [*or as the Case may be*], and that I am legally or equitably seised as of Freehold for my own Use and Benefit of Lands or Tenements held in Free and Common Socage [*or seised or possessed for my own Use and Benefit of Lands or Tenements held in Francalleu or in Roture (as the Case may be)*,] in the Province of Nova Scotia [*or as the Case may be*] of the Value of Four thousand Dollars over and above all Rents, Dues, Debts, Mortgages, Charges, and Incumbrances due or payable out of or charged on or affecting the same, and that I have not collusively or colourably obtained a Title to or become possessed of the said Lands and Tenements or any Part thereof for the Purpose of enabling me to become a Member of the Senate of Canada [*or as the Case may be*], and that my Real and Personal Property are together worth Four thousand Dollars over and above my Debts and Liabilities.

THE SIXTH SCHEDULE

PRIMARY PRODUCTION FROM NON-RENEWABLE NATURAL RESOURCES AND FORESTRY RESOURCES

1. For the purposes of section 92A of this Act,

(*a*) production from a non-renewable natural resource is primary production therefrom if

(i) it is in the form in which it exists upon its recovery or severance from its natural state, or

(ii) it is a product resulting from processing or refining the resource, and is not a manufactured product or a product resulting from refining crude oil, refining upgraded heavy crude oil, refining gases or liquids derived from coal or refining a synthetic equivalent of crude oil; and

(*b*) production from a forestry resource is primary production therefrom if it consists of sawlogs, poles, lumber, wood chips, sawdust or any other primary wood product, or wood pulp, and is not a product manufactured from wood.

B Constitution Act, 1982

Schedule B to the *Canada Act 1982* (UK), 1982, c 11

TABLE OF CONTENTS

1   PART I   CANADIAN CHARTER OF RIGHTS AND FREEDOMS

  1   Guarantee of Rights and Freedoms

  2   Fundamental Freedoms

  3   Democratic Rights

  6   Mobility Rights

  7   Legal Rights

  15   Equality Rights

  16   Official Languages of Canada

  23   Minority Language Educational Rights

  24   Enforcement

  25   General

  32   Application of Charter

  34   Citation

35   PART II   RIGHTS OF THE ABORIGINAL PEOPLES OF CANADA

36   PART III   EQUALIZATION AND REGIONAL DISPARITIES

37   PART IV   CONSTITUTIONAL CONFERENCE

37.1 PART IV.I   CONSTITUTIONAL CONFERENCES

38   PART V   PROCEDURE FOR AMENDING CONSTITUTION OF CANADA

50   PART VI   AMENDMENT TO THE CONSTITUTION ACT, 1867

52   PART VII   GENERAL SCHEDULE TO THE CONSTITUTION ACT, 1982

PART I

CANADIAN CHARTER OF RIGHTS AND FREEDOMS

Whereas Canada is founded upon principles that recognize the supremacy of God and the rule of law:

GUARANTEE OF RIGHTS AND FREEDOMS

Rights and freedoms in Canada

1. The *Canadian Charter of Rights and Freedoms* guarantees the rights and freedoms set out in it subject only to such reasonable limits prescribed by law as can be demonstrably justified in a free and democratic society.

FUNDAMENTAL FREEDOMS

Fundamental freedoms

2. Everyone has the following fundamental freedoms:

(*a*) freedom of conscience and religion;

(*b*) freedom of thought, belief, opinion and expression, including freedom of the press and other media of communication;

(*c*) freedom of peaceful assembly; and

(*d*) freedom of association.

DEMOCRATIC RIGHTS

Democratic rights of citizens

3. Every citizen of Canada has the right to vote in an election of members of the House of Commons or of a legislative assembly and to be qualified for membership therein.

Maximum duration of legislative bodies

4(1) No House of Commons and no legislative assembly shall continue for longer than five years from the date fixed for the return of the writs at a general election of its members.

Continuation in special circumstances

(2) In time of real or apprehended war, invasion or insurrection, a House of Commons may be continued by Parliament and a legislative assembly may be continued by the legislature beyond five years if such continuation is not opposed by the votes of more than one-third of the members of the House of Commons or the legislative assembly, as the case may be.

Annual sitting of legislative bodies

5. There shall be a sitting of Parliament and of each legislature at least once every twelve months.

MOBILITY RIGHTS

Mobility of citizens

6(1) Every citizen of Canada has the right to enter, remain in and leave Canada.

Rights to move and gain livelihood

(2) Every citizen of Canada and every person who has the status of a permanent resident of Canada has the right

(*a*) to move to and take up residence in any province; and

(*b*) to pursue the gaining of a livelihood in any province.

Limitation

(3) The rights specified in subsection (2) are subject to

(*a*) any laws or practices of general application in force in a province other than those that discriminate among persons primarily on the basis of province of present or previous residence; and

(*b*) any laws providing for reasonable residency requirements as a qualification for the receipt of publicly provided social services.

Affirmative action programs

(4) Subsections (2) and (3) do not preclude any law, program or activity that has as its object the amelioration in a province of conditions of individuals in that province who are socially or economically disadvantaged if the rate of employment in that province is below the rate of employment in Canada.

LEGAL RIGHTS

Life, liberty and security of person

7. Everyone has the right to life, liberty and security of the person and the right not to be deprived thereof except in accordance with the principles of fundamental justice.

Search or seizure

8. Everyone has the right to be secure against unreasonable search or seizure.

Detention or imprisonment

9. Everyone has the right not to be arbitrarily detained or imprisoned.

Arrest or detention

10. Everyone has the right on arrest or detention

(*a*) to be informed promptly of the reasons therefor;

(*b*) to retain and instruct counsel without delay and to be informed of that right; and

(*c*) to have the validity of the detention determined by way of *habeas corpus* and to be released if the detention is not lawful.

Proceedings in criminal and penal matters

11. Any person charged with an offence has the right

(*a*) to be informed without unreasonable delay of the specific offence;

(*b*) to be tried within a reasonable time;

(*c*) not to be compelled to be a witness in proceedings against that person in respect of the offence;

(*d*) to be presumed innocent until proven guilty according to law in a fair and public hearing by an independent and impartial tribunal;

(*e*) not to be denied reasonable bail without just cause;

(*f*) except in the case of an offence under military law tried before a military tribunal, to the benefit of trial by jury where the maximum punishment for the offence is imprisonment for five years or a more severe punishment;

(*g*) not to be found guilty on account of any act or omission unless, at the time of the act or omission, it constituted an offence under Canadian or international law or was criminal according to the general principles of law recognized by the community of nations;

(*h*) if finally acquitted of the offence, not to be tried for it again and, if finally found guilty and punished for the offence, not to be tried or punished for it again; and

(*i*) if found guilty of the offence and if the punishment for the offence has been varied between the time of commission and the time of sentencing, to the benefit of the lesser punishment.

Treatment or punishment

12. Everyone has the right not to be subjected to any cruel and unusual treatment or punishment.

Self-crimination

13. A witness who testifies in any proceedings has the right not to have any incriminating evidence so given used to incriminate that witness in any other proceedings, except in a prosecution for perjury or for the giving of contradictory evidence.

Interpreter

14. A party or witness in any proceedings who does not understand or speak the language in which the proceedings are conducted or who is deaf has the right to the assistance of an interpreter.

EQUALITY RIGHTS

Equality before and under law and equal protection and benefit of law

15(1) Every individual is equal before and under the law and has the right to the equal protection and equal benefit of the law without discrimination and, in particular, without discrimination based on race, national or ethnic origin, colour, religion, sex, age or mental or physical disability.

Affirmative action programs

(2) Subsection (1) does not preclude any law, program or activity that has as its object the amelioration of conditions of disadvantaged individuals or groups including those that are disadvantaged because of race, national or ethnic origin, colour, religion, sex, age or mental or physical disability.

OFFICIAL LANGUAGES OF CANADA

Official languages of Canada

16(1) English and French are the official languages of Canada and have equality of status and equal rights and privileges as to their use in all institutions of the Parliament and government of Canada.

Official languages of New Brunswick

(2) English and French are the official languages of New Brunswick and have equality of status and equal rights and privileges as to their use in all institutions of the legislature and government of New Brunswick.

Advancement of status and use

(3) Nothing in this Charter limits the authority of Parliament or a legislature to advance the equality of status or use of English and French.

English and French linguistic communities in New Brunswick

16.1(1) The English linguistic community and the French linguistic community in New Brunswick have equality of status and equal rights and privileges, including the right to distinct educational institutions and such distinct cultural institutions as are necessary for the preservation and promotion of those communities.

Role of the legislature and government of New Brunswick

(2) The role of the legislature and government of New Brunswick to preserve and promote the status, rights and privileges referred to in subsection (1) is affirmed.

Proceedings of Parliament

17(1) Everyone has the right to use English or French in any debates and other proceedings of Parliament.

Proceedings of New Brunswick legislature

(2) Everyone has the right to use English or French in any debates and other proceedings of the legislature of New Brunswick.

Parliamentary statutes and records

18(1) The statutes, records and journals of Parliament shall be printed and published in English and French and both language versions are equally authoritative.

New Brunswick statutes and records

(2) The statutes, records and journals of the legislature of New Brunswick shall be printed and published in English and French and both language versions are equally authoritative.

Proceedings in courts established by Parliament

19(1) Either English or French may be used by any person in, or in any pleading in or process issuing from, any court established by Parliament.

Proceedings in New Brunswick courts

(2) Either English or French may be used by any person in, or in any pleading in or process issuing from, any court of New Brunswick.

Communications by public with federal institutions

20(1) Any member of the public in Canada has the right to communicate with, and to receive available services from, any head or central office of an institution of the Parliament or government of Canada in English or French, and has the same right with respect to any other office of any such institution where

    (*a*) there is a significant demand for communications with and services from that office in such language; or

    (*b*) due to the nature of the office, it is reasonable that communications with and services from that office be available in both English and French.

Communications by public with New Brunswick institutions

(2) Any member of the public in New Brunswick has the right to communicate with, and to receive available services from, any office of an institution of the legislature or government of New Brunswick in English or French.

Continuation of existing constitutional provisions

21. Nothing in sections 16 to 20 abrogates or derogates from any right, privilege or obligation with respect to the English and French languages, or either of them, that exists or is continued by virtue of any other provision of the Constitution of Canada.

Rights and privileges preserved

22. Nothing in sections 16 to 20 abrogates or derogates from any legal or customary right or privilege acquired or enjoyed either before or after the coming into force of this Charter with respect to any language that is not English or French.

MINORITY LANGUAGE EDUCATIONAL RIGHTS

Language of instruction

23(1) Citizens of Canada

    (*a*) whose first language learned and still understood is that of the English or French linguistic minority population of the province in which they reside, or

    (*b*) who have received their primary school instruction in Canada in English or French and reside in a province where the language in which they received that instruction is the language of the English or French linguistic minority population of the province,

have the right to have their children receive primary and secondary school instruction in that language in that province.

Continuity of language instruction

(2) Citizens of Canada of whom any child has received or is receiving primary or secondary school instruction in English or French in Canada, have the right to have all their children receive primary and secondary school instruction in the same language.

Application where numbers warrant

(3) The right of citizens of Canada under subsections (1) and (2) to have their children receive primary and secondary school instruction in the language of the English or French linguistic minority population of a province

(*a*) applies wherever in the province the number of children of citizens who have such a right is sufficient to warrant the provision to them out of public funds of minority language instruction; and

(*b*) includes, where the number of those children so warrants, the right to have them receive that instruction in minority language educational facilities provided out of public funds.

ENFORCEMENT

Enforcement of guaranteed rights and freedoms

24(1) Anyone whose rights or freedoms, as guaranteed by this Charter, have been infringed or denied may apply to a court of competent jurisdiction to obtain such remedy as the court considers appropriate and just in the circumstances.

Exclusion of evidence bringing administration of justice into disrepute

(2) Where, in proceedings under subsection (1), a court concludes that evidence was obtained in a manner that infringed or denied any rights or freedoms guaranteed by this Charter, the evidence shall be excluded if it is established that, having regard to all the circumstances, the admission of it in the proceedings would bring the administration of justice into disrepute.

GENERAL

Aboriginal rights and freedoms not affected by Charter

25. The guarantee in this Charter of certain rights and freedoms shall not be construed so as to abrogate or derogate from any aboriginal, treaty or other rights or freedoms that pertain to the aboriginal peoples of Canada including

(*a*) any rights or freedoms that have been recognized by the Royal Proclamation of October 7, 1763; and

(*b*) any rights or freedoms that now exist by way of land claims agreements or may be so acquired.

Other rights and freedoms not affected by Charter

26. The guarantee in this Charter of certain rights and freedoms shall not be construed as denying the existence of any other rights or freedoms that exist in Canada.

Multicultural heritage

27. This Charter shall be interpreted in a manner consistent with the preservation and enhancement of the multicultural heritage of Canadians.

Rights guaranteed equally to both sexes

28. Notwithstanding anything in this Charter, the rights and freedoms referred to in it are guaranteed equally to male and female persons.

Rights respecting certain schools preserved

29. Nothing in this Charter abrogates or derogates from any rights or privileges guaranteed by or under the Constitution of Canada in respect of denominational, separate or dissentient schools.

Application to territories and territorial authorities

30. A reference in this Charter to a province or to the legislative assembly or legislature of a province shall be deemed to include a reference to the Yukon Territory and the Northwest Territories, or to the appropriate legislative authority thereof, as the case may be.

Legislative powers not extended

31. Nothing in this Charter extends the legislative powers of any body or authority.

APPLICATION OF CHARTER

Application of Charter

32(1) This Charter applies

(*a*) to the Parliament and government of Canada in respect of all matters within the authority of Parliament including all matters relating to the Yukon Territory and Northwest Territories; and

(*b*) to the legislature and government of each province in respect of all matters within the authority of the legislature of each province.

Exception

(2) Notwithstanding subsection (1), section 15 shall not have effect until three years after this section comes into force.

Exception where express declaration

33(1) Parliament or the legislature of a province may expressly declare in an Act of Parliament or of the legislature, as the case may be, that the Act or a provision thereof shall operate notwithstanding a provision included in section 2 or sections 7 to 15 of this Charter.

Operation of exception

(2) An Act or a provision of an Act in respect of which a declaration made under this section is in effect shall have such operation as it would have but for the provision of this Charter referred to in the declaration.

Five year limitation

(3) A declaration made under subsection (1) shall cease to have effect five years after it comes into force or on such earlier date as may be specified in the declaration.

Re-enactment

(4) Parliament or the legislature of a province may re-enact a declaration made under subsection (1).

Five year limitation

(5) Subsection (3) applies in respect of a re-enactment made under subsection (4).

CITATION

Citation

34. This Part may be cited as the *Canadian Charter of Rights and Freedoms.*

PART II

RIGHTS OF THE ABORIGINAL PEOPLES OF CANADA

Recognition of existing aboriginal and treaty rights

35(1) The existing aboriginal and treaty rights of the aboriginal peoples of Canada are hereby recognized and affirmed.

Definition of "aboriginal peoples of Canada"

(2) In this Act, "aboriginal peoples of Canada" includes the Indian, Inuit and Métis peoples of Canada.

Land claims agreements

(3) For greater certainty, in subsection (1) "treaty rights" includes rights that now exist by way of land claims agreements or may be so acquired.

Aboriginal and treaty rights are guaranteed equally to both sexes

(4) Notwithstanding any other provision of this Act, the aboriginal and treaty rights referred to in subsection (1) are guaranteed equally to male and female persons.

Commitment to participation in constitutional conference

35.1 The government of Canada and the provincial governments are committed to the principle that, before any amendment is made to Class 24 of section 91 of the "*Constitution Act, 1867,*" to section 25 of this Act or to this Part,

(*a*) a constitutional conference that includes in its agenda an item relating to the proposed amendment, composed of the Prime Minister of Canada and the first ministers of the provinces, will be convened by the Prime Minister of Canada; and

(*b*) the Prime Minister of Canada will invite representatives of the aboriginal peoples of Canada to participate in the discussions on that item.

PART III

EQUALIZATION AND REGIONAL DISPARITIES

Commitment to promote equal opportunities

36(1) Without altering the legislative authority of Parliament or of the provincial legislatures, or the rights of any of them with respect to the exercise of their legislative authority, Parliament and the legislatures, together with the government of Canada and the provincial governments, are committed to

(*a*) promoting equal opportunities for the well-being of Canadians;

(*b*) furthering economic development to reduce disparity in opportunities; and

(*c*) providing essential public services of reasonable quality to all Canadians.

Commitment respecting public services

(2) Parliament and the government of Canada are committed to the principle of making equalization payments to ensure that provincial governments have sufficient revenues to provide reasonably comparable levels of public services at reasonably comparable levels of taxation.

[Parts IV and IV.1 omitted.]

PART V

PROCEDURE FOR AMENDING CONSTITUTION OF CANADA

General procedure for amending Constitution of Canada

38(1) An amendment to the Constitution of Canada may be made by proclamation issued by the Governor General under the Great Seal of Canada where so authorized by

(*a*) resolutions of the Senate and House of Commons; and

(*b*) resolutions of the legislative assemblies of at least two-thirds of the provinces that have, in the aggregate, according to the then latest general census, at least fifty per cent of the population of all the provinces.

Majority of members

(2) An amendment made under subsection (1) that derogates from the legislative powers, the proprietary rights or any other rights or privileges of the legislature or government of a province shall require a resolution supported by a majority of the members of each of the Senate, the House of Commons and the legislative assemblies required under subsection (1).

Expression of dissent

(3) An amendment referred to in subsection (2) shall not have effect in a province the legislative assembly of which has expressed its dissent thereto by resolution supported by a majority of its members prior to the issue of the proclamation to which the amendment relates unless that legislative assembly, subsequently, by resolution supported by a majority of its members, revokes its dissent and authorizes the amendment.

Revocation of dissent

(4) A resolution of dissent made for the purposes of subsection (3) may be revoked at any time before or after the issue of the proclamation to which it relates.

Restriction on proclamation

39(1) A proclamation shall not be issued under subsection 38(1) before the expiration of one year from the adoption of the resolution initiating the amendment procedure thereunder, unless the legislative assembly of each province has previously adopted a resolution of assent or dissent.

Idem

(2) A proclamation shall not be issued under subsection 38(1) after the expiration of three years from the adoption of the resolution initiating the amendment procedure thereunder.

Compensation

40. Where an amendment is made under subsection 38(1) that transfers provincial legislative powers relating to education or other cultural matters from provincial legislatures to Parliament, Canada shall provide reasonable compensation to any province to which the amendment does not apply.

Amendment by unanimous consent

41. An amendment to the Constitution of Canada in relation to the following matters may be made by proclamation issued by the Governor General under the Great Seal of Canada only where authorized by resolutions of the Senate and House of Commons and of the legislative assembly of each province:

(*a*) the office of the Queen, the Governor General and the Lieutenant Governor of a province;

(*b*) the right of a province to a number of members in the House of Commons not less than the number of Senators by which the province is entitled to be represented at the time this Part comes into force;

(*c*) subject to section 43, the use of the English or the French language;

(*d*) the composition of the Supreme Court of Canada; and

(*e*) an amendment to this Part.

Amendment by general procedure

42(1) An amendment to the Constitution of Canada in relation to the following matters may be made only in accordance with subsection 38(1):

(*a*) the principle of proportionate representation of the provinces in the House of Commons prescribed by the Constitution of Canada;

(*b*) the powers of the Senate and the method of selecting Senators;

(*c*) the number of members by which a province is entitled to be represented in the Senate and the residence qualifications of Senators;

(*d*) subject to paragraph 41(*d*), the Supreme Court of Canada;

(*e*) the extension of existing provinces into the territories; and

(*f*) notwithstanding any other law or practice, the establishment of new provinces.

Exception

(2) Subsections 38(2) to (4) do not apply in respect of amendments in relation to matters referred to in subsection (1).

Amendment of provisions relating to some but not all provinces

43. An amendment to the Constitution of Canada in relation to any provision that applies to one or more, but not all, provinces, including

(*a*) any alteration to boundaries between provinces, and

(*b*) any amendment to any provision that relates to the use of the English or the French language within a province,

may be made by proclamation issued by the Governor General under the Great Seal of Canada only where so authorized by resolutions of the Senate and House of Commons and of the legislative assembly of each province to which the amendment applies.

Amendments by Parliament

44. Subject to sections 41 and 42, Parliament may exclusively make laws amending the Constitution of Canada in relation to the executive government of Canada or the Senate and House of Commons.

Amendments by provincial legislatures

45. Subject to section 41, the legislature of each province may exclusively make laws amending the constitution of the province.

Initiation of amendment procedures

46(1) The procedures for amendment under sections 38, 41, 42 and 43 may be initiated either by the Senate or the House of Commons or by the legislative assembly of a province.

Revocation of authorization

(2) A resolution of assent made for the purposes of this Part may be revoked at any time before the issue of a proclamation authorized by it.

Amendments without Senate resolution

47(1) An amendment to the Constitution of Canada made by proclamation under section 38, 41, 42 or 43 may be made without a resolution of the Senate authorizing the issue of the proclamation if, within one hundred and eighty days after the adoption by the House of Commons of a resolution authorizing its issue, the Senate has not adopted such a resolution and if, at any time after the expiration of that period, the House of Commons again adopts the resolution.

Computation of period

(2) Any period when Parliament is prorogued or dissolved shall not be counted in computing the one hundred and eighty day period referred to in subsection (1).

Advice to issue proclamation

48. The Queen's Privy Council for Canada shall advise the Governor General to issue a proclamation under this Part forthwith on the adoption of the resolutions required for an amendment made by proclamation under this Part.

Constitutional conference

49. A constitutional conference composed of the Prime Minister of Canada and the first ministers of the provinces shall be convened by the Prime Minister of Canada within

fifteen years after this Part comes into force to review the provisions of this Part.

[Part VI omitted.]

PART VII

GENERAL

Primacy of Constitution of Canada

52(1) The Constitution of Canada is the supreme law of Canada, and any law that is inconsistent with the provisions of the Constitution is, to the extent of the inconsistency, of no force or effect.

Constitution of Canada

(2) The Constitution of Canada includes
>   (*a*) the *Canada Act 1982*, including this Act;
>   (*b*) the Acts and orders referred to in the schedule; and
>   (*c*) any amendment to any Act or order referred to in paragraph (*a*) or (*b*).

Amendments to Constitution of Canada

(3) Amendments to the Constitution of Canada shall be made only in accordance with the authority contained in the Constitution of Canada.

Repeals and new names

53(1) The enactments referred to in Column I of the schedule are hereby repealed or amended to the extent indicated in Column II thereof and, unless repealed, shall continue as law in Canada under the names set out in Column III thereof.

Consequential amendments

(2) Every enactment, except the *Canada Act 1982*, that refers to an enactment referred to in the schedule by the name in Column I thereof is hereby amended by substituting for that name the corresponding name in Column III thereof, and any British North America Act not referred to in the schedule may be cited as the *Constitution Act* followed by the year and number, if any, of its enactment.

Repeal and consequential amendments

54. Part IV is repealed on the day that is one year after this Part comes into force and this section may be repealed and this Act renumbered, consequentially upon the repeal of Part IV and this section, by proclamation issued by the Governor General under the Great Seal of Canada.

54.1 Repealed.

French version of Constitution of Canada

55. A French version of the portions of the Constitution of Canada referred to in the schedule shall be prepared by the Minister of Justice of Canada as expeditiously as possible and, when any portion thereof sufficient to warrant action being taken has been so prepared, it shall be put forward for enactment by proclamation issued by the Governor General under the Great Seal of Canada pursuant to the procedure then applicable to an amendment of the same provisions of the Constitution of Canada.

English and French versions of certain constitutional texts

56. Where any portion of the Constitution of Canada has been or is enacted in English and French or where a French version of any portion of the Constitution is enacted pursuant to section 55, the English and French versions of that portion of the Constitution are equally authoritative.

English and French versions of this Act

57. The English and French versions of this Act are equally authoritative.

Commencement

58. Subject to section 59, this Act shall come into force on a day to be fixed by proclamation issued by the Queen or the Governor General under the Great Seal of Canada.

Commencement of paragraph 23(1)(*a*) in respect of Quebec

59(1) Paragraph 23(1)(*a*) shall come into force in respect of Quebec on a day to be fixed by proclamation issued by the Queen or the Governor General under the Great Seal of Canada.

Authorization of Quebec

(2) A proclamation under subsection (1) shall be issued only where authorized by the legislative assembly or government of Quebec.

Repeal of this section

(3) This section may be repealed on the day paragraph 23(1)(*a*) comes into force in respect of Quebec and this Act amended and renumbered, consequentially upon the repeal of this section, by proclamation issued by the Queen or the Governor General under the Great Seal of Canada.

Short title and citations

60. This Act may be cited as the *Constitution Act, 1982*, and the Constitution Acts 1867 to 1975 (No. 2) and this Act may be cited together as the *Constitution Acts, 1867 to 1982*.

References

61. A reference to the "*Constitution Acts, 1867 to 1982*" shall be deemed to include a reference to the "*Constitution Amendment Proclamation, 1983.*"

SCHEDULE TO THE CONSTITUTION ACT, 1982

(Section 53)

MODERNIZATION OF THE CONSTITUTION

Item	Column I Act Affected	Column II Amendment	Column III New Name
1.	British North America Act, 1867, 30-31 Vict., c. 3 (U.K.)	(1) Section 1 is repealed and the following substituted therefor: "1. This Act may be cited as the *Constitution Act, 1867*." (2) Section 20 is repealed. (3) Class 1 of section 91 is repealed. (4) Class 1 of section 92 is repealed.	Constitution Act, 1867
2.	An Act to amend and continue the Act 32-33 Victoria chapter 3; and to establish and provide for the Government of the Province of Manitoba, 1870, 33 Vict., c. 3 (Can.)	(1) The long title is repealed and the following substituted therefor: "*Manitoba Act, 1870*." (2) Section 20 is repealed.	Manitoba Act, 1870
3.	Order of Her Majesty in Council admitting Rupert's Land and the North-Western Territory into the union, dated the 23rd day of June, 1870		Rupert's Land and North-Western Territory Order
4.	Order of Her Majesty in Council admitting British Columbia into the Union, dated the 16th day of May, 1871.		British Columbia Terms of Union
5.	British North America Act, 1871, 34-35 Vict., c. 28 (U.K.)	Section 1 is repealed and the following substituted therefor: "1. This Act may be cited as the *Constitution Act, 1871*."	Constitution Act, 1871
6.	Order of Her Majesty in Council admitting Prince Edward Island into the Union, dated the 26th day of June, 1873.		Prince Edward Island Terms of Union
7.	Parliament of Canada Act, 1875, 38-39 Vict., c. 38 (U.K.)		Parliament of Canada Act, 1875
8.	Order of Her Majesty in Council admitting all British possessions and Territories in North America and islands adjacent thereto into the Union, dated the 31st day of July, 1880.		Adjacent Territories Order

Item	Column I Act Affected	Column II Amendment	Column III New Name
9.	British North America Act, 1886, 49-50 Vict., c. 35 (U.K.)	Section 3 is repealed and the following substituted therefor: "3. This Act may be cited as the *Constitution Act, 1886.*"	Constitution Act, 1886
10.	Canada (Ontario Boundary) Act, 1889, 52-53 Vict., c. 28 (U.K.)		Canada (Ontario Boundary) Act, 1889
11.	Canadian Speaker (Appointment of Deputy) Act, 1895, 2nd Sess., 59 Vict., c. 3 (U.K.)	The Act is repealed.	
12.	The Alberta Act, 1905, 4-5 Edw. VII, c. 3 (Can.)		Alberta Act
13.	The Saskatchewan Act, 1905, 4-5 Edw. VII, c. 42 (Can.)		Saskatchewan Act
14.	British North America Act, 1907, 7 Edw. VII, c. 11 (U.K.)	Section 2 is repealed and the following substituted therefor: "2. This Act may be cited as the *Constitution Act, 1907.*"	Constitution Act, 1907
15.	British North America Act, 1915, 5-6 Geo. V, c. 45 (U.K.)	Section 3 is repealed and the following substituted therefor: "3. This Act may be cited as the *Constitution Act, 1915.*"	Constitution Act, 1915
16.	British North America Act, 1930, 20-21 Geo. V, c. 26 (U.K.)	Section 3 is repealed and the following substituted therefor: "3. This Act may be cited as the *Constitution Act, 1930.*"	Constitution Act, 1930
17.	Statute of Westminster, 1931, 22 Geo. V, c. 4 (U.K.)	In so far as they apply to Canada, (*a*) Section 4 is repealed; and (*b*) Subsection 7(1) is repealed.	Statute of Westminster, 1931
18.	British North America Act, 1940, 3-4 Geo. VI, c. 36 (U.K.)	Section 2 is repealed and the following substituted therefor: "2. This Act may be cited as the *Constitution Act, 1940.*"	Constitution Act, 1940
19.	British North America Act, 1943, 6-7 Geo. VI, c. 30 (U.K.)	The Act is repealed.	
20.	British North America Act, 1946, 9-10 Geo. VI, c. 63 (U.K.)	The Act is repealed.	
21.	British North America Act, 1949, 12-13 Geo. VI, c. 22 (U.K.)	Section 3 is repealed and the following substituted therefor: "3. This Act may be cited as the *Newfoundland Act.*"	Newfoundland Act

Item	Column I Act Affected	Column II Amendment	Column III New Name
22.	British North America (No. 2) Act, 1949, 13 Geo. VI, c. 81 (U.K.)	The Act is repealed.	
23.	British North America Act, 1951, 14-15 Geo. VI, c. 32 (U.K.)	The Act is repealed.	
24.	British North America Act, 1952, 1 Eliz. II, c. 15 (Can.)	The Act is repealed.	
25.	British North America Act, 1960, 9 Eliz. II, c. 2 (U.K.)	Section 2 is repealed and the following substituted therefor: "2. This Act may be cited as the *Constitution Act, 1960.*"	Constitution Act, 1960
26.	British North America Act, 1964, 12-13 Eliz. II, c. 73 (U.K.)	Section 2 is repealed and the following substituted therefor: "2. This Act may be cited as the *Constitution Act, 1964.*"	Constitution Act, 1964
27.	British North America Act, 1965, 14 Eliz. II, c. 4, Part I (Can.)	Section 2 is repealed and the following substituted therefor: "2. This Part may be cited as the *Constitution Act, 1965.*"	Constitution Act, 1965
28.	British North America Act, 1974, 23 Eliz. II, c. 13, Part I (Can.)	Section 3, as amended by 25-26 Eliz. II, c. 28, s. 38(1) (Can.), is repealed and the following substituted therefor: "3. This Part may be cited as the *Constitution Act, 1974.*"	Constitution Act, 1974
29.	British North America Act, 1975, 23-24 Eliz. II, c. 28, Part I (Can.)	Section 3, as amended by 25-26 Eliz. II, c. 28, s. 31 (Can.), is repealed and the following substituted therefor: "3. This Part may be cited as the *Constitution Act (No. 1), 1975.*"	Constitution Act (No. 1), 1975
30.	British North America Act (No. 2), 1975, 23-24 Eliz. II, c. 53 (Can.)	Section 3 is repealed and the following substituted therefor: "3. This Act may be cited as the *Constitution Act (No. 2), 1975.*"	Constitution Act (No. 2), 1975

Glossary

Aboriginal law   sub-area of Canadian public law involving rights, land claims, and other legal issues concerning Indigenous peoples in Canada *(p. 44)*

actus reus   "guilty act" or objective physical part of a criminal offence *(p. 275)*

administrative agency   government bodies created under various federal, provincial, and territorial statutes with the purpose of administering particular statutory regimes *(p. 251)*

administrative tribunal   administrative agency that fulfills quasi-judicial functions as part of its mandate *(p. 256)*

adversarial system   system, used in common law courts, whereby the primary responsibility for the presentation of cases lies with the opposing litigants and their counsel, not with the judge presiding over the case *(p. 36)*

affinity   the relationship that a person has to the blood relatives of his or her spouse *(p. 218)*

affirmative action   policy, particularly in relation to education or employment, intended to assist groups who have suffered past discrimination *(p. 167)*

aggravating circumstance   factor in the case that causes the judge to impose a harsher sentence on the convicted person than he or she would otherwise *(p. 293)*

alternative dispute resolution (ADR)   process used instead of a court trial to help settle a dispute *(p. 336)*

annulment   the legal cancellation or invalidation of a marriage *(p. 218)*

appeal (of decisions by administrative bodies)   process whereby a court is authorized by legislation to hear an appeal of an administrative decision, which is generally less restrictive than the judicial review process *(p. 259)*

appearance notice   document given to a person, usually at the scene of the crime, requiring that person to come to court on a certain date and time to answer to a charge *(p. 287)*

appellant   individual, corporation, or other entity who lost at trial and who initiates an appeal to a higher court *(p. 156)*

arbitration   dispute resolution process whereby the parties agree beforehand on an arbitrator to assist them and on whether the arbitrator's decision will be advisory or binding *(p. 337)*

arraignment   procedure by which the charge is read to the accused in open court and the accused is asked how she wishes to plead *(p. 289)*

arrest   detaining or holding a person by legal authority *(p. 280)*

articles   apprenticeship under a practising lawyer *(p. 307)*

assault   psychological tort involving one person's apprehension of harmful physical contact from another person *(p. 186)*

banns of marriage   the public announcement in church of an impending marriage *(p. 219)*

battery   tort requiring actual occurrence of harmful or offensive physical contact *(p. 187)*

benchers   lawyers (and some non-lawyers) who are responsible for administering and governing a provincial or territorial law society *(p. 306)*

bicameral   legislature with two houses involved in the passage of legislation *(p. 91)*

bijural   term describing the operation of two legal systems in one jurisdiction, such as the common law and civil law systems in Canada *(p. 29)*

Bill of Rights (1689)   English statute that formally ended the power of the Crown to legislate without the consent of Parliament *(p. 36)*

bill   draft version of a proposed new statute *(p. 101)*

binding   term used to describe a higher court decision that a lower court in the same jurisdiction must follow according to the principle of *stare decisis* *(p. 33)*

bona fide occupational requirement   in the context of employment, a bona fide (Latin for "in good faith") requirement is one that exists for a legitimate reason—for example, safety—and that cannot be removed without undue hardship on the employer *(p. 166)*

bright line rule strict rule that a lawyer or law firm cannot represent two current clients whose interests are directly adverse to each other unless both clients consent after receiving full disclosure from the lawyer *(p. 321)*

builders' (or construction) lien charge against land that builders use to secure amounts owed them for work done on landowners' property *(p. 238)*

called to the bar formal ceremony whereby a law student becomes entitled to practise law *(p. 308)*

case brief summary of a case, with the constituent parts of the court's reasons for judgment arranged in a set order *(p. 157)*

case depending on context, refers to the reasons for judgment (where the court provides them), to the court process more generally, or to the entire dispute from beginning to end *(p. 156)*

cession transfer of a colony from one country to another *(p. 62)*

Chancery department of state established by English monarchs to assist with legal matters and to issue writs *(p. 30)*

chattels tangible, movable objects such as furniture, equipment, and cars *(p. 213)*

Civil Code of Quebec (Code Civil du Québec) Quebec's current civil code, which came into effect on January 1, 1994, and which replaced the *Civil Code of Lower Canada* that had been in force since 1866 *(p. 40)*

civil code authoritative legislative encoding of a country's private law *(p. 37)*

civil law system of law based on codified rules; may also refer to private law *(p. 29)*

civil liberties rights and freedoms protected by the Charter and other sources *(p. 160)*

civil wrong wrong that occurs in the context of relationships between persons and is addressed by one of the areas of private law *(p. 186)*

codes of conduct written sets of rules regulating the ethical behaviour of professionals *(p. 315)*

Commissioner in Executive Council official name for a territorial Cabinet *(p. 114)*

commissioner federally appointed official who is the formal head of the territorial executive government *(p. 114)*

common law system of law, based on the English legal tradition, that relies on precedent rather than on codified rules; may also refer to rules as distinguished from equitable principles, or case law as opposed to legislation *(p. 29)*

cones of silence institutional mechanisms used by law firms to secure confidential information so that lawyers working at the same law firm are prevented from accessing information that could prejudice a former client; sometimes also called Chinese walls *(p. 321)*

Confederation coming together of the three British North American colonies of Nova Scotia, New Brunswick, and the Province of Canada (Ontario and Quebec) to form the Dominion of Canada in 1867; the term later included all the provinces and territories that have joined Canada since that date *(p. 64)*

confidence convention convention requiring the government to resign if it loses the support of the majority of the elected representatives in the House of Commons and, if a new government cannot be formed, to call an election *(p. 113)*

consanguinity a blood relationship between relatives *(p. 218)*

constitutional law law dealing with the distribution of governmental powers under Canada's Constitution *(p. 83)*

constitutionally entrenched describes a statute that falls within the definition of the Constitution of Canada as set out in section 52 of the *Constitution Act, 1982* *(p. 92)*

convention established and traditional "rules" on which our system of responsible government is based and which qualify many of the rules of government set out in constitutional legislation, such as the *Constitution Act, 1867*, but which are not, technically, legally binding *(p. 110)*

conviction judge or jury's finding an accused person guilty of an offence *(p. 289)*

corporation company or group of people authorized by statute to act as a single entity (legally a person) and recognized as such in law *(p. 235)*

Corpus Juris Civilis comprehensive codification of Roman civil law, compiled by the emperor Justinian (483–565 CE) *(p. 39)*

corrective justice theory of justice according to which (1) a person has a moral responsibility for harm caused to another, and (2) the latter's loss must be rectified or corrected *(p. 9)*

Court of Chancery English court, existing separate from common law courts, established to provide equity *(p. 32)*

Court of King's (or Queen's) Bench English court that decided criminal matters *(p. 31)*

court state-sanctioned forum where disputes between opposing litigants are formally adjudicated *(p. 128)*

critical legal studies theory of law largely concerned with exposing law as an instrument of the rich and powerful *(p. 17)*

critical race theory theory of law that focuses on race-based inequities; an offshoot of critical legal studies *(p. 17)*

Crown attorney lawyer, also known as a Crown prosecutor or Crown counsel, who is an agent of the attorney general and who represents the Crown in court, particularly in criminal matters *(p. 270)*

Crown immunity covering term for the various protections afforded the Crown, including Crown privilege, the presumptions of legislation not applying to the Crown, and (formerly) immunity from tortious liability *(p. 115)*

Crown sovereign (currently the Queen), whose authority in Canada has been formally delegated to the governor general (federally) and to the lieutenant governor (provincially) but is actually exercised by the executive branch of government *(p. 110)*

decision depending on context, refers to the outcome or disposition of a case, to the holding in the case, or (where the court provides them) to the entire set of reasons the court gives for its judgment *(p. 156)*

deed formal document showing ownership of property *(p. 212)*

defamation tort involving allegations of impropriety that injure a person's reputation *(p. 195)*

defendant individual, corporation, or other entity who defends a non-criminal lawsuit initiated by the plaintiff *(p. 156)*

delegatus non potest delegare principle that a person or body to whom power is delegated cannot subdelegate that power (Latin: "one to whom power is delegated cannot himself further delegate that power") *(p. 107)*

deontological theories that focus on the inherent rightness or wrongness of behaviour, without regard to the behaviour's consequences or outcomes *(p. 9)*

devolution legislative arrangement whereby a central authority grants power to regional authorities that are subordinate to the central authority *(p. 105)*

discrimination prejudicial treatment of people on the ground of race, age, sex, disability, or other recognized ground; prohibited by human rights legislation *(p. 164)*

dissent refers (in the context of a split decision on appeal) to the judgment of one or more justices in the minority *(p. 138)*

distinguishable term given to a precedent from a higher court that a lower court decides not to follow, usually on the grounds that the facts in the cases differ *(p. 34)*

distributive justice theory of justice concerned with appropriate distributions of entitlements, such as wealth and power, in a society *(p. 10)*

division of powers refers to the divided jurisdiction—between Parliament, on the one hand, and the provinces, on the other hand—to make legislation in a federal state such as Canada *(p. 93)*

domestic law law of a particular state or society *(p. 20)*

double-aspect law law whose subject matter falls within a federal subject area and a provincial one *(p. 101)*

duty of competence lawyer's obligation to provide services that meet the standard of a reasonably skilled lawyer *(p. 320)*

duty of confidentiality lawyer's obligation not to divulge information concerning a client's affairs that has been acquired in the course of the professional relationship unless the client authorizes the lawyer to divulge this information *(p. 320)*

duty of disclosure Crown's mandatory disclosure to the accused, before the trial, of the evidence against him *(p. 284)*

duty of loyalty lawyer's obligation to avoid conflicts of interest between clients and between lawyer and client *(p. 321)*

equity discretionary legal decisions offered by judges in the Court of Chancery, based on fairness and providing relief from the rigid procedures that had evolved under common law courts *(p. 32)*

essential validity concerns a person's capacity to marry and the substantive requirements of a valid marriage *(p. 216)*

ethics standards of right and wrong, often applied to specific groups—for example, professions *(p. 7)*

executive branch of government that is responsible for implementing or administering the laws in Canada and whose authority, in this country, is divided between the federal, provincial, and territorial governments *(p. 109)*

expectation damages remedy for contract disputes that attempts to place the innocent party in the position she would have been in if the contract had been performed as promised and all of the contractual representations had been true *(p. 205)*

facta (sing. factum) written legal arguments to be presented on an appeal *(p. 136)*

fairness (also procedural fairness or natural justice) principle that fairness requires that certain "rights" be accorded to persons engaged with an administrative process, such as the right to notice, the right to be heard and to respond, the right to representation, and the right to an adjudicator who is free from bias or an appearance of bias *(p. 264)*

false imprisonment tort whereby one person totally restrains the movement of another person *(p. 187)*

federal paramountcy doctrine doctrine according to which, in the event of conflict between a federal law and a provincial law in an area over which both levels of government have jurisdiction, the federal law governs and overrides the provincial one *(p. 101)*

federal superior courts (or federal courts) comprising the Federal Court, the Federal Court of Appeal, the Tax Court of Canada, and the Court Martial Appeal Court *(p. 132)*

federalism in Canada, the division of state powers between the federal Parliament in Ottawa and the legislatures of the provinces and territories *(p. 72)*

fee simple interest or estate in land that is the closest to absolute ownership an owner can have, entitling her to possess the property, build on it, and transfer it to others during her lifetime or in a will at her death *(p. 210)*

feminist theories of law theories of law that generally concern the legal, social, and economic rights of and improving opportunities for women *(p. 17)*

feudalism socio-political system in medieval Europe based on relationships of obligation and allegiance among king, nobles, and subjects, with land given to subordinates in return for loyalty and military support *(p. 30)*

fiduciary duty in the context of a partnership, the responsibility to act carefully and reasonably in the best interest of the firm *(p. 232)*

fiduciary obligations trust-like obligations, such as loyalty and good faith, that apply in certain contexts, including lawyer–client dealings *(p. 319)*

formal validity concerns the formalities or ceremonial requirements of a marriage *(p. 216)*

general partnership business structure in which two or more persons carry on business in common with a view to profit *(p. 232)*

governor general Queen's representative in Canada, formally authorized to exercise her powers as head of the executive government in Canada but who, by convention, exercises these powers only on the advice of the prime minister and federal Cabinet *(p. 112)*

Governor in Council official name for the federal Cabinet *(p. 112)*

historic treaties treaties between Indigenous peoples and the Government of Canada made between 1701 and 1923, under the terms of which Indigenous people surrendered large tracts of land in exchange for reserve lands and other benefits *(p. 51)*

human rights rights that respect the dignity and worth of an individual *(p. 163)*

hybrid offence dual procedure offence, meaning that the Crown attorney has the option of choosing whether to prosecute it as a summary conviction offence or an indictable offence *(p. 279)*

imperial statute law passed by the English Parliament applying specifically to an overseas English colony *(p. 62)*

indictable offence most serious type of offence in the *Criminal Code* (for example, murder), carrying the most serious sentences *(p. 279)*

indictment written document, used in superior court, describing the offences with which the accused is charged *(p. 289)*

Indigenous law law of Indigenous peoples within states, as distinct from states' laws in relation to them *(p. 30)*

inferior courts provincial and territorial courts whose jurisdiction is limited to the less serious criminal matters, family and youth matters, and small claims disputes; the federal courts martial, part of the military court system, are also inferior courts *(p. 130)*

information written document, used in provincial court, describing the offences with which the accused is charged *(p. 289)*

Inns of Court professional associations for lawyers in England and Wales, with supervisory and disciplinary functions over their members and authority to call law students to the bar; the four Inns of Court today are Inner Temple, Middle Temple, Lincoln's Inn, and Gray's Inn *(p. 33)*

inquisitorial system feature of civil law proceedings whereby trial judges actively assist lawyers in presenting their cases and are free to call and question witnesses and to order investigations into other evidentiary matters; contrasts with the adversarial system used in common law courts *(p. 41)*

instrumentalist theories that focus on something—for example, justice or the law—as a means to an end *(p. 9)*

intellectual property property derived from the intellect or mind—works of art, inventions, and designs *(p. 214)*

intervener party, other than the original parties to a court proceeding, who does not have a substantial and direct interest in the proceeding but has interests and perspectives helpful to the judicial determination and whose input is accepted by the court *(p. 346)*

joint tenancy form of co-ownership that features the right of survivorship as well as the "four unities" of *possession* (each co-owner has an equal right to possess the entire property), *interest* (each co-owner has an identical interest in the property), *time* (the co-owners receive their interests at the same time), and *title* (the co-owners receive their interests under the same instrument, such as a will) *(p. 211)*

judgment final outcome or disposition of the dispute heard before the court or, when the court provides reasons for its judgment, the entire set of reasons *(p. 156)*

Judicial Committee of the Privy Council highest appeal authority for colonies in the British Empire; exercised final appeal for Canada until 1949 *(p. 75)*

judicial independence principle that judges should be free to make decisions based on the law and free from outside interference *(p. 150)*

judicial interim release formal name for bail; the release of an accused prior to her trial *(p. 288)*

judicial review (of decisions by administrative bodies)   process by which a superior court can review the decision of an administrative body or inferior court on two main grounds: substantive review (review of the merits of the decision) and procedural review (review of the process followed in making the decision) *(p. 259)*

judicial review on Charter grounds (or Charter challenge)   process by which a court reviews the constitutionality of legislation on the basis that it infringes the Charter *(p. 94)*

judicial review on federalism grounds   process by which a court reviews the constitutionality of legislation based on a division-of-powers analysis, that is, by determining whether one level of government has attempted to enact legislation in an area assigned to the other level under the Constitution *(p. 75)*

jurisdiction   refers (in the context of legislative power under the Constitution) to the specific subject areas over which the federal Parliament and the provincial legislatures have been assigned authority *(p. 96)*

jurisprudence   also known as "philosophy of law" or "science of law"; concerns theories that are used to describe, explain, or criticize the law *(p. 12)*

king's peace   the ideal peace and well-being of a nation that the English monarch was obliged to uphold and protect *(p. 31)*

law and society   kind of legal study that looks at law from a broadly social, interdisciplinary perspective *(p. 17)*

law society   governing body of lawyers in a province or territory *(p. 306)*

lawyer–client privilege   lawyer's obligation not to divulge confidential information concerning a client's affairs that has been communicated to the lawyer by the client and is connected to the giving or receiving of legal advice *(p. 321)*

leasehold interest   form of property ownership that implies an obligation to pay rent *(p. 210)*

legal aid   government funding of lawyers who provide legal assistance to persons with low income *(p. 333)*

legal ethics   rules of conduct that govern the legal profession, the primary purpose of which is to protect clients, the public, and the administration of justice *(p. 313)*

legal positivism   theory that the only valid source of law is the principles, rules, and regulations expressly enacted by the institutions or persons within a society that are generally recognized as having the power to enact them *(p. 14)*

legal realism   theory, developed in the United States and Scandinavian countries, that encouraged a more thoroughly empirical study of the process by which laws are made and applied *(p. 15)*

legislation   written laws made by legislative assemblies *(p. 91)*

legislative intent   legislature's express or implied intent in passing a statute *(p. 124)*

legislature   representative assembly charged under a constitution with making laws for a particular region or state *(p. 90)*

libel   kind of defamation that involves defamatory language in writing, such as in a newspaper article or book, whether in print or online *(p. 195)*

Lieutenant Governor in Council   official name for a provincial Cabinet *(p. 113)*

lieutenant governor   formal head of the provincial executive government who, by convention, exercises executive power on the advice of the provincial premier and Cabinet *(p. 112)*

limitation period   period in which a legal action must be taken or the ability to do so is lost *(p. 277)*

limited liability partnership   partnership structure used by certain professions in Canada (accountants and lawyers, for the most part) whereby partners are not liable for the professional negligence of other partners *(p. 233)*

limited partnership   partnership structure involving at least one general partner, who operates the partnership and is liable for any partnership debts, and at least one limited partner, who invests in the partnership but does not operate it or take part in managing its business and is not personally liable for its debts and obligations *(p. 233)*

lobbying   organized effort to influence legislators on behalf of a particular interest *(p. 345)*

majority   refers (in the context of a split decision on appeal) to the group of justices who form the majority and whose decision becomes the decision of the court *(p. 138)*

Marxist theories of law   legal theories, based on the writing of the communist philosopher Karl Marx, that are concerned with the distribution of wealth in a society; related to distributive justice theories *(p. 17)*

mediation   dispute resolution process whereby the parties try to reach a settlement with the assistance of a third party *(p. 336)*

mens rea   "guilty mind" or subjective mental element of a criminal offence (such as, depending on the offence, intending to bring about the consequences of one's actions or simply intending to perform the *actus reus*) *(p. 275)*

military law   constitutionally separate and relatively self-contained system of law regulating the Canadian Forces *(p. 23)*

misrepresentation   false representation made during contract negotiations *(p. 203)*

mitigating circumstance   factor in the case that causes the judge to impose a milder sentence on the convicted person than he or she would otherwise *(p. 293)*

modern treaties treaties between Indigenous peoples and the Government of Canada made after 1973 when Aboriginal title was recognized *(p. 51)*

morality standards of right and wrong, often associated with personal character *(p. 7)*

mortgage kind of charge against land that secures a debt owed by the landowner *(p. 210)*

municipal by-laws form of subordinate legislation passed by municipalities *(p. 107)*

natural law source of law that is higher than human-made (or positive) law and with which human-made law must comply in order to be valid *(p. 13)*

negligence area of tort law that addresses harm caused by carelessness, not intentional harm *(p. 189)*

negotiable instrument document that promises the payment of a specific amount of money to the payee, on demand or at a set time, and that can be transferred to a third party *(p. 237)*

negotiation dispute resolution process whereby the parties talk to each other directly and seek a mutually acceptable solution to their problem *(p. 336)*

nuisance in law, either public or private nuisance *(p. 195)*

occupiers' liability liability of occupiers of land for injuries that visitors sustain while on the occupiers' property *(p. 193)*

open court principle principle that judicial proceedings should be administered in public *(p. 149)*

parliamentary sovereignty doctrine that Parliament has ultimate and complete power to pass any law *(p. 108)*

patriate to remove a nation's legislation or constitution from the control of the mother country and bring it under the control of the nation itself *(p. 77)*

personal property security creditor's security based on the debtor's personal property *(p. 214)*

personal property tangible, movable objects as well as intangible interests, such as shares in a company *(p. 213)*

persuasive describes a precedent that a court is persuaded to give some weight to but is not bound to follow because the precedent is from another jurisdiction or is otherwise not binding *(p. 34)*

plaintiff individual, corporation, or other entity who initiates a non-criminal lawsuit *(p. 156)*

plea bargain agreement between the Crown and the defence on how the accused will plead in court and on the sentence he will receive *(p. 288)*

plead to answer to a criminal charge in ways permitted by the *Criminal Code* *(p. 288)*

POGG power general residuary power given to Parliament—in other words, the power to fill in the gaps left by the specifically enumerated areas of jurisdiction assigned to the two levels of government *(p. 96)*

positive law human-made law, as opposed to a higher law (natural law) that transcends persons or institutions *(p. 15)*

practice norms ethical standards and legal skills that legal practitioners must follow and possess to deliver legal services effectively *(p. 20)*

precedent court decision that, under the doctrine of *stare decisis*, is binding on lower courts in the same jurisdiction *(p. 33)*

preliminary inquiry hearing before a provincial court judge to determine whether the Crown has sufficient evidence for the accused to stand trial for the offence *(p. 289)*

premier political head of a provincial or territorial government who leads the party with control of the majority in the Legislative Assembly (in Nunavut, there are no political parties, but the premier must command the support of the majority in the Assembly) *(p. 113)*

prerogative writs special common law remedies for administrative infractions *(p. 266)*

pre-sentence report report, prepared by a probation officer, that provides information about the background and character of the offender to assist a judge in sentencing *(p. 294)*

prime minister political head of state in Canada who leads the party with control of the majority in the House of Commons *(p. 113)*

private bill bill dealing with a private matter that relates, for example, to a particular individual, corporation, or charity *(p. 102)*

private law law that concerns the relationships between persons *(p. 22)*

private nuisance tort that involves one person's using her property in such a way as to substantially interfere with another person's enjoyment or use of his property, but without any actual trespass occurring *(p. 195)*

pro bono term applied to legal work that lawyers do at no charge to help the public (from the Latin *pro bono publico*: "for the public good") *(p. 334)*

procedural law law relating to the process by which core rights and obligations are determined and enforced *(p. 20)*

proclamation special government order bringing a statute into force *(p. 102)*

prorogue to formally close a legislative session *(p. 95)*

provincial superior courts provincially constituted courts with inherent jurisdiction to hear all matters (unless taken away by legislation) and with two levels, a trial level and an appeal level; sometimes refers just to the trial level *(p. 131)*

public bill   bill dealing with a matter of public policy *(p. 101)*

public international law (or international law)   law relating primarily to international treaties and customs and to interstate relationships *(p. 20)*

public law   law dealing with the legal relationship between a state and individual members of the state *(p. 22)*

public nuisance   occurs when a public interest is interfered with—for example, when a highway is obstructed or a river is polluted through the defendant's actions *(p. 195)*

puisne   term applied to describe judges who rank below another judge or judges on the same court—for example, the judges below the chief justice on an appeal court *(p. 134)*

quasi-criminal offences   less serious offences, such as pollution or traffic offences, that do not fall under the federal criminal law power; they may be passed by all levels of government but are frequently created under provincial legislation *(p. 274)*

quasi-legislative materials   non-legislated written rules that relate to and affect a legal process *(p. 108)*

Queen's Privy Council for Canada   formal advisory council of the governor general, the active portion of which is the federal Cabinet *(p. 113)*

ratio* or *ratio decidendi   Latin phrase ("the reason for the decision") referring to the governing rule in a case or the way it was applied to the facts *(p. 33)*

reading   bill's formal presentation to the legislature before it becomes a statute *(p. 102)*

real property (or real estate)   land and anything attached to the land, such as buildings and resources *(p. 207)*

reference   special case in which the executive branch of government refers a question of law to a court of appeal, usually a question concerning the constitutionality of a statute or course of action the government is considering *(p. 136)*

regulations   form of subordinate legislation passed by a person or body (frequently the government Cabinet) to expand on or fill out a statute's legislative scheme *(p. 107)*

reliance damages   remedy for contract disputes that compensates the innocent party for expenses he incurred preparing for the performance of contractual obligations *(p. 206)*

reserve   to postpone rendering its decision, after a hearing has concluded, so that the court can carefully prepare the reasons for its judgment *(p. 137)*

respondent   individual, corporation, or other entity who won at trial and is responding to the appellant on an appeal to a higher court *(p. 156)*

responsible government   system of government in which the members of the executive branch are drawn from the elected members of the legislative branch and in which their power continues only so long as they enjoy the support of the majority in the legislature *(p. 110)*

restitution damages   remedy for contract disputes that compensates the innocent party for moneys usually paid over to the other party (deposits and part payments, for example) *(p. 206)*

retributive justice   theory of justice based on *lex talionis*, or the law of retaliation *(p. 9)*

royal assent   formal approval of a bill by the Queen's representative *(p. 102)*

royal prerogative   powers and privileges given by the common law to the Crown; a source of limited executive power *(p. 115)*

rule of law   key legal concept whose central tenets are that everyone is equal before the law and that power under the law should not be used arbitrarily *(p. 17)*

search warrant   warrant, issued by a justice of the peace or a provincial court judge, authorizing police to conduct a search *(p. 281)*

section 96 courts   provincial superior courts, so called because their judges are federally appointed under section 96 of the *Constitution Act, 1867 (p. 131)*

section   basic unit of a statute *(p. 122)*

sentence   punishment the judge imposes on a person convicted of a criminal offence *(p. 291)*

separation-of-powers doctrine   doctrine according to which separate powers are assigned to the legislative, executive, and judicial branches of government *(p. 90)*

slander   kind of defamation transmitted via oral or other transitory forms of communication *(p. 195)*

sociology of law   kind of sociological study that looks at law from a broadly social, interdisciplinary perspective *(p. 17)*

sole proprietorship   business that is owned and operated by an individual and that is not a legal entity separate from the owner *(p. 231)*

specific performance   remedy for contract disputes whereby the court orders the party in breach to perform his obligations as promised *(p. 206)*

standard of review   defines the level of deference the court pays to the tribunal when conducting a judicial review *(p. 261)*

stare decisis   Latin phrase ("to stand by decided matters") referring to the common law principle that a precedent is binding on lower courts in the same jurisdiction *(p. 33)*

statutes   primary form of legislation *(p. 91)*

statutory interpretation   process of interpreting legislation to resolve any ambiguities regarding its meaning or effect *(p. 122)*

strict liability tort   tort for which the defendant is held responsible even if the damaging action was neither intentional nor a result of negligence *(p. 193)*

style of cause   name of the case or title of the proceeding, consisting of the names of the parties to the dispute *(p. 157)*

subordinate (or delegated) legislation   legislation passed pursuant to a statute whereby the principal law-making power has delegated authority to another body to make laws *(p. 106)*

substantive law   law that deals with core rights and obligations *(p. 20)*

substantive review   review of an administrative decision's merits that considers both the legal and factual bases of the tribunal's analysis *(p. 261)*

summary conviction offence   least serious type of offence in the *Criminal Code* (for example, trespassing or disturbing the peace), tried only in provincial court and subject to the lightest sentences *(p. 277)*

summons   document served personally on an accused person requiring her to be in court at a certain date and time *(p. 287)*

superior court of criminal jurisdiction   highest court in each province and territory to hear criminal matters, sometimes with a jury, its designation varying by province and territory *(p. 279)*

supremacy clause   section 52(1) of the *Constitution Act, 1982,* which provides that the Constitution is the supreme law of Canada and empowers the courts to find that laws that are inconsistent with the Constitution are of no force and effect *(p. 93)*

Supreme Court of Canada   Canada's highest court and final court of appeal *(p. 132)*

tenancy in common   form of co-ownership that does not involve the four unities or the right of survivorship, meaning that a co-owner can transfer his interest to others during his lifetime or leave it to others in his will *(p. 211)*

territorial superior courts   federally constituted superior courts with jurisdiction in the territories *(p. 132)*

Torrens system (or land titles system)   system for registering property ownership that eliminates the transfer of title by deeds and replaces them with statutory transfer forms, meaning that the title is guaranteed (or indefeasible) *(p. 212)*

tort   type of civil wrong for which damages can be obtained by the person wronged *(p. 186)*

trespass to goods (or trespass to chattels)   tort whereby one person intentionally interferes with another's rightful possession of movable property *(p. 187)*

trespass to land   tort involving the physical intrusion by one person onto land occupied by another *(p. 187)*

trespass to person   intentional tort encompassing three subcategories of tort: assault, battery, and false imprisonment *(p. 186)*

undertaking (by an accused)   promise by an accused to the court, usually to appear back in court at a certain date and time *(p. 288)*

undertaking (by a lawyer)   clear statement of intention by a lawyer that is reasonably relied on by another person (often another lawyer) and amounting to a solemn promise that must be kept or the lawyer giving the undertaking will be liable for misconduct *(p. 319)*

unicameral   legislature with one house involved in the passage of legislation *(p. 91)*

unified family courts   special divisions of the trial level of a provincial superior court with complete jurisdiction over family law matters, including matters that would otherwise be heard in a provincial inferior court *(p. 140)*

unitary government   form of government whereby one supreme authority governs the whole country *(p. 72)*

verdict   finding of a jury on the matter before it—for example, whether the accused is guilty or not guilty *(p. 290)*

vicarious liability   the strict liability of one party for the fault of another due to the special relationship between them (typically, an employer–employee relationship) *(p. 194)*

writ   court document, obtained by a plaintiff, by which the defendant was informed that a particular type of action had been started against him *(p. 32)*

Index

Aboriginal law, 45
  see also Indigenous law
Aboriginal legal systems, 50, 62
Aboriginal peoples
  Charter and, 165-66,
    171, 175, 176, 367
  Constitution Act, 1867
    provisionre, 73
  Constitution Act, 1982
    provisionre, 83, 167, 171,
    175, 176, 208-9, 367, 368
  criminal law system and,
    see criminal law
  patriation of Constitution
    and, *see* patriation
    of Constitution
  sentencing, 292-93
  treaty rights and, 175, 367, 368
Aboriginal title, 80, 208-9
abuse of power, 18
access to justice, *see* legal
  services, access to
actus reus,
  example, 6
  defences, 291
  defined, 275
administrative law agencies, *see*
  administrative agencies
  generally, 250-51
  tribunals, *see* administrative
    tribunals
administrative agencies
  administrative function, 253
  appeal of decisions, 259, 260
  Constitution Act, 1867
    provisions re, 252
  constitutional basis of, 252

constitutional limitations
  on, 252-53
cross-delegation, 253
defined, 251
delegated power of, 253-57
  administrative
    functions, 254-56
  cross-delegation, 253
  generally, 251
  interdelegation, 253
  legislative functions, 254
  permissible–impermissible,
    chart, 255
  quasi-judicial functions,
    253, 256
  redelegation, 253
  subdelegation, 254
described, 251-52
executive function, 253
functions
  administrative, 253
  executive, 253
  legislative, 253
  quasi-judicial function, 253
interdelegation, 253
judicial review
  defined, 259
  jurisdiction of superior
    courts, 260
  privative clauses, 261
legislative function, 253
prerogative writs, 266
privative clauses, 261
procedural rules of, 258
public's interaction with, 258
quasi-judicial function, 253
redelegation, 254

remedies on review, 266
review of decisions
  discretionary decisions
    of, 264-65
  grounds for, 261-65
  procedural fairness
    issues, 264-65
  procedural review, 264
  standard of review, 261
  substantive review, 261, 265
section 96 court, deemed as, 253
subdelegation, 254
substantive rules of, 258
tribunals, *see* administrative
  tribunals
administrative tribunals
  challenging decisions, 259-66
    appeals, 259
    judicial review, 259, 260
  defined, 256
  independence, 256
  jurisdiction, 256
  subject–jurisdiction chart, 257
adversarial system, 36
affinity, defined, 218
affirmative action, 167, 174
aggravating circumstance, 293
alimony, *see* family law
alternative dispute
  resolution, 306, 336-38
  arbitration, 337
  comparison of forms, 338
  defined, 336
  mediation, 336-37
  negotiation, 336
annulment, 218
appearance notice, 287

appellant, defined, 156
arbitration, 337
arraignment, 289
arrest, 280
articles, defined, 307
assault, 186-87
assent, 102, 103, 105
assizes, 31
attorney/attorney-at-law, 308
automatism, 291

banns of marriage, 219
barrister, 308
battery, 187
behaviour, norms or standards, 5
benchers, 306, 322
bicameral, 91, 95
bijural, defined, 28, 29
bill, defined, 101
Bill of Rights (Canada), *see*
    Canadian Bill of Rights
Bill of Rights (UK), 36,
    73, 74, 115, 161
bills of exchange, 237
binding, defined, 33, 145
Bitumen Reference Case, 99-100
bona fide occupational
    requirement, 166, 167
bright line rule, defined, 321
British North America Act, see
    Constitution Act, 1867
browse-wrap agreement, 201
builders lien, 238
business law
    builders/construction liens, 238
    business structures, 231-36
    business transactions, 237-38
    corporations, 234-36
        advantages and
            disadvantages, 236
        Charter application to, 236
        creation of, 236
        directors, 235
        generally, 234-35
        liability, 235
        name, 236
        NUANS search, 236
        officers, 235

piercing/lifting the
    corporate veil, 235
private, 236
public, 236
generally, 230
negotiable instruments, 237
partnerships, 232-34
    advantages, 233-34
    comparison of types,
        chart, 234
    disadvantages, 233-34
    fiduciary duty, 232
    firm, 232
    general partnership, 232
    liability, 233
    limited liability
        partnership, 233
    limited partnership, 233
sole proprietorships, 231-32
    advantages, 232
    business name, 231
    disadvantages, 232
    liability of owner, 231
    licences, 232
    permits, 232
    registration, 231
    taxes, 231

called to the bar, meaning of, 308
Canada Act 1982, 82, 93
Canadian Bill of Rights,
    81, 82, 173, 178
*Canadian Charter of Rights
    and Freedoms*
    Aboriginal and treaty rights,
        83, 171, 175, 176, 208-9, 367
    application of, 167, 175-76
    arbitrary detention, 172, 364-65
    constitutional patriation, 93
    corporations, application to, 236
    criminal law, 271
    cruel and unusual
        punishment, 173, 365
    democratic rights, 170, 364
    detention, 172, 364-65
    enforcement, 175, 367
    equality rights, 11, 173-74, 365
    fundamental freedoms, 168, 364

fundamental justice, 172
general provisions, 175
generally, 167
guarantee of rights and
    freedoms, 168, 364
infringement–justification
    analysis, 169-70
judicial review on Charter
    grounds, 94
legal rights, 173-74, 364-65
minority language rights,
    174-75, 366-67
mobility rights, 171-72, 364
notwithstanding clause,
    176, 367-68
Oakes test, 169-70
official languages,
    174-75, 365-66
override clause, 176, 367-68
parliamentary power and, 109
presumption of
    innocence, 173, 365
proclamation of, 162
reasonable limits clause, 169-70
self-incrimination, 173, 365
sexual orientation as analogous
    prohibited ground, 173, 174
text of, 364-68
unreasonable search and
    seizure, 172, 364
Canadian Constitution, *see also*
    patriation of Constitution
    constitutional exemption, 93
    convention, 78
    division of powers, 93
    executive power, *see*
        executive power
    exhaustiveness, principle of, 109
    frozen concepts, 100
    judiciary, *see* judiciary
    legislative power, *see*
        legislative power
    legislative void, 109
    living tree, 100
    principle of
        exhaustiveness, 109
    reading down, 93
    reading in, 93, 174

separation-of-powers
  doctrine, 90
  severance of, 93
  striking down, 93
  temporary suspension, 93
  watertight compartments, 100
Canadian Judicial Council, 151, 152
Canadian law, *see also*
  Canadian Constitution
  civil law, *see* civil law
  common law, *see* common law
  generally, *see* law
  history of, *see* historical
    development
case brief, 157
cases
  briefing, 157
  citation, 157
  decision, 156
  defined, 156
  judgment, 156
  law reports, 156-57
  neutral citation, 157
  reading, 156
  source of law, 37
  style of cause, 157
  terminology, 156
  understanding, 156
causation
  criminal law, 6
  tort law, 6, 189, 192
caveat emptor, 239
cession, 62
Chancery, 30, 32, 210
charge, *see* mortgages; property
Charlottetown Accord, 94-95
Charter, *see Canadian Charter
  of Rights and Freedoms*
Charter challenge, 94
charters (royal), 31
chattels, 213
cheque, 237
  drawee, 237
  endorsement in blank, 237
  parties, 237
  payee, 237
  payer, 237
  restrictive endorsement, 237

Chinese wall, 321
Civil Code of Lower Canada, 67
Civil Code of Quebec (*Code
  civil du Québec*)
  defined, 40, 66-67
  historical origins, 65-66
  revised, 67
  topics of, 40
civil law, *see also* common law;
  historical development
  alternative meanings, 41
  Code of Hammurabi, 38
  common law, comparison
    with, 41-43
  Dark Ages, during, 39
  defined, 28, 29, 37
  harmonizing with Canadian
    common law, 43
  inquisitorial system, as, 41
  meanings, 23
  origins of, 37-41
  post-Renaissance
    period, in, 39-41
  Roman era, 38-39
civil liberties
  Canadian Bill of Rights, 161, 162
  *Canadian Charter of Rights
    and Freedoms*, *see
    Canadian Charter of
    Rights and Freedoms*
  civil rights versus, 160
  defined, 160
  evolution of, 161-62
  future of, 176-77
  human rights, *see* human rights
  implied bill of rights, 161
  US civil rights movement, 161-62
civil rights, 160-62
civil wrong, 186
click-wrap agreement, 201
Code Civil (France), 40
Code of Hammurabi, 10, 38
Code of Ur-Nammu, 38
codes of conduct, 315, 316
Colonial Laws Validity Act, 1865, 92
commissioner
  defined, 114
  territorial, 105

Commissioner in Executive
  Council, 114
common law, *see also* civil law;
  historical development
  adversarial system and, 36
  alternative meanings, 41
  applying versus making law, 35
  Bill of Rights, 36
  Chancery, 30
  civil law, comparison
    with, 41-43
  Court of Chancery versus, 32
  defined, 28, 29, 37
  equity versus, 32
  feudalism and, 30
  harmonizing with
    Canadian civil law, 43
  judge-made rules, 129
  Judicature Acts, 32-33
  judicial immunity, 152
  meanings, 23
  origins of, 30-33
  pre-Norman England, law in, 30
  precedents, use of, 33-37
  royal court system,
    development of, 31
  stare decisis, *see stare decisis*
  statutes, 129
  writ system, 31-32
competence, duty of, 320
cones of silence, 321
Confederation, defined, 64
confidence convention, 113
confidentiality, duty of, 320
conflict of interest, 322
congress, 90
conjunctive elements, 6
consanguinity, 218
consent, 188, 290
constitution, *see* Canadian
  Constitution
Constitution Act, 1791, 66, 67
Constitution Act, 1867
  Aboriginal peoples and,
    47, 51, 52, 53, 54, 73
  administrative agencies and, 252
  criminal law and, 271, 273, 285
  enactment, 70-71

Constitution Act, 1867 (continued)
  executive power provisions,
    112-13, 352-53
  judiciary provisions, 129-30, 360
  legislative power, 353, 357-58
  patriation of Constitution
    and, 82-83
  private law provisions, 185
  text of, 351-62
Constitution Act, 1982
  Aboriginal peoples and, 83,
    171, 175, 176, 208-9, 368
  Charter provisions, *see*
    Canadian Charter of
    Rights and Freedoms
  constitutional amendment
    provisions, 94, 368-70
  constitutionally
    entrenched, 91-92
  generally, 91
  patriation of Constitution
    and, 82-83
  statutes, entrenchment, 82-83
  supremacy clause, 93, 370
  text of, 363-74
constitutional law, defined, 83
constitutionally entrenched,
  defined, 92
construction lien, 238
consumer law
  advertising standards, 244-45
  Canada Consumer
    Protection Act, 242
  Competition Act, 240
    bid-rigging, 240
    multi-level marketing
      plans, 240
    price-fixing, 240
    pyramid schemes, 240
  federal legislation, 240-42
  Food and Drugs Act, 241-42
  news and media
    monopolies, 241
  offences, punitive
    damages, 243-44
  protection law, generally, 238-39
  provincial legislation, 243
  Sale of Goods Acts, 239-40

contract law
  arbitration clauses, 202*n*
  bargaining power, 204
  breach of contract, 203
  choice of law clause, 202*n*
  condition, 202, 203
  condition precedent, 202
  contingent agreement, 202
  contractual negotiations,
    198, 200
  counteroffer, 198
  damages, 205-6
    causation, 206
    expectation damages, 205
    general damages, 205
    liquidated damages, 206
    mitigation, 206
    monetary, 32
    punitive damages, 206
    reliance damages, 205, 206
    remoteness, 206
    restitution damages,
      205, 206
    special damages, 205
    wrongful dismissal, for, 206-7
  duress, 204
  duty of good faith, 199-200
  duty of honesty, 199-200
  electronic contracts, 201
  exclusion clauses, 202
  express term, 202
  formation of contract, 197-99
    acceptance, 197, 198
    certainty of terms, 197, 199
    consideration, 197, 198-99
    formal requirements,
      197, 199
    intention to contract,
      197, 199
    offer, 197, 198
  forum selection clause, 202*n*
  generally, 197
  illegality, 205
  implied terms, 202
  incapacity, 204
  inequality of bargaining
    power, 204
  injunctions, 32, 206

  misrepresentation, 203
  mistake and frustration, 203-4
  non-performance,
    excuses for, 203-5
  pervasiveness of contracts, 197
  privity rule, 205
  promises, 202
  rectification, 32
  remedies, 205-6
    damages, *see* contract,
      damages
    injunction, 206
    rescission, 203
    specific performance, 32, 206
  representations, 202
  restraint of trade, 205
  revocation of offer, 198
  serious breach of contract, 203
  specific performance, 32, 206
  standard form contracts, 200
  terms and terminology, 201-3
  third-party beneficiaries, 205
  unconscionability, 204
  undue influence, 204
  unfair bargain, 204
  warranty, 202, 203
  weaker parties, 204
convention, defined, 110, 111-12
conviction, 289
copyright, 215
corporations, *see* business law
Corpus Juris Civilis, 39, 40
corrective justice, 9
court, defined, 128
Court Martial Appeal Court,
  see military courts
Court of Chancery, 31,
  32, 143, 210, 211
Court of Common Pleas, 31
Court of King's (or
  Queen's) Bench, 31
courts, *see also* judiciary
  criminal courts, *see* criminal law
  domestic violence court, 141
  drug treatment court, 141
  equitable jurisdiction, *see*
    equitable jurisdiction
  federal courts, *see* federal courts

first instance, 128
general jurisdiction, 128
Indigenous courts, 141
inferior, *see* inferior courts
inherent jurisdiction, 128
judges, *see* judges
mental health courts, 141
military courts, *see*
    military courts
origins of, *see* common law
overview, 129, 133
provincial, *see* provincial courts
section 96 courts, 131, 132
small claims court, *see*
    small claims court
superior, *see* superior courts
Supreme Court, *see*
    under judiciary
Tax Court, *see* Tax Court
territorial, 129
trial, *see* trial courts
wellness court, 141
coutumes, 39, 40
Covid-19 pandemic, 204
credit card, 237
Criminal Code, *see* criminal law
criminal law
    Aboriginal people and,
        292-93, 295-98
        justice principles, 296
        sentencing principles,
            292-93
        traditional practices,
            adapting, 296-97
    abortion, 7
    absolute liability offences, 274
    actus reus, see actus reus
    assisted dying, 7, 277
    burden/standard of
        proof, 275-76
    community shock test, 281
    Constitution Act, 1867
        provisions, 271, 273, 285
    correctional system, 294
    Criminal Code
        basis of, 271-73
        classification of offences
            in, 276-79

organization of, 276-77
    sentencing provisions,
        291-94
criminal courts
    original jurisdiction re, 285
    specialized courts, 285-87
criminal versus quasi-
    criminal offences, 273-75
Crown election offence, 279
defences
    automatism, 291
    consent, 290
    duress, 291
    intoxication, 291
    mental disorder, 291
    mistake of fact, 291
    mistake of law, 291
    necessity, 291
    provocation, 290-91
    self-defence, 290
domestic violence
    courts, 286-87
drugs, 7, 273
drug treatment courts, 286
dual procedure offence, 279
elements of criminal
    offence, 275
generally, 270-71
hybrid offences, 279
indictable offences, 279
Indigenous courts, 287
limitation period, 277, 279
mens rea, see mens rea
mental health court, 285-86
Oakes test, 169
overview chart, 272
pleas
    autrefois acquit, 288
    autrefois convict, 288
    guilty, 288
    not guilty, 288
    pardon, 288
police investigation, 279-83
    arrest, 280
    confessions, voluntary
        requirement, 281
    detention, 280
    disclosure duty, 283, 288

generally, 279-80
    search and seizure, 280-82
    search warrant, 281
presumption of
    innocence, 169, 275
pretrial hearing conference, 288
prostitution law
    changes to, 7
    constitutionality of, 278
provincial offences, 274
racism, 282-83
reasonable limits, 169
reverse onus, 169
sentencing, 291-94
    Aboriginal offenders, 292-93
    aggravating
        circumstances, 293
    Criminal Code provisions
        re, 291-94
    defined, 291-92
    Gladue principles,
        292-93, 296
    mitigating
        circumstances, 293
    pre-sentence report, 294
statutory sources of, 271-73
strict liability offences, 274
summary conviction
    offences, 276, 277, 279
superior court of criminal
    jurisdiction, 279
systemic racism, 282-83
trial process and procedure
    appearance notice, 287
    arraignment, 289
    conviction, 289
    courts, 285-87
    defences, 290-91
    election, 289
    indictment, 289
    information, 289
    judicial interim release, 288
    plea, 288
    plea bargain, 288
    preliminary inquiry, 289
    pretrial procedures, 287-89
    sentencing, *see* criminal
        law, sentencing

criminal law (*continued*)
summons, 287
undertaking, 288
verdict, 290
unreasonable search
and seizure, 172
voir dire, 280
*Youth Criminal Justice
Act*, 273, 294-95
critical legal studies, 17
critical race theory, 17
cross-delegation, 253
Crown
defined, 110
title to land, 209
Crown attorney, 270, 308*n*
Crown counsel, 270*n*
Crown immunity, 115, 116
Crown prosecutor, 270*n*, 283-84
Crown privilege, 115
curia regis, 30, 31, 39
customary law, 28
customs, 39

damages
compensatory, 196
contractual, *see* contract law
elements of remedies, 6
exemplary, 244
general, 196
monetary, 32
punitive, 10, 196, 243-44
special, 196
wrongful dismissal, 206-7
debit card, 237
deceit claims, 188*n*
decision, defined, 156
deeds, 212
defamation, 195
hyperlinking, 196
justification, 195
privilege, 196
responsible journalism, 195
truth, 195
defendant
defined, 156
origins, 32
private law, 185

delegated legislation, 106
delegatus non potest delegare, 107, 254
denunciation, 10
deontological, defined, 9
deterrence, 10
devolution, 105
disclosure, duty of, 283-85, 288
discrimination, 164, 166-67, 173
disjunctive elements, 6
dissent, defined, 138
distinguishable, defined, 34, 145
distributive justice, 10-11
division of powers, 93
divorce, *see* family law
domestic law, 20, 184
domestic violence court, 141
double-aspect law, 101
drug treatment court, 141
duress, 204, 275, 291

equality, 11
equitable jurisdiction, 41, 203, 204
equitable owner, 211
equitable title, 211
equity, 32
"equity follows the law" maxim, 32
equity prevails, 33
mortgages, 210
essential validity, 216
ethics, defined, 7
ethics, professional, *see
under* legal profession
Exchequer, *see* Chancery
Exchequer Court, *see*
Court of Chancery
executive, defined, 109-10
executive power
conventions, 110, 111-12
Crown immunity, 115, 116
Crown/sovereign, 110, 111
dual executive, 110
elected office, 111
executive influence,
limits of, 116-17
generally, 109-10
offices, 113-14
responsible government
and, 110-12

royal prerogative, 115-16
sources of, 112-16
common law, 115-16
Constitution Act, 1867
provisions, 112-13
conventional practice, 113-14
offices, 113-14
statute law and
common law, 116
expectation damages, 205-6
extrajudicial remedies, 196

factum/facta, 136
fairness, 264
false imprisonment, 187
family law
child support, 221, 223
common law marriage, 222-23
courts, *see* judiciary,
provincial courts
divorce, 220-22
children, custody,
and access, 221
division of family assets, 222
grounds for, 221
support obligations, 221, 223
generally, 216
maintenance, 221
marriage, 216-20
affinity, 218
age requirement, 219
annulment, 218
banns of marriage, 219
common law marriage,
222-23
consanguinity, 218
consent requirement, 219
consummation ability, 218
essential validity, 216-19
formal validity, 216, 219-20
polygamy, 217
rights and
responsibilities, 220
sham marriages, 219
shotgun wedding, 219
two persons
requirement, 217
unmarried requirement, 218

marriage breakdown, 220
matrimonial property, 220, 222
spousal support, 221
federal courts, 129, 143
  defined, 132
  divisions, 143
  Federal Court of
    Appeal, 132, 143
  inferior courts, 131
  generally, *see* judiciary
  inferior, 131
  military, *see* military courts
  superior courts, 132
  Tax Court of Canada, *see*
    Tax Court of Canada
federal paramountcy doctrine, 101
federalism, 72, 75, 76, 78, 83, 108-9
fee simple, 210
feminist theories of law, 17
feudalism, 30
fiduciary duty, 233
fiduciary obligations, 319
firm, *see* business law,
  partnerships
First Nations, *see* Aboriginal;
  Indigenous law/people
foreclosure, 211
formal validity, 216-19
frozen concepts, 100

garnishment, 238
general partnership, 232
Germanic laws, 30
globalization, 28
governor general, defined, 112, 113
Governor General in Council, 113
Governor in Council, 112

habeas corpus, 74, 172
historical development
  Aboriginal legal systems, 50, 62
  Alberta, 69
  British Columbia, 69
  British North America Act, 70
    division of powers
      under, 72-73
    interpretation of, 75-76
    omissions in, 73-75

Chief Dan George, lament for
  Confederation, 74-75, 79
*Civil Code of Quebec (Code
  civil du Québec)*, 66-67
Confederation
  conferences, 70-71
English law, common law
  rules of reception, 60-62
    adoption, 62
    conquest/cession, 62
    imperial statutes, 62
    settlement, 62
English settlement,
  legal effect of, 62
federalism
  choice of, 72
  judicial review on
    grounds of, 75-76
  Judicial Committee of the
    Privy Council, role of, 75
  Manitoba, 67-68
  New Brunswick, 65
  Newfoundland and
    Labrador, 63-64
  Northwest Territories, 70
  Nova Scotia, 64
  Nunavut, 70
  Ontario, 67
  patriation of Constitution, *see*
    patriation of Constitution
  post-Confederation issues, 73-76
  Prince Edward Island, 64-65, 70
  Quebec, 65-66
  reception dates of
    English law, 63
  Saskatchewan, 68
  Yukon, 70
human rights
  affirmative action
    programs, 167, 174
  bona fide occupational
    requirement exceptions,
    166, 167
  *Canadian Human Rights
    Act*, 164-66
    Aboriginal people
      and, 165-66
  defined, 163

  discrimination, defined, 164
  provincial/territorial
    legislation, 164
hybrid
  offence, 279
  structure of rules, 6
hyperlinking, 196

illegality, 205
imperial statute, defined, 62
incapacity, 204
indictable offence, 279
indictment, 289
Indigenous law/people, 28, 30
  Aboriginal law, 45
  access to justice, 341, 343
  *Canadian Human Rights
    Act*, 165-66
  colonial context, 44
  constitution, 78-80, 83
  Constitution Act, 51, 52, 83
  courts, 141 287
  criminal courts, 287
    see also criminal law
  custom, 50
  defined, 45
  duty to consult, 53
  First Nations, 45
  freedom of religion, 171
  Gayanashagowa, 49
  historic treaties, 51
  human rights, 165-66
  Indian, 45
  Indian Act, 51, 165-66
  Inuit, 45
  Iroquois Confederacy, 49
  land claims, 51, 52, 80
  Métis, 45
  Métis Law of the Hunt, 50
  modern treaties, 51
  nature of, 48-50
  new directions, 54-55
  patriation process, 78-80
  religious freedom, 171
  Royal Commission on
    Aboriginal Peoples, 296-98
  Royal Proclamation of 1763, *see*
    Royal Proclamation of 1763

Indigenous law/people (*continued*)
   Sparrow test, 52
   title to property, 51, 52
   Truth and Reconciliation
      Commission, 296-98
   Van der Peet test, 52
industrial design, 215
inferior courts, 128, 130-31
   federal, 132
   provincial, 130-31
information, 289
injunction, 32, 196
Inns of Court, 33
inquisitorial system, 41
instrumentalist, defined, 9
intellectual property, 215
intention, criminal law, 6
intentional torts, *see under* torts
interdelegation, 253
international law, 20, 184*n*
international trade, 28
intervener, 346
intoxication, 291
intrusion upon seclusion, 188*n*
invasion of privacy, 188*n*
Islamic law, 28

joint tenancy, 211
judges, *see also* courts
judgment, defined, 156
Judicial Committee of the
   Privy Council, 75-76
     see also Privy Council
judicial independence, 150-52
judicial interim release, 288
judicial process, 15
judicial review, *see under*
   administrative agencies
judicial review on Charter
   grounds, 94
judicial review on federalism
   grounds, 75-76
     good behaviour, 151
     inferior court, 149
       appointment process, 149
       constitutional
          jurisdiction, 149
       qualifications, 149

judges affair, 117*n*
judicial immunity, 152
judicial independence, 152
military, 149
National Judicial Institute, 146
patronage, 147
role of, 15
statutes, 129
superior court, 146-48
   appointment authority,
     145, 146-47
   appointment process,
     145, 147
   qualifications, 148
   training, 145
tenure, 151
territorial, 149
judiciary
   case law, reading and
     understanding, 156-58
   common law, 129
   constitutional protection, 151
   court
     Constitution Act, 1867
       provisions re, 129-30
     defined, 128
     types, 128-29
   federal court system
     features of, 142
     Federal Court, 142-43
     Federal Court of
       Appeal, 142-43
     Tax Court of Canada, 144
   federal courts, 131, 132
   generally, 128-29
   hierarchy, chart, 133
   inferior courts, 130-31, 132
   judges, *see* judges
   judgments, reading and
     understanding, 156-58
   judicial appointments,
     see judges
   judicial immunity, 152
   judicial independence,
     150-52
   military court system, 144
   open court principle, 149-50
   precedents, system of

binding authority,
   33, 129, 145
distinguishable, 34
persuasive authority,
   34, 145
ratio decidendi, 33, 145
stare decisis, 33,
   129, 144, 145
provincial court systems
   family courts, 140
   generally, 138
   inferior courts,
     130-31, 140-41
   superior courts,
     131-32, 138-39
   unified family courts, 140
provincial courts, 130-31
puisne judges, 134
role of, 129
superior courts, 130, 131-32
Supreme Court of Canada,
   132, 133, 134-38
   appeal to as of right, 136
   composition, 43
   described, 43, 134-35
   judges of, 134, 136-37
   judgments of, 137-38
   leave to appeal to, 135
   references to, 136
territorial court systems,
   141-42
   inferior courts, 130-31, 142
   superior courts,
     131-32, 142
territorial courts, 130-31
jurisdiction, defined, 96
jurisprudence, defined, 12
just society, 11, 77
justice
   access to, *see* legal
     services, access to
   corrective, 9
   definitions of, 8-9
   distributive, 10-11
   image of, 10
   law and, 8-11
   rectificatory, 9
   retributive, 9-10

justices of the peace, 306
Justinian Code, 39

Kinder Morgan pipeline, 99
king's peace, 31

laissez-faire, meaning of, 239
land claims, 80
land titles system, 212-13
law
    bijural jurisdiction, 28, 29
    civil, *see* civil law
    common, *see* common law
    defined, 5
    divisions of, 20-23
        chart, 21-22
    domestic law, 20, 184
    economics and, 17
    ethics and, 6-7
    international law, 20, 184*n*
    justice and, *see* justice
    legislation, *see* legislation
    military law, 23
    morality and, 6-7
    private law, 22, 184
    procedural law, 20
    public law, 22, 184
    religion and, 11-12
    retaliation, 10
    rule of, *see* rule of law
    rules and, 5-6
    sources of, 36-37
    substantive law, 20
    terminology, 23
    theories of
        analytic, 12
        critical legal studies, 17
        critical race theory, 17
        feminist theories, 17
        jurisprudence, 12
        legal positivism, 4, 14-15
        legal realism, 4, 15-16
        Marxist theories, 17
        natural law theory, 4, 13-14
        normative, 12
        rule of law, *see* rule of law
        sociology of law, 17
        utilitarianism, 16

law and society, defined, 17
law clerk, *see* legal profession
Law of the Twelve Tables, 38-39
law reform commissions, 343-44
law reports, 156-57
law society, 306
lawyer–client privilege, 321
lawyers, *see* legal profession
lay benchers, 306
leasehold interests, 210
legal aid, 333
legal information, public
    access to, 338-39
legal positivism, defined, 14-15
legal profession
    conflict of interest, 322
    disciplinary proceedings, 322-23
    educational requirements, 307-8
    ethical duties, 315-25
        client, to, 319-22
        competence, 320
        confidentiality, 320
        court, to, 317-18
        fiduciary obligations, 319
        general public, to, 318-19
        lawyer–client privilege, 321
        loyalty, 321
        notaries, of, 324-25
        paralegals/clerks/
          assistants, re, 324
        profession, to, 318-19
        state, to, 317
    ethics, professional, 313-25
        advocacy and, 317-18
        CBA Code, 315-16
        codes of conduct, 315, 316
        duties, *see* ethical duties
        FLSC Model Code, 316
        generally, 313
        integrity, 316
        judges, 314-15
        lawyers, 315
        undertakings, 319
    generally, 304
    integrity, 316, 317
    judges/adjudicators, 306
    law clerks, 308
    law firms, 307

    law-related positions, 312-13
    law societies, 308, 315
    lawyers, 307
    legal assistants, 310-11
    notaries, 311-12
    origins of, 305
    paralegals, 308-10, 324, 335
    professionalism, 316
legal realism, defined, 15-16
legal services, access to
    ADR, *see* alternative
        dispute resolution
    government measures
        to enhance, 339-43
    legal aid plans, 333
    legal scholarship, 336
    ombudsman, office of, 341, 342
    paralegals, role of, 335
    prepaid plans, 335-36
    pro bono legal services,
        334, 335
legislation, *see also* statutes
    defined, 91
    interpretation, 122, 124
    reading, 122-25
    source of law, 37
    understanding, 122-25
legislative assembly, 90
legislative intent, 124
legislative power
    generally, 90-91
    legislation, defined, 91
    legislative void, 109
    legislature, defined, 90-91
    municipal by-laws, 107-8
    parliamentary power
        Charter and, 109
        constitutional amendment
          and, 109
        federalism and, 109
    parliamentary sovereignty,
        doctrine of, 108, 109
    quasi-legislative materials, 108
    regulations, 107
    statutes, *see* statutes
    subordinate legislation, 106-7
legislative void, 109
legislature, defined, 91

lessee/lessor, 210
letter of credit, 237
letters patent, 115
lex talionis, 10
LGBTQ2+, 277
libel, 195
Lieutenant Governor in
    Council, 112, 113
limitation period, 277, 279
llmlted liability partnership, 233-34
limited partnership, 233
living tree, 100
lobbying, defined, 345
loyalty, duty of, 321

Magna Carta, 74, 115, 161
majority, defined, 138
manifest destiny, 71
marriage, *see* family law
Marxist theories of law, 17
McGill Guide, 157
McLachlin, Right Honourable
    Beverley, 146
M-commerce, 201
mediation, 336-37
medical assistance in dying, 7, 277
Meech Lake Accord, 94
mens rea, 172, 273, 275, 291
mental disorder, 291
mental health court, 141
military courts, 129
    Court Martial Appeal
        Court, 132, 143, 144
    General Court Martial, 131, 144
    judges, appointment of, 147
    Standing Court Martial,
        131, 144
military law, 23
misrepresentations, 203
mistake of fact, 291
mistake of law, 291
mitigating circumstance, 293
morality
    defined, 7
    descriptive, 7
    ethics and, 6-7
    laws, relation to, 6
    normative, 7

mortgages, 210-11
    foreclosure, 211
    redemption, 211
multiculturalism, 28
multidisciplinary practices
    (MDPs), 307
municipal by-laws, 107-8
murder, 6

Napoleonic Code, 40
National Judicial Institute, 146
natural justice, 264
natural law, 13-14
necessity, 291
negligence, *see* tort law
negotiable instrument, 237
negotiation, 336
neighbour principle, 11-12, 319
neutral citation, 157
Nicomachean Ethics (Aristotle), 9, 13
norms, 5
nuisance, 195

occupiers' liability, 193
ombudsperson, 341, 342
open court principle, 149-50

paralegals, 308-10, 335
parlement, 39
Parliament, 90-91, 95-96, 101-2
parliamentary power, 109
parliamentary sovereignty, 37, 108-9
partnerships, *see* business law
patents, 215
patriate, defined, 77
patriation of Constitution
    Aboriginal land claims, 80
    Aboriginal peoples and, 78-80
    Aboriginal rights, 83
    Constitution Act, 1867, 82-83
    Constitution Act, 1982, 82-83
    constitutional law, effects on, 83
    domestic amending formula, 78
    federalism versus
        separatism, 77-78
    generally, 77
    "persons" case, 81
    Trudeau, Pierre, 77-78

women and, 81-82
patronage, 147
personal property, *see*
    property law
personal property security, 214
persuasive, deflned, 34, 145
pith and substance, 96, 100
plain language movement, 23
plaintiff
    defined, 156
    origin of, 31
    private law, 185
plea bargain, 288
plead, 288
POGG power, 73, 96, 103
police, *see* criminal law
pollution offences, 274
positive law, 15
practice norms, 20
pre-sentence report, 294
precedent
    civil law, 41
    common law, 37, 129
    comparative analysis, 36
    defined, 33, 144-45
    developing, 35
    distinguishable, 34, 145
    flow of, 34
    new, 35
    persuasive, 34
    policy, 36
precedents, system of, *see* judiciary
preliminary inquiry, 289
premier, 113
prerogative writs, 266
pretrial hearing conference, 288
prima facie, 190
prime minister, 113
private bill, 102
private law
    burden/standard of proof, 185
    civil law, 41
    Constitution Act, 1867
        provisions, 185
    constitutional basis of, 185
    contracts, *see* contract law
    defined, 22
    family law, *see* family law

property law, *see* property law
torts, *see* tort law
private nuisance, 195
privilege, lawyer–client, 321
Privy Council, 75-76, 81
pro bono, defined, 334
procedural fairness, 18, 264
procedural law, 20
proclamation, 102
promissory note, 237
property law
   intellectual property, 214-15
      copyright, 215
      described, 214
      industrial design, 215
      patents, 215
      trademarks, 215
      types of, chart, 215
   personal property, 213-14
      chattels, 213
      corporeal interests, 213
      described, 213
      incorporeal interests, 213
      intangible interests, 213
      personal property security
        legislation, 214
      possession, 213
      security interests, 214
      tangibles, 213
   real property, 207-13
      Aboriginal title, 208-9
      co-ownership, 211
      condominium, 211
      deeds, 212
      described, 207-8
      equitable owner, 211
      equitable title, 211
      escheat, 209
      fee simple ownership, 210
      interests in land, 209-11
      joint tenancy, 211
      land title registry
        system, 212-13
      leasehold interests, 210
      legal versus equitable
        title, 211
      mortgages, 210-11
      registry systems, 212-13

rights and obligations, 212
riparian rights, 212
strata lot, 211
tenancy in common, 211
title insurance, 213
Torrens system, 212-13
townhouse, 211
trustee, 211
types of ownership, 209-11
prorogued, 95
provincial courts, 129
provincial statutes, *see*
  statutes, provincial
    inferior courts, 130-31, 140-41
    superior courts, 131-32, 138-39
      inherent jurisdiction,
        138, 139
      precedent, 139
provocation, 290-91
public advocacy offices, 340-41
public bill, 101
public demonstrations, 345
public inquiries, 344-45
public interest groups, 346
public international law, 20, 184*n*
public law, 11, 22, 29, 41, 44, 45
public nuisance, 195
puisne, defined, 134

quasi-criminal offence, 273-75
quasi-judicial functions, 256
quasi-legislative materials, 108
Quebec Act, 1774, 65
Queen's Privy Council
  for Canada, 113
    see also Privy Council

ratio decidendi, 33, 145
reading, defined, 102
reading down, 93
reading in, 93, 174
real estate, 207-8
real property, *see* property law
rectification, 32
reference, 136
regulations, 107
remedies, *see under* contracts; torts
rescission, 203

reserve, 137
responsible government, 110-12
retributive justice, 9-10
reverse onus, 169
royal assent, 102, 103, 105
Royal Commission on the
  Status of Women, 81
royal courts, 32
royal prerogative, 115
royal prerogative of mercy, 115
Royal Proclamation of 1763,
  51, 61, 64, 65, 80, 83, 208
royal proclamations, 115
rule in *Rylands v Fletcher*, 193-94
rule of law
    defined, 17
    international context, 20
    judicial independence
      and, 150-52
    Magna Carta and, 18
    origins, 17-18
    principles of, 18-19
Rule of Law Index, 20
rules
    condition rules, 5
    law and, 6
    power conferring, 6
    structure of, 6
    types of, 5-6

search warrant, 281
section 96 courts, 131, 132, 253
section, defined, 122
self-defence, 290
sentencing, *see* criminal law
separation-of-powers doctrine, 90
severance, 93
sharia, 28
sheriffs, 31
shrink-wrap agreement, 201
slander, 195
small claims court, 139, 140
sociology of law, 17
sole proprietorship, 231-32
    advantages, 232
    business name, 231
    disadvantages, 232
    liability of owner, 231

sole proprietorship (*continued*)
    licences, 232
    permits, 232
    registration, 231
    taxes, 231
solicitor, 308
solicitor–client privilege, 321
solicitor of record, 308*n*
sovereignty association, 78
specific performance, 32, 206
standard of care, 6
standard of review, 261
standards of behaviour, 5
stare decisis, 33, 37, 41, 42, 129
Statute of Westminster, 1931, 92, 93
statutes
    bills, 101-2, 103
    citation of, 124-25
    common law, 129
    Constitution Act, 1982
        constitutional amendment
            provisions, 94-95
        supremacy clause, 93
    constitutionally
        entrenched, 91-94
        Constitution Act, 1982
            provisions, 92
    defined, 91
    division of powers, 92
    enactment procedure,
        101-2, 103
    federal jurisdiction,
        72-73, 96-101
        double-aspect laws, 101
        POGG power, 73, 96, 103
        proclamation, 102
        readings, 102
        royal assent, 102
        section 91 powers,
            97-98, 100-1
    federal paramountcy
        doctrine, 101
    federal statutes, 95-96
    generally, 91
    House of Commons, 95
    parliamentary sovereignty,
        doctrine of, 108-9
    provincial jurisdiction, 73, 103, 104

    proclamation, 103
    readings, 103
    royal assent, 103
    section 92 powers, 73, 104
    provincial statutes, 102
    structure of, 122, 123
        coming into force
            section, 122
        commencement section, 122
        consequential amendment
            sections, 122
        definition section, 122
        enabling sections, 122
    territorial jurisdiction, 105
    territorial statutes, 105-6
statutory interpretation, 122, 124
strict liability tort, 193-94
striking down, 93
style of cause, 157
subordinate legislation, 106-7
substantive fairness, 18
substantive law, 20
substantive review, 261, 265
summary conviction
    offence, 276, 277, 279
summons, 287
superior court of criminal
    justice, 279
superior courts, 128
    jurisdiction to review
        administrative decisions, 260
supremacy clause, 93
Supreme Court of Canada,
    see under judiciary

Tax Court of Canada, 132, 143, 144
tenancy in common, 211
territorial courts, 129
title insurance, 213
Torrens system, 212-13
tort, defined, 186
tort law
    act of God, 193
    capacity to commit tort, 189
    civil wrong, 186
    consent, 188, 192
    defamation, 195, 196
    generally, 186

    illegality, 192, 193
    intentional torts
        battery, 187
        deceit claims, 188*n*
        defences to, 188-89
        false imprisonment, 187
        interference with economic
            interests, 188
        interferences with persons/
            property, 186-87
        intrusion upon
            seclusion, 188*n*
        invasion of privacy, 188*n*
        trespass to land/goods/
            chattels, 187
    legal authority, 188
    negligence
        breach of duty, 189, 191
        but for test, 192
        causation, 189, 192
        contributory negligence, 192
        damages, 189, 192
        defences to, 192-93
        defined, 189
        duty, 189, 190
        elements of claim, 189-92
        foreseeability, 192
        generally, 189
        material contribution
            test, 192
        misfeasance, 189
        neighbour principle,
            11-12, 190
        nonfeasance, 189
        proximate cause, 192
        reasonableness
            standard, 191
        remoteness, 192
        standard of care, 6, 189, 191
        unborn child, mother's
            duty to, 191
    nuisance, 195
    occupiers' liability, 193
    remedies, 196-97
        abatement of nuisance, 196
        compensatory damages, 196
        damages, 196
        extrajudicial, 196

general damages, 196
injunctions, 196
punitive damages, 196
recapture of goods, 196, 197
special damages, 196
rule in *Rylands v
Fletcher*, 193-94
self-defence, 188
strict liability torts, 193-94
vicarious liability, 194
trade, 28
trademarks, 215
Trans Mountain Expansion
Project, 99
Treaty of Paris, 1763, 64, 65
Treaty of Utrecht, 64, 65
trespass to chattels, 187
trespass to goods, 187
trespass to land, 187
trespass to person, 186-87
trial courts, 128
trial, criminal, *see* criminal law

Truth and Reconciliation
Commission, 44, 45,
46-48, 53, 54, 341

ultra vires, 76
unconscionability, 204
undertaking, defined, 288, 319
undue influence, 204
unfair bargain, 204
unicameral, 91, 102
Unified Family Court, *see*
judiciary, provincial court
Uniform Law Conference
of Canada, 201
Union Act, 1840, 66, 67
unitary government, 72
United Nations, 20, 201, 215, 307
*United Nations Declaration
on the Rights of Indigenous
Peoples* (UNDRIP), 44, 45, 46,
47-48, 53, 54, 298, 341
utilitarianism, 16

verdict, 290
vicarious liability, 194

wahkohtowin, 49
watertight compartments, 100
wellness courts, 141
wire transfer, 237
women
Aboriginal women, 82
patriation of constitution,
81-82
workplace safety, 274
World Bank, 20
World Justice Project, 20
writ
defined, 32
general, 31-32
prerogative writs, 266
wrongful dismissal, 206-7

*Youth Criminal Justice
Act*, 273, 294-95

Credits

CHAPTER 1

Chapter-opening photo: Xtock Images/Alamy Stock Photo

Box 1.3: Duncan Walker/iStock

Box 1.4: Alain Le Garsmeur Canada/Alamy Stock Photo

Box 1.5: Heritage Image Partnership Ltd/Alamy Stock Photo

Box 1.6: Glasshouse Images/Alamy Stock Photo

CHAPTER 2

Chapter-opening photo: North Wind Picture Archives/Alamy Stock Photo

Box 2.3: EmmePi Travel/Alamy Stock Photo

Box 2.5: DARMAP0021/Darlington Digital Library, University of Pittsburgh

CHAPTER 3

Chapter-opening photo: Content courtesy of the Department of Canadian Heritage. © All rights reserved. Department of Canadian Heritage. Reproduced with the permission of the Minister of Canadian Heritage, 2020.

Box 3.1: Royal Proclamation, King George III of England Issued October 7, 1763/Library and Archives Canada, e010778430

Figure 3.1: Benjamin West, The Death of General Wolfe (detail), 1770, oil on canvas, 152.6 x 214.5 cm (National Gallery of Canada)

Figure 3.2: Courtesy of Canadian Geographic.

Figure 3.3: Courtesy of Canadian Geographic.

Figure 3.4: G. P. Roberts/Library and Archives Canada, C-000733

Box 3.2: Everett Collection Inc/Alamy Stock Photo

CHAPTER 4

Chapter-opening photo: robertharding/Alamy Stock Photo

Figure 4.1: WorldStock/Shutterstock

Box 4.2: Photo courtesy of Trans Mountain.

Figure 4.4: The Canadian Press/PA/Andrew Milligan

CHAPTER 5

Chapter-opening photo: Karl Kost/Alamy Stock Photo

Figure 5.2: Dennis MacDonald/Alamy Stock Photo

Box 5.2: GerryRousseau/Alamy Stock Photo

Box 5.4: Roy Grogan/Supreme Court of Canada Collection

CHAPTER 6

Chapter-opening photo: Edgars Sermulis/Alamy Stock Photo

Figure 6.1: American Photo Archive/Alamy Stock Photo

Figure 6.3: Joe Ng/Alamy Stock Photo

Box 6.2: Photo courtesy of Trevor Florence and Invermere Soaring Centre Ltd.

Box 6.3: The Canadian Press/Tom Hanson

CHAPTER 7

Chapter-opening photo: Andriy Popov/Alamy Stock Photo

Box 7.2: Ievgen Chabanov/Alamy Stock Photo

Box 7.5: Olha Khorimarko/Alamy Stock Vector

Box 7.8: Jonathan Hayward/The Canadian Press

CHAPTER 8

Chapter-opening photo: SeventyFour Images/Alamy Stock Photo

CHAPTER 9

Chapter-opening photo: DWD-Comp/Alamy Stock Photo

CHAPTER 10

Chapter-opening photo: Lars Hagberg/Alamy Stock Photo

Box 10.3: Luke Durda/Alamy Stock Photo

Table 10.1: Adapted from James S Frideres & Rene R Gadacz, Aboriginal Peoples in Canada, 9th ed (Toronto: Pearson, 2012).

CHAPTER 11

Chapter-opening photo: Cultura RM/Alamy Stock Photo

CHAPTER 12

Chapter-opening photo: Darryl Dyck/The Canadian Press